A HISTORY OF SOUTH AFRICA

A History of South Africa

from the DISTANT PAST to the PRESENT DAY

Editor
Fransjohan Pretorius

An initiative of the History Commission of the Suid-Afrikaanse Akademie vir Wetenskap en Kuns (South African Academy for Science and the Arts).

PROTEA BOOK HOUSE
Pretoria
2022

A History of South Africa: From the Distant Past to the Present Day
Fransjohan Pretorius

First edition, first impression in 2014 by Protea Book House
First revised edition, first impression in 2022

PO Box 35110, Menlo Park, 0102
1067 Burnett Street, Hatfield, Pretoria
8 Minni Street, Clydesdale, Pretoria
info@proteaboekhuis.co.za
www.proteaboekhuis.com

Translator: Bridget Theron
Editor: Danél Hanekom
Proofreaders: Carmen Hansen-Kruger and Carla Lang
Cover design: Sharon Bredenkamp/Marketing Support Services
Cover images: Gallo Images/Thinkstockphotos
Cartographer: Ingrid Booysen
Indexer: George Claassen
Typography: 11.25 on 14 pt Adobe Caslon Pro by Ada Radford
Printed and bound: Shumani RSA, Parow

© 2014 Fransjohan Pretorius (compilation and introduction)
© 2014 Individual authors (contributions)
© 2014 Ingrid Booysen (maps)

ISBN: 978-1-4853-1385-4 (printed book)
ISBN: 978-1-4853-1386-1 (e-book)

All rights reserved. No part of this book may be reproduced or transmitted in any form or by any electronic or mechanical means, including photocopying and recording, or by any other information storage or retrieval system, without written permission from the publisher.

Contents

List of maps ... 7
Introduction ... 9
1. South Africa's primeval past
   Andrie Meyer ... 17
2. The Dutch era at the Cape, 1652–1806
   Johan de Villiers ... 41
3. People of bondage
   Robert Shell ... 68
4. Cape colonial society under British rule, 1806–1834
   Johan de Villiers ... 79
5. Migration and the societies north of the Gariep River
   Jan Visagie ... 105
6. The emigration of the Voortrekkers into the interior
   Jan Visagie ... 125
7. State formation and strife, 1850–1900
   Jackie Grobler ... 155
8. The mineral revolution
   Wessel Visser ... 188
9. An economic history of the nineteenth century
   Grietjie Verhoef ... 205
10. Afrikaner nationalism, 1875–1899
    Hermann Giliomee ... 223
11. Everyone's war: the Anglo-Boer War (1899–1902)
    Fransjohan Pretorius ... 239
12. Post-war race relations, 1902–1948
    David M. Scher ... 260
13. Afrikaner nationalism, 1902–1948
    Hermann Giliomee ... 281
14. Black political awakening, 1875–1949
    Jackie Grobler ... 313

15. The consolidation of the apartheid state, 1948–1966
    David M. Scher   328
16. B.J. Vorster and separate development
    Kobus du Pisani   349
17. Black resistance against apartheid, 1950s–1980s
    Jackie Grobler   374
18. "Adapt or die", 1978–1984
    Hermann Giliomee   396
19. Uprising, war and transition, 1984–1994
    Hermann Giliomee   411
20. Apartheid: a different angle
    Hermann Giliomee   434
21. The South African economy in the twentieth century
    Grietjie Verhoef   448
22. The development of trade unions and organised labour
    Wessel Visser   478
23. South Africa after apartheid, 1994–2004
    Japie Brits   493
24. The troubled teens: South African democracy, 2004–2013
    Jan-Jan Joubert   525
25. Coloureds: a complex history
    Cornelius Thomas   547
26. The Indians in South Africa
    Goolam Vahed   574
27. English-speaking South Africans: uncertain of their identity
    John Lambert   588
28. The South African churches and apartheid
    J.W. (Hoffie) Hofmeyr and J.A. (Joan) Millard   610
29. An environmental history of South Africa
    Elize S. van Eeden   633
30. From state capture to Covid: the decline of the ANC, 2014–2020
    Jan-Jan Joubert   664

Bibliography   675
Authors' biographies   687
Index   691

List of maps

1. Southern Africa: from 3600 million years ago to current	16
2. The Cape Peninsula in 1795	63
3. The Cape Colony in 1835	78
4. Voortrekker routes, 1835–1838	129
5. The Boer Republics	173
6. The Boer Republics during the Anglo-Boer War	238
7. Black homelands	348
8. South Africa's provinces after 1994	492

Introduction

"Then we should write a history ourselves."

This explosive remark by Prof. Jacques van der Elst, chief executive officer of the Suid-Afrikaanse Akademie van Wetenskap en Kuns at a symposium organised by the History Commission in 2006, caused me many sleepless nights.

On this occasion the discussion turned to the fact that the content of South African history presented these days, particularly at school level, basically emphasises the country's struggle history, specifically the history of black South Africans. The conclusion reached was that whereas in the apartheid years the emphasis tipped too heavily towards an Afrikaner or white-centric approach to the past, the pendulum has now swung too far to the other side, with an undue focus on struggle history.

In the apartheid era the struggle and its endeavours did not really feature in the history of South Africa. Black people were considered a "problem", as evident in themes such as the "Native question" and "Coloured question". The existence of black concentration camps set up by the British authorities during the Anglo-Boer War, for example, did not feature either because they were not seen as part of the Afrikaner nationalists' close identification with the suffering of Boer women and children. Nor, indeed, were the black concentration camps mentioned in British histories of the Anglo-Boer War at the time.

However, with the dawn of the New South Africa in 1994, black resistance became the central theme in school history syllabuses. Just as it had in the Afrikaner-centric approach of earlier years, when Afrikaner heroes and their travails were presented as the authentic history of South Africa, now the victory of the black resistance movements were presented as being the only true history of South Africa. It was all too easy to allow the pendulum to swing towards the struggle side to show how destructive and pernicious apartheid had been for the country's black, coloured and Indian people – which indeed it was.

Afrikaner republicanism features seldom, if at all, in black struggle history. In one work the suffering and death of black people in the concentration camps of the Anglo-Boer War is discussed, while there is mute silence on the similar fate of white inmates. Their respective roles are reversed after 1994. In the same work, a single short sentence mentions President Paul Kruger of the Zuid-Afrikaansche Republiek – one of the most influential figures in South African history of the nineteenth century – and it merely indicates that he did not see eye to eye with the mine magnates.

As a result, at the 2006 symposium the need was expressed for an all-embracing, comprehensive history of South Africa that would move the pendulum back towards the centre in a spirit of reconciliation and mutual understanding between different cultural and political groupings. The Akademie's History Commission was asked to launch this ambitious project. The objective was an inclusive approach – certainly not an exclusive one – to the history of South Africa.

As far back as 1969 the *Oxford History of South Africa*, edited by Monica Wilson and Leonard Thompson, paved the way for a wider perspective on South African history. Unlike earlier works, neither the presence of the Portuguese at the end of the fifteenth century nor the arrival of Jan van Riebeeck on the southern tip of Africa in 1652 were seen as the beginning of South Africa's history. An interdisciplinary approach which included the work of experts in the fields of archaeology and social anthropology has ensured that the precolonial period has also enjoyed wider attention.

Ever since, a general history of South Africa has been unthinkable without a discussion of the first people in southern Africa and the various precolonial groups that comprised this complex society. In this vein, *South Africa: A Modern History* by T.R.H. Davenport (1978, and later editions together with C.C. Saunders); *An Illustrated History of South Africa*, edited by Trewhella Cameron and S.B. Spies (1986); and the *Reader's Digest Illustrated History of South Africa* (1988) included chapters on the precolonial history of South Africa. The same can be said of *New History of South Africa* edited by Hermann Giliomee and Bernard Mbenga (2007); and

The Cambridge History of South Africa, edited by Carolyn Hamilton, Bernard Mbenga and Robert Ross (2010).

With this in mind, our first chapter is one by ethno-archaeologist Andrie Meyer, who shows that South Africa's history can be traced back millions of years to the origins of the universe and the earth. Meyer tells of the treasure trove of relics that still remain and date back to those early times. He goes on to explain how the genesis and development of South Africa during different historical eras have influenced the course of colonial history and our recent past, right up to the present.

No history can lay claim to being absolutely objective. Nor do we assume to do so. Nevertheless, we declare our intention, as far as possible, to present an equitable and unbiased history of South Africa. To achieve this we provide divergent points of view on specific periods side by side, with the emphasis still firmly on group interaction. The Netherlands era at the Cape from 1652 to 1806 is therefore not seen only from the perspective of the colonists. The chapters by Johan de Villiers and Robert Shell discuss the fate of the slave society as well as that of the Khoekhoen (who were previously known as the Khoikhoi or Hottentots).

As far as the period 1750 to 1854 is concerned, Jan Visagie unravels the motivations that spurred the migrations of the white trekboers and the Voortrekkers. In doing so, he also discusses the role played by other groups in the interior – the Bushmen, Korana and the Griqua; and how the Sotho-Tswana and Nguni-speakers and the Voortrekkers were influenced by the Mfecane.

Jackie Grobler looks at state formation and fields of conflict in the second half of the nineteenth century and takes up the story begun by Visagie of the different black societies. Grobler also investigates the constitutional, political and agricultural development in the Cape Colony and Natal and the establishment of a number of Boer republics, of which the Republic of the Orange Free State and the previously divided Zuid-Afrikaansche Republiek (ZAR) were the most important. His chapter, that of Wessel Visser on the mineral revolution, and Grietjie Verhoef's contribution on the economic history of South Africa in the nineteenth century, complement each other particularly well, as does Hermann Giliomee's chapter on Afrikaner nationalism in the last decades of the nineteenth century.

This brings us to the turn of the nineteenth century. Here the point of departure is that the Anglo-Boer War was, in the first place, a confrontation between the Boer republics and Great Britain. Furthermore, it was also a war which affected and involved all South Africans – white, black and coloured (written by Fransjohan Pretorius). Reference is also made to an alternative name for the war, the South African War, which also implies the participation of all population groups.

Our quest to place the experiences of all different groupings in perspective reaches its high point in the twentieth century. Indeed, most of the chapters in this book focus on this period. Alongside the customary political history that revolves around powerful leaders from 1902 to the present (written by David Scher, Giliomee, Kobus du Pisani, Japie Brits and Jan-Jan Joubert) attention is given to the ambient economy of the time (Verhoef); the trade union movement (Visser); Afrikaner nationalism (Giliomee); black resistance (Grobler); the white English-speaking experience (John Lambert); and also a brief look at the Chinese society in South Africa (Karen Harris). On the coloured and Indian experience, see more below. In a new and innovative theme, Elize van Eeden discusses the significance of environmental history.

No single interpretation of history can stand alone in its claim to be valid. Scher and Giliomee, for example, differ in their opinions on the role that apartheid played in the National Party's victory in 1948. In contrast to Scher's explanation of events under the apartheid government between 1948 and 1966, Giliomee provides a different view on apartheid by attempting to find answers to questions such as: Was apartheid entirely different from the segregation policy pursued between 1902 and 1948? And: Could South Africa have fared better economically had there not been apartheid?

We have followed a chronological approach, but this book also has a strong thematic element in each of the particular periods. We hope that this work will be useful to high school learners and teachers, but are confident that historians and the interested general reader will have much to gain from its chapters.

Since the appearance of the Afrikaans edition of this book with the title *Geskiedenis van Suid-Afrika: Van voortye tot vandag*, published by Tafelberg in 2012, we have come to the realisation that we have not entirely achieved the balance we hoped for. This English version (and future Afrikaans editions) therefore has a number of important changes and additions. Visagie's two chapters on the causes and the course of the Great

Trek have been shortened and appear as a single chapter, while the same process was followed with Hermann Giliomee's two chapters on Afrikaner Nationalism in the periods 1902–1924 and 1924–1948. Jan-Jan Joubert's chapter on the democratic puberty 2004–2011, becomes "The troubled teens: South African democracy, 2004–2013"; there are two welcome new chapters on the complex histories of the coloured and Indian people by Cornelius Thomas and Goolam Vahed respectively; and Hoffie Hofmeyr, this time with co-author Joan Millard, have written a dynamic new chapter on the South African churches and apartheid which replaces the previous chapter on the Afrikaans churches in the twentieth century.

This second edition gives us the opportunity to extend the period under scrutiny, and Jan-Jan Joubert has kindly added a chapter on the political history of South Africa from 2014 to the announcement of the lockdown due to Covid on 26 March 2020. His contribution was added as a final chapter.

Although the book is a project of the History Commission of the Suid-Afrikaanse Akademie vir Wetenskap en Kuns, and prominent authors were indeed drawn from that particular group of historians to make their contributions to this publication, we also, where necessary, approached experts in their specific fields from outside the ambit of the Akademie. What we present here is therefore not the work of authors who have any particular ethnic, language, or ideological affinity. They are quite simply a group of historians who wish to contribute positively to the field of historical writing. Drawing on the work of such a wide range of authors inevitably means that the central theme – interaction between all population groups – does not necessarily show the same intensity throughout and that individual interpretations may differ, but we trust that our earnest objective to achieve a better balance has in some measure been achieved.

I identify closely with the remarks made by the editors of *The Cambridge History of South Africa*, when they admit in the Introduction of volume 1:

> We are neither under the illusion nor do we pretend that what we have written will endure free from criticism. Indeed, we are certain that the changing composition of the South African historical profession and the inclusion in it of many people from backgrounds or orientations that were previously marginalised or excluded will lead to a whole variety of new emphases and approaches.

New times will no doubt continue to bring to the fore new perspectives and interpretations on the changeable nature of South African society.

A special word of thanks to the exceptional and exceptionally large team who participated in this project. I was time and again struck by the support and enthusiasm of my co-workers. This made my task far easier. Each chapter was also subjected to careful peer evaluation.

My thanks to Hermann Giliomee and Tafelberg for permission to use the piece from *New History of South Africa*, namely Robert Shell's work on the slaves.

Prof. Jacques van der Elst made an enormous contribution to the publication of the Afrikaans edition. The same can be said of Dr Dionē Prinsloo, the current chief executive officer of the Suid-Afrikaanse Akademie vir Wetenskap en Kuns, with regard to this English version. Their positive support was highly appreciated. Linda Brink, senior administrative officer of the Akademie, also earns my sincere thanks for the selfless and valuable help she provided.

My thanks also to Ingrid Booysen who compiled the maps with such skill and attention to detail.

A forbearing Dr Bridget Theron deserves the greatest praise for the English translation which is testimony to her distinctive flowing style of writing.

Finally, my sincere thanks to Dr Nicol Stassen of Protea Book House who was aware of the significance of publishing an English translation of our work, and to Danél Hanekom, who proved supremely efficient and composed in her duties as final editor.

Fransjohan Pretorius
Editor
October 2021

Timeline

Million years ago (approximately)

#		
1	3600–3100	Kaapvaal Craton
2	3000	Zimbabwe Craton
3	2700	Kaapvaal Craton – Zimbabwe Craton contact zone
4	3400	Barberton rocks
5	2500–1500	Phalaborwa Complex and Bushveld Complex
6	2023	Vredefort Dome and surrounding asteroid crater
7	1200	Pilanesberg volcano
8	1600–90	Kimberlite containing diamonds in volcano pipes
9	182–180	Drakensberg and Maluti mountains
10	160–65	Southern African coast line and primeval rivers
11	20 & 5	Southern Africa plateau and rivers
12	4–1	Australopithecenae and first humans

Years ago (approximately)

#		
13	220 000	Tswaing Meteorite Crater
14	10 000–current	Current biomes: **14a** Savannah; **14b** Grasslands; **14c** Nama Karoo
15	10 000–200	Late Stone Age – San people and rock art
16	1500–300	Iron Age kingdoms and mines
17	300–current	Bantu-speaking tribes and kingdoms
18	150–current	Colonial and post-colonial mines

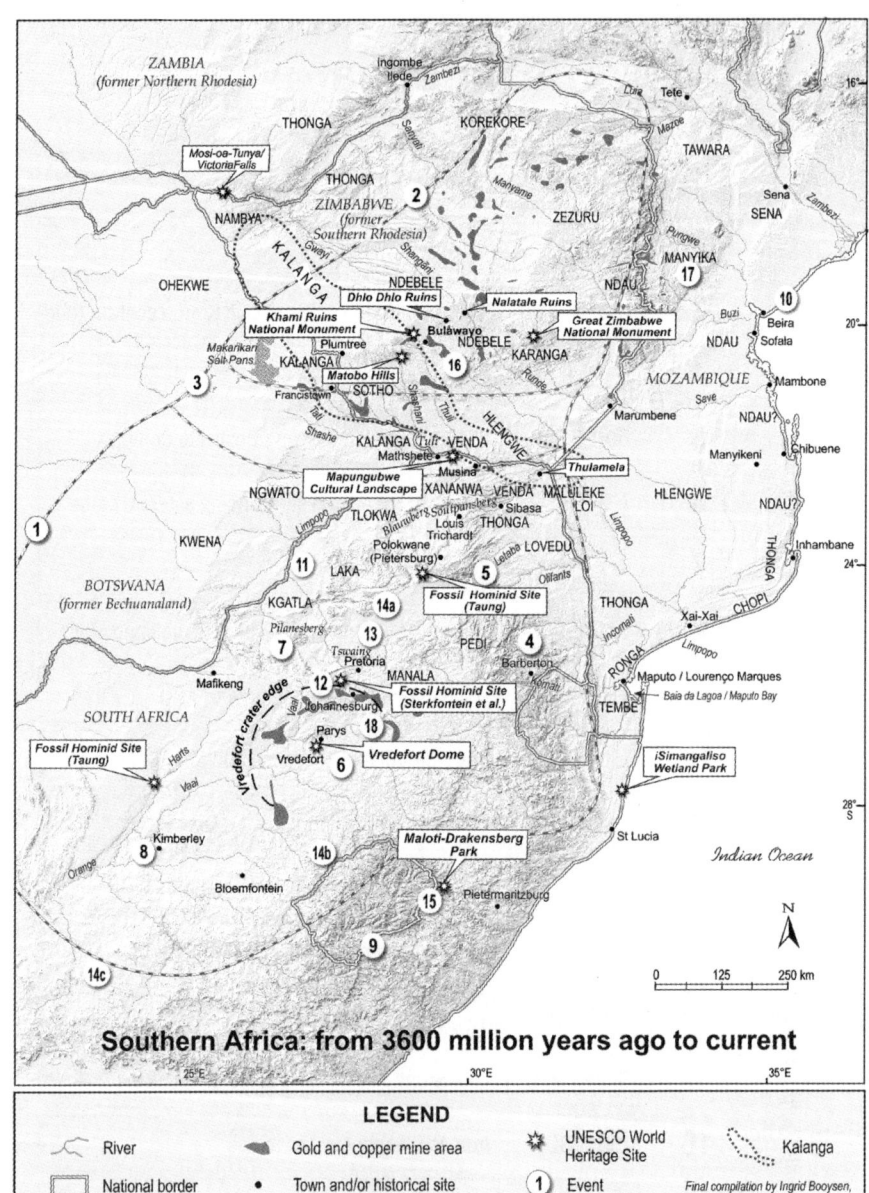

1
South Africa's primeval past
Andrie Meyer

The landscapes of South Africa are a legacy of the origin and evolution of the Earth, including the formation of the first land mass, the first forms of life and the emergence of humankind right up to the present landscapes and their human inhabitants. South Africa's evolution during various prehistoric periods not only influenced the course of colonial history, but also the recent past and even the present. The remains of earlier southern African natural and cultural landscapes, human inhabitants and their traditions are therefore a heritage treasure and an intact record of the past.

History including the human past began with the formation of the Universe, the galaxies and planet Earth which, according to scientific calculations, originated between 13 700 million (13,7 billion) and 4600 million (4,6 billion) years ago. Various techniques in the natural and human sciences are used for the dating, description, reconstruction and interpretation of our past. Among the natural sciences and human sciences that are used to study the past are physics, astronomy, geology, palaeontology, geography, anthropology, archaeology, history and cultural history.

The history of the Earth is divided into major divisions of geological time called eons. Eons are in turn divided into smaller periods of time. The oldest major time period was the Archaean Eon which, according to scientific calculations, began about 4600 million years ago with the origin of the Earth, and lasted until 2500 million years ago. During this eon the basic geological composition, as well as the core, mantle and crust of the Earth were formed. At this time the hydrosphere (the waters on the Earth's surface) began to take shape as early oceans, lakes and rivers and the atmosphere also began to form around the Earth. These environmental elements, together with sunlight and definitive weather and climatic conditions, provided the necessary sources of nutrition and environmental conditions for the development and survival of life forms. The first elementary forms of life, such as bacteria, developed in seawater during the Archaean Eon.

The second major geological time period was the Proterozoic Eon, which according to scientific calculations lasted from about 2500 million years up to about 545 million years before the present. This eon is divided into three consecutive eras. The Proterozoic Eon is most notable for the formation and fragmentation of various successive primeval continents and the origin of life forms such as bacteria and algae.

The Phanerozoic Eon is the current eon and is calculated to have begun about 545 million years ago. This eon is divided into different eras that are again divided into periods; the periods are then sub-divided into various epochs. During the Phanerozoic Eon today's continents, oceans and climatic conditions developed; a great variety of life forms evolved and humankind appeared on the Earth. During the last 65 million years – the Cenozoic Era of the Phanerozoic Eon – the present landscapes, plant and animal life (flora and fauna) gradually took shape, while other plant and animal species became extinct.

The earliest human-like beings (hominins) and the first people emerged about 7 to 2 million years ago in East Africa and southern Africa, at the end of the Pliocene Epoch and the beginning of the Pleistocene Epoch. Thereafter, during the Pleistocene Epoch and Holocene Epoch, the present landscapes and humankind developed and people gradually spread throughout the world.

The origin of the Universe

Space telescopes and space photographic documentation of the characteristics and movements of the galaxies and solar systems have given rise to different astronomical theories on the origin and development of the Universe. The Universe is the entire celestial space including all the galaxies and space phenomena. According to the Big Bang theory the Universe and time originated about 13 700 million years ago as a result of the explosion of a single source of immensely high-density matter – possibly a massive neutron particle.

Just after the Big Bang, the newly born Universe was extremely dense and hot. Scientific research indicates that during the subsequent cooling down of the Universe an invisible energy field – known as the Higgs Field – came into existence throughout the Universe. The Higgs Field is believed to be accompanied by an elementary type of particle called the Higgs Boson, which continuously interacts with other particles passing through the Higgs Field by transferring mass to these passing particles during a process known as the Higgs Effect. This process makes the passing particles heavier and slower. Conditions became just right for the rise of quarks and electrons – the building blocks of matter. A quark is an elementary particle and a fundamental constituent of matter. Quarks aggregated to form protons and neutrons which then became combined as the very dense nucleus of an atom. Electrons – subatomic particles with a negative elementary electric charge – became trapped in orbits around these nuclei, thus forming the first atoms which are basic units of matter. These are mainly helium and hydrogen atoms which are regarded by scientists as the most abundant elements in the Universe. Without this process, there would be neither atoms nor life.

This newly formed matter – the building material of celestial bodies – was hurled in the form of gas and dust from the centre of the explosion into the surrounding space. All matter began to gravitate further outwards, initiating the continuous growth and expansion of the Universe.

In time, because of the effect of gravity, the gases formed nebulous clouds of concentrated matter. This densification of matter led to the release of heat energy and nuclear fusion, from which the first stars were formed about 200 million years after the Big Bang. Astronomical observations show that stars are formed out of clouds of gas, known as nebulous clouds or nebulae. Due to gravity conditions and processes of condensation, a nebula which comprises various forms of matter increasingly rotates around its own axis and develops inherent gravitation. This again causes the nebula to rotate faster, to shrink, become denser and hotter to eventually form an increasingly glowing star.

The rest of the matter revolved around the star or sun in a primitive protoplanetary disk in which the condensation of matter formed prototype or primitive planets which developed later into mature planets and their moons. In time, countless such solar systems and galaxies emerged and the Universe was formed. As time passed, old solar systems burnt out and new ones developed. According to one view on the origin of the Universe it comprises groups of stars that formed galaxies which then again formed new groups and super groups of stellar systems. The movement of celestial bodies is influenced by unidentified "dark energy" (a form of imperceptible energy which is widely present in space and causes the Universe to expand rapidly outwards) and "dark matter". According to scientific theory, dark matter comprises matter particles which do not give off or reflect electromagnetic radiation and as a result are not directly observable. The presence or force of gravitation of dark matter exercises a notable influence on the movement of visible stars and galaxies. Antimatter also contributes to the release of energy. Antimatter comprises tiny antiparticles, for example a positron with a positive electrical charge, which is the opposite of matter particles such as an electron, which has a negative charge. When similar matter particles and antimatter particles come into contact with each other, they are thought to interact in a process of mutual destruction during which they are transformed into energy.

The spiral-shaped Milky Way Galaxy – in which the Earth, within its solar system, is located on the outside fringe – according to estimates comprises 100 000 million stars and has a total diameter of 100 000 light years. (A light year is the distance light travels in one year at a speed of 300 000 km per second.)

Meteorites from outer space which are found on the Earth's surface are a valuable source of information on the origin, existence and composition of matter in the Universe. A meteorite is a particle of natural material that has fallen to the Earth from outer space, comprising rock and metal and is smaller than an asteroid. An asteroid, which is also known as a planetoid or small planet, also consists of rock and metals and orbits around the Sun, such as the asteroid belt between the planets Mars and Jupiter.

One of the many meteorites that are studied by scientists is the Yamato 691 meteorite that was found in 1969 in Antarctica. According to scientific calculations, this meteorite is 4500 million years old and is presumed to come from an asteroid in orbit in the vicinity of the planets Mars and Jupiter. This meteorite comprises minerals that have never been observed before, including a mineral called wassonite which is made up of a combination of titanium and sulphur.

The formation of the Earth

The solar system, comprising the Sun and the planets of which the Earth is one, was formed about 4600 million years ago. Asteroids also orbit in the solar system. There is an asteroid belt between Mars and Jupiter which consists of between 1,1 and 1,9 million asteroids with a diameter of more than a kilometre, together with millions of smaller asteroids. This asteroid belt is possibly the remains of a protoplanetary disc around the Sun.

The Earth with its one moon is one of eight planets that orbit around the Sun. These planets are, in sequence (distance from the Sun), Mercury, Venus, Earth, Mars, Jupiter, Saturn, Uranus and Neptune. Pluto, previously referred to in earlier literature as the ninth or furthest planet from the Sun, is currently classified as a dwarf planet in the Kuiper Belt. According to more recent information, the Kuiper Belt comprises smaller celestial bodies which were formed at the time of the origin of the solar system.

The position of the Earth as the third planet at about 150 million km from the Sun was and still is an important factor in the development and continued existence of life forms. It is far enough from the Sun to be neither too hot nor too cold and the size of the Earth ensures that there is enough gravitational pull for the preservation of the hydrosphere and atmosphere. The fact that the Earth rotates on its own axis (which accounts for day and night) and the tilt of the planet's axis (which brings seasonal changes and accompanying weather conditions) are also important requirements for earthly forms of life.

At the time the Earth was formed, its surface was a hot, melted mass which gradually cooled over time and formed three concentric layers. The outer, solid crust is 10 to 50 km thick and consists mainly of granite and basalt, although granite, as far as we know, does not occur on the ocean floor. Beneath the crust is the mantle. It is about 2900 km thick and consists of hot earth matter which is forced upwards and cooler matter which is forced downwards in a phenomenon that is called convection currents. In the centre of the Earth is the core, which due to high pressure from the earth layers covering it, is extremely hot. It has a melted outer layer and an inner layer which is apparently solid as a result of the pressure of the earth from above. The continuous interaction between the Earth's mantle and crust, together with the surrounding atmosphere and hydrosphere, causes the formation of various rock types. Melted rock from the mantle that cools down to form igneous (eruptive) rock, as well as magma or lava which as a result of pressure from below rises to the Earth's surface, forms sediments and sedimentary rocks which are then transformed into metamorphic rock by the pressure of earth and heat. This process of rock formation is known as the rock cycle.

After the cooling and hardening of the outermost layers of the Earth, water vapour and carbon dioxide began to form in the early atmosphere, but oxygen (which is vital for life forms) was not yet present. Water vapour which had condensed from the atmosphere, began to fall as rain from about 3900 million years ago and formed the oceans. Between 3800 and 3500 million years ago, the first living organisms developed in seawater from a primitive ancestral organism and by about 3400 million years ago they diversified as microbes such as bacteria and fungi. Cyanobacteria began to produce oxygen by using sunshine, water and carbon dioxide during the process of photosynthesis. Fossils of these microbes have been found in rocks at Barberton in South Africa and at a prehistoric beach at Strandley Pool in western Australia. The early multi-cellular predecessors of animals, plants and fungi developed from these primary life forms.

The formation of cratons (stable parts of the Earth's crust that have not changed significantly over time) that rose as rock domes from the mantle of the Earth to above the level of the sea, eventually formed the first small continents. In the course of time, due to the processes of rock formation, they became core sections of larger continents. The development of these land masses, together with topographic characteristics, the formation of the atmosphere, hydrosphere, climate and weather conditions, gradually contributed to the development and changing of ecological conditions that were favourable for the development and diversification of life forms on Earth.

The first land mass was the mineral-rich Kaapvaal Craton which appeared above the level of the sea during the Archaean Eon between 3600 and 2700 million years ago. The oldest fully fledged continent was Ur which developed between ca 3500 and 1500 million years ago and by 3000 years ago amalgamated with the Kaapvaal Craton and other land masses.

During the Proterozoic Eon, the development and fragmentation of a sequence of continents involved Arctica (ca 2500 to 1500 million years ago); Atlantica (ca 2000 million years ago); Nena (ca 1600 to 1300 million years ago); Rodinia (amalgamation of Ur, Atlantica and Nena about 1100 to 700 million years ago) and Pangaea (assembled fragments of Rodinia and other continental fragments which formed Gondwana in the south-east and Laurasia in the north-west of Pangaea, between 600 to 300 million years ago).

Finally, during the Phanerozoic Era, Gondwana and Laurasia fragmented around 182 to 65 million years ago to form the present continents of the world. During this process of continent formation, the earliest known continental land mass, the Kaapvaal Craton, became a core substance of South Africa.

Timeline

DEVELOPMENT OF THE EARTH AND LIFE FORMS (IN YEARS BEFORE THE PRESENT)
Ca 13 700 million:
• The Big Bang: Origin of the Universe. • The galaxies start to form, including the Milky Way Galaxy and solar systems.
Ca 4600 million:
• Formation of the sun and the solar system in which the Earth is a planet, in the Milky Way Galaxy.
Archaean Eon, ca 4600–2500 million:
• Formation of the Earth, atmosphere, hydrosphere and first life forms.
Ca 4600–3900 million:
• The surface of the Earth begins to cool; origin of the first rock formations; early tectonic plate formation occurs. • Atmospheric gases and water vapour are formed; rain falls and oceans form. • First living organisms appear in shallow seawater near hot springs.
Ca 3900–2700 million:
• Early cyanobacteria develop widely in seawater, using sunshine, water and carbon dioxide during photosynthesis to produce carbohydrates and oxygen.
Ca 3600–2700 million:
• Formation of the Kaapvaal Craton, the oldest known continent, and its minerals.
Ca 3500–1500 million
• The continent Ur forms from the amalgamation of cratons and other land masses.

Ca 3400–2700 million:
• Origin of the Barberton rock formations which become part of the earliest land mass, the Kaapvaal Craton. • Early forms of life, microbes in shallow seawater, are fossilised in Barberton rocks.
Ca 3200–2700:
• Origin of the Zimbabwe Craton.
Ca 2700 million:
• The Zimbabwe Craton collides and consolidates with the Kaapvaal Craton.
Proterozoic Eon, ca 2500–545 million:
• Formation of continents and development of early life forms.
Ca 2500–1300 million:
• Formation of the continents Arctica, Atlantica and Nena. • Mineral-rich geological formations such as the Bushveld Complex and the Phalaborwa Complex emerge in the Kaapvaal Craton.
Ca 2023 million:
• An asteroid collides with the Kaapvaal Craton and forms the Vredefort Dome and asteroid crater.
Ca 2000 million:
• Living organisms which are the ancestors of animals, fungi and plants develop.
Ca 1600–90 million:
• Kimberlite magma containing diamonds forms in volcano pipes.
Ca 1200 million:
• A volcano forms the Pilanesberg.
Ca 1100–700 million:
• The continents Nena, Ur and Atlantica fuse to form the supercontinent Rodinia which thereafter breaks up into land fragments.
Ca 600–300 million:
• Fragments of the earlier supercontinent Rodinia reassemble to form the continent Pangaea. • North-western Pangaea is formed by Laurasia and south-eastern Pangaea is formed by Gondwana.

Phanerozoic Eon, ca 545 million – present:	
• Gondwana and Laurasia fragment and form the present-day continents. • Development of an extensive range of life forms.	
Ca 540 million:	
• Multi-cellular living organisms evolve.	
Ca 400 – 200 million:	
• Many plant and animal types evolve in oceans and on land.	
Ca 220 000:	
• A falling meteorite forms the Tshwaing Meteorite Crater.	
Ca 182 – 65 million:	
• A mantle plume rises beneath the southern African part of Gondwana and vast quantities of lava pours through ruptures in the crust to the surface. • Gondwana fragments and forms the present-day continents of Africa, South America, India, Antarctica and Australia, as well as the island Madagascar.	
Ca 65 million – present:	
• The Cenozoic Era and development of the present landscapes of the Earth. • Dinosaur species die out; rapid development of mammals.	
Ca 25 million:	
• Heyday of the great apes.	
Ca 20 and 5 million:	
• Pressure from below the Earth's crust lifts southern Africa and forms its plateau character.	
Ca 7 – 1 million:	
• Hominins (human-like primates) evolve in East Africa and southern Africa.	
Ca 2,6 million:	
• The first representatives of the genus *Homo* emerge in East Africa and southern Africa. They make and utilise primitive bone and stone implements.	
Ca 2 million – present:	
• Glacial periods in the northern hemisphere cause deserts in southern Africa • The present landscapes of the Earth develop. • Humankind and distinctive peoples and cultures develop and spread throughout the world.	

The Kaapvaal Craton and the origins of southern Africa

The origin of South Africa can be traced back to the Kaapvaal Craton, the first known continent in the Earth's history. The Kaapvaal Craton originated 3600 to 3100 million years ago, long before Africa existed as a continent. Granite rocks of the Barberton mountain landscape formed in the Kaapvaal Craton between 3400 and 2700 million years ago and provide geological evidence of the development of the Kaapvaal Craton. New rock formations were continuously formed in and on the weathered Kaapvaal Craton with the associated formation of minerals such as gold, iron and manganese. This was followed between ca 2061 and 2049 million years ago by the development of the world-renowned Bushveld Complex which comprises different consecutive rock types such as granitic and volcanic lavas and a variety of minerals such as chrome, platinum and vanadium, and the Phalaborwa Complex with copper, phosphorous and vermiculite.

About 2023 million years ago an asteroid collided with the outside expanse of the Kaapvaal Craton. According to estimates, the force of this collision was comparable to that of 100 million megaton of TNT. It made an impact crater of 300 km in diameter, the oldest and largest known impact crater on planet Earth. The impact caused a rebound dome, presently known as the Vredefort Dome, in the middle of the crater and shockwaves that rippled outwards leading to the elevation, fragmentation and tilting of the surrounding geological formations. The outer edge of the crater stretches past the location of the present-day Johannesburg. In the west and north-west of the crater there were geological layers with rich gold-bearing rock exposed in tilted layer fragments. With time the asteroid crater largely weathered away, but in the late nineteenth century prospectors discovered the remaining gold deposits in the rim of the crater. These finds gave rise to the development of the extensive Witwatersrand gold-mining industry.

The Vredefort Dome, which is listed by UNESCO as a world heritage site, comprises the weathered remains of the rebound rocks in the middle of the asteroid impact crater or astrobleme, the oldest known astrobleme on the Earth. The semicircular series of mountains of the Vredefort landscape are the remains of the edge of the original rebound dome and are visible on satellite photographs from outer space. The Vaal River, which flows in a south-westerly direction through this mountainous landscape, came into being much later during the formation of the present-day continents.

As a result of the tectonic movements and transformation of the plates in the Earth's crust, various consecutive supercontinents were formed and fragmented, only to reassemble again and consolidate as new continents. During these episodes of continent formation, the Kaapvaal Craton formed part of a succession of a variety of such continents, each episode of which added significant continent collision impact effects and land mass to the Kaapvaal Craton. The mineral-rich Zimbabwe Craton arose further north, collided with the Kaapvaal Craton and formed a permanent single land mass together with the Kaapvaal Craton around 2700 million years ago. With time, they became part of the continent Ur which formed as the oldest fully fledged continent between 3500 and 1500 million years ago.

While the Kaapvaal Craton was part of Ur, the Soutpansberg and Waterberg rock systems heaved up on the Kaapvaal Craton and there are indications in the rock that oxygen was already present. A volcano that was apparently about 7 km high formed on the Kaapvaal Craton 1200 million years ago and gradually weathered to form the Pilanesberg range near Rustenburg.

During the existence of Ur, the other continents which developed were Arctica between 2500 and 1500 years ago; Atlantica from 3000 to 1500 million years ago; and Nena 1600 to 1300 million years ago. Between 1100 and 700 million years ago the continents Ur, Atlantica and Nena assembled to form the supercontinent Rodenia, with the Kaapvaal Craton positioned in the south-western extremity of Rodinia.

Around 700 million years ago Rodinia broke up and eventually reassembled again between 600 and 300 million years ago to form the supercontinent Pangaea. While Laurasia formed the north-western part of Pangaea and Gondwana, its south-eastern part, the Kaapvaal Craton, was positioned in the south of Gondwana. By 500 million years ago Gondwana was made up of all the future continents of the southern hemisphere.

While southern Africa was still part of Gondwana, extensive geological layers formed on and around the Kaapvaal Craton. The Agulhas sea with its sediments formed over southern Gondwana; and Agulhas sediments formed the Cape super-group rock formations and the Cape mountains between 450 and 310 million years ago. Large-scale climate changes and an extensive development of plant and animal life also occurred. Fossil remains of these plants and animals were preserved in layers of rock. As time went by, dense vegetation growth present in the marshes and river deltas of Gondwana formed coal deposits between 310 and 180 million years ago. Between 1600 and 90 million years ago diamondiferous kimberlite magma also pushed up in volcanic pipes such as those at Kimberley and Cullinan.

A mantle plume rose beneath the southern African part of Gondwana and vast quantities of lava poured through ruptures in the crust to the surface between 182 and 180 million years ago. When Gondwana fragmented between 182 and 65 million years ago, the existing mainlands of Africa, South America, Antarctica, India and Australia, as well as the island of Madagascar were formed in the southern hemisphere, and drifted away from one another. Together with the new northern continents of North America and Eurasia they formed the continents that we know today, along with the present-day coastlines, oceans, ocean currents, winds as well as climatic and weather patterns that developed. These phenomena had a great influence on the development and continued existence of life forms. Another fundamental impact on the African landscapes was the southern African land mass which lifted for the first time approximately 20 million years ago and did so again about 5 million years ago. This gave southern Africa its plateau character and the associated unique topography, climate, plant and animal life as well as the lifestyles of the people who later lived in the region.

During the Pleistocene Epoch, between 2 million and 10 000 years ago, climate variations with associated glacial (ice age) periods in the northern hemisphere caused extremely dry climatic conditions in the interior of southern Africa. During these consecutive ice ages the lowering of atmospheric temperature caused the ice sheets in the polar regions and particularly those from the North Pole, to spread out over a vast area. An enormous quantity of water was therefore trapped in the form of ice sheets, some of which were kilometres thick and covered extensive areas of the Earth's surface. The resultant lowering of water levels in the oceans reduced the level of the sea around the southern African coastline by as much as 130 m.

These changing climatic conditions together contributed to the formation of extensive desert regions in the southern African interior. The Kalahari Desert and the remains of the sand deposits elsewhere in southwestern Africa is today evidence of this primeval desert. During the inter-ice age periods temperatures rose again, the ice sheets in the polar regions decreased in size and the melting ice caused the ocean level to rise. The rainfall in parts of the southern African interior then increased once more and, with this, so did the plant and animal life. These variable environmental changes also influenced the distribution and adaptation to the environment of the Stone Age people in the region. Approximately 220 000 years ago a meteorite which according to scientific interpretations must have been some 30 to 50 m in diameter crashed into the Earth just north of present-day Pretoria and caused the Tswaing impact crater of about 1,13 km wide and 100 m deep.

Approximately 10 000 years ago, after the end of the last ice age and the beginning of the present Holocene Epoch, the present climatic conditions developed. Southern Africa's plateau character, as well as its ocean currents and wind patterns, led to today's climatic, seasonal and weather conditions and the natural environment of the southern African continent. Typical characteristics are the summer rainfall in the north; the winter rainfall in the southern Cape; and higher rainfall in the east and south compared to the arid climatic conditions in the west. Different biome systems that have developed in this period are the present-day fynbos in the Western Cape; the forest biome of the southern Cape coast; the savannah biome in the warmer north; the grassland of the central Highveld; and the succulent Karoo, Nama Karoo and deserts of the arid west.

Timeline

LANDSCAPE ELEMENTS OF SOUTH AFRICA (IN YEARS BEFORE THE PRESENT)
Ca 3600 – 1300 million:
• Earth crust from under the surface of the sea develops as the Barberton mountainous landscape. • Increasing land formation and origin of the Kaapvaal Craton in South Africa. • Extensive mineral deposits form in layers of rock of the Kaapvaal Craton. • Origin of the primeval continents Ur, Arctica, Atlantica and Nena.
Ca 2700 million:
• The mineral-rich Zimbabwe Craton and the Kaapvaal Craton form a single land mass.

Ca 2061 and 2049 million:	
• Origins of the mineral-rich Bushveld and Phalaborwa igneous complexes.	
Ca 2023 million:	
• An asteroid collides with the Kaapvaal Craton and causes the Vredefort Dome and impact crater.	
Ca 1900–1700 million:	
• Origin of the Waterberg group and the Soutpansberg group rock formations; indications in these rocks that oxygen is present at the time of their formation.	
Ca 1600–90 million:	
• Kimberlite magma in volcanic pipes from the Earth's mantle forms diamonds, such as those at Postmasburg, Cullinan (Premier Mine) and Kimberley.	
Ca 1300–500 million:	
• Origins of the supercontinents Rodinia, Pangaea and Gondwana. • The Pilanesberg volcano forms the Pilanesberg mountain range.	
Ca 700–500 million:	
• The Kaapvaal Craton forms part of the developing supercontinent Gondwana.	
Ca 450–310 million:	
• The Agulhas sea with its sediments form over southern Gondwana. • Agulhas sediments form the Cape super-group formations and Cape mountains.	
Ca 310–180 million:	
• North of the Cape mountains an inland lake, rivers and marshes form. • Dense plant growth in the marshes and river deltas form coal deposits. • Dinosaur species emerge and flourish. • Silt deposits form in which, over time, animal and plant fossils are preserved. • Dry climatic conditions cause widespread deserts. • The silt and sandstone deposits form the Karoo super-group rock formations.	
Ca 182–180 million:	
• Basaltic lava covers the ground surface and forms the Drakensberg and Maluti mountain ranges. • Large-scale and long-lasting soil erosion begins to occur.	
Ca 180–65 million:	
• Gondwana fragments and the southern continents, including Africa, are formed. • The southern African coastline, continental shelf and early rivers form. • The mineral-rich Kaapvaal Craton remains a core part of South Africa. • Deep, tropical soils develop.	

Ca 90–20 million:
• The Falkland plateau breaks away from the Cape region and drifts westwards. • The origin of the prehistoric Limpopo River, Kalahari River and Karoo River. • The upper reaches of the Limpopo River are cut off from the rest of the Limpopo River by lifting of the land mass and form an inland lake known as Makgadikgadi. • The Karoo River and Kalahari River merge to form the Orange (Gariep) River.
Ca 20 million:
• Because of pressure from below the crust of the Earth, southern Africa is lifted and develops a plateau character. • Cold ocean currents develop on the west coast and cause arid and desert conditions in the adjacent interior.
Ca 5–2 million:
• The interior plateau is lifted even higher, especially in the east. • Rainfall increases on the eastern plateau ridge. • Dry conditions develop in the western interior. • Origin of the Kalahari Desert.
Ca 2 million–10 000:
• The Pleistocene Epoch, during which ice ages occur in the northern hemisphere and deserts in southern Africa.
Ca 220 000:
• Meteorite collision forms the Tswaing Crater.
Ca 10 000–today
• The Holocene Epoch, during which the present-day climatic conditions, vegetation biomes and animal life develop.

The first people of South Africa

The first hominins (members of the superfamily *Hominoidea* who were upright-walking, human-like primates) existed between 7 and 5 million years ago in East Africa. They are at present known as *Orrorin tugenensis* in Kenya, *Sahelanthropus tchadensis* in Chad and *Ardipithecus ramidus* in Ethiopia.

The Australopithecines (southern apes) were pre-human primates, who lived between about 4,5 million and 1 million years ago on the grass plains and savannah regions of East and southern Africa. They walked upright because their thighs were longer than those of apes, while their arms were shorter and their pelvic skeleton was suited to an upright body position. Different variations of the *Australopithecus* genus were *Australopithecus robustus* and *Australopithecus africanus*. The earliest Australopithecines apparently still lived partially in trees. They lived a simple nomadic lifestyle in the veld searching for edible plants.

The first true humans were hunters and gatherers who had the ability to produce stone tools. Of these the first that have been identified from fossil remains are known as *Homo habilis* ("handy man"); they lived in the Early Stone Age between about 2,5 million and 1,5 million years ago in East Africa and southern Africa. They were hunters and gatherers of veld foods but were physically and intellectually able to apply elementary technology to manufacture and use stone tools. The stone utensils produced by *Homo habilis* were crude stone chopper-like tools and stone flakes which are collectively known as the Oldupai industry (previously known as Olduvai) because some of these ancient tools were first found in the Oldupai Gorge in northern Tanzania.

Important fossil remains of Australopithecines, the first human-like primates and their handmade tools, have also been found in South Africa. Scientists have discovered fossilised parts of Australopithecines' skeletons and their stone tools dating back to 4,5 to 1 million years ago at the world heritage sites which are listed by UNESCO as the Fossil Hominid Sites of Sterkfontein, Swartkrans, Kromdraai and environs, and the Makapan Valley and Taung Skull Fossil Site. The Fossil Hominid Sites of Sterkfontein, Swartkrans and Kromdraai are also known as the Cradle of Humankind. The skeletal remains include those of *Homo habilis* and *Australopithecus sediba*, who lived at Sterkfontein 1,9 million years ago and show evidence of human physical characteristics such as hand, pelvic and foot bones.

Homo erectus, or "erect man" were hunters and gatherers of veld foods who lived in the Early Stone Age between 1,7 million and 250 000 years ago in large parts of Africa. With time they spread to southern Europe, the Near East and Asia. Many of their implements have been found in Africa, for example on the Cape south coast, in gravel layers on the banks of ancient rivers, and in pans in the vicinity of the Gariep and Vaal rivers. They made stone tools which are classified as the Acheulian industry (named after the type site in France). These tools were not only manufactured by hand but were also hand-held when used. Different types of stone tools that were developed during this period were hand-held axes or cleavers and crude stone flakes which were used as knives and scrapers.

Homo sapiens ("wise man") also known as archaic man, lived throughout Africa, southern Europe and Asia from between 5 000 000 and 800 000 years ago to about 100 000 years ago. Physically and intellectually, they were to a large extent comparable to modern humankind. They made specialised stone implements such as knife blades, scrapers and spear tips. An example of the archaic *Homo sapiens* is seen in the fossilised skeletal remains of one such person who lived 260 000 years ago in the vicinity of present-day Florisbad, near Bloemfontein.

Homo sapiens sapiens developed from the archaic *Homo sapiens* between about 250 000 and 20 000 years ago and was already physically and intellectually comparable with modern humankind. They were Stone Age hunters and gatherers in Africa, Europe and Asia. From there their descendants gradually spread to the Americas, Australia and Tasmania. During the Middle Stone Age in South Africa these people were already making advanced stone implements. In Blombos Cave on the Cape south coast sea shells with holes made through them were found that must have been used as body adornment. There were also engraved patterns on ochre – evidence of the oldest prehistoric art dating back some 75 000 years ago.

During the Late Stone Age in South Africa, which lasted from about 20 000 to approximately 200 years ago, nomadic specialised hunters and gatherers were found throughout southern Africa; they used a variety of stone tools for different uses. They were the ancestors of the Khoesan people of southern Africa.

The Khoesan

The people known historically as the Khoesan comprise two related main groups: the San, or Bushmen; and the Khoekhoen (previously Khoikhoi). The Khoesan are descendants of the people of the Late Stone Age and have in part preserved their cultural traditions right up to the present. However, in the last century they have virtually disappeared from large parts of southern Africa.

The San were traditionally nomadic hunters and gatherers of edible veld food and traditionally lived in small family groups in their hunting areas, sheltering under rock overhangs (rock shelters) or in shallow caves or making rudimentary shelters from branches and grass. Their typical hunting weapons were bows and poisoned arrows. Rock paintings on the walls of rock shelters and engravings on rocks in the open veld depicting people, animals and abstract symbols are found throughout southern Africa and are associated with the San. Some of the richest San rock art sites up to some 4000 years old are located in the uKhahlamba Drakensberg National Park in South Africa, which together with the Sehlathebe National Park in Lesotho form the trans-boundary Maloti-Drakensberg Park world heritage site. The surviving San communities currently live in the arid north-west of southern Africa, particularly in the Kalahari region in Botswana.

The Khoekhoen lived in traditional family groups in makeshift reed huts. The framework of wooden canes was covered with plaited reeds (reed mats) and this basic building material was carried on pack-oxen from one campsite to the next. Skeletal remains of domesticated sheep dating back about 2000 years have been found in Late Stone Age settlement deposits in the rock shelters on the Cape coast and are attributed to the early Khoekhoe hunters. These hunters were already nomadic herders of small livestock and gradually acquired cattle, presumably from Bantu-speaking Iron Age subsistence farmers. Until the onset of the colonial period, these Khoekhoe groups became fairly prosperous livestock pastoralists. A Khoekhoe society, which today still maintains a traditional pastoral lifestyle, are the semi-nomadic Nama of the Richtersveld and the Richtersveld Cultural and Botanical Landscape world heritage site.

Timeline

PRE-HUMAN PRIMATES AND EARLY PEOPLE OF EAST AND SOUTH AFRICA (IN YEARS BEFORE THE PRESENT)
Ca 7–6 million:
• The first hominins appear in East Africa: *Orrorin tugenensis* in Kenya and *Sahelanthropus tchadensis* in Chad. Hominins are extinct members of the superfamily *Hominoidea*: upright-walking, human-like primates.
Ca 5 million:
• *Ardipithecus ramidus* appears in Ethiopia.

Ca 4 million:	
• *Australopithecus anamensis* emerges in Ethiopia.	
Ca 3.8–3 million:	
• *Australopithecus afarensis* emerges in Kenya and Tanzania.	
Ca 3,3 million:	
• *Kenyanthropus platyops* appears in Kenya.	
Ca 3 million:	
• *Australopithecus africanus* emerges in South Africa.	
Ca 2,6 million:	
• *Australopithecus robustus* and the first handmade stone tools appear.	
Ca 2,6 million–200 000:	
• Early Stone Age cultures of southern Africa.	
Ca 2,5–1,5 million:	
• *Homo habilis* ("handy man") appears in East Africa and South Africa. They make some of the first stone implements in South Africa.	
Ca 2 million–10 000:	
• Pleistocene Epoch and ice ages.	
Ca 1,9 million:	
• *Australopithecus sediba* with human-like characteristics lives at Sterkfontein.	
Ca 1,7 million–250 000:	
• *Homo erectus* appears in East and southern Africa and expands into Eurasia. They make stone implements known as the Acheulian industry.	
Ca 800 000–500 000:	
• Early archaic *Homo sapiens* ("wise man") emerges.	
Ca 250 000–20 000:	
• *Homo sapiens sapiens* develops and spreads throughout the world.	
Ca 10 000–present	
• Holocene Epoch • Present climate, landscapes and human populations develop.	

The Iron Age and the Bantu-speaking societies

Indigenous early farming and metal working communities were already present 2000 years ago in North Africa; in the Sudan region; in Cameroon; and in East Africa. From there they spread southwards via the East African Great Lakes region and the coast.

The skeletal remains of cattle, goats, sheep, poultry and dogs, as well as the identifiable remnants of grain and bean crops, have been found in many Iron Age settlements. Evidence of mixed subsistence farming in the Iron Age is still apparent on many sites, with Mapungubwe as one of the most important examples. Mapungubwe was the capital of an early southern African kingdom or small state in the Limpopo river valley in the northern part of South Africa between AD 1000 and 1300. Today it is part of the Mapungubwe National Park and the Mapungubwe Cultural Landscape world heritage site.

The origin of domesticated animals kept by Iron Age people can be traced back to East and North Africa, the Near East and Asia. The domesticated goat (*Capra hircus*) evolved from the west Asian goat (*Capra aegagrus*) and together with Iron Age people they spread southwards from Egypt as far as South Africa. The domesticated sheep (*Ovis aries*) has evolved from a wild Asiatic predecessor (*Ovis orientalis*), while both thin-tailed and fat-tailed sheep (which feature in rock art in Zimbabwe) spread via the west coast of southern Africa to the Cape south coast. The origin of African cattle goes back to the humpless *Bos taurus* of Eurasia; *Bos indicus* of Asia (which had a hump); and the indigenous *Bos primigenius* of North Africa. The domesticated fowl (*Gallus gallus*) comes from India and south-eastern Asia, from where it spread to northern, western and southern Africa. The domesticated dog (*Canis familiaris*) appears to have evolved from the south-east Asian wolf (*Canis lupus arabs*).

The grain crops cultivated by the Iron Age people also originated in north-eastern and East Africa. Drought and environment resistant sorghum varieties developed from *Sorghum verticilliflorum* from East Africa and *Sorghum bicolor* from north-eastern Africa. Millet varieties that were grown include *Pennisetum glaucum*, which grows wild in the Sahara region, and *Pennisetum typhoides* from East Africa. The bean (*Vigna unguiculata*) was one of several species of the widely grown drought-resistant genus *Vigna* in the arid savannah regions south of the Sahara.

Some of these subsistence-farming communities who made iron tools and adornments of iron and copper, settled in the savannah regions of the northern and north-eastern parts of southern Africa in the Early Iron Age between AD 400 and 800. By the Middle Iron Age, i.e. between AD 800 and 1600, communities were tending to live in larger, more permanent settlements. Their economy, which was based on mixed subsistence farming with cattle, goats, sheep and chickens as well as crops such as sorghum, millet and bean varieties, was closely associated with the development of their specific technology, settlement patterns and social life. Their cultural traditions included more socially complex community structures and their kingdoms often developed into small African states.

An early example of this was the inland tribal kingdom of Mapungubwe which is distinguishable, among other things, for the crafting and possession of gold cultural objects. This, as well as the settlement pattern (the layout of the site, terraced stone walls and stone steps) also indicate the residents' royal status. According to African tribal tradition, the little gold rhinoceros and remains of a gold sceptre or royal staff which archaeologists found at Mapungubwe were symbols of the social status and the power that is attributed to a king. Gold cultural objects and royal staffs are also associated with similar, still existing kingdoms in south-eastern Africa.

Similar sites of later indigenous kingdoms are Great Zimbabwe and Khami in the present-day Zimbabwe. The people of those kingdoms exchanged gold, copper and iron – which they discovered in their natural form and mined – and also ivory, to seafaring Swahili traders from the East Coast of Africa, and to Arabian and Portuguese traders for goods such as glass beads and Chinese ceramics that were manufactured outside Africa. The Great Zimbabwe National Monument and Khami Ruins National Monument are listed by UNESCO as world heritage sites.

The Iron Age societies in southern Africa of the Late Iron Age (between AD 1500 and AD 1800) were the predecessor societies of the kingdoms which later in the historical period became known as the Bantu-speaking societies. Their settlement sites with middens or domestic refuse dumps, stone ruins, graves, remnants of metalworking and sherds of clay pots, are widely scattered in the northern, eastern and central parts of South Africa, from the sub-tropical East Coast and the savannah region of the Lowveld to the grass plains of the Highveld and the mountainous regions of the present-day Swaziland and Lesotho. Their characteristic societal structures developed into tribal kingdoms. A tribal kingdom is a kin-based population group with its own identity and a hierarchical sociopolitical ranking structure. It also has a communal lifestyle, traditions, a feeling of solidarity and an own geographical residential and subsistence-farming area.

The Bantu-speaking indigenous African societies of southern Africa are historically identified collectively, on grounds of their language, as the south-eastern Bantu speakers. They can further be divided into the Nguni and the Sotho-Tswana peoples of South Africa and Botswana; the Tsonga people of Mozambique (some of whom live in the north-east of South Africa); the Shona of Zimbabwe; the Venda of South Africa (who are related to the Shona); and the Lemba, most of whom live in small groups with other communities such as the Venda and Sotho in the Limpopo region.

In prehistoric times the Nguni belonged to one language group, but over the centuries they divided into smaller groups, each of which developed their own cultural character and language dialect. As a result of this division of the original Nguni groups, by the nineteenth century various Nguni kingdoms were scattered in the vicinity of Swaziland; to the east into present-day KwaZulu-Natal; and southwards towards what is now the Eastern Cape. Some of these groups also moved into a region northeast and east of present-day Pretoria and further north in the Limpopo Province.

By the seventeenth century the northern Nguni comprised three related groups, the Lala, Mbo and Ntungwa. The northern Nguni later split up into various kingdoms who by 1800 had settled in the area north of the Mzimvubu River and south-east of Swaziland and the Drakensberg range. As far as we know, the southern Nguni have lived in the vicinity of the Mzimvubu River since 1600. Among the most prominent groups are the Mpondo, Mpondomise, Thembu and Xhosa. A characteristic of traditional Nguni settlements were their dome-shaped huts which were arranged in a half-circle around the central cattle kraal.

According to tradition, by the seventeenth to the nineteenth century the Ndebele people were already living in the vicinity of the present-day Gauteng, Mpumalanga and Limpopo. The Manala Ndebele apparently lived in the northern and eastern part of what is now the greater City of Tshwane municipal area, while the Ndzundza Ndebele could be found further to the east and into the present-day Steelpoort region in Mpumalanga. The Kekana Ndebele and Langa Ndebele settled in the south of what is now the Limpopo Province. A more recent settlement characteristic of the Ndebele of the north-eastern Highveld is the brightly coloured geometric patterns painted on the walls of their homes. Some of these motives are inspired by everyday contemporary objects and structures. The Ndebele in the northern provinces of South Africa are differentiated from the Matabele who were the followers of Mzilikazi. The Matabele are often also categorised as Ndebele, but they left the Zulu area in the nineteenth century and formed the Matabele kingdom north of the Vaal River before eventually moving to the western part of today's Zimbabwe.

The Sotho are residents of the inland plateau of South Africa and Botswana. Some of their predecessors' villages are recognisable as ruined stonewall settlements. The original Sotho eventually divided into a number of core groups and later spread out in the interior of South Africa and eastern Botswana. Extensive Iron Age residential sites dated from AD 700 to 1300 at Moritsane and Tautswe Hill in south-east Botswana are regarded as the capital of predecessors of the Kgalagadi, while prominent Kgalagadi groups were inhabitants of the Molopo region.

The Fokeng and the Digoya were early residents in the Highveld in the Vaal River area – the Digoya in the area south of the Vaal, and the Rolong in the area between the Vaal, Harts and Molopo rivers. Breakaway groups of the original Tswana are the Hurutshe, who settled on the upper reaches of the Marico River; the Kwena of the Marico and Crocodile River regions; and the Kgatla of the Witwatersrand area. An important breakaway group of the Kgatla is the Pedi in the region near the Steelpoort River in Mpumalanga. Examples of Sotho societies with a colourful history and distinguishing cultural characteristics like well-preserved examples of rondavel architecture and traditional practices such as social etiquette, clothing, food and household artefacts, are the Hananwa of Blouberg and the Sotho of Lesotho.

Tsonga groups such as the Nhlanganu, Tshangana, Nkuna and others of the eastern Lowveld area in the Limpopo Province and Mpumalanga and northern KwaZulu-Natal are offshoots of the Tsonga of southern Mozambique. For centuries, Tsonga societies such as the Tembe were involved in the ivory trade and apparently also traded gold with seafarers such as the Portuguese, who by the early sixteenth century had established a trading post at Baía da Lagoa, now known as Maputo. Their traditional settlement areas provide evidence of various building styles including rondavel-type dwellings and grain storage huts.

The Venda is a separate group. According to tradition, they moved from the north to settle in the Limpopo and Soutpansberg regions towards the beginning of the eighteenth century. As far as language and culture are concerned, they appear to be related to the Shona of Zimbabwe, but some scholars maintain that the Venda originally descended from the Makonde of Lake Malawi. According to language research, the Venda language is more closely related to that of the Kalanga, who are also known as the Western Shona, a group that lives in the western parts of Zimbabwe and the eastern border area of Botswana. The Kalanga possibly migrated via the Shashi and Limpopo river valleys in a south-easterly direction during or after the era of the Mapungubwe Kingdom. After their arrival in present-day South Africa, the Venda gradually divided into various kingdoms. Notable Venda settlement characteristics are the rondavel architecture, often on stone terraces against mountain slopes, and their colourful traditional ceremonies accompanied by music, dance and colourful clothes.

Some historians are of the opinion that the Lemba, who according to tradition arrived in South Africa together with the Venda, earlier came under the cultural influence of the Moslem traders on the east coast of Africa. They are skilled craftsmen and traders and often serve as dignitaries at traditional ceremonies.

2

The Dutch era at the Cape, 1652–1806

Johan de Villiers

Patterns of modern South African society became established when different groups of people in the subcontinent came into contact with one another during the seventeenth century. The South African society of today developed out of this melting pot.

South Africa's geographical location made contact with the outside world difficult. It is possible that Arab and Indian traders along the east coast did not travel further south than Delagoa Bay. It was a remarkable achievement when Portuguese navigators rounded the southern tip of Africa at the end of the fifteenth century.

Bartholomew Dias (1488) and Vasco da Gama (1498) both sailed in small vessels that were exposed to the fierce winds and high seas of the South Atlantic Ocean and the rugged, inhospitable Cape coast. It must have been idealism that made Dias change his original name of Cape of Storms (*Cabo Tormentoso*) to Cape of Good Hope (*Cabo da Boa Esperança*) in his report to King João II. He sailed around the southernmost point of Africa in a howling gale and reached the coast of Africa near what is now Mossel Bay.

In order to survive, the indigenous residents of the subcontinent made distinctive adaptations to the changing climatic conditions, topography and available natural resources. The wide spread of small self-sufficient communities over a large area limited mutual contact, but did not rule it out completely. The local coastal dwellers were startled and apprehensive at the arrival of unfamiliar foreign visitors who wished to barter fresh water and meat. They could not understand one another's language and customs. In some instances this led to clashes such as in 1510 when the Viceroy of Portuguese India, Francisco d' Almeida, died in an incident in

Table Bay. Thereafter Portuguese seafarers tried to avoid landings on this coast. A permanent legacy of the Portuguese navigators to South Africa is their naming of certain coastal features and places such as St Helena Bay, Saldanha Bay, St Francis Bay, Infanta River and Natal territory.

Sporadic contact between the indigenous residents and seafarers from other Western European countries such as Denmark, England, the Netherlands and France continued during the course of the sixteenth and early seventeenth century. They were for the first time able to experience one another's distinctive languages, clothes, daily articles, music and dance. In 1620 Augustin de Beaulieu noted that the indigenous people's characteristic dancing songs always repeated the word "hautitau". And in 1623 the Dane Jon Olafsson confirmed the repetitive word "hottentots" in their typical dancing chant. By word of mouth visitors such as Nicolaus de Graaff (1640) and Jean-Baptiste Tavernier (1649) began to use this word as a general name for the local inhabitants.

On 25 March 1647 the cargo vessel *Nieuwe Haerlem* went aground in the vicinity of the later Blaauwberg, north of the Salt River mouth. The crew members were saved and much of the cargo was salvaged, but there was not enough room for everyone on the ships that were departing on the return voyage. Junior merchant Leendert Jansz and 62 of the shipwrecked men had to wait more than a year for an opportunity to return to the Netherlands. In 1649, now back home, Jansz and Matthijs Proot compiled a *remonstrantie* (report) in which they argued that a permanent refreshment station in Table Bay would be of great convenience to vessels on their voyages to and from the commercial stations of the Dutch East India Company (*Vereenigde Oost-Indische Compagnie*, abbreviated VOC). They experienced that the indigenous people were peaceable when they were well treated. The local people were prepared to learn the Dutch language and to engage in barter. Moreover the soil around Table Bay was suitable for cultivation and adequate water was available for irrigation.

> **THE VOC**
>
> In 1602 various small trading companies based in the Netherlands merged to form the Dutch East India Company (the VOC). It comprised six autonomous managerial bodies, namely the trading chambers of Amsterdam, Zeeland, Rotterdam, Delft, Hoorn and Enkhuizen. All the chambers were under the management of a council comprising seventeen directors - called the Here XVII (Council of Seventeen) which usually met in Amsterdam.

> In March 1602 the States General, the highest governing authority in the Netherlands, granted a charter to the VOC which gave it the monopoly of all its trade east of the Cape of Good Hope and west of the Straits of Magellan. In 1619 a governor general and a Council of India were appointed to act on behalf of the VOC in respect of all local matters; they were to be headquartered in Batavia, on the island of Java.
>
> Thereby the VOC with its charter gained virtually sovereign control over all its trading posts and in practice it was only responsible to its shareholders. This made the Company a highly profitable body. The VOC was in reality the first large stock exchange or stock market in the world. Shareholders received a dividend which was initially in the form of goods supplied.
>
> Eventually the Company was liquidated after 196 years due to chronic mismanagement and an enormous debt burden of 110 million guilders.

Settlement at the Cape

In 1650 the Council of Seventeen decided in principle to set up a refreshment post at the Cape. The choice of a commander for this task eventually fell on Johan Antoniszoon van Riebeeck. His previous experience in service of the Company (in Batavia, Japan and Tonkin) as well as his personal impressions of the Cape of Good Hope in 1648, proved decisive.

On 6 April 1652 Van Riebeeck arrived in Table Bay with three ships, named the *Drommedaris*, *Goede Hoop* and *Reijger*. The rest of his party only arrived a month later in two additional ships, *Walvis* and *Oliphant*.

The orders from the Council of Seventeen were clear: Only a small area was to be developed as a refreshment post for the visiting vessels of the VOC. The main purpose was to provide the Company's ships with fresh meat, vegetables and water. About 90 people were assigned this task. For safety reasons Van Riebeeck was instructed to build a fort (Fort de Goede Hoop), but preferably peace was to be maintained with the indigenous people and visitors from other countries. The Company's main purpose was that the refreshment post should not only limit expenses, but at the same time be profitable to the VOC. Local government was run by a political council which comprised Van Riebeeck as chairperson, his deputy commander, the sergeant and the bookkeeper. The first meeting on 8 April 1652 made practical decisions about the security of the small settlement and the relationship with the indigenous people.

The Khoekhoen in the vicinity of the Cape Peninsula were cattle herders and were important for providing a regular supply of meat to the Company's ships in Table Bay. To supply meat to some thirty ships at a time meant that about 300 cattle and 300 sheep had to be acquired by bartering. Copper disks, iron objects, tobacco and red glass beads were popular items of exchange. The Khoekhoen also enjoyed bread, wine and arrack (rice brandy). Van Riebeeck and his officials needed an interpreter to avoid any misunderstanding. Consequently, successful use was made of Autshumao (alias Herry, the beachcomber), his sister's child Krotoa (alias Eva), Doman (alias Anthonie) and Dorha (alias Claas Das).

Despite several attempts Van Riebeeck could not resolve the shortage of meat. The Khoekhoen were not prepared to barter cattle for various exchange articles if this meant a drastic decrease of their own herds. There was also internal division and a lack of trust among them. The communities in the vicinity of the Cape Peninsula were the Goringhaicona (also called Strandlopers, under Autshumao), the Goringhaiqua (also called Kaapmans, under Gogosoa), the Gorachouqua (also called Tabakdiewe, under Choro and Ankaisoa) and the Cochoqua (under Oldasoa and Gonnema). Further north were the Namaqua.

Van Riebeeck's patience with the Khoekhoen was tested to breaking point. On 19 October 1653 Autshumao and his followers stole virtually all the Company's livestock and killed the herd-boy, David Jansz. When Autshumao showed up again at the fort in June 1655, Van Riebeeck had to accept all his excuses and apologies. The interpreter Doman, who took over Autshumao's task, meanwhile advised the Kaapmans to steal the livestock from the refreshment station in rainy weather because with damp fuse igniters and gunpowder Van Riebeeck's people would not be able to use their flint-lock firearms effectively.

In July 1659, when the Kaapmans stabbed the herdsman Sijmon in 't Velt to death and took 68 head of cattle and 67 sheep, Van Riebeeck called up the local soldiers and burghers. The Kaapmans reacted with evasive action, but in a skirmish that followed, three Khoekhoen were killed. It was only in April and May 1660 that peace was brokered with the various leaders after a fixed border and specific entry routes for both groups had been laid down. Thereafter the official policy of appeasement was resumed.

As livestock herders and in their bartering transactions the Khoekhoen became more accustomed to the Dutch language, lifestyle, clothing and daily articles. During the refreshment station's first decade of existence, there was only one Christian convert among the Khoekhoen, namely Krotoa. She was taken into Van Riebeeck and his wife Maria's home in the fort as a housekeeper when still a young girl and everyone called her Eva.

> **THE NAMING OF THE KHOEKHOEN**
>
> Most of the indigenous coloured residents of the Cape were known in the seventeenth and eighteenth centuries as "Hottentots", although they were divided into smaller groups or communities, each with a particular name. The general name Hottentot had attained documentation status by Van Riebeeck's time. Only in the nineteenth century was "people of colour" used as an alternative name by, among others, the British governor Richard Bourke.
>
> Because of the negative connotations associated with the word "Hottentot", researchers, particularly those in the latter half of the twentieth century, began to use the more innate ethnonym "Khoekhoen" as an alternative spelling. This double-stemmed name literally means "person of people".

Free burghers and expansion at the Cape

In 1657, in order to improve the provision of especially vegetables and tobacco at the refreshment post, Van Riebeeck granted small farms along the Liesbeek River in the vicinity of Rondebosch to nine members of Company staff and their families. The Company would buy all the produce of the free burghers and they were not permitted to trade with the Khoekhoen.

Visiting VOC commissioner, Rijckloff van Goens, agreed that the number of free burghers could increase and that they should be given Company assistance in the form of ploughs and draught oxen. The property of the Company and the free burghers was demarcated and protected by a number of small forts (Kijkuyt, Duinhoop, Keert de Koe, Coornhoop, Ruyterwacht and Houd den Bul), palisades and a row of wild almond trees some of which can still be seen in Kirstenbosch Botanic Gardens). The free burghers experienced many difficulties and Van Riebeeck had to handle their complaints circumspectly, without damaging the Company's interests.

In time, the free burghers were also permitted to follow careers other than agriculture. Some made a living as skilled tradesmen, entrepreneurs and professional people. They originated mainly from the Netherlands and the surrounding German- and French-speaking regions.

The introduction of free burghers in 1657 changed the original refreshment post into an expanding colony. At the same time the Company officials who saw their work at the Cape as temporary came up against free burghers who regarded the Cape as their permanent home. Between 1657 and 1702 the free burghers grew in number from 14 to 1368.

> **VAN RIEBEECK'S SIGNIFICANCE**
>
> Jan van Riebeeck (1619-1677) was a devoted Company official during his ten years at the Cape. His business sense, adaptability and skill as a negotiator in various areas made him a pioneer. As leader of the society in Table Valley he acted reasonably and fairly.
>
> He reached a provisional agreement with the Khoekhoen and promoted exploratory expeditions. His experiments in the agricultural sector provided his successors with a valuable legacy. His thankless task as a commander in times of crisis was not duly recognised by his contemporaries (local employees as well as his colleagues overseas). And yet the successful establishment of the Company's refreshment station at the Cape under his leadership became a symbol of hope amidst much frustration and disillusionment.

Slaves and free blacks

Van Riebeeck regarded the local Khoekhoen as physically unsuitable for land cultivation and other means of manual labour. His suggestion to supplement the labour supply by using sailors from visiting ships in a temporary capacity was rejected by the Council of Seventeen. However, Van Riebeeck was given permission to import slaves. The first slaves, from Angola and Guinea, arrived at the Cape in 1658 aboard the ships *Amersfoort* and *Hasselt*. In this way a new element was added to the composition of the society at the Cape.

Thereafter more slaves were brought in from Madagascar and Asia. They were from widely different regions and bound to learn the language of the Company officials and their Dutch owners. Desertion of slaves was severely punished. By 1693 there were 322 slaves (including men, women and children) in the service of the Company at the Cape. Subsequently, the number of slaves in the service of free burghers began to exceed those of the Company. The slaves certainly made an enormous contribution to the economic development of the Cape, particularly in the agricultural sector, but also as accomplished tradesmen and domestic workers. Malay slaves were especially sought after because of their skills in the trade and building industry.

Emancipation of slaves and/or their children by owners created a distinctive minority group in Cape society which became known as "free blacks". Examples of economically active free blacks in the seventeenth century were Louis from Bengal and Anthonie from Angola both of whom had small farms in the Jonkershoek Valley near Stellenbosch.

The Huguenots

When Simon van der Stel took office in 1679 as commander of the Cape, the first free burghers had already moved over the Cape Flats to the Eerste River. Meanwhile, the Company also set up cattle posts in the regions of Hottentots-Holland, Tygerberg and Saldanha Bay. In the same year of his arrival Van der Stel established the first inland town, Stellenbosch, named after himself. In 1687 a second settlement on the Berg River was named Drakenstein.

Van der Stel's plans to colonise were promoted when the King of France, Louis XIV, revoked the Edict of Nantes in 1685. This robbed the French Protestants of their religious freedom and thousands of these Huguenots fled to neighbouring countries, including the Netherlands.

Between 1688 and 1692 the Council of Seventeen sent about 200 of these Huguenots to the Cape to boost the free burgher population. They represented about 23,5% of the free burgher population of 856 people. In their interaction with the free burghers the relatively small number of Huguenots exercised a significant influence on developments at the Cape.

Van der Stel scattered the Huguenots on small farms between the Dutch free burghers in Stellenbosch, Drakenstein, Franschhoek (Olifantshoek), Paarl and the Wagenmakersvallei (present-day Wellington) in order to promote their assimilation. However, in 1691 they were permitted to have their own minister of religion, the Rev. Pierre Simond, and their own schoolmaster, Paul Roux, in Drakenstein.

The Huguenots became the founders of the wine industry in the Cape Colony and helped to increase wheat production. Furthermore, their Calvinist attitudes strengthened the free-burgher population's outlook on life. Well-known Voortrekkers such as Piet Retief and Sarel Cilliers were descendants of the Huguenots.

Resistance against the governor

In 1699 Simon van der Stel handed over the rule at the Cape to his eldest son, Willem Adriaan van der Stel. An increased level of unity among the burghers and a greater variety of agricultural activities were the hallmarks of the Van der Stel era (1699–1707).

W.A. van der Stel encouraged progressive farming methods and particularly sheep farming in the Land van Waveren (north of the Drakenstein Mountains in the vicinity of today's Tulbagh). Without the knowledge of the Council of Seventeen he farmed privately on the farm Vergelegen near present-day Somerset West and used the Company's labour and implements to make it a prosperous model farm. Other highly placed officials followed his example, including the second-in-command Samuel Elsevier, the minister of religion Petrus Kalden, and W.A. van der Stel's younger brother Frans (jokingly called Don Francisco).

Dissatisfaction among the free burghers reached crisis proportions when the governor's favourite, Johannes Phijffer, gained full control of the Cape wine concession. Adam Tas, Henning Hüsing and other angry free burghers submitted a petition to the Council of Seventeen in 1705 in which they complained about the governor's misuse of power. Van der Stel, who suspected trouble was brewing, drew up a positive testimonial absolving himself of all blame. He then set about trying to identify the leaders of the resistance.

When asked who had forced him to sign the alleged petition against the governor, the Huguenot Guillaume du Toit answered in all honesty: "My conscience, my Master!". On 25 February 1706 the governor had Adam Tas arrested and took possession of documents from his desk. The burghers Jacques de Savoye, Pieter Meyer and Jakobus van der Heiden were even held in the notorious "Dark Hole" in the Castle at Cape Town.

In the meantime the Council of Seventeen in the Netherlands appointed a commission of inquiry as soon as it received the burghers' petition. Word of this positive development reached the Cape on 20 February

1707 with the arrival of the frigate *Peter and Paul*. The following night the burgher Albert van Emmenes rode through the streets of Stellenbosch shouting loudly: "Victory! Victory!"

Shortly afterwards, on Sunday, 4 March, a number of excited youths ran amok in the streets of Stellenbosch, near the town's mill. When the magistrate, Johannes Starrenburg, arrived to find out what the noise was all about, he confronted two of the culprits who could not get away in time with a cane. One of them was the unruly 16-year-old Hendrik Biebouw. According to eye witnesses he uttered the following meaningful words (translated): "I will not back down, I am an Afrikaner; even if the magistrate beats me to death or throws me into jail, I shall not be silenced!"

This is the first contemporary evidence of a burgher identifying himself as an Afrikaner. Thereby the bewildered Biebouw apparently expressed his sense of belonging to an emerging South African nationhood and his dissatisfaction with the Company's officials. In the broader context these events were an indication of increasing competition between some burghers and officials in the small community of Stellenbosch.

The eventual outcome of the burghers' resistance was that the Council of Seventeen relieved the governor, his deputy Elsevier, magistrate Starrenburg and minister of religion Kalden of their posts. The two Van der Stel brothers and the guilty officials left for the Netherlands in April 1708, never to return.

Colonial expansion and the Khoekhoen

The Khoekhoen were not particularly warlike towards the burghers. Only a few groups were involved in repeated theft of livestock and attacks on burghers. The so-called Second Khoekhoen War (1673–1677) was no more than a number of skirmishes. The punitive expeditions also launched by the authorities against the Cochoquas under Gonnema were not very successful against such an elusive enemy.

Various factors were responsible for the detribalisation and the dwindling number of Khoekhoen in the eighteenth century. Unequal bartering for livestock with Company officials and free burghers, inter-group rivalry and conflict, theft of livestock and loss of animals to disease all played a role in the decline of the Khoekhoen. In order to survive, many of them worked for burghers as cattle herders or wagon drivers. Contagious disease also took its toll in detribalisation. The dreaded smallpox epidemics of 1713, 1755 and 1767 totally wiped out some groups of Khoekhoen and drastically reduced the number of others. The first signs of smallpox were noted on 18 April 1713 at the Slave Lodge in Cape Town. This contagious and deadly disease was apparently passed on by the washing that was brought ashore from visiting ships. The Khoekhoen were very susceptible to this disease and before long it was reported to the authorities that Khoekhoen who had fled into the interior caused the epidemic to spread even more rapidly.

There are no exact statistics, but the visiting author François Valentijn confirmed that the epidemic wiped out literally hundreds of Khoekhoen in some districts of the colony. The Swedish traveller Anders Sparrman also found that in 1776 an unknown "gall fever" caused great loss of life especially among the Khoekhoen. According to the census of 1805, there were only about 20 000 Khoekhoen left in the Cape Colony. By this time they had become a landless proletariat and had to a large extent sacrificed their own language and traditional lifestyle in order to comply with Western lifestyle and norms.

On the question of to whom the farming lands in the colony belonged, there are divergent opinions. The Khoekhoen laid claim in communal context to residential and grazing land in certain regions. Their nomadic lifestyle was to a large extent dependant on the availability of water. Within the restricted official borders of the initial Cape settlement, ownership of farms was granted to burghers. They could apply annually for grazing licences in uninhabited areas. By 1714 there were already about 400 farms made available for wheat and wine production. The Khoekhoen's traditional lifestyle brought them into contact with these landowners. After the smallpox epidemic of 1713, when independent livestock farmers officially also obtained loan farms, the traditional lifestyle of many of the detribalised Khoekhoen within the expanded colonial borders came under increasing pressure.

Initially, the Company officials and burghers simply differentiated themselves from the Khoekhoen on grounds of religious considerations, namely as Christians and distinct from heathen. However, by the mid-eighteenth century this differentiation became ever more dependent on race and a markedly different status in the social hierarchy at the Cape. As early as 1661 a school teacher was appointed in Cape Town to educate the Khoekhoen in the Dutch language and Christian religion. Some burghers in the isolated interior did not exclude their workers from their family devotions, but the standard of living of the Khoekhoen did not benefit a great deal from this. Generally speaking, they were poorly paid and lived in their traditional reed huts near the homestead of the farmer. Organised missionary activity among the Khoekhoen in the colony met with opposition in 1742 when the Moravian missionary Georg Schmidt was forbidden by the Cape authorities – after complaints were received from ordained ministers of religion and some church members – to administer the sacraments to converted Khoekhoen at Baviaanskloof.

However, by the end of the eighteenth century, many burghers had adopted a new, more positive outlook on Christian mission stations among the Khoekhoen. This can be attributed to the spirit of philanthropy at the time and the zeal of ministers and missionaries. In 1799 the Zuid-Afrikaansche Zendelings Genootschap (South African Missionary Society) was formed in Cape Town to work with overseas missionary societies to promote mission work, particularly among the Khoekhoen. In 1792 the Moravians re-opened the Baviaanskloof mission station and in 1805 it was renamed Genadendal. This soon proved an example to be followed; it set a standard of integrity which inspired respect from the authorities and burghers alike.

In the military sphere there was close co-operation between the burghers and the detribalised Khoekhoen. Among the workers there were those individuals who learnt to shoot accurately with the old muzzle loaders. This was necessary when hunting game, but also for better protection of livestock against thieves and wild predators. Because of the limited number of soldiers in the Cape garrison, a unique commando system developed in the interior. It was dependent upon the close co-operation between mounted burghers, free blacks and experienced Khoekhoen, with the approval of the magistrate (landdrost) of the relevant district.

In 1781 a Corps Bastaard Hottentotten (ethnically mixed Khoekhoen) was established in Cape Town to assist in defence against a possible outside attack on the colony. The force of 400 troops was under the command of two burgher officers, Hendrik Eksteen and Gerrit Munnik. When a group of French mercenaries were sent to the Cape shortly afterwards, the Khoekhoe soldiers were able to return to the farms from where they were drafted. In 1793 it became necessary to establish a Corps Pandoeren (Pandour Corps) comprising 200 Khoekhoen under command of a burgher officer, Captain Jan Cloete. This was the beginning of a long period of professional military service by Khoekhoen and people of mixed parentage in the Cape Colony.

The fate of the Bushmen

The Bushmen were the closest descendants of the primeval inhabitants of southern Africa. Company officials and visitors of the seventeenth century gave them the descriptive name "Bosjesmannen" (people of the bushes) because they often hid away from strangers, timidly sheltering behind shrubs and bushes.

The hunting way of life of the Bushmen meant that they were involved almost continually in a struggle with livestock owners in the interior. The best grazing lands were also the best hunting areas. In this regard the Khoekhoen and free-burgher stock farmers were natural allies in skirmishes against Bushmen hunters, with their deadly poisoned arrows, who desperately attempted to protect their hunting areas from increasing penetration by livestock farmers.

In 1688 the Bushmen attacked several cattle herders in the Drakenstein region. Simon van der Stel then ordered that this "enemy" be attacked. By 1700 livestock farming in the interior increased even more and the struggle against Bushmen grew even fiercer. In 1715 garrison soldiers in the Drakenstein region were for the first time replaced by exclusively burgher commandos. Armed burghers were also placed in the passes over the Hex River Mountains, Piekenierskloof and in the Witzenberg to trap fleeing Bushmen. Several Bushmen and two burghers were killed in these commando deployments. In 1739 another large commando was sent out against plundering Bushmen in the Roodezand and Piketberg vicinities. And in 1754 a similar commando sent into the Bokkeveld and Roggeveld managed to retrieve a considerable number of stolen cattle and concluded a temporary peace with that particular Bushman community.

By 1770 livestock farmers (both Khoekhoen and burgher herders) had spread to the central highlands of the colony. Between 1786 and 1795 Bushmen from the Roggeveld, Hantam, Nuweveld and Sneeuberg stole large numbers of cattle and killed no less than 276 herd-boys and farmers. In skirmishes with burgher commandos many Bushmen perished. In a single commando operation at the end of 1774 some 503 Bushmen were shot dead and 241 women and children taken captive. In certain cases the total annihilation of Bushmen seemed to be the objective.

By 1795 it seemed evident that any concerted struggle between the livestock farmers and Bushmen had become largely a thing of the past. The remaining Bushmen spread out northwards into the Gariep (Orange) River region. In 1798 the Cape authorities sent *veldwagmeesters* (local civil and military representatives) to the remaining groups of Bushmen between the Sak River and Kareeberg with a gift of sheep and an offer of peace. The conflict of the Khoekhoen and burghers against the Bushmen during the eighteenth century is a tragic history of suffering in an open frontier situation, where the weakest party had to bow to the superiority of the strongest power.

> **THE NAMING OF THE SAN AND KHOESAN**
> The Khoekhoen called the small fleet-footed hunter-gatherers who often stole their sheep by the derogatory name "San" or "Sana". The names "Sonqua" or "Obiqua", which they also used for these people, literally meant "bandits" or "murderers".
> The term "Khoesan" (Khoisan) is a relatively new formulation derived in the twentieth century. It attempts to capture the common characteristics of the Bushmen and Khoekhoen, but there are also valid reasons for recognising the unique identity of each of these groups separately.
> In contrast to the Khoekhoen, the Bushmen lived in small family groups and had no societal power structure such as a chieftain or tribal leader. They were small in stature and lived a nomadic lifestyle to make the best use of hunting areas and available veld foods. They used stone tools and hunted with bows and arrows. They lived in caves or under makeshift shelters covered with branches. Their unique rock art, comprising drawings and engravings, apparently had religious connotations.

Slaves and their half-caste offspring

Although slavery was unquestionably a social evil, it was practised widely throughout the world in the eighteenth century. In the Cape Colony slave labour was regarded as essential for the local economy. Able and hard-working slaves were a financial asset and investment for their individual owners, while slave labour was also financially advantageous for the Company as a whole. However, it also led to the situation that many slave owners considered it beneath their dignity to do any manual labour for themselves. The traveller Cornelis de Jong remarked at the end of the eighteenth century that very few burghers were willing to put their own hands to the plough or were prepared to use their own limbs in the packing shed.

Slaves who were owned by the Company were generally less accomplished than those who belonged to private individuals. The Company slaves were housed in the Slave Lodge in Cape Town which was built in 1679. The day-to-day supervisors were themselves also slaves, known as mandoors (foremen). The Company kept a reasonably constant number of slaves: in 1714 it had 445; 605 in 1742; 625 in 1784 and 509 by 1793.

Privately owned slaves were usually better clothed and educated. They were often better treated than those in Company possession. Their jackets and trousers were made of rough cloth. They worked barefoot, but were permitted to wear a hat if they were able to speak Dutch. The slaves from West Africa and Madagascar were physically strong, but relatively cheap due to their limited communication skills. Slaves from the East, who were known as Malays, usually were proficient craftsmen and highly sought after. Slaves born at the Cape were considered most reliable because they were less likely to run away.

Prominent slave owners in and near Cape Town owned as many as ten to twenty slaves, while Governor W.A. van der Stel had no less than 200 slaves on his farm Vergelegen. The average number of slaves per owner was three adults. By 1710 there were about as many slaves as free burghers in the colony, but soon afterwards the number of slaves exceeded that of the burgher population.

Desertion was an ongoing problem and was often accompanied by theft, murder and arson. Slaves who deserted and were found again were punished heavily. However, there was also recognition for loyal service in the form of money, greater latitude and even emancipation (freedom from slavery). Slaves were sometimes virtually treated as members of the owner's family.

In 1685 a part of the Slave Lodge in Cape Town was equipped as a school for the children of slaves. Later some of these children also attended public schools. In 1779 there were 84 slave children in schools in Cape Town. However, in the course of the eighteenth century, slaves were increasingly barred from Christian churches in part because of the terms of an ordinance in 1721 that prohibited slaves to present their children for baptism. Malay slaves were mostly followers of Islam and free to practise their religion unhindered.

In the Cape settlement children of mixed parentage, i.e. mostly the offspring of slaves and Europeans, gave rise to an additional population group, commonly known as Basters (half-castes). From the earliest years of the Cape refreshment station there was a shortage of marriageable women. In 1658 the burgher Jan Zacharias married the slave Maria from Bengal, although there were very few such marriages. In 1685 the visiting commissioner, H.A. van Reede, placed a total ban on marriages between burghers and slaves, however extra-marital relationships between slaves and visiting sailors, garrison soldiers and free burghers persisted. In 1681 a male slave, Cupido from Bengal, who had sexual relations with a white woman, was burnt alive at the gallows.

In 1685 there were 58 children with "German" fathers, that is to say men of European origin, in the Slave Lodge. The visiting commissioner, Van Reede, proposed that such children be qualified in a trade and set free at the age of 25 years. In contrast, in terms of the Roman Dutch Law children born out of wedlock would inherit the status of the mother (in this case a slave) and consequently remain a slave. Only in 1775 was it officially regulated that a slave owner could not sell a slave woman and her illegitimate children. They were to be set free after the owner's death.

These half-caste children were not really at home with any other group at the Cape. In the eighteenth century they were a minority group and because of prevailing prejudice were often looked down upon. Nevertheless, some of them were successful and prosperous, for example J.A. Vermaak. Although his mother was a slave, in 1803 he was elected as a member of the Community Council (the local management body) of Cape Town. By the end of the eighteenth century there were about 2000 persons of slave parentage who were also accepted as baptised Christians. Most of this group married other free blacks, but they rarely intermarried with the Khoekhoen. These people of mixed blood were liable for tax and served in the commandos against the Bushmen. Some of them left the colony in the eighteenth century; one such group under the leadership of Adam Kok moved northwards over the Gariep River and by 1813 became known as the Griqua. Their lifestyle was similar to that of the pioneer trekboers, livestock farmers who had moved over the colonial borders in search of grazing for their herds.

In the aftermath of the French Revolution which popularised the principles of freedom and equality, slavery eventually came to an end on 1 December 1834 in the Cape Colony. This was the most notable humanitarian step taken by the British throughout its vast colonial empire in the nineteenth century, although there were already signs of steps to lighten the fate of the slaves during the Dutch era at the Cape.

Pioneer women

Extraordinarily high demands were made on the physical and emotional resources of the relatively small number of white women during the establishment and expansion of the Cape settlement. To adapt to and survive these pioneering circumstances demanded exceptional resourcefulness, dedication and a variety of practical skills.

Maria de la Quellerie, Jan van Riebeeck's wife, was loved and widely respected by all. She is described as being attractive, soft-natured and determined. Her French background and Protestant convictions impressed all those who visited the Cape. In 1653 she took the intelligent young Khoekhoe girl Krotoa (also known as Eva) into her household and gradually familiarised her with the language, lifestyle and religion of the Dutch settlement. In this way Eva was equipped to become a skilful interpreter, a baptised Christian (1662) and marriage partner for the Company official and surgeon, Pieter van Meerhoff (1664). Maria and her family departed for Batavia in 1662 where her husband was the commander at Malacca. There, two years later, Maria tragically died of smallpox.

The illiterate Annetje Boom, also known as Annetje de Boerin, displayed remarkable initiative in the early Cape settlement. She was the wife of Hendrik Boom, head gardener of the Company at the Cape. She was contracted to provide milk, butter and buttermilk to the local community. In addition she ran an inn that offered paid accommodation to visitors. Despite many setbacks (storms, fire, desertion of workers, theft and war) her hard work was rewarded with success. In 1665 she was able to return to the Netherlands with her family. Other well-known pioneer women in the farming community were the German woman Catharina (Trijn) Ras in the Steenberg vicinity and the highly principled Huguenot, Sara de Clercq (later du Toit) of Stellenbosch.

Because of the chronic shortage of marriageable white women in the early colony, some burghers married free black women. The children of such unions were readily accepted into society of the time. Angela (Ansiela) from Bengal, a freed slave, married the burgher Willem Basson. After the death of her husband in 1689 she became a successful businesswoman. Her daughter Anna de Koning married the well-known captain of the Cape garrison, Olof Bergh.

In the absence of medical practitioners, some women provided a valuable nursing service in Cape society. For example, in the early eighteenth century Maria Buisset was a respected midwife and a pioneer in the medical field.

The wives of Cape governors such as Maria (wife of W.A. van der Stel), Elizabeth (wife of Rijk Tulbagh) and Reinet (married to Cornelis van de Graaff) were prominent in their support of their husbands, but were not necessarily well liked. Other well-known women in the late eighteenth-century Cape society were Johanna Duminy of the farm Bokrivier near Swellendam; Anna Maria Truter, wife of the traveller John Barrow; and Lady Anne Barnard, who was married to the colonial secretary of the Cape during the first British occupation of the colony. Without the diaries kept by these women, we would know far less today about everyday life in those days at the Cape.

Augusta, daughter of Commissioner General J.A. de Mist, is well known for her diary, written in French, which she kept while on a journey with her father in 1803/1804. The town and district of Uitenhage were named after their early family name. Another eminent woman was the remarkable Catharina, sister of the minister of religion, Helperus Ritzema van Lier, who was very active in missionary and evangelical circles. Her prose and poetry were typical of the rising mysticism and philanthropy of the late eighteenth century.

The church and Cape society

The Reformed Church played a significant role and was involved in various spheres of society for almost the entire one and a half centuries of the Dutch era in the Cape Colony. Already at the establishment of the refreshment post in 1652, the religious tradition of the Reformed Church was ensconced at the Cape. In particular, the church provided hope to a remote and largely isolated white community.

The official request of the Council of Seventeen, given to Van Riebeeck, made it clear that Christianity had to be established and consolidated at the new refreshment station. Initially the *siektetrooster* (sick-comforter) Willem Wijlandt and his successors were responsible for meeting the spiritual needs of the local community, including the Khoekhoen and slaves. The first ordained minister of religion of the Cape congregation, Joannes van Arckel, began his ministry in 1665, but died a few months after his arrival. Sick-comforters and ministers of religion were all salaried officials in the service of the VOC. Initially, regular church services were held in Fort de Goede Hoop and thereafter in the Kat of the Castle until the Rev. Petrus Kalden dedicated a new church building in 1704 on a site near the Company's garden where the Groote Kerk (Dutch Reformed Church) stands today. Sick-comforters continued to serve workers at the many outlying posts of the Company in the colony.

The free burghers were not compelled to attend church services on Sundays. Because of the great distances involved, many of them had to go to great lengths to receive the sacraments of baptism and Holy Communion. New congregations were gradually established: Stellenbosch (1686), Drakenstein (1691), Roodezand (1743) and Swartland (1745). Elders and deacons were appointed from among the officials and free burghers. They served as members of the church councils. A total of about 45 ministers officiated at the Cape during the lengthy VOC era. Before their appointment they were strictly selected by the presbytery of Amsterdam and the Council of Seventeen.

The first combined church meeting or convocation of the five congregations in the colony met in 1746 under the chairpersonship of the Rev. Franciscus le Sueur to consider mutual issues. In 1759 the Political Council suddenly banned these meetings because it was of the opinion that they might threaten its local authority. Although the superior power of the Company was maintained over the Cape church, for example by the appointment of ministers of religion and sick-comforters, individual religious freedom was permitted. There were various Lutherans, Roman Catholics and adherents of other religions among the officials and free burghers. Protestant Huguenots who made their homes in the colony were gradually assimilated into the local church. Muslim slaves and political exiles from the East retained their own identity as a religious community in Cape society.

The traditional beliefs of the local Khoekhoen were in time replaced by European-oriented acculturation and the religious convictions of other residents in the colony. Early in the eighteenth century, missionary work among the Khoekhoen was informal and sporadic, such as was conducted at Petrus Kalden's home at Zandvliet. However, with the arrival of the Moravian missionary Georg Schmidt in 1737, missionary endeavours began in earnest at Baviaanskloof (the later Genadendal). In 1744, due to local opposition, Schmidt was obliged to return to Europe and it was only in 1792 that the Moravians resumed their work with renewed vigour. It was for the most part due to the missionary zeal of the Rev. H.R. van Lier that by 1788 there was a great spiritual revival among Christians at the Cape which led to more active evangelising among the slaves and Khoekhoen.

During the Dutch era at the Cape, church and education were closely integrated. Basic literacy was necessary for children in pioneering circumstances to enable them to read the Bible and master the catechism. The sick-comforter Pieter van der Stael opened a slave school in 1658 and in 1663 his successor, Ernestus Back, ran the first public school in the settlement on a part-time basis. The first person appointed specifically as a teacher was Daniel Engelgraaf. Following this, a small school was opened in Stellenbosch in 1683 to meet the educational needs of the growing local community. By 1714, Governor De Chavonnes appointed a *Kommissie van Skolarge* (Commission of Scholastics) that organised and controlled the running of schools and the remuneration of all school teachers in the colony.

By the end of the eighteenth century, various European missionary societies had made headway with schooling for slaves, free blacks and Khoekhoen. During the Batavian administration (1803–1806) Commissioner General J.A. de Mist's progressive School Ordinance made provision for the separation of the church's responsibility for the running of public schools. Similarly De Mist's Church Ordinance was also comprehensive and liberal, but upheld the authority of the state over the church.

Confrontation and transformation, 1750–1806

In about the last fifty years of the Dutch era, the Cape society was characterised by remarkable growth and progress despite certain inhibitory factors. The boundaries of the colony were extended despite the Company's restrictive and monopolistic trade policies. The burghers were becoming increasingly aware of their identity, interests and their vision for the future. Local officials and free burghers alike were attempting to use new economic opportunities for individual gain.

In 1752, on the orders of Governor Rijk Tulbagh, August Beutler moved eastwards to explore the interior. When he reached the Keiskamma River he reported that for all practical purposes this river separated the Khoekhoen's grazing lands, specifically those of the Gonaqua herders, and the grazing areas used by the black herders (the Southern Nguni or Xhosa). However, it was only 26 years later in 1778 that another governor, Joachim van Plettenberg, concluded an agreement with certain Xhosa leaders whereby the Great Fish River was to be respected as the eastern frontier of the Cape Colony. In a fluid and open-frontier situation it was difficult to apportion blame, and herders on both sides were guilty of crossing this boundary with impunity. Skirmishes and cattle raiding eventually culminated into three frontier wars during the eighteenth century, namely in 1779, 1793 and 1799.

Meanwhile, in 1739, Pieter de Bruyn led an unofficial expedition to the area north of the Gariep River and returned with livestock from Great Namaqualand. Much later, in 1760, the enterprising elephant hunter Jacobus Coetzee crossed the Gariep River at Guados (also known as Skaapdrif) and pushed on to the present Warmbad (originally known as Aigams) in southern Namibia. Another expedition to the same region, this time under Captain Hendrik Hop, was unsuccessful and brought no financial rewards for the Company. In 1779 Robert Jacob Gordon renamed the Gariep the Orange River in honour of the royal house of the Netherlands.

THE HEROIC DEED OF WOLRAAD WOLTEMADE

In the height of a violent storm in Table Bay on 1 June 1773 the vessel *De Jonge Thomas* ran aground on a sand bank near the mouth of the Salt River. When the news of the tragedy reached the Castle, 30 soldiers were sent to guard any goods that were likely to be washed ashore. While the storm continued to rage, there was nothing that could be done to rescue the 203 people on board the stricken vessel.

> The elderly father of one of the soldiers doing duty on the beach, a poor dairy farmer called Wolraad Woltemade, had brought food for his son. When he saw the desperate plight of the crew and passengers on board the ship, he immediately mounted his white horse, plunged into the surging waves and made his way to the wreck. In this way he brought two people at a time safely back to the shore. Fourteen were rescued but when the exhausted rider and his horse reached the sinking ship for the eighth time, six near-hysterical people jumped onto the horse at the same time. All of them disappeared under the icy waves together with Woltemade and his horse. The ship soon broke apart and only 53 people eventually managed to reach the shore clinging to pieces of wreckage.
> According to the Swedish traveller Anders Sparrman, Woltemade's heroic deed was all the more significant because he was apparently unable to swim. His dauntless and death-defying rescue mission made him the first hero of the European settlement at the Cape.

In 1779 and 1782 organised resistance by the Cape burghers against the VOC's economic restrictions and the Company officials' lack of empathy for their grievances led to the submission of comprehensive petitions to the Council of Seventeen. The Patriots, as the Cape burghers called themselves, formed a front against the wealthy, privileged group they nicknamed the "Mamelukes" (so-called after the ruling class of former slaves in Egypt).

The Patriots were influenced by the ideals of liberty and equality that were the vogue in Europe, and by the American War of Independence (1775–1783). Their efforts only met with limited success, but they did gain greater representation for burghers on the Council of Justice and the dismissal of the unpopular and stubborn fiscal (bailiff) Willem Boers.

Meanwhile, the war between the Netherlands and Britain in 1781 brought temporary economic relief for the farming producers in the colony. A large French fleet under Commander Pierre André de Suffren arrived in Table Bay and strengthened the Cape garrison with two additional regiments. The increase in shipping traffic also ensured the sale of the colony's surplus agricultural products. Cape Town soon had the nickname "Petit Paris" (Little Paris) and the residents appeared more dynamic and prosperous.

In 1785 under a new governor, Cornelis Jacob van de Graaff, significant extensions were begun to the fortifications in and around the Cape

Peninsula and construction began on a large new hospital. In general, this encouraged a more extravagant lifestyle. During this governor's term of office, the colony's expenditure was four times that of the previous Van Plettenberg era. As a result, in 1791 the Council of Seventeen recalled Van de Graaff to the Netherlands.

In 1792 and 1793 respectively, two visiting commissioners general of the VOC, Sebastiaan Nederburgh and Sijmon Frykenius, announced drastic cost-cutting measures; proportionally spread tax increases; free trade with the Netherlands; and restrictions on the extensive powers of the fiscal. Their implementation was left to the next commissioner general, Abraham Josias Sluysken, but his intervention was too little and too late.

The Cape Patriots' resistance in the remote outlying districts of Graaff-Reinet and Swellendam gave a new dimension to their dissatisfaction. On 6 February 1795 angry burghers chased away the unpopular magistrate of Graaff-Reinet, Honoratus Maynier, and rejected the Company's authority. They announced that from that time onwards all office bearers would be appointed by popular vote and that the Patriots would only recognise the authority of the States General, the highest ruling body in the Netherlands. In Swellendam on 18 June 1795 the Patriots also rejected the authority of the Council of Seventeen. The Swellendam burghers elected Hermanus Steyn as their national landdrost (magistrate) and Petrus Delport as national military commander.

Colourful individuals in the colonial frontier regions

The remote northern and eastern frontier regions of the colony were characterised by interaction between the various groups of people who lived there. Each community was responsible for its survival and this depended largely on its own initiatives and available resources. All the communities strove for sustainable subsistence and local dominance, but in an open frontier zone nothing was ever certain or stable. Under these circumstances a unique commando system developed and natural leaders came to the fore. The motives and actions of these leaders were often not in strict accordance with those laid down by the Cape authorities or the Council of Seventeen.

One example is Adam Kok (c. 1710–c. 1795), a freed slave who lived in the vicinity of present-day Piketberg. By the middle of the eighteenth century he had grazing rights on the farm Stinkfontein. A number of Basters (half-castes) and Khoekhoen grouped around him. By 1771 he and his followers spread out towards the Kamiesberg and Gariep River regions to hunt elephants and were actively involved in the ivory trade. He always maintained cordial relations with the Cape authorities and acted as the patriarch of his adherents. In 1813, on the advice of the missionary John Campbell, his descendants were persuaded to call themselves by the distinctive name Griqua and their headquarters at Klaarwater was re-named Griquatown.

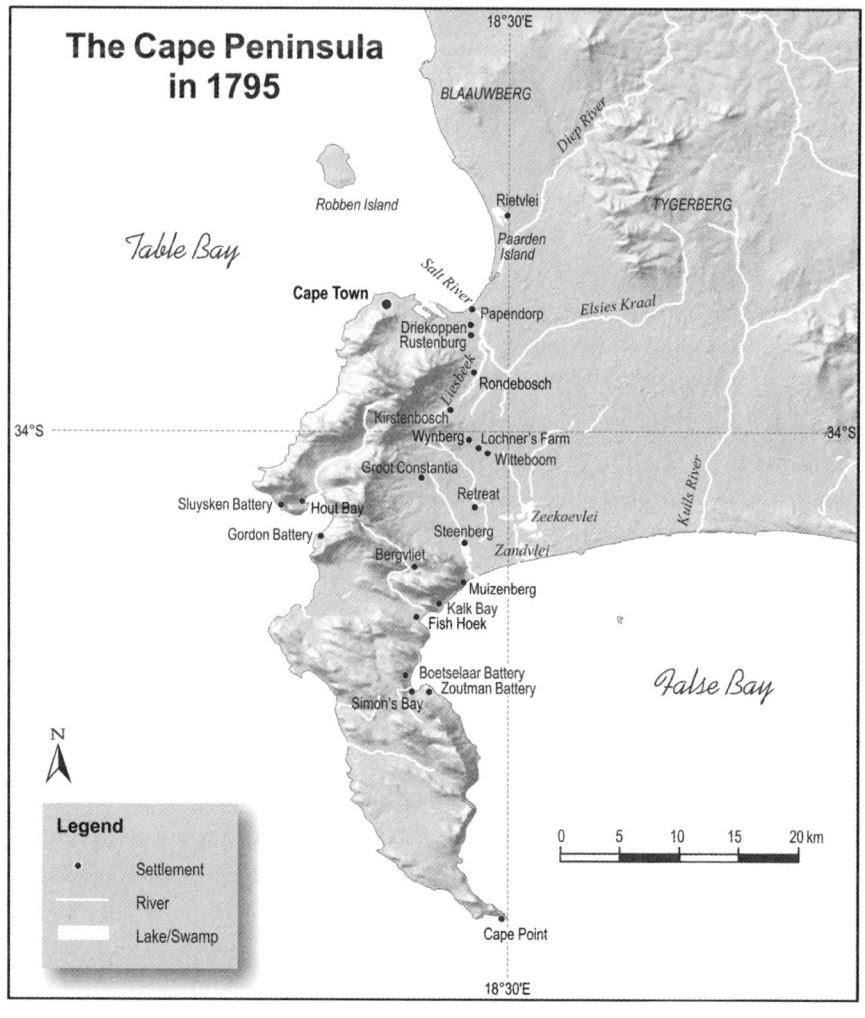

Adriaan van Jaarsveld (1746–1801) was another prominent frontier figure. He was also born and bred in the Piketberg area. By 1770 he had established himself as a livestock farmer in the Sneeuberg region. He was soon appointed as a field corporal and subsequently as a *veldwagmeester* (local civil and military functionary) to take action with the commandos against plundering Bushmen. After the first Eastern Frontier War (1779–1780) he settled in the Kamdeboo area and was appointed as field commander. His commando acted against Xhosa cattle raiders and ultimately took possession of 5300 head of cattle in restitution. Although Van Jaarsveld was a brave and resourceful military leader, he was also reckless and individualistic.

He was appointed as heemraad (member of the landdrost's council) in the new district of Graaff-Reinet (1785), but soon clashed with Maynier's liberal opinions. In 1795 Van Jaarsveld participated in the resistance staged by the burghers against the authoritarian measures of the VOC in Graaff-Reinet. Four years later he was accused of falsifying a receipt and was arrested. On the way to Cape Town to face this charge, he was set free by a group of burghers led by Marthinus Prinsloo, but was eventually re-arrested. Along with other burgher rebels he was held in captivity in the Castle, where he subsequently died.

Petrus Pienaar (1750–1796), another frontier figure, came from the vicinity of Tulbagh. He gained prominence as a hunter, guide and adventurer who operated beyond the borders of the colony. He participated in at least two expeditions to the as yet unknown interior, the first in 1779 with Colonel R.J. Gordon to the Gariep (Orange) River and another in 1793 with Sebastiaan and Dirk van Reenen to the Swakop River in what is now Namibia. In 1790 Pienaar acted as spokesperson for the burghers and other law-abiding residents of the Hantam region. Although he eventually became a *veldwagmeester*, he was not popular as an organiser of commandos against Bushmen plunderers. By 1790 Pienaar, with the help of a man called Jager Afrikaner (not to be confused with naming the burghers as Afrikaners) and his Khoekhoe and half-caste followers, was in charge of the most effective fighting unit in the northern frontier region. Pienaar provided weapons and ammunition to his allies to encourage them to join the commandos, but in the end they turned against him. In March 1796 he, his wife and daughter were murdered by members of the Jager Afrikaner clan on his farm Elandsdrift near present-day Calvinia.

The leader of the Afrikaner clan, Jager Afrikaner (c. 1750–1823), was certainly the most controversial marginal figure in Little and Great Namaqualand. He was of mixed slave and Khoekhoe ancestry. After the murder of Pienaar, Jager and his followers fled to the lower reaches of the Gariep to escape retribution. They soon became a band of robbers who conducted a reign of terror in the northern frontier regions of the colony. They extended their herds of livestock and also absorbed other fugitives. Eventually their main settlement was at Hamis, east of present-day Warmbad in southern Namibia.

Jager Afrikaner temporarily stopped his plundering after representatives of the London Missionary Society (LMS) arrived in his region. The German Johannes Seidenfaden provided education for his children and those of his followers. Afrikaner began to realise that as far as trade and political matters were concerned, it would be advantageous for him and his adherents to be on good terms with the missionaries and Cape authorities. This positive image was improved when the missionary Johann Ebner baptised Afrikaner and his family in 1815.

In 1819 when Jager Afrikaner went to Cape Town in the company of the missionary Robert Moffat, the authorities provided him with an ox-wagon and granted him permission to conduct trade at the Cape markets. After his death he was succeeded by his son Jonker Afrikaner (1790–1860).

A new administration

In June 1795 the sandglass virtually ran dry for the Company when a large British fleet under command of Admiral George Keith Elphinstone and troops on board led by Major General James Craig arrived in Simon's Bay. Meanwhile, the Netherlands was under French rule and the Prince of Orange escaped into exile in England. Commissioner General Sluysken and members of the Political Council could not be persuaded that the British only had honourable motives when they requested, on behalf of the Prince of Orange, that they protect the colony temporarily against French annexation.

When initial negotiations failed, the British resorted to military action. The half-hearted local defence of Muizenberg on 7 August and the arrival of British re-enforcements under command of Major Alured Clark eventually forced Sluysken to sign a treaty of surrender on 16 September 1795. The temporary administration of the colony by the British had a bridging character. Keeping the peace and maintaining the status quo took precedence and many problems remained unresolved. Unrest and simmering societal grievances, particularly in the eastern frontier zone, were not adequately addressed.

In Europe the Treaty of Amiens, signed on 25 March 1802, gave the Batavian government of the Dutch control of the Cape Colony. A year later J.A. de Mist (commissioner general) and Jan Willem Janssens (governor) began their quest to put the colony's affairs back on track. De Mist's liberal outlook was evident in the re-shaping of the general administration. For example, local matters were handled in Cape Town by a Community Council instead of the old Burgher Senate; and an efficient postal service was introduced to improve communication with the interior.

Two new districts, Tulbagh and Uitenhage, were created. Field-cornets, who were appointed from among local residents, were introduced in each ward. The landdrost (magistrate) and heemraden (community councillors) were also assigned the duty of solemnising burgher marriages. De Mist's Church Ordinance of 1804 guaranteed equal acceptance of the various Christian religious beliefs and the followers of Islam. Similarly, De Mist's School Ordinance introduced state control of education, which meant that equal educational opportunities and amenities were made available to all burghers. The first-hand knowledge De Mist and Janssens acquired about the unique circumstances of people who lived in the interior helped them to devise realistic measures and inspire trust.

In addition, the colony received an independent judiciary, with the right of appeal to The Hague. The post of the fiscal was replaced by an attorney general and a Council of Justice comprising qualified jurists. An independent Board of Executors was charged with handling all estates. In the economic sphere free trade and agricultural production made progress, but intermittent success with crops and turnover problems continued. The colonial treasury controlled all public funds. The Batavian authorities regarded slavery as undesirable in the colony, but felt that it had to be phased out gradually. Employers had to provide written service contracts for their Khoekhoe workers to protect the interests of all parties concerned. The policy in the border regions was to maintain mutual peace. All available means had to be pursued to defend the colony against a possible external enemy.

In January 1806 the short-lived Batavian administration suddenly came to an end. On the morning of 8 January a British force under Major General David Baird and a naval fleet under Admiral Home Popham attacked the pride of the Batavian garrison on the plains at Blaauwberg. When General Janssens's line of defence was breached, he retreated strategically to the Hottentots-Holland mountain pass (called the Gantouw by local Khoekhoen) with the largest part of his armed forces. He quickly realised that further resistance against the superior numbers of the British invaders would be fruitless. After negotiations with the British commanders, a mutually acceptable treaty on the transfer of governmental powers was signed on 18 January.

The second British occupation was destined to bring a new dimension to the composition and nature of the population in the colony. Thereby the contours of society irreversibly changed. Nevertheless, many Dutch institutions and practices survived for many years in the Cape Colony.

3
People of bondage
Robert Shell*

Almost from the start the Cape was a slave society. Bereft of freedom and status, slaves defined the liberties and status of others. They were the colony's most important source of labour. In Cape Town the men worked in the market gardens and provided artisan skills; on the farms they worked in the fields and vineyards. The women served as cooks, nannies and wet nurses in the houses. The children were the playmates of their masters' children. The incorporation of domestic slaves into the colonists' "family" laid the basis for the kind of society that developed in the colony.

Most slaves were to be found in the urban and peri-urban areas, and the probability of slaves being sold was always highest in Cape Town, where slaves were sold almost every week in the popular auctions in Church Square. These were held under a large tree, next to the Company's Slave Lodge and facing the rear of the Dutch Reformed Church. Between 1652 and 1808, when the slave trade was stopped, about 63 000 slaves were imported. In all, 26,4% of the colony's slaves were from Africa, 25,1% from Madagascar, 25,9% were brought in from India and 22,7% from Indonesia.

Officials and burghers perceived each group of slaves differently, attributing skills and character to the country of origin and engaging in crude racial and geographical stereotypes. Slaves from Bengal or the Coast of Coromandel, Surat and Macassar, had a reputation as skilful needlewomen and were used in this capacity. Slaves from Mozambique were deemed to be mild and patient, but Malays were viewed as treacherous and

---
*Chapter 3 has been transposed from Hermann Giliomee and Bernard Mbenga (eds), *New History of South Africa*, Tafelberg, Cape Town, 2007, pp. 53–59.

inclined to run amok. Highly sought-after slaves were Cape-born mulattoes – the offspring of liaisons between Europeans and slaves – who were called Afrikanders by the British. A commentator noted: "The Afrikander women are the favourite slaves of the mistress, arranging and keeping everything in order, and are entrusted with all that is valuable – more like companions than slaves; but the mistress rarely and the slave never, forget their relative situations, and however familiar in private, in the presence of another, due form prevails."

There were four groups of slaves: those in the employ of the company; those owned by the Company officials; and those owned by the colony's burghers – representing the overwhelming majority of the slaves – while a fourth and very minor group of slaves was owned by the free blacks. For more than a century Cape slavery was predominantly urban. As late as 1767, more than 40% of all the colony's slaves lived in Cape Town.

The Slave Lodge

The most prominent group of slaves was those who belonged to the Company. Almost all were housed in the Slave Lodge. The Company used hundreds of slaves for various tasks such as running the Company's market garden plantation; working in the hospital; building the port's considerable fortifications and performing the town's unattractive chores, such as removing slurry to the beach. Slaves also acted as a special police force which dispensed rough justice. After a century the Company's slave force had grown to 1000.

The Lodge, usually called the "Loots" or the "Logie" was a large, windowless building. It was located at the top of the main thoroughfare, next to the Company's nine-acre vegetable garden and across the street from the large Company hospital. The Lodge was virtually a fortress run by the Company officials on a military system.

Few Europeans entered the Lodge by choice, except during one hour each night when it became an active brothel for the local garrison. There were almost as many slave women as men in the Lodge, sometimes more. A couple from the Slave Lodge could get permission to be placed on the "marriage list", but the Dutch Reformed Church never sanctioned or even recorded such slave marriages. Slaves owned by the colonists were not permitted to marry until 1823.

Mortality for the slaves in the Lodge was high. Throughout the period of slavery there were more deaths in the Lodge than there were births or slaves who ran away. It was nothing short of a demographic sinkhole.

Some of the slaves in private hands qualified as artisans. The three leading trades were those of mason, blacksmith and carpenter. Most of the owners lived in Table Valley and ran small businesses there.

Life was particularly tough for slaves who worked on the farms near Cape Town that were intensively cultivated; wine, wheat, rye and barley were the predominant crops. Hard work throughout the year was the slaves' lot. So indispensable was slave labour to these farms that it was generally thought the economy would collapse if slavery were abolished. Slaves lived out their lives on wine and wheat farms, separated from one another and rarely visiting the few towns and villages of the interior. Katie Jacobs, a slave born in the Malmesbury district in the nineteenth century, was separated from her Malagasy-speaking mother by sale to an owner in the next valley and neither saw nor heard from her again.

There were also a few slaves on extensive sheep and cattle farms that the colonists carved out in the eighteenth century. Typically, on such a farm an overseer of the son of the owner supervised a few Khoekhoe herdsmen, or a few older slaves who had been "farmed out" were there on their own. Here they lived out their lives in great isolation.

Nannies and wet nurses

Almost all female slaves lived in the house and were part of the household. Their role was that of servant, cook, nanny, surrogate mother and sometimes wet nurse as well. Slave women also busied themselves with crocheting, embroidering, sewing, knitting and laundering. In Cape Town the female slaves in the ubiquitous boarding houses ministered to all the needs of the revitalised sailors and officers.

A single slave woman often performed the roles of midwife, wet nurse and nanny. The slave nurse-nanny was there to assist at the birth; she suckled the child; she carried the settler's infant to be baptised; and she was the child's companion when it was time to go to school. "Such a slave is very well treated," Otto Mentzel, an astute contemporary observer, noted. "In addition to good food, she gets many presents with the prospect of manumission for good service in the bringing up of several children."

In this way slave women were not only brought into the bosom of the family, so to speak, but also actually became, in a literal sense, the bosom of the burgher family. Wet-nursing was frowned on in metropolitan Holland at this time, but settler women had slaves to employ to feed their infants. Cape settler women clearly perceived that there was some sort of link between lactation and ovulation. The Cape wet nurse, by lactating for the biological mother, ensured that the biological mother would be ovulating again sooner than if she were breastfeeding. Therefore the birth intervals between her children would be shorter.

So important was the wet nurse to the slave society that two terms entered the colonial creole language: *minnemoer* or *mina* (love-mother) and *aiya* (old nursemaid). These words have survived, as has the nanny herself.

Punishment and paternalism

Slaves convicted of serious offences – and this included lifting a hand against a master, setting a house on fire or making advances to a European woman – were commonly punished harshly: impaled, branded and quartered. The extreme penalty was death preceded by torture. Convicted slaves were broken alive on the wheel, their flesh was pulled off with red-hot tongs; they were mutilated, impaled or slowly strangled. The bodies of the executed slaves were left hanging on gibbets, or exposed after mutilation in Cape Town or on farmsteads. By 1727 there were so many disfigured or mutilated living slaves that the government decided to brand escaped slaves on the back to spare the feelings of the colonists, particularly pregnant women.

But while these gruesome punishments acted as a kind of deterrent, this does not mean that the masters' control of slaves depended in the first place on whips and chains. Physical coercion alone can never explain why slavery as a system worked in South Africa. This is particularly true of the isolated farms, far removed from police and military force stationed in Cape Town.

The authority limited punishment of privately owned slaves to "domestic correction", the same type of punishment a husband and father could apply to his wife and children. Chains and whips were forbidden. The wording of the relevant statute is clear: "The owner is allowed, in the case of a slave making a mistake, to correct such a slave with domestic punishment, it is not permitted to set a slave in irons, or worse, to torture or otherwise maltreat the slave."

A "sort of child of the family"

The main method private owners used to control their slaves, especially the slaves in the household, was by incorporating them into their extended families in a system the historians of slavery call paternalism. The household or the "family" provided the only "home" there was for slaves who had been uprooted from their own culture and kin. The slave remained an outsider in all civic and legal matters, but the slave owner always insisted that the slave was part of the larger "family", which was presented to the slave as a poor but tangible consolation.

Travellers to the Cape in the eighteenth and nineteenth centuries increasingly referred to this phenomenon. In the final years of the eighteenth century, Lady Anne Barnard, a newly arrived English socialite, wrote that she was unsure whether she should give a necklace to a slave woman who belonged to her hosts *before* handing out gifts to the natural members of their family. In reply, both women laughed and said that she (Lady Anne) should not be concerned at all. The slave woman had been "born in the same house", and was a "sort of child of the family". Lady Anne was encouraged to give the woman the beads right away.

The phrase "born in the same house" invariably referred to a slave's special status in the slave-owning family. Cape slave owners went to considerable lengths to keep slaves, especially female slaves, as "part of the family". To sell such slaves to outsiders would be to undermine paternalism. The slaves of deceased slave owners tended to go to relatives rather than strangers.

Paternalism never entailed equality with the other members of the household. Even the young daughters were allowed to punish adult household slaves. At some point in every slave's life, usually at the young master's or mistress's maturity, there arose a simultaneous realisation that while the young master or mistress was bound for adulthood, the slave – in the settlers' eyes – was scheduled for perpetual childhood and dependence, and the demeaning obscurity that went with that fate. No matter what their age – or status – all Cape slaves remained "boys" or "girls".

Naming a slave

All Cape slaves were known in the community by their first names. The slave trader or the new owner gave slaves new names, and the legal transfer of ownership was the opportunity to rename a slave. The daily, community-wide repetitious use of the first name and no other was an important part of the process of socialising slaves into their status of unending childhood. The names could be facetious (Clever or *Slim*; Sweet Potato or *Patat*), or were taken from calendar months (April or September) or the Old Testament (Solomon or Moses). Classical names (Cupido or Titus) and indigenous names were also given. Only rarely was the name that of the owner or his children.

The dispute over baptism

The question whether and when slaves should be baptised kept the church and the colonists occupied until well into the nineteenth century. Baptism was an important ritual, acting as a condition for the exercise of many rights. At the Synod of Dordt in 1618/1619 the Reformed Church in the Netherlands agreed that all heathen children in a houschold whether slave or free, should enjoy the right of Christian instruction. But it was the head of that household, not the church and not the parents of the child, who had the primary responsibility for deciding about baptising slaves and heathens.

It was also decided that baptised slaves "should enjoy equal rights with other Christians". Baptised slaves could not be sold to heathens but could be passed to other Christians by inheritance or gift. There was no clear agreement on the proper age at which a slave should be baptised and no mention of how these measures should be enforced. All these matters were left to the head of the household.

By about 1725 it had become clear that some owners were denying their infant slaves the right to baptism. Otto Mentzel, writing in the 1740s, noted: "It is a matter for regret that the children born in slavery are neither baptised nor given any religious instruction. There is a common and well-grounded belief that Christians must not be held in bondage; hence only such children as are intended for emancipation are baptised." The church records show a clear trend towards fewer baptisms over the century. Most slave owners did not bother with their slaves' baptism at all. By the late eighteenth century, pews especially built for slaves in the Mother Church (*Moederkerk*) of Cape Town were empty Sunday after Sunday.

While no slave owner, no matter how cynical, would dare claim that slaves had no right to baptism, the owner could justify a delay in baptism by arguing that slaves should be instructed before they were baptised. Then the slave owner could, by endless domestic ruses, postpone bringing the slaves into the Christian community and thereby avoid any risk of reducing the marketability of slaves. Put in purely materialistic terms: slaves were safer investments if they were not Christian, a conviction that continued until emancipation.

Of the 2543 slave baptisms from 1652 to 1795, as many as 1715 were of slave children belonging to the Dutch East India Company – an average of one per month. These Lodge slaves were considered part of the "household" of the Company, and all slaves born into the household of the Lodge. This meant that private owners baptised a total of 828 slaves – and an average of less than nine a year. Of the few slave owners who did baptise their infant slaves, most were wealthy individuals.

Mixed relationships

During the early years, the situation was fluid enough for some children born outside wedlock from unions of non-European parents to be accepted into the European community. The slave Armosyn Claasz gave birth to the children of four different fathers in the Company's Slave Lodge, some described as half-caste, which means that the father was white. Many of these children and their descendants were absorbed into what became prominent Afrikaner families.

During his 1685 visit to the Cape, High Commissioner H.A. van Reede prohibited marriages between Europeans and full-blooded slave women (that is, of pure Asian or African origin). He did, however, permit marriages with half-caste women, with the intention of assimilating such half-castes into the European population. Fathers generally would not own up to their liaisons with slaves, and therefore they did not help their children by slave mothers to gain their freedom – a fact of Cape life that Van Reede's regulations were meant to address.

In the period of Company rule, just over 1000 ex-slaves and indigenous women married free burghers of European descent (and only two male ex-slaves married free women of European descent). When one considers that 65 000 slaves were imported into the Cape, and almost an equal number were born into slavery, it is clear that the chances of a slave entering the ranks of colonial society were small and highly gendered and, moreover, that they declined with time as the price of slaves rose. No one could marry a slave: she first had to be manumitted (freed). At the end of the eighteenth century Willem Klomphaan tried to manumit his slave mistress and his two children but died before he could pay the full sum.

The quest for freedom

All slaves yearned for freedom but few managed to escape. They could run away to places where fugitive slaves hid. There were such communities at Faure, Hangklip and on Table Mountain itself. Several small, stable fugitive societies in the colony offered shelter to runaway slaves, and these havens survived throughout the period. The 60-slave Hangklip community that lived in a cave lasted for a century, virtually undisturbed until slavery was abolished in 1834.

The other route to freedom was through manumission and becoming what was known as a "free black". Freedom was not a right conferred by the state but a favour granted within the household. Manumitted people were termed *vrijzwarten*, free blacks, even if descended from a European parent. The manumission regulations were framed more in cultural than legal terms. The ability to understand, speak and write Dutch headed the established list of manumission requirements.

From 1715 to 1791, the Council of Policy received a total of 1075 manumission requests, of which only 81 involved Company slaves. The manumission rate in the colony was low, indeed extremely low. The average per year was only 0,165% of the slave force. The figure for Brazil and Peru was six times higher than that at the Cape.

The fact that the proportion of the free population at the Cape remained very small in the 1820s and 1830s, except in Cape Town, had momentous consequences for future race relations. Virtually all people who were desperately poor and had no status were black; all the richer people were white. An association between whiteness and success arose.

Freed male slaves at the Cape began their freedom with a combination of formidable disadvantages. Among these were prejudice, poverty, the inability to obtain credit, and also the extreme difficulty of obtaining gainful employment. Free blacks were excluded from most occupations as early as 1727. Burgher councillors even forbade free blacks to sell small sundries like "toast and cakes" on the streets. Many were forced to turn to the precarious occupation of fishing the most dangerous waters of the South Atlantic. Although some free slaves had to be helped by the poor fund of the church, most found succour among the sympathetic free black Muslim community, many of whom owned slaves themselves and were regular manumitters.

Population of the Cape Colony

Year	European free burghers	Burghers' slaves	Free blacks
1670	125	52	13
1690	788	381	48
1730	2540	4037	221
1770	7736	8200	352
1798	c.20 000	25 754	c.1700

*Slavery as an international phenomenon**

In the seventeenth and eighteenth centuries slavery was in use throughout the world. A slave was the property of the individual or institution for whom he/she had to work and to obey implicitly. Slaves occupied the lowest level of the social hierarchy. They could be acquired in four ways, namely from among the ranks of prisoners of war; people who were unable to pay their debt; children whose parents were so indigent that they sold their offspring as slaves; and children who were born into slavery. The price paid for a slave depended on his/her physical strength, health, age, race and special skills.

Various European countries imported slaves from western and central Africa into their colonies to ease the labour shortage in the production of crops such as sugar, coffee, cotton and rice in North America and the Caribbean, as well as in the silver and gold mines of Peru and Mexico. By about 1600 Portuguese traders were importing approximately 4000 slaves annually from Africa to Brazil. The British Royal African Company's trading vessels based in Liverpool, Bristol and London transported thousands of slaves from the Gold Coast (Ghana), Benin and Gambia to the British colonies in North America and the Caribbean Islands. Similarly, the French colonies in the Caribbean lapped up a large number of slaves. Conditions on board the transatlantic slave ships were shockingly

---

*This sub-section was written by Johan de Villiers.

bad. The restricted space available and the scanty rations provided were responsible for great loss of life. About 10–15% of the slaves perished at sea.

Recent research by P.D. Curtin provides a conservative estimate of the number of imported slaves in the New World during the seventeenth and eighteenth century as follows:

Portuguese-Brazil	3,6 million
British colonies	2 million
French colonies	1,6 million
Spanish colonies	1,5 million
Netherlands-Suriname and the Antilles	0,5 million
Danish colonies	28 000

In addition, about six million slaves were taken from Africa to Asia, while some eight million people were enslaved in Africa itself.

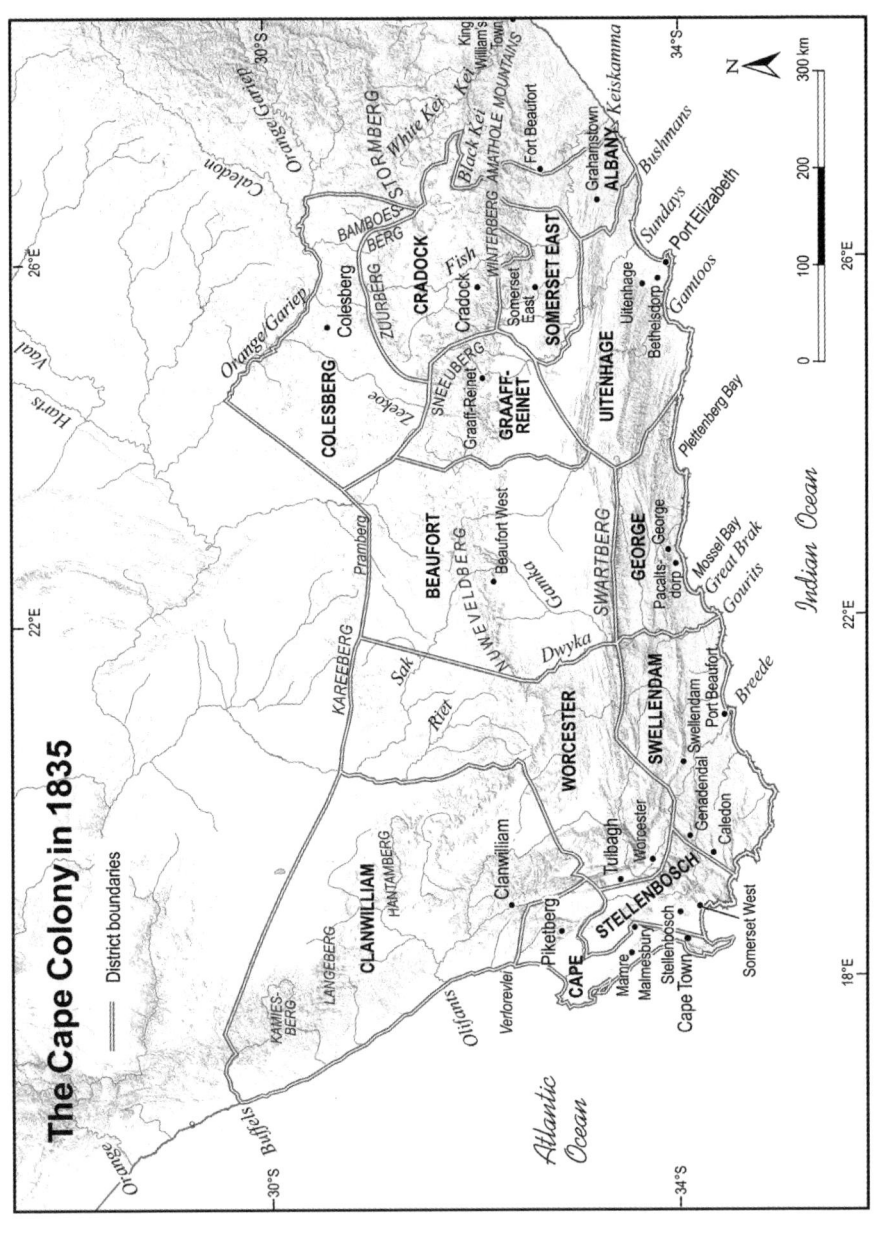

4
Cape colonial society under British rule, 1806–1834

Johan de Villiers

At the beginning of the nineteenth century Cape society was characterised by a strictly demarcated class division. These were the autocratic ruling class, wealthy property owners, business associates, free workers (those who were not slaves), contracted labourers and slaves. This kind of social hierarchy was typical of society in many countries at the time, particularly in Western Europe. In addition to this class division there prevailed an increasing awareness of race at the Cape. To a great extent therefore, race and class influenced the status of individuals and groups.

Additional polarising factors in Cape society, such as freedom versus enslavement, power versus weakness and wealth versus poverty, were balanced out by general community needs and expectations which led to a greater sense of solidarity, particularly when there was an external threat. It is therefore understandable that the colonial community was traumatised by the British military takeover in 1806.

Developments at the Cape were closely linked to events in Europe. Just over a year after the Peace of Amiens in 1802 between Britain and France, the British government under William Pitt once again declared war against Napoleon Bonaparte in May 1803. This was after French troops occupied the German city of Hanover in retaliation for the British delay in withdrawing from the island of Malta as required in terms of the Amiens treaty. In the naval battle of Trafalgar on 21 October 1805, the French fleet was destroyed. This affirmed British naval supremacy and opened the way for a relatively easy British military occupation of the Cape Colony. The residents had to choose between open resistance and submissive acceptance of the new dispensation.

Why was the Cape Colony important for Britain? In the first place the Industrial Revolution in Britain had created a demand for raw materials from overseas and new markets. The strategic location of the Cape on the important sea route between Britain and the British trading posts in Asia was crucial. The Cape Colony could serve as a military outpost to protect British trade interests, particularly those in India. In the second place, natural harbours on the coast of southern Africa were extremely limited. This being so, British control of the harbours of the Cape Peninsula (Table Bay and Simon's Bay) would prevent foreign powers making use of the local facilities. Thirdly, during the first British occupation of the colony (1795–1803), British officials, travellers, traders and missionaries had formed positive impressions of the local residents and the vast potential of the Cape. Thanks to the descriptions of their travel by people such as John Barrow, British policy makers in London were aware of the value of an established infrastructure and available human resources that were at the disposal of British entrepreneurs in the colony.

> **COLONIALISM**
> Colonialism is the policy or endeavour on the part of major powers to gain and maintain control over subordinate powers elsewhere in the world. Examples of great European powers who from the fifteenth century onwards established colonial empires far beyond their borders are Spain, Portugal, Britain, France and the Netherlands. The entire social, economic and political development of the colonists was subjected to the supremacy of the distant motherland. Colonies had to give the motherland priority as far as a source of raw materials and agricultural products were concerned and also provided new markets for industrial products from the motherland. In addition, the colonies could also provide an alternative place of residence for unemployed workers and frustrated entrepreneurs from the motherland. The concept imperialism is closely aligned to colonialism. It describes the desire or urge on the part of great powers to expand their empires on a worldwide scale.

New brooms sweep clean

The British military takeover of the Cape Colony was decided by an effective strategy and firepower, but to win over the hearts of the conquered residents was a far greater challenge for the new rulers. Initially

General David Baird was the acting governor and he had two important goals. Firstly, he wanted to protect the colony militarily against a possible French occupation force. To achieve this he had 6000 British troops at his disposal. Secondly, he aimed to manage civil matters in the colony in an orderly manner to serve the interests of Britain and the local residents. The terms of the peace treaty of Rustenburg (1806) were reasonable, but the promises had to be addressed by means of reliable implementation. Baird had to win over the hearts and minds of various groups in Cape society in favour of British rule.

The Cape Regiment that was formed gave some detribalised Khoekhoen and "Basters" (people of mixed blood) the opportunity to follow a military career. For their part, the burgher population was well disposed by Baird's continuation of tried and trusted governmental institutions from the Dutch era at the Cape. Most of the functionaries from the Batavian administration were retained for the time being. With thousands of British soldiers in Cape Town the mother city of the colony soon developed an English character, but in the outlying areas and the countryside Dutch was retained.

For the sake of keeping good order, Baird only made a few necessary changes. He did away with De Mist's civil marriage law, postal services were speeded up and the customs duty on British goods was relaxed. To bridge expected food shortages he imported grain and rice from Madras in India and supplies from St Helena. At the request of the Burgher Senate he also allowed American vessels to deliver coffee and Indian calico. Baird was in favour of local agricultural development, but this was only directed at providing immediate requirements. All these measures made him popular amongst the burgher population.

With the arrival in May 1807 of the new governor, the Earl of Caledon, the British reconciliation policy began. Various pro-British supporters from the burgher population were appointed to key positions in the local government, including Olof Gotlieb de Wet (judge), Willem van Ryneveld (state prosecutor), Johannes Truter (fiscal) Abraham Fleck (orphan master) and Christoffel Brand (post-holder or manager, at Simon's Bay). To these can be added respected Cape families such as the Cloetes, Van der Bijls and Mijburghs, who became completely anglicised. Another issue which promoted the image of British rule among the burghers was the appointment of accomplished multilingual magistrates (landdrosts) such as Jacob Cuyler (Uitenhage), Adriaan van Kervel (George) and Daniël van Ryneveld (Jan Disselsvlei, later named Clanwilliam). This improved the administration in the outlying districts appreciably and made it more accessible to the residents.

Another of Caledon's far-sighted measures was the introduction in 1811 of a travelling circuit court for the outlying districts. This meant that at least two judges visited the various landdrost offices annually and could also pay attention to the interests of slaves. In addition, Caledon was also an avid supporter of missionary work among the Khoekhoen. During his governorship the Moravian mission station at Mamre was established. His contribution to the regulation of labour to bring about greater stability was also of considerable significance (see the following section).

Caledon's re-organisation of the Lombard Bank (which in 1793 became the first banking institution established at the Cape) and other financial measures placed the economy of the colony on a sound footing. He tried to encourage the production of wine, grain and wool by the residents, but only had limited success. The functioning of the administration was also improved by the construction of several new government buildings.

Caledon gained first-hand knowledge of the outlying districts by sending Major Richard Collins on two inspection tours. The British officer's reports emphasised the seriousness of the Bushman threat in the northern districts and the Xhosa raids in the Zuurveld. Caledon's border policy was tentative, because he did not want to implement any drastic measures while the Napoleonic wars were raging in Europe. He also wanted to limit government spending. He had sympathy for the residents of the colony with regard to their loss of livestock, but left the problem to be dealt with by his successor.

Eventually Caledon, a nobleman without a military background, came into conflict with General Henry Grey, the commander of the Cape garrison. Grey insisted on the highest executive military power without interference from the civil governor. This division of power was a serious dilemma the British government had to pronounce upon. To prevent a similar problem in future, the imperial government wisely decided that all Caledon's successors should be British generals.

Under the next governor, Sir John Cradock, further conciliation took place from 1811 onwards between the British authorities and local residents. It was Cradock's task to organise the Fourth Frontier War in the aftermath of enormous loss of life and material goods suffered by the colony's residents during the previous three years as a result of increasing attacks by some Xhosa groups. A combined offensive by British troops and burgher commandos managed to stabilise the Fish River boundary. The impressions Cradock gained from his investigative journey in 1813–1814 and the measures that he implemented thereafter also strengthened mutual ties between the burghers and the government.

Cradock's most enduring contribution was the introduction of hereditary quitrent land tenure to replace the old system of loan farms. This meant that burghers had more security about the right of succession. The governor also instituted a system of free schooling. In the course of nine years the new British authority succeeded in establishing a paternalistic, but stable relationship with the various residents of the colony.

CAPE TOWN, THE MOTHER CITY

Under British rule Cape Town made steady growth as an administrative and commercial centre. By 1815 the number of permanent residents in the city was about 15 600. Just over a decade later it was already 26 000. About half of the residents were slaves and free workers of colour, while the other half comprised government officials and business people.

During the Napoleonic wars thousands of British soldiers were stationed in Cape Town to defend the colony against possible enemy occupation. This benefited the local market by creating a profitable market outlet. The lowering of customs duties facilitated the export of the colony's somewhat erratic wine and grain production via Cape harbours. Visitors to the city could find accommodation in many inns and various taverns provided liquor to travellers and residents alike. The most prominent residents lived in the valley below Table Mountain on large properties with workers' quarters, stables and enough land for gardening.

The most impressive building in Cape Town was the five-pointed Castle built in the early VOC era. On the coastal side it was supported by the artillery batteries of Fort Knokke, Roggebaai, Amsterdam, Chavonnes and Mouille. The parade ground alongside the Castle and the military barracks for 2000 soldiers completed the military facility. Other impressive landmarks in the city were the governor's residence beside the old Company garden (his summer residence was at Rustenburg in the region of Newlands), the Groote Kerk in Keizersgracht (later called Adderley Street), the Burgerwachthuis on Green Market Square, the Latin School, the Slave Lodge and the prison.

> By 1834 Cape Town's modern appearance was also enhanced by the addition of a public library, museum, a planetarium, a lighthouse and improved hospital facilities. Although the gravel roads and disorderly traffic left much to be desired, under British rule there was better street lighting (oil lanterns), provision of water (a piped system) and cargo-loading facilities at the anchorage in Roggebaai.

The burghers and the Khoekhoen under British rule

Under the British administration the different population groups in the colony continued their long-established pattern of existence. Apart from the Cape officialdom and the business class, the large majority of the white population were Dutch-Afrikaans-speaking burghers who made a livelihood as cultivators and livestock farmers. They were about 26 000 in number (men, women and children) and formed the proverbial backbone of the colony's agricultural economy. The reasonably well-to-do grain and wine farmers were settled in the south-western part of the colony.

In the expansive northern and eastern border regions the poorer sheep and cattle farmers lived a semi-nomadic life. These farmers were very individualistic. They were weaned in Europe and rooted in Africa – hence the growing tendency to call themselves "Afrikaners". In order to survive, this population group had to adapt to the often harsh climate, inhospitable environment and other hostile elements. Poverty forced them to be enterprising, hardworking and self-sufficient. They were obliged to help one another in times of crisis. They were usually hospitable to strangers, but were not inclined to take well-intentioned advice from outsiders. To foreigners their farming methods often appeared primitive and inefficient. They were largely dependent on others to do their unskilled manual labour.

Most of the Dutch-Afrikaans-speaking burghers were outwardly phlegmatic and even apathetic towards the British conquerors of the Cape, but in their hearts they were anti-British. Their affinity to the Netherlands persisted long after the British takeover and was seen in typical practices and expressions. Although most burghers had not received advanced education, they were proficient in the basic skills of reading, writing and arithmetic. Because they lived in relative isolation, together with the other residents of the colony, they gradually developed an early form of the Afrikaans language which they used at home and in the workplace.

For the most part the burghers were religious people and their devotion to the Bible was the guiding principle in their lives. The livestock farmers in the remote interior were far away from churches and ministers and were exposed to moral decline. They were particularly prejudiced towards the indigenous people of the colony and regarded them as being of a lower social standing.

The burghers did not take an active part in politics, but they kept informed of local affairs at the district drostdy which later became known as the magistrate's office. The first periodicals in Dutch were *Het Nederduitsch Zuid-Afrikaansche Tijdschrift* (1824) and the newspaper *De Zuid-Afrikaan* (1830). These provided the opportunity for authors from among their own ranks, such as Meent Borcherds, Christoffel Brand, Abraham Faure and Jacques Smuts, to become a critical mouthpiece for the burghers.

In addition to the burghers, the detribalised Khoekhoen and half-breed (coloured) community formed a second component of the labour force in the colony. With the British takeover in 1806 approximately 20 000 of them lived scattered throughout the colony. This number included all people of mixed ancestry, but not the Khoekhoen who lived outside the colony's borders. When Caledon was appointed as governor, in terms of the law the Khoekhoen were officially free and independent. They paid no taxes to the authorities and were not obliged to perform military service. They were free to live where they chose, providing they did not trespass on the private property of burghers.

The leaders of remaining Khoekhoe clans exercised no real power any longer over their people. Examples of such tribal chieftains who in 1809 were still financially remunerated by the colonial government were Christlief Booda and Paulus (Daalie) Haas of Genadendal, Hans Klapmuts who lived in Groenekloof, and Hans Mozes and Claas Kees of Swellendam. Caledon realised that the traditional system of tribal authority was outmoded and had served its purpose. Only a small number of Khoekhoen still lived as livestock farmers in recognised areas or reserves within the colony. Most of the Khoekhoen made a living as temporary or permanent workers in the service of the burghers. Still others found a means of livelihood at the mission stations (such as Genadendal, Mamre and Bethelsdorp) or as soldiers in the Cape Regiment at Wynberg. The rest were landless squatters or vagrants who lived by begging or petty theft.

By 1809 the legal position of the Khoekhoen in the colony was still uncertain. For this reason the governor decided to accept the recommendations made earlier by the fiscal, Willem van Ryneveld. This decision was realised by Caledon's proclamation of 1 November 1809 which placed the Khoekhoen fully under the jurisdiction of the colony's courts. This meant that their citizenship was legally recognised and that in future all Khoekhoen were required to have a permanent place of residence. When the Khoekhoen entered the employment of burghers a proper service contract had to be drawn up in triplicate so that the worker, the employer and the landdrost (resident magistrates after 1827) all had a record of the agreement. The aim was to protect the interests of all parties. In addition, a written letter of permission (a pass) was required when the Khoekhoen wished to travel to other parts of the colony. This measure was effective in limiting theft and vagrancy.

The negative outcome of Caledon's proclamation was that the freedom of movement of the Khoekhoen was drastically reduced and workers were of necessity linked to their employers. It also put the status of Khoekhoe workers at a lower level than that of the burghers. From the point of view of the government the measure created greater work stability at a time when the colony was undergoing a chronic shortage of labour. It again emphasised the necessity of a stable workforce for economic development. However, the proclamation made no provision at all to help the Khoekhoen to gain private ownership and become independent livestock farmers. Without capital the only alternative open to enterprising Khoekhoen was to move beyond the borders of the colony and follow a lifestyle very similar to that of the trekboers.

Cradock extended Caledon's proclamation in 1812. All Khoekhoe children between the ages of eight and 18 were formally *ingeboek* (apprenticed) to approved burghers so that the youngsters could learn sound working methods. They had to be provided with food and clothes and be brought up in accordance with Christian principles. It was only in 1828 that a new ordinance (No. 50) passed by Governor Richard Bourke improved the position of the Khoekhoen. This measure stipulated that they were free people of colour with full citizenship rights. Work contracts would no longer tie them to a particular place of residence. The letter of permission to travel (pass) was done away with and individual ownership of property was henceforth allowed. However, the major shortcoming of this ordinance was that it still did not promote economic equality.

The merit of sustained labour among the Khoekhoen was also promoted by the various Christian missionary societies in the colony. The Moravian Missionary Society did pioneering work at Genadendal and about three quarters of the approximately 800 residents were baptised. They were trained in one or more trades, for example as wagon makers, farriers, coopers, transport drivers, merchants, millers, brick layers, postmen and midwives. However, most residents of Genadendal were still workers on nearby farms.

In December 1807 Caledon gave his approval to grant some land (on the west coast close to Cape Town) for a second Moravian mission station, Mamre. In 1816 another, Enon, was opened in the Uitenhage district. The Moravian missionaries established an institute for lepers, Hemel-en-Aarde (Heaven and Earth) on the Onrust River, and another mission station at Elim (near Cape Agulhas). In 1830 the Rhenish Missionary Society from Germany also opened Wupperthal in the Cederberg range and Ebenezer on the Olifants River, both of which were based on the agricultural and trades pattern practised at Genadendal. In addition, missionaries of the Berlin Society established stations in Transorangia and the Little Karoo in 1834.

The Bethelsdorp mission station run by the London Missionary Society (LMS) was situated in the Uitenhage district. In 1809 Lieutenant Colonel Richard Collins reported that the dwellings occupied by the Khoekhoe residents were dirty and squalid. The inhabitants looked dejected and apathetic. They lived on the meagre yield of their wheat fields and livestock. Only 66 of the 639 residents were baptised and only 43 were involved in profitable trades, although the missionaries James Read and J.T. van der Kemp had tried to teach them basic reading and writing skills. The missionaries also sent reports to the directors of their mission society which mentioned that the Khoekhoen were being gravely mistreated by the burghers.

As a result, the British government charged the Cape governor with looking into these complaints. Van der Kemp died in December 1811 before the circuit court, also known as the Black Circuit, could investigate the allegations. Eventually, 17 cases of murder and 15 of assault were investigated as well as a number of complaints of withholding of wages by employers. None of the murder charges could be proven and only a few perpetrators were eventually fined. This court hearing stirred up unprecedented tension in the mutual relationships between the burghers, the government, the Khoekhoen and the missionaries.

Dr John Philip, who was appointed as superintendent of the LMS in the Cape Colony acted as the political spokesperson for the Khoekhoen and championed their interests. His book *Researches in South Africa*, published in 1828, caused a sensation in the Cape and in Britain. It also exposed the complexity of the divergent societal relationships in the colony. Other mission stations run by the LMS during the first decades of British rule were Zuurbraak (1811), Pacaltsdorp (1813), Theopolis (1814) and Hankey (1822).

The brothers Albrecht and William Anderson who were LMS missionaries also worked outside the colony, north of the Gariep, at Warmbad and Klaarwater. At these places they ministered to the Nama and Griqua people respectively.

As far as military life was concerned, between 1806 and 1817 the Cape Regiment offered a promising career for Khoekhoe men and from 500 to 700 were accepted as part of the regiment. Although this exacerbated the shortage of labour in the colony, it ensured a better quality of life for the soldiers concerned. The regiment played an important role on the eastern frontier of the colony, where it was used in offensive operations and defensive deployment. The first leader of the regiment was the experienced Lieutenant Colonel John Graham. The field preacher of the regiment was a missionary from the Netherlands, Aart van der Lingen, who was able to communicate easily with the soldiers in their common patois.

After this regiment was disbanded for financial reasons in 1817, a new but smaller unit was formed, the Cape Corps of Infantry and Cavalry, under command of Major George Sackville Fraser. In this corps, Khoekhoe soldiers were for the first time officially trained as mounted infantry, armed with carbines. In 1827 this colonial corps was replaced by the Imperial Cape Mounted Riflemen under command of Lieutenant Colonel Henry Somerset.

Freedom for the slaves

The slaves were the third important component of the labour structure at the Cape. With the British occupation in 1806 there were already 29 000 slaves in the colony. The British government's decision in 1807 to ban all slave trade per ship to its colonies did not bring an end to slavery in the colony, but it did mean that new slaves could no longer be imported.

Almost a third of the slaves lived in Cape Town while the rest worked mainly in the wheat and wine producing regions of the Western Cape. Slave labour formed the cornerstone of the entire agricultural economy of the colony. The nature of slave labour did not really change much under British rule. Some slaves were used for unskilled labour, while others were skilled tradesmen.

The traveller William Burchell observed that slaves with a Malaysian background who were born in Cape Town were the most valuable investment. They were used as skilled tradesmen and were hired out by their owners for the highest fee. These male slaves were trained as carpenters, horse-shoers, wagon makers, brick layers, etc., as well as other practical skills. Women slaves were often trained as dressmakers, nurses, cooks and domestic workers. A slave's financial worth was determined by the intrinsic value of his/her labour. Sought-after slaves often enjoyed more freedom and responsibility than others. Slaves who had given years of faithful service to an owner were sometimes very devoted and close to the owner and the family. They were then freed from slavery after the owner's death, especially if they were baptised as Christians. During British rule of the colony about 1000 slaves were voluntarily set free by their owners. Nevertheless, by 1834 there were still about 39 000 slaves registered in the Cape Colony.

For the most part, the life of a slave was very difficult and demanding. There were heavy restrictions placed on their personal lives and they were committed to their owners in all respects. Slave children were sometimes separated from their parents and family ties were ignored. In the courts, evidence presented by slaves was not readily accepted. Any transgressions committed by slaves were cruelly punished, because it was reasoned that the imposition of punishment served as a warning to others.

In 1820 the Dutch traveller Marten Teenstra described the lifestyle of the typical Overberg farmer as *"lui en lekker"* (lazy and pleasurable), because all the work was done by slaves. He went on to liken the slaves to *"tamme huisdieren"* (tamed household animals). According to Teenstra some Cape burghers argued that slavery was condoned by the Bible and that slaves were better off being cared for body and soul by their owners than to allow them the freedom to die in abject poverty.

That not all slaves lived peacefully and carefree during the British rule at the Cape is evident in the slave uprising that took place on 27 October 1808. Two local slaves, Louis from Mauritius and Abraham, were encouraged by two Irishmen, the day-labourer James Hooper and a sailor, Michael Kelly, to stage an uprising. They eventually gathered 331 slaves from about 34 farms in the vicinity of Koeberg, Tygerberg and Swartland to join them to demand that the fiscal in Cape Town grant them their freedom. During their march they seized twelve wagons and four saddle horses and also looted various firearms and gunpowder. The elderly Adriaan Louw was struck on the head and Christiaan Storm was bundled virtually naked onto a wagon and robbed of his personal possessions. The procession then divided into two groups and approached the Sout River where more horses, wagons and ammunition were looted.

Governor Caledon immediately ordered a division of cavalry and foot soldiers to cut off the marchers and they surrendered without offering any resistance. Eventually 51 of the insurgents were tried and sentenced. Five of the leaders, including the slave Abraham and the Irish worker, Hooper, were sentenced to death, while another 34 slaves were sentenced to imprisonment and corporal punishment. This uprising showed that their freedom was more important to the slaves than the restricted protection which they enjoyed in the service of their masters. It is also worth noting that the uprising was not directed at specific slave owners, but developed as a desperate attempt on the part of the slaves to gain their freedom by appealing to the authorities.

From 1815, in the aftermath of the French Revolution and Enlightenment, the influence of philanthropists increased in Britain. Among other things they wanted to improve the lot of slaves in the British colonies. In the British parliament politicians such as William Wilberforce and Thomas Buxton became the main champions of more progressive slave legislation. From 1816 onwards there had to be a slave register in every district of the Cape Colony so that the number and sale of slaves could be monitored at the drostdy. The sale of slaves was also taxed by the government.

On 10 September 1822, when the slave Joris was cruelly tortured and beaten to death at the farm Simonsvlei near Klapmuts, a charge was laid against the owner, 22-year-old Wilhelm Gebhart, and legal steps were taken against him. In the high court he was found guilty without extenuating circumstances and sentenced to death. Even a letter from John Philip of the LMS to Governor Somerset appealing for mercy was in vain. The execution of Gebhart on 15 November was an unprecedented event, but served to remind slave owners once again that their slaves had to be handled in a humane manner.

In 1823 an important slave proclamation followed. It limited the working hours of slaves to a maximum of twelve hours per day in the summer and ten hours per day in the winter. On Sundays slaves could not be forced to work. Marriages between slaves were officially recognised and the separate sale of individuals in slave families was prohibited. Furthermore, slaves were allowed to have private possessions. They also had to be properly fed and adequately clothed. Corporal punishment for misdemeanours was limited to 25 lashes. Slave children in Cape Town and the larger towns were compelled to receive basic school education.

Despite these progressive measures a slave uprising broke out in 1824 in the district Worcester (previously Tulbagh). A slave called Galant encouraged a number of others to demand their freedom and to use force if necessary. In this conflict two burghers were killed and several wounded. The slaves involved were eventually arrested and sentenced to death. It is doubtful whether this uprising can be specifically attributed to the 1823 slave legislation.

In 1826 another slave ordinance (No. 19) laid down that any slave who was seriously mistreated had to be set free immediately. A slave protector was appointed in Cape Town, with assistant protectors in the various districts. This move encouraged slaves to come forward with alleged offences by owners. Slave owners were highly upset by all this and held a public meeting in July in Cape Town. They declared that they were in favour of gradual emancipation, but were strongly against any loss of control over their slaves. A similar meeting was held in Graaff-Reinet in October where it was recommended that slave children should be set free at birth. For such male infants it was suggested that the government should pay compensation to the owners, but for female babies no fee was deemed necessary.

After 1830, under increasing pressure from leading philanthropists of the time, the British government consolidated slave legislation in its colonies and laid down even more stringent measures. This legislation focused particularly on slavery in the West Indian islands, but was also applicable to the Cape Colony. Henceforth slaves were not required to do more than nine hours of work per day. Corporal punishment for female slaves was prohibited and male slaves who were guilty of offences could not be punished by means of whipping. Every slave owner had to keep a punishment book which was inspected twice a year. Slave owners throughout maintained that their inherent instinct to act with appropriate humanity was the guiding principle in the treatment of their slaves. After strenuous opposition in 1831 the inspection requirements were relaxed and only remained applicable in the vicinity of Cape Town and Grahamstown. About 2000 owners nevertheless gathered in Cape Town on 17 September 1832 to protest against the British government's interference in the colony.

Slavery could never be morally justified. It was an evil that had to be eradicated, because it violated the dignity, personal freedom and responsibility of the people involved. Eventually, in August 1833, the British parliament decided officially to end slavery in all its colonies, effective from 1 December 1834. Thereafter the freed slaves were contracted to remain in the service of their former owners as apprentices for a period of four years. It was also decided that owners would be compensated, but this was at a level below the actual price paid for the slave. In addition, the payments were only payable in London in the form of British debentures. The result was that slave owners suffered great financial losses and were sometimes cheated by unscrupulous agents.

Although most burghers in the colony were not against the principle behind the emancipation of slaves, they supported the idea of a more gradual process. The slaves naturally welcomed their freedom with great joy, but were soon disillusioned by the reality that they had to support themselves. Many slaves were only equipped to do unskilled work, but now had to compete with other prospective employees on the open market. However, the chronic labour shortage in the colony meant that most of those who had been freed were at least ensured of poorly paid work.

The troubled eastern frontier region

In the first decade of British rule the situation on the eastern frontier region of the colony was highly unsettled by the divergent claims and needs of different interest groups. The Zuurveld, an area between the official Fish River border (1780) and the Bushmans River, was the focus of intense conflict, with the regular occurrence of unauthorised attacks, theft and murder. There was indeed sometimes also reasonably peaceful interaction between different groups in the form of negotiation and bartering. Four important role players dominated the scene. These were the governing colonial authorities (represented in the region by civil officials and the military command), the white rural citizens (who were for the most part cattle and sheep farmers), the detribalised Khoekhoen (including the Gonaqua) and the numerous Xhosa communities (all of whom were livestock owners).

The colonial authorities had to maintain their supremacy over the eastern frontier region at all costs, but had to keep expenditure as low as possible. Where negotiations and agreements failed, regular troops under British officers were merely required to act as a reserve force. The primary responsibility for the security of the eastern frontier region rested mainly with the rural citizens and loyal Khoekhoen. They were called up for commando service in times of emergency. The enemy was usually the nomadic Bushman hunters on the colony's northern border regions and the Xhosa infiltrators in the eastern frontier zone. The dire shortage of workers in these distant regions meant that in periods of relative peace some burghers took the opportunity to recruit illegal farm workers from among the Xhosa and to engage in barter. Meanwhile, the Xhosa stock farmers increasingly encroached into the fertile Zuurveld in search of better grazing and also because of overpopulation (especially grazing for cattle) in the areas east of the colony's Fish River border.

Caledon was aware of the increasing occurrence of stock theft and loss of life in the eastern frontier zone. The Xhosa paramount chief, Ndlambe, had access to an army of some 3000 warriors and was the most powerful military factor in the Zuurveld. His arch rival, Ngqika, paramount chief of the Rarabe, was established in the Tyumie Valley east of the Kat River, situated outside the colonial border. Other Xhosa headmen in the disputed Zuurveld region included the elderly Chungwa, Ngqueno, Habana, Kassa and Galata. They were unable to prevent their followers from indulging in stock theft. Some Xhosa also encroached into the regions of Bruintjeshoogte, Winterhoek, Zwagershoek and Tarka in search of grazing. In 1810 more than 1000 head of cattle were stolen from white farmers in the Uitenhage district.

The burgher Isaac Joubert, twelve Khoekhoe herd-boys and two slaves were killed by the Xhosa raiders. Landdrost Major Jacob Cuyler was convinced that the stolen cattle had been taken eastwards over the border and would not easily be retrieved. In addition, theft and acts of violence were increasing in the Graaff-Reinet district. Based on the recommendations of Lieutenant Colonel Richard Collins, the colonial government only had one solution. If peaceful persuasion proved unsuccessful, the Xhosa offenders would have to be driven permanently out of the Zuurveld and surrounding areas and over the Fish River border by military force. This had to be done with the least possible shedding of blood. Captain Abiathar Hawkes, commander of a number of British dragoons, reported to the landdrost of Graaff-Reinet in June 1811 that large numbers of burghers had vacated their farms in the Bruintjeshoogte district for fear of the prevailing violence and plundering.

The unavoidable Fourth Frontier War broke out in December 1811. This was after British military reinforcements were sent by the new Cape governor, Sir John Cradock, from Cape Town to the eastern frontier region. The capable Lieutenant Colonel John Graham of the Cape Regiment was appointed commissioner and local commander of the armed forces. The reserve force was under command of Major Thomas Lyster in Graaff-Reinet. The offensive force was divided into three sections. The right wing was under Major Cuyler, the left wing under Landdrost Anders Stockenström snr. The central force was led by Captain George Fraser. In all these detachments armed burghers were divided up for combat together with the regular troops under British command, but the burghers remained under direct control of their own field-commanders and field-cornets.

Meanwhile, Stockenström, on the orders of his superiors, gained an assurance from Ngqika that he would not prevent Ndlambe's followers from settling east of the Fish River, outside the colony. Graham distrusted Ngqika's promise, but for the British authorities this was a positive turn of events. It offered all Xhosa who had settled in the Zuurveld an alternative place of refuge outside the colony and away from the disputed Zuurveld. However, on 29 December 1811 at Doorn Nek in the Zuurberg, Stockenström, a coloured interpreter and eight burghers of his escort were attacked and killed by Chief Kassa's followers when they tried to persuade them to move back over the Fish River.

Early in 1812 a combined colonial task force, about 800 soldiers and burghers under command of Graham, launched a campaign against Ndlambe. Within two months about 20 000 Xhosa were driven out of the colony, but this did not mean peace in the frontier zone. To prevent possible encroachments over the Fish River boundary, at least 22 guard posts were set up and regular patrols were carried out. A permanent military and administrative centre was established in the Zuurveld and named Grahamstown. It soon became the headquarters of the new sub-district of Albany.

The relative peace was of short duration. Cattle theft resumed along the extended Fish River boundary. The new governor, Lord Charles Somerset, held discussions in April 1817 with Ngqika and his uncle, Ndlambe, in the presence of a number of headmen from the Kat River Valley. On this occasion Somerset announced the controversial "spoor system" (also called the reprisal system) whereby the kraal (local settlement) to which the tracks of the stolen cattle led, had to make full compensation to the colonial claimants, regardless of whether the missing cattle were found at that place or not. Because the colonial government only recognised Ngqika as paramount chief, it was he who had to take the final responsibility for all offences committed by the Xhosa – a responsibility which he was highly loathe to accept. His dilemma was that Xhosa sub-chieftains and headmen normally exercised independent authority over their followers.

Dissatisfaction and internal disputes in Xhosa ranks grew worse when Ngqika hesitated to react to the colonial government's demands that compensation be paid for alleged stock theft. The upshot was that in January 1818, Major G.S. Fraser took possession of more than 2000 head of cattle belonging to Ndlambe's followers. The wave of robbery and plundering increased among the various Xhosa communities. This was the ideal opportunity for Ndlambe to extend his power at the expense of Ngqika.

In June 1818 a bloody battle took place between the forces of Ndlambe and those of Ngqika on the Amalinde plains near Debe Nek in the Zuurberg. Ngqika's force was utterly defeated. From his hiding place in the Winterberg, Ngqika pleaded with the British authorities to provide him with military assistance. Governor Somerset thought it was an ideal opportunity to stabilise the eastern frontier zone. Lieutenant Colonel Thomas Brereton advanced into Ndlambe's territory with a mixed force of regular infantry and mounted volunteers. This marked the beginning of the Fifth Frontier War. Some 23 000 head of cattle were looted, but

Ndlambe and his followers avoided direct confrontation and hid away in the forests. Ngqika was compensated with 9000 head of cattle and the rest were used to meet colonial expenses.

Ndlambe's military power was by no means broken. Under the influence of the legendary medicine man, Nxele, also known as Makhanda or Lynx (due to his left-handedness) large numbers of Xhosa warriors gathered to attack the colony. Meanwhile, Lieutenant Colonel Thomas Willshire made military preparations for an offensive against Ndlambe, but before these plans could be implemented, about 10 000 Xhosa warriors attacked Grahamstown in the full light of day on 22 April 1819. It was a town of scarcely 350 white residents of whom most were military personnel. Coincidentally, also in Grahamstown on that day, there were 130 Khoekhoe hunters from the mission station at Theopolis with their leader Boesak.

After two-and-a-half hours the battle came to an end. Eventually the outcome did not merely depend on numbers, but on firepower, tactical expertise and the calm, purposeful action of the defenders. The attackers suffered great losses. About 1000 Xhosa warriors were killed or wounded. In the ranks of the defenders, only three were killed and five were wounded.

The successful defence of Grahamstown motivated Willshire to launch a colonial counter-offensive with all guns blazing against Ndlambe on 22 June. The commando comprised 500 infantry and dragoons, together with commandeered burghers under the leadership of the young Andries Stockenström (see box). Thousands of cattle were looted from the retreating Xhosa. On 15 August 1819 Nxele gave himself up after Ndlambe and most of his followers had moved away towards the Kei River. His military power was broken and this meant the end of the Fifth Frontier War. Hintsa, the paramount chief of the Gcaleka, offered refuge to Ndlambe. On orders from Governor Somerset the region between the Fish and the Keiskamma rivers was declared a neutral buffer zone. In reality the eastern boundary of the Cape Colony was thereby extended to the Keiskamma, although this region was not officially annexed.

The greatest loser was Ngqika who had to forfeit a large amount of his land although he was an ally of the British authorities. The neutral area was often, for various reasons, violated by the burghers, Khoekhoen and Xhosa respectively. The eastern boundary of the colony was officially shifted in 1825 to the Koonap River and in 1829 to the Kat River. This increased the Xhosa's sense of injustice over the loss of land where they had formerly lived.

ANDRIES STOCKENSTRÖM JUNIOR

Andries Stockenström, jnr, son of Landdrost Anders Stockenström, was born in Cape Town. At 16 years of age he accompanied Lieutenant Colonel Richard Collins as interpreter on an inspection journey to the eastern frontier zone where he gained significant insight into the lifestyle of the residents of the interior.

In 1811 he was appointed as standard bearer in the Cape Regiment. He distinguished himself as leader of the burgher commandos during the Fourth Frontier War. His practical intelligence and deliberation were recognised by Governor Cradock when he was appointed as deputy landdrost of the small newly established town of Cradock. In May 1814 he was promoted to lieutenant in his regiment and the following year Governor Somerset appointed him, at the tender age of 22 years, as landdrost of the district of Graaff-Reinet. He therefore served simultaneously in civil and military posts.

Stockenström was undoubtedly an extremely talented and ambitious leader. He was individualistic and had no qualms about criticising government policy and the actions of representatives of the London Missionary Society. This made him a controversial, but exceptional leader in the uncertain circumstances of the eastern frontier region. During the Fifth Frontier War he was in command of the Graaff-Reinet burghers who were deployed for operations in the Kat River Valley. They were supporting the paramount chief Ngqika, against Ndlambe and the Gcaleka. Afterwards, Stockenström scoured the woods near the Fish River to make the region safe. In acknowledgement of his leadership he was promoted in October 1819 to captain of the Cape Corps of Infantry and Cavalry.

Stockenström was soon involved in a spat with Captain Henry Somerset, son of the governor and recipient of a Waterloo medal for services rendered in the Napoleonic wars. He served in Grahamstown in the same corps as Stockenström. In 1820 this disagreement led to Stockenström's resignation from the corps, but he remained on as landdrost of Graaff-Reinet.

Meanwhile, Stockenström's administrative expertise and his experience of conditions in the eastern frontier zone were recognised in 1828 by the new governor, Richard Bourke, and he was appointed as commissioner general of the eastern districts. Stockenström's creation of the Kat River settlement in May 1829 was a breakthrough in better security on the eastern frontier. He settled detribalised Khoekhoen and people of mixed descent there as a buffer against the Xhosa. Headman Maqoma and his followers were forced to vacate their permanent place of residence in the Kat River region.

> Stockenström's task as commissioner general was made more difficult by the disagreement between him and Henry Somerset on the implementation of the spoor system beyond the colony's borders. In June 1830 Stockenström gave orders for a punitive expedition against one of the Xhosa headmen, Tyali, in reaction to his people's alleged stock theft. In the course of this commando action an unarmed headman by the name of Zeko was shot dead. Thereafter, Stockenström was sceptical about repeating such punitive raids by the commandos, especially if these were to be led by Henry Somerset, who was commandant of the frontier region. With the outbreak of the Sixth Frontier War in 1834, Stockenström's leadership in the frontier region was again indispensable. In 1836 the British government appointed him as lieutenant governor of the Eastern Cape. This prepared him for his subsequent involvement in local politics and also as a member of the Cape parliament. In 1856 he retired from public life and died eight years later in London with the title of baronet.

The Slagtersnek rebellion

By 1815 antagonism among members of the burgher population in the eastern frontier districts against the British authorities took on serious proportions. The findings of the circuit court of 1812 were still fresh in the memory of the burghers. In 1815 a Khoekhoe farm worker by the name of Booy lodged a complaint of mistreatment at the office of the landdrost in Graaff-Reinet against his employer, Cornelis Frederik (Freek) Bezuidenhout, who lived along the Baviaans River. When Bezuidenhout failed to turn up at the court despite repeated warnings, Lieutenant Rousseau and Ensign MacKay with twelve soldiers of the Cape Regiment were sent to arrest him. This group, accompanied by two officials of the court, arrived on Bezuidenhout's farm on 10 October 1815.

Bezuidenhout, his son Hans, of mixed origin, and the 18-year-old Jacob Erasmus, a chance visitor, took up a position behind a few rocks near the homestead. He began to fire at the soldiers and they returned the musketry. Bezuidenhout and his two helpers then sought better shelter in a crevice under a rocky ledge beside the Baviaans River. After many requests to surrender, Rousseau ordered the soldiers to storm the hiding place. Bezuidenhout's two helpers gave themselves up without any further resistance. In the shooting that followed, Bezuidenhout was mortally wounded and was buried the following day on his farm.

At the graveside, his brother Johannes (Hans) swore that he would avenge his brother's death. Hendrik Frederik (Kasteel) Prinsloo was also fired up by this incident to organise a burgher rebellion against the British authorities, who according to the records of the high court case that followed, he labelled as "God forsaken tyrants and scoundrels" (*"Godvergete tiranne en skelms"*). Hans Bezuidenhout reportedly said that the burghers of the eastern frontier region could no longer endure the "heavy burdens and injustice" (*"swaar laste en onreg"*) of the British authorities. He believed that his dead brother had been blameless and that the burghers should "fight their country free again" (*"weer vry moes veg"*). Rousseau's military post, he said, should be attacked and the burghers should seize all the ammunition. Another burgher, Cornelis Faber, should be sent to solicit help from Ngqika for a simultaneous attack of all the military posts along the border. It would be "an encounter in which blood would be shed" (*"oorlog des bloedkuils"*) and no mercy would be shown. Hans Bezuidenhout believed that the Khoekhoe soldiers received more privileges at the hands of the British authorities than did the burghers in the eastern frontier districts. He was prepared to offer the entire Zuurveld right up to the Bushmans River as compensation for Xhosa assistance against the British colonial government.

Captain Caesar Andrews of the Cape Regiment immediately sent soldiers to arrest Hendrik Prinsloo. This prevented the leaders of the rebellion from persuading more burghers to take up arms. About 60 rebels turned up on 14 November at Andrew's military post and demanded that Prinsloo be set free. Major Fraser arrived and insisted that any grievances should be submitted in writing to the authorities in the proper manner. This calmed the emotions. The rebellious burghers gathered on 18 November at Slagtersnek, but were confronted by a military force of 40 soldiers and 39 loyal burghers. Commandant Willem Nel and field-cornet Adriaan de Lange persuaded some of the rebels to give themselves up.

However, the rebel leaders Hans Bezuidenhout, Cornelis Faber, Stephanus Bothma, Abraham Bothma and Andries Meyer fled northwards and were followed by Fraser. By 29 November most of them were forced to surrender in the Tarka River region near the Winterberg by troops of the Cape Regiment. Hans Bezuidenhout, his wife Martha and eleven-year-old son Gerrit offered resistance at Madoers Drift (Spring Valley). Bezuidenhout was killed in the skirmish and his wife and son lightly wounded.

The question of the real motives of the leaders of the uprising and the attitude of some burghers on the eastern frontier against the British authorities remains controversial. Governor Somerset was of the opinion that the burghers had grown accustomed to regarding the Khoekhoen as inferior and that because of this, the death of Freek Bezuidenhout by soldiers of the Cape Regiment aroused a general feeling of antipathy among them. In a letter to Lord Bathurst, British secretary of state for the colonies, Somerset declared: "Independent of the great distinction between Christian and Heathen, which they look upon the Hottentots to be, the difference between Black and White ... will take much time to do away [with] in the feelings of this people."

The high court found the six leaders of the uprising guilty of high treason. They were sentenced to death by hanging. They were Prinsloo, Faber, the two Bothma brothers, Theunis de Klerk and Willem F. Krugel. The latter was subsequently reprieved by the governor for his valuable service in the Fourth Frontier War, but he was banned from the eastern frontier region for life.

The public execution of the other five condemned men took place on 9 March 1816 on the farm of Willem van Aardt. The hangman was summoned from George, but he took only one new gallows noose with him. This meant that weathered ropes were used for the simultaneous execution, and four of the condemned fell to the ground. They begged Landdrost Cuyler for mercy, but Cuyler was not empowered to make changes to the decision of the courts and the procedure was repeated. For many years these tragic events served as a grave warning for dissatisfied burghers; they realised all too well that armed resistance against the authorities was doomed to fail.

The events at Slagtersnek also convinced Cuyler that the Khoekhoen was the only element of the population that the British authorities could rely upon in a crisis. Field-cornet Abraham Greyling of Zwagershoek confirmed that the burghers of Bruintjeshoogte were convinced that the British authorities were more inclined to protect the Khoekhoen than the burghers. However, the commissioners of justice who visited the eastern frontier region found that: "The cause of the Rebellion may be clearly traced to a few discontented inhabitants of the neighbourhood of the Baviaans River, the relatives and friends of C.F. Bezuidenhout, whose uniform disobedience to the laws of years past, and at last violent resistance to them, led to his own destruction."

In contrast, years later Louis Meurant, editor of *Het Kaapsche Grensblad*, declared that the use of Khoekhoe soldiers was a controversial and not to be forgotten decision. Many Xhosa chieftains had shed a great deal of blood and caused enormous misery in the eastern frontier zone, but came off scot-free.

It is clear that although most of the burghers did not approve of the Bezuidenhouts' actions, they sympathised with their motives. For some burghers in the frontier districts the uprising became a symbol of their oppression by the British, but there were also loyal burghers who helped to end the rebellion quickly and with as little violence as possible. The Slagtersnek rebellion eventually only had a limited influence on those who decided to move away from the eastern frontier region as part of the Great Trek some two decades later.

The British settlers

In 1820 the number of residents in the Cape Colony increased significantly with the arrival of about 4000 British settlers. This meant that the total civilian population rose within a few months from some 42 000 to about 46 000. Why did these British settlers decide to move to the Cape?

By 1815 the Napoleonic wars were over and unemployment increased in Britain. To make matters worse, levels of British trade decreased due to international competition and industries cut down on the number of workers because modern technology and mechanisation called for fewer, but better-skilled operators. The Cape Colony offered a rosy livelihood for British emigrants. After the Fifth Frontier War there was relative peace and the neutral buffer zone and border posts gave the impression of effective security for colonial residents.

A project initiated by Benjamin Moodie to encourage Scottish apprentices and tradesmen to the colony was successfully carried out in 1817. These new immigrants were settled near Grootvadersbosch in the Swellendam district. In the same year Governor Somerset issued a plea to the British government to allow selected settlers to establish themselves as stock farmers in the depopulated Zuurveld. The result was that in 1819 the British government made funds available for an ambitious emigration scheme. Prospective settlers in groups of at least ten adult men, with wives and children would be sent free of charge by ship to the Cape and supported once there. Each settler would be given a small farm of about 40 hectares on a quitrent basis and exempted from levying during the first ten years. Agricultural implements such as English ploughs and seed-wheat, as well as food rations at cost price, were promised to all settlers.

In 1820 approximately 4000 settlers under 57 leaders arrived in Algoa Bay. The first of 21 ships carrying settlers were the *Chapman* and *Nautilus*. Somerset was on leave in England when they arrived and the acting governor, Sir Rufane Donkin, had to make local arrangements for the reception and placement of the settlers. They came from all levels of British society and from various rural and urban areas. Donkin had instructions to place the English, Scottish and Irish apart from one another.

It was no easy task to settle the 4000 newcomers in appropriate groups in their respective destinations. The largest single group was 344 people under their leader Hezekhiah Sephton, while the smallest group was 23 people under Miles Bowker. John Bailie's group required about 100 ox-wagons to reach their destination near the mouth of the Fish River. Khoekhoe wagon leaders and experienced burghers were used as guides. Thomas Pringle's group of Scottish settlers had to embark on a journey of 16 days to reach their small farms along the Baviaans River.

The settlers were poorly prepared for the new challenges. Not all of them were experienced farmers and they were unfamiliar with local conditions. It was a tough learning curve. Initially they lived in temporary wattle-and-daub huts and soon found that the light English ploughs were not well suited to till the ground in the Zuurveld. In addition, the farms were too small to be economically viable. The wheat crops were destroyed by rust, caterpillars, locusts and unseasonable floods. The market was also limited. Many settlers eventually turned to other means of making a living as merchants, officials, stock farmers and fishermen.

Some settlers had significant success as livestock farmers. Among the pioneers in merino sheep farming were Richard Daniell, Miles Bowker and Thomas Philipps. Other settlers followed the example of experienced colonial cattle farmers when they were able to buy larger farms. Then there were those who made their mark in the civil service and successful commercial undertakings. A typical example was the versatile John Centlivres Chase who became a merchant and official, as well as a politician and writer.

On his return to the colony in 1822, Somerset raised a number of objections about Donkin's efforts, but his autocratic managerial style soon drew criticism from all sides. The crown colony status of the Cape Colony made the governor virtually untouchable as far as the colonists and their complaints were concerned. Somerset was only responsible for his decisions to the imperial government in London. His direct contact there was the current secretary of state for the colonies, Lord Bathurst. The Council of Advice which was introduced in the colony in 1825 did nothing to curb the governor's monopoly on local decision making. It was nevertheless a body which paved the way for a greater voice for the colonists as far as governance was concerned. A representative government organ, the Legislative Council, was introduced in 1834. These changes were largely the result of settler agitation.

The struggle for freedom of the press was an example of the settlers' criticism of the governor's interference and his prohibition of any public expression of opinion. The report on a libel case in Thomas Pringle and John Fairbairn's weekly paper, *The South African Commercial Advertiser*, raised Somerset's ire. In May 1824 he banned all further editions of the paper. Pringle and the printer, George Greig, went to London to submit a complaint about the unwarranted limits placed on the free expression of public opinion. Bathurst reacted sympathetically and ruled that the weekly could resume publication subject to certain conditions. Only in 1828 was the struggle for freedom of the press won in the colony. The governor and his council could now no longer step in to forbid responsible journalistic reports and critical commentary.

Another area in which the settlers knowingly made an impression was the notable anglicisation of colonial society. It was the explicit ideal of Somerset and his predecessors to make the local population proficient in spoken and written English as soon as possible. Somerset's aim was to serve the interests of the British Empire by re-shaping all the residents of the colony in the British-born image. The idea was created that British culture and institutions were far better and of higher calibre than any other. The arrival of the British settlers and their typical character and way of life strengthened this perception.

In consultation with Bathurst, Somerset allowed a number of Scottish Presbyterian ministers such as George Thom (Caledon), Andrew Murray (Graaff-Reinet) and Henry Sutherland (Worcester) to come to the Cape to fill vacancies in the Dutch Reformed Church. Despite opposition, a bilingual policy was permitted in the church. At the synod of 1834, twelve of the 22 ministers were Scottish. Teachers were also brought in from Scotland to anglicise the youth, but the Afrikaans-speaking youths were not fully anglicised. Examples of these capable imported teachers were James Rose-Innes (Uitenhage) and William Robertson (Graaff-Reinet).

Somerset's language proclamation of 1822 outlined the gist of his anglicisation policy. He announced a three-part time schedule for its official implementation. From 1823 English was to be the only official language in the colony. By 1825 it had to be the only language in the records of all government offices and two years later English would be the only language used in the judicial courts of the colony. On the positive side, Somerset did make an important contribution in creating certain institutions such as the jury system and the appointment of civil commissioners and justices of the peace. These replaced the old Burgher Senate, heemraden and landdrosts.

The settlers undoubtedly gave a permanent British character to the white population of the Eastern Cape and this was an asset to the colony as a whole. Their descendants adapted these traditions to changing times and circumstances.

By 1834, on the eve of the Sixth Frontier War and the emigration of thousands of Afrikaans-speaking burghers during the Great Trek, Cape society had all the social ingredients which would eventually characterise the so-called rainbow nation of South Africa. In the century that followed many polarising factors, but also ideals that united the people, formed the seedbed for countless changes in South Africa.

5
Migration and the societies north of the Gariep River
Jan Visagie

The movements of black people in southern Africa in the period 1750–1835 during the Mfecane were for the most part enforced migrations. Broadly speaking, what are the causes of migration? One interesting theory refers to the push-and-pull factors that motivate people to move. The push factors include occurrences in a country which as it were force people out; these factors are usually aggressive in nature. In other words, certain circumstances "pushed" people out and made them move away. Push factors which might prompt thoughts of moving include shortage of employment opportunities; lack of land; political censure or fear; grievances with regard to culture and language; disillusionment about certain legislation, etc. As for pull factors, these are usually positive aspects in another country that attract people and persuade them to move there. These could be factors such as better work opportunities; better living conditions; political and religious freedom; security; better education facilities; better medical care; family ties; and the availability of cheap labour and land.

The migrations in southern Africa such as the Mfecane and the Great Trek were in fact very small in comparison with migration streams elsewhere in the world, for example the resettlement of 400 000 Jews in Palestine in the early 1900s. Another example in the twentieth century is the migration of three million Russians, Poles and Germans out of the Soviet Union in the wake of the Russian civil war.

Migrations in southern Africa

This chapter will first provide a brief discussion of the origin, composition, grouping, migrations and lifestyles of the various population groups who lived north of the Gariep River (as the Khoekhoen called the Orange River) in the period from 1750 to 1835. This background information will promote a better understanding of the Mfecane and Great Trek.

By about 1800 there were various Khoekhoe, Bushman, coloured and Bantu-speaking communities north of the Gariep. In addition there were already a few whites and some coloured residents such as the Griqua and the Korana who had moved out of the Cape Colony in search of a livelihood.

Further east in the regions that are today known as Mpumalanga, the eastern parts of Limpopo, Free State, KwaZulu-Natal, the eastern part of the Eastern Cape and the kingdom of Swaziland, there were Bushman, Sotho, Tswana, northern Nguni and southern Nguni societies, as well as the Venda and Lemba. Among these groups it was largely the Griqua and Korana between the Gariep, Harts and Vaal rivers; the rising Zulu kingdom under Shaka in Natal; the Basotho under Moshoeshoe at Thaba Bosiu; and the Ndebele (also called Matebele) under Mzilikazi on the western Highveld (west of present-day Pretoria), who formed new power blocs in the interior.

Further "ingredients" in this pot which within a decade or three would threaten to boil over, were the white trekboers who had moved in these years out of the Cape Colony and over the Gariep. At the same time a number of missionaries settled there. Also in the mix was the British government; it was slowly beginning to take an interest in this region and exercise its authority there. It is true to say that the Cape Colony was "overflowing" and its northern border was in effect being pushed further north.

CAPE BORDER REGIONS

What is understood by the names given to the Cape northern border, northeastern border and eastern border regions in the first half of the nineteenth century?

Normally a border is merely an imaginary line or geographical landmark (rivers or mountains) which delineates a region. In the Cape documents of that time it was often also used for the name of the region/area or districts that lay along this border.

In the period from 1800 to 1850 the Cape borders were changed often, but in broad terms the *northern border* ran from the west coast to about just west of the town of Colesberg (at the Seekoei River). Initially this boundary line was far further south of the Orange River. For example, in about 1800 the border ran from the west coast along the Buffels River, over the Nuweveld Mountains to the Plettenberg beacon on the Seekoei River. At the time, the districts south of this border, such as Stellenbosch and Graaff-Reinet, were the northern border districts. Stellenbosch was later sub-divided into various districts such as Tulbagh and Clanwilliam, while from Graaff-Reinet the districts of Somerset (East), Beaufort West and others were formed.

In later years the *northeastern border* ran southwards from the mouth of the Stormberg Spruit (a tributary of the Orange River) all along the Stormberg Spruit to the Stormberg range and then southwards following the Klaassmits and Swartkei rivers to the Winterberg Mountains. The large districts of Cradock and Somerset (East) lay along the northern border.

By about 1825 the *eastern border* south of the Winterberg followed the Koonap and Great Fish rivers to the coast. The district of Albany (Grahamstown) was situated on this boundary line.

The Bushmen

Expansion to the north and north-east from the Cape Colony, as well as the expansion from the Eastern Cape, Transgariep and Natal, meant that the Bushmen groups living there were either pushed out or were subjugated. Bushmen who were not integrated into the economy of white farmers or those of the various black communities, dispersed to beyond the colony's northern and northeastern borders where they joined up with other hunter gatherers.

In the interior the relationship between the Bushmen and black groups deteriorated sharply when black people encroached on their hunting areas. The Bushmen reacted to their settlement by attacking them and stealing their livestock. This was a repetition of their reaction against the white farmers who had settled in their hunting grounds in the colony a decade or two earlier. The eventual outcome was that the Bushmen were either driven off by the black communities or incorporated into their social structure as people of lower status.

These clashes between the Bushmen and their rivals, the southern Nguni and northern Nguni, eventually meant that the Bushmen fled to the mountainous regions of the Eastern Cape and to the Drakensberg. However, the small Bushmen groups who struggled to survive in the Drakensberg were attacked and virtually wiped out in the 1820s and 1830s by desperate fugitive groups who were victims of the Mfecane.

The area between the northern border (which in about 1800 was still south of the Gariep River) and the Gariep River, and also north of it, was occupied by the Griqua from about 1780. They drove the Bushmen away from their fountains and hunting grounds in an aggressive and cruel manner. The second group of arrivals in the region, the white trekboers, also drove the Bushmen purposefully from the north-west, an area known as Bushmanland, in the years between 1800 and 1825. There were also some reasonably successful efforts on the part of the white farmers to hire the Bushmen as workers, and to befriend others by giving them food and livestock. Many Bushmen became herdsmen and workers on the white burghers' farms and thereby surrendered their independence.

The Korana

The Korana were among the earliest residents of the Transgariep. Some historians believe that they were part of the Khoekhoe communities who migrated northwards very early and established themselves just north of the Gariep River. They were nomadic livestock farmers and were constantly in search of water and grazing. The Korana, like the Khoekhoe groups, showed a lack of cohesion and by the 1830s there were at least twenty separate groups, each under its own *kaptein* (captains or chiefs). These groups were in time strengthened by the northwards expansion of small Khoekhoe groups who moved out of the Cape Colony and over the Gariep in the early eighteenth century. Even white burghers, slaves and free blacks who for one or another transgression had to leave the colony, joined the Korana groups.

Certain Korana communities grew strongly such as the Swart Volk (black people) under the leadership of the white fugitive Jacob Kruger, who had several Korana wives. His propensity for violence, along with his possession of firearms, soon split the group into two. The Regshande (right-handed ones) under Kruger settled in the vicinity of the later Griekwastad (Griquatown), while the Towenaars (wizards) lived in the southern Transgariep. There was also a group under white leadership in the person of Jan Bloem; and another that was led by Koos Taaibosch. The Korana groups moved around a great deal and later, with the help of their firearms, launched marauding raids on the Bushmen, Griqua, Sotho, Tswana and Ndebele. By the end of the eighteenth century they were notorious for their constant plundering expeditions in the interior. Smaller

Sotho chieftaincies between the Gariep and Vaal were virtually wiped out by the Korana.

In the 1820s and 1830s the Korana often teamed up with splinter groups and victims of the Mfecane to plunder other communities. For example, they connived with the Taung and Rolong in 1828 and again in 1831 to attack the Ndebele of Mzilikazi. Both attacks failed miserably. The Bushmen were constantly under pressure from the Korana and later particularly from the Griqua. Many Bushmen were integrated into the ranks of the Korana in the process and some Korana groups even served under Bushman captains such as Dawid Danster. The Griqua under Andries Waterboer and Adam Kok often formed alliances with the Korana and together they attacked the formidable Ndebele. The Griqua chiefs wanted to bring the Korana under their control but could never really succeed in doing so.

The Griqua

The Griqua were the first of the groups who assumed a more or less Western lifestyle to settle permanently in reasonably large communities north of the Gariep. Their migration to the north and north-east was to a large extent motivated by their quest for available and easily attainable land, although in some cases they also sought freedom from domination, discrimination and harsh colonial laws.

Among the disintegrating Khoekhoe groups there was a large group which refused to enter the service of white farmers. They lived in small scattered groups on the borders of the colony and tried to make a living as hunter gatherers, livestock farmers and even stock thieves. Their membership was gradually strengthened by escaped slaves, free blacks, "Basters" (half-breeds) and a few white people. Their spoken language was Dutch and their apparel, weapons and certain aspects of their lifestyle were largely similar to those of the white farmers. During a meeting on 7 August 1813 at the small town of Klaarwater, this mixed group of people decided to assume the name Griqua and that Klaarwater would henceforth be known as Griekwastad (Griquatown). The Rev. John Campbell, inspector of the London Missionary Society (LMS) who was present at the meeting, recorded this interesting event in his book *Travels in South Africa*.

In about 1800 two important Griqua communities settled between the colonial northern border and the Gariep. One was under Cornelius Kok, son of Adam Kok, who had just died, and Cornelius's sons Adam II and Cornelius II. The second group was led by Barend Barends and comprised mostly of "Basters". By 1805 both chiefdoms lived north of the Gariep: Kok and his group at Klaarwater (later Griquatown) and Barends and his followers at Daniëlskuil. The authority of these captains or chiefs was recognised by the colonial government. In the exercise of his power, each chief was supported by a council that passed the necessary laws. Judicial power was in the hands of magistrates who were usually members of the chiefs' families. Local administration was carried out by field-cornets; in time of war they also acted as military commanders.

The Griqua chiefs Cornelius Kok, his son Adam Kok II, and Barend Barends were restless people who moved around a great deal, making a steadfast administrative system very difficult. Furthermore, the relationship between the chiefs and the missionaries of the LMS, who had been working among the Griqua since 1801, was a troubled one because the missionaries interfered in Griqua affairs by among other things favouring the introduction of an elected chieftainship in place of the existing hereditary system. Another issue that caused instability was that many of the new arrivals who were absorbed into Griqua ranks, namely "Basters", Korana and Khoekhoe groups, were not always prepared to accept the authority of the captains. Chiefly power was also weakened by some of their subjects who through trading activity had become relatively wealthy and had acquired firearms. This increasingly made them feel secure in their independence of the captains' authority.

In time there was a further division between various Griqua chiefdoms which had a negative impact on unity. Cornelius Kok decided to relinquish his chieftaincy in favour of his son Adam Kok and return to his earlier home in the Kamiesberg. Meanwhile, the missionaries persuaded the Griqua to introduce an elected chief and Adam Kok was duly elected as their leader. This election was fully recognised by the colonial government and Kok received the official mace from the Cape governor. In 1816 Cornelius Kok returned to Griquatown and reclaimed the chieftainship. However, his influence had waned during his absence and he and his followers were forced to move off and settle in Campbell. Shortly before his death he appointed his other son, Cornelius II, as his heir to the chieftaincy.

Adam Kok II eventually resisted the political interference of the missionaries and this caused further division among the chieftaincies. A Griqua group called the Hartenaars rose against him and formed an independent authority near the Harts River. Adam Kok II was so disconcerted by this development that he resigned, and shortly before his departure from Griquatown he handed over the reins of government to his son, Kort Adam. The missionaries again interfered and organised an election in which Andries Waterboer, the missionaries' favourite, was chosen as chief. Waterboer had been trained by the missionaries and had even stood in for a short while as assistant missionary. The missionaries had chosen him above the illiterate Adam Kok, but some Griqua were dissatisfied because Waterboer was not a member of the Kok family and was partly of Bushman descent. The instability and division among the Griqua grew even worse with Waterboer's election and the possibility that the four chiefs might unite became even more remote.

The missionary William Anderson and his colleagues worked tirelessly in Griquatown and established a firm base of Christianity there. The missionaries also played an important role in many other spheres. They even handled the colonial government's correspondence with the Griqua and thereby unofficially represented the British government. However, Anderson's political interference and his attempts to force ethical norms upon the Griqua eventually undermined his authority and in 1820 he left Griquatown. Shortly after his departure the British government began to make its authority north of the Gariep felt by placing a British resident in Griquatown. He was John Melvill, a former government land surveyor who also had an interest in missionary work. Melvill's attempts to unite the Griqua under Waterboer caused great dissatisfaction among the other chiefs and in 1826 he returned to the Cape Colony without having accomplished anything.

Meanwhile, through the intercession of Dr John Philip, superintendent of the LMS, Adam Kok II established himself on the old Bushman mission station at Philippolis. Here Kok and his group of about sixty Griqua families set up a system of governance comprising a council of twelve members as well as magistrates and field-cornets. His secretary and right-hand man was the intelligent Hendrik Hendriks who also handled the correspondence with the British government. Other residents who lived there with the Griqua were Tswana, Sotho and Korana families. They too, along with newcomers from the colony, were accepted into the community. In the early 1830s a few Khoekhoen, former residents of the Kat River settlement just north of Fort Beaufort in the Cape Colony, also joined

Kok's people. Adam Kok died in 1835 and after many disagreements and upheavals he was succeeded by his son Adam Kok III.

So it was that in the first decades of the nineteenth century the Griqua state grew rapidly and became significantly stronger; with time they also extended their land holdings at the expense of the Bushmen and other communities. The Bushmen were chased out of their hunting grounds and killed, while Korana groups in the vicinity were forced into submission. The Griqua economy was based mainly on livestock farming, but the cultivation of grain and more particularly the conduct of trade in cattle, skins, ivory, salt and grain with neighbouring communities such as the Tlhaping, Basotho and Korana, took precedence. By acting as the middlemen between the colony and the black communities north of the Gariep in the 1820s and 1830s, the trade in these products brought good profits for the Griqua, which served to increase their living standards appreciably.

In June 1823 the Tlhaping town of Dithakong was threatened by a group of Phuting, Fokeng and Hlakwana. They were fugitives who had been attacked by other groups and then – typical of the Mfecane period – planned to attack the next group. Robert Moffat, the LMS missionary, rushed to ask the Griqua to help defend Dithakong and Adam Kok, Barend Barends and Andries Waterboer, together with about a hundred armed men, helped to beat off the attack.

Mzilikazi's Ndebele made their influence felt on the western Highveld from 1826 and subjugated most of the Tswana chieftaincies. The result was that the Griqua trade routes with their northern neighbours were blocked and made more tenuous. In reaction to this, in 1829 a combined Griqua, Korana and Tswana force under Jan Bloem advanced against Mzilikazi, but after initial successes the Ndebele launched a counter-attack and more than fifty of Bloem's men were killed.

Barend Barends made determined efforts to unite all the Ndebele's enemies so that they could be forced out of Griqua territory. In June 1831 a combined Griqua, Tlhaping and Rolong force advanced on Mzilikazi; about half of the approximately 1000 men were Griqua. After they had looted 6000 head of cattle from the Ndebele, they made the acquaintance of Mzilikazi's full and terrible might; Barends's camp was attacked in the dead of night and about 400 Griqua were killed.

The Voortrekkers who were moving into the region soon awakened the interest of the Griqua, who saw them as suitable allies against Mzilikazi. In 1836, together with a commando of Voortrekkers and Rolong, the Griqua advanced confidently against Mzilikazi at Mosega. The attack prompted Mzilikazi's decision in 1837 to leave the Marico district and his retreat effectively split the Ndebele into two groups. One moved into what is today Zimbabwe, while the other under Mzilikazi himself settled in the Okavango area in the north of present-day Botswana. Only later did Mzilikazi and this group rejoin his other followers. However, the Griqua played only a small role in Mzilikazi's decision to move to Zimbabwe.

The Griqua's knowledge and possession of firearms and horses meant that in the 1820s and 1830s they were largely spared the chaos of the Mfecane in the interior and were able to avoid direct attacks. But as we have seen above, they were involved to some extent. The historian H.J. van Aswegen (1988) notes that the settlement of the Griqua in the Transgariep created a new open frontier region where colonised groups came into contact with one another. The Griqua settlement, amidst the destruction and violence surrounding them, did succeed in their relatively small area in creating a sense of calm which made the white farmers' occupation of the region easier, but which ironically enough was to the detriment of the Griqua.

White trekboers

Even before 1700, white livestock farmers from the Cape Colony slowly began to move northwards and later eastwards into the interior in search of better grazing for their herds. Most white livestock farmers were settled on their loan-farms in the colony, but there was a group who for financial reasons moved around and in time they became known in history as the trekboers. The systematic possession of farms in the eighteenth century was spontaneous expansionism and not part of the Vereenigde Oost-Indische Compagnie's (VOC) policy. Despite the fact that the VOC had no wish that it should do so, the Cape Colony expanded enormously between the years 1700 and 1780. The Western Cape district of Stellenbosch could for several years until the Graaff-Reinet district came into being in 1785, similarly be called an Eastern Cape district because the Lower Fish River formed part of its eastern border.

In about 1780, when the migration of the cattle farmers was checked by the Great Fish River and the Bantu-speaking societies, the migration stream swung towards the north. By 1778, the northernmost point of the northern border region was the Plettenberg beacon near Colesberg, but the livestock farmers soon moved further north as far as the Gariep River and laid claim to farms. One outcome of this expansion process was that the Cape government had to continuously and systematically move the boundary to keep the white population within its borders. In the first decades of the nineteenth century the expansion continued and even before 1820 a few white farmers moved beyond the Gariep River at certain times of the year in search of grazing for their livestock. In the years 1822 to 1824 the northern boundary was moved to the Orange (Gariep) River, but even this did not stop the white farmers.

The periodic droughts, particularly in the border districts of the Cape Colony, were among the most important reasons why livestock farmers had to go in search of better grazing for their herds in certain years and seasons. There were also factors such as migratory antelope and locusts that from time to time destroyed the available grazing. The carrying capacity (number of sheep per hectare) of land in the Karoo districts was low and far bigger farms were necessary to provide sufficient grazing and water for an average-sized herd. Even the largest Karoo farms were inadequate to meet these needs in times of drought. At such times, the farmers in the northeastern border regions regularly crossed to the other side of the Stormberg stream with their herds, while those in the northern border area moved across the Gariep River.

In this way the trekboers developed mobility. While on the move their wagons were their homes and their protection against wind and weather; they also served as a means of refuge when they were under enemy attack. Because their seasonal migrations were by and large economically motivated they did not initially want to settle permanently in the Transgariep, but once they had done so they consistently tried to maintain their ties with the Cape Colony as befits dutiful citizens, and paid their state dues such as the annual *rekognisiegelde* (recognition fees) on loan farms to the relevant local government bodies. It was important for them to remain registered on the district *opgaafrol* (tax roll) and to keep their links with the Cape NG Church.

The livestock farmers in the border districts, particularly those in Colesberg (an offshoot of the Graaff-Reinet district) and Cradock did not all possess their own farms. Some of these farmers, those who were not *bywoners* (white tenant farmers), had to move around in search of grazing and water. Families without fixed property were among the first to leave the colony and settle permanently in the Transgariep. By the early 1830s more than 200 families who by their own admission did not own ground, already lived beyond the border. In 1834 they informed the government that they were unable to find land in the colony and that if the authorities refused to give them permission to take possession of land north of the Gariep, they would be obliged to live an independent existence in the Transgariep.

In the 1830s many other trekboers who owned land in the colony also decided to make the Transgariep their permanent home although they were reluctant to relinquish their citizenship. By 1834 there were 1000 white trekboer families in the Transgariep. Some were perhaps still seasonal migrants but a large percentage was permanently settled there. A year or two later, some of the farmers in the Transgariep were already so strongly anti-British that they joined up with the Voortrekkers who were passing by on their way into the interior.

The trekboers' isolated existence made them individualistic as far as exercising their own authority in their environment and over their families and workers was concerned. In doing so they were often heavy-handed in their treatment of their workers (Khoekhoen, slaves or black people). Furthermore, they soon started to resist the authority of the distant Cape government and that of their neighbours in the region. Because of dangers in the border region they were forced to protect themselves and to use firearms if necessary.

In the 1820s when the trekboers arrived in the area north of the Gariep River, the Bushmen were already involved in clashes with the Korana and Griqua. Attempts by the Cape government and the missionaries failed to protect the Bushmen and offer them alternative means of subsistence. A few white trekboers tried to collect cattle for the Bushmen and to give them a more stable and independent lifestyle, but this too came to nothing. Livestock farmers complained that Bushmen stock thieves from the mission station at Philippolis were depleting their herds. Eventually the Bushmen were driven away from their hunting grounds by white trekboers and the Griqua.

Despite Adam Kok's attempts to remove the incoming white livestock farmers from his land along the Riet and Modder rivers, his Griqua followers did not always co-operate. Indeed, many Griqua sold or hired out their farms to the trekboers and Kok's authority was not assertive enough to prevent this. These transactions later caused problems on the validity of land rights; added to which it should not be forgotten that despite Adam Kok's claims to the land, it was in fact the traditional property of the Bushmen.

The trekboers' occupation of the southeastern Transgariep in the years 1825 to 1836 was also characterised by individuals who began to expand into the western Transgariep. After 1836 their interaction with the Griqua deteriorated substantially.

Until 1836 the trekboers' contact with the Basotho in the eastern Transgariep, that is the Caledon River valley, was limited. Because of the upheavals of the Mfecane, Moshoeshoe of the Basotho was obliged to remain in his stronghold on Thaba Bosiu. He and his people feared attacks from two fierce competitors, the Tlokwa and Mzilikazi's Ndebele, who until 1836 had regularly wreaked havoc among nearby communities. After 1836, when the turmoil of the Mfecane had abated, the trekboers' settlement in the Caledon valley became even more of a land-rights problem, one which later led to a great deal of conflict. And this was only the beginning, because the white expansion into the interior was now about to get into full stride.

The Mfecane/Difaqane

Our knowledge of the migration, groupings and residential areas, as well as the political and social structure of the black societies in southern Africa prior to 1700 is limited. It is however clear that they made knowledgeable and advantageous use of their environment and the available resources. From the eleventh to the eighteenth century the population growth of these societies increased exponentially and their settlement and grouping also began to take on a fixed pattern.

For practical reasons, anthropologists divide the Bantu-speaking communities of South Africa into two main groups, namely the Nguni speakers and the Sotho/Tswana speakers. Each of these groups is then sub-divided, although anthropologists emphasise that these divisions are somewhat artificial because African people do not use the terms *Nguni* and *Sotho/Tswana* in such a broad context and it is indeed smaller groupings that are thus named. The sub-division of the Nguni and Sotho/Tswana into northern, southern and western groups has been created by anthropologists for practical reasons. Furthermore, the terms *Nguni* and *Sotho/Tswana* do not imply that they are homogenous groups. Indeed, with time intermixing took place, which means that a clear differentiation between the two groups is not always possible.

The northern Nguni group comprises the Zulu and Swazi, while the southern Nguni group includes the Xhosa, Mpondo, Thembu and Mpondomise. The western Sotho/Tswana comprises, among others, the Rolong, Hurutshe, Kwena, Fokeng and Kgatla, while the major northern Sotho society is the Pedi. The southern Sotho included a variety of smaller communities before they were incorporated in the nineteenth century into the Basotho. Societies such as the Venda, Lemba and Tsonga do not fall under the major divisions mentioned above but are nevertheless influenced by nearby groups as a result of their close interaction with them.

In the period of about 1750 to 1835 a process of transformation took place among black societies in southern Africa that is known as the "Mfecane" in Zulu and the "Difaqane" by the Sotho/Tswana people. In the light of the fact that these terms were included in at least one dictionary of the late nineteenth century, they must have been in reasonably wide use by that time. The German missionary Albert Kropf defines the word "im-Fecane" in his Xhosa dictionary as "Marauders, free-booters, bandits, lawless tribe, especially the followers of Matiwana [Matiwane], who were defeated and broken up at the Umtata [Mthatha River] in 1829". It is however more correct to note that in Sotho/Tswana the word "Difaqane" literally means "enforced migration" and that this refers to events in the period from 1750 to 1835. For practical reasons in this chapter the events will be referred to as Mfecane, the Zulu equivalent.

This transformation can be described as a series of dramatic events because it changed the composition of black societies, their settlement patterns and indeed the entire demography of southern Africa. Outwardly, it had the appearance of waves of violence that rippled outwards. When one community attacked a neighbouring group and subjected them and/or put them to flight, the victims were evicted from their traditional settlement areas and in order to survive attacked other communities. In this way a chain of clashes and incidents of looting and carnage took place which eventually led to the displacement of living areas, the formation of new communities and the origin of new power blocs.

The conflicts were widely dispersed and their influence was felt from present-day Tanzania, Zimbabwe and Mozambique in the north, to the Cape eastern border region in the south; and from today's Botswana in the west to the Basotho settlement areas and then the coastal area in the east.

According to research undertaken in the last few decades, the Mfecane was not simply triggered by the Zulu king Shaka and his destructive campaigns of conquest but began many years before his time in an area to the north of Zululand. The argument is that the Mfecane can be attributed to ground-breaking changes of a socio-economic nature within the black societies.

But Shaka's part in the causes of the Mfecane cannot be entirely ignored. More recent research indicates that although he did not play as big a role as was first thought, he and his overwhelming military might were responsible for a great deal of unrest and shedding of blood. Indeed, it could be argued that he gave momentum to the whole process of violence at the time in what is today KwaZulu-Natal. However, elsewhere in Zululand there were also flash points of violence and Shaka and his Zulu force was only one of these. For instance, as early as about 1750 and in the decades thereafter there was a fierce internecine war raging between various communities in and around the area of today's North West Province.

Research has also shown that groups such as the Griqua, Korana, white trekboers, white hunters, hawkers, slave traders in Delagoa Bay and even missionaries played an insignificant, yet disruptive role – if at all.

There is however also the so-called "Cobbing theory" named after the historian Julian Cobbing. He argues that white people from the Cape Colony and the Portuguese colony of Mozambique were initially responsible for the unrest. According to him, the problem was caused by white raiding groups supported by the Griqua and Korana, who came to seize slaves for labour in the South African interior. According to Cobbing, missionaries such as Robert Moffat and John Melvill were simply slave traders (wolves) in sheep's clothing. They put calculated pressure on black groups near the northern frontier to go and work in the Cape, and in this way exacerbated the unrest in the interior. The Cobbing theory means that the Zulu's role in the Mfecane was less pervasive and that the militaristic Zulu kingdom was structured on self-defence. Be that as it may, the final word on the causes of the Mfecane has yet to be written.

The origin of the Mfecane can also be traced back to the Sotho/Tswana-speaking communities who from 1750 onwards were embroiled in widespread internecine conflict. In the vicinity of the present-day North West Province, societies such as the Kwena, Kgatla, Rolong, Fokeng and Hurutshe were involved in conflicts which, as elsewhere, were characterised by fierce rivalry. Only after 1800 did the Ngwaketse break the Hurutshe's supremacy on the Madikwe River. South of the Molopo River the Tlhaping gained control over the Rolong; and the Kgatla and Pedi became the strongest societies on the Mashishing (Lydenburg) plateau. The typical pattern of the Mfecane conflicts – attacks, fragmentation, fugitive groups and consolidation – was also seen among the Sotho/Tswana communities. Thereby strong kingdoms were sometimes decimated and new alliances were made.

In the last quarter of the eighteenth century a number of communities in the area between the Thukela River in the present-day KwaZulu-Natal and Delagoa Bay (Maputo) became stronger and larger. The chieftainship of Mabhudu in southern Mozambique is an example of this. Neighbouring weaker groups were defeated and absorbed or were put to flight.

To the north of today's KwaZulu-Natal on both sides of the Mfolozi River, the Ndwandwe and Mthethwa communities also expanded and sought alliance partners even further afield. Further west, at the foot of the Drakensberg range, were the Hlubi who were also growing stronger.

Chieftaincies such as the Ngwane under Matiwane who were able to avoid the conflicts taking place around them were quick to flee. They migrated westwards, attacked the Hlubi and killed their leader. One group of Hlubi fled and the other was absorbed by the Ngwane. Matiwane, now considerably strengthened by the integration of weaker groups, settled in the vicinity of present-day Bergville and rapidly became the strongest chieftain in the Upper Thukela River region.

In the second decade of the nineteenth century the Mthethwa under Dingiswayo grew even stronger due to the subjugation and absorption of other groups. One of Dingiswayo's alliance partners was the Zulu under Senzangakhona. When the latter died, Shaka became leader of the Zulu with Dingiswayo's help.

By 1818 the power struggle in northern Zululand between the Mthethwa under Dingiswayo and the Ndwandwe under Zwide reached breaking point. Dingiswayo was killed by Zwide, and Shaka took over the leadership of the Mthethwa. He then proceeded to unite the neighbouring communities and the conflict against Zwide began. Zwide's second attack on the Zulu/Mthethwa penetrated deep into the Thukela area and Shaka retaliated, putting the Ndwandwe to flight. Some of the Ndwandwe's allies retired via Delagoa Bay and then went further north, while Zwide's remaining units consolidated in the region north of the Phongola.

Although Shaka's enlarged Zulu kingdom expanded strongly both north and south of the Mfolozi River and also exercised authority in the vicinity of the Thukela and Mzinyathi rivers, his sphere of influence did not extend as far as Delagoa Bay. Furthermore, his southern border was so vulnerable that he had to rely on his dependent communities to protect it.

During the Mfecane fugitives and splinter groups were spread out over a wide area. Former Ndwandwe groups such as those under Zwangendaba and Nxaba eventually settled in southern Tanzania. Soshangane migrated with his followers to the south of Mozambique and founded the Gaza kingdom. Zwide finally settled in what is today known as Swaziland. Two years after Zwide's death in 1824, Shaka launched an attack on Zwide's son and defeated the Ndwandwe north of the Phongola. Some Ndwandwe splinter groups joined the Ndebele who were now growing ever stronger, while other groups were absorbed into Zulu ranks.

The Ndebele (sometimes referred to as the Matebele) were members of the Khumalo clan and lived among the Zulu and Ndwandwe. Their leader Mzilikazi had a fall out with Shaka and moved with a reasonably small group of followers to the Highveld, where in about 1823 he set up his headquarters, ekuPumuleni, close to present-day Groblersdal. The smaller chieftainships of the Pedi and the Kgatla in this area were no match for the well-trained Ndebele. They were defeated and splinter groups were absorbed into the Ndebele. Similarly, hundreds of fleeing members of the Ndwandwe from what is today KwaZulu-Natal were also integrated into the Ndebele. By 1825 the Ndebele had moved north of the Magaliesberg in the vicinity of the Apies River. Mzilikazi's headquarters, emHlahlandlela, was now on the Crocodile River. From here he gained control over a large area north of the present-day Pretoria and Rustenburg. In this region he defeated a number of groups including the Kgatla and the Hurutshe. As already mentioned, in 1828 and 1831 the Korana, Griqua and Taung launched unsuccessful raids on the Ndebele. In 1832 it was the Zulu, this time under Shaka's successor, Dingane, who attacked Mzilikazi's impis, but they too had only limited success. At this stage Mzilikazi once again moved his headquarters, this time to Mosega and eGabeni (Kapain) in the vicinity of the Marico River. Within a few years he was in control of the entire western Highveld and by the early 1830s there was recognition of his powerful influence as far afield as the Cape Colony.

The conflicts and marauding raids likewise spread to the southern

Highveld, where the Hlubi under Mpangazitha attacked the Tlokwa under their female leader, Manthatisi. She in turn fell upon other groups who were settled near the Vaal and Sand rivers. Eventually the Tlokwa, the Hlubi and the Ngwane went to settle in the Caledon River valley south of the Drakensberg. In 1825 the Tlokwa overpowered the Hlubi and absorbed some of them. Other Hlubi splinter groups migrated southwards via the settlement areas of the Thembu and Xhosa and they either joined up with the Mfengu or with Matiwane's Ngwane.

In the 1820s fugitives (victims of the Mfecane) caused disruption in virtually the entire interior including the Caledon River valley with their marauding raids. In this way the Rolong and Tlhaping were continually ravaged by hostile attacks between 1823 and 1826. Communities such as the Fokeng and Sebetwane succeeded in sidestepping such raids and established the Kololo kingdom in the present western Zambia. Similar dispersal occurred south of Zulu territory, and groups such as the Thembu moved into areas settled by the Mpondo under Faku where some of them were accepted while another faction disintegrated as a result of Faku's attacks.

The Mfecane can be regarded as one of the most significant revolutionary movements in southern Africa in the eighteenth and nineteenth centuries. From the Great Lakes region of central Africa through the Kalahari to the Cape border regions, the extraordinary mobility of black communities caused their complete transformation.

The most noticeable and immediate result was the enormous loss of life and disruption of the daily lives of those involved. After being forced to flee and going through untold human suffering, many people found that they had no livestock for their subsistence and that for a long time there would be no question of organised crop cultivation. It is not known how many people perished, but it must have been thousands. A number of communities were completely wiped out.

The settlement pattern of the majority of societies was radically changed. Large parts of the Transgariep and areas north of the Vaal were almost depopulated. Survivors of earlier chieftaincies sometimes returned to their previous settlement areas only to find that there was no ordered societal life of which they could become part.

Another significant result of the Mfecane was the rise of strong, centralised states. The numerous small chieftaincies of earlier times, so prevalent prior to the Mfecane, were now replaced by or integrated into large power blocs. It is true that the development of large unified polities was in progress before Shaka's time. Shaka's organisational ability continued this trend and his wars of conquest also promoted the rise of new centralised states elsewhere. The leaders at the head of these emerging states included Moletsane of the Taung; Sekwati of the Pedi; Manthatisi and her son Sekonyela of the Tlokwa; Montshiwa of the Rolong; Moshoeshoe of the Sotho; Mzilikazi of the Ndebele and Shaka of the Zulu.

Together with the political transformation, there were also social changes. Shaka made important alterations to the structure of his kingdom. An elite group was built up under the guidance of the chieftain/king who had control over the means of production and the position of power which his indunas enjoyed. He also intervened in the sexual relations of his subjects by for example stipulating when they were permitted to marry. The *amabutho* (working groups) initially had to render services to the chieftain – later they were obliged to hunt and tend the livestock – and in the case of the Zulu they became a permanent part of the king's household. They were marshalled according to age and not as units from a specific area, so that local predisposition was avoided and loyalty to the unitary state was promoted.

The enormous flood of outsiders, that is to say homeless victims of the Mfecane towards the borders of the Cape Colony in the late 1820s and early 1830s, and more particularly the surge of people who arrived in the colony, was another significant outcome of the Mfecane. This translated into a rapid increase in the number of unemployed vagrants in the eastern frontier districts. The accompanying heightened level of insecurity in the border districts came at a crucial time – just when white eastern frontier farmers' dissatisfaction over a variety of issues reached crisis proportions.

In the aftermath of the Mfecane, parts of the Transgariep and areas north of the Vaal River were reasonably uninhabited. Travellers' reports, and in particular Erasmus Smit's diary, tell of the devastation that had occurred there. The settlement of the trekboers who were moving into the interior and thereafter the arrival of the Voortrekkers in many of these areas therefore took place without any noteworthy opposition in regions that in the previous few centuries had been populated by black groups who were now seeking shelter in the mountains and ravines. From the point of view of the black groups, however, at no stage had they ever permanently abandoned what they saw as their traditional land.

Inevitably the settlement of the white farmers in the interior became an additional destabilising factor and a threat for the existing and newly formed black societies.

The origin of new black states after the Mfecane

The Taung: During the Mfecane, Moletsane at the head of the Taung also had to plunder in order to survive, but he succeeded in keeping his people together. For example, they had sought refuge with Adam Kok at Philippolis, with the Rev. Samuel Rolland at Beersheba and Moshoeshoe at Mkwatleng. While they were under Moshoeshoe's protection, a number of other wandering groups joined them. Although under his authority, Moletsane and his people lived a reasonably independent existence and later even became one of Moshoeshoe's valued allies.

The Tlokwa: After the death of her husband in about 1815, Manthatisi acted as regent of the Tlokwa on behalf of her underage son Sekonyela and proved to be a particularly popular leader. She was so widely respected that the Tlokwa community became known as the Manthatisi. Furthermore, all the fugitives who fled to the borders of the Cape Colony, regardless of the fact that they were of different ethnic backgrounds and came from a mishmash of communities, were known as the Mantatees or Makatees by the white and coloured farmers in the border regions. Despite the turmoil of the Mfecane, the Tlokwa managed to stay in their territory although they had to change their locality several times. Their secure location atop a mountain near the present-day Ficksburg became a place of refuge for other fugitives. In addition, Sekonyela became known as a wily commander who plundered a large number of cattle over the years. By about 1833 membership of the Tlokwa had increased to 24 000 people.

The Sotho: The Sotho was led by the accomplished Moshoeshoe, who achieved particular fame on account of his diplomacy with societies and chieftains who crossed his path. The Sotho seldom participated in the marauding raids which were so typical of the Mfecane period; Moshoeshoe chose instead to remain in his mountain fortresses – initially Butha-Buthe (in 1822) and later Thaba Bosiu. His gifts to influential chieftains such as Matiwane of the Ngwane; Sekonyela of the Tlokwa; and Shaka of the Zulu, were indicative of his careful diplomacy and ensured that he eventually had more friends than enemies. Negotiations and alliances were key tactics which ran like a golden thread through Moshoeshoe's interaction with other black societies.

Chieftains who did indeed attack him such as Matiwane of the Ngwane, had to deal with the full force of the Sotho's cleverly planned counter-attacks. Matiwane was defeated and migrated towards the eastern Cape frontier region, where he was defeated again in 1828 at the battle of Mbholompo on the Mthatha River by Xhosa and colonial forces.

Missionaries of the Paris Evangelical Society, notably Thomas Arbousset, François Daumas, Eugène Casalis and Constant Gosselin, introduced the Sotho to the Western way of life. Casalis later settled at Thaba Bosui on Moshoeshoe's invitation to fulfil the role of the king's advisor.

The Tswana: The Tswana communities did not manage to form a closely knit, unified state either before or after the Mfecane. One of these societies, the Rolong, had to change its place of residence frequently during the Mfecane to avoid plundering raids. In their flight they were separated from one another and eventually there were only small, scattered groups who remained behind trying to subsist on the available arable land and grazing. In 1833 an Ndebele military force attacked the western Rolong's capital, Khunwana, near today's Mahikeng and killed many people. This revenge attack was on account of the murder of two of Mzilikazi's Ndebele representatives. As a result of this a large number of homeless people roamed the countryside.

The same fate befell the Kwena community under Khama. The Hurutshe under their chieftain Mokgatlha were Mzilikazi's vassals and were not attacked, but as a result of the decimation of the Rolong, the Kwena panicked and fled southwards. Dispersal and starvation became the order of the day. However, many of the Tswana groups remained under Mzilikazi's authority and paid him tribute.

European missionaries took some Tswana groups under their protection and a measure of rebuilding took place among these communities. In this way the Tlhaping, Tlharo and Kgalagadi largely escaped the violence of the Mfecane thanks to the Rev. Robert Moffat's intercession and presence at Dithakong, the Tlhaping capital. Similarly, Moroka's Rolong bo-Seleka survived on account of the timely action of the missionaries. In 1833 James Archbell persuaded this Rolong group to move to Thaba Bosiu. It was also here that the Voortrekkers came into contact with them.

6
The emigration of the Voortrekkers into the interior
Jan Visagie

In the years 1835 to 1845 more than 2500 heads of white families took part in the emigration of the Afrikaners from the Cape Colony to the northern and north-eastern parts of South Africa – the so-called Great Trek. The approximately 17 000 emigrants represented about one fifth of the white population and one third of the Afrikaners in the Cape Colony at the time. In addition, it is estimated that each white family was accompanied by at least two or more black employees. These workers possibly included ex-slaves, people of Khoekhoe and Bushman origin or members of the black communities from the border areas. This would have brought the number of emigrants by 1845 to at least 23 000.

Over the years historians have provided different evaluations of the Great Trek. It has variously been described as a desperate protest against foreign (British) rule; and a protest against the equalisation of white and black people. According to the historian W.M. Macmillan in 1927, the Great Trek was "the great disaster of South African history"; but in contrast, his contemporary, E.A. Walker, was of the opinion that this emigration was a "central event" in the history of South Africa.

The culture of the Afrikaner trekboers (itinerant livestock farmers who moved around in search of grazing for their animals) in the eighteenth and early nineteenth century was also characteristic of the later Voortrekkers. But the Great Trek was not simply an accelerated continuation of the trekboer movement – the motivation was completely different. One of these differences was particularly far-reaching in character. Because the Voortrekkers crossed beyond the country's borders in large groups and without permission; and because they were determined to set up their own independent republic, free of British control and never to return, they were indeed part of a rebellion, albeit of a peaceful nature.

The Afrikaners' emigration did not emerge spontaneously and the idea to move had to be promoted actively to persuade enough people to participate. In most cases it was a combination of grievances which made the Voortrekkers decide to leave. In the fifteen years prior to the start of the Great Trek the Afrikaner frontier farmers had to deal with a series of experiences which made them more convinced than ever that as far as their economic wellbeing was concerned they could no longer remain in the Cape Colony. At the same time they were exposed to political and social changes which threatened their status and security and limited their freedom. All these issues culminated in a feeling of estrangement towards the British government at the Cape, and a negative disposition developed among the Afrikaners. They increasingly began to feel as if moving away was the only solution.

The many and varied causes of the emigration did not necessarily affect all the farmers with equal severity. It is even possible that one issue or aspect was crucial in making an individual decide to join a Voortrekker group. There were certainly cases where households were not planning to move at all, but later decided to do so under pressure from family members. Like others elsewhere, Afrikaners in the eastern districts often lived in large, closely-knit family groups on neighbouring farms where patriarchal authority played a decisive role.

The causes of the Great Trek that are discussed below have been divided into categories under two broad headings: economic factors and social factors, although it is clear that more often than not, these were closely interrelated.

Economic factors

Landownership and the administration of land affairs

On the eve of the Great Trek, the Great Fish River had already been declared the eastern border of the Cape Colony some 50 years earlier. Financial and philanthropic reasons made it necessary for the government to forbid all further expansion of colonial boundaries. However, Afrikaner frontier farmers could only make a living from stock farming and for this, large farms were required. Furthermore, because of drought and other factors, the quality of grazing had deteriorated markedly in the ten years before the emigration. Young farmers therefore found that their future prospects were becoming severely limited; in the 1820s there was already a shortage of cheap, suitable land. The increase in population, the arrival of more people from the western districts, and the settlement of thousands of British settlers in Albany made the acute shortage of land in the eastern frontier region even worse and pushed up the price of land.

Up until 1813 much of the land in the interior was occupied on the loan-farm system. In addition to many advantages for the government and the farmers, this system of land tenure promoted rapid expansion because such farms could not be sub-divided and the sons of livestock farmers simply had to move further afield in search of their own farms. Loan farms served their purpose in pioneering circumstances, but with a denser population it became increasingly obvious that it was an inappropriate method of land distribution.

In 1813 the British government decided that loan farms would no longer be made available and that all new land grants were to comply with the terms of the perpetual quitrent system. On application, existing loan farms could be transferred to the new system but they first had to be surveyed to meet the requirements of quitrent farms. This new quitrent system of land tenure was devised to bring order and consistency to land distribution but various circumstances meant that its implementation was extremely inefficient.

The quitrent system cost the farmer much more and he had to wait for years before the farm was registered in his name. Proof of this is that by 1828 there were more than 4000 applications for land that were still outstanding. Even until 1840 and for years thereafter, there was large-scale disorder in the colony's administration of land affairs. Delays in the issue of title deeds caused great uncertainty among farmers about their landownership. Excessive valuation of their land without adequate consideration of its fertility and carrying capacity also meant that the annual quitrent became extremely expensive. Furthermore, incorrect surveys and high levels of corruption led to further delays and additional costs for the farmer.

In the two decades before the Great Trek, financial losses and uncertainty about property ownership were two components of the administration of land that caused great dissatisfaction, particularly among the frontier farmers. The decisions and developments mentioned above left them despondent about their future in the colony; the result was bitterness and a deep distrust of the British-run government at the Cape. It is significant that it was specifically from areas such as the East Riet River and Koonap (now the districts of Bedford, Adelaide and Fort Beaufort), where complaints about land administration were particularly prevalent, that more than 300 families decided to join the Great Trek, and that Voortrekker leaders such as Louis Tregardt and Piet Retief came from these parts.

Wartime losses

The Afrikaner frontier farmers suffered great financial losses in the frontier wars of 1812, 1819 and particularly the war of 1835. The Sixth Frontier War (1835) brought enormous losses. In the first months of the war the invading Xhosa force caused extensive damage to property which amounted to more than £290 000. A completely inadequate sum was granted as compensation for war losses. Furthermore, because of the ongoing stringency measures which the Cape government had to apply, there were far too few permanent force soldiers stationed in the eastern frontier zone as a peace-keeping force and as in the past, this had to be bolstered by burgher commandos. In addition to these wartime sacrifices by the farmers, the government also requisitioned provisions, wagons, cattle and horses from burghers in the western and eastern districts – for which they later received woefully inadequate payment. The fact that the losses suffered in the Sixth Frontier War are mentioned by virtually all the witnesses as being among the most important causes of the Trek underlines their importance.

Vagrancy

In the decade before the Great Trek many nomadic gangs in the eastern and north-eastern districts lived by launching periodic marauding raids and stealing livestock. In peacetime, black groups crossed the border almost daily to seize animals from the farmers' herds. After the passing of Ordinance 50 of 1828 and the scrapping of the pass system, the number of vagrant Khoekhoe groups also increased. One contemporary writer claimed in 1836 that of the approximately 32 000 coloured people in the colony, between 8000 and 10 000 wandered around without fixed employment.

The number of unemployed vagrants in the colony increased even more with the influx of homeless people who were fleeing from the ravages of

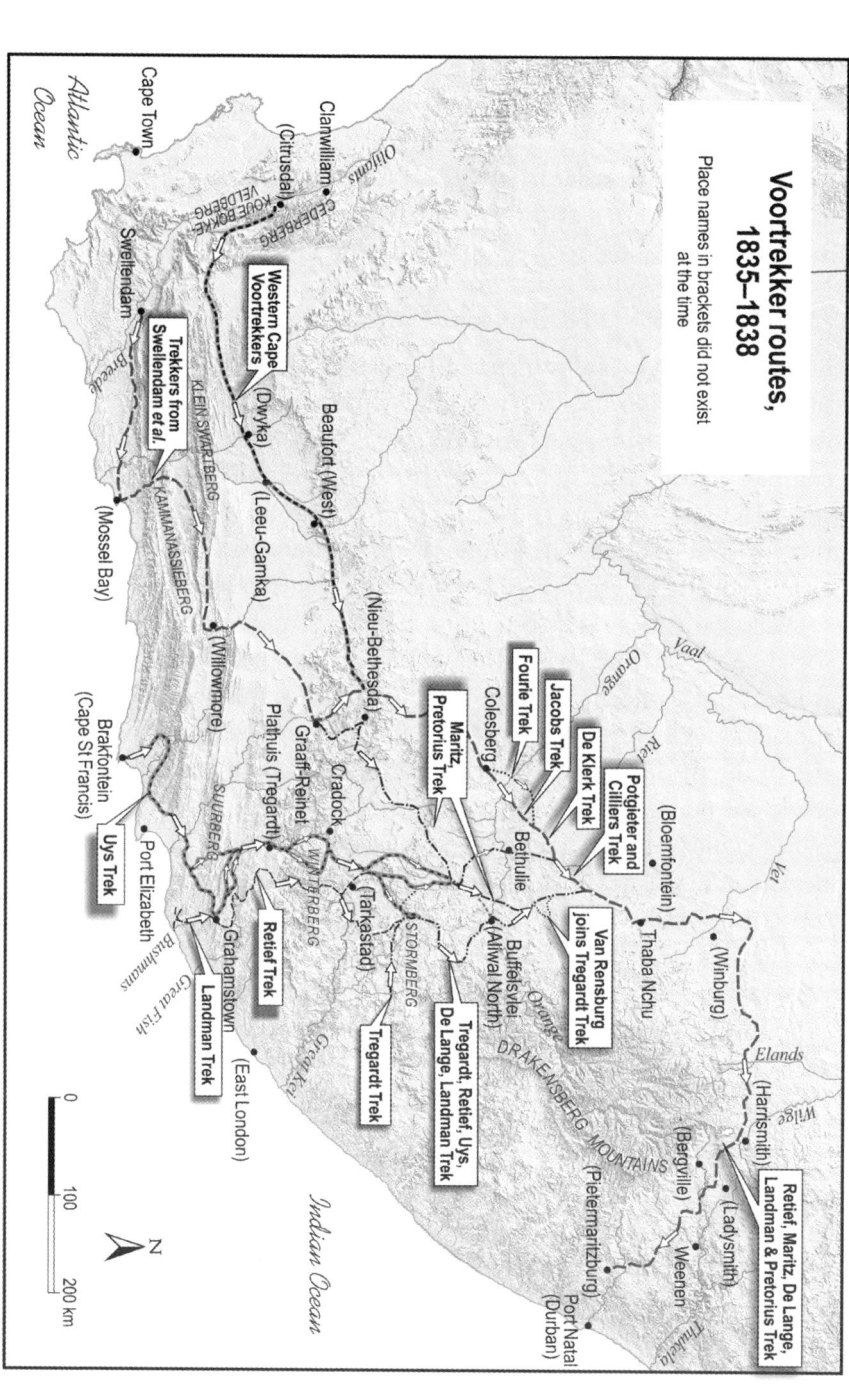

the Mfecane (see chapter 5). The government allowed a limited number of "mantatees" (as the fugitives were called) to be employed by the frontier farmers, but apparently the majority wandered about without fixed work and had to steal in order to survive. It is clear that the many vagrants created a security problem for the frontier farmers on their isolated farms. This also contributed to their determination to leave.

Labour legislation: Khoekhoe communities

Labour laws such as Ordinance 50 released free coloured and Khoekhoe servants from enforced labour. For all contracts of longer than one month which a farmer had signed with his servant, the farmer had to register the contract with a justice of the peace. In most cases the farmer had to make a special journey, usually a considerable distance from his home, to complete this registration, and it had to be renewed annually. The pass system was also scrapped and vagrancy was no longer a punishable offence.

Very soon, these laws brought a transformation in the colony at both social and economic levels. The philanthropic objective was to place the worker and cattle herder on an equal footing with the employer, but thereby the employer lost a great deal of authority. Furthermore, the duties of the worker were not clearly defined and insufficient provision was made for punishment if duties were neglected. This meant that an employer could not easily discipline or lay a charge against an employee who neglected his or her duties, damaged employer's property or showed any form of resistance.

The changed labour legislation made a radical difference to the traditional relationship between employer and employee. In 1836, Piet Retief, a prominent Voortrekker leader, summarised the impact of these new laws when he declared that:

> The increasing insubordination and desertion ... of the Coloured Classes, on entering into service are other grievances of great magnitude ... the great distance of the seat of the magistracy from [the farmers'] habitations ... has a powerful effect in producing this insubordination, it being impossible that the masters for every offence ... can undertake a journey of 2 or 3 days ... The only alternative is they are deprived in most cases of the services of their Servants ...

Retief went on to say that if the farmers were unable to get workers, they would have to leave their farms.

Labour legislation: slaves

British philanthropists achieved an important victory with the passing of the law which emancipated all slaves in the British Empire. The stipulation was that slaves would officially be freed on 1 December 1834. For the next four years, until 1 December 1838, they were still required to work for their former owners as indentured (apprenticed) servants. This legislation also affected the white Afrikaners and their employees and had certain economic and social consequences.

According to one source, on 1 December 1834 there were 30 287 slaves in the seven western districts of the Cape Colony, while in the four eastern districts, Graaff-Reinet, Somerset (East), Uitenhage and Albany, there were only 5458 slaves. Another source gives the number of slaves slightly higher, as 33 277 and 5744 respectively. In the seven western districts there was an average of 6,5 slaves per owner, while the comparative number in the eastern districts was 4,5 slaves per owner. In the past some authors have reasoned that the higher number of slave owners in the western districts were more heavily impacted by the inadequate compensation for their freed slaves than the smaller number of slave owners in the eastern districts. The question then arises: If the issue of the freedom of slaves was a cause of the Great Trek, why did so few people from the western districts join the emigration?

The three-part answer to this question is that other grievances that were not present in the western districts also played a role in the eastern districts; that more people moved from the western districts than earlier historians realised (a significant number apparently came from the Clanwilliam and Swellendam districts); and that the average slave ownership in these two parts of the colony did not really differ a great deal. It is also true to say that the frontier farmers were far poorer than their counterparts in the western districts. A slave in the eastern districts represented an average outlay of £100 which in the 1830s was a great deal of money. The twelve adult slaves who were the property of Voortrekker leader Gert Maritz, were valued at £1540, but eventually he only received about £632 as compensation.

Maritz could count himself lucky. On average the slave owners in the colony only received one fifth of the value of their slaves. When all the costs were deducted and many irritating regulations and provisions met on how to receive the compensation, slave owners heard that the downgraded compensation amount would only be paid in London. Needless to say, agents took good advantage of the situation. The discouraged owners' compensation certificates were bought up by the agents at an even lower price, prior to their going to London to claim on them. Many slave owners were so bitter about the whole procedure that they decided not to claim at all; they simply let the matter drop and did not sell their certificates to agents. Apparently many of these Afrikaners were members of the group who left the colony shortly afterwards. As late as 1854, unclaimed compensation money in London that had still not been paid out amounted to £5906-18s-4d.

The second result of the changed legislation with regard to slaves was socio-economic in nature. Between 1823 and 1831 the proclamation of one law after another reduced the usefulness of slave labour for the Afrikaner farmers. This series of laws meant that slaves could not be forced to work on Sundays; limited working hours were laid down and later reduced even further; if the stipulated working hours were exceeded extra payment had to be made; a slave protector was appointed; and the slave owner had to keep a punishment book. These restrictions meant that the owners' control and authority over their slaves, whom they regarded as their private property, was seriously curtailed.

A part of the slave-owning community of the time was already concerned about the inhumanity of slavery. Farmers in Graaff-Reinet suggested a method which would lead to the gradual phasing out of slavery without incurring such great financial loss to the owners. But the Cape government had to follow the decisions taken in London and simply ignored these proposals; all slaves were suddenly emancipated in 1834. The practical outcome of this was that it caused a great deal of tension between owner and slaves. Good relationships on both sides were compromised and the loss of their patriarchal authority was a severe psychological blow to the farmers. In terms of the law, slaves could now challenge their erstwhile owners in court if they felt their rights had been violated. At face value this was an acceptable procedure, but slaves often laid false claims which meant that farmers had to travel long distances to defend themselves in court. A head clerk in the office of the Cape colonial secretary thus described the "interference with their slaves by the appointment of Guardians and Special Justices" as one of the main causes of the Great Trek.

Social factors

The Afrikaner community at the time, and particularly the white farmers in the eastern districts, regarded themselves as being at a higher social level than the indigenous population. Firstly, they saw themselves as Christians and the black people as heathens. Secondly, they used skin colour and physical characteristics as criteria to differentiate between people. Thirdly, they ascribed to rigid class differences and believed that white people were supposed to assume a dominant role while people of colour were destined to be subordinate. Before long, the British government's legislation curtailed the Afrikaners' patriarchal position of dominance and interfered with their spiritual outlook. Decades later Afrikaners still harboured these grievances.

In the first place the equalisation laws such as Caledon's Khoekhoe proclamation of 1809 and Ordinance 50 of 1828 clashed with the conception some Afrikaner farmers had derived from the Bible. Furthermore, Afrikaners considered the equalisation laws as an affront; they felt that the governor and the government were placing the Khoekhoe people above the Afrikaner farmers and their interests. This made them feel increasingly estranged from the Cape government.

Since the days of Company (VOC) rule and until 1827, the Afrikaner farmers had grown accustomed to certain local government bodies in which they had been given a measure of political influence. These included the board of the landdrost (magistrate) and heemrade (county court) who met approximately every three months. The members of the heemrade were prominent burghers of the particular district; they represented the interests of the residents. In addition there was a veldkornet (field-cornet) for every ward in a district; he was appointed by the government from among the burghers and was usually well-respected among the residents of that ward. With the scrapping of the magistrates, heemraad system and the restriction of the duties of the field-cornets in 1827, the burghers lost their last vestiges of representation in a local government body.

Until that time, most of the magistrates and heemrade were influential Afrikaners who inspired trust among the residents of the district. However, they were then replaced by one official who was known as a civil commissioner and resident magistrate. If the district warranted it, the post was filled by two officials. Thereby an old tradition that dated back to the time of VOC rule was broken, and for the most part government officials were replaced by English speakers. These changes were part of a process of transformation that was focused on running a more efficient government, but it made the Afrikaner farmers feel that they were being marginalised in their own country. There is plenty of evidence that the frontier farmers were highly aggrieved about the loss of their representation in local government structures.

The Sixth Frontier War of 1835, in addition to the serious losses which the frontier farmers suffered, caused further bitterness towards the government over a range of events. During the war there were various incidents between members of the Afrikaner civilian force and troops of the British permanent force which made it clear that the Afrikaners were far from satisfied with the high-handed and arrogant attitude of the British soldiers towards them. The Afrikaner farmers' contempt for the life of a professional soldier became clear later in 1835 when the governor, Sir Benjamin D'Urban, announced that he was planning the introduction of a permanent citizen force or militia in the colony. The proposed law immediately caused great dissatisfaction among Afrikaner farmers. Their main complaint came down to the fact that their rights as free burghers were being infringed and they would be forced into a system which would be very close to that of a professional soldier. Together with the financial losses and requisitioning of their cattle and beloved saddle horses (for which they had received inadequate compensation or in some cases were not compensated at all), this emotional issue again caused a sense of being victimised, which lasted for many years; in some cases it came to the fore years later in the memoirs of former Voortrekkers. Although the militia system was never implemented, the emotional damage had already been done and the deep distrust of the government increased.

The administrative neglect of the eastern districts and particularly the north-eastern districts made the frontier farmers feel that the government was only aware of them when they collected their taxes. One should also mention that in the 1820s and 1830s these districts were exceptionally large, with far too few officials to cope with the administration. In 1825, when the district Somerset (East) was eventually separated off from the huge, unwieldy district of Graaff-Reinet, it was still an enormous expanse of land stretching from the Zuurberg (north of the present Kirkwood) to the Orange (Gariep) River. Indeed there was a sub-district Cradock which administered the far north-eastern wards such as Tarka and Brakrivier, but as was the case with other towns, there were only one or two officials and the small group of field-cornets who carried out the official duties of the ward. In the districts of Graaff-Reinet, Albany and Uitenhage the under-staffing and shortage of funds also applied.

The main reason for this was again the stringency policy of the imperial government in Britain; successive Cape governors were consistently warned about over-spending. However, this policy brought with it higher costs for the farmers. They had to travel up to 100 km to the nearest magistrate's office if they wanted to lay a charge. Possibly the most significant result of this was once again a feeling of mistrust and estrangement towards a government they no longer knew; which they no longer wanted; and which was not able to protect or was interested in protecting them; and laws that were forced upon them.

The question of whether nationalism was a cause of the Great Trek has received considerable attention from historians. Today most agree that there was a latent undercurrent of national feeling among frontier farmers on the eve of the Trek, but that nationalism was in fact a result of the Trek rather than one of its causes. However, there must have been a desire for freedom and independence among the Voortrekkers, because they did not simply move aimlessly into the interior. There was also a clear intention to establish their own self-sufficient state. But other than in the correspondence of a few leaders of the frontier farmer community, the desire for independence did not come strongly to the fore.

Reconnaissance of the interior and the east coast

The Afrikaners' determined efforts to find out more information about the interior in the five years previous to the Great Trek was both a cause and a result of the emigration. In contrast to what was previously thought, in the early 1830s the interior of South Africa was fairly well known through information relayed back to the colony by early travellers, missionaries and farmers who hunted game. A few travellers such as Dr Andrew Smith published maps on their return which provided cartographical information on the interior albeit, at this early stage, rather rudimentary.

The reconnaissance of the interior by the Afrikaner farmers took place primarily in the period from 1830 to 1834 when journeys were undertaken to Damaraland (Namibia), Natal, and the present-day Limpopo respectively. Because none of the subsequent trekker parties went to Damaraland, it can be accepted that the reports on the farming prospects there were unfavourable. The scouting party that went to Natal was a larger group comprising about 21 white farmers and approximately the same number of coloured people. They were under the leadership of Uitenhage farmer and later Voortrekker leader, Piet Uys.

The expedition to Natal took place from September 1834 to March 1835 and to all accounts the members of the group reported back with high praise for the farming prospects there. For example, some members of the expedition told an English-speaking frontier farmer, Thomas Bowker, that they "had seen, between the Orange River and the country of Natal, an immense and fertile country, destitute of inhabitants, in which they might find a refuge".

Leaders of the Great Trek

A number of trekker leaders and their treks may be singled out.

Louis Tregardt

Although Tregardt's group was the first to leave, his party was in many respects outside the mainstream of the Great Trek. They had no contact at all with the other Voortrekkers, except with the group under Lang Hans van Rensburg, who trekked together with the Tregardt party for a short distance; and Hendrik Potgieter, who visited them at Soutpansberg.

Tregardt kept a diary while on their epic journey to the north. Although he wrote in Dutch, his text already shows a distinct transition to Afrikaans.

He lived originally in the present district of Bedford, and from there, in 1834–1835, after a short stay near Indwe River in Gcalekaland, he moved to the north with a small group of about seven families. It seems probable that in September/October 1835 or shortly afterwards, he joined up with Lang Hans van Rensburg and his party of 49 white people at Zevenfontein (north of the present Rouxville). From there they set off together, moving through the Transorangia and over the Vaal River, before continuing west of the present Middelburg until they reached the Soutpansberg.

Near Strydpoort the Van Rensburg party went ahead and then lost contact with the Tregardt group. Later researchers have come to the conclusion that the entire Van Rensburg party was murdered in July 1836 after a clash with one of Manukozi's impis at the Djindispruit near the Limpopo River.

In June 1836, the Voortrekker leader Hendrik Potgieter led an expedition to the north and visited Tregardt near the Soutpansberg. Apparently the arrangement was that Tregardt would wait there for Potgieter and his group to return. In August 1837, when Potgieter had still not arrived back after a year, Tregardt and his people decided to continue their journey to Lourenço Marques (now Maputo) in Delagoa Bay. In the vicinity of the Soutpansberg, disaster struck the Tregardt group when at least six people, including three of Tregardt's young children, died of malaria.

After an extremely hazardous journey over the Drakensberg, Tregardt and his remaining people finally reached Delagoa Bay, where they were welcomed by the Portuguese governor. However, in Delagoa Bay another 20 members of the group, including Tregardt and his wife, died of malaria. This brought to an end Tregardt's dream of making a new beginning at a neutral port far away from British influence.

A small group of 25 survivors from Tregardt's group, mainly children and widows, were fetched by the Natal Vootrekkers and taken back to Port Natal (now Durban) by ship, arriving there safely on 19 July 1839.

Andries Hendrik Potgieter and Sarel Cilliers

Hendrik Potgieter was a respected and influential person in the Tarka ward near the north-eastern border of the colony. His father and grandfather had been frontier pioneers since the late eighteenth century. He had a strong personality and was very conservative and religious.

Potgieter left his farm at the end of 1835 or early in 1836 with a small party of families, but as was often the case with other leaders, many people joined the group at a later stage. Tarka provided more Voortrekkers than any other ward, and Potgieter soon headed one of the largest Voortrekker groups. He and his people probably crossed the Orange (Gariep) River at the Boesmanspoort drift just west of where the Caledon River flows into the Orange.

Early in 1836 the Potgieter group made the first formal plans to set up a system of government. At a gathering north of the Orange River the men who were present elected Hendrik Potgieter as commandant in a democratic manner. By the end of 1836, together with the Maritz party, a decision was taken at Thaba Nchu (called Blesberg by them) east of the present-day Bloemfontein, on the first Voortrekker government.

Sarel Cilliers trekked from the Nuwe Hantam ward in the Colesberg district. On the way he was joined by a number of other families. It was only at the Boesmansberg in Transorangia that his party of Voortrekkers joined up with Potgieter's people.

At Thaba Nchu the headman of the Rolong community, Moroka, and the Rev. James Archbell of the Wesleyan mission, received the Voortrekkers in a friendly manner. The Voortrekkers exchanged cattle and wheat and shot game for the Rolong. At the Great Vet River, more or less where Winburg is today, the Voortrekkers met the remnants of the detribalised Taung community under Makwana. Potgieter made an agreement with Makwana in terms of which the large area between the Vet and the Vaal rivers was given to the Voortrekkers in exchange for a number of cattle. This was the first of several agreements concluded between the Voortrekkers and the black communities in the interior. As a result of this transaction, groups of Vootrekkers spread out in this stretch of land, and the Liebenberg family even set up camp on the northern side of the Vaal River.

From the vicinity of the Vet River Potgieter led an exploratory expedition of eleven people to the Soutpansberg; and from there they went further north-east to investigate the farming possibilities of the region. They also wanted to establish whether there was an accessible route to the sea. The expedition departed in May 1836 and, as already mentioned, made contact with the Tregardt party. Almost at the east coast, they turned back when they were seemingly convinced that access to the Portuguese harbour in Delagoa Bay was feasible.

On their return on 2 September 1836 a scene of complete devastation awaited them at the wagons. In Potgieter's absence the Voortrekkers had been attacked on 23 August 1836 in the vicinity of the Vaal River near the present-day Parys by an Ndebele impi under Mkaliphi, Mzilikazi's foremost commander. It is possible that unwittingly the Voortrekkers had encroached on Mzilikazi's land, and he apparently also saw their horses and their rifles as a threat. About twenty Voortrekkers and an unknown number of coloured cattle herders were killed, while possibly as many as 150 Ndebele warriors perished in this clash which is known as the Battle of Vaal River.

Potgieter found the dejected trekker party at the Renoster River, scattered around a hill 24 km south of the present Heilbron. Meanwhile, Mzilikazi sent Mkaliphi out against them again but this time with the full military might of the Ndebele – between 3000 and 5000 men. However, Potgieter received prior warning from local black people of the advancing

Ndebele force, and a Voortekker patrol confirmed that a huge force was approaching. It was impossible for the Vootrekkers to flee; the only way out for the 36 able-bodied men was to entrench themselves defensively. They resorted to a barricade of wagons (also called a "laager"), a method of defence that had previously been used with some success at the Vaal River clash several months before. About 50 wagons were drawn together in a circle formation at the base of the hill. To protect the women and children, four wagons were placed together in a square in the centre of the laager. All openings between the wagons were closed with thorn tree branches and the wagons were bound together with leather thongs and stakes that were driven securely into the ground.

On 20 October 1836 the Battle of Vegkop took place. After about half an hour the Ndebele suddenly decided to retreat. The Voortrekkers pursued them until sundown, but were unable to retrieve any of the livestock the Ndebele had plundered. The battle was a victory for the Voortrekkers, but the significant amount of booty the Ndebele had taken was a decided setback. Virtually all their sheep, cattle and draught oxen had been looted, amounting to about 6000 head of cattle and 41 000 sheep; fortunately for them their horses had been inside the laager and were not taken. Two of the Voortrekkers were killed and an unknown number were injured. It is estimated that the Ndebele lost about 400 men.

For some weeks after the battle the Voortrekkers had to struggle to survive without milk cows and slaughter animals. Relief came when the Rolong headman, Moroka, agreed to loan them some draught oxen. The Voortrekkers with their 50 wagons eventually returned to Thaba Nchu where the missionary Archbell also loaned them some provisions. A few days later the group under Gert Maritz arrived in Thaba Nchu and strengthened the Voortrekker ranks considerably.

Gert Maritz and Piet Retief

Gert Maritz, a prosperous wagon maker and businessman, was only 40 years old when in September 1836 he led his Voortrekker party out of Graaff-Reinet. He and his sister Susanna Maria (who later married the Netherlands-born missionary, the Rev. Erasmus Smit) had apparently received a good education. Maritz was to find his law books particularly useful during the migration. While on their journey, and later in Natal, Maritz was the one who set the rules as far as law and order were concerned; these he based on the value system of his fellow Voortrekkers.

The Maritz group crossed the Orange River at Sand Drift, west of where the town of Aliwal North is today, and arrived at Thaba Nchu on 19 November 1836. Smit was the only minister of religion who accompanied the emigrants but many of them, to Smit's dismay, also attended the Rev. Archbell's services at Thaba Nchu.

On 2 December 1836 the Voortrekkers under Potgieter and Maritz held the first people's gathering. A governing body of seven members, known as the Burgher Council, was elected. This council was the highest legislative, executive and judicial authority in the trekker society. It is notable that the Voortekkers guarded against the misuse of power by ensuring that a single individual did not hold too much authority; for this reason no one was named head of the Burgher Council. From this stage onwards the Voortrekker government was elected in a democratic manner by means of a secret ballot, and the Burgher Council was responsible to the people at large.

Meanwhile, another prominent Voortrekker came to the fore. During his years as a resident of Grahamstown, Piet Retief was a man of many skills, but his inability to manage his financial matters properly, and to run the building contracts he had with the government, brought him to the brink of bankruptcy in 1824. He appeared a number of times before the courts on account of his debts and in 1832 even spent a short time in gaol (euphemistically called the "debtors yard") in Grahamstown. Eventually he was declared bankrupt in March 1834. However, these setbacks did not detract from Retief's character in the eyes of his fellow burghers and a few months later with the outbreak in December 1834 of the Sixth Frontier War, the government appointed him as acting commandant in the Winterberg. There is no indication that the failure of his business dealings played a role in his decision to trek.

In February 1837 Retief left the Winterberg ward in the district of Albany, with a large company of Vootrekker families. He announced the reasons for his emigration in the form of a Manifesto which was published in the *Graham's Town Journal* of 2 February 1837. In the compilation of this document Retief was possibly assisted by the newspaper's editor, L.H. Meurant, although the essence of the statement would have been his own work. Among the reasons he touched upon were the resentment of the Afrikaner farmers over the inadequate protection provided in the frontier region; the irritating laws and capital losses suffered because of the emancipation of slaves; and the slur the philanthropists had cast upon the frontier farmers' character. He went on to assure the government that the emigrants planned to practise the principles of freedom in the interior and would see to it that "proper" relations were maintained between master and servant. The emigrants hoped for a more peaceful life in the interior and would neither molest nor rob anyone they came into contact with. Retief also undertook to inform the communities in the interior of the Voortrekkers' intention to live in peace and harmony; but they would defend their property should they be attacked. Finally, he declared that the emigrants were leaving the colony in the full assurance that the Cape government had nothing more to require of them and that the Voortrekkers would be permitted to rule themselves without any interference.

Retief's group crossed the Orange River at Buffelsvlei (later Aliwal North) and early in April 1837 crossed the Orange River and camped alongside the Vet River where most of the other Voortrekkers were already waiting.

Shortly before Retief's arrival, Potgieter and Maritz decided to launch a punitive expedition against Mzilikazi, because the Ndebele chief was still an ever-present danger to the Voortrekkers. It was also felt that Mzilikazi should be called to account for his marauding and shedding of blood. Furthermore, Potgieter was determined to reclaim the Voortrekkers' plundered livestock. The arrival of increasing numbers of emigrants from the colony provided added encouragement for such an expedition. Early in January 1837, Potgieter, Maritz, 107 white men and about 100 men from among the black communities in the area left for Mosega. At dawn on the morning of 17 January, the commando attacked the Ndebele and by 11:30 about 15 dwellings near Mosega were in ruins and 7000 head of cattle were plundered. Their exhausted horses made the men decide not to press on to attack the Ndebele headquarters at eGabeni (Kapain) further north, where both Mzilikazi and Mkaliphi were present at the time. The battle was therefore indecisive.

The arrival at the Vet River of Piet Retief and his company made a revision of the existing government structures necessary. At a public gathering on 17 April 1837 Retief was elected as "governor", while Maritz retained his position as chairman of the Council of Policy (Raad van Politie) and also his judicial powers.

The reason why Potgieter was not elected to any of these senior posts was apparently because he purposely withdrew on account of a difference of opinion with Retief on the direction the Trek should take. Retief wanted to go to Natal, while Potgieter was of the opinion that it was inevitable that the British would expand their influence to Port Natal. For this reason from the outset he had his eye on the interior Highveld, in other words north of latitude 25° south, and therefore beyond the reach of the declared British jurisdiction.

Although Retief carried out his leadership duties in an efficient manner, he sometimes acted without consulting members of the management council such as Maritz. For example, Retief corresponded with the British governor in the Cape without informing the Council of Policy. He also acted against the advice of Maritz by going with a group of Voortrekkers to visit Dingane, the Zulu king, to negotiate about the transfer of land.

Meanwhile, Piet Uys, from the Gamtoos River ward in the Uitenhage district, also arrived with his group and joined the Voortrekker community. Potgieter and Uys launched a second expedition against Mzilikazi. In the battle which began on 4 November 1837 and lasted nine days, the Ndebele force in the north-west was utterly defeated and Mzilikazi and his followers were forced to flee the region.

Natal as destination

Retief finally took the decision to trek to Natal when a gathering of the people held on 13 September 1837 failed to reach agreement on the most suitable destination. He left his wagons on the western side of the Drakensberg and with 15 men and four wagons set off to meet Dingane to negotiate with him about a grant of land for the Voortrekkers. At Port Natal (the present-day Durban) he asked an English trader, Thomas Halstead, to accompany him as an interpreter. On 5 November 1837 Retief, in the company of the Rev. Francis Owen, the English missionary at Dingane's stronghold, held discussions with Dingane.

The Zulu king listened to Retief's request, but told him that some of the king's cattle had been stolen by a mounted commando wearing Western clothing. Dingane promised to grant the stretch of land between the Thukela and the Mzimvubu River to the Voortrekkers if Retief first traced and returned his stolen cattle to him. Retief surmised, correctly, that the livestock thieves were not the Voortekkers as Dingane had suggested, but were in fact the Tlokwa under Sekonyela. He readily agreed to comply with Dingane's conditions. With little difficulty Retief managed to recapture the cattle from Sekonyela by tricking and handcuffing him. Without any shedding of blood he rounded up Dingane's 700 head of cattle and retuned them to the king. By way of punishment, Retief also saw fit to seize between 60 and 70 horses and about 30 rifles from Sekonyela.

Accompanied by about 60 volunteers and 30 coloured servants, Retief then set off for a second visit to Dingane's headquarters, Mgungundhlovu. He and his men arrived there on 3 February 1838, seemingly unaware that Dingane distrusted their motives. Retief was convinced of Dingane's good intentions and because of this he even delayed his departure for a few days after the king had granted the Voortrekkers the area between the Thukela and Mzimvubu in a document dated 4 February 1838, known as the Retief-Dingane treaty. On the morning of 6 February 1838, a young boy, William Wood, who lived with the Rev. Owen among the Zulu and knew the Zulu language well, warned the small group of Voortrekkers that Dingane was hatching a plot against them, but none of the party took the warning seriously.

The treaty was only signed on 6 February and Retief and his men were about to leave when Dingane asked them to bid him farewell. As was customary, they approached the king unarmed, drank beer together, and watched a group of Zulu warriors performing a traditional dance. Suddenly Dingane gave the order that the "wizards" should be killed. The entire group, including their servants, were dragged to a nearby hill, KwaMatiwane, where they were killed.

Dingane's motives

While Retief was retrieving Dingane's cattle from Sekonyela, and possibly even prior to that, the Zulu king's complex attitude towards the missionaries and Voortrekkers was becoming increasingly fraught with uncertainty. The problem was compounded because he no longer trusted the missionaries enough to ask for their advice about Retief. The fact that the missionary A.F. Gardiner wrote to Dingane to remind him that the region he had promised to Retief had already been granted to the Voortrekkers in terms of the treaty, surely added to the king's irritation. Furthermore, his two advisers, Ndlela and Dambuza Nzobo, were unable to set his mind at rest; both were apparently against the missionaries and felt that Retief's request for land should be refused.

According to Zulu oral tradition, Dingane felt that the Voortrekkers' easy victory over Mzilikazi's Ndebele; their accomplished horsemanship;

accurate marksmanship; and the cunning way Retief had outsmarted Sekonyela, had to be wizardry. Zulu tradition also has it that Dingane considered Sekonyela a wizard, and therefore in the king's eyes Retief was an even greater, more powerful wizard than Sekonyela. This was why Dingane had used the words "kill the wizards!" when he gave the order to kill Retief and his party.

Dingane had also grown wary of other actions on the part of the Voortrekkers that made him feel threatened. There was, for example, Retief's untactful letter to Dingane in which he told the king that Mzilikazi fully deserved his punishment and that God did not allow bad kings to live for long. Dingane grew even more suspicious when Retief refused to hand over to the king the "punishment" rifles and horses he had seized from Sekonyela when he returned Dingane's cattle. Importantly, it must also have been decidedly unsettling to the Zulu king that the Voortrekkers had already moved into Natal, crossed the Thukela, and had set up camp over a wide area even before agreement over the land grant had been reached and the treaty signed.

Because the Zulu knew exactly where the Voortrekker encampments were, Dingane decided to use the element of surprise and to close in on Retief's company. He ordered his impis to attack the scattered Voortrekker laagers near the Bushmans and Bloukrans rivers. Along these two tributaries of the Thukela and other streams such as the Moordspruit and Rensburgspruit, there were many trekker families who were waiting for Retief's return. The ever-cautious Maritz had set up a proper laager beside the Bushmans River not far from where Estcourt is today. The Potgieter and Uys groups were still for the most part on the other (western) side of the Drakensberg, but some of them were already busy struggling down the mountainsides into Natal.

At dawn on 17 February thousands of Zulu attacked the unsuspecting, vulnerable Voortrekker families and many Voortrekkers were killed. The first victims were those who were camped along the Bloukrans River and Moordspruit, where defensive laagers had not been formed. Maritz's laager was also attacked, but by this time the element of surprise was no longer a factor. On the one hand the Zulu warriors were becoming fatigued, and on the other, Maritz's preparedness, the brave defence by his men, and the strongly flowing Bushmans River meant that the Zulu eventually retreated. However, on their way back they seized thousands of livestock that belonged to the Voortrekkers.

The attacks on Retief's group and on the scattered Voortrekker camps were a grave setback. Including Retief and his party, about 350 whites and approximately the same number of coloured and black people were killed. In total 600 people perished.

A commando of about 350 men under the joint command of Potgieter and Uys departed in early April on a punitive expedition against the Zulu. On 11 April they were trapped in a Zulu ambush beyond the Buffels River and eleven trekkers were killed, including Uys and his son Dirkie. This defeat in what became known as the Battle of Italeni, was yet another setback for the Voortrekkers in Natal. Potgieter had had enough. He left Natal and reverted to his original plan to trek to the Highveld, as far as possible away from British influence.

WAS THE RETIEF-DINGANE TREATY AN AUTHENTIC DOCUMENT?

In 1923 the well-known South African historian, George Cory, queried the authenticity of the Retief-Dingane treaty. This subsequently led to the University of Stellenbosch inviting Professors Cory and W. Blommaert and Dr Gustav Preller to engage in an academic debate on this document. The help of handwriting experts was also called in to examine the extant copies of the treaty.

One of Cory's misgivings was that the original treaty was lost during the Anglo-Boer War and that the lithographic copies could not be compared to the original. However, these copies and other reproductions of the treaty were so accurate that it could be proved that the signatures of Retief and the Boer witnesses were in fact authentic. Cory's other misgiving on whether the document was genuine or not was also cleared up, and in a public address in December 1923 he acknowledged that the handwriting on the copies proved that it was made from the original Retief-Dingane treaty and that the document could indeed be regarded as fully authentic.

The value of this historic document lies in the fact that for Retief and his followers the agreement meant that the area between the Thukela and Mzimvubu rivers was granted to the Voortrekkers and belonged in perpetuity to them and their descendants. But according to traditional oral evidence, as far as Dingane and his followers were concerned, the treaty implied merely that the Voortrekkers could occupy this land – it was not their property. All land on which the Zulu communities lived was communal land which was the property of the king or, as Dr Oscar D. Dhlomo, a recognised expert on Zulu traditional practices, put it in 1988, in terms of the treaty the Voortrekkers could "occupy the land without necessarily owning it – as all land was owned by the King as trustee on behalf of his subjects".

The Battle of Blood (Ncome) River

The year 1838 brought one catastrophic event after another for the Voortrekkers. Suddenly they were without their foremost leaders, because not only did Retief and Uys perish, but Potgieter trekked back over the Drakensberg and Maritz died on 23 September 1838. But the year did take a turn for the better when Andries Pretorius arrived at the Voortrekker laager in November 1838. An increasing number of people had also turned up in the previous few weeks from Transorangia and the Cape Colony to strengthen Voortrekker ranks.

After paying an investigative visit to the Voortrekkers at the end of 1837, Andries Pretorius and his group left Graaff-Reinet in October 1838. On 22 November he arrived at the main laager at the Little Thukela. Here he was immediately appointed as commandant general of the punitive expedition (later called the "Wenkommando" because it was victorious) against Dingane. Two days later he left with his commando and moved to the north-east in the direction of Zululand. On the way the Voortrekker leader Karel Landman with his followers joined them so that the expeditionary force comprised 470 men. Included in this number were three Englishmen, one of whom was Alexander Biggar, a former British officer and settler.

Pretorius planned the campaign with great precision. On the way he discussed with his commanders and the members of the commando the idea of taking a vow, and he gained their approval. This done, Sarel Cilliers took the lead and made the vow on behalf of the men in a prayer on Sunday 9 December 1838 at the present-day Wasbankspruit. Thereafter, each evening, right up to the evening before they clashed with the Zulu, they renewed their vow. The promise made was that if God granted them a victory, the day would be commemorated each year by them and their descendants, and that a church would be built to remind them of the vow they had taken.

While the commando moved through Zululand they received a report that the main Zulu force was on its way in their direction. Shortly after sunrise on 16 December 1838 about 10 000 Zulu warriors under the command of Dambuza and Ndlela repeatedly stormed the Voortrekker laager, but time and again the men managed to withstand the onslaught. After about two hours Pretorius ordered the gates of the laager to be opened so that the mounted Voortrekkers could storm the Zulu warriors. The horsemen were driven back into the laager twice, but when they stormed out a third time the Zulu were put to flight.

Pretorius was part of the group which pursued the fleeing warriors; while on the chase he received a painful stab wound in his left hand from an assegai. By about midday the pursuit was called off. After a period of rest Pretorius again sent out a mounted commando, but the fleeing Zulu could not be overhauled.

On the side of the Voortrekkers there were only three men injured, but the next day more than 3000 Zulu corpses were counted around the laager. Because of the great loss of life, this clash beside the Ncome River, or Blood River as the Voortrekkers called it afterwards, was the greatest single battle ever fought on South African soil. Throughout the punitive campaign Pretorius proved himself to be a good organiser, a sound judge of people and an outstanding strategist. He was indeed regarded as the hero of Blood River and virtually overnight his fame spread far beyond the borders of Natal.

Blood River was a serious setback for the Zulu, but their power was by no means broken. Pretorius and his Wenkommando then moved towards Mgungundhlovu, about 60 km south-east of the battlefield. There, on 20 December, they found the burnt-out and deserted ruins of what had once been the Zulu headquarters. Nearby, on KwaMatiwane, they discovered the remains of Retief and his group of men, as well as Retief's badly weathered leather bag. The Retief-Dingane land grant document was still there.

The Republic of Natalia, 1838–1843

Now settled in Natal, despite all their trials and tribulations the Voortrekkers could at last establish their own republic. Thus the Republic of Natalia was born. The borders of the republic were in accordance with the Retief-Dingane treaty, namely the Mzimvubu and Thukela rivers. To the east it was the Indian Ocean, but the western boundary was not delineated. In the course of 1838 the Voortrekkers began to compile a new constitution and elected a Volksraad of 24 members.

The Volksraad was the highest governing body in the republic and held legislative, executive and judicial powers. Members of the Volksraad had to be men between the ages of 25 and 60 years and were elected annually by all male burghers over the age of 21 years. (Throughout the world at that time it was only men who had the franchise.) The Voortrekkers were still wary of entrusting too much power to a single individual, particularly in the light of Retief's tendency to take ill-advised decisions on his own. As a result, there was no head of state and supreme authority was vested in the Volksraad.

The absence of a head of government at the helm of the executive authority was clearly a weakness. While the Volksraad was not in session, there was no one to deal with the implementation of the laws. A new body, the Kommissieraad (Commission Board) which could act as an executive authority if the Volksraad was in recess, was a partial solution to the problem.

Meanwhile, the Voortrekkers occupied the land which had been granted to them according to the Retief-Dingane treaty. Local government was introduced and the republic was divided into districts each headed by a landdrost (magistrate) and heemrade that dealt with the administration of justice and other administrative functions respectively. However, judicial matters were subject to the authority of the Volksraad, which acted as an appeal court. This local government system was important to the Voortrekkers and the system put in place by De Mist, the commissioner general during the Batavian administration (1804), was used as an example. The sub-division into districts and these into wards (each under a field-cornet) were also a logical progression of those the Afrikaner farmers were accustomed to. Pietermaritzburg (named after Pieter Retief and Gert Maritz) became the capital of the new republic.

The closer union of the Voortrekker communities in Natal and those under Potgieter at Potchefstroom was an important priority for the Natal Volksraad. With this goal in mind, Pretorius was delegated to go to Potchefstroom to hold discussions with Potgieter. After talks in 1839 and 1840, the Voortrekkers were eventually united into one republic on 2 February 1841. The Republic of Natal now also included the district of Potchefstroom-Winburg which would be represented by an Adjunct Council of twelve members. Potgieter was acknowledged as the military commander (the chief commandant) of the Voortrekker region west of the Drakensberg. The considerable distance between the two communities made regular interaction difficult and the two councils operated largely independently.

In September 1840 the Volksraad requested the Cape governor, Sir George Napier, to recognise the young Voortrekker republic as a free and independent state, but the British government refused to do this, indicating that it envisaged expanding British authority to include Natal. The Voortrekkers' request for assistance from the king of the Netherlands also failed to bear fruit. The young republic was therefore unable to gain international recognition.

In May 1842 the British occupied Port Natal when troops under command of Capt. T.C. Smith arrived there and hoisted the British flag. The British action was largely in reaction to the Voortrekkers' military aggression towards the Zulu and their attack on the Bhaca under Ncapayi. The British were afraid that the Voortrekkers' aggression against the black communities on the east coast would cause further problems and might place pressure on the black communities on the eastern frontier region of the Cape Colony.

The Voortrekkers resisted what they saw as unwarranted British intrusion into their republic and besieged the British force at Congella, demanding their surrender. However, after a siege that lasted a month and several skirmishes, the British received reinforcements and on 5 July 1842 the Volksraad decided to back down. Ten days later a peace treaty was signed in terms of which the British authority over Natal was recognised. The official annexation of Natal only took place a year later, on 9 August 1843, when Henry Cloete was sent as commissioner to declare Natal a British territory. In May 1844 Natal was made a separate district of the Cape Colony.

Although the Voortrekkers' republic in Natal was of short duration, it signified a milestone for the Afrikaner farmers. Despite all the shortcomings of this first attempt to establish their own state, it was a learning exercise in democracy and a process in which their national realisation developed further.

The Voortrekkers at Potchefstroom-Winburg

In 1838, after Potgieter and his followers had settled down in Potchefstroom, they elected their own government structure which became known as the Council of Hendrik Potgieter. This was appropriate because Potgieter was the acknowledged leader of the community and had jurisdiction over all the Voortrekkers in the northern Transorangia (Winburg) and the western region beyond the Vaal River (Potchefstroom and surrounding areas).

When the community of Potchefstroom-Winburg agreed to join the Republic of Natal in 1841, the usual organisation of districts and wards (each with a field-cornet) was introduced. With the British annexation of Natal, Potgieter finally severed all his ties with the Natal Voortrekkers; the Adjunct Council was dissolved and revived as a Burgher Council, and the constitution of Natalia was taken over without any changes.

Potgieter's fear that British domination was advancing ever closer, made him decide to move from Potchefstroom with a group of Voortrekkers to Ohrigstad, north of the present Mashishing (Lydenburg). J.J. (Kootjie) Burger, former secretary of the Natal Volksraad, and his supporters had also trekked to Ohrigstad which meant that by the end of 1846 there were two governments in Ohrigstad, both of which claimed that they had legitimate authority over the region.

Potgieter was bitterly disappointed when the Burger group refused to recognise his leadership and in 1848 he trekked further north to settle in Schoemansdal (west of the present-day Louis Trichardt, now also known as Makhado).

The dissent among the Voortrekkers grew even more prevalent when Andries Pretorius and his party settled near the Magaliesberg Mountains. His considerable influence and wide popularity meant that he immediately began to play a leading role among the Voortrekkers in Transorangia and Potchefstroom. His strong opposition to the extension of British authority over Transorangia reached such a pitch that in August 1848 he clashed with Sir Harry Smith's troops at Boomplaats. Pretorius was defeated, but his opposition to British expansionism increased his influence among his own people. In contrast, the Potgieter supporters believed that Pretorius's confrontation with the British might place the independence of the region across the Vaal River in jeopardy. They also felt threatened by Pretorius's growing influence among the Voortrekkers.

Therefore, by 1849 there were three Voortrekker factions north of the Vaal River. Firstly, there were the Potgieter supporters in the north with their own government; they regarded Potgieter as the chief commandant and leader of all the Voortrekkers north of the Vaal. Secondly, there was the group under Kootjie Burger at Ohrigstad and Lydenburg who did not recognise Potgieter's authority, but were unable to exercise any authority beyond their own district. Thirdly, there was the group in Southern Transvaal who recognised Pretorius's authority.

Pretorius focused his attention on establishing a single, united Voortrekker state. Despite a number of public gatherings held to resolve their differences, the disputes continued. At a meeting of the Volksraad in Rustenburg in September 1851 where his opponents from Lydenburg were not present, Pretorius gained full authority to negotiate with the British government on the recognition of independence.

The Sand River Convention

Pretorius immediately informed Major Henry Warden, the British resident in the Orange River Sovereignty (the area between the Orange and Vaal rivers that had been declared a British territory in 1848 by Sir Harry Smith) in writing that he wished to negotiate an "agreement".

The British immediately took up Pretorius's suggestion that they engage in talks because they were experiencing serious problems in the South African regions under their control. Since 1850 the Cape Colony had been involved in an Eighth Frontier War against the Xhosa. Furthermore, with the limited military and financial resources at his disposal, the British resident in the Orange River Sovereignty could not sustain his position vis-à-vis Moshoeshoe and other indigenous societies. A shortage of resources meant that the British government was unable to enforce adherence to its boundaries and led to Warden's defeat at the hands of the Basotho at Viervoet in June 1851.

On 17 January 1852 the Sand River Convention was signed by Pretorius and a few delegates and commissioners W.S. Hogge and C.M. Owen on behalf of the British government. In terms of this agreement, Britain officially recognised the independence of the Voortrekker republic north of the Vaal River. Thereby, the Voortrekkers had reached one of their greatest ideals. It was the beginning of the Zuid-Afrikaansche Republiek (ZAR). For the British government at the Cape it was a necessary financial and security measure, because now the Voortrekkers, in a certain sense their allies, could be used to protect the borders of the British colonies.

The Bloemfontein Convention

In the 1840s the heterogeneous composition of the population of the southern Transorangia region (see chapter 5) had prompted Britain to extend its influence there too. The Griqua lived in the south under Adam Kok; in the east were the Rolong under Moroka; and further east Moshoeshoe ruled over the Basotho, who had laid claim to the fertile land west of the Caledon River.

The various groups of white farmers in the region included the trekboers under Michiel Oberholzer and the republican Voortrekkers in the vicinity of Winburg. The trekboers were inclined to be loyal to the British government and distanced themselves from the Voortrekkers, most of whom lived in the area between the Vet and Vaal rivers. After the annexation of Natal, this group of Voortrekkers set up their own government and under Potgieter's leadership were part of the Potchefstroom-Winburg community. In fact, Potgieter and the Burgher Council claimed that their authority stretched as far as the Orange River.

Soon afterwards the British expanded their influence over Transorangia. Governor Napier declared the entire region up to the latitude 25° south as British territory. He wanted to protect the Cape northern frontier region with buffer states at the least possible cost and therefore tried to exercise indirect control over Transorangia. To accomplish this he entered into agreements with Adam Kok and Moshoeshoe which laid down, among other things, that the signatories would remain trusted friends of the Cape Colony. They also undertook to maintain law and order in their respective regions; to extradite criminals; and to warn their allies against possible hostilities.

The Voortrekkers and the loyal trekboers were not prepared to be placed under the authority of these black leaders. White resistance against Adam Kok increased until British troops defeated an armed group of Voortrekkers at Swartkoppies in May 1845. Governor Maitland came to an agreement with Adam Kok that the territory south of the Riet River would be retained as an inalienable and exclusively Griqua reserve. In the north, British subjects could buy or rent land, but the land was to remain under the sovereignty of the Griqua leader.

An important step was the placing of a British resident at Bloemfontein, Major Henry Warden. This was the first appointment of a British official in Transorangia. With virtually no support, Warden had to do his best to cope in the midst of growing unrest among the various population groups. This eventually led to direct British intervention. In February 1848 Sir Harry Smith annexed the entire region between the Orange and Vaal rivers and the Drakensberg on behalf of Britain, to be called the Orange River Sovereignty.

Until this stage, Andries Pretorius was hoping to engage in peaceful negotiations to gain independence for the Voortrekkers. However, the annexation of Transorangia made him resort to resistance. With the biggest commando he had yet led, Pretorius advanced against Smith in the southern Transorangia, but on 29 August 1848 he was defeated at the Battle of Boomplaats. Once again the endeavours of the Voortrekkers had reached a low point. The only path to freedom now lay north of the Vaal River.

Even before the signing of the Sand River Convention in January 1852, the British government had decided to pull out of the region between the Orange and the Vaal. Meanwhile, the Basotho under Moshoeshoe had delivered a telling blow to British prestige when they successfully withstood a British attack at Bereaberg. A special commissioner, Sir George Clerk, was then sent to the area. Despite opposition from many British traders, missionaries and loyalist trekboers, the Bloemfontein Convention was signed on 23 February 1854 by Josias Hoffman and six other former Voortrekkers. In terms of this agreement, the British government recognised the independence of the territory between the Orange and Vaal rivers, and the Orange Free State (OFS) Republic came into being. This was a particularly significant event because the British government had withdrawn from a territory which it had previously annexed.

The significance of the Great Trek

With the emergence of the two independent Voortrekker states in the interior of South Africa, the Afrikaner farmers had achieved one of their long-cherished ideals – their freedom. Thereby the country was divided into two British colonies on the coast and two Afrikaner states in the interior. The Great Trek can therefore be regarded as one of the most significant events in the history of the Afrikaners. It was also a decisive turning point in the history of South Africa, because it had spread white influence throughout the entire region.

With the Great Trek, private Afrikaner initiative took the lead relatively successfully for the first time in the 1830s. The emigration was accompanied by a great deal of hardship and grief, but gave rise to a stronger feeling of solidarity and identity. At the end of the nineteenth century the Afrikaners could look back with pride at what their forebears had accomplished. Their emigration can be seen as an accelerated process of white expansion. Thereby numerous new opportunities were opened up in Africa for wealthy entrepreneurs, traders, businessmen and other professionals.

The Voortrekkers broke away completely from the monarchical state system and apart from the initial shortcomings, created a new republican system of governance. Indeed the significance of the Great Trek and the forms of government which have since emerged, have their basis in the principles that the Afrikaners improvised for their republican state. This was while the British parliamentary system in the Cape Colony was still in the process of unfolding. The Voortrekker republic in Natal was indeed the first republic in Africa.

The principles of the Voortrekker racial policy have lived on in the political ideas adopted by later generations and were often misused by politicians in the twentieth century for political gain. The emergence of racial prejudice and the later policy of apartheid is, however, very complex and cannot simply be traced back to a single event such as the Great Trek.

The Cape church disapproved of the Great Trek and not a single minister of the Gereformeerde Kerk (Reformed Church) accompanied the Voortrekkers. Although this was only a temporary loss for the Voortrekkers, it later led to division among the churches in the Boer republics.

The emigration of the Voortrekkers and their settlement in the interior led in a dramatic manner to the rise of the Afrikaners. As the historian C.W. de Kiewiet once remarked, the Great Trek linked the future of the entire South Africa inextricably to the Boers.

7
State formation and strife, 1850-1900
Jackie Grobler

Between 1850 and 1900, South Africa experienced a dramatic transformation due to large-scale political, economic, cultural and demographic upheavals. In this period the constitutional unit which became known as South Africa early in the next century took on its unmistakeable shape.

In the beginning of this period there were about twenty societies that were more or less independent living in this southernmost part of Africa. Fifty years later the entire area was divided into two British colonies (the Cape Colony and Natal) and two Boer republics, the Zuid-Afrikaansche Republiek, or ZAR, and the Orange Free State (OFS). All the black societies were under their administrative control.

In 1850 farming was by far the most important economic activity of the vast majority of South Africans and there was no talk of a healthy money-driven economy. By 1900 a thriving mining industry was well underway and there were stock exchanges, banks and tens of thousands of wage-earners. In 1850 the ox-wagon was the main means of transport and there were virtually no roads, bridges or mountain passes, especially in the northern parts of the country. By the 1890s, railways crisscrossed the land and motor cars were beginning to make their appearance.

In 1850 there were a mere handful of schools in South Africa. Tertiary education was limited to a modest institution in Cape Town – while in the United States of America, Harvard College had been founded more than a century earlier. By 1900 there were schools scattered throughout the country and there were various colleges for post-school training. In 1850 Cape Town was the largest town in South Africa and was the only metropolis with more than 10 000 inhabitants; most South Africans lived in the rural areas on farms or in small, undeveloped villages. By 1900 about 15% of the total South African population had moved to urban areas and Johannesburg had a population of more than 100 000.

What were the reasons behind these sweeping changes in South Africa and its dramatic transformation in the second half of the century?

Black societies under pressure

The Bushmen (San)

For the Bushmen, or San, the second half of the nineteenth century brought no prospect of progress. The few independent Bushmen communities that were still eking out a meagre existence in inhospitable regions such as the Cederberg and Drakensberg Mountains, Bushmanland and the Kalahari Desert, came under increasing pressure in this period. Their hunter-gatherer way of life was becoming more precarious due to the spread and population growth of herder communities and mixed farming societies, whose search for grazing necessitated that they expand into the more arid and inhospitable regions occupied by the Bushmen hunter-gatherers. By the end of the century there were no longer any Bushmen clans in the Drakensberg; now poverty-stricken, they were obliged to become wage labourers and livestock herders for their stronger neighbouring societies.

The Khoekhoen (Griqua, Korana, Nama)

By 1850 there were still some independent or at least semi-independent Khoekhoe groups in South Africa. Furthermore, there were various South African societies that developed from the Khoekhoen, such as the Griqua. But for these groups too, the second half of the nineteenth century was a period of hardship.

The Khoekhoen and others who were not seen as white and who lived in the Kat River settlement in the Eastern Cape increasingly began to feel like second-class citizens. The reason for this was that the local British officials and white farmers in the vicinity placed restrictive measures on them and tried to force them to work as labourers on white-owned farms. When the Eighth Frontier War (the Mlanjeni War) broke out in 1850, their dissatisfaction boiled over. The majority of the settlement's residents, including those of the Khoekhoe garrison based at Fort Armstrong, who staged a mutiny against their white officers, joined the ranks of the Xhosa in this war. Before long the Khoekhoen at the Shiloh and Theopolis mission stations showed their solidarity by joining the Kat River rebellion. Meanwhile, the British authorities called up coloured troops based in the present-day Western Cape and sent them to the eastern frontier to end the war and the associated rebellion. However, these soldiers were reluctant to fight against fellow members of their racial group, and were eventually sent back to the Cape.

The Griqua who had settled along the banks of the Gariep River in the present-day Free State under the leadership of Adam Kok III, fared relatively well. Some became part of the mainstream economic activity, farming successfully with merino sheep. However, those who sold their land to white farmers remained impoverished. With the establishment of the republic of the OFS in 1854, the Griqua were accorded no political rights at all. With the full agreement of the British, they came under the control of the Boers (which is the name assigned to the burghers or citizens of the ZAR and the OFS). The Griqua simply had to accept that the independent status they had enjoyed had been brought to an abrupt end. Their only remaining options were to fight for their independence, or find somewhere else to live. They decided to move away to find another home.

Towards the end of the 1850s, the Griqua heard about an unoccupied region south-east of the Drakensberg between the Mzimkulu and the Mzimvubu rivers, an area called No-Man's-Land (later named Griqualand East). With the blessing of the British governor of the Cape Colony, they sold off their land and moved there in 1860. At first, all went well in their new home and they established a well-ordered society based in their capital, Kokstad. However, from 1872 the British began to make steady inroads into Griqualand East. After the death of Adam Kok in 1875, the unity in Griqua ranks began to crumble and many sold off their land to outsiders. Three years later, in 1878, Griqualand East was annexed by Britain, thus ending the independence of the Griqua society and consigning it to history.

In addition to the Griqua of Adam Kok III, there was another branch of Griqua people, members of the Waterboer family, living along the lower reaches of the Gariep River in the vicinity of Griekwastad. Their undisturbed independent existence came to end in the 1870s when diamonds were discovered in the region. The British government took over their land and named it Griqualand West. In 1880 it was incorporated into the Cape Colony. The majority of the Griqua sold off their land and their claim to the riches of the diamond fields to white people; soon they declined into poverty.

By 1850 the Gariep River valley even further downstream near the Augrabies waterfall was inhabited by a group of Khoekhoe herders who spoke the same language as the Korana and included people of mixed blood. In time they acquired rifles and horses and used these to their advantage in cattle raids on white-owned farms. The white farmers had moved into this area with their stock in the second half of the nineteenth century and had registered their farms with the Cape government. Two wars between the Korana and the Cape authorities followed in 1868–1869 and 1878–1879 respectively. The Korana were defeated and their leaders sentenced to imprisonment on Robben Island. The area where the Korana had lived was re-named Gordonia and was opened up for white settlement. Thereby, the independent existence of these groups also came to an end.

The last Khoekoe society that was largely independent between 1850 and 1900 was the Nama of Namaqualand and the Richtersveld. Encroachment by white farmers meant that many of the Nama fled to the safety of mission stations at places such as Leliefontein, Kommagas, Steinkopf and Richtersveld.

The southern Nguni

The southern Nguni – Xhosa-speaking societies living in the south-eastern parts of the country – began a war against the Cape colonial authority in the second half of the nineteenth century. The confrontation was the direct outcome of British colonial expansion in that region and the establishment of British Kaffraria, which included the land inhabited by the Ngqika and the Ndlambe.

The war was precipitated in 1850 when the British authority in the Cape dethroned the Ngqika leader, Chief Sandile, to the anger of his people. A Xhosa prophet by the name of Mlanjeni predicted that the Xhosa ancestors would assist the people against the white invaders. The Eighth Frontier War, or Mlanjeni War, began in December 1850 when the Ngqika destroyed three British military bases in the border district of Victoria. It took the British three years to re-establish their supremacy over the Xhosa.

In 1856 and 1857 a devastating tragedy befell the Xhosa in the form of an event that came to be known as the Xhosa cattle killing. A young girl by the name of Nongqawuse prophesied that a warrior-ancestor would intervene on behalf of the Xhosa against the British. The ancestors would also provide the people with food, but the Xhosa had to show their commitment by killing all their livestock and destroying their food reserves. Some of the chiefs, including the Xhosa paramount, Chief Sarhili, supported the prophecy and ordered their subjects to comply. The overwhelming majority of Xhosa in the region west of the Kei River obeyed the command. Being victims of colonialism and subjection by the British, the Xhosa were desperate for any help that might improve their lot.

All the sacrifices were in vain and the ancestors did not arrive to offer their assistance at the appointed time. The outcome was that the majority of the Xhosa became the victims of dire starvation. Tens of thousands died and tens of thousands of others crossed the border into the Cape Colony to beg for food and to search for a new means of livelihood. It has been estimated that about a third of the Xhosa either died or fled into the Cape Colony.

The British authority used the chaos that followed the cattle killing to their advantage, speeding up the subjugation and detribalisation of the Xhosa. Governor George Grey deliberately settled white farmers among the Xhosa not only to "civilise" them but also to accelerate their detribalisation. He succeeded on several counts. Xhosa headmen who had inherited their rank now had to make way for elected chiefs; and tribal-held land was replaced by individual title holding. Traditional African religion was increasingly supplanted by Christianity. In addition, Xhosa peasants were supplied with ploughs and wagons and began to farm to supply the markets. Those who enjoyed the franchise began to vote for white politicians in the Cape parliamentary elections.

The Xhosas' final attempt to retain their independence led to the outbreak of the Ninth Frontier War of 1878–1879. The Gcaleka were initially reasonably successful, but British colonial troops defeated them and soon thereafter firm administrative measures were enforced in their settlements. In 1881, a short-lived uprising against these restrictions was snuffed out by Cape troops. By 1894 the entire Transkei region, in other words the region north-east of the Kei River (beyond the river as seen from Cape Town) including Pondoland, Thembuland and Griqualand East, was placed under white control.

It can be argued that some Xhosa communities were to an extent responsible for the loss of their independence. In 1875 when Ngangelizwe, a Thembu headman, came off second best in a skirmish with the Gcaleka Xhosa under Chief Sarhili, he demanded the protection of the British government – which therefore justified British interference. The Xhosa in the Transkei were permitted to some extent to retain their traditional systems but local councils headed by white magistrates were introduced to oversee the administration of the Xhosa.

When minerals were discovered later in the nineteenth century, the circumstances of the Xhosa changed again. In 1894 the Cape parliament passed the so-called Glen Grey Act which brought an end to the equal political status of the Xhosa with white residents of the Cape Colony. A special landownership system was introduced for the Xhosa whereby an individual could only own four hectares of land. Furthermore, such ownership was not valid as property qualification for the franchise.

The northern Nguni

The northern Nguni comprise mainly the Zulu and the Swazi people. By 1850 the Zulu had formed an independent society which was broadly speaking resident in the region north of the Thukela River in the present KwaZulu-Natal. Their king was Mpande. Until his death in 1872, he safeguarded the independence of his kingdom by using diplomatic means to avoid confrontation with the British and the Boers. At the same time he maintained the strong military system of the Zulu.

In 1856 a fierce difference of opinion arose between Mpande's sons over who would succeed their father. Cetshwayo eventually emerged as the most suitable candidate and became the most powerful political figure in the Zulu kingdom. However, Mpande retained his hold on the kingship until his death almost sixteen years later. After Cetshwayo became king, he rapidly built up the Zulu military machine until it comprised a formidable force of 40 000 warriors who were divided into regiments, or *amabutho*, according to age. The British considered the presence of this powerful force on the northern border of Natal, a British colony, as a distinct threat to its supremacy in southern Africa.

STATE FORMATION AND STRIFE, 1850–1900 161

To create an excuse to attack and destroy the Zulu army, Sir Bartle Frere, the British high commissioner, sent an ultimatum to Cetshwayo making a number of unreasonable demands. The Zulu king was unable to meet all the terms and the British promptly took the opportunity to invade Zululand, leading to the Anglo-Zulu War of 1879. The Zulu defended their land courageously and on 22 January they famously gained an emphatic victory over the British at Isandlwana. However, the British succeeded in defending a second Zulu attack on the same day at the mission station at Rorke's Drift. Over the next few months a number of indecisive skirmishes took place.

In July 1879 the British marched on Cetshwayo's capital, Ulundi. The Zulu defended bravely but their spears, shields and knobkerries were no match for the British firearms and the Zulu were defeated. Cetshwayo was taken prisoner and placed in captivity in Cape Town. Zululand was divided into thirteen districts, each of which was placed under a chief appointed by and responsible to the British authorities. A Zulu civil war followed which led to further chaos. The British eventually allowed Cetshwayo to return to Zululand, but he was no longer the king of a united, independent Zululand. He died a broken man in 1884.

Cetshwayo's named successor, his son Dinizulu, was only fifteen years old at the time. He was soon involved in a bitter struggle with Chief Zibhebhu, another claimant to the throne. In desperate straits, Dinizulu approached a group of Boers who agreed to help him gain the upper hand. In exchange for their help and their recognition of him as the Zulu king, Dinizulu gave the Boers a large piece of land on the north-western border of Zululand. Here the Boers established what became known as the New Republic. However, in Zululand itself the British authority did not recognise Dinizulu as king and the disorder and unrest continued. In 1887 the British used the widespread unrest as an excuse to annex the whole of Zululand. Ten years later it was incorporated into Natal and thus became an integral part of a British colony, ending the independence of the Zulu kingdom.

One of the few northern Nguni groups that still enjoyed a more or less independent existence in the second half of the nineteenth century was the Hlubi. In 1873 their chief, Langalibalele, refused to obey the instruction issued by the Natal colonial government that the members of his community had to register their firearms. A military force was sent to discipline him. The Hlubi were routed and their livestock and land was taken over by the British. Langalibalele tried to flee, but he was captured, tried and found guilty of a number of misdemeanours. Thereafter he was banned and among other punishments spent a while on Robben Island. His people, the Hlubi, lost their independence, never to regain it.

In the meantime the Swazi peoples had under the leadership of King Mswati II, the son of Sobhuza I who was the founder of the Swazi nation, successfully managed to maintain their independence for most of this period. In the process they turned to whites in the Zuid-Afrikaansche Republiek (ZAR, or Transvaal) as potential allies. However, by the end of the century the Swazi kingdom was severely undermined by concessions extracted from the Swazi rulers by both the Transvaal and the British authorities in South Africa.

The Sotho

In the nineteenth century the history of the Basotho who were resident in what is today Lesotho was so closely integrated with the broader South Africa that they warrant discussion here. In 1850 Moshoeshoe, still the king of the Basotho, was already in his sixties. The heartland of the Sotho kingdom was in the vicinity of Thaba Bosiu, Moshoeshoe's mountain stronghold.

Because there was not enough land near Thaba Bosiu to accommodate all the Basotho and enable them to farm successfully, Moshoeshoe and his followers laid claim to the entire eastern part of the Orange River Sovereignty (approximately the present Free State province), an area over which Britain had assumed control in 1848 and administered from Bloemfontein. On two occasions Moshoeshoe had been involved in military confrontations over what he considered unreasonable boundaries between his kingdom and the Orange River Sovereignty; in both clashes the Basotho had proved too strong for the British troops sent out against them. And yet, the border remained where it was – and still today separates South Africa from Lesotho.

In 1854 the British decided to withdraw from the sovereignty and to hand over control to the Voortrekkers who had settled there. The Voortrekkers established their republic and called it the Orange Free State. From the outset the Basotho began to pressurise the government and the residents of the newly formed republic to accede to their demands for land. But the Free Staters were equally determined – they wanted to maintain the border which they had inherited from the British.

Josias Hoffman, the first president of the Orange Free State, was on quite good terms with Moshoeshoe. Hoffman went out of his way to make regular personal contact with him and to maintain cordial mutual relations with the Sotho kingdom. For example, he invited Moshoeshoe to Bloemfontein where he received a hearty welcome and a banquet was held in his honour. Hoffman also visited Thaba Bosiu, and on one occasion gave Moshoeshoe a small barrel of gunpowder as a gift. However, this gesture stirred up so much public opposition among the white Free Staters that in 1855 Hoffman was forced to resign as president. The Boers firmly believed that in all dealings with black people, great care had to be taken to ensure that they did not gain access to firearms.

The next president of the Orange Free State, Jacobus Boshof, also failed to resolve the border issue between the republic and the Sotho kingdom. In 1858 the ongoing tension on the border reached such a pitch that the republic declared war against the Basotho. Free State commandos moved in on Thaba Bosiu but were unable to take the mountain fortress. Meanwhile Basotho warriors penetrated deep into republican territory and plundered farms. Boshof was forced to recall his commandos from Thaba Bosiu to meet this new challenge. He also appealed to both the ZAR and the Cape governor, Sir George Grey, to come to his assistance. Eventually, Grey acted as mediator between the Free Sate and the Sotho kingdom. The negotiations which followed led to the signing of the Treaty of Aliwal North, which broadly speaking reconfirmed the existing boundary line.

Although the Basotho were still dissatisfied with the border arrangements, a few years of peace ensued. But the problem was still far from solved; indeed it escalated because the Basotho population grew apace and there was less and less land available for young aspirant farmers. The Basotho still had their eye on land that the OFS regarded as theirs.

In 1865 war broke out again, but this time the Basotho did not fare as well. The Orange Free State was now much stronger and furthermore, in the first phase of the war, commandos from the ZAR came to their aid. Added to this, Moshoeshoe was more than 70 years of age and his sons were embroiled in a succession struggle, which meant that the Sotho kingdom was no longer united. Nevertheless, the republic's commandos, despite the courageous actions of commanders such as Louw Wepener, were still unable to take Thaba Bosiu. The Free Staters then took the desperate measure of destroying the Basotho's means of subsistence, burning all their crops in an attempt to force them to surrender. In 1866, Moshoeshoe finally agreed to peace. The Treaty of Thaba Bosiu was signed, in terms of which many of the fertile regions of the Sotho kingdom had to be handed over to the Free State.

The next year conflict flared up again and this time the Free State commandos brought the Basotho to the brink of collapse. Moshoeshoe, who still occupied Thaba Bosiu, pleaded for British assistance. Early in 1868 the British government gave the Cape governor, Sir Philip Wodehouse, permission to declare the Sotho kingdom a British protectorate. This he duly did in March 1868. The second Treaty of Aliwal North was signed and the boundaries of the Sotho kingdom were again demarcated. The Basotho lost large tracts of land that they had occupied before the 1865 war, including the entire western portion of the Caledon River valley which the Free Staters now called the "conquered territory".

The British annexation of Basotholand (which they originally named Basutoland) was in many respects a significant event. It ensured the survival of the Basotho people but they paid with the loss of their independence. For three years Basotholand was administered directly by the British high commissioner in South Africa, but in 1871 it was incorporated into the Cape Colony. In 1880 the Cape government introduced measures to disarm the Basotho but they objected strenuously to this and the so-called Gun War broke out. Peace was only signed in 1884 when the British government again took over the governance of Basotholand from the Cape Colony. Because of the shortage of arable land in their country, many Basotho had by this time spread into the neighbouring OFS where they became poorly paid wage labourers or share-croppers on farms owned by white settlers.

The Bapedi

In the second half of the nineteenth century the Bapedi lived in a region which today forms part of the provinces of Mpumalanga and Limpopo. Chief Sekwati, their leader, had built up his power by diplomacy and alliances with nearby communities. It was on occasion necessary for the Bapedi to defend themselves against northern Nguni societies such as the Swazi and the Zulu. In 1851, for example, Mpande's Zulu army launched two attacks on the Pedi polity, but on both occasions they were able to defend themselves successfully.

Another problem for the Bapedi was the arrival of the Voortrekkers. When Hendrik Potgieter's trekker party of about 100 families settled themselves in the vicinity of Ohrigstad (north of the later Lydenburg) Chief Sekwati was prepared to conclude a peace treaty with them. But the Voortrekker numbers increased rapidly and relations between them and the Bapedi deteriorated; in August 1852 war broke out. Potgieter called up a commando and launched an attack on Phiring, Sekwati's headquarters, but he was unable to get the upper hand.

Five years later, in 1857, the Pedi polity signed an agreement with the Voortrekkers whereby the Steelpoort River would serve as the boundary between them, with the trekkers agreeing to remain south of the river. After Sekwati's death in 1861, his son Sekhukhune took over after he had overthrown the rightful successor, Mampuru. During his rule, Sekhukhune had to fight off the frequent incursions of white farmers from the ZAR into Pedi territory. Furthermore, the Swazi often joined forces with the Boers. In 1876 the differences between the Bapedi and the Boers escalated into a full-blown war, in which the Bapedi were initially able to defend themselves with ease. However, early the next year they were flagging and had to plead for peace.

After the British had annexed the ZAR in 1877, they advanced on the Pedi polity in 1878 and 1879 with a large military force strengthened by Swazi warriors. Sekhukhune's power was broken and his territory considerably reduced in size. He was imprisoned in Pretoria but was set free in 1881, only to be murdered in 1882 when he returned home to his people. The re-instated ZAR government undertook a campaign against the Bapedi and inflicted a heavy defeat on them, which finally brought an end to their independence.

The Tswana

In the early phase of the Great Trek there was often co-operation between the Voortrekkers and the Tswana, particularly because they had both experienced the might of Mzilikazi's Ndebele and perceived and fought them as a common threat. However, with time and for various reasons, relations between the two groups soured. The Voortrekkers' claim that they were entitled to supreme authority over the entire interior because they had driven the Ndebele out of South Africa was one important bone of contention. According to this view, all black societies were legally subordinate to the trekkers, which meant that indigenous societies such as the Tswana were obliged to adhere to the rules laid down by the white Voortrekkers.

Shortly after 1850 there were clashes over such issues. In 1851 the Tswana chieftain, Kgosi Montshiwa of the Barolong, complained that the trekkers were contravening in his territory. Discussions about the boundary line between the Barolong and the Boers were initially successful but after the conclusion of the Sand River Convention (1852), whereby Britain recognised the independence of the Boers north of the Vaal River, tension escalated. Piet Scholtz, the Boer commander on the western boundary of the Transvaal, now not only demanded that black communities recognise the authority of the trekkers, but also that black people had to provide labour in exchange for the right to settle on certain tracts of land. In addition, the Boers began to take steps to prevent black people from gaining access to firearms.

These measures soon led to active resistance from the Batswana. By mid-1852 Kgosi Mosielele of the Bakgatla refused point blank to accede to demands that he force his followers to provide labour for the Voortrekkers. Furthermore, his people began to plunder the trekkers' cattle. Scholtz reacted by raising a commando to punish Mosielele who took refuge with Kgosi Sechele of the Bakwena. In August 1852 this led to a confrontation at Dimawe between the Boers and the combined forces of the Bakwena and the Bakgatla. Scholtz gained the upper hand and about 100 Batswana were killed. In addition to large herds of cattle taken as booty, the Boers captured a number of Batswana women and children who were subsequently *ingeboek* (indentured) as workers. Sechele complained in vain about this to the British authorities in the Cape.

In this period, the most south-westerly Tswana society living in the present North West Province was the Batlhaping. After the discovery of diamonds in the confluence of the Gariep and Vaal rivers in the late 1860s, their territory was rapidly taken over by the British. Although the Batlhaping tried to resist this subjugation on two occasions, the first in 1878 and again in 1896, they too had to surrender their independent status.

In 1885 the British colonial government decided to protect the Tswana from the inroads of the Boers in the ZAR by declaring a protectorate over the Tswana territories. However, the Bechuanaland Protectorate was incorporated into the Cape Colony in 1895, which meant that the Tswana societies south of the Molopo River finally lost their independence.

Smaller communities north of the Vaal River

By 1850 a number of independent Ndebele communities lived north of the Vaal River, but all were destined to lose their independent status in the course of the next 50 years. In a few cases they were wiped out by the white authorities – sometimes in reaction to attacks on the Boers.

In the northern part of the ZAR the Kekana Ndebele under Mokopane launched an attack in 1854 on a party of white travellers at a drift over the Nyl River, south of the Strydpoort mountain range. The entire group, including children, were murdered. At the same time, a party of white hunters was wiped out by the Langa Ndebele. Two Boer commandant generals, M.W. Pretorius and Piet Potgieter, called up their followers and the commandos hurried to the site of the attacks, the present Moorddrif. The Ndebele took refuge in a cave in the mountains which has since become known as Makapansgat. The burghers surrounded the cave and besieged the fugitives, demanding that Mokopane be surrendered to them, but the Ndebele refused.

Potgieter was killed during the siege but very few burghers were injured. In contrast, the Kekana Ndebele suffered heavily and the majority died from hunger and thirst. Mokopane was never found. Shortly after the incident, the ZAR Volksraad established a new village in the vicinity and called it Piet Potgietersrus.

The Ndzundza Ndebele lived in the present Mpumalanga and were reasonably successful in preventing white encroachment into their region for a number of years. But by 1882 enmity between a Ndzundza sub-chief called Nyabela and the white authorities developed into a full-scale war. After several months the Boers managed to gain the upper hand; Nyabela was captured and sentenced to life imprisonment, but was released in 1898. The land on which his community had previously lived was divided up into smallholdings and given to the Boers who had participated in the campaign.

In the second half of the nineteenth century the Lobedu lived in the mountains near the present town of Modjadjiskloof. They were ruled by a queen by the name of Modjadji. She supposedly had power over rainfall and was accorded great respect not only by her followers but also by other communities. After her death she was succeeded by other "rain queens".

The Venda

By 1850 the Venda were living in the district near the fertile Soutpansberg Mountains in the northern parts of what is today the Limpopo Province; they were loosely divided into groups under headmen. When a small party of Voortrekkers under Hendrik Potgieter arrived in about 1848, they settled down in the southern foothills of the Soutpansberg and laid out a small town that later became known as Schoemansdal. Some of the Venda formed close ties with the new arrivals; these links benefited both communities.

There were also Venda who worked for the Boers on their farms, while others were employed as hunters or ivory-carriers by white hunters. However, in time, the rapid increase of hunting activity by white settlers became cause for concern among the Venda because they too were hunters. This sense of alarm and suspicion soured relations between them. When the Boers vacated Schoemansdal in 1867, inter alia because of the tsetse fly hazard, the Venda community of Chief Makhado was able to protect itself against white interference for a period of almost 30 years. However, in 1898 a strong Boer force from the ZAR launched an assault against them and forced them from their strongholds in the Soutpansberg. Driven by necessity, Chief Mphephu and about 10 000 of his followers fled across the Limpopo River. The conquest of Venda meant that the land belonging to the last remaining independent black society in South African territory had been taken over by the whites.

State formation

The Cape Colony

By 1850 the Cape Colony had already been part of the British colonial empire for more than 40 years. Executive control over the colony was in the hands of a governor appointed by the colonial office in London. At the time, Sir Harry Smith held this position. The year 1834 saw some limited advancement of the system of governance in that a legislative council was introduced to assist the governor. Five nominated colonists who were then appointed at the discretion of the governor, and four prominent officials, served on this council.

In 1854 after a seven-year period of concerted effort on the part of the colonists, the British agreed that the legislative council should become an elected body, and a representative government was duly put in place. However, the executive was still not directly responsible to the legislative council. This was the position until 1872 when it was agreed that a responsible government be introduced in the Cape Colony. This meant that the executive authority – the prime minister and his cabinet – were responsible for their actions to the elected legislative council, and thereby to the colonists. This also implied that the members of the executive had to resign if they lost the confidence of the legislature. However, the Cape parliament was still subordinate to the British parliament and the British monarch (king or queen) was officially the head of state. The British government was represented in the Cape Colony by the governor and he had to sign all the colony's legislation and proclamations before they could take effect.

A system of qualified franchise was in place. This meant that any male citizen who was above a certain age and who met the prescribed education and economic requirements, was entitled to vote. Initially, every male colonist of 21 years or older who earned more than £50 sterling per year, or who occupied property worth at least £25 sterling, was able to register as a voter. This meant that it was mainly the white residents of the colony who had the vote. These stipulations were changed from time to time.

The Cape political scene was for the most part dominated by English-speaking colonists. John Charles Molteno, who came from the Eastern Cape, was the first prime minister. Most Afrikaners initially chose to remain aloof from the political process. Although comprising about 75% of the total white population of the Cape in 1872, less than a third of the Cape's members of Parliament were Afrikaners.

Towards the end of the 1870s things began to change. Afrikaner nationalism had gradually grown stronger in reaction to the British policy of anglicisation. As early as 1875 this had led to the formation of the Genootskap van Regte Afrikaners (GRA, the Society of True Afrikaners), which stood for *"ons taal, ons nasie en ons land"* (our language, our nation and our country). In 1876 the GRA launched the first newspaper in Afrikaans, *Die Afrikaanse Patriot*. The founding of the Afrikaner Bond at the Cape in 1879 was another indication of the rise of Afrikaner nationalism. The leading figure in this political movement, which in time became a political party, was Jan Hendrik ("Onze Jan") Hofmeyr.

However, the majority of Cape Afrikaners remained loyal to the British Empire until well into the 1890s and were often referred to as "Victoria's Afrikaners". It was with the backing of this group of Afrikaners that Cecil John Rhodes became prime minister of the Cape in 1890. This support was reflected in the trend of his policies, which catered for the interests of the Cape Afrikaners. Firstly, they demanded that Dutch be recognised as a parliamentary language alongside English, that this be actively promoted and that there be legislation passed to this effect. Secondly, Rhodes was sympathetic to their negative attitude about the unrestricted extension of the franchise to black residents in the Cape Colony, and thirdly, he made sure that as far as possible the interests of farmers were considered when formulating government policy.

It was only after the Jameson Raid in 1896 that the large majority of Cape Afrikaners turned their back on Rhodes; soon thereafter he resigned as prime minister. This opened the way for the Afrikaner Bond and shortly before the turn of the century, it came to power in the Cape, with W.P. Schreiner as prime minister. By this time war clouds were gathering over South Africa. Schreiner did all he possibly could to promote reconciliation between the ZAR and Britain, but his efforts were in vain. He tried to keep the Cape neutral, but the British government would not allow this because the Cape was a British colony. Some Cape Afrikaners stood strongly behind their fellow Afrikaners in the republics and chose to take an active part in the Anglo-Boer War.

Whites and Indians in Natal

From a white perspective, in the second half of the nineteenth century Natal was an almost exclusively English-speaking colony. Between 1847 and 1851 about 5000 immigrants from Britain and Ireland arrived and as a result most of the white residents spoke English. However, in 1851 Britain stopped all assisted emigration to Natal.

Natal experienced much the same constitutional development as the Cape Colony. In 1857 it was granted representative government and in 1893 this progressed to responsible government. In theory, all adult male residents of Natal, as in the Cape Colony, were entitled to vote, but the franchise qualification for black people was so complicated that only three black residents had registered as voters by 1893.

From 1846, Theophilus Shepstone was responsible for the administration of blacks who lived within the borders of Natal. He placed this group of people, most of whom were Zulu speakers who had decided to break away from their traditional communities, in ten locations or reserves and appointed African chiefs, indunas and headmen to deal with local affairs. For example, Shepstone appointed black headmen to keep order and collect taxes. The most important tax was a hut tax, and black people had to pay it to finance the British administration of the reserves. White magistrates, with the assistance of a black police force, were appointed above the African authorities to keep the whole system running smoothly. This so-called Shepstone System brought decades of peace and order, but not all blacks in Natal accepted the authority of the headmen who were forced upon them. Furthermore, the system failed in one of its primary aims – to ensure that there were enough black workers who were prepared to offer their labour to white farmers.

Nor did agricultural development in Natal run smoothly. Mealies were grown with some success, although not on large scale because there were few marketing opportunities. Attempts to cultivate cotton failed, but the prospects for sugar production appeared to be more promising. However, sugar cane is an exotic crop that had to be planted and harvested by hand. This intensive farming called for a large number of workers who would be satisfied with low wages. The local black people were not prepared to perform this trying work because they could maintain an independent subsistence relatively easily in the reserves or on farms which they could hire cheaply.

A solution to the labour question was found in the importation of unskilled contract labourers from India; thus the basis was laid for South Africa's Indian population. Between 1860 and 1911 more than 150 000 contract labourers were shipped to Natal, with the Natal government paying their travelling costs. On the sugar plantations they were treated little better than slaves. They worked long hours, their living quarters were poor, their rations were meagre and social services were virtually absent. On completion of their ten-year contracts, their passage back home was paid or they could elect to remain in Natal where (at least until 1890) they were given a small plot of land free of charge. More than half of the Indian contract workers remained and decided to stay on in Natal.

The majority made a living as small-scale farmers, fishermen, merchants or peddlers. In addition to the sugar-cane workers, other Indians, some of whom paid their own passage, came to Natal. Indians subsequently moved throughout South Africa with the exception of the OFS where for many years they were forbidden either to live or to work.

The two Boer republics

After Britain had recognised the independence of the Voortrekker societies north of the Vaal River and those who had settled north of the Gariep (or Orange) River, in 1852 and 1854 respectively, these disunited communities had to begin the difficult task of forming viable states. In the Transgariep this process went relatively smoothly and the OFS came into being on 23 February 1854, with Bloemfontein named as its capital. At this stage there were about 15 000 Afrikaners living in the republic.

The signing of the Sand River Convention on 17 January 1852 did not mean that a free, united Afrikaner state (or Boer state) north of the Vaal River came into being immediately. Indeed, the process of state formation took all of twelve years, because many of the divisions of the 1840s still persisted. At the time the Sand River Convention was concluded, the trekker communities in the Transvaal divided politically into the following groups: In the west and south-west (the Potchefstroom, Magaliesberg and Marico region) the large majority of Voortrekkers supported Commandant General Andries Pretorius, while in the far north Commandant General Hendrik Potgieter at Soutpansbergdorp (later called Schoemansdal) had the most support. In the east, where the town of Lydenburg had become the centre of Voortrekker activity, the belief was that power should be vested in the Volksraad rather than a military leader. Elsewhere in Transvaal, including the Apies River valley in the central part; the Suikerbosrand in the south-east; and the Buffels River in the far south-east, where the residents founded a village named Utrecht, there were isolated communities who lived a sparse, precarious existence.

The different groups in the Transvaal were only able to succeed in establishing the Zuid-Afrikaansche Republiek (ZAR) in 1857. However, a further period of altercation and discord followed in the early 1860s which at times even led to armed conflict and civil war. A relatively stable, unified state was only formed in 1864.

Although the exact composition and powers of these two republics and their high councils and functionaries differed, the members of their legislative bodies and the presidents of both republics were elected in a democratic manner by adult male burghers. It was therefore the Voortrekkers who established the republican form of government in the interior.

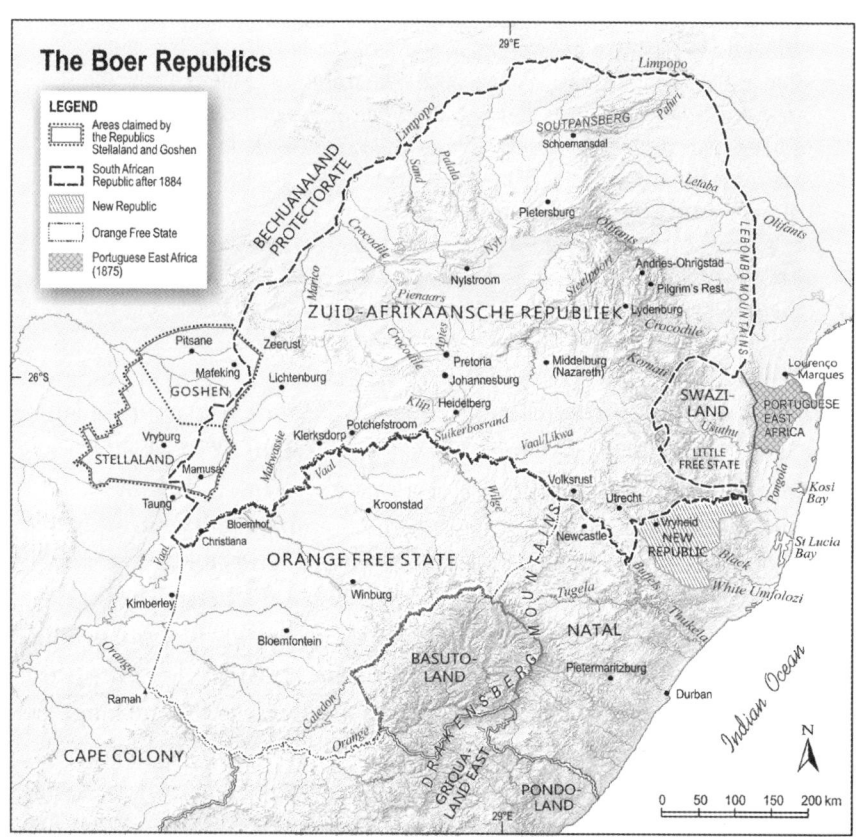

> **BLACK SOCIETIES IN THE BOER REPUBLICS**
> Black societies were not involved at governance level during or after the Great Trek when the Voortrekkers gained political control in certain parts of the country. Over the years, the leaders of the ZAR and OFS implemented their traditional policy of separation (segregation) in regions which they saw as theirs. According to this policy, each group was entitled to rule itself as it saw fit in its own territory, although certain boundaries and dividing lines had to be maintained. In the colonial period, policies of this nature were no exception – nowhere were the "local" people fully integrated into the governance of the country. Nor did these communities make any claim to participation in the highest organs of government.
>
> Within Free State territory, black people were permitted to remain in their traditional strongholds and their territories later became identified as "reserves". Although they were liable to pay tax, they were not asked to perform any civic duties, and within the reserves there was political self-governance.
>
> On many occasions the Voortrekkers and other white residents in the Boer republics conducted cordial negotiations with neighbouring black societies about their respective possession of land near the boundaries. This meant that as time went by, black communities were restricted to these areas. The trekkers began farming on the land along these boundaries and gradually small groups of blacks and their families settled there as farm workers. Generally speaking, the attitude of the Boers towards their black workers was one of guardianship (sympathetic supervision).
>
> It was also part of the republican Afrikaners' outlook that blacks should not be allowed to possess firearms. Paul Kruger, who later became president of the ZAR, firmly believed that whites simply could not afford to take this risk because of the overwhelming number of black people.

In the first 20 years after the Sand River Convention, the political landscape in the Transvaal was dominated to a large extent by M.W. Pretorius, the son of the Voortrekker leader Andries Pretorius. After his father's death in 1853, M.W. Pretorius became the commandant general in the Potchefstroom, Magaliesberg and Marico region. In the north a similar change of leadership took place at this time, when the Voortrekker leader Hendrik Potgieter died in December 1852 and his son Piet followed in his late father's footsteps as commandant general. After Piet Potgieter's death in 1854, Stephanus Schoeman came to the fore as the most important leader in the north.

The disunity in the Transvaal grew worse in 1853 with the arrival of Rev. Dirk van der Hoff as the first permanent minister north of the Vaal

River. He was a Hollander, belonged to the Hervormde Kerk (Reformed Church), and attached himself for the most part to the Pretorius group. It was primarily the more conservative group, the so-called Doppers, who were reluctant to accept Van der Hoff. One of the leaders of the Doppers was the young Rustenburg commandant, Paul Kruger. They soon acquired the services of their own minister, Rev. Dirk Postma of the Gereformeerde Kerk (Reformed Church) based in the Netherlands. In the 1860s the Cape Nederduitse Gereformeerde Kerk (Cape Dutch Reformed Church) was also established in the Transvaal.

By 1857, M.W. Pretorius had succeeded in uniting all the regions and factions and had drawn up a constitution for the republic. He was duly elected as president and head of the executive authority. Pretoria, which had been founded in 1855 and was named after Andries Pretorius, became the capital of the ZAR a few years later.

At the end of 1859, Pretorius's efforts to unite the ZAR and the Orange Free State led to his election as president of the OFS as well. However, this proved unacceptable to his opponents in the ZAR and he was compelled to choose between the two republics. His choice fell on the OFS, leaving the Transvaal leaderless once again.

In the wake of Pretorius's resignation, the political disunity in the Transvaal reached new heights. His supporters refused to accept that he was no longer president and intimated that the Volksraad no longer represented the will of the *volk* (the people). They argued that they now represented the will of the *volk* and called themselves the Volkslaer (People's Laager). In opposition to this group, the members of the Volksraad stood their ground and insisted that the authority of the state had to be upheld. They became known as the Staatslaer (State's Laager) and their most prominent leader was Paul Kruger. Early in 1864 the two groups were embroiled in a shoot-out but the skirmish ended indecisively. In the aftermath of this confrontation, Pretorius turned up in Pretoria and announced that he had resigned as president of the Free State. The two opposing factions then agreed to hold new elections; Pretorius was re-elected president, while Paul Kruger was chosen as commandant general.

In 1871 the Volksraad again forced Pretorius to resign, this time because of his inept handling of the dispute that arose over the ownership of the diamond fields. On the advice of President J.H. (Jan) Brand of the Free State, in 1872 the Transvalers elected Rev. T.F. Burgers, a Cape Afrikaner, as their new president. This was a mistake because as a liberal minister of religion, Burgers was unable to consolidate the support of the conservative Transvalers behind his presidency. Both Kruger, the vice-president, and Piet Joubert, who was the commandant of Wakkerstroom, were at times during Burgers's term of office only lukewarm in their support. Indeed the disunity in the republic ran so deep that in 1877 the Transvaal Boers were totally powerless when British imperialism again threatened their independence.

There was a marked revival of British interest in South Africa after the discovery of diamonds in 1867, and the first step towards what Lord Carnarvon, the British secretary of state for the colonies, hoped would become a federation of South African states, was the annexation of the ZAR. On 12 April 1877, Sir Theophilus Shepstone read out a proclamation to this effect on Church Square in Pretoria. In reaction, the Boers merely raised a complaint through Burgers, but did absolutely nothing to resist. They were too demoralised and disunited to contemplate any forceful action. After the annexation, Burgers left the Transvaal.

But soon afterwards, a stubborn sense of resistance began to stir among the Boers. In 1877 and again in 1878, they sent deputations to Britain to plead for the reversal of the annexation. Paul Kruger led both deputations; neither was successful. This made the burghers even more determined to regain their independence. Elsewhere in South Africa a growing number of Afrikaners began to identify with the Transvalers' aspirations, which in itself was another indication of the awakening of Afrikaner nationalism. The Transvaal Boers also held a series of public meetings and emotional rallies to discuss their grievances and express their antagonism to British rule.

The last of these rallies took place in December 1880 on the farm Paardekraal (where the town of Krugersdorp was later laid out). About 3000 burghers attended. It was decided on 11 December that the remaining members of the previous government of 1877 should be re-instated in their positions. This represented the first step towards active resistance. The members of the Volksraad who were present at Paardekraal instructed the government that a triumvirate be formed under the leadership of Paul Kruger, the vice-president.

The First War of Independence

The Transvaal burghers presumed that the British would not yet be expecting an attempt to restore the republic and at Paardekraal they began to plan for war. Piet Joubert was chosen as commandant general. He made good use of the right accorded to him under martial law to appoint generals and commandants for specific tasks. While he departed with the biggest commando for Heidelberg, which was to serve as a temporary capital, another commando went to Potchefstroom, where a large British garrison was stationed. On 16 December the first shots of the Transvaal War of Independence (otherwise known as the First Anglo-Boer War) rang out in Potchefstroom.

Although the British had a number of military garrisons in the Transvaal, including a force of more than 1000 men in Pretoria, these troops struggled to suppress the uprising. This became clear on 20 December 1880 when the Boers claimed a decisive victory over a British taskforce near Bronkhorstspruit, east of Pretoria. The governor of Natal, General George Colley, immediately began to raise a force in Natal so that he could move in for an attack on the Transvaal. Joubert was informed of this and moved with his main commando to the Laingsnek pass, where the wagon trail from Natal snaked its way through the mountains of the Drakensberg range.

Because the British in Natal were not well prepared to wage a war, Colley had some difficulty in raising a force and only managed to reach the Drakensberg at the end of January 1881. The Boers were waiting for him; they pounced on his troops and defeated them in the Battle of Laingsnek on 28 January. Colley suffered heavy losses and had to postpone his planned march into the Transvaal to lift the Boer siege of the garrisons until he had received reinforcements. The Boers also emerged as victors in the second confrontation on the Natal front, the Battle of Schuinshoogte, on 8 February 1881.

THE GLORIOUS VICTORY AT MAJUBA

Towards the end of February 1881, a large group of British troops joined Colley's force. Although there was already talk of peace negotiations, Colley decided to attack to rescue his reputation.

He wanted to use the surprise element and planned his attack in great secrecy. On Saturday evening of 26 February after the evening meal, he ordered a force of 570 men to advance in the dark and in dead silence. Acting on his orders the soldiers climbed to the top of the Majuba Mountain during the night – an extremely arduous task in the pitch darkness and across unknown terrain. The last exhausted soldier only reached the south-westerly point of the

> mountaintop shortly before daybreak the following morning. They then spread out along the summit's edge which was some 1300 m in circumference.
> The Boers saw the soldiers just before sunrise and Joubert ordered that burghers be sent to attack them. Several hundred burghers quickly began to climb up the steep mountainside. The British fired down on them from the top but this did not deter the Boers. They made clever use of all possible hiding places and did this so effectively that the British did not realise that they were climbing ever higher. The British were cruelly disillusioned when the first group of Boers clambered over the edge of the northerly crest at about one in the afternoon and began firing on them at close range.
> The struggle for the summit of Majuba lasted only between ten and twenty minutes. The British defence simply disintegrated. Many of the soldiers and officers began to run to the ridge of the southern crest. Some of them were shot, including Colley himself who was mortally wounded when he walked back, apparently in a dazed state. The soldiers who had reached the edge of the crest unharmed rushed down the steep decline and fled back to Colley's camp at Mount Prospect. A few tumbled down the steep cliffs and fell to their death. The Boers occupied the entire summit and fired down at the soldiers who were trying to get away. However, a thick mist suddenly descended on the mountaintop and ended the Battle of Majuba.
> The British force had suffered a crushing defeat. Six officers and 86 troops died and nine officers and 125 troops were wounded. Two Boers were killed and five were lightly wounded.
> For the British, Majuba became a symbol of defeat – a defeat that had to be avenged. Nineteen years later, in 1900, they succeeded in doing so when during the Anglo-Boer War, on the anniversary of Majuba Day, Lord Roberts forced General Piet Cronjé to surrender at Paardeberg. On the very same day, but on the Natal front, General Redvers Buller and his troops broke through the Boer defensive line.
> The famous victory at Majuba was an important step in the Transvalers' struggle to regain their independence. A few days after the battle, Joubert and Sir Evelyn Wood, Colley's successor, signed a ceasefire agreement at Laingsnek.

The Pretoria Convention was signed on 3 August 1881, but did not fully restore the ZAR's independence. The Boer republic was still under British suzerainty – a vague term which basically meant that the British government had supervisory powers over the ZAR's external affairs and its domestic legislation concerning black people. Five days later, the governance of the ZAR was handed over to a triumvirate under the leadership of Kruger. A new Volksraad was duly elected which ratified the Pretoria Convention.

The implementation of the convention gave rise to many problems and the Boer leaders decided to approach the British government about making certain amendments. Paul Kruger, Nicolaas Smit and Rev. S.J. du Toit, the superintendent of education, left in November 1883 for London. Early the next year, lengthy discussions were held with Lord Derby, the then secretary of state for the colonies. A new agreement, the London Convention, was reached; this was signed on Majuba Day of 1884. This time there was no mention of suzerainty; the ZAR was again recognised as an independent state. The only stipulation was that no treaty could be signed with a foreign state without the consent of the British monarch.

The Transvaal War of Independence became an important stimulus for Afrikaner nationalism and Paul Kruger came to the fore as the symbol of the Afrikaner spirit of independence.

SHORT-LIVED BOER REPUBLICS

The British interference in Zululand and its resultant breakdown as a political unit was not without side effects for Afrikaner society. Cetshwayo's downfall meant that his successor, his son Dinizulu, made a desperate appeal to a group of Afrikaners to provide him with support in a civil war against other Zulu chieftains. In exchange he gave them a large portion of land, where they set up the New Republic in 1884, with Vryheid as the capital and Lukas Meyer as president. The New Republic was incorporated into the ZAR as the Vryheid district in 1888.

On the western boundary of the ZAR in the early 1880s, similar disturbances to those in Zululand broke out among the Tswana groups. This also led to requests for the Boers to provide help and again the Boers were given land for their services. Two separate republics were established here, namely Stellaland, with Vryburg as capital; and Goshen, with Rooigrond as capital. These two small republics had an even shorter lifespan than the New Republic, because both were disbanded by Britain in 1884. The eastern portion of these republics was incorporated into the ZAR, while the more extensive western parts were incorporated into the newly formed British Bechuanaland.

The discovery of diamonds

Officially, the first diamond was discovered in the Hopetown district in 1867. Shortly afterwards a far bigger diamond was picked up by a Griqua shepherd in the Gariep River valley. This set off the diamond rush and thousands of people streamed into the northern Cape to seek their fortune.

By 1870 there were 10 000 diggers – local people as well as foreigners – all searching for diamonds. Prospectors also began to move away from the rivers looking for the precious gems and in 1871 on a rocky outcrop on the farm Vooruitzigt between the Vaal and the Gariep rivers, a very large deposit was discovered. Because there were literally thousands of diamonds found there, crowds of diggers descended on the farm. Before long there was a huge, deep hole where the *koppie* (rocky outcrop) once was – and still the diggers were finding diamonds.

The village that sprung up around this "big hole" was named Kimberley in honour of the British secretary of state for the colonies, Lord Kimberley. By 1873 the diggers' corrugated-iron shacks were replaced by more permanent structures; entrepreneurs opened businesses; and lawyers set up agencies. South Africa's first modern mining town had become a reality. The majority of Kimberley's white residents were English speaking, but many Afrikaners settled there as well. The mining town also attracted crowds of black South Africans, although they were only permitted to work in the burgeoning mining industry as labourers.

This vibrant new population of local people and foreigners from overseas meant that the farmers in the western Free State (and later also those further afield) suddenly had new markets for their agricultural products. The majority of these farmers were Afrikaners. Black farmers also made good profits, the best example being the Basotho who supplied wheat; and initially at least, the Batlhaping, who sold firewood to the diggers. At the same time, the opportunity arose for enterprising Afrikaners to make a good living as transport riders; two such men, who later became famous generals in the Anglo-Boer War, were Koos de la Rey of Lichtenburg in the then Western Transvaal, and Christiaan de Wet from the southern Free State.

One unforeseen outcome of the establishment of the diamond mining industry and the huge demand for labour was that thousands of black labourers purchased firearms with the money they earned on the mines. Many white burghers grew increasingly concerned that a widespread black uprising against white supremacy was on the cards. One of the results of this supposed threat – in the British colonies as well as the Boer republics – was the introduction of strong measures to restrict the movement of black people, including the implementation of various versions of the pass system.

Another result of the large-scale mining of diamonds was the implementation of a closed compound system to house black contract workers; this was in complete disregard of the basic rights of the workers.

Diamond mining also kick-started the industrial revolution in South Africa and the discovery of rich gold deposits some years later propelled this to new heights. Gold had been mined in the precolonial period in South Africa, but the richest gold reef in the world was discovered on the Witwatersrand in 1886.

Prospectors and gold seekers had been crisscrossing the entire Transvaal since the 1850s. From time to time they found small, uneconomic quantities of alluvial gold, but these were scarcely enough to keep alive the hope of finding substantial deposits of the precious metal. Gold fever really fired the imagination in the Transvaal following discoveries of that precious metal at Tati, in present-day Botswana (1867), at the Murchison Hills near present-day Tzaneen (1868), on the farm Eersteling near what later became Pietersburg (now Polokwane) (1871) and near Lydenburg and in hills and valleys north-east and east of that town (1873). The mining town of Pilgrim's Rest in the present Mpumalanga lies in the valley around the small stream where a few million pounds worth of alluvial gold were mined.

In 1883 the Struben brothers, Fred and Harry, systematically began their search for gold on the Witwatersrand. However, it is generally acknowledged that either George Harrison (an Australian digger) or his friend George Walker (a Briton) discovered what was to become the richest gold reef in the world, the main reef on the farm Langlaagte (where Johannesburg's central business hub is today). Suddenly two large mining camps appeared virtually overnight on the Witwatersrand; tent towns mushroomed and were later replaced by a makeshift hotchpotch of corrugated-iron shelters.

The once poor Transvaal was suddenly assured of prosperity and accelerated progress. Businesses flourished; new markets were opened up for agricultural products; and there were more job opportunities on the mines, factories and farms. The diverse backgrounds of this new conglomeration of people unavoidably led to clashing outlooks on life and values. Cultural and political differences also gave rise to much friction. It was the 10 000 Uitlanders (foreigners), specifically the British citizens who came to live on the Witwatersrand, who in time became a political factor and had a marked influence on the course of history.

The discovery of mineral wealth on their borders and later within the confines of the two Boer republics soon led to fierce disagreement. Neither Britain nor the Cape Colony had any legal claim to ownership of the diamond fields. Nicolaas Waterboer's Griqua, backed by Waterboer's legal adviser David Arnot, laid claim to virtually the entire area where the diamonds had been found. The government of the OFS had no doubt that at the very least the whole area between the confluence of the Vaal and Gariep (Orange) belonged to the Free State; it was unquestionably part of the republic. The ZAR, for its part, claimed the diamond-rich area north of the Vaal River, east of its confluence with the Harts River. The chiefs of the Batlhaping, Barolong and Korana also registered claims to parts of the region north of the Vaal River. All the claimants believed that their respective claims were based on solid ground and no one was prepared to back down.

The irony of the so-called diamond fields debate is that, in the end, none of these claimants were successful, because in May 1871 the British government decided to make the disputed territory part of the British Empire. The Transvaal president, M.W. Pretorius, made it easy for the British when he agreed to arbitration on the issue. The final arbiter was Robert Keate, the British lieutenant governor of Natal. In October 1871 he found that the largest part of the diamond fields belonged to the Griqua, and that a portion north of the Vaal River was the property of the Barolong. Barely ten days later, the Cape governor, Sir Henry Barkly, proclaimed British authority over the territory which had been awarded to the Griqua, ostensibly to protect their interests. The British then took over, renamed the region Griqualand West and for all practical purposes annexed the diamond fields.

The diamond fields dispute had sensational results. In the Transvaal, Pretorius was forced to resign because of his inept handling of the ZAR's claim. President Jan Brand of the OFS had acted with far more wisdom. He made it clear that he was only prepared to accept the arbitration of a neutral arbiter, someone of the calibre of the president of the United States of America or the king of the Netherlands. The British government refused to permit this; they would not countenance outside interference in South Africa. After the Keate Award and the British annexation of Griqualand West, the Free State Volksraad protested strenuously, but without success. A total of 143 farms that belonged to Free State burghers were now suddenly under the British flag. Some of these farm owners went to the Griqualand West land court to receive confirmation of their right of ownership. To the great embarrassment of the British government, the court ruled in favour of the farm owners.

Shortly after this ruling, Brand went to London for discussions with the new secretary of state for the colonies, Lord Carnarvon. He refused to accept Brand's consistent argument on the validity of the Free State's claim. However, as a gesture of reconciliation Carnarvon offered the Free State £90 000 as compensation, at the time a small fortune. Brand accepted this on behalf of the residents of his republic, and thereby the matter was settled, although the Free Staters still felt aggrieved.

Another important outcome of the discovery of diamonds was that it rekindled Britain's interest in the two Boer republics. The British government used several different tactics in their attempt to regain control over the Transvaal and the Orange Free State, including the incorporation of Griqualand West into the Cape in 1871; declaring Griqualand West a crown colony in 1872; and the annexation of the Transvaal in 1877. This latter event (as seen earlier in this chapter) led to the Transvaal War of Independence of 1880–1881.

The way Britain handled the diamond fields dispute led to the strengthening of ties between the two Boer republics. Brand was of the opinion that the two republics should stand together against Britain and in 1872 the Transvaal and Free State signed a treaty of friendship, trade and extradition.

Barkly's annexation of the diamond fields took place shortly after the granting of responsible government – parliamentary self-government – in the Cape Colony. To the governor's great shock and consternation the Cape parliament refused to accept responsibility for Griqualand West. This was but one way the Cape Afrikaners were able to express their sympathy for the Boer republics at the outcome of the diamond fields debacle. In the course of the next three decades this sympathy grew in reaction to events such as the British annexation of the Transvaal in 1877 and the Jameson Raid in 1896. By the turn of the century there were closer ties than ever before between the Cape and the Boer republics.

The prelude to the Anglo-Boer War

After the Transvaal had regained its independence in August 1881, vice-president Paul Kruger took up residence in Pretoria so that he could give his full attention to matters of state. He particularly wanted to improve the education system in the ZAR and to stimulate the economy by promoting the establishment of industries. In 1883 the Transvalers held their first presidential election since the War of Independence. The foremost candidates were Kruger and Piet Joubert. Kruger gained a decisive victory and was sworn in as president in May 1883.

One of Kruger's greatest dreams was to become totally free of British control by building a railway line to link Pretoria and Delagoa Bay (today Maputo). To achieve this he held talks in 1884 with the Portuguese government, because Delagoa Bay was in the Portuguese colony of Mozambique. However, it took more than ten years before the Nederlandsche Zuid-Afrikaansche Spoorweg-Maatschappij (NZASM), which was specially established for this project, finally completed the so-called Eastern line at the end of 1894.

Other railways, including those between the Cape and the Transvaal via the Orange Free State, were also constructed in Kruger's presidency and made a substantial contribution to the development of the ZAR. Johannesburg and Pretoria were linked by rail and in 1899 the line was extended to Pietersburg (now Polokwane). The so-called Rand Tram crossed the Witwatersrand from east to west and in the far east the eastern line to Delagoa Bay was linked to the mining town of Barberton.

The discovery of gold and the prosperity this brought was something of a mixed blessing for the ZAR. The gold was valuable and was sold for high prices on overseas markets. Furthermore, the mining companies paid high taxes that went into the ZAR government coffers. Whereas prior to 1886 the Transvaal was bankrupt, there was now money to pay officials; services such as education could be rendered; a government artillery was established; and impressive government buildings such as the Raadsaal (council chamber) and the Palace of Justice were built on Church Square in Pretoria.

Thousands of diggers streamed into Johannesburg from all over the world to mine the gold. The sudden arrival of a sprawling, growing urban population provided a stable and ever-expanding market for agricultural produce in the heart of the republic; this provided a substantial income for many Transvaal farmers. But most of the diggers had an urban culture and an outlook that was completely out of sync with the Transvaal burghers. For this reason they called these new people in their midst Uitlanders (foreigners).

Poverty-stricken Afrikaners who did not own farms drifted into the mining camps where they accepted unskilled work on the goldfields and managed to survive. Educated Afrikaners, mainly from the Cape, also went to the Witwatersrand and made a good living as agents, lawyers and so on. One example is that of Christiaan Beyers, later a Boer general, who settled in Boksburg and opened a law practice.

For the Transvaal government, the biggest challenge was that the Uitlanders rapidly increased in number, so much so that they became a threat to the existence of the state as a Boer republic. Some Uitlanders – particularly those who came from Britain – began to complain that they were paying too much tax and that the government was treating them badly. They wanted Britain to take over the Transvaal again and to remove the Boer government. They regarded the Afrikaner culture as inferior and the Afrikaners as backward.

In 1894 there were already 75 000 Uitlanders compared to about 150 000 burghers in the republic. Kruger was afraid that eventually there would be more Uitlanders than burghers. He was convinced that if the Uitlanders were granted the franchise they would eventually take over political control of the Transvaal and hand it over to Britain. He regarded them as money-grabbing materialists and refused to grant them the vote. This negative attitude explains why in a speech in 1894, Kruger referred to the Uitlanders as "thieves, murderers and fortune seekers".

In 1895 the Uitlander issue degenerated into violence. Cecil John Rhodes was not only the prime minister of the Cape Colony; he was also one of the wealthiest men in South Africa with extensive financial involvement in the gold-mining industry on the Witwatersrand. He was convinced that British control over the goldfields would be in the best interests of the mining industry – but this would mean Kruger's government giving up its authority in the Witwatersrand. Rhodes was fully aware that this would not be accomplished voluntarily and peacefully. He therefore conspired, with the full knowledge (and thus complicity) of the British secretary of state for the colonies, Joseph Chamberlain, to organise an uprising. The Uitlanders on the Witwatersrand, including his brother, Frank Rhodes, were also involved in the plot. Cecil Rhodes planned to send a number of hired soldiers under the orders of his friend and confidant, Leander Starr Jameson, into the republic from outside the border. When

Rhodes gave the signal, Jameson and his men would move in and overthrow Kruger's government. The raid was planned for the end of 1895.

Rhodes's plans went awry from the outset. The Uitlanders and their Reform Committee in Johannesburg suddenly felt hesitant about playing their part in the uprising. Meanwhile, an impatient Jameson decided to act on his own initiative and just after Christmas, without waiting for the order to do so, he and his 500-man force galloped across the Transvaal western border at Marico.

Kruger's reaction was to call up a commando under Piet Cronjé. Jameson and his attackers had almost reached Roodepoort when Cronjé and his burghers overwhelmed them at Doornkop. This was the end of the Jameson Raid.

Although the Jameson Raid had been put down successfully, the danger threatening the Boers was far from over. On the contrary, Britain felt humiliated. It was under these circumstances that early in 1897 the British government decided to send Sir Alfred Milner to South Africa as the new high commissioner. From the British side, Milner was apparently the individual who should be apportioned the greatest blame in the outbreak of the Anglo-Boer War in 1899. Judging from his actions it seems that he made it his mission to end the ZAR's independence. More particularly, he focused his attention on the Uitlander issue, harping on it out of all proportion and using this to put pressure on the ZAR.

Milner realised that Kruger was his biggest stumbling block. As for Kruger, he was fully aware of Milner's plans. For this reason he signed an offensive and defensive agreement with President M.T. Steyn of the Orange Free State in 1897 in terms of which the two Boer republics would support each other if the survival of either state was under threat.

Kruger began to have forts built around both Pretoria and Johannesburg and purchased quantities of arms and ammunition; he realised war was looming. From Germany he imported thousands of 7mm Mauser rifles – the best rifles available at the time. From France he ordered 155mm Creusot guns which were recognised worldwide. These were to defend the forts. The Boers gave the name "Long Toms" to the four heavy Creusot 155mm guns. In addition, the Boers had the use of various other types of artillery including the light rapid-firing 1-pounder automatic machine guns (or "pom-poms").

Meanwhile, Kruger negotiated with Milner in the hope of preventing a war. On 31 May 1899 they were together in Bloemfontein, where both Milner and Kruger put their demands on the table. Milner insisted that after five years of residence in the republic the Uitlanders had to be given the vote, because he believed that they would defeat the Boers in an election. Kruger replied: "You don't want the franchise; you want my country!" And yet he did, to some extent, agree to Milner's demands. This was not good enough for the British and they began shipping imperial troops to South Africa. It was clear to Kruger and his government that a war was inevitable because they were not prepared to simply give in to the British.

8

The mineral revolution

Wessel Visser

Historians see the mineral revolution as a watershed in nineteenth-century South Africa because of the sweeping economic, social and political changes it set in motion. The discovery of diamonds and gold shifted the hub of economic activity to the north of the country and became the mainspring for progressive industrialisation and the rise of vibrant new cities such as Kimberley and Johannesburg in the interior.

South Africa, which prior to 1910 comprised the British colonies of the Cape and Natal as well as two independent Boer republics, moved from an economy dominated by agriculture with a subsistence economy to a modern industrial state. This dramatic development over the course of a few decades was possible largely because of the technological inventions and progress of the Industrial Revolution in Western Europe and Britain. From about 1750 to 1850 many important technological advances were made, including those in the field of electricity, mining, metallurgy and engineering, and these in turn served as the driving force of economic growth. Without this technological progress and industrial renewal, it would have been impossible to mine the gold-bearing ore, especially the deep-level mining process on the Witwatersrand.

There is evidence that as early as 500 BC black societies were mining iron, gold and copper in southern Africa and that the Batlhaping were trading in diamonds years before white diggers arrived in the Gariep (Orange)–Vaal region to mine the precious stones. Early black societies found alluvial gold in riverbeds in the Tati region north of the Limpopo River in the present Botswana; in what is now Zimbabwe; and also in South Africa's present-day Mpumalanga province. They processed the metal and used it to barter for goods they needed, initially in their dealings with the Arab and Indian traders and later with the Portuguese on the east coast of Africa. In 1685 the governor of the Cape, Simon van der Stel, discovered rich deposits of copper ore near the present-day Springbok in Namaqualand, but this was only mined on a large scale after 1850.

The discovery of diamonds

On a day in 1867 a farmer called Schalk van Niekerk was given a shiny stone by a boy from a neighbouring farm, De Kalk, on the southern bank of the Gariep River in the district of Hopetown. His suspicion that it was a diamond was soon confirmed; it was established that it was indeed a diamond and that it weighed an impressive 21,25 carats. This gemstone was later called the Eureka diamond. Soon afterwards, a Griqua shepherd named Swartbooi picked up an even bigger diamond in the Gariep valley; he sold it to Van Niekerk for a horse, ten head of cattle and 500 sheep. Van Niekerk then sold it for £11 200, which overnight made him a very rich man indeed. This diamond, weighing 83,5 carats was later named the Star of South Africa.

Over the next two years travelling merchants bartered for diamonds with the local Batlhaping, Griqua and Korana. The big diamond rush began early in 1870 after rich deposits of the gems were discovered at Klipdrift on the Vaal River. By July 1870 as many as 800 diggers were camped on the banks of the Vaal and by October the number had swelled to 5000.

The early mining activity was in and along riverbeds to find alluvial (or sedimentary) diamonds. These diggings soon covered an area of 160 km along the Vaal from its confluence with the Gariep as far as small riverside towns such as Klipdrift (later Barkly West) and Delportshoop. The whole region was soon swarming with diggers and fortune seekers, white and black, from every level of society and every corner of the country. There were also those who came from further afield – from Britain, Europe, America, Brazil and Australia.

Before long there were far richer dry diggings between the Vaal and the Modder River at Du Toitspan and Bultfontein. In 1871 more gems were found on the farms belonging to the De Beer brothers. But the excavations on the nearby Colesberg *koppie* rendered the greatest concentration of diamonds ever discovered. There was an extraordinarily rich diamond-bearing pipe in volcanic rock, also known as kimberlite. Thousands of diggers descended on the *koppie* and staked out their claims. Soon there was a huge gaping hole where the Colesberg *koppie* had once stood.

> **A DIAMOND CLAIM**
>
> As soon as a new deposit of diamonds was discovered, a horde of prospective diggers would immediately rush to the site. For example, the Kimberley mine was initially known as the New Rush mine. Before he could begin mining, a digger had to register his claim (for which he paid 10 shillings a month); he then marked out his claim by driving four stakes into the ground in a square of about 10 x 10 m in size.

In 1873 it was decided to call the Colesberg *koppie* area by the name of Kimberley, in honour of the British secretary of state for the colonies. The four Kimberley mines (Bultfontein, Du Toitspan, Kimberley and De Beers) soon became the hub of the diamond fields. Later, two other diamond mining areas, Jagersfontein and Koffiefontein, were discovered in the south-western Orange Free State, but they were nowhere near as profitable as the mines in the Kimberley region.

Because there was uncertainty about the exact borders of the diamond fields, a number of claims were made to ownership of the land. Despite submissions by the Orange Free State, the South African Republic (ZAR), as well as the Griqua chief, Nicolaas Waterboer, the Tlhaping, Rolong and the Korana, it was Britain that eventually gained control of the diamond fields. Robert Keate, who acted as arbiter in the dispute, ruled in 1871 that the largest part of the diamond-rich land belonged to Nicolaas Waterboer and his Griqua followers, and that a portion north of the Vaal was in territory occupied by the Barolong. Shortly after the Keate Award, the Cape governor, Sir Henry Barkly, engineered control of the diamond fields by Britain when he announced that Nicolaas Waterboer and his Griqua followers had been declared British subjects. In 1872 Griqualand West was declared a British crown colony, and in 1880 it was incorporated into the Cape Colony.

Initially the diggers lived in rudimentary sacking and reed shelters, huts, wagons or tents. Later, these were replaced by temporary wood and corrugated-iron buildings. Because of the lack of roads and other infrastructure, transport was difficult and goods very expensive. The growth of trading posts in digger villages, of which Kimberley was the biggest and most progressive, also attracted artisans, businessmen, diamond buyers and professional people such as attorneys and doctors. As the population mushroomed, Kimberley grew in size and brick buildings were constructed for shops, offices and canteens.

Once the diamond diggings expanded, many were bought out and absorbed by large companies and diamond mining became an industry in its own right. A capitalistic wage economy (based on the wages which the workers earned) developed and this in turn created a greater need for unskilled labour. Although black people such as the local Batlhaping were initially permitted to own claims and work them as individual diggers, most workers in the diamond mines were black contract workers who were recruited from other parts of the country. This led to the migrant labour system.

Black workers usually covered the distance from their rural homes to the diamond mines on foot, worked their contract and then returned home, unless their contracts were renewed. The most numerous ethnic groups on the diamond mines were the Bapedi, the Tsonga from Mozambique and the Basotho from present-day Lesotho. For the Bapedi in particular, the availability of firearms, useful items such as blankets and bicycles, and money to increase their livestock holdings, were all important in luring them to the mines. The Basotho often used their wages for *lobola* and to pay for traditional weddings, while the weak economy, ecological disasters and wars in Mozambique were enough to make many Tsonga workers choose to become contract workers on the diamond mines.

The compound system was introduced to provide black contract workers with food and accommodation. In this way, capitalist mine owners were able to maintain control over the workers and ensure that the labour force, on which their profits depended, remained constant.

Initially, the compounds or dormitories were "open" and workers could come and go as they pleased, with reasonable freedom of movement. By the early 1880s the open compounds accommodated as many as 20 000 workers. However, in 1885 "closed" compounds were introduced to prevent the theft of diamonds, but also to maintain more stringent control over workers, thereby increasing production, cutting costs, and generally making the labour force more malleable. The closed compounds were self-contained units which cut off the workers completely from the outside world for the duration of their contracts. The compounds were strictly guarded, securely fenced and covered overhead with wire netting to prevent parcels of gems from being thrown over the enclosure. Closed corridors led directly to the adjacent mine.

Conditions in these compounds, quite apart from the enforced isolation, left much to be desired. They were cramped and housed far too many men; the beds were usually cement bunks; and the amenities were poor and unhygienic. Sickness, especially respiratory ailments such as pneumonia, were the order of the day and medical care was far from satisfactory. In addition, food was insufficient and of poor quality. These conditions meant that there was a high death rate in the compounds. Conditions only improved from about 1903 when mining companies were forced to make improvements to their compounds.

From about 1874, as the mining operations grew deeper and flooding of the "big hole" became a problem, it became impossible for individual workers to continue mining their claims. Expensive machinery was needed and because the diggers did not have the capital, the expertise or the necessary business acumen to compete with large companies, most of them sold their claims. Cecil John Rhodes realised that the consolidation of the diamond-mining industry by merging the biggest companies was the only way the industry could progress. In 1888 he succeeded in buying out the diamond holdings of other wealthy capitalists such as Charles Rudd and Barney Barnato and merging them with his own holdings to form a new giant in the diamond-mining industry, De Beers Consolidated Mines. By 1890 De Beers produced about 90% of the diamonds mined in Kimberley.

The discovery of gold

By 1850 fortune hunters and prospectors had already traversed the entire Transvaal searching for gold. When P.J. Marais was appointed official ZAR prospector in 1853, prospecting for gold gathered momentum and in October of that year he discovered traces of alluvial gold in the Jukskei River.

From about 1867, prospectors such as the German-born Karl Mauch found small deposits near the Olifants River in Eastern Transvaal (now Mpumalanga). Alluvial gold was also found north of Lydenburg in 1869; in the vicinity of the Klein Letaba and Groot Letaba rivers (1870); on the farm Eersteling near Marabastad (1871); at Pilgrim's Rest (1873); and on Sheba Reef in the mountains above Barberton (1884). The alluvial gold at

Barberton soon lured hundreds of prospectors, including diamond magnates such as Alfred Beit and Sammy Marks. However, the gold deposits in the Eastern Transvaal were not very profitable or sustainable.

On the Witwatersrand – the area between Springs in the east and Randfontein in the west – there had been ongoing prospecting for gold since 1880. It had been so named because of the streams and springs which flowed over the sun-bleached chalk boulders of the high-lying ridge. In 1881 Jan Bantjes sank a shaft at Kromdraai north of Krugersdorp and the brothers Fred and Harry Struben uncovered a rich quartz reef beside the Wilgespruit in 1884. In 1886, either the Australian George Harrison or the Briton George Walker (it is debatable who made the initial find) discovered the Witwatersrand's main gold reef on the farm Langlaagte. The news spread like wildfire and as had happened in the case of the diamond fields, hundreds of prospectors and fortune seekers descended on the Witwatersrand.

In September 1886 the ZAR government declared the farms Langlaagte, Randjeslaagte, Turffontein, Doornfontein, Elandsfontein, Driefontein, Roodepoort, Paardekraal and Vogelstruisfontein – all of which were in possession of Afrikaner farmers – officially open as public diggings. This was the stimulus which led to the establishment of the richest gold-mining industry in the world. The first mines were opencast or surface mines. After 1887 mining activity also began at Germiston, Benoni and Nigel on the East Rand.

Coal for the increased production of electrical power was discovered in nearby Vereeniging and Boksburg, which meant that the gold mines could be mechanised far quicker than the diamond mines.

It soon became clear that the gold-mining process on the Witwatersrand was going to be both difficult and expensive. The gold content of the ore was low which meant that many tons of gold-bearing conglomerate had to be brought to the surface to extract a small amount of gold. Although initially the thin upper layer could be mined, the 30 km long gold reef went far deeper which meant that the mining process demanded expensive equipment, explosives, technological knowledge and a great deal of capital expenditure. Because of a lack of expertise and capital, the owners of the gold-bearing land soon sold their farms to wealthy investors.

In the 1890s deep-level mining began. It was an expensive and labour-intensive undertaking; individual diggers and small companies simply could not compete. By 1889 no less than 44 small gold-mining companies went bankrupt, but from 1890 to 1892 the industry was saved by mining magnates who combined their capital to form so-called mining houses which were also heavily backed by overseas capital. These powerful mine owners or mining magnates became known locally as the Randlords.

By 1893 there were ten large mining houses that were active on the Witwatersrand, including Rand Mines Limited comprising mine magnates Alfred Beit, Hermann Eckstein and Lionel Phillips; Consolidated Goldfields of South Africa owned by Cecil Rhodes; the Johannesburg Consolidated Investment Company formed by Barney Barnato; and the Anglo-French Company run by the George Farrar group. These powerful capitalist entrepreneurs who were the driving force behind the establishment of the gold-mining industry in South Africa came from Britain, Germany and France and this gave a strong European influence to the rapidly developing economy.

Johannesburg and its residents

In 1886 the ZAR government appointed a two-man commission to lay out a town to accommodate the thousands of fortune seekers on the Witwatersrand. The commission comprised vice-president Christiaan Johannes Joubert and Johann Rissik of the ZAR land surveyor general's office. Their choice fell on Randjeslaagte, a triangular piece of *uitvalgrond* (land unaccounted for) between the farms Braamfontein, Doornfontein and Turffontein. The new town was called Johannesburg, using the names of the two commissioners, Joubert and Rissik.

The residents of the Witwatersrand at the time can be loosely grouped into three categories, which accounted for the cosmopolitan society in the new mining camps. Firstly, there were the skilled miners and artisans from Britain, the USA, Europe, Russia and Australia who were attracted to the goldfields by the relatively good wages on offer. It was they who initiated trade unionism in South Africa. The labour unions exerted great pressure for the implementation of legislation on job reservation which would protect the skilled workers with scarce competencies from the threat of unskilled labour. Then there were others including bankers, shopkeepers, chemists, bakers, hotel owners, and bottle-store owners; also Italian, Portuguese and Jewish vegetable and dairy farmers. The Transvaal burghers called this whole group, which included the Randlords, the Uitlanders.

Secondly, there was a group of semi-skilled or unskilled rural Afrikaners who were share-croppers (*bywoners*) and were labelled "poor whites".

Most had suffered dire economic hardship and were forced to seek a better livelihood in Johannesburg. The rinderpest epidemic of 1896–1897; crop diseases and drought; the devastation of the Anglo-Boer War; and the larger-scale agricultural methods of farmers with financial resources, all meant that subsistence farmers were gradually being absorbed, which drove many *bywoners* to the cities.

For poor, unskilled Afrikaners there were very few opportunities for formal employment in the mining industry on the Witwatersrand. As a result, many of them had to use their inborn natural abilities and their experience as entrepreneurs to make a living. Until Johannesburg was linked to the coast by railways, many Afrikaner entrepreneurs were involved in transport riding. Goods were moved over long distances from the harbours to the Witwatersrand by ox-wagon. Over shorter distances, scotch-carts (small two-wheeled carts with a box-like tipper that were drawn by horses or oxen) were used between the towns on the Witwatersrand. After railway lines to Johannesburg were opened up, the transport riding business declined.

A second type of business that offered opportunities to Afrikaner entrepreneurs was public transport. Before Johannesburg boasted an electrical tram system, some Afrikaners made a living as Cape cart drivers (the predecessor of the taxi business). These carts were also drawn by horses. By the middle of the 1890s more than 1500 licences per annum were issued to Cape cart drivers.

Brick-making was a third means of employment for many Afrikaners. In the rapidly developing Johannesburg there was a huge demand for building bricks. In 1887 the ZAR government purchased part of the farm Braamfontein so that burghers could manufacture bricks for a living. The terrain was initially called Brickfields, but by 1897 it was known as Burghersdorp. By the 1890s, modern brick-making factories, like Sammy Marks's Vereeniging Brick & Tile Company, which mass produced bricks of a better quality, systematically superseded this form of early Afrikaner entrepreneurship on the Witwatersrand.

Unskilled black workers, including people of Indian descent, coloured people and Chinese made up the third and largest group of the Witwatersrand workforce. The gold-mining industry was even more labour intensive than diamond mining and created a huge demand for cheap labour. Many black people, poverty stricken for the same reasons as the Afrikaners, but also as a result of British and ZAR expansionism, were also forced to move into the cities. The poorer they became, the more prepared they were to accept work on the mines. The migrant labour and compound systems to house black workers (used in the diamond industry) were similarly applied on the Witwatersrand, although black people also lived in shanties on the outskirts of the city in areas that were demarcated for them, named locations. The black workforce on the Witwatersrand goldfields comprised mainly the Tsonga from Mozambique, the Basotho from Basotholand and the AmaZulu from Natal. They were recruited by recruitment agencies set up by the Chamber of Mines, an organisation established to represent the interests of the mining houses. Black people also worked as washermen, domestic servants and police constables.

> **THE "AMAWASHA": EARLY BLACK ENTREPRENEURS**
> As was the case with unskilled Afrikaner poor whites and bywoners, it was exceedingly difficult for many unskilled black people to find formal employment and make a living on the Witwatersrand other than working as contract workers on the mines. This led to the development of a male Zulu washermen's guild, the so-called AmaWasha, who worked in Johannesburg between 1890 and 1914. There was a great need for those who took in washing, particularly for the city's white residents who at first were almost all single men. The money which the washermen earned was usually invested in land and cattle back at their homes.
> Initially, the AmaWasha did their washing in streams in Johannesburg's outlying areas but later washing was done in Braamfontein, Auckland Park, Elandsfontein, Booysens and Concordia. By 1896 more than 1200 washermen were registered with the Johannesburg health authorities. However, when modern steam washers were introduced and the authorities ruled that the AmaWasha had to move from the city centre to beyond the town borders, this entrepreneurial initiative came to an end.

The compounds on the Witwatersrand were far bigger and housed many more workers than those on the diamond fields. However, they were not closed completely like those at Kimberley, primarily because the danger of theft was not as great. In addition, the gold-mining companies had to compete with one another, and they also had competition from the capitalist merchants in Johannesburg who wanted the workers to have freedom of movement so that they could spend their wages in nearby shops.

Initially, the mining companies even tried to control the black workforce with alcohol which was sold in beer halls on mine property. This also brought in additional revenue from the sale of alcohol.

To prune their costs, thereby improving their profits and gaining tighter control over the black labour force, between 1889 and 1890 the gold-mining companies tried to cut workers' wages. They argued that deep-level mining needed expensive equipment to extract the ore and bring it to the surface. Black trade unions were forbidden, so workers were unable to bargain for improved wages in an organised manner. Resistance by black mine workers was kept under control by the use of a strengthened mine police force and by pass laws that were strictly applied. This meant that breaking of one's contract in the form of desertion was made a criminal offence.

Economic results

Before the discovery of minerals, geographical South Africa's economy was based largely on subsistence agriculture and farmers only produced enough for their own requirements. The discovery of diamonds and gold led to a more vibrant cash economy with an emphasis on market-oriented production and wage labour. By far the largest part of the money accrued from diamond and gold production was paid out in the ZAR and elsewhere in South Africa as salaries and wages, and was also used to purchase local products.

This large, concentrated buying power necessarily also brought prosperity for farmers and industries, and to other parts of South Africa. After the discovery of minerals the ZAR became part of the world economy and South Africa gained acceptance in international economic circles. Transvaal gold shares were traded on stock exchanges in London, Paris and Berlin.

As the production of gold increased, many of the world's foremost trading nations adopted the so-called gold standard in use in Britain. It became easier to accept gold as the standard against which the world's currencies were measured. This placed London, the Bank of England and the British pound sterling at the very epicentre of international trade.

The gold standard was a monetary standard whereby the exchange rate of a country's currency was measured against a fixed amount of fine, or pure gold. In other words, currencies were measured against the value of gold, because the price of gold was fixed. After the Napoleonic wars of the nineteenth century, Britain accepted a monetary system whereby one gold pound was equated to 113,0016 grain of pure gold. By law, the Bank of England and other commercial banks had to be in a position, upon request, to exchange banknotes and deposits for their value in gold. Gold therefore served as a reserve guarantee for the value of a country's monetary holdings such as banknotes. The amount of gold held by the Bank of England, determined how much credit the bank could issue in the form of banknotes and its deposits.

The flow of gold in and out caused fluctuation in the supply of money held (monetary stock). This then caused the prices of goods to change. Because of Britain's leading role in world trade at the time, virtually all countries were affected by its economic fluctuations. Furthermore, British capital represented the largest of all the international investments in the new South African gold-mining industry. When the huge significance of the ZAR's gold deposits was first realised, the inflow of its gold into the world's gold markets meant that the problem of international liquidity (the immediate availability of money) became less pressing.

The ZAR welcomed the development whereby capital that had arisen from the diamond-mining industry could be made available for investment in the gold-mining industry. The mining capitalists of Kimberley not only had the money to invest in the gold mines, but could also apply the experience and technological expertise they had gained there. In many ways, Kimberley's diamond industry was the forerunner for the Witwatersrand's gold mining industry. The production and export of diamonds grew rapidly. Between 1866 and 1870 the average annual export of diamonds was only £35 700, but between 1881 and 1885 it increased to £3 242 000 (of the total exports from South Africa of £8 021 000). Gold production also accelerated very quickly. Whereas the value of production in 1885 was only £6010, by 1898 it had risen to £16 241 000. In that year the ZAR was the largest single producer of gold and contributed 27,5% of the world's gold supply.

Trade and industry suddenly increased as a result of the mineral revolution. A lively import trade began with goods coming in from Britain, the USA, France and Germany. Johannesburg soon developed into a large city with a highly diversified economy, mainly because of the widening scope of the mining industry. The ZAR was transformed from the poorest to the richest state in South Africa and Kruger now had the economic means to improve the Transvaal administration. Schools, transport and public works all received attention.

The state revenue of the Cape Colony, Natal and the Orange Free State likewise rose sharply. Industries developed in the Cape Colony and to a lesser extent in Natal, particularly at the Durban harbour. Cape Town had the financial infrastructure, the harbour, banks and commercial houses necessary to support the new industrial development, but to maintain its economic status the city had to keep abreast of the diamond and gold industries and their markets. The Cape Colony therefore spent a great deal of money on constructing new railways.

The diamond industry was an important economic stimulus for the Orange Free State because it bordered on the Kimberley diamond fields. General dealers and other businesses such as Fichardts opened branches in Bloemfontein and other towns. In the 1870s the average monthly turnover of these businesses was between £4000 and £5000.

The lack of infrastructure in the interior, which meant that goods such as mining equipment and food could only be delivered irregularly and unreliably over long distances by ox-wagon to the diamond and goldfields, did however offer opportunities as far as agriculture was concerned. There was an upsurge in trade to and from Kimberley and the Witwatersrand, with both white and black farmers supplying agricultural produce for the new mining communities. As the demand for food on the diamond and goldfields grew, inland markets blossomed and the farmers adjusted their production accordingly. There was a new emphasis on intensive agriculture and many black and white farmers changed from subsistence agriculture to commercial farming with great success. Dairy products, chickens, vegetables, wheat and mealies were in great demand. The Batlhaping, for example, increased their agricultural production to supply the needs of the Kimberley mining community.

Wood was initially the only source of energy on the diamond fields. Due to the shortage of firewood there was a vibrant trade for this commodity, from which the Batlhaping made good profits. The Basotho wheat farmers also contributed positively to the increased agricultural productivity in the central interior.

In the Eastern Cape the Mfengu were highly successful cattle, grain and wool farmers and offered strong competition to white farmers, while black farmers in the Herschel district produced large quantities of sorghum and wheat. In the Cape Colony the production of crops, wine and brandy increased with the demand, and wagon makers in Wellington were far busier than usual. In the Oudtshoorn district ostrich farming also expanded because fashion-conscious women wanted ostrich feathers.

One of the immediate results of the mineral revolution was that infrastructure such as roads, railways, harbour facilities and telegraphic links had to be upgraded and expanded. Railways were constructed from Cape Town, Port Elizabeth and East London to Kimberley. The line from Cape Town reached Kimberley in 1885.

The expansion of railways to the diamond fields caused a sharp drop in the prices of food, other goods and fuel. These commodities could now be transported quickly and cheaply to Kimberley. This had a negative affect on the Batlhaping and Basotho farmers. Cheap coal from Wales arrived regularly in Kimberley, bringing an abrupt end to the Batlhaping's profitable trade in firewood; and imported American wheat was cheaper than wheat produced by the Basotho. This economic setback, together with the shortage of available land and ecological problems, meant that the Basotho who had previously been relatively prosperous, became impoverished. For the mine owners this was a positive development because it meant that economic necessity would force the Batlhaping and the Basotho to fill the need for cheap labour on the mines. Railway lines from Delagoa Bay (now Maputo), Durban and the Cape harbours also reached the Witwatersrand by the mid-1890s. However, this brought an end to the income that white and black transport riders had enjoyed.

The mineral revolution also led to the development of secondary industries. To provide in the needs of the people on the diamond and goldfields, there was industrial development in the harbour cities. Secondary industries, some of which were large capitalist companies, were established throughout South Africa and gradually provided the necessary equipment, clothes and luxury goods that the growing population required. In the Orange Free State, which bordered on the diamond fields and was an important link in the produce and transport network, there was a leather tannery, a number of smithy shops and a construction company that specialised in building bridges.

In the ZAR the expansion of secondary industries accompanied the implementation of President Paul Kruger's notorious concession policy. Concessions for the provision of water supplies, sanitation, electricity and dynamite were awarded on a monopoly basis to specific companies or individuals who had won over the president's favour. Industrialists such as

Alois Nellmapius and Sammy Marks were permitted to erect factories which produced a wide range of goods such as boots, glass bottles, canned fruit, meat and alcoholic beverages. Marks and his brother-in-law, Isaac Lewis, also owned companies that mined coal at Witbank (now Emalahleni) and Vereeniging to provide the mines with fuel.

However, Kruger's concession policy earned him the anger of the Randlords because they argued that it impeded free enterprise. As a result of the republic's improved financial position Kruger was also able to enforce closer control over the black societies in the ZAR and was better able to draw them into the growing economy as wage labourers.

The development of secondary industries led to a great demand for electrical power. As early as 1882, Kimberley had electric street lighting while gas lights were still in use in an international city such as London. On the Witwatersrand a private company, the Rand Central Electric Works Limited, even built its own power stations. The first coal-fired power station went into production in Brakpan in 1897.

When the mining industry resumed production after the Anglo-Boer War, the demand for power stations increased and a consortium, the Victoria Falls & Transvaal Power Company (VPF) was formed, from which Eskom was to develop later. The VPF was responsible for the construction of a number of power stations, notably the one in Vereeniging in 1912.

Social results

A direct result of the mineral revolution was the massive increase of the population on the diamond and goldfields. Accelerated urbanisation, particularly in the ZAR after 1880, led to the depopulation of the rural areas. Urbanisation brought various social problems and divisions.

From 1870 onwards Kimberley, with a population of more than 50 000, was divided socio-geographically on the basis of race. In addition to those in the compounds, there were many black people living in the demarcated locations outside the town. In 1879 an official policy was accepted whereby residential segregation between black and white was implemented. The greatest social evils were alcohol misuse – there were bars on every corner and at every turn; gambling, which often led to fighting, assault and murder; and prostitution. The latter was linked to the fact that at first there were very few women who accompanied their men to the diamond diggings.

Diamond smuggling, or illicit diamond buying (IDB) was also a significant problem and usually took the form of dishonest white men buying stolen diamonds illegally from black workers.

Hotels were opened in Kimberley where local residents could buy meals and where dance parties and concerts were held. There were also theatres where concerts, revues and melodramas were presented. Kimberley's racecourse was opened in 1872 and various social clubs were formed, including a horse-racing club and a tennis club. Local newspapers were distributed and a public library, churches, mosques and a synagogue were built. Kimberley's municipal council was formed in 1878.

In Johannesburg the first corrugated-iron shelters soon made way for brick buildings. Residential areas for black and white followed much the same pattern of segregation as in Kimberley and mirrored the marked class difference between rich and poor. By 1896, only ten years after the shanty town had appeared on the bare Highveld plains, Johannesburg already had a population of 10 000 souls of whom at least two thirds were men between the ages of 20 and 40 years. White workers boarded in the many boarding houses near the mines or lived in working-class residential areas such as Fordsburg, Jeppe, Malvern, Mayfair, Vrededorp, Burgersdorp, Troyeville, Turffontein, Booysens and Langlaagte. Initially, thousands of poor whites, black people and Indians lived together in derelict slums like Ferreirasdorp and Brickfields (Burghersdorp) where the standard of living and health conditions were appalling.

As in Kimberley, there were social evils such as overcrowded buildings, unhygienic conditions, poor-quality housing, alcohol misuse, prostitution and immorality. There was also a loss of traditional values, racism, firearm smuggling, and other criminality. These evils seemed to be more prevalent in Johannesburg because the city had a bigger and more cosmopolitan population and there was a greater demand for cheap labour.

The wealthier residents lived in suburbs such as Doornfontein, Ophirton, Yeoville, Houghton and Berea, while the Randlords chose to live in the elegant Parktown, far from the mineshafts and factories.

Many schools and churches were built once the temporary mining camps had evolved into the city of Johannesburg. A variety of social clubs and societies were established for recreation purposes and at the Wanderers Club there were facilities for sports, including cricket, rugby, athletics and cycling. The exclusive Rand Club became a popular meeting place for the wealthy.

The comparatively rapid increase of the South African population reflected the tempo of economic development. The white population, which stood at a mere 328 000 in 1875, had already grown to 1 276 242 by 1911, an average increase of 3,9% per year. The very rapid growth of the white population between 1875 and 1904, an average of 4,3% per annum, was to a large extent because of immigration, particularly to the Witwatersrand goldfields. By comparison, the country's black population grew by 1,9% per year between 1904 and 1951.

The mineral revolution also stimulated city development. While in 1845 there were only about 45 towns and cities in South Africa, this number had risen to 369 by 1921 and by 1951 it had gone up to 603.

Political results

Since 1806 Britain had actively tried to maintain its supremacy in southern Africa, but the discovery of diamonds threatened this position. Britain was well aware that other European powers also wanted colonial possessions in Africa and was determined to defend its dominant position in southern Africa. Any sign of interference in South Africa by one of these powers was immediately checked by Britain. This geopolitical jostling for power was particularly evident in the uneasy relations between Britain and Germany, especially after Germany declared a protectorate over German South West Africa in 1884.

The discovery of diamonds ushered in a period of confrontation between Britain and the Boer republics. Because Britain was determined to maintain its supremacy over the subcontinent, the Free State's claim for ownership of the diamond fields had to be nullified for strategic reasons; the "road to the north" linking the Cape Colony and the interior had to be kept open for possible British expansion. In addition, the financial implications and advantages of having the diamond fields in British possession were considerable. To this end, the Keate Award was explained away in Britain's favour; the diamondiferous land was duly re-named Griqualand West and was eventually incorporated into the British-controlled Cape Colony. The Free State was fobbed off with a British payout of £90 000.

It was also clear that if Britain wanted to utilise the gold discovery and the massive profits to be had on the Witwatersrand to form a British-oriented state to support the gold-mining industry, it would have to gain political authority over the ZAR. The political confrontation for control of the gold caused tension between the Uitlanders and the Transvaal burghers. Conspiracies by mine magnates such as Rhodes (the Jameson Raid of 1895–1896 for example) and attempts by British imperialists like Joseph Chamberlain and Alfred Milner to bring down the Kruger government failed initially. But eventually the growing British pressure on the ZAR led to the outbreak of the Anglo-Boer War (1899–1902) and Britain was the victor. Thereby British supremacy was established throughout South Africa and British control of the gold-mining industry and black labour was finally achieved.

The need for cheap labour was to a large extent responsible for the subjugation of black societies. Industrial capitalists put persistent pressure on them to provide this labour. British expansionism and the gradual encroachment of the Boer republics into the territories where traditional black societies were living led to their subjugation and the loss of their political independence. Oppressive legislation soon followed, such as the reserve system, measures to restrict their movement and the implementation of hut tax and head tax. Before long these communities were detribalised and poverty stricken and their only alternative was to seek poorly paid work on the mines. The mineral revolution gave the ZAR the necessary economic stability and resources to subjugate black South Africans, which tipped the scale in favour of white dominance over the entire country.

Finally, the mineral revolution led to another surge of Afrikaner nationalism and black nationalism. The Orange Free State and the ZAR moved closer to each other economically and politically. Afrikaner nationalism which had been aroused by the British annexation of the Transvaal in 1877, the First Anglo-Boer War, the victory of 1880–1881 and the ill-fated Jameson Raid, experienced a prosperous period.

Black nationalism was stimulated by the industrial revolution in the sense that black people, particularly the educated black elite in the Eastern Cape, identified with British aims. They developed a moderate, participatory approach and an unshakable belief in British fair play. In the confrontation between imperialism and republicanism they strongly supported Britain; they cherished expectations that if Britain emerged victorious from the Anglo-Boer War, all black people would have a much better chance in life.

9
An economic history of the nineteenth century
Grietjie Verhoef

At the beginning of the nineteenth century South Africa was an agricultural region and economic development revolved around its unique resources. The interaction between the country's natural and human resources created an environment in which individuals, groups, institutions and ideologies influenced the course of the economy.

After 1806 the Cape Colony was under British control and the interior was inhabited and cultivated by indigenous people. With the northward expansion of the Voortrekkers and with the onset of the British occupation, political control of this region changed hands. Although the economy did not change with these new political circumstances, it is true to say that economic development in later years often led to political change.

Although the Industrial Revolution in the first half of the nineteenth century established a new economic order in Europe (with mass production, the development of international industries and world markets), it appears that a large portion of the farming population on the southern tip of Africa withdrew from interaction with the wider world and competitive markets, moving back to a simple economic environment without a monetary economy, using a barter system. At the time South Africa was on the periphery of developments in the world metropolis – the heart of economic progress was in Europe. However, this benefited the USA and the colonies because the colonial authorities and the settler populations became part of this progress by means of trade and other economic activity.

The late nineteenth century was a time of extensive colonial expansion. Britain, France, Germany, Belgium and Italy all established colonies in

Africa and in this way these regions became drawn into economic activity in Britain and Europe. Most of the initiative for the expansion and modernisation of colonies came from the immigrant population which gradually settled there. The contact with their countries of origin was strengthened by the "open" character of the local economy. Economic activities were dependent on trade with the rest of the world and, therefore, after an initial period of stagnation, developments in the mother countries began to take effect in the colonies. The economic activity of nineteenth century South Africa was largely an extension of developments in Europe and the USA.

Three features of the region played a decisive role in South Africa's economic progress. The first was that a large number of people of different indigenous ethnic entities lived in the country before the Europeans settled there. The second feature was the large number of European settlers who in time considered the country their fatherland. Thirdly, the rich deposits of a variety of minerals presented a vital factor in economic progress. The diamond and gold deposits in particular transformed the structure of the South African economy. The close interaction of human and mineral-rich natural resources formed the basic ingredients of a rapidly growing economy.

> **HUMAN CAPITAL**
> At the beginning of the nineteenth century the population in the area that was to become South Africa was made up primarily of cultivators and pastoralists. In 1820 approximately 4000 white British immigrants settled in the Eastern Cape, but three years later the British government terminated state aid for emigration to the Cape Colony.
> The Great Trek was responsible for the spreading of the white population into the interior, although the number of people involved in this migration was small. After 1837 about 5000 English and Irish tradesmen, again with state support from Britain, came to the colony.
> The majority of the Voortrekkers who still lived in Natal left this colony after 1848 to join the other trekkers in the interior. In the following three years Britain sent about 4500 colonists to Natal to supplement the number of settlers there; and between 1858 and 1870 the British government settled another 12 000 immigrants in the eastern part of the country, in both Natal and the Eastern Cape.

> This group of immigrants, together with the indigenous black people, the Khoekhoen and the Bushmen, developed the country's economy. Most of the wage labour was performed by the black, Khoekhoe and (until their emancipation) slave population. The white people were primarily farmers, businessmen or tradesmen. In 1838 slaves were emancipated and they joined the labour market in the Cape Colony as free people. This broad division of labour remained unchanged for the rest of the century.
> By 1900 the total population of the area was just over one million people.

The most notable event of nineteenth century South Africa was the discovery of minerals – diamonds in 1867 and substantial amounts of gold in 1886. Within a few decades the predominantly agricultural economy, with its strong features of a subsistence economy and barter, was completely transformed. A modern, capitalist mining industry developed and with it a market economy and credit market. Whereas in most developed countries the transition from an agricultural economy to an industrial, market economy evolved gradually, this transition in South Africa was extremely rapid. The mineral revolution meant that both mining and industrial development in general occurred rapidly.

Despite these radical changes, a large portion of the black population remained land-based and dependent on the land for their subsistence. However, there was a gradual increase in wage labour by black and other population groups. Many of the black people were still actively involved in subsistence farming, but others entered into wage labour on white-owned farms or took part on a small scale as independent farmers in the burgeoning market economy.

After the turmoil of the Mfecane many black people returned to establish themselves in the eastern frontier region and began to participate actively in the capitalist markets which had developed after the arrival of the British settlers. Indeed, these black communities who had settled in the Eastern Cape after the Mfecane were less beholden to traditional tribal authority and research has shown that they competed very successfully with white farmers in capitalist markets when they began to produce more than they needed for their own consumption.

In other parts of the country where traditional authority was still strictly observed, production took place as part of communal landownership and produce was redistributed in terms of traditional practice.

The various black ethnic communities such as the Zulu in Natal, the Pondo in the Eastern Cape and the Sotho in the Free State, continued their independent existence in their various regions until the discovery of diamonds and gold prompted a massive demand for unskilled labour. Thereafter many black people considered the option of wage labour so that they could earn the money demanded by the colonial authorities.

The colonial government introduced various forms of taxation to encourage indigenous people into wage labour. Furthermore, attracted to the potential of increasing their wealth, traditional leaders were persuaded to put pressure on their subjects to enter into wage labour. Traditional leaders also developed an appetite for European consumer goods that could only be purchased if these traditional leaders had hard currency or money. The white authorities experienced endless challenges to entice black people away from their subsistence lifestyle into wage labour in the mines and industries. This endeavour took on even greater and more dynamic proportions in the twentieth century.

The Cape's economy

Early Cape farmers cultivated the land to meet their own needs and those of passing ships in Table Bay. One of the important guarantees given to the farmers after the British occupation in 1795 was that colonists' rights and privileges would be recognised and private property respected. Farmers also sold more of their produce to visiting vessels. The export from the Cape increased from £637 253 in 1850 to more than £7,6 million in 1900.

These exports also gave the colony the buying power to import a reasonable amount of goods. However, the main reason for the impressive export figures was the export of diamonds since 1867. Before the discovery of diamonds, more than 94% of the exports comprised agricultural and animal husbandry produce.

Agricultural development was severely limited by the small local demand for farm produce. What was not used locally had to be exported or went to waste.

The arrival of the British settlers in 1820 was an important landmark and meant that people with new skills and knowledge were added to the population. There now was a healthy trade environment in the Eastern Cape in which black farmers also took part. Merchants and shopkeepers helped with the export of agricultural produce and also imported consumer goods for the rapidly growing population of the eastern frontier region. Prosperous black farmers, who produced grain, vegetables or meat in excess of their own demand, sold this produce to the merchants. They also cultivated new crops and by 1868 they sold large quantities of mealies, sorghum, wheat, oats, beans and potatoes on local markets.

The purchasing power of the Eastern Cape was enhanced by the rising exports. The black farmers acquired money for their surplus production which created a demand for provisions and other necessities sold by the British shopkeepers. In this way the Eastern Cape became an important centre of economic activity in the last half of the nineteenth century, which positioned the region well to provide the necessary provisions for the burgeoning new market in Kimberley.

The most significant economic activity in the southern part of the Cape Colony was agriculture. By 1865 as many as 78,9% of the Cape population worked in the agricultural sector. Farmers cultivated fruit, wheat, winter grains such as barley, rye and oats; they also planted vineyards to make wine, and grew a little sugar and mealies. In addition, there was livestock and sheep farming. It was only with the expansion to the Eastern Cape that wide-scale sheep farming was practised. Wool-bearing sheep were initially imported in 1795 by the governor during the Batavian rule, but wool farming only took off after the 1830s. The production costs of food were high because the Cape was so far from European markets. It was virtually impossible to export on a large scale to those countries and the local market was therefore small.

Wine production was rather more successful: Britain gave preference to Cape wines, which meant that it could be exported duty free to Britain and Europe. (A duty is a charge, or tax, levied on goods transported from one country to another – either as imports or exports.) The Cape wines were not for end use but were to be blended with European wines. This meant that there was a strong demand for Cape wine, but not necessarily for wine of high quality. Between 1825 and 1831 Britain systematically phased out preferential treatment and that brought the export of Cape wine to an end.

From the late 1860s there was a strong demand for ostrich feathers which were very fashionable at the time. However, when this fad blew over and Europe fell into a depression between 1879 and 1882, the fortunes of many farmers who had suddenly grown wealthy by supplying the fashionable feathers were plunged into poverty.

The export of wool experienced a boom period in the 1850s and 1860s and increased from 1,2 million kg of wool (with a value of £212 166) to 8,8 million kg (valued at £1,2 million). This was a huge injection for the Cape economy. The nature of exports changed; whereas previously the emphasis had been on foodstuffs and wines this now changed to raw materials such as wool, hides and skins. However, at the end of the 1860s wool prices plummeted due to a recession in Europe; and as a result an even more dire recession hit the Cape economy.

In the last half of the nineteenth century the Cape could be described as industrially progressive. Manufacturing was as yet somewhat elementary, but there were brickworks, fish processing plants for export purposes, grain mills, soap and candle factories, snuff manufacturing and iron and copper foundries. Compared to industrialisation in Europe the Cape was far behind, but in comparison with other smaller regions, the Cape was reasonably advanced. There was also an extensive financial services sector with small local banks, trust companies and insurance enterprises. In the Eastern Cape there were wholesale companies which imported consumer goods and capital equipment and exported agricultural produce.

With the expansion of economic activity the demand for money increased and businessmen needed credit. Small banks emerged and were able to meet local requirements. Examples of such banks were the first savings bank, the Cape of Good Hope Savings Bank which was formed in 1831; the Eastern Province Bank (1838) in Grahamstown; and the Port Elizabeth Bank (1847). The first insurance company in the Cape and in South Africa was the South African Fire and Life Assurance Company (1831) and the first Board of Executors was established in 1834 by 22 residents of Cape Town. Between 1834 and 1899 no fewer that 30 trust companies were formed in the Cape. A monetary economy developed, which is evidence of the advanced nature of the Cape economy at that stage. The same could not be said of the other colony, Natal, or the Boer republics.

This dramatic expansion of economic activity in the Cape caught the attention of British banks. In 1861 the first so-called imperial bank, the London and South African Bank (LSAB) opened a branch in Cape Town. The following year Standard Bank opened for business, and in 1873 the Oriental Bank Corporation. The depression of the late 1860s caused severe problems for many of the small local banks. Clients had little or no money to deposit and the banks had limited capital to survive this difficult period. Most of the small banks were taken over by Standard Bank or the LSAB and as a result the imperial banks dominated the financial sector.

The first railway line was constructed in the years 1860 to 1863 and ran between Cape Town, Wellington and Worcester. All transport of goods was therefore by road in ox-wagons or in horse-drawn carts. The discovery of diamonds in Kimberley in 1867 changed this fundamentally. After the drought of the late 1860s and the depression that followed the collapse of the wool price, there was a sudden upsurge thanks to the mining of diamonds. This stimulated secondary industrial activity because there was a rising demand for consumer goods, food, clothing, footwear and tools, all of which stimulated food production and the rise of small industries.

It also became vital to build rail links to the nearest seaports – Durban, Port Elizabeth and East London. The Cape government immediately took control of the construction of railway lines (the short line at Cape Town was initially under private ownership) and by 1885 the railway from Cape Town reached Kimberley. Because of the high costs involved it was decided to opt for a line 1065 mm wide, compared to the 1433 mm of European and American railways. This later caused serious difficulties for South Africa when railway carriages were imported from overseas.

The discovery of gold on the Witwatersrand in 1886 accelerated the railway construction programme. But this surge of economic development caused a political conundrum: the Zuid-Afrikaansche Republiek (ZAR) refused permission to the British-controlled Cape authority to extend its direct railway line from Kimberley across the Vaal River to Johannesburg, because this would give the British control over a very strategic stretch of railway line which ran across Boer territory to the Witwatersrand goldfields. Instead the ZAR wanted to complete the railway line to Delagoa Bay to secure cheaper exports directly through the nearest harbour without British interference. Eventually, the Cape government was granted permission by the Free State to build its railway through Bloemfontein. This line was completed at the end of 1892 and the Transvaal line to Delagoa Bay in 1894. The railway line from Durban through Volksrust reached Johannesburg in 1895.

This railway development was vital for economic progress. Not only was the transportation of goods speeded up dramatically and made more efficient, but people and goods could now reach the interior easily. The railway network also linked local markets more effectively. Imports and exports were simplified significantly and economic fluctuations in world markets began to influence the local economy more directly.

Diamonds brought economic prosperity to the Cape Colony. Many new work opportunities were created for unskilled labour. The gross domestic product of the Cape rose from £3,2 million in 1867 to more than £13,5 million in 1881. The production of copper, which was discovered in Namaqualand in 1852, remained marginal on production of just more than £261 110. The most significant injection was the demand for consumer and production goods by the rapidly growing population in Kimberley and vicinity. The railway construction programme stimulated urbanisation and consequently also created new demand – and a wild speculation erupted. The banks extended credit to their clients too easily without insisting on adequate security. This caused the so-called "diamond crisis" of 1881 (see below).

Smaller-scale diamond prospecting companies and individual diggers were gradually bought out by the large mining companies. After the discovery of the rich diamond pipes at Jagersfontein and Kimberley, these big corporations jumped in with vast capital resources and squeezed the smaller diggers out of the market. Soon the major companies were mining large quantities of the gems which created a surplus, leading to a drop in the price of diamonds. Cecil John Rhodes realised that it was necessary to have centralised control over the supply of diamonds and he forced Barney Barnato (the other major player in the diamond industry) out of the market with the formation of De Beers Consolidated Mines in 1888. De Beers therefore gained a monopoly over the diamond-mining industry and was able to exercise full control over the release of diamonds into the market so that the price could remain high.

In 1881 there were 65 diamond mining companies and more than £12 million was invested in the industry. Of this, £6,5 million came from the Cape Colony itself. The liberal credit extension by banks, sometimes only against the security of claims, began to change by mid-1881. Credit extension was contracted and uncertainty developed in stock exchanges; the fact that the First Anglo-Boer War had broken out was added cause for concern. Soon afterwards the worst depression yet in the history of the Cape Colony followed – and lasted from 1882 until 1886. It was eventually the discovery of gold on the Witwatersrand that came to the rescue of the Cape economy.

The various conflicts in which British forces were involved in South Africa also provided a boost to the economy. The nineteenth-century frontier wars meant that British officials and troops had to be sent to the conflict areas. These soldiers were remunerated and they created a demand for food and other consumer goods, which in turn stimulated agricultural production and commercial enterprise. In the same way the annexation of the Transvaal in 1877, the Anglo-Zulu War of 1879, and the First Anglo-Boer War (1880–1881) all injected money into the local economy. However, the destruction caused by the Second Anglo-Boer War of 1899 to 1902 was so extensive that it was not until 1906 that the South African economy entered an upward cycle of recovery.

The economic history of the Cape Colony shows how business cycles move upwards and downwards in response to climate and natural conditions, new money and speculation in anticipation of prosperity.

Natal's economic development

The colony of Natal really only began to play a role in the local economy after the Voortrekkers settled there in 1838. After their departure in the 1840s the new British immigrants began to develop an economy that was linked to British economic interests in the Cape. Until 1856 Natal was administered as an extension of the Cape Colony.

The other inhabitants of Natal were the Zulu people, some of whom cultivated crops such as mealies and sorghum, but they were primarily livestock farmers. Cattle played an important role in their traditional life and were regarded as an indication of wealth and status. Land belonged to the chief and headmen and was cultivated on a communal basis. It was the traditional leader's right to provide his people with food and cattle. Food production was not intended for surplus trading. The Zulu did not trade surplus production outside their own traditional areas. There is evidence of the bartering of cattle and basic farm implements with neighbouring black groups, but no extended market exchange in food or consumer goods developed.

After the Anglo-Zulu War of 1879, Britain extended colonial administration to the Zulu territory. Although they continued their rural lifestyle, increasing pressure was exercised on the Zulu people to supply wage labour in the British colony. The practice of providing wage labour on white farms did indeed develop, but during the nineteenth century the

Zulu kingdom retained basic economic independence and the people adhered to their traditional way of life.

When white settlers arrived, they brought with them the Western capitalist market approach. Initially the Voortrekkers cultivated the land for their own consumption but they also bartered for goods that they were unable to produce for themselves. The British immigrant farmers introduced a variety of new crops such as coffee and tea plants from India and sugar from Mauritius. They also cultivated mealies successfully and by 1891 produced more than were grown in the Free State. Cotton cultivation failed because of insufficient labour to pick the cotton. The Zulu people were reluctant to engage in agricultural wage labour, because they were successful subsistence farmers. The settler farmers were also hampered by plant and cattle diseases against which there was at the time no effective control.

In 1850 sugar cane was introduced and soon proved successful. A protective duty was imposed to shield the local industry and assist its establishment. This duty placed a "tax" on imported sugar which made it more expensive than local sugar. By 1859 the shortage of workers in the sugar industry led to the agreement by the Natal colonial authority to indentured labour from India. The first Indian workers arrived in Natal the following year. By 1866 there were 5600 Indian contract labourers in Natal, but for financial reasons it was decided not to finance further importation. It was not until 1911 that the practice was resumed.

Sugar production stood at an impressive 82 000 tons by 1910 and was worth £1,23 million. Indian workers made up 70% of the labour force in the sugar industry. After the expiry of their contracts the majority decided to remain in Natal as vegetable farmers, peddlers or shopkeepers. This group of Indians, as well as independent Indian businessmen who immigrated to South Africa at the end of the nineteenth century, became prosperous businessmen, some of whom set up businesses in the Transvaal. They played a significant role in the development of retail and wholesale business in South Africa.

Although the Natal economy focused largely on agriculture, small trading enterprises developed in the vicinity of Durban harbour. The Natal Fire and Trust Company of Durban began to offer insurance services in the town in 1849, which shows that a solid money economy was taking shape. Furthermore, there was enough money in circulation for the Natal Bank to be formed in 1854 in Pietermaritzburg. Shortly afterwards

Standard Bank and the LSAB also opened branches in Natal and in 1881 the Natal Bank opened a branch in the Transvaal. By 1902 the Natal Bank had eleven branches. It conducted business until 1914 when it was taken over by the National Bank.

As was the case of wars in other colonies, the Anglo-Zulu War of 1879 boosted the Natal economy. It was almost as if capital had been imported without the obligation of interest payment!

The Orange Free State and the Transvaal

The two Boer republics which were established in the 1850s also depended primarily on agriculture. The Transvaal was not very progressive prior to the last decade of the nineteenth century. Agricultural activity was limited, with food production and the livestock farming mainly for own consumption. Hunting produced goods for which there was a demand in the south. Railway links with the two republics only developed after the discovery of diamonds. Up to the last decade of the nineteenth century transport was conducted by transport riders using horse-drawn wagons to move merchandise from one place to another.

Until late in the nineteenth century the burghers of the ZAR lived in relative poverty. Most farmers had few, if any, farming implements; they lived in simple wattle-and-daub homes and largely depended on cattle and sheep farming. Herds of between 400 and 600 cattle and between 300 and 400 small livestock (sheep and goats) were occasionally found. Cattle were kept for their meat, milk and as draught animals. Butter was made, but not cheese. Wood was used for furniture and as building material. By 1866 the government introduced restrictions on tree felling and deforestation to conserve the natural vegetation.

Some farmers hunted more than they farmed, because hunting was fairly profitable. In 1880 hunters collected almost 100 000 kg of ivory in the Soutpansberg region alone. Buffalo horns, rhino horns, hippo teeth and honey were exported. Finally, hunting activity had to be banned by law to protect the game from extinction. Salt was mined in the so-called "soutsee" (salt sea) between the present-day Bela-Bela (previously Warmbaths) and Rustenburg. The salt was used to preserve the meat that was hunted. The Soutpansberg salt pans produced about 1000 bags of salt annually.

Other mineral resources were also mined in the region – coal from 1861 on the Eastern Transvaal Highveld and small volumes of lead near Pretoria and Marico. The lead was used to make ammunition. The discovery of small deposits of gold in the Lydenburg district of the Transvaal (mentioned in the previous chapter) between 1874 and 1880 proved to be disappointing. The value of these gold deposits was only between £197 000 and £1 million. Small deposits of silver, cobalt, copper and iron were also mined.

The farmers experimented with sorghum, mealies and other types of grain, but did so only for their own consumption. Fruit, particularly oranges, and vegetables were also planted in the Rustenburg area. However, stock farming was dominant. Most farmers owned more than one farm and moved around with their stock in search of grazing.

Manufacturing enterprises were simple and focused largely on the farming community's needs. There was a wagon-making industry, wheat mills near Potchefstroom and a cigar factory that processed tobacco grown in the Rustenburg district. Before 1880 the hub of trading activity was at Potchefstroom. In 1867 the first agricultural show was held there.

The Transvaal depended on peddlers, most of them Jews, and on traders to transport goods from the republic and to bring in dire necessities from the harbour towns to the northern regions. Free State farmers later sold their wool in Johannesburg and bought wheat and flour there. Potchefstroom and Rustenburg were the most prosperous areas in the region. Judging by the number of trading licences issued in the Transvaal by 1870, a vibrant internal market had developed in the republic.

In districts such as Lydenburg, Waterberg, Wakkerstroom, Heidelberg, Utrecht and Bloemhof, various trading licences were issued. In 1870 ostrich feathers, wool, cattle, grain and leather products to the value of £133 500 were exported. This was very little in comparison with the total value of exports from the Cape Colony which in 1850 was already more than £637 235.

By 1883 it was estimated that trade had increased to about £1 million. This was largely attributed to the opening of the first food processing factory just outside Pretoria. Appropriately named Eerste Fabrieken, it was opened by President Paul Kruger on 6 June 1883. There was also the normal artisan work and the manufacturing of wagons and footwear, but no manufacturing production to compare with similar industries in Europe at that time.

Although Transvaal had an internal market, the connection with metropolitan markets was extremely limited. Therefore, fluctuations in the business cycles in Britain and Europe had significantly less effect on the Transvaal than in the two British colonies.

Roads were generally fairly good, but there were very few of them. Passengers had to travel in wagons between the diamond diggings and coal was transported to and from Delagoa Bay in the same manner. With a white population of barely 25 000 in 1870, Transvaal was economically isolated and dependent on a limited internal market. There was no talk of notable foreign trade or participation in international goods traffic with the European metropole. Furthermore, there were no local banks, only branches of Standard Bank and the LSAB. The ZAR only established its own bank in 1888.

In the Orange Free State the economy gradually showed signs of improvement. After the signing of the Bloemfontein Convention in 1854 and the departure of the British troops, the financial wellbeing of the white population of about 15 000 was so weak that trade virtually came to a standstill and exchange resorted to bartering. Roads were poor and a journey in a wagon from Bloemfontein to Durban took more than three weeks; to Port Elizabeth it took eight weeks.

The export of wool gradually brought in foreign exchange. Wool production increased from 50 bales of merino wool in 1850 to more than 5000 bales in 1856. Farmers in the southern Free State also benefited from the rapid growth in the wool industry in the 1850s and 1860s. They sold wool to the wholesalers in the harbour towns, from where it was exported. Towns such as Bloemfontein, Fauresmith, Smithfield and Harrismith were powerful and prosperous trading centres.

Farmers were primarily involved in general agricultural activities, but by 1860 mealies, wheat and other varieties of grain were cultivated on a reasonable scale. The farmers sold their produce themselves. In addition, an active internal market in hides, skins and game developed. In one year a business in Kroonstad sold 152 000 blesbok and wildebeest hides. The trade in ostrich feathers was also fairly brisk.

On the Free State Highveld and in the Southern Transvaal, farmers made extensive use of black labour. In time, legislation was passed which made it possible for black people to live as sharecroppers on white-owned farms. The sharecroppers provided labour and paid part of what they produced to the farmer in exchange for the right to farm on his land.

Because of the collapse of markets during the diamond crisis, farmers who had large mortgages on their farms suffered badly. They were unable to pay for labour and became dependent on the produce grown by black farmers, which meant that sharecropping became increasingly popular. The practice also grew more prevalent as the competition for land increased. Black sharecroppers farmed with great success both before and after the discovery of diamonds and contributed to the agricultural development in the Free State. Concurrently, the Basotho farmed independently and were highly successful with mealies, wheat, wool and mohair. They sold their surplus production on the markets. By the time that a huge demand for food developed at the diamond mines, the Free State had already bought large volumes of grain, sheep and wool from their Basotho neighbours and then sold it on the diamond fields.

Trade was so successful that some of the Cape banks opened branches in the republic. In 1862 the first two Free State banks were also established, namely the Bloemfontein Bank and the Fauresmith Bank. The prospects were so good that the LSAB and Standard Bank also opened branches, but in 1864, after conflict with the Free State government, all foreign banks were banned from operating in the republic. In 1877 the National Bank of the Orange Free State was established. This bank had an excellent reputation and was widely regarded as a model bank.

The Free State economy expanded steadily but it was the discovery of diamonds which eventually stimulated the demand for food and all kinds of consumer goods, and with this improved demand came prosperity.

Minerals and growth

To a degree it seemed as if the economies of the two colonies and the two republics waited for an external injection to unite into a more successful market that could participate significantly at international level. The discovery of diamonds in 1867 did just that. The rapid acceleration of diamond mining led to a massive inflow of capital. It brought hordes of people into the country and this in turn increased the demand for provisions and served as the economic stimulus for the entire region.

The diamond-mining industry developed rapidly. The export of diamonds rose from an average value of £35 700 per annum between 1866 and 1870 to £3,2 million per annum between 1881 and 1886. This massive new buying power translated into employment opportunities, the need to expand transport links, and an almost insatiable market for farm produce. It also earned foreign exchange which meant that the necessary capital equipment and modern technology could be imported to increase the efficiency and profitability of diamond mining. The result was an unmistakable upswing in economic activity in the colonies and the republics.

Speculation in diamond shares was widespread and banks granted credit less responsibly. By 1881 the danger signs were looming. Banks gradually restricted credit and speculators had to sell off their shares. This forced the price of these shares down and the euphoria of making quick money changed to despair – the "bubble" had burst. This so-called "diamond crisis" plunged the entire region into a depression. Goods traffic via the Cape and Natal harbours collapsed; state revenue dropped sharply and insolvencies in the Cape rose from 259 in 1880 to more than 1000 in 1883. Suddenly the region was in a sharp downward cycle. To make matters worse, there was a severe drought in South Africa and Europe was similarly caught in the grip of a depression.

These events were evidence that an integrated capitalist market had developed in South Africa, with stock trading (the sale of shares in listed companies), speculation, an elastic credit system (the granting of credit on request, or the restriction of credit if economic activity decreased) and an integrated "organic" entity of economic crises and cycles. The larger economic connectedness of the entire country emerged strongly after the discovery of gold. The structure of the economy changed rapidly from predominantly agricultural to one of agriculture and mining.

When large deposits of gold were discovered on the Witwatersrand in 1886, the demography and economy of the country changed dramatically. A fair degree of business expertise had developed, especially in the Cape and Natal. The diamond industry put the basic industries in the colonies and republics on the road to greater sophistication. Capital was coming into the region more regularly, labour was readily available and enough food was being produced by the black and white farmers.

The discovery of gold helped to lift the entire country to emerge from the depression of the 1880s and lead the economy into a new phase of growth. Although part of the yield from gold was paid out in dividends to foreign shareholders, the bulk was spent in South Africa. This massive buying power meant greater prosperity for farmers and industrialists throughout southern Africa. The structure of total exports also changed: In 1885 the value of gold exported was £35 300 (of total exports of £8 021 000), but by 1910 this had escalated to £35 million (of total exports of £47 574 000). Indeed, by 1910 at the time of Union, gold played a dominant role in South Africa's economy, comprising about 64% of the country's total exports.

The discovery of gold triggered various radical changes. On the one hand, the population in the Transvaal took on a cosmopolitan character with many foreigners from Europe, the USA, Britain, Australia and other parts of the world. On the other hand, economic traffic displayed a more international character and restrictive political and social arrangements in the Transvaal caused tension between the different groups of residents. Various other sectors also grew with rapid strides. Banks such as Standard Bank strengthened their position with the takeover of the LSAB in 1877 and in 1888 De Nederlandsche Bank voor Zuid-Afrika (the Netherlands Bank of South Africa, later Nedbank) opened for business in the Transvaal. By 1890 there were eleven banks with 66 branches in the country.

Just as had happened after the discovery of diamonds, the general speculation in gold shares and land on the Witwatersrand was accompanied by excessive credit extension. By March 1890 the collapse known as the "gold crisis" began and the market value of joint-stock companies was virtually halved overnight. Depositors rapidly withdrew their money. Without deposits a bank cannot lend money, so access to credit came to an abrupt halt. This led inevitably to less economic activity and the onset of a depression from the last few months of 1890.

In 1896 a rampant disease that attacked hoofed animals, the rinderpest, was a further setback to the economy; and three years later the Anglo-Boer War broke out. This bitter conflict completely destroyed the economic resources of the Boer republics – their people, productive lands and means of survival. Between 1903 and 1909, on the eve of Union, the country was caught in the throes of a serious depression.

However, the gold-mining industry stimulated industrial production and between 1890 and 1910 the number of factories in the Transvaal increased from 550 to 1500. Although industrial output prior to Union had reached a total value of £17 million, this was only rudimentary and was largely because of the processing of agricultural products. In the Cape there were more than 2000 "factories", but this industrial production could only be described as basic. Most of these "factories" were grain mills, bakeries, sawmills, wagon-making establishments, leather tanneries, furniture factories and printing shops. They were small manufacturing enterprises which provided the direct needs of the farming community. There was no talk of using new technology to produce technically advanced goods as was the case in Britain or Europe. The manufacture of machinery and engineering equipment only developed later to serve the interests of the mining industry.

In the Cape, the production of manufactured goods was protected by the introduction of an *ad valorem* import duty (tax) on goods that competed with local products. In Natal there was also limited manufacturing and in the Free State virtually nothing. In the Transvaal it gained momentum with the mineral revolution. Nevertheless, one cannot really talk of industrial or manufacturing production at the turn of the century. The value of manufacturing in the Cape was about £7,4 million; in Natal £4,4 million; in the Transvaal £4,6 million; and in the Free State £749 000.

The value of the gold exports by 1910 was £35 million. The value of imports was more than £27 million, which meant that excluding gold, the imports exceeded the exports by far. South Africa did not produce nearly enough in its own industries to export goods; it used the foreign exchange earned with its gold exports to pay for its imports. This was an unhealthy situation which continued until the 1960s.

The reason why manufacturing production developed so slowly was because the export of certain goods such as gold, diamonds and wool had a relative advantage, but also because local industries were virtually unprotected against competition of cheaper products from more developed markets overseas.

The indirect protection of these local industries by the introduction of high transport duties eventually led to the customs agreement of 1906. Before the Anglo-Boer War the Transvaal government charged extremely high rates on the transportation of goods on its section of the railway and this pushed up the costs of exports and imports in the British colonies. After the war the British high commissioner, Lord Alfred Milner, hoped to reduce the rates on the railway to the other colonies to assist the recovery of agricultural production and to ensure greater economic co-operation. However, the Portuguese government threatened that if Milner did not retain the preference position on the Johannesburg to

Delagoa Bay railway, Portuguese workers from Mozambique would no longer be permitted to do contract work on the gold mines. Faced with this threat, Milner backed down and the agreement between the Transvaal and the Portuguese authority in Mozambique on the Delagoa Bay line remained in force. This was despite the fact that he had to forfeit income for the imperial authority from transport rates on the Natal line.

Eventually, in 1906, Lord Selborne, the new British high commissioner, succeeded in brokering a customs agreement (involving the four British colonies, the British High Commission Territories and Southern Rhodesia) which scrapped duties within South Africa as well as to and from neighbouring territories. At a conference of the Customs Union in 1908, the hope was expressed for the first time that tariff protection would be granted to the emergent South African industrial sector. It was clear that the four colonies were beginning to develop common interests.

The eventual consolidation of railway lines into a single network was a positive move towards the economic development of South Africa. It clearly shows how transport and communications were the incentive to integrate the emerging economy, now based on money and goods traffic, fully into the capitalist system. The customs union promoted further co-operation between the four colonies which were in effect already functioning as an economic entity.

10
Afrikaner nationalism, 1875-1899
Hermann Giliomee

On 13 August 2000 *Rapport* wrote that the 18-year-old Carina Carshagen, who had just won the debating competition run by the Afrikaanse Taal- en Kultuurvereniging (ATKV) had said (translated): "The Afrikaners are swaddled in a dreamless sleep. They do not know who they are, nor what an Afrikaner is; and furthermore they have no dream to strive for... We Afrikaners have unfortunately always built our dream around an ideology, but this ideology has now collapsed." She ended with the words: "If the Afrikaners want to have a dream again, the concept Afrikaner must be re-defined. The Afrikaner must know who he is and be prepared to make a difference in the new South Africa."

The dream Carina referred to are the ideals that Afrikaner nationalists aspired to after 1875, more than a century ago. In that year the first nationalist organisation – the Genootskap van Regte Afrikaners (GRA, the Society of True Afrikaners) – was formed in Paarl. A hundred years later, in 1975, Afrikaner nationalism reached its pinnacle of success: Afrikaners controlled the state and the government and had a share of some 20% of the economy. Afrikaans was one of the two official languages and was generally well established.

In the century between 1875 and 1975 Afrikaner nationalists persuaded their fellow Afrikaners to unite in a party to take political control; to promote Dutch initially and later the Afrikaans language and culture; and to work for the economic wellbeing of Afrikaners and South Africa. However, it was only in the second and third decade of the twentieth century that a nationalist movement took shape among Afrikaners. This chapter looks at the development in the last quarter of the nineteenth century when it was suggested for the first time that Afrikaners should form their own party.

The name Afrikaner

By the year 1700 "Afrikaners" referred to slaves who were born in Africa. In the course of the eighteenth century people of mixed origin moved to the north-west of the colony where they lived under leaders such as Jonker Afrikaner and Jager Afrikaner. However, in the same period, burghers of mainly Dutch, German or French origin who lived in the south-west of the colony began to refer to themselves as Afrikaners. For a long time some white Dutch- and Afrikaans-speaking people also referred to themselves as "Christians".

After Britain occupied the Cape, first in 1795 and again in 1806, many Cape Afrikaners wanted local English speakers to regard themselves as Afrikaners too. When *De Zuid-Afrikaan*, the first Dutch newspaper, appeared in 1830, the editor wrote: "All those who live in the country and make a living from it, are Afrikaners." He also said that those who criticised the colony should be strongly opposed by "all Afrikaners, both the English and the Hollanders".

In the late nineteenth century there were also coloured people, especially those who were politically active, who used the name Afrikaner. In 1883 an Afrikaner League (Coloured) was established in Kimberley. The founder was Pieter Johannes Daniels, originally from Stellenbosch. In the first decades of the twentieth century some National Party (NP) candidates also called for the vote for "coloured Afrikaners".

An Afrikaner society in the making

In the course of the nineteenth century Afrikaners began to form a clearly identifiable group based on their origin, language and religion. Gradually they also accepted the name Afrikaners. Although nationalist associations and newspapers were only set up from 1875, an Afrikaner community was therefore already a reality. This society developed largely in reaction to British authority and what was experienced as an attitude of British superiority. English dress, architecture, social etiquette and behaviour set the norm. English speakers generally regarded their language as far more "progressive" or "civilised" than Dutch. Afrikaans was usually seen as an unrefined language.

Once Britain had assumed final control over the Cape in terms of a peace treaty signed in 1814, the governors and administration were keen to "improve" and "refine" the Cape. One of the first steps in this process was a new language policy. In 1822 the government under Lord Charles Somerset announced that English would be phased in over the next five years as the language of the government and in the courts.

In the 1820s Somerset's administration also tried to anglicise the schools and the church. In free government schools the only medium of instruction was English. The burghers were keen to have their children learn English but were against the idea that Dutch would be excluded; they wanted schools that taught the children in both languages. Once the British authority became firmly established, the parents' insistence on Dutch became less insistent. When the Athenaeum (later the South African College, and even later the University of Cape Town) was established, the parents and the NG Church ministers did not object that most of the teachers were English and Scottish. However, the church ministers were worried when the college wanted to provide religious instruction, because they were afraid that the youth might decide to join an English church.

It was difficult for the Cape burghers to challenge British superiority. Until the 1820s there were as yet no Dutch newspapers, periodicals, books, paintings or inventions which they could claim as their own. The Cape Dutch houses that were built from about that time were indeed a cultural creation of which the Afrikaans colonists became justifiably proud.

NATIONALISM

Nationalism describes a certain way in which people think and act politically about society. Nationalists believe that society largely comprises peoples or peoples-in-the-making, who stand together on the basis of their history, language and culture. In contrast, liberals emphasise the individual and his/her rights and freedoms, while communists focus largely on class formations, for example the working class and their interests.

Nationalists place their greatest trust in their people – they believe that what is "unique to their culture" and the "bonds of blood" bind members of a people together and that they are "almost like a family". "We are not about self-gratification, we stand together for the wellbeing of the people", is a typical nationalist message. Nationalism arises almost always from a feeling of injustice, for example when an imperial empire (such as the British Empire) or a wealthy community looks down upon a people's language, culture and history,

> or if they are excluded from the best job opportunities. The leaders of a nationalist movement try to persuade people to unite against prejudice and humiliation.
>
> To build up a nationalist movement is very difficult because it is seldom clear who actually belongs to the movement and who does not; or even what the movement is called. In the case of the Afrikaners this is strikingly illustrated.

The movement that has become known as the Great Trek was not caused by nationalist sentiments among the Boers living in the Cape eastern border districts but by a lack of land, labour and adequate security. Yet the Voortrekkers did feel that the British officials treated them as inferior beings. Olive Schreiner, an English author, who worked among the border farmers in the Eastern Cape, wrote: "What embittered the colonists most was the cold indifference with which the government handled them and the knowledge that they were regarded as a subject and inferior race."

After the Great Trek and the formation of respectively the Zuid-Afrikaansche Republiek (ZAR, also known as the Transvaal) in 1852 and the Orange Free State (OFS) in 1854, by 1860 there were about 200 000 Afrikaners living in the area that later came to be known as South Africa. Of them, approximately 136 000 were in the Cape Colony where they comprised three quarters of the white population. In each of the two republics there were about 30 000 Afrikaners. Approximately 3000 had made Natal their home.

By 1850 nobody spoke yet of an Afrikaner people who had spread across South Africa's borders. Often it is an outsider who first recognises the possibility that a people, a *volk*, is in the process of developing. In 1860 Sir George Grey, Governor of the Cape Colony, wrote that the Afrikaners formed a single society: "They have the same surnames as the people of the Cape Colony and have close family ties with them. They talk the same language (Dutch and not English); belong to the same church (the NG Church); have the same legal system (Roman-Dutch law); and have the same sympathies, prejudices, habits and feelings about the indigenous races."

The republics were for years overshadowed by the Cape Colony. Nevertheless, burghers in the Transvaal and the Free State developed a loyalty to their respective republics. They were republicans rather than nationalists. In contrast, many of the prominent Cape Afrikaners were loyal to the British Empire and Queen Victoria.

The British annexation of the Transvaal in 1877 caused great dissatisfaction among Afrikaners throughout the country. The Transvaal burghers asked the colonial Afrikaners to help them. In June 1880, the Pretoria-based newspaper, *De Volksstem*, made a typical nationalist call on Afrikaners outside the Transvaal to come to their aid: "We are after all one nation, one blood, one bone and one flesh." At meetings, Afrikaners in the Free State and the Cape expressed strong support for the Transvaal cause.

In December 1880 the Transvaal burghers rose in opposition against the British authority and early in 1881 gained a resounding victory over the British forces at Majuba. In Bloemfontein *De Express* enthused about the military triumph: "Despite all previous differences, the feeling stirs in us that we are one people with the same love of freedom and the same hatred of tyranny."

Before the uprising the Transvaal burghers made a covenant, as the Voortrekkers had done in 1838 before the Battle of Blood River (Ncome River). Sarel Cilliers had led the Voortrekkers in making a solemn vow that they and their descendants would honour the day each year with a memorial service and would build a church, if God would grant them a victory over the Zulu force. The idea of being a chosen people – which was fostered by the victory at Blood River – is one of the strongest myths of nationalism. A myth is a belief or a fable which is usually about the origin of a people or a nation, but cannot be proven. Such cultural myths can only be widely dispersed when people begin to read books and newspapers and establish political and cultural organisations. In the 1830s there was no question of that as yet.

In carrying out the vow made at Blood River the Voortrekkers built a church in Pietermaritzburg. However, the practice of observing a special day of remembrance fell into disuse. In 1877, after Britain annexed the Transvaal, the burghers began to commemorate the day again. On 16 December 1880, between 5000 and 9000 armed burghers at Paardekraal near the present-day Mogale City (Krugersdorp) made a covenant with God and affirmed their promise with a stack of stones.

Paul Kruger, who became president of the reinstated ZAR in 1883, addressed the burghers every year on 16 December. On each occasion he delivered the message that there was a bond between the Voortrekkers and the Hebrews of old. He called his burghers "God's people" and emphasised the idea of their calling. His message was that the republic would remain independent for as long as the burghers remained faithful to this calling.

After the First Anglo-Boer War a new political consciousness arose in the Transvaal. As J.G. Kotzé, who had just been appointed as judge, remarked: "This promoted a strong national feeling among the Boers and they united in solidarity behind the state." The Transvaal of individualistic pioneers who were largely unconcerned about the central government and its authority was a thing of the past. Kruger, himself a pioneer, had persuaded them to support the state. He also attached great value to schools where the medium of instruction was Dutch.

A political party for the Afrikaners

In 1853 the Cape already had a parliament, but it would be more than twenty years before Afrikaans- and Dutch-speaking burghers began to organise themselves into political parties. Although there were more Afrikaans-speaking than English-speaking voters, there were more English speakers in Parliament.

By the early 1870s the Cape Afrikaners began to shake off their political apathy. In 1872 the Cape received responsible government which meant that the colony had been given more autonomy from the British government to develop and administer the colony and to secure its borders. Furthermore, the discovery of diamonds in the Kimberley area stimulated the economic development of the Cape; a great deal more revenue was made available for the government. Importantly, the members of Parliament were now in a position to advance the interests of their constituencies and specific support groups.

One of the support groups was the Afrikaner nationalists. However, without an energetic political party or organisation, people who had nationalist tendencies found it difficult to promote their cause. The eight Afrikaners who formed the Genootskap van Regte Afrikaners (GRA) in Paarl on 14 August 1875 fully realised this. Their leader was S.J. du Toit, a young NG minister in the town.

At this juncture, many Afrikaners were dissatisfied because English was the only official language. Furthermore, at school their children had to learn a history that glorified the British Empire and had little that was good to say about Afrikaners. Gradually a need arose for a history of Afrikaners that would be taught in schools.

By the 1870s there was also a great need in the Cape for an Afrikaans Bible because so many poor Christians of all race groups did not understand Dutch or English. In the early 1870s two Dutch immigrants, Arnoldus Pannevis and C.P. Hoogenhout, suggested that there should be an Afrikaans translation of the Bible. The British and Foreign Bible Society, which had already helped to produce translations into indigenous languages, approached S.J. du Toit about the project.

Du Toit convened a meeting to discuss the issue, but it was decided that the time was not yet ripe for an Afrikaans translation of the Bible. At the same meeting the GRA was established. This organisation aimed to serve the interests of all Afrikaners who had "Afrikaans hearts" rather than "Dutch or English hearts".

The GRA instilled in Afrikaners the determination to regard Afrikaans as their own language; to write in Afrikaans and speak it in public. However, it was not, as the GRA claimed, a language that was only created by Afrikaners or belonged exclusively to Afrikaners. Afrikaans had taken shape because burgher and slave; farmer and worker; Boer woman and domestic worker, all needed a language to communicate easily with one another. The Muslim community of Cape Town was indeed the first group which used Afrikaans in a book when Afrikaans prayer books were printed in the 1840s in Arabic script.

The GRA launched its own newspaper, *Die Afrikaanse Patriot*, to spread its message, and also published a nationalist history, entitled *Die geskiedenis van ons land in die taal van ons volk*. It was highly critical of the government and the "English" and said that the Afrikaners were heroic, honest and true to their Christian faith. In his writings, Du Toit propounded the idea that God had placed the Afrikaners in Africa and had given them the Afrikaans language.

For a brief period in the 1880s *Die Patriot* had the largest circulation of all Dutch or Afrikaans newspapers. The style was clear, concise and fresh, with simple sentences and for the most part using words of one syllable.

Many people did not agree with the strange way the newspaper spelt certain Afrikaans words (other than "ni" and "di" there were also "gen" for "geen" [none] and "ferkeerd" for "verkeerd" [incorrect].) Afrikaners who had a higher level of education, especially those in the Cape Colony, preferred English as their written language and wanted Dutch to be used in church. They read Dutch newspapers and English books.

The NG Church was strongly opposed to Du Toit and his *Die Patriot*. He went against many things the NG Church stood for, such as revival services, special prayer hours, English-medium schooling, and an exaggerated submissiveness to the government of the day. The church was also strongly loyal to the queen and the British Empire. In 1880 the Cape synod discussed *Die Patriot* over three days, one speaker after another criticising the paper's "pernicious influence", particularly its tendency to cast suspicion on the government, the church and its office bearers. Du Toit defended himself and his newspaper, but in a vote of 114 to 2 the synod condemned the paper in the strongest terms.

Later historians labelled the activities of the GRA as the First Afrikaans Language Movement. The GRA printed 93 650 copies of Dutch books and 80 000 copies of Afrikaans books. But in 1890 the movement ground to a halt. Du Toit lost his support because he threw his political weight behind Cecil John Rhodes, who was an avid proponent of the British Empire.

A second group, comprising the farmers in the Cape, also sought political representation. In the beginning of the 1870s it was especially the wine farmers in the south-western Cape, almost all of whom were Afrikaners, who began to grow dissatisfied because they felt that the government was favouring the merchants, who were mostly English speakers. The wheat farmers were also angry about low prices and cheap wheat that was being imported from overseas.

The refusal of their Transvaal counterparts to accept British supremacy underlined the necessity for Afrikaners in the Cape to form their own party. However, it was their resistance to a new tax that was imposed on wine farmers that was the strongest motivation to do so. Nationalism often offers another advantage: members of a group can advance their economic interests if they stand together politically.

In 1879 S.J. du Toit called for the formation of an Afrikaner Bond to promote Afrikaners' culture and interests. The next year, people began to form branches in the Cape Colony and a few branches were also set up in the Boer republics. The Afrikaner Bond was not only for Afrikaners, but for "everyone who recognises Africa as their fatherland ... whether they are of English, Dutch, French or German origin." This was the first political party in the history of South Africa and soon became the largest party in the Cape parliament.

Early in the 1880s Jan H. ("Onze Jan") Hofmeyr took over the control of the Afrikaner Bond after Du Toit accepted a position in the Transvaal. Hofmeyr was a newspaper editor who was active in promoting the interests of the wine farmers. He was not a nationalist and was against the idea that Afrikaans should replace Dutch but he identified closely with the Afrikaner community. At the same time he wanted to build a new nation from the two white communities by encouraging "enlightened English" to join the party.

Because the Afrikaner Bond soon had the support of almost all the Afrikaners, Hofmeyr came to the point when he said he would rather have five Englishmen sign up as members than a hundred Afrikaners. He was determined to attract both Afrikaners and English – the Afrikaans farmers as well as the English merchants. He was also careful not to antagonise the NG Church, which was strongly in favour of the British Empire and did not want any Afrikaans in the church or schools.

Hofmeyr must have been worried about the declining culture and language of the colonial Afrikaners and was able to gain greater recognition for Dutch as an official language. However, he wanted to avoid making this a point of dissent. He was very careful not to give the impression that the Cape Afrikaners were disloyal to the British Empire. Although he did not sing the praises of the empire per se, he believed that the British fleet was necessary to protect the Cape Colony in an era of competition between the great powers.

He also tried to win support among the coloured and black voters. The Cape Colony had a non-racial constitution, while there were many black voters in the Eastern Cape, and in the area of the present Western Cape a number of coloured people also had the franchise. The Afrikaner Bond did what it could to attract these votes in elections but, like the other parties, was not prepared to accept coloured or black people as party leaders. At election time the fact that Afrikaners had earlier been slave owners on a far greater scale than English speakers was used against the Afrikaner Bond. Some candidates even warned the coloured voters that the Afrikaner Bond wanted to restore slavery again, which was untrue.

The Orange Free State as a model republic

In the Orange Free State, British interference in matters north of the Orange River caused feelings of anti-imperialism that eventually gave way to a form of nationalism. In 1868 Britain annexed what they called Basutoland (now Lesotho) and three years later, the rich diamond fields. After diamonds had been discovered in 1867, a British arbiter accepted the claims of the Griquas and the Barolong above those of the Free State and the Transvaal.

The Free State regarded the manner in which Britain had seized the diamond fields as a great injustice. Jan Brand, Free State president from 1864 to 1888, handled the issue with considerable diplomacy. He succeeded in persuading the British government to pay £90 000 in compensation to the Free State for the loss of the diamond fields. Brand then put this money to good use by setting up a state bank which made the republic more independent with regard to its finances. He also laid emphasis on a strong legal system to attract trade and investment and acted against corruption.

However, the diamond fields still held advantages for the Free State. In Kimberley, which was just across the Free State border, there was now a massive market for farm produce and goods of every kind, which provided an economic injection. Wool was also exported, but on a limited scale.

This small republic was ambitious and wanted to attract immigrants with good qualifications. A Scot, John Brebner, reformed the education system; and in Bloemfontein, C.L.F. Borckenhagen, a German, became editor of *De Express* in 1877. An avid proponent of republican independence, Borckenhagen exercised a significant influence on both sides of the Vaal River.

British cultural influences remained strong. From its founding until the last years of the republic, Bloemfontein was essentially an English town and English was the most widely used language not only in private schools but also in the farm schools that were set up by wealthy farmers. In 1888 a member of the Volksraad declared disparagingly that the preference given to English in the best-known Bloemfontein school, Grey College, would "teach the children to scorn and forget their own language and to disparage their nation".

Nevertheless, a republican spirit developed rapidly among the burghers, which was in sharp contrast with the "colonial patriotism" of the Cape Afrikaners. According to Cape leader Jan Hofmeyr, in the Free State there was a lively feeling that "government and community are one", something that was completely absent in the south, or at best was uncertain.

By 1890 the Free State was regarded as the part of South Africa which had the most efficient administration. James Bryce, a British constitutional commentator, labelled it a "model republic". The rural character, relatively homogenous voter body and the absence of concentrations of wealth made this republic a stable one. English speakers and a few Germans dominated the trade and professional life in the towns. The state welcomed immigrants and its republicanism was linked to nationhood which included all white people.

Marthinus Theunis Steyn (1857–1916) was the first Free State president who was born in the republic. His father's farm was just outside Bloemfontein and from an early age, together with his parents, he mingled with the predominantly English elite in the capital – the Brands, Fichardts, Fischers and Frasers. Steyn married Tibbie Fraser and corresponded with her in English.

In the Netherlands where he wanted to study law, his Dutch was so poor that he decided to go to London instead. In 1889 Steyn was appointed as judge in Bloemfontein and in 1896 he was elected president of the Free State. One of the reasons for his election was the Free State Afrikaners' moral support for the Transvaal after the Jameson Raid. He was well known for his courage, charm, strong character and sound judgement and is sometimes labelled the first modern Afrikaner. The kind of politics that he and other Free Staters stood for, Steyn described as follows: "A person can be a good Afrikaner and genuine republican regardless of the language one speaks."

As a republican, Steyn maintained close ties with the ZAR, but culturally he identified more readily with the Cape Afrikaners. He tried to build up the Free State as a society of freedom-loving farmers. He favoured a more direct form of democracy by means of referendums and gave increasing attention to the question of language and culture which he saw as expressions of Free State nationhood. He believed that if the Dutch language fell into disuse, the decline of the nation would follow. He instructed his officials to use Dutch in correspondence with Free State burghers and with the Natal and Cape governments. People who were fluent in Dutch were given preference in appointments to the civil service. His government also exercised pressure on schools, most of which used English as a medium of instruction, to introduce Dutch.

Cape and Transvaal Afrikaners

The discovery of rich gold deposits on the Witwatersrand in 1886 made the Transvaal prosperous within a decade. The Cape government was miffed that the colony increasingly had to play second fiddle to the ZAR. The Transvaal's plans to expand its borders also conflicted with Cecil John Rhodes's desire to see the British flag flying over territories to the north of the Cape Colony and the Transvaal.

In 1890 Hofmeyr and the Afrikaner Bond helped Rhodes to become prime minister of the Cape Colony and Rhodes wanted to follow this up by using the Afrikaner Bond's political support to colonise new regions. This brought him into conflict with Paul Kruger and the Transvalers; Kruger was keen to expand the republic's borders by opening up more land for the farmers.

Another source of conflict between the ZAR and the Cape Colony was import duties. When the Transvaal republic was still struggling financially, it had to pay high rates to the Cape Colony for goods that were imported through Cape harbours. All complaints about this to the Cape government fell on deaf ears. When the Transvaal grew wealthy after the discovery of gold, the republic began to establish local industries. Higher import duties were therefore levied on products that the Cape exported to the Transvaal. The Cape protested vehemently, but to no avail.

Although Kruger prioritised Transvaal interests, he also used the language of a nationalist. He insisted that Afrikaners throughout southern Africa should support the two republics against British imperialism.

The spirit of political solidarity between Afrikaners in the north (Transvaal and the Free State) and the south (the Cape Colony) had however waned because their respective governments had followed their own paths and had prioritised their own interests. In 1887 a committee of the Afrikaner Bond wrote a letter to Kruger which read (translated):

> We must acknowledge with regret that we detect a cooling off of the warm feeling of fondness in the case of our Transvaal brothers. We fear that unless matters take a different turn it will soon be impossible to receive as much sympathy again from the Cape Colony as was previously the case [during the First Anglo-Boer War of 1880–1881].

For Cape Afrikaners who went to settle in the Transvaal it soon became clear that there was a marked difference between the "colony" and the "republic". The two republics laid far greater emphasis on the language and culture of their burghers than did the Cape Colony. M.E. Rothmann, who became known in the next century as the esteemed writer M.E.R., wrote of her school days in Swellendam in the 1880s and 1890s: "From early childhood thousands of impressions were brought to bear upon me that whatever was English was good; whatever was Afrikaans, was less good."

M.E.R. writes as follows in the introduction to *Oorlogsdagboek* on Dr William Robertson, NG minister in Swellendam in the 1880s and 1890s (translated):

> He saw it as his duty to force the English language and practices upon us. The state was after all, or so such enforcers argued, under English control and to inculcate the English language and practices was the best way to cultivate unity and strength. Was this then a disgrace? This never occurred to them in the slightest. Quite the contrary.
>
> The answer to this question was simply this – that to make the English stamp permanent, the Afrikaners had to be made to believe that their practices, their language and their outlook on life was wrong and had to be replaced by something better ... Such an attempt created lasting and extremely damaging emotional confusion. It does a child great harm to feel that his mother and father's language and their way of life should be seen as less worthy, when in fact it is merely different from the language and outlook of those who gave him his lessons at school.

It was in resistance to this message of English superiority that many Afrikaners became increasingly nationalistic. In the 1890s, when Rothmann went to work in the Transvaal, she found that her own language was neither pushed aside nor downgraded, but was used everywhere in the Volksraad, courts, schools and civil service. She wrote (translated): "Instead of coming across the history of our own people as a laughable and contemptuous scrap in an English schoolbook, it is studied as a worthy possession."

"An electric shock to the national heart"

Britain could not abide the fact that the ZAR had full control over the richest goldfields in the world at a time when gold was the lifeblood of the international economy. The famous author George Bernard Shaw expressed this sentiment when he referred disparagingly to "a little community of border farmers who were totally incapable of controlling the mineral wealth of South Africa".

The British government thought that the ZAR's strengthened economic position held an ever greater threat for Britain. Joseph Chamberlain, the British secretary of state for the colonies, believed that if Britain did not intervene, its international image would be undermined. As Lord Salisbury, the British prime minister, summed it up, "[We], and not the Dutch, are Boss [in South Africa]".

British imperialists such as Chamberlain and Rhodes therefore set about devising ways of gaining control of the goldfields. At the end of December 1895, with the full knowledge and support of these two men, Dr Leander Starr Jameson invaded the Transvaal with a small force. The aim was to incite an uprising among the so-called Uitlanders (foreigners who did not have the franchise or citizenship but who worked in the Transvaal) and with their help overthrow the ZAR government. The plan failed miserably.

The Jameson Raid caused a surge of Afrikaner nationalism throughout the country. In Cape Town, F.S. Malan, young editor of the newspaper *Ons Land*, wrote: "The dagger thrust used in an attempt to paralyse Afrikanerdom forever in the republics sent an electric shock through the national heart. Afrikanerdom awakened with all earnestness and consciousness … a new wave of feeling infused the entire South Africa."

The raid ended the co-operation between Rhodes and Hofmeyr's Afrikaner Bond. The rift widened when Rhodes fought tooth and nail against the Afrikaner Bond in the election of 1898. However, the Cape Afrikaners were lukewarm about helping the Transvaal burghers in concrete ways. Many of them had a superior attitude towards their fellow burghers in the two republics. However, they were more than prepared to give the northern Afrikaners advice, even if was uncalled for. Very few of them regarded Kruger as a competent politician.

The Cape Afrikaners were mainly colonial burghers of the British Empire. They wanted the Transvaal to break down its tariff walls; they were hoping that the republics and colonies could be united into a single state under the British flag. Republican independence, to which Kruger attached so much importance, was of no interest to the Afrikaner Bond; nor was the idea of uniting all Afrikaners throughout the country into a single party. Yet Hofmeyr wrote to the British prime minister saying that the southern and northern Afrikaners felt a bond because of all the ties of common origin, language and religion. They trusted one another and were friends. "Their wrongs are our wrongs and services rendered to them are services rendered to us."

Alfred Milner, who arrived in Cape Town in May 1897 to take up the post of British governor and high commissioner, brought matters to a head. He believed that if the ZAR were not dealt a swift defeat over the matter of the Uitlander franchise, British authority and its image in South Africa might soon decline. To place pressure on London, Milner exaggerated the question of the Uitlander franchise and other grievances out of all proportion. He gained the support of certain mine magnates because they were impatient about some of the ZAR's policies and its administrative ineptness, which hampered their production. Milner painted a picture for the British government of a traitorous Afrikaans society in the Cape Colony which would be prepared to help Kruger by undermining British authority.

The Afrikaner leaders did their best to persuade Milner that there was no question of a countrywide plot against British interests and that they and their followers were blameless in this regard. According to J.T. Molteno, son of a previous prime minister of the Cape Colony, Milner often insulted the Afrikaners and questioned their loyalty. When the Graaff-Reinet branch of the Afrikaner Bond handed him a written declaration of their loyalty in 1898, his answer was: "Of course you are loyal. It would be monstrous if you were not." If they wanted peace, he continued, they should put pressure on Kruger for reform and choose which side they wanted to be on. He wrote to Chamberlain to say that the English press in South Africa had applauded him loudly for these statements.

Britain would have been cautious about waging war if there was any possibility of a mass uprising of Cape Afrikaners, but the Cape people were caught up in multiple identities. As colonial patriots they were loyal to the Crown and their own colony. If they had a preference for republicanism it was merely an ideal for the distant future. They also believed that the Cape Colony should be the basis of a future white nation under the British flag.

Milner soon realised that the leaders of the Cape Afrikaners wanted to avoid war at all costs and would thus do their best to persuade Kruger to make the necessary concessions. The relatively weak feelings of Afrikaner nationalism among Cape Afrikaners made it easier for Milner to stir up a war against the Boer republics.

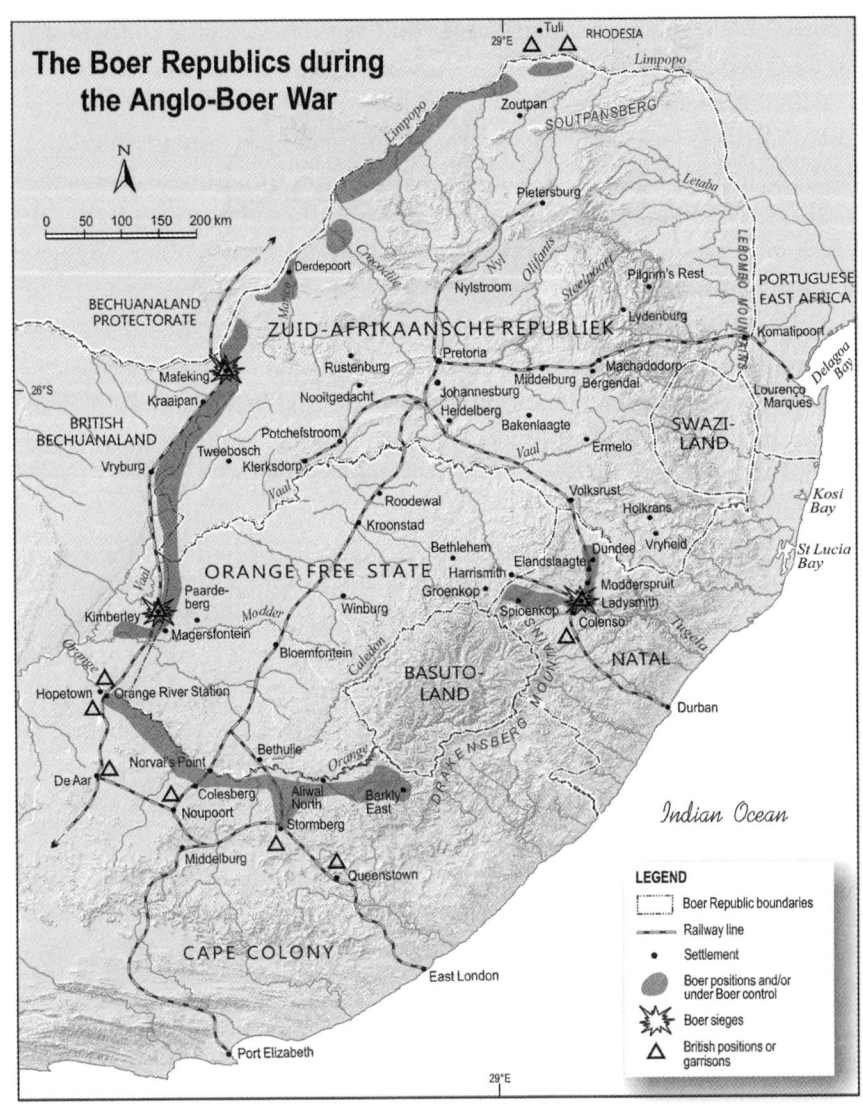

11
Everyone's war: the Anglo-Boer War (1899-1902)

Fransjohan Pretorius

By 1875 Lord Carnarvon, the British secretary of state for the colonies, was determined to bring about a federation of South African states under the British flag. Britain annexed the Zuid-Afrikaansche Republiek (ZAR, or Transvaal) in 1877 and at the same time planted the seed of Afrikaner nationalism. The Transvalers – who dearly wanted their independence back – defeated the British forces in the First Anglo-Boer War of 1880–1881, which ended in victory at Majuba on 27 February 1881.

The Pretoria Convention of 3 August 1881 did not fully restore the Transvaal's independence, but placed it under British suzerainty. This vague notion meant that Britain retained supervisory control over the Transvaal's external policy as well as its legislation affecting the black communities living within its borders. The London Convention which followed on 27 February 1884, gave the Transvaal full independence (sovereignty) as far as domestic matters were concerned, but the limitations on its foreign policy remained in place.

Prior to the discovery of gold on the Witwatersrand in 1886, the Transvaal led a somewhat precarious existence. Gold, however, had the potential to make the Transvaal a very real political and economic threat to British supremacy in South Africa, just at a stage when Britain was involved in a race with France and Germany for colonies in Africa.

Thousands of Uitlanders (foreigners), most of them British subjects, streamed to the goldfields to seek their fortune. Motivated by fear that the Uitlanders' presence would threaten the Boers' independence, in 1890 President Paul Kruger increased the period of residence required before gaining Transvaal citizenship (and therefore the right to vote) from five years to 14 years. Most of the Uitlanders had no intention whatsoever of forsaking the citizenship of their fatherland and replacing it with ZAR citizenship, but some of the mine magnates demanded a voice in the management of the Transvaal because Kruger's policy of concessions made the mining industry expensive to run. The concession policy meant that the Transvaal government sold the right, for example to produce dynamite, to an individual; this made free competition impossible and pushed up the price.

Cecil John Rhodes, prime minister of the Cape Colony, who wanted a united South Africa under the British flag, made sure that by 1890 the Transvaal was encircled by British territory on its western, northern and south-eastern sides. In 1895, once the railway line between Pretoria and Delagoa Bay in Mozambique had been completed, giving Transvaal greater economic independence from the British colonies, Rhodes organised the Jameson Raid. The plan was that the Reform Committee, comprising Uitlanders, would instigate an uprising in Johannesburg. Dr Leander Starr Jameson would then rush to their aid with a force raised in Bechuanaland (today Botswana) and together they would oust the Transvaal government and take control. The poorly planned Jameson Raid of New Year 1896 failed when General Piet Cronjé forced the attackers to surrender before they could reach Johannesburg.

Historians agree that the British secretary of state for the colonies, Joseph Chamberlain, knew of Rhodes's conspiracy and, furthermore, that he supported it. The raid and the suspicion that Britain was closely involved in the plot led to a surge of nationalism among Afrikaners living in the Boer republics as well as those in the British colonies. Under President M.T. Steyn the Free State strengthened its political alliance with the Transvaal in March 1897. In terms of this agreement the republics would support each other if the independence of one or both was under threat. Both republics now also began to purchase weapons and ammunition on a huge scale from Germany and France.

In May 1897 Chamberlain appointed Sir Alfred Milner as high commissioner in South Africa. This proved to be a turning point in relations between Britain and the Transvaal. Milner, like Chamberlain, was a strong proponent of a federation of South African states under the British flag. Transvaal – the bastion of Afrikaner nationalism – had to be eliminated.

How well-grounded was Milner's fear that Afrikaner nationalism was a threat to Britain's position in South Africa? Generally speaking, Afrikaner leaders did not support the idea of a unified South Africa. As for

Kruger, he was indeed open to closer co-operation between the South African republics and colonies, but when the independence of Transvaal was at stake, he dug in his heels. To Milner's dismay, Kruger was re-elected as president in February 1898 with an overwhelming majority. Thereupon an exasperated Milner wrote to Chamberlain: "There is no way out of the political troubles of S[outh] Africa except reform in the Transvaal or war."

Milner then proceeded to use the matter of voting rights for the Uitlanders to interfere in the Transvaal's domestic politics. He announced that British suzerainty had not been lifted by the London Convention and went on to claim, erroneously, that this afforded him the opportunity to become involved in the Transvaal's domestic affairs. In co-operation with Chamberlain he influenced the British press and public opinion on the issue of the Uitlanders' grievances and on the possibility of war if a satisfactory solution could not be found. With Milner's encouragement, in March 1899 the Uitlanders sent a petition bearing 22 000 signatures to Queen Victoria; the signatories demanded that they be given the vote and called upon Britain to intervene on their behalf. To add even more weight to the Uitlanders' petition, Milner maintained in his "helots" telegram of 4 May 1899 to Chamberlain that thousands of British subjects were being treated as mere helots (slaves) in the Transvaal.

Through President Steyn's intercession, Kruger and Milner met in Bloemfontein on 31 May 1899. Kruger was prepared to give Uitlanders the vote after residence of seven years. However, to compensate for this concession he came up with new demands which placed the success of the conference in jeopardy. Among other things he wanted the incorporation of Swaziland into the Transvaal and arbitration (decision by a third party) on the London Convention. Milner would not agree to these terms and insisted on a franchise qualification of five years. When Kruger could not see his way to agree, Milner ended the negotiations on 5 June.

The political tension mounted. Britain was in a powerful position because as the strongest maritime power she could prevent overseas goods from reaching the Transvaal. Furthermore, with the whole British Empire on her side, Britain had access to a virtually unlimited number of troops, weaponry and food supplies. On 8 September the British government sent 10 000 troops to South Africa. This would bring the number of troops at the ready on the republican borders to 22 000 men.

The Transvaal and its ally the Orange Free State anxiously watched the growing number of British troops massing on their borders. On 27 September 1899 Commandant General Joubert called up about 60% of the Transvaal burghers and ordered them to advance to the borders. Six days later Steyn gave his burghers the same directive.

> **ONE WAR, DIFFERENT NAMES**
>
> The war that took place between 1899 and 1902 has various names, some of which are more acceptable than others. The name the British gave it, the Boer War, is just as one-sided and subjective as the names the Afrikaners used: the Engelse Oorlog (English War) and the Tweede Vryheidsoorlog (Second War of Independence).
>
> Currently, the name South African War enjoys wide support. Its adherents argue that it was a war fought on South African soil and that both white and black people were involved or were affected by the war. The problem with this name is that Great Britain, the power which is now generally accepted as having been the instigator of the war, does not feature in this name. After all, the Vietnamese do not speak of the Vietnam War.
>
> Those who support the use of the name Anglo-Boer War argue that it is more appropriate because it is representative of the parties who were involved in the diplomatic, political and military conflict. The official declaration of war was between Great Britain and the two Boer republics and it was also these two parties that officially ended the war. Criticism of this name is that it does not reflect black people's participation in the war and that "Anglo" is too limited because it only refers to English involvement. It does not recognise the part played by the Scots, Welsh, Irish, Cape colonists, Natalians, Australians, New Zealanders and Canadians who fought on the British side.
>
> Regardless of which name is chosen, it should be clearly understood that officially it was a war between Britain and the two Boer republics and that black people became involved in and were affected by this war.

The military course of the war

On 9 October 1899 the Transvaal government issued an ultimatum to Britain. It demanded that all the problems between the two states should be resolved by arbitration; that the British troops on its borders be withdrawn immediately; and that the troops which were on their way to South Africa by ship should not step ashore. The British government ignored the ultimatum after which, two days later, on 11 October, the Anglo-Boer War began.

For the first five months of the war it was characterised by set-piece warfare. In other words the British and Boer forces faced one another on the battlefield in direct confrontation and each used artillery and rifle fire in attempting to defeat the other. In the initial encounter on 12 October at Kraaipan on the western front, the Boers under General Koos de la Rey put a British armoured train out of action. The first major battles were at Talana and Elandslaagte in Natal, where the British gained victories on 20 and 21 October respectively. At Talana the British commander, General Penn Symons, was fatally wounded, while the same fate befell General Jan Kock, the Boer commander at Elandslaagte.

The Boer forces besieged (i.e. took up a tactical defensive position) around the towns of Ladysmith in Natal; and Kimberley and Mafeking (nowadays Mahikeng) in the Cape Colony. The British forces naturally tried to relieve their garrisons in these towns and this led to several important battles. However, despite the British numerical superiority, the Boers gained significant victories from their concealed positions. On 11 December 1899 at Magersfontein, south of Kimberley, General Piet Cronjé defeated Lord Methuen when the British forces were outmanoeuvred by Boer forces in concealed trenches in front of, instead of on top of, the nearby rocky outcrops. This was an ingenious plan devised by Koos de la Rey, Cronjé's second-in-command. He realised that Methuen was fully expecting that the Boers were hidden on top of the hills.

> **THE BRITISH SOLDIER IN THE VELD**
>
> For the British soldier (or Tommy, as he was generally known) the conditions in South Africa were extremely difficult. In May 1900 Frederick Tucker of the 1st Rifle Brigade was a member of General Sir Redvers Buller's force that was preparing to advance into Transvaal from Natal. On 18 May he wrote in his diary:
> "We find the weather bitterly cold. The troops are busy almost the whole day digging trenches and erecting defensive ramparts so that we are well prepared for an attack. There are reports that a large number of Boers are well entrenched and are lying in wait on Majuba hill and Laingsnek. For the past two days there has been a dire shortage of rations. We are now eating our draught oxen - their meat is more suitable to repair boots than for human consumption."

On 15 December General Louis Botha defeated General Buller at Colenso in Natal when the British once again failed to see Botha's camouflaged entrenchments just on the other side of the Tugela River. On 24 January 1900 at Spioenkop near Ladysmith Buller suffered one of the most humiliating defeats of the war. The 17-year-old Deneys Reitz wrote on his experience of the Battle of Spioenkop:

> "We were sustaining heavy casualties from the English schans [entrenchment] immediately in front of us, and the men grew restive under the galling point-blank fire, a thing not to be wondered at, for the moral effect of Lee-Metford volleys at twenty yards must be experienced to be appreciated. The English troops lay so near that one could have tossed a biscuit among them, and whilst the losses which they were causing us were only too evident, we on our side did not know that we were inflicting even greater damage upon them."

On the other hand, a British soldier, Herbert Unwin of Thorneycroft's Mounted Infantry wrote about Spioenkop in a letter home:

> "I was laid (sic) in one position nearly all day, cramped, and parched with thirst; the trenches piled with dead and dying men. One poor fellow in our trench had his arm blown off close to his shoulder. He picked it up with the other hand, saying 'My arm, my arm. Oh God, where's my arm!' Quite mad with pain, he jumped out of the trench, and was instantly shot again, and saved further pain."

The end of February 1900 brought a turn in the fortunes of the war with the simultaneous collapse of all the Boer fronts. On 15 February the siege of Kimberley was lifted by British forces and twelve days later Cronjé and 4000 burghers surrendered to Lord Roberts at Paardeberg in the western Free State. These setbacks put the Boers' positions around Colesberg in danger and as a result the southern front also disintegrated. In Natal, Buller eventually broke through Botha's thin line on 27 February at Pieter's Heights and relieved Ladysmith the next day. Mafeking was only relieved on 17 May 1900. When this finally happened, the joyful bonfires in London leapt high in celebration of the heroic feats of endurance exhibited by Colonel Robert Baden-Powell and his men.

FOREIGNERS IN THE WAR

In the course of the war the British army was strengthened by volunteer contingents from Canada, Australia, New Zealand, the Cape Colony and Natal. On the other hand, about 13 000 Cape and Natal rebels took up arms on the Boer side against Britain.

> Approximately 2000 foreign volunteers joined the Boer forces. They wanted to show their support for the Boers in their resistance against British imperialism, but many of them were also drawn to South Africa because of their love of adventure. Most went back home when it became apparent before the middle of 1900 that the tide of the war had turned against the Boers.
>
> Among the foreign volunteers there were many colourful figures such as Colonel Georges de Villebois-Mareuil of France and Yevgeny Maximov of Russia, both of whom earned the accolades and admiration of the Boers for their bravery. In April 1900 near Boshof in the Free State, De Villebois-Mareuil perished while commanding the Vreemdelingekorps (Foreigners' Corps).

For the Boers, the six months after the setbacks of February 1900 was a period of great confusion and disarray. They had to fall back everywhere. Roberts occupied Bloemfontein on 13 March 1900 and by 5 June Pretoria was also under his control. Indeed, the British commander-in-chief annexed the Free State as British territory on 24 May and the Transvaal on 1 September 1900. This was not recognised by either the Transvaal or the Free State governments who continued to function "in the field". A large number of burghers laid down their arms in response to British promises of peace and protection.

Meanwhile, after the death of General Piet Joubert on 27 March 1900, Louis Botha was appointed as commandant general of the Transvaal forces. Over the next few months he and other dynamic officers such as Christiaan de Wet and Koos de la Rey took over from the older guard of incompetent generals such as Lukas Meyer, Kooitjie Snyman, Daniël Erasmus and Hendrik Schoeman.

De Wet, now chief commandant, led the Boer resistance in the Free State and ushered in the guerrilla phase of the war with surprise attacks on isolated British columns and on Roberts's straggling line of communication. His victory on 31 March at Sannaspos, east of Bloemfontein, was the first sign that the guerrilla phase of mobile warfare was at hand. As if he was engaged in a hunt for wildlife, De Wet and some of his burghers took up a concealed position in the bed of a stream to the west of the British camp at Sannaspos. The Boer cannons were set up on the eastern side of the British camp and when they opened fire on the camp, the soldiers – just as De Wet expected they would – rushed headlong towards the west, directly into the hands of De Wet's burghers waiting in the stream.

On 7 June at Roodewal station, north of Kroonstad, De Wet launched a surprise attack and seized a large amount of ammunition and provisions, the most valuable booty taken in the entire war. A severe setback for the Boers the following month was the surrender of Marthinus Prinsloo with 4400 Free Staters to the British forces on 30 July 1900 in the Brandwater Basin south of Bethlehem.

> **DANIE THERON**
> This leading Boer scout was born in Tulbagh in the Cape Colony in 1872 and qualified for Transvaal citizenship after his participation in the campaign against Mmalebôgô.
> Theron distinguished himself in the battles of Colenso and Spioenkop in Natal before he was sent to the western front in February 1900. One of his most daring feats was when he crept through the British lines (and returned safely) to deliver a message from General Christiaan de Wet to General Piet Cronjé who was trapped at Paardeberg.
> Early in March 1900 a special scouting corps, the Theron Verkennings-korps (TVK) was formed with Theron as captain. It was an elite corps of a hundred men that soon doubled in size. The corps became the eyes and ears of the Boer force by keeping close tabs on the British forces and often even penetrating their lines. In this way they were able to provide the Boer officers with valuable information.
> Between June and August 1900 the TVK undertook important scouting duties for De Wet when the British were making a concerted effort to catch him. The TVK often formed the rearguard and held back the pursuing enemy. On 22 July Theron was promoted to commandant after he and his corps captured a train and ensured that the Boer force was able to cross the railway line in safety.
> On 5 September 1900 Theron was killed on the Gatsrand in the Western Transvaal when he decided to scout the area on his own and ran into a British force. With his determination and strict sense of justice Theron enforced iron discipline. Yet he was popular among the members of his corps and he inspired them by his example. On Theron's death De Wet wrote: "Men as lovable or as valiant there might be, but where should I find a man who combined so many virtues and good qualities in one person?"

The last set-piece battle of the war took place on 27 August 1900 at Bergendal (Dalmanutha), near Machadodorp, when Roberts succeeded in driving the Transvalers further eastward. Thereafter, Botha in the Eastern Transvaal, like De Wet in the Free State and De la Rey in the Western Transvaal, began applying guerrilla tactics. When the occasion presented itself the Boer generals combined the scattered commandos, attacked isolated British columns and then quickly galloped away.

For almost two years the *bittereinders* (bitter-enders, Boer die-hards) kept up the fight in this manner. Meanwhile, President Kruger departed for Europe in October 1900 where he tried unsuccessfully to seek the diplomatic intervention of European governments on behalf of the republics. When he arrived in Europe the general public welcomed him enthusiastically; by and large they sympathised with the Boer cause. In this the press played an important role as opinion former, by depicting Britain as the "oppressor of nations".

Pro-Boer committees collected money to relieve the suffering of needy Boers. Ambulance teams, especially those from the Netherlands, Germany and Russia, were equipped and sent to the war front. In the Netherlands the empathy for the Boer cause was the strongest. As for the French, the Germans and the Russians, they were in the first place anti-British – and thus pro-Boer.

However, the governments of European countries were too afraid to antagonise the powerful Britain by actively assisting the Boers. Germany, France and Russia were particularly tentative of taking action, because each feared that the other European powers would team up with Britain against the one that chose to side with the Boers. Kruger died in 1904 in exile in Switzerland.

Kitchener intervenes in the war

In November 1900 Lord Horatio Herbert Kitchener took over the reins from Roberts as British commander-in-chief. He adopted a three-part strategy to end the war. Firstly, he continued to pursue Roberts's scorched-earth policy which had been in operation since June 1900. The republics were subjected to deliberate and systematic devastation. Some towns and thousands of farm homesteads were burnt to the ground, food supplies were destroyed and livestock was killed in their thousands.

Secondly, the concentration camp system started by Roberts in September 1900 was extended, whereby civilians, particularly women and children from destroyed homesteads were removed and placed in camps. Kitchener believed that in this way the burghers on commando would no longer be able to survive on the food provided for them by the women on the farms and that, furthermore, they might well lay down their arms to be re-united with their families. In addition, black people were gathered into separate concentration camps so that they were unable to provide the commandos with any assistance such as information and provisions.

Thirdly, Kitchener began his "drives", a means of flushing the commandos out and trapping them against lines of blockhouses erected for this purpose in a network spanning the entire theatre of war. By the end of the war there were about 8000 blockhouses over a distance of some 5600 km. (Today there are about 50 of them still standing.)

In the long term Kitchener's strategy was successful. The Boers still achieved a number of significant victories, such as De la Rey's on 13 December 1900 at Nooitgedacht; Botha's on 30 October 1901 at Bakenlaagte; De Wet's on 25 December 1901 at Groenkop; and De la Rey's on 7 March 1902 at Tweebosch. But eventually the superior numbers of the British forces were simply overwhelming. By March 1902 there were still about 20 000 Boers in the veld – ten times less than the British force which in addition had the assistance of about 30 000 armed black people in the British army. Black groups had by this time also taken over large parts of remote areas of the republic and were a threat to poverty-stricken, homeless Boer women and children who were wandering in the veld, as well as to the remnants of scattered commandos. Additionally, because of the scorched-earth policy, in large parts of the republic, particularly in the north-eastern Free State and virtually the entire Eastern Transvaal, there was no food. Furthermore, the Boers were divided: about a third of the burghers had laid down their weapons in the course of the war, and another third was in prisoner-of-war camps – most of them overseas.

After discussions at Vereeniging when all these issues were considered, the Boer delegates decided on 31 May 1902 by 54 votes to 6 to surrender. That night the Peace of Vereeniging was signed at Melrose House in Pretoria. The two defeated republics lost their independence and were incorporated into the British Empire as the Transvaal Colony and the Orange River Colony.

PRISONERS OF WAR

From the outset both the British and the Boers took prisoners of war.

More than 20 000 Boers were held in prisoner-of-war camps in the course of the war. Many boys, a few as young as eight years old, were captured with their fathers as prisoners of war and sent to the camps. Mass surrenders by the Boers, for example those by General Piet Cronjé at Paardeberg on 27 February 1900 and General Marthinus Prinsloo in the Brandwater Basin on 30 July 1900 meant that the prisoner-of-war camps in the Cape Colony and Natal soon became too small. Camps were thus set up on St Helena, Ceylon (today Sri Lanka), the islands of Bermuda and in India. About a thousand

> Boers, as well as approximately 50 women and 100 children were also interned in Portugal after they had crossed over the border into Mozambique in September 1900.
> Officially, about 400 British officers and 9200 troops were taken as prisoners of war. However, the true number is far higher because not all those who were captured were recorded in the guerrilla phase. In addition, more often than not in this mobile warfare phase the Boers immediately freed their prisoners because they did not have the facilities to house them. British troops that were captured were initially held on the racecourse in Pretoria (today the showgrounds) and the officers were taken to the Staats Model School (it was from here that the young Winston Churchill famously escaped). In December 1899 the prisoners of war were moved to Waterval, north of Pretoria; and they were moved once again, this time to Nooitgedacht near Nelspruit in the Eastern Transvaal, as Roberts advanced towards Pretoria. It was here that they were eventually freed by General Ben Viljoen at the end of August 1900 when the British forces were approaching.
> For both British and Boer prisoners of war the provision of food was generally insufficient and of poor quality. Strict discipline was maintained, although the treatment of the inmates depended on the goodwill of the specific camp authority. Organised sport such as rugby, cricket, athletics and tennis – and also traditional *boeresport* (country sports) for the Boers – provided a welcome diversion for bored prisoners of war. There were also lively cultural activities such as debates and musical evenings.
> For the Boer prisoners of war the news of the signing of the Peace of Vereeniging came as a great shock. They had to swear an oath of allegiance to the British crown before they were allowed to return to their fatherland.

The concentration camps

When the war broke out most Boer women and their children remained on the farms to take care of the farming. Others moved to the towns because of a shortage of food supplies or for fear of neighbouring black groups.

Early in 1900 there were already incidents of Boer homesteads being burnt down by the British forces. Because of the continual attacks on his rail connections, particularly by General De Wet in the Free State, Lord Roberts officially launched his scorched-earth policy on 16 June of that year. He initially ordered that the farmsteads nearest to where railways had been destroyed should be burnt down.

In September, Roberts extended the scope of the policy by ordering that in addition to burning down homes, all food supplies within a radius of 16 km had to be destroyed. This meant that an area of 547 km² was devastated after every Boer attack on the British lines of communication. Not surprisingly, the British officers gained the impression that they had Roberts's official approval to burn down and utterly devastate everything at will. Under Kitchener the scorched-earth policy was even more stringently applied and as many as 30 000 farm homesteads were burnt down.

Meanwhile, by September 1900 Roberts had begun to place all the Boers who had laid down their arms, along with their families, in camps – the so-called refugee camps. The intention was to prevent them from being re-commandeered by the Boers. However, a growing number of Boer women and their children whose homes had been burnt down and had fled into the veld were also forcibly taken to these camps. The British called these women and children the "undesirables" and before long they comprised the majority of people in the camps; in their case, therefore, the camps were not "refugee" camps at all, but concentration camps. This term should however not be confused with the concentration camps established by Nazi Germany to house Jews during the Second World War. The Nazis had an entirely different objective in setting up their "death camps"; this cannot be compared with the motives of the British with their concentration camps.

By September 1901 there were 34 concentration camps for white people, with about 110 000 inmates. This number did not increase much afterwards because from December 1901 very few Boer civilians were sent to the camps.

From the outset there were deaths in the camps, but in the period from August to October 1901 these reached a dreadful climax, with 3205 deaths in October alone. After the war P.L.A. Goldman, a former archivist from the Transvaal, established that 27 927 white people died in the concentration camps – 26 251 women and children (of whom more than 22 000 were younger than 16) and 1676 men older than 16 years of age. In the aftermath of the war the bitterness Afrikaners felt towards the British revolved to a large extent around the high death toll in the concentration camps.

This high mortality rate can be ascribed to the generally unhygienic wartime conditions across the country, including the pollution of water in particular, but also to the unhygienic habits of some Boer families who were backward in their living standards; and to the poor management by British camp administrators. Inept camp administration can be further sub-divided. It was inefficient in its choice of suitable sites for the camps; there was a low standard of order and cleanliness on the part of some camp officials; the poor food provided to inmates meant that their resistance to disease was lowered; medical personnel were on the whole unskilled and too few in number; and finally, it proved to be highly unwise for the camp authorities to insist on the enforced grouping together of large numbers of rural people who over the years had not built up immunity against contagious diseases such as measles and had no knowledge of how to keep them under control. Kitchener must be accorded most of the blame for this because he was responsible for extending the concentration camp system without due regard for the implications.

There was a significant lowering of the death toll after Lord Milner, the British high commissioner, took over the camp administration in November 1901 from an indifferent Kitchener whose main preoccupation was military matters. This drop in the number of deaths was also in great measure because of the intervention of a British woman, Emily Hobhouse, who visited South Africa and publicised the bad conditions in the camps when she returned home. In reaction, the British government named a commission of women under the leadership of Millicent Fawcett to make an official investigation of conditions in the camps. Their suggestions for improvements – including better qualified doctors and nurses, better hospital facilities, and food of better quality – had the desired effect. By May 1902 the mortality rate in the camps had dropped to 196 for the month.

In the course of the twentieth century Afrikaner leaders used the suffering and deaths of the Boer women and children in the concentration camps to promote Afrikaner nationalism. However, it should also be borne in mind that even before the war, at least one out of every ten children in the rural areas died at a young age. Although the poor British camp administration was by far the major reason for the high death toll, it cannot necessarily be held responsible for all the deaths in the camps.

Fearing the dangers of life in the concentration camps, a number of women simply wandered around in the veld with their children for the duration of the war. In the Eastern and Western Transvaal and the eastern Free State especially, they found shelter on the mountainsides in ravines and caves. Their suffering was also extreme. Because of the scorched-earth policy, lack of food became a huge problem. The increasing antagonism of some black groups also presented great danger. By the end of the war about 14 000 Boer women and their children were still in the veld.

Handsuppers and joiners

In the course of the war about a third of the available members of the Boer fighting force, that is about 20 000 burghers, laid down their arms and took an oath of neutrality. The Boer die-hards who continued to fight referred to them as *hendsoppers* (from the English word "hands up"). Some handsuppers were burghers who had never joined the commandos at all.

The laying down of arms was particularly prevalent in the aftermath of severe military setbacks such as the surrender of General Piet Cronjé at Paardeberg and the British occupation of Bloemfontein and Pretoria. These Boers were war weary and demoralised; they felt that continuing the struggle was unrealistic or hoped that their action would bring a swift end to the war so that their property would no longer be exposed to devastation.

The joiners (from the English word "join") went even further than the handsuppers; they served actively on the British side as members of the so-called burgher corps or as guides. Most of them were poverty-stricken *bywoners* (tenant farmers) who were enticed to join up by the prospect of payment and vague British promises of a privileged position after the war. From October 1901, Kitchener incorporated the National Scouts and the Orange River Colony Volunteers officially into the British army. Their leaders were prominent former Boer officers such as General Piet de Wet, brother of General Christiaan de Wet, and General Andries Cronjé, brother of General Piet Cronjé. By the end of the war there were 5464 joiners in British military service.

After the war, the bitter-enders openly rejected the handsuppers and joiners. They were outcasts from Afrikaner society and excluded from political circles and the church. Generals Louis Botha, Jan Smuts and Koos de la Rey made attempts to effect a measure of reconciliation, but these were only partially successful.

Cape and Natal rebels

Afrikaners in Natal and the Cape Colony adopted an attitude of loyal protest. In general, they were loyal to the British crown, but their cultural and political affinity to the Boers of the two republics meant that most of them supported the ideal of republican independence. In contravention of the terms of martial law, many Afrikaners in the British colonies provided the invading Boer commandos with food. The rebels went a step further and joined the Boer force as combatants. Sometimes they were pressurised to do so by the Boer commandos.

The Cape Colony experienced two waves of invasion by the Boer forces. The first was when the war broke out; the second began in December 1900 and also included General Smuts's invasion of September 1901. About 10 000 Cape rebels, mainly from the districts bordering on the republics, joined the Boers in the first wave. With the disintegration of the fronts in March 1900, some of the rebels returned to their homes, while others accompanied the commandos to the republics. Mainly because of a shortage of weapons and a drop in morale, only about 3000 Cape rebels joined the Boers with the second wave of republican invasion. The Cape districts of Murraysburg, Graaff-Reinet, Middelburg and Cradock were the focus of activity because the Kamdebo, Tandjiesberg, Sneeuberg and Zuurberg mountain ranges offered the ideal terrain in which to hide. The commandos under General Wynand Malan, commandants Gideon Scheepers, J.C. Lötter and Willem Fouché, were comprised almost entirely of Cape rebels.

Natal was the only region where the Afrikaners were in the minority compared to English-speaking residents and there were therefore fewer rebels in Natal than the Cape Colony. Furthermore, the Boer forces were only in Natal between October 1899 and June 1900, and this was in northern Natal, where most of the rebels came from.

Eventually, 1012 Cape rebels were sentenced to imprisonment; 360 were banned to Bermuda as convicts with hard labour; and 379 were sentenced to death (of whom 44 were executed and the others reprieved). After the war 10 577 Cape rebels lost the vote for five years. In Natal, 409 rebels were found guilty of high treason but only one was executed. Natal rebels also lost the franchise for a period of five years.

Black people and the war

The Anglo-Boer War was in the first instance a struggle between Boer and Brit, but the conflict also closely involved the black population groups in the country. Black and coloured people participated in the war in a combatant as well as a non-combatant capacity. Black people made up the majority of people within the borders of both the republics. In the Transvaal there were 289 000 whites compared to 755 000 blacks and in the Free State it was 78 000 whites compared to 130 000 blacks.

In the nineteenth century all the black groups were under the political control of white authorities. Britain annexed Basutoland (present-day Lesotho) in 1868; announced a protectorate over Bechuanaland (present-day Botswana) in 1885; incorporated Zululand into Natal in 1897; and the administration of Swaziland was transferred to the Transvaal in 1894. In the Transvaal the black groups were subjugated one by one and large areas were taken over for white settlement. Thereby black population groups lost their economic self-sufficiency. A migrant labour system was introduced which involved white people becoming dependent on black labour; black people, in turn, grew dependent on the white economy and industries.

By far the majority of black people were hoping for a British victory. The black, coloured and Indian elite hoped that Britain would extend the Cape franchise qualifications – in terms of which black people who had certain educational and property ownership qualifications could apply for the vote – to the north. When the war broke out the later well-known Indian leader Mohandas Gandhi initially called upon his fellow Indians to support Britain to show their loyalty to the British crown although he felt that justice was on the side of the Boers. During the war the role of Indians was limited to that of stretcher bearers in the aftermath of battle on the Natal front. Gandhi himself was involved in this capacity after the Battle of Spioenkop.

There was a tacit agreement between the British and Boer leaders that this was a "white man's war" and that black people would not be armed in the conflict – the Boers because they were so heavily outnumbered by the black population groups; and the British because they did not want to arouse resentment among the Cape and Natal white people or pave the way for a social revolution in South Africa. As it turned out neither of the two parties kept to this unspoken agreement.

From the beginning of the war both the British and the Boers used black and coloured people for non-combatant purposes. In the British army they served mostly as wagon drivers or general workers in the camps. However, in the guerrilla phase, black scouting corps under command of white officers provided valuable military assistance to the British army.

In the first year of the war, on instructions from the British government, Lord Roberts gave orders that black people were not to be armed for active service against the Boers. When General Pieter Kritzinger, who was fighting with his Free Staters in the Cape Colony, warned Lord Kitchener in July 1901 that black people in service of the British army would be executed regardless of whether they were armed or not, Kitchener, with the sanction of the British government, decided that the black scout corps should receive firearms for self-protection. This also included those who were on guard in the blockhouses.

The Liberal opposition in the British parliament was highly critical of this policy. After many inquiries from the War Office, Kitchener eventually admitted in March 1902 that there were 10 000 armed black men in the British army. However, this number was inaccurate because it did not include those who had provided their own weapons. Lloyd George's remark in the British parliament that there were as many as 30 000 armed black men in British military service was nearer to the truth.

During their operations in the Cape Colony there was a great deal of tension between the Boer commandos and the local coloured people. In February 1901, a coloured leader from Calvinia, Abraham Esau, who had demonstrated his opposition to the Boers, was tortured to death by a Boer commando under Commandant T.K. Nieuwoudt. A low point in these fraught relations was when General Manie Maritz and his men attacked Barnabas Links and his Basters at the Leliefontein mission station in January 1902, inflicting many deaths and casualties. The attack was in retaliation to the hostile behaviour of the Basters and particularly the antagonism of Links, who refused to take orders from Maritz.

In other respects the black population groups also posed a threat to the Boers. In the guerrilla phase, the Transvaal government basically lost control over the black communities within its borders. Boer families were driven out of large parts of the Western Transvaal by the Tswana; and the Pedi did the same in the Eastern Transvaal. Black people also looted livestock from the Boers and drove the animals to the British army where they fetched good prices. In addition, they co-operated with the British army by preventing the Boer commandos from moving through their territories. This meant that the Boers' mobility, which was already being restricted by Kitchener's drives towards the blockhouse lines, was limited even further.

On the morning of 6 May 1902 near Vryheid, a Zulu community, the Qulusi, killed 56 burghers of the Vryheid commando at Holkrans (Mthashana). This was part of a long history of friction between Boer and Zulu over land and livestock. The Boer delegates who negotiated on peace terms at Vereeniging fully realised what a significant role armed black people played in the war. The threat posed by black groups was an important consideration for the closure of the peace agreement. Other issues included the suffering of the Boer women and children in the concentrations camps; the widespread destruction in the republics; and the unequal struggle against the overwhelming British force.

Notwithstanding the government's official policy, in a few cases black people took up arms on the Boer side. During the siege of Mafeking, for example, General Snyman armed the local Tswana "for security reasons". When President Kruger came to hear of this, the black people were immediately disarmed and sent away.

> **MATHAKGONG AND "GENERAL" WINDVOËL**
> Black people's involvement in the Anglo-Boer War certainly made for extremes. On the one hand there was someone like Mathakgong, a Rolong hero during the siege of Mafeking. He stole a hundred head of cattle from Boer farms around Mafeking and managed to drive them into the town. In so doing he relieved the desperate shortage of food for black and white alike. For the Boer families in the vicinity, Mathakgong was no doubt a frightening figure. In his diary the author and politician Sol Plaatje describes him as "one of the unsung heroes" of the siege of Mafeking.
> Then there was also "General" Windvoël, an *agterryer* (literally, an afterrider, someone riding behind), a servant in the employ of the Du Plessis brothers of the Rustenburg commando. He had his own horse and rifle and was determined to help defend the republics along with the Du Plessis's. On patrol he took it upon himself to take the lead and the burghers allowed him to have his way because he had the sharp eyes of a hawk. When he spotted the British forces he more often than not came up with some ingenious plan. For this reason the burghers nicknamed him "General" Windvoël. During the Battle of Vlakfontein on 29 May 1901, facing great personal danger, he rescued a burgher who was having trouble with an unwilling horse and brought him back to safety.

The Boer forces used black people predominantly in a non-combatant capacity such as digging trenches and driving wagons. Many Boers took their farm workers along with them to serve as *agterryers* while on commando. They took care of the horses (also during the fighting), were water carriers and made the fires for cooking purposes. There was usually a good relationship between a Boer and his *agterryer*, based on a paternalism that was readily accepted by the *agterryer*. There were probably as many as 11 000 of these servants on commando, although the number dropped sharply after the British occupation of Bloemfontein and Pretoria. Only in a very few cases were *agterryers* involved with the Boers in the fighting.

From the second half of 1900, the British army began to put black people into concentration camps. Some of them had sought the protection of the British authorities, but the removal of black communities from the theatre of war was not in the first place for humanitarian reasons. Kitchener wanted to prevent the Boers from receiving food or information from them and he wanted to employ the men as wartime workers. With their pay, these men could then support their families in the camps. Other than in the case of white people, black people were sent to concentration camps until the end of the war. In total there were about 66 black camps, some of which were temporary. They housed approximately 115 000 people.

In mid-1901 the Native Refugee Department took over the control of the black camps from the superintendents of the white camps in an attempt to improve the conditions. A more important reason for the change was that in the camps black workers could be recruited for the British army; they could be used to replace the black mineworkers who in many cases had returned to the gold mines.

The camp inmates had to erect their own dwellings and were permitted to plant crops for their subsistence. Salt and milk was distributed free of charge. Those who worked and could afford it, could buy mealie meal and luxury articles such as sorghum, sugar, coffee, tea, syrup and tobacco.

As in the white concentration camps the death toll in the second half of 1901 took on grim proportions. December 1901 was the worst month when 2831 deaths were recorded. Similar to the white camps, children were by far the main victims, comprising 81% of the deaths. The official statistics are definitely inaccurate, and it is surmised that as many as 18 000 died.

The majority of deaths among black inmates were as a result of chickenpox, measles and dysentery. This can be largely attributed to the dreadful conditions in the overcrowded camps. Huts and tents were placed far too close together and did not provide enough protection from wind and weather. Water was often in short supply or polluted; medical facilities were rudimentary; and there was a lack of fuel to make fires. The quality of food was dreadful and the rations were even smaller than those for the white camps. So much so that most of the inmates were forced to become self-sufficient.

At the beginning of 1902 improvements were made to the black camps, especially regarding the quality of food. This brought the death toll down considerably, but by then it was a case of too little too late.

> **SOL PLAATJE**
>
> This exceptional and accomplished Rolong journalist, politician and author was born in 1876. He grew up as a Christian on the Berlin Missionary Society mission station of Pniel, north-west of Kimberley. Through private study he gained the Cape Civil Service Certificate. He was fluent in eight languages and this stood him in good stead when he was appointed as an interpreter in the Mafeking magistrate's office.
>
> In the Anglo-Boer War, Plaatje was among those trapped in the town during the Boer siege of Mafeking (October 1899–May 1900) where he continued his interpreting work for the British authorities. However, it is his diary which links him so closely to the Anglo-Boer War. It was discovered 70 years after the war and was published for the first time in 1973. The diary entries begin on 29 October 1899 and continue until the end of March 1900. It provides significant insight into the experiences and opinions of an educated black man of the time and also tells of the woes of the ordinary black people as they struggled to survive under siege conditions. This is the only Anglo-Boer War diary written by a black man that has so far been discovered. After the war, Plaatje turned to journalism and published the first Tswana/English weekly newspaper, *Koranta ea Becoana*.
>
> Plaatje was dismayed that the Peace of Vereeniging in 1902 did not make provision for the extension of the qualified franchise applicable in the Cape Colony and Natal to the conquered republics. He was also dissatisfied with the Natives Land Act of 1913 which in effect reduced the status of black people from small-scale farmers to farm labourers. In 1912 he became correspondence secretary of the newly formed South African Native National Congress (after 1923 known as the African National Congress).
>
> In addition to his book *Native Life in South Africa* (1916) and translations into Tswana of various Shakespeare dramas, Plaatje is perhaps best known for his novel *Mhudi* (1930).

In conclusion, the Peace of Vereeniging established British supremacy in South Africa. However, Lord Milner's imperial policy, which was based on the complete anglicisation of the Afrikaner people failed shortly after the war when Sir Henry Campbell-Bannerman's Liberal Party came to power in Britain in 1905. Indeed, Milnerism had the opposite effect – it ignited Afrikaner nationalism. In the economic sphere, however, the British presence provided the foundation for the rise of South African industries in the twentieth century.

The war destroyed the Afrikaners economically and psychologically. It contributed to the poor-white question and speeded up urbanisation. Countless Boers had lost their farms and had no alternative other than to seek work on the gold mines. However, in the course of the twentieth century the Afrikaners would take over political control of South Africa. They were determined to be independent of British influence. This shaped them as race patriots and aroused an aggressive nationalism which motivated them to strive for self-determination and complete control of South Africa. These aspirations, together with their fear of the black majority, can in part explain the implementation of the apartheid policy in the second half of the twentieth century. With the birth of the Republic of South Africa in 1961, Vereeniging was finally avenged.

Black people were also battered and demoralised by the war; they too struggled with abject poverty and many drifted to the towns; black men streamed to the mines to work as unskilled labourers. In addition, the occupation of white-owned land by black communities during the war was not recognised in the terms of the Peace of Vereeniging. Nor was the qualified franchise extended to the north. The Transvaal Colony gained responsible government in 1906 and the Orange River Colony in 1907, but black ambitions on the franchise were frustrated.

This occurred once again with the formation of the Union of South Africa in 1910 and prompted black South Africans to establish the South African Native National Congress in 1912. In 1923 it became known as the African National Congress. The black struggle for liberation was therefore set in motion and it endured throughout the twentieth century until success was achieved with the formation of a democratically elected South African government in 1994. For black people too, Vereeniging was at last avenged.

12
Post-war race relations, 1902–1948
David M. Scher

During the Anglo-Boer War it was tacitly agreed that this particular armed struggle was between two white parties and that black people would not be involved in a military capacity. Apart from a number of important exceptions this agreement was for the most part honoured.

Most black people hoped for a British victory and the burghers of the Boer republics were well aware of this. For example, at the peace discussions at Vereeniging in May 1902, the representatives from various Boer commandos complained of harassment and hostile conduct on the part of black groups during hostilities. Black opposition in the war to the Boer cause strengthened the Afrikaners' conviction that they were potential allies with British imperialism against Afrikanerdom.

This fear was not unfounded. In 1901 Lord Alfred Milner, the British high commissioner in South Africa, received a group of delegates that apparently represented 100 000 coloured people in the Cape Colony. Members of this group were pleased that the two Boer republics were to be absorbed into the British Empire; they were convinced that "only under the British flag and British protection" would they "enjoy justice, equality and freedom".

This faith in the virtues of British imperialism was equalled by the Boers' conviction that in the eyes of the black population they had been defeated in a humiliating manner.

Boer and Brit: a relationship of convenience

In the reconstruction of South Africa after the Anglo-Boer War, black people were most probably the greatest losers. The British felt that reconciliation between the Afrikaners and the English was the most urgent matter at hand. Before the war Milner spoke of Britain's "pledged undertaking" to give black people a fair deal. However, the crux of the South African situation was that both white groups were determined to maintain their dominant position. As for the British authority, it wanted to postpone the question of the black franchise until self-government had been granted to the former Boer republics, since the Cape Colony and Natal had acquired their responsible government in 1872 and 1893 respectively.

Once colonial responsible government was in place (in 1906 in the Transvaal and in 1907 in the Orange River Colony – the former Orange Free State), elections were held. In the Transvaal the political party Het Volk gained the most votes and General Louis Botha became prime minister with General J.C. (Jan) Smuts as colonial secretary. Both supported a policy of reconciliation. This meant that the so-called bitter-enders and handsuppers should reconcile, that there should be conciliation between Afrikaners and English speakers, and that all South Africans should accept the link with the British Empire. It was expected that Afrikaners and English speakers would unite to form a new, larger South African unitary state which would be accorded self-government by the "magnanimous" British conquerors.

In the Orange River Colony the Orangia Unie political party easily won the general election of November 1907. Abraham Fischer became prime minister and General J.B.M. Hertzog was appointed as attorney general and Minister of Education. The Fischer cabinet included both Afrikaners and English speakers. However, Hertzog was undoubtedly the dominant figure in the cabinet and began to formulate his own political philosophy. In contrast to the policy proffered by Botha and Smuts in the Transvaal, Hertzog's emphasis was on a white South African nation comprising two separate components. He wanted Afrikaners and English-speakers to evolve separately; each group should retain its own particular culture and identity.

In the Cape Colony in February 1908, the South African Party under John X. Merriman came to power with the support of J.H. ("Onze Jan") Hofmeyr's Afrikaner Bond. In Natal Frederick R. Moor became prime minister.

At the time, the constitutional union of the four British colonies in South Africa was being widely discussed in white circles. The Selborne Memorandum of 1907, named after Lord Selborne, the British high commissioner in South Africa and Milner's successor, was drawn up by Lionel Curtis and was backed by the British government. The memorandum emphasised the advantages of unification. It would, it was claimed, provide a uniform and manageable solution to the customs and railway problem, clarify the position of black people, and address related labour issues.

Merriman and Smuts had a great deal of correspondence on this matter. Their exchange of letters shows clearly how these two architects of the later Union of South Africa viewed the racial issue in relation to the Afrikaner-English question. Merriman realised that the race policy would be a major question in any future unification. He defended the existing Cape franchise with its limited participation by coloured and black people. Merriman's Cape liberalism was based on the presumption that granting people of colour the franchise would channel the simmering grievances of coloured and black people in an acceptable manner. As William Porter, former attorney general of the Cape Colony, expressed it in the previous century, Merriman preferred to meet a coloured man at the polls rather than to confront him "in a ravine or a cleft with a rifle at his shoulder".

However, Smuts did not believe that such a policy would promote the cause of a united South Africa. He preferred to leave the "untenable burden" of finding a solution to the race question to the greater wisdom of future decision makers. Merriman tried to persuade Smuts to accept a countrywide non-racial voting system to prevent imperial intervention. Merriman did concede that it would possibly be unwise if opposing white political parties tried to garner black votes, but felt it would be far worse if black people became the foster children of the imperial power because this would lead to ongoing imperial intervention in South Africa.

Smuts, however, would not be persuaded. The future constitution of the unitary state, in the interests of unification and reconciliation, made provision for the different colonies to retain their own electoral systems. According to Smuts the question of the black franchise would be best addressed after constitutional union. Public leaders who rose above the crude racist attitudes of ordinary white citizens would then tackle the question in a responsible manner in the best interests of South Africa. At all costs Smuts wanted a union and he admitted that the establishment of the Union of South Africa was more important to him than the matter of black political rights.

A series of meetings were held between October 1908 and May 1909 in Durban, Bloemfontein and Cape Town with delegates from all four colonies. During the National Convention, as these meetings were collectively called, a constitution had to be drawn up for the proposed Union of South Africa and the matter of the Afrikaner-English relationship was discussed. The greatest achievement as far as the Afrikaner delegates were concerned was the recognition of language equality between Dutch and English. However, it was clear that the success of the unification process was fully dependent on decisions about the voting system and the issue of the franchise. The delegates soon realised that differences of opinion and the colonies' divergent legislative measures on black political rights would make the franchise issue highly controversial.

The crisis was averted when it was decided that the existing electoral systems in the different colonies would be retained. It was agreed that no black, coloured, or Asian person could become a member of Parliament in the new unitary state. On the insistence of the Cape delegates it was decided that no changes would be made to the Cape electoral system without a two-thirds majority vote at a joint sitting of both houses of the central Parliament.

The two white language groups, the Afrikaners and the English speakers, did not really differ on racial outlook. As early as 1900 the English journalist and author J.A. Hobson had come to the conclusion that both groups were "strongly opposed to the liberation and upliftment of the 'native'". That English speakers were just as hard-hearted in their stance towards other races was apparent in their attitude to indigenous groups in Natal, where about 85% of the white population was English speaking. The Natalians implemented a segregation policy which was later mirrored in the Union of South Africa. Furthermore, at the National Convention the Natal representatives were against any extension of the black franchise. In the Transvaal, English-speaking leaders of the Labour Party also supported segregation. They demanded that white labour be protected and therefore co-operated comfortably with Botha's Het Volk political party.

The reality of consensus among the white population on the matter of black people's political rights and the racial question in general is underlined in the overwhelming evidence gleaned by various commissions, including the South African Intercolonial Native Affairs Commission (or as it is better known, the Lagden Commission). Naturally there was not full consensus, but white people certainly agreed that they should retain political power in South Africa. Although the so-called "native problem" had already come up for discussion prior to the formation of the Union, it was generally felt that the interests of black people should be handled on a national basis.

In the light of this conviction, the Lagden Commission of 1903 to 1905 undertook a comprehensive investigation of the matter. The commission was the brainchild of Lord Milner and most of its members were English speaking. It submitted an in-depth report on how the former Boer republics could be re-built and also addressed the provision of black labour for the mines. Wide-ranging recommendations were made on the division of land according to white and black territories; these were later embodied in the Natives Land Act of 1913. In many ways the Lagden Commission's report became the blueprint for the course taken by the segregation policy in South Africa.

One of the commission's departure points was that the black vote should not be permitted to upset the balance between the two white population groups in South Africa. The commission warned that political parties could easily misuse the voting power of black people in the Cape Colony and cause a fierce election tussle between white voters. Black people's votes would then become the determining factor in differences of opinion between white political parties. According to the commission the number of black voters might before long exceed the white voters in some parts of the country and this would "create an untenable situation which would be unwise and even dangerous".

THE BAMBATHA REBELLION

A few years after the close of the Anglo-Boer War, white supremacy in southern Africa was shaken by the so-called Bambatha rebellion. Possibly influenced by other colonial insurrections, notably by the Herero in German South West Africa (now Namibia) in 1904–1905, smouldering black discontent in Natal flared up to become a full-scale rebellion.

The roots of the rebellion lay in the imposition by the Natal colonial authorities of a highly unpopular poll tax on the black population payable from 1 January 1906. By the end of the month, opposition to the measures reached breaking point. On 10 February two white policemen were killed in the Richmond district in a clash which followed the refusal of followers of a minor chef, Mveli, to pay the tax. Convinced that insolent "agitators" from the growing separatist Ethiopian church were behind the deaths, an angry white community called for revenge. Faced with growing settler hysteria, the governor declared martial law. The Natal militia, supported by volunteers from

> other parts of South Africa, destroyed crops and kraals, and deposed recalcitrant chiefs. Twelve of the participants in the Richmond fracas were court-martialled and shot.
> Matters came to a peak when, in April 1906, Bambatha, the Zondo chief, supported by other chiefs, created a Zulu military force which engaged in guerrilla activities. On 10 June 1906 Colonel Duncan McKenzie, leading a colonial force, heavily defeated the rebels. Bambatha was killed and his head cut off (supposedly for identification purposes). Despite denying involvement in the rebellion, Dinuzulu, the son of Cetshwayo, the last Zulu king, was arrested and tried for high treason and other charges. Released from imprisonment in 1910, he was later exiled to the Transvaal.
> The impact of the rebellion was significant. More than 3000 black people and 30 white people died in what was essentially a traditional peasant revolt against the colonial authority. Although the newly formed black political movements were not involved in the rebellion, the events heightened political consciousness and unity among black people who now turned to other means of resistance.
> The Bambatha rebellion was the last major armed rebellion by black people against white supremacy until the 1960s. Henceforth, the struggle for black rights would be fought primarily in the political, economic and legal fields.

The formation of the Union of South Africa

The final sitting of the National Convention took place in Bloemfontein between 3 and 11 May 1909. The draft constitution for a unitary state, or union, was approved the following month by the parliaments of the Cape Colony, Transvaal and Orange River Colony. In Natal the draft constitution was accepted by means of a referendum.

On 20 September 1909 the British parliament passed the South Africa Act which then led to the official establishment of the Union of South Africa on 31 May 1910. The aspirations of black people were simply sidelined. Although the overwhelming majority of white people supported the South Africa Act, many politically aware black, coloured and Indian people registered their opposition to certain aspects of the draft constitution as embodied in the South Africa Act.

In *Vukani Bantu! The beginnings of black protest politics in South Africa to 1912* (1984) André Odendaal writes of how, in the aftermath of the Anglo-Boer War, black people fostered certain expectations because of promises made to them by the British authority. Nothing came of these expectations. Their disappointment led to greater political awareness among black people in all four colonies. They began to react with ever increasing urgency to the white groups' growing support for segregation; newspapers made their appearance at this time and black organisations were formed.

However, the approach of black leaders remained moderate and they still showed their loyalty to the British crown, adopting a careful and moderate strategy in the fond hope of gradual constitutional change. Although more recent black leaders have interpreted these early attempts as extremely conservative, timid and naïve, at the time many of the black leaders in the Cape Colony had the vote. According to Odendaal, it was perhaps to be expected that they would first try to explore conventional channels to air their grievances before adopting a more confrontational attitude.

There were eventually a multitude of objections from black, coloured and Indian ranks about the stipulations of the draft bill compiled at the National Convention. On 24 March 1909 black delegates from all four colonies were invited to attend a South African Native Convention at Waaihoek, a township outside Bloemfontein. The Cape Coloured Association and the African Political (later People's) Association also held a protest meeting in Cape Town's town hall on 5 March. The black and coloured groups' respective congresses decided to appeal to the British government to make amendments to the draft bill.

William Schreiner, a prominent liberal and former premier of the Cape Colony, led the delegation of black and coloured leaders that went to London. Mohandas (Mahatma) Gandhi, later a revered Indian statesman, also went to London to appeal on behalf of the Indian people in South Africa. A number of white politicians were highly critical of the Schreiner delegation. According to Merriman, Schreiner's message was one of the most unfriendly gestures as far as the black people of South Africa were concerned. General Louis Botha, who shortly afterwards became the first prime minister of the Union of South Africa, insisted that the issue of political rights for black, coloured and Indian people would be addressed within the country and not by Britain. He believed that in the past most South Africans had shown a sense of justice and reasonableness towards black people. According to him, South Africans could similarly be relied upon to deal equally with this matter in the future.

Although some British members of Parliament criticised the ethnic restrictions in the draft bill, and the British premier, Herbert H. Asquith, requested that white South African politicians should change the restrictive franchise qualifications, the Westminster Parliament made no amendments to the draft bill on the proposed union. The system of exclusive political power for white people was duly confirmed with the establishment of the Union of South Africa in 1910. This situation remained in place until 1984 when the constitution was amended to give coloured and Indian people parliamentary representation in separate chambers of Parliament. In the aftermath of Union many changes were made to the constitution; these eventually dispossessed black and coloured people in the Cape Province and Natal of the vote and ended their representation in the central Parliament.

According to Leonard Thompson, historian and scholar of the unification process in South Africa, the removal of direct imperial control over South Africa was regarded as justified because it was expected that this would heal the breach between Afrikaners and English speakers. It was hoped that white people would act with increasing goodwill towards black, coloured and Indian people and that the Union would become a liberal democracy in the British tradition. However, this was not to be. On this Thompson writes: "Consequently, besides being a striking example of the operation of political forces in a multiracial society, the story of the unification of South Africa provides a salutary reminder of the limitations of human foresight."

More comprehensive independence for the Union

Until the 1920s the constitutional status of the Union of South Africa and its relationship with Great Britain was uppermost in the minds of white politicians. Botha and Smuts envisaged that the Union would become a member of the Commonwealth of Nations (a name which Smuts used for the first time in 1917). However, for Hertzog and followers of the National Party (NP), the republican past and the independent diplomacy of the old Boer republics were still fresh in the memory; their goal was a republic.

Smuts's philosophy of holism led him to believe that South Africa should not only be sovereign and independent, but also part of a wider international community, the British Commonwealth of Nations (later the British Commonwealth). In 1921 and again in 1923, Smuts, by now prime minister, attended the Imperial Conferences in London. These conferences were held to clarify the constitutional relationship between Britain and the Dominions because there was confusion over the juridical status of the Dominions and their constitutional position as self-governing states. In practice the Dominions had a great deal of equality with Britain but the question was whether their position was legally entrenched. According to Smuts, although they were accorded a great deal of freedom, the Dominions were still "subject provinces" of Britain.

In 1924 the Pact government comprising the NP and the Labour Party, with Hertzog as prime minister, came to power. Prior to the election Hertzog concluded an agreement with F.H.P. (Fred) Creswell of the Labour Party in terms of which he undertook not to change the constitutional relationship between the Union and the British crown. However, this did not deter Hertzog from trying to clear up the uncertainty about the legal and constitutional status between the Dominions and Britain. Hertzog wanted the Union's position to be set down in clear legal terms, including whether or not the Union, if it so wished, had the right of secession from the Commonwealth.

Hertzog attended the Imperial Conference of 1926 in London and with great perseverance paved the way for the acceptance of the Balfour Declaration. Lord Alfred Balfour, chairperson of the sitting, acceded to Hertzog's request and issued an official declaration on the status of the Dominions:

> [The dominions] are autonomous Communities within the British Empire, equal in status, in no way subordinate to one another in any aspect of their domestic or external affairs, though united by a common allegiance to the Crown, and freely associated as members of the British Commonwealth of Nations.

The Balfour Declaration and the Imperial Conference of 1926 were regarded as a significant diplomatic achievement. Britain, which has no written constitution, was initially reluctant to commit the relationship between Britain and the Dominions to writing. However, Hertzog who was supported in his drive by his Irish and Canadian counterparts, refused to back down and insisted upon a written declaration. On his return home, Hertzog enthusiastically claimed that the Balfour Declaration had brought the centuries-old struggle for national freedom for South Africa to a happy conclusion. However, future events were to show that this was not necessarily so simple.

Few other questions on the country's sovereignty seemed to divide people as much as the decision on a national flag. In 1926 the Minister of Internal Affairs, Dr D.F. Malan, tabled a draft bill which made provision for a South African flag. A bitter dispute flared up immediately on what the flag should look like. Those who supported imperialism were determined to retain the Union Jack. The pro-imperial group in Natal even threatened that the province would withdraw from the Union of South Africa if the Union Jack was rejected. On the other side of the political spectrum, were the fiery republican-oriented members of the NP. Malan supported the idea of a "clean flag", that is an entirely new flag with no British symbols at all. Neither of the groups was prepared to accept a compromise.

The flag controversy also threatened to divide the Pact government. Under pressure from Creswell, leader of the Labour Party, and Tielman Roos, leader of the NP in the Transvaal, Hertzog agreed to delay the designing of a new flag.

Smuts, as leader of the opposition, suggested that the future flag of the Union should comprise a combination of the Union Jack, the Transvaal Vierkleur, and the Free State republican flag. This concept was seen as so exorbitant that even some members of Smuts's own party refused to support it. Nevertheless, the senate, in which Smuts's South African Party (SAP) had the majority of support, approved the suggestion. At the request of Roos the governor general took the unusual step of asking Hertzog and Smuts to agree to a compromise. After a crisis in the Cabinet, during which Malan threatened to resign, a compromise was at last reached.

The eventual solution was that the Union had two official flags. On the national flag the Union Jack and the flags of the two former republics were incorporated together in the centre against the background of three horizontal bands of orange, white and blue. The Union Jack was the second official flag and fluttered alongside the national flag. These flags were flown at prescribed places such as outside Parliament and on other state buildings. The new national flag was officially brought into use on 31 May 1928. The use of two flags was in force until 1957, after which the Union Jack was no longer flown; South Africa then had only one official flag as is the international norm.

While the flag controversy was still raging, efforts were made to clarify the legal inconsistencies in the Balfour Declaration. Although the Dominions' equal status with Britain had been legally acknowledged, they still could not pass laws that were in conflict with a British law, nor could the Dominions develop their own independent foreign policy. Furthermore, the Dominions were still legally subordinate to the British Privy Council, and the governors general in the Dominions – who represented the King, but were advised by the British government – could theoretically still reject parliamentary legislation if they so chose.

These legal inconsistencies could only be removed by an Act of the British parliament. This was eventually achieved. In 1930 the official status of the governor general as representative of the British King in South Africa, was removed. Thereafter he only represented the King, no longer the British government. From then onwards the British government was only represented in Pretoria by a high commissioner who had exactly the same status as the South African high commissioner in South Africa House on Trafalgar Square in London. The governor general was also thereafter appointed on the exclusive advice of the Union's ministers. This took place for the first time in 1937 when Patrick Duncan was appointed as governor general.

The Union Parliament passed the new Union Citizenship Act, which gave South Africans their own nationality in addition to their status as British subjects. After another Imperial Conference in 1930, the British government, on the insistence of the Dominions, gave legislative authority to the Balfour Declaration by passing the Statute of Westminster (1931). With this statute, the source of South Africa's sovereignty was transferred from the Westminster Parliament in London to the Union Parliament in Cape Town. The political and constitutional status of the Dominions was thereby at last clarified, largely thanks to the efforts of Smuts and particularly Hertzog.

Segregation in the statute book

In the two decades after Union, there was overwhelming consensus among white political parties on the race question and there was growing support for restrictive legislation in this regard. As early as 1910 Louis Botha, premier at the time, called for racial issues to be given priority over party politics. Both the Unionists and the Labour Party were in favour of segregation and it was also supported by the National Party, which was formed in 1914. A far as the so-called Indian question was concerned, white political parties also agreed on the principle of limited Indian immigration, the active promotion of Indian repatriation and the maintenance of separate residential areas.

The consensus among white parties and the white voters in general is clear from the manner in which discriminatory legislation was received in Parliament. In 1911 the Native Labour Regulation Act and the Mines and Works Act were passed in Parliament virtually without any opposition. Furthermore, in 1913 the Natives Land Act, which was tabled by Jacobus W. Sauer, a prominent Cape liberal politician and Minister of Native Affairs, was duly passed. In the parliamentary debate on its terms, Sauer praised the new Act saying that 99% of the members of Parliament and even the "friends of the natives" had readily accepted the basic principles of the new law.

The Natives Land Act (No. 27 of 1913) in fact laid the foundation for the later homelands policy. In terms of this legislation, existing reserves, mission reserves (in Natal), traditional tribal lands, and some farms that were in private or tribal possession, were identified for black people's exclusive possession. However, black people were not allowed to buy land outside these demarcated areas unless specific permission to do so was granted by the governor general. An important clause in this Act was that there was to be no intervention in black people's right to qualify for the franchise. (This was with reference to the common voters' roll in the Cape Province.) Furthermore, the governor general could grant additional land to black people if the need arose; in the years that followed this became a fairly common practice.

The Natives Land Act (1913) did not apply to black people in the cities and therefore the Urban Areas Act of 1923 was passed. This Act was preceded in 1922 by the Transvaal Commission for Local Government (the Stallard Commission). From the outset this commission took the view that white people had the exclusive right of residence in urban areas and that black people were merely there to "meet the needs" of the whites. This stance was embodied in the Group Areas Act (1923) which laid the foundation for residential segregation and bolstered the idea that black people did not have the right to live permanently in the towns.

The Natives Land Act and the Urban Areas Act therefore became the pillars of the segregation policy. These laws were then supplemented by the Industrial Conciliation Act of 1924 which excluded black people from membership of recognised trade unions. The entire legislative process was duly passed by Parliament without any significant objections by any of the parties.

Prior to the general election of 1929 the racial question had not really played a major role in the election campaign, but this did not mean that the issue would not rear its head at a later stage. During the First World War, NP supporters objected to the fact that black people were sent to Europe to provide backup military service and other wartime services. According to them, it was wrong to involve black people in a war between white combatants – this would disturb the natural order of race relations in South Africa. Louis Botha tried to calm these fears by assuring members of Parliament that the black people overseas would be accommodated in compounds and would therefore by no means be exposed to any unwarranted influences.

The coloured vote

The South Africa Act of 1909 effectively removed all hope the coloured people had of gaining political power. In 1910 only 2,5% of the total coloured population had the franchise (compared to 21% of the white population who had the vote) and in addition, coloureds could not be elected to Parliament.

In reaction to this, Dr Abdullah Abdurahman, president of the mainly coloured African People's Organisation (APO), worked towards political unity between coloured and black people. Although coloured leaders such as Abdurahman and prominent black leaders of the time like the writer John Tengu Jabavu, founder of the newspaper *Imvo Zabantsundu*, both protested against oppression, the political ties between their respective followers were far from strong. Geographic isolation, differences in language and race, divergent customs, economic differences, and unequal status prevented them from joining forces in a single political organisation.

The APO's management, which was comprised largely of intellectuals and small businessmen, avoided any form of mass action, preferring to send petitions and delegations to the government or to launch election campaigns to air their grievances. The Union government often received the APO representatives positively, in marked contrast to the reception accorded the leaders of the African National Congress (ANC) which had been formed in 1912 as the South African Native National Congress.

Although the number of coloured and black people who had the vote was limited, they were a significant factor in various constituencies in the Cape. In 1909 they formed about 14,8% of the voters in the Cape and by 1929 this had grown to almost 20%. If the coloured voters had chosen to cast their votes as a block, they could have played a telling role in a struggle between white political parties. In the 1920s coloured voters were the decisive factor in about eight to twelve constituencies in the Cape Province.

In the early years of the Union most of the coloured and black voters supported the pro-imperialist Unionist Party. When this party was absorbed into the South African Party (SAP), many of the coloured voters also supported the SAP. In the general election of 1924 the ANC vacillated between open support for the SAP and boycotting the election. Clements Kadalie's Industrial and Commercial Union (ICU) came to the fore as supporters of the Pact parties. Although in 1924 the Cape Native Voters' Association still supported the SAP, by 1929 it was not officially affiliated to any political party. Instead it encouraged its voters to vote for candidates who were in favour of retaining the qualified vote for black people in the Cape Province.

To its later embarrassment, the NP also tried to recruit black voters (Hertzog even made a donation to Kadalie's ICU). However, in the 1920s Hertzog concentrated on gaining the support of coloured voters. The NP's policy towards black people and Indians was outlined in its Programme of Principles issued in 1914 and 1921 respectively, but it had no specific policy as far as the coloureds were concerned. Hertzog's first public statement on coloureds in his capacity as NP leader was issued in 1918 and declared that coloureds should have the same political and economic rights as white people. He reiterated this opinion at the congress of the Free State branch of the NP in 1919, adding (translated): "They don't see themselves as blacks. They were born and bred in the midst of white society and especially that of Dutch-speaking Afrikaners, and they feel that the interests of the Dutch-speaking Afrikaners are also their interests."

Some coloured voters did indeed support the NP. After the general election of 1924 a group of coloured supporters carried W. Bruckner de Villiers of the NP into Parliament as representative of the Stellenbosch constituency. Although there was relatively little support for the NP in coloured ranks, Hertzog continued his efforts to canvass for their votes. After the Pact government came to power in 1924, he tried to extend limited political rights for coloureds to the northern provinces. His most significant statements on coloured rights are summarised in a speech he made in 1925 in his own constituency of Smithfield:

> It should not be lost sight of that in the case of the Cape Coloured we are dealing with a class of our population that in many ways is close to the European; and in almost every aspect except colour, basically differs from the native... Economically, industrially and politically, he should be integrated with us. Socially it is his desire, just as it is ours, that he will keep to himself and not seek any association with the whites... As far as the vote is concerned, in the Cape he stands on the same footing as the European and he has thus already been accepted alongside the white man.

The phrase "he should be integrated with us" was ambiguous. It was unclear exactly what Hertzog meant. Should coloureds be placed on equal footing with white people in every aspect? Or should they, as in the Cape Province, take up a position somewhere between white and black people? And if they were in all other aspects equal to white people, why then should they be segregated socially?

Hertzog was not a very proficient public speaker and his utterances were often ambiguous and open to different interpretations. He did indeed try on two occasions, in 1926 and again in 1929, to extend the franchise to coloureds resident in the other provinces who met certain educational and economic requirements. They would then theoretically have had the opportunity to elect one white representative to Parliament (the lower house). Hertzog's motivation was perhaps to drive a wedge between coloured and black people to prevent the existence of a united non-European (black, coloured and Indian) opposition. He also wanted to gain support for the NP from coloured voters in the Cape. In any case, his suggestions on the extension of the coloured vote were not received favourably in the northern provinces and there was even talk of dissatisfaction among some Cape NP members about the coloured vote in the province. Hertzog wanted to avoid a possible clash in NP ranks and let the matter drop.

Although Hertzog was prepared to consider giving the vote to "civilised" coloured women in 1928, he received little support for the idea.

Some members of the NP insisted that the franchise rather be given to white women in order to mitigate the significance of the coloured vote. This in fact happened in 1930 when members of Parliament voted by an overwhelming majority in favour of the franchise for white women.

The coloured and black vote in the firing line

After 1929 the NP's policy on coloured people changed. Why did this happen?

During its first term in office (1924–1929) the NP's policy on coloureds rested mainly on three principles. Firstly, coloureds had to be separated from black people; secondly, they should not be politically and economically segregated; and thirdly, coloureds' economic and political status should be raised to the same level as that of white people. Many NP supporters believed that coloureds could be persuaded to cut their ties with English speakers and the South African Party (SAP) and to vote for the NP.

The NP was in any case prepared to give this possibility a fighting chance and there were valid reasons why the party felt it might succeed. For example, the NP had worked closely with its coloured counterpart organisation the Afrikaanse Nasionale Bond (ANB) which had attracted a significant number of prominent coloureds. However, the general election of 1929 did not bring the expected swing of coloured voters away from Smuts's SAP to the NP. The NP underestimated the influence of Abdurahman and the APO; nor did it give enough consideration to the coloureds' loyalty to the British Empire and symbols such as the Union Jack. Abdurahman placed great emphasis on loyalty to the British, pointing out that it was they who had ended slavery. He accused the NP of disloyalty to the Union Jack.

It is important to keep in mind that it was only in 1929 that the NP gained an absolute majority of seats in Parliament. In previous years the party had to cast about to gain as much support as possible from any group of voters to consolidate its position in Parliament. After the franchise was extended to white women in 1930, the proportion of coloured voters in the Cape Province dropped appreciably. This prompted some members of the NP to agitate for the removal of coloured men from the common voters' roll. In 1932 at the NP's Cape provincial congress it was proposed that coloured voters should be removed from the common voters' roll and that a system of separate representation in Parliament (by white representatives) be created for them. However, Hertzog would not accept this proposal before there was an opportunity "to ask the people" how they felt about this in the next election, which was due in 1934. However, this election and the opportunity to "ask the people" did not eventuate because of the changes that took place in the South African political scene in the next two years.

Early in 1933 Hertzog and Smuts decided to form a coalition. They ruled together until December 1934, when the NP and the SAP fused to form the United Party (UP). Hertzog continued as prime minister and Smuts became his deputy. In reaction to this fusion, the more radical NP members under D.F. Malan's leadership broke away to form the new Gesuiwerde (Purified) National Party. This disruption and repositioning of the main political parties pushed the question of disenfranchising coloureds into the background until the 1950s, when Malan's NP was in undisputed power and the matter could easily be pushed through.

The fusion provided Hertzog with a fresh opportunity to attempt to solve the so-called "native question" by taking black people off the common voters' roll in the Cape Province and giving them white representatives in the parliamentary lower house and in the senate. Hertzog believed that this would remove the issue of race from party politics and promote harmony between Afrikaners and English speakers.

To remove black people from the common voters' roll Hertzog needed a two-thirds majority vote in a joint sitting of both houses of Parliament. It was mainly the SAP which supported the black franchise, but at the beginning of the 1930s even Smuts admitted that the franchise for black people in the Cape Province was a lost cause. Growing differences of opinion over this issue led to tension within the SAP; the overwhelming majority of Natal and Transvaal members were in favour of removing black voters from the common voters' roll. Hertzog was aware of the dissension in the ranks of the SAP and used it to his own advantage.

After the fusion of the NP and the SAP, Hertzog softened his previous hardline stance on British imperial links, compulsory bilingualism in the civil service, and the status of provinces. By doing so he hoped to win over the English-speaking Natal SAP hotheads and they would eventually help him to implement his race policy.

In 1936 Hertzog achieved this when the Native Representation Act was passed. In terms of this Act the 10 628 registered black voters in the Cape Province were placed on a separate voters' roll and they could elect three white representatives to Parliament. All enfranchised black South Africans could also elect four white senators by means of an electoral college. This Act also made provision for a Native Representative Council which would serve as an advisory body. The Native Trust and Land Act was passed at the same time. This made provision for a trust fund which could purchase an additional 7,2 million morgen of land to add to the existing black reserves. This meant that the reserves now comprised 13,7% of the total surface area of the country.

Although the years 1934–1939 are sometimes described as the highpoint of co-operation between Afrikaners and English speakers, there were still differences between the two language groups. The ruling United Party under Hertzog included a series of divergent and often opposing groups, from liberalists like Jan Hendrik (Kleinjan) Hofmeyr to those like Oswald Pirow who supported segregation. This made the UP extremely vulnerable to attacks by its opponents, such as the Purified NP, which began to play the different factions in the UP off against one another.

The two most important matters which the Purified NP focused upon were the race question and the Union's relationship with Britain. At an NP congress in Bloemfontein in 1938, Malan spoke out against those who were only concerned about imperial interests and maintaining ties with Britain. He went on to say:

> It is those interests that from the outset gave the native and coloured the vote on an equal basis with the white man. Not on merit or on principle – because nowhere else in the British Empire is this the case – but here [it has been done] for the specific reason of using it as a counterweight against the emerging nationhood of the Boer people.

Matters of racial differences were at the crux of the Purified NP's attacks on the government. The general election of 1938 was for example notable for the use by the NP of the so-called "Baster Plakkaat" (Bastard Poster) which depicted the alleged evils of mixed marriages. It showed a racially mixed family (a black man and white woman) with two coloured children playing in the dust outside the ghetto-like family home. With this illustrated pre-election poster the NP wanted to emphasise the UP's lack of responsibility in failing to implement stricter laws against mixed marriages. The NP's anti-black and anti-Semitic propaganda after the rise of Adolf Hitler in 1933 in Germany struck a chord with some Afrikaners in South Africa who sympathised with the nationalist-socialist doctrines of Nazi Germany.

As leader of the opposition, Malan submitted a petition to Parliament in 1939 that was signed by 230 619 people; it appears that it was also signed by many UP supporters. Firstly, the petition called for the introduction of separate residential areas according to race. Secondly, all mixed marriages had to be legally banned. Thirdly, the petition demanded that sexual relations between white and black persons, or as it was put, "admixture of blood", should become a punishable offence. Finally, the signatories wanted the implementation of political and economic segregation between white and coloured people.

Hertzog refused to comply with any of these demands. He also steadfastly maintained that the coloured people's franchise rights should not be tampered with.

The outbreak of the Second World War in 1939 led to renewed polarisation between Afrikaners and English speakers and also caused bitterness and tension in Afrikaner ranks over the issue of nationalism. Smuts was appointed as prime minister in that same year.

To the great dissatisfaction of the NP the Smuts government not only entered the war alongside Britain but also recruited coloured and black people to serve in an assistant capacity. Black volunteers were not provided with firearms, but were used as semi-military helpers on the war front. From opposition ranks, Frans Erasmus remarked that many of the coloured soldiers had previously been "skollies" and that they now formed part of the government's "voters' factory". The NP was also dissatisfied about the legislation on active military service which was tabled in Parliament in 1941. It laid down that absent voters who were involved in military service could also cast their votes.

In the war years and thereafter, the Smuts government realised that major changes would have to be made to the race policy. However, little was done in this regard and the structure of South African society remained essentially the same. Although Smuts said that segregation "had fallen on evil days", for the most part his government merely made minor policy shifts; greater structural transformation that might diminish white power was not considered.

Although in 1937 the Wilcocks Commission, a commission of inquiry into the socio-economic position of the coloured people in the Union, recommended that the Cape electoral system should be extended to include the other provinces, neither Hertzog nor Smuts introduced legislation in this regard. But the Smuts government realised that the coloured community needed a better channel to air their opinions and grievances and as a result the Coloured Advisory Council was established in 1943. The main aim of the council was to advise the government on coloureds' economic, political and social interests. As far as possible, the council also had to assist the Smuts government to implement the recommendations of the Wilcocks Commission.

However, the Coloured Advisory Council led to great political division among coloureds. Opponents of the council insisted that it represented little else than yet another division on racial grounds in a constitutional framework. According to them it created a precedent that supporters of segregation could use to exercise further pressure, for example, that coloured voters be removed from the common voters' roll and that separate residential areas be created for white and coloured people. These fears became reality in the decades that followed.

In this period coloured politics took on a far more resolute, but also a more frustrated character. The well-known educationist Prof. Richard van der Ross wrote in his memoirs:

> For at least the next twenty years politics became the politics of protest. Indeed, they [the coloureds] did little else other than protest – they did not resort to action. There was also division in coloured ranks – there were those who wanted to take overt action, while others held back. The moderate groups also organised themselves and searched for a constructive approach.

The strong racial consciousness of the 1940s cannot be overemphasised. The NP's demands for increased segregation and the pressure for the removal of coloured voters from the common voters' roll, caused growing tension. When the UP won a by-election in the constituency of Cape Town Castle, the NP's official publication, *Die Kruithoring*, described the result as a "triumph" for coloureds. The NP was particularly critical of the UP's alleged neglect of racial and colour differences.

The fierce dispute between the NP (at the time the opposition) and the UP (the government) over racial issues is evident in the following parliamentary debate of January 1947. From the opposition benches T.E.

Dönges interrupted the UP member for Soutpansberg, S.A. Cilliers, by asking him if he would put up with it if coloured people came to sit beside him on the train. Cilliers's honest reply was that he did not want to travel with coloured people. He added that they should be kept in their place but that the reason for this should be clearly explained to them.

In the same debate E.R. Strauss, opposition member for Harrismith, asked Cilliers whether he and his wife would be prepared to ride in a bus with coloured people and the "dirtiest" of black people. In response Cilliers retorted that Strauss allowed black people to bake his bread for him. Strauss replied that he would only allow this if the baker was clean; if he could possibly prevent it he would certainly not allow the baker in his bed or in his car.

In his reply, Cilliers pointed out certain contradictions in Strauss's argument: How could someone bake his bread and yet not be allowed to ride with him in a bus? Strauss in turn reiterated the basic contradiction in the governing circle's reasoning. When a member of the government discussed segregation, they were not against the house-help boiling the kettle in the kitchen, but on the other hand they did not want white people during the day or in the night, to have to ride in the same train carriage as people of colour.

In the light of the NP's relentless standpoint on race and the UP's ambiguous reaction, it is understandable that many coloured and black people expected the worst when the political alliance of the NP, under the leadership of D.F. Malan, and the Afrikaner Party, under N.C. (Klasie) Havenga, won the general election on 26 May 1948.

Historians differ over the degree to which the politics of race played a role in the NP victory. I am inclined to agree with Bernard Friedman who writes in his book *Smuts: A reappraisal* (1975) that Malan decided upon a strategy that would ensure that the racial issue took centre stage in the run-up to the election. The NP relegated the question of republicanism to the background and replaced it with a strategy of "black peril". Indeed, in an important speech on 20 April 1948 in Paarl, Malan earnestly asked the voters whether, in the future, the European race would and could retain its racial purity, or whether it would continue to drift along until it disappeared into the black sea of the non-European population.

13
Afrikaner nationalism, 1902–1948
Hermann Giliomee

Afrikaner nationalism had its origins in the Anglo-Boer War and the great bitterness that it caused in the hearts and minds of Afrikaners throughout the country. These feelings flared up again after the outbreak of the First World War when South Africa aligned itself with Britain and declared war against Germany. Secondly, Afrikaner nationalism was fostered by the economic system which was completely dominated by English speakers other than in the agricultural sector. The average income per head of English speakers was almost twice that of Afrikaners. Afrikaner nationalists argued that only by standing together could this gap be bridged. Thirdly, the secondary position which Afrikaans had to overcome when compared to English, encouraged nationalists to develop the Afrikaans language at various levels and to accept it as the symbol of their identity. Lastly, Afrikaner nationalists wanted South Africa to be as independent as possible of Britain. South Africa's participation in both the First and Second World Wars caused great division in the ranks of the National Party, the political party which most Afrikaners supported.

The aftermath of the war

In the Anglo-Boer War (1899–1902) Britain crushed the republics militarily but in the longer term the war stimulated Afrikaner nationalism. Afrikaners throughout the country were deeply shocked by the British military tactics, particularly the scorched-earth policy, the death of 26 000 Boer women and children in the concentration camps and the execution of a number of Cape rebels.

They admired the *bittereinders* (bitter-enders, Boer die-hards) who had prolonged the struggle for two years under exceptionally difficult circumstances after Bloemfontein and Pretoria had been occupied. In his *Memoirs of the Boer War* General Jan Smuts praised their contribution to the struggle, saying it meant that for generations to come, "every child to be born in South Africa was to have a prouder self-respect and a more erect carriage before the nations of the world". Afrikaner nationalists would later describe the bitter-enders as the first freedom fighters of the twentieth century.

The plans laid by Lord Milner, the British high commissioner in South Africa, to re-build the defeated republics were also highly controversial. He afforded English the status as the only official language. Schools had to use English as the only medium of instruction and the history of the British Empire and the wider world was taught to the children. His policy inspired the nationalists to such an extent that by 1905 Milner himself wrote that ministers of the church, doctors, attorneys, law agents and journalists were all spreading the "message of Afrikanerdom" in the conquered republics.

However, nationalism can only really flourish when organisations are established that extend beyond district and provincial borders. The Afrikaanse Christelike Vrouevereniging (ACVV) (Association of Afrikaans Christian Women) which was formed in Cape Town in 1904 is the country's oldest welfare organisation. Their work originally focused on impoverished Afrikaans families. In the same year the first branch of the Suid-Afrikaanse Vrouefederasie (Federation of South African Women), which had the same aims as the ACVV, was formed in Pretoria. The following year the Suid-Afrikaanse Onderwysunie (South African Teachers' Union) came into being with the objective of uniting Afrikaans-speaking teachers into a single organisation. The Het Volk Party was established in the Transvaal and the Orangia Unie in the Orange River Colony (Free State).

In reaction to Milner's education policy, and with financial contributions from the Netherlands, the defeated Boer leaders set up private schools for Christelik-Nasionale Onderwys (CNO) (Christian National Education) in the Free State and the Transvaal. These schools advocated a combination of the nationalistic and Christian message. By 1903 there were already 228 such schools in the Transvaal with more than 9000 pupils. In the Orange River Colony the number was slightly lower.

Initially, Generals Louis Botha and Jan Smuts, the most important

Boer leaders in the Transvaal, supported the CNO schools, but they later abandoned the idea after the British government decided in 1906 to introduce self-government in the former republics. With Afrikaners making up only about half of the voters in the Transvaal, Botha and Smuts called for reconciliation between the two white communities. They merely wanted symbolic equality between Dutch and English. In practice, they envisaged that English would eventually become the main language, and later the only official language.

Botha and Smuts's other great priority was to promote economic growth to provide employment for the large number of unemployed Afrikaners. To ensure economic development it was necessary for British investors to see South Africa as having lucrative investment possibilities. A strong nationalistic movement would frighten off investors.

In the Transvaal, the heart of resistance against the phasing out of the CNO schools was based at the theological college of the Gereformeerde Kerk (Reformed Church) in Potchefstroom. At the time the college was the only institution for higher education in the country which still used Dutch as the medium of tuition. Because of financial straits the members of the Reformed Church, or the "Doppers" as they were also called, were compelled to scrap the idea of the CNO schools. However, they continued to convey the message that the power of the Afrikaners lay in the necessity of organising themselves into a separate community.

Whereas Smuts, as Minister of Education in the Transvaal, only made provision for mother-tongue education until the fifth school year, General J.B.M. Hertzog, who was Minister of Education in the Orange River Colony, laid down that Dutch and English would both be used in the classrooms right up until the highest standard. Three subjects had to be taken in the medium of Dutch, and three in English. For Hertzog, language equality and mother-tongue education were both sound principles.

THE LION AND THE LAMB

In response to the plea that Afrikaans and English, in the interests of "reconciliation", be used together in the same school, the Afrikaans author, C.J. Langenhoven, wrote this satirical letter (translated here) to his English counterparts: "Friends, let us make peace and maintain peace. Let the leo and the lamb graze together: the lamb on the grass and the leo on the lamb. All of you can be the leo and I will be the lamb. Then I too will become part of the leo. That will honour the lamb and delight the leo."

Unity through a language

For Afrikaner nationalists the big question was: For which language should they demand their rights? For Dutch? For simplified Dutch, or for Afrikaans?

The two most senior Afrikaner leaders in the Cape, J.H. ("Onze Jan") Hofmeyr and F.S. Malan, chose a simplified version of Dutch. In 1905 Hofmeyr gave an important address with the title: "Is 't ons ernst?" (Is it our earnest?) He said that the instruction the children were receiving in Cape schools in Dutch was so poor that they could not even write an intelligible letter in the language. He asked the "Dutch-Afrikaans" people whether they were serious in their efforts to retain Dutch as their language.

Gustav Preller, a journalist with *De Volkstem* in Pretoria, took the opportunity to take up the cudgels for Afrikaans. Under the heading "Laat 't toch ons ernst wezen" (Let it be our earnest) he wrote an article in which he argued that Afrikaans should be taken seriously. His view was that Afrikaans was the only language which could stand alongside English. It had become ingrained amongst the Afrikaners; it had the "greatest and the best chance to survive in the future". The Afrikaners should make it their own spoken and written language.

Preller made reference to the poem "Winternag" (Winter night) by Eugène Marais which was published in 1905. In this poem the expressive phraseology and creative potential of Afrikaans became apparent for the first time. The opening stanzas describe the icy whisper of a breeze in the gloom ... in Afrikaans that is so starkly yet gently expressive that it leaves no doubt that the language had indeed moved from its infancy and had come of age.

A key figure in the new national movement was Dr D.F. Malan. In 1904, when he was still a student in Utrecht in the Netherlands, he wrote that the Afrikaners would only become strong if they were united. The best defence against anglicisation, he said, was the realisation that they had their own legacy, grounded on their "own nationality, language, religion and character". Like Smuts, Malan had grown up in the tradition of the Afrikaner Bond. Whereas Smuts had been drawn to the holistic vision of the unity and interdependence of humankind and nature, Malan saw the smaller unity of the *volk* (the Afrikaner people) with its own specific calling and destination as the most important concept. In 1908 Malan made the following call (translated): "Elevate the Afrikaans language to a written language; make her the bearer of our culture, of our history, our national ideals, and thereby you will also raise up the people who speak the language." By 1907 there were already language societies in Pretoria, Cape Town and Bloemfontein which promoted Afrikaans.

Initially, those who supported the idea of a simplified version of Dutch were opposed to the movement for Afrikaans, because they felt that it would merely weaken the struggle against the domination of English; but eventually the pro-Afrikaans and pro-Dutch groups moved closer together. The pro-Dutch group increasingly accepted that the attempt to retain Dutch was a lost cause. The promoters of Afrikaans realised the necessity of strategic action. Before Afrikaans could take over from Dutch in South Africa, it would first have to be standardised (use consistent spelling and sentence structure); and there had to be a sound body of published literature in Afrikaans.

Both groups took part in the establishment in 1909 of the Zuid-Afrikaanse Akademie voor Taal, Letteren en Kunst (later called the Suid-Afrikaanse Akademie vir Wetenskap en Kuns, South African Academy for Science and the Arts) which recognised both Dutch and Afrikaans and had the promotion of Afrikaans as its aim. In 1915 the Academy published the first Afrikaans spelling rules.

The struggle for the recognition of Afrikaans could not be won by debates or emotional appeals. There had to be impressive poetry, novels, biographies, newspapers and periodicals in Afrikaans.

Totius (J.D. du Toit) produced simple but nevertheless popular poetry. He used one of his poems against the message of certain church and political leaders. Their slogan "vergewe en vergeet" (forgive and forget) advised Afrikaners to get the war out of their heads as quickly as possible and immediately begin to re-build the country. The poem "Vergewe en vergeet" (1908) used the image of a small trampled thorn tree to symbolise the Boers' shattering defeat at the hands of Britain in the war. However, it suggests that the Afrikaners, like the tiny tree, would recover from the cruel setback and would grow ever stronger.

C.J. Langenhoven came to the fore as the most popular writer in Afrikaans. He made a range of Afrikaans people read books on a large scale with his *Die hoop van Suid-Afrika* (1913), *Sonde met die bure* (1921) and others. Popular periodicals such as *Die Brandwag* (1910) and later *Die*

Huisgenoot (1916) and *Die Boerevrou* (1919) also began to take an important place in people's lives. Their aim was to make people aware of their environment and the wider world in their own language. People were encouraged to regard themselves as Afrikaners, and Afrikaans as the symbol of their identity.

By 1913 Gustav Preller's book on the Voortrekker leader Piet Retief had already seen ten editions. It was clear evidence of the strong need for a nationalistic history.

Language equality in the Union

The big breakthrough for Afrikaans was the language clause that was laid down in the constitution of South Africa. At the National Convention (1908–1909) – where a constitution for the proposed Union of South Africa was compiled – the two Free State leaders, Hertzog and former president M.T. Steyn, insisted that Dutch and English had to have equal official status in practice. This had to form the basis for the unity of the two white communities.

The most dramatic moment at the Bloemfontein deliberations in 1909 was when Steyn joined the debate. He was greatly admired by the delegates because during the war, despite ill health, he had remained with his burghers in the veld until the bitter end. In his speech, as was usual in those times, he referred to the Boers and the British as different "races". He asked the delegates to erase the "devil of racial hatred" which had plagued the country for so long. The way to do this, he said, was to "place the two languages on an absolutely equal footing everywhere – in Parliament, the courts, the schools and the civil service."

Article 137 of the constitution complied fully with Steyn's demand: The two languages not only had to be symbolically equal; in practice they had also to enjoy equal treatment. All the government publications, including the laws, had to be in both official languages and there was now the reasonable expectation that state officials also had to serve the public in Dutch or Afrikaans. Nationalists later used the language clause to set up Dutch (later Afrikaans) schools and universities and to create job opportunities for Afrikaners in the civil service.

The language equality caused great consternation among some English speakers. They were convinced that in practice English would become the only official language in the country and that there was therefore no need for children to receive instruction in Dutch. Certain editors even accused Hertzog, saying that his insistence on equality for Dutch was a form of racism aimed at the English speakers. Another argument was that Afrikaans children would gain a distinct advantage if they received their schooling in English because, after all, English was the language of the economy and of the wider world of the British Empire.

The establishment of the National Party

In the first year after the Union of South Africa became a reality, a political struggle developed in the cabinet between supporters of the British Empire and Afrikaner nationalists. In particular, Louis Botha, prime minister and leader of the South African Party (SAP), and his great ally Jan Smuts, were inspired by the thought that South Africa should be a loyal member of the British Empire. This implied that all member states would have a great measure of freedom and trade advantages, but they also had to fulfil the duties of the empire. The member states had to make war together and could not break away from the British Empire. Smuts saw the "British connection" as vital for the reconciliation between the two white communities and for the economic progress of South Africa. In contrast, Afrikaner nationalists supported a policy of "Suid-Afrika Eerste" (South Africa First), whereby South Africa should put its own interests first, above those of the British Empire.

The issue was brought to a head by the looming war in Europe. Some experts thought that South Africa would be obliged to enter the war on the side of Britain. However, Hertzog was opposed to this. He said: "Imperialism is only acceptable as long as it is to South Africa's advantage." He wanted to know what use self-government was to South Africa if the country could not decide for itself whether it wanted to declare war or not. Hertzog expressed this opinion in typically nationalistic language: "In South Africa the Afrikaner is the 'boss' and will play the role of the 'boss'." By "Afrikaner" he meant people whose ultimate loyalty was to South Africa, but this statement caused great consternation, particularly among English speakers.

Both leaders were proponents of "South Africa First", but Botha expressed his views more diplomatically. He was careful not to do or say anything which would cause antagonism between the two white groups.

For his part, Hertzog believed that leaders should speak their mind because there were people in the party who still clung to Britain and British interests. His speeches became increasingly less compatible with his membership of the Botha cabinet. Convinced that Hertzog's pronouncements were causing considerable damage to the image of the SAP, in 1912 Botha left Hertzog out of his cabinet.

While Hertzog was still a member of the cabinet he did not make too much of the fact that the government was not strictly speaking adhering to the constitutional directive that there be absolute equality for English and Dutch. However, once he had been expelled from the cabinet he no longer held back. At a language festival organised by students at Stellenbosch in 1913, he read out a telegram from M.T. Steyn which said: "The language of the conqueror in the mouths of the conquered is the language of slaves."

According to the distinguished author and literary critic M.E.R. (M.E. Rothmann) this caused a dramatic turnabout. Until that stage it had been an "uphill battle" to maintain "our language and identity". Then, at "a critical time a word was uttered. This lit a veld fire among us." One source claims that there were people who promptly stopped speaking English in public.

At a congress of the *volk* held in Bloemfontein from 7 to 9 January 1914, attended by 450 delegates, the National Party of the Free State was formed with Hertzog as leader. From the outset, "South Africa First" and the language issue enjoyed priority in the party.

Hertzog's first supporters came from young ministers of religion, especially those of the Reformed Church (Doppers) and from the ranks of teachers. They refused to forgive Botha and Smuts for leaving the CNO schools in the lurch. Their slogan of "our strength lies in isolation" clashed directly with the SAP's attempt to reconcile the two white communities.

It took more than eighteen months before nationalists in the other provinces established a party based on the same principles as the NP in the Free State. The Transvaal NP was formed on 26 August 1914 in Pretoria; the Natal NP on 17 June 1915; and the NP in the Cape Province on 15 September 1915. Dr D.F. Malan became leader of the Cape party. He was at the same time also editor of *De Burger*, which first appeared on 26 July 1915.

The NP leaders believed that reconciliation between the two white groups could only be possible if the English speakers respected the Afrikaners. The best way to show the Afrikaners this was to respect their language and culture.

In 1917 Malan declared that in his view Afrikaners countrywide were being treated as inferior, particularly in the way their language was being denigrated – "in the civil service, in schools and on every notice board". The outcome of this, in his opinion, was that the Afrikaners themselves tended to think they were less worthy. The NP encouraged its supporters to stand up for their rights. Hertzog said that the Afrikaners should "fight a language struggle so that they no longer felt they were lagging behind like henchmen".

Languages seldom allow one another much living space if they have to survive in the same country. And when a smaller, newer language such as Afrikaans has to compete against an international language like English, the struggle is particularly merciless. However, the English speakers were in the minority among the white voters. Their leaders tried to make English out to be the language of people who were "progressive" and "cultured". They hoped that the rich abundance of English literature and the success of the large English companies such as the Anglo-American Corporation and South African Breweries would prove so magnetic that people would feel drawn to the English culture.

English-language newspapers were inclined to label the nationalists' insistence on Afrikaans as "rascist". They often referred to the two white communities as separate races and made attempts to regard schools or organisations such as the Voortrekker movement that were organised on the basis of Afrikaans, as a form of rascism. However, they had no problem with separate English private schools or the Boy Scouts, an English youth organisation. This kind of attitude made C.J. Langenhoven ask an English-speaking acquaintance: "Why is my politics always racism and your racism always politics?"

By the early 1920s Afrikaans began to replace Dutch in the public realm. Whereas the English-language newspapers still respected Dutch as an official language, many of them had no time for Afrikaans, which was rapidly taking over from Dutch. *The Star* and *The Cape Times* described Afrikaans as "dreadful", "stupid" and a "bastard language". In reaction to this, Langenhoven said in a speech in 1914 that Afrikaans was not something one had to be ashamed about, but proud: "Afrikaans places us higher than the Englishman on the national and patriotic levels, yes, higher than any other white resident of our country, because it is the only 'white-man's language' which does not come directly from overseas."

By describing Afrikaans as a "white-man's language" instead of recognising that white, coloured and black people were all involved in the creation of Afrikaans, Langenhoven was making a great mistake, just as S.J. du Toit had done 40 years earlier. Both made this error against the background of certain English speakers, and also certain middle-class Afrikaners who rejected Afrikaans as inferior. Du Toit and Langenhoven wanted Afrikaners to be proud of Afrikaans. But in later years many coloured people held this attempt to regard Afrikaans as a white "creation" or "possession" against the Afrikaner nationalists.

An own newspaper and university

In December 1914 a group of prominent Afrikaners in Stellenbosch decided to establish a publishing company, De Nationale Pers, which would be used as a vehicle to spread the nationalistic message. The newspapers they planned to publish would have to compete with *Ons Land*, the most important Dutch newspaper in Cape Town, which was a stalwart supporter of the cabinet's wartime decision to invade German South West Africa. The leading figure in this new publishing enterprise was Jannie Marais, a farmer in the Stellenbosch district. He bought a quarter of the first issue of 20 000 shares at £1 each. In June 1915 the first edition of *De Burger* appeared in Cape Town with D.F. Malan as editor.

Despite divisions within the NP, according to *De Burger* there were signs that the "national heart has begun to beat again ... throughout the entire country there is a murmur of the need for a new way forward, which is becoming ever stronger. It is the determination to become a *volk*."

The newspapers published by Nasionale Pers (*De Burger* in Cape Town and *Het Volksblad* in Bloemfontein); its periodicals (*Die Huisgenoot* and *Landbouweekblad*); and its publications, soon had people reading in their own language throughout their county and in the wider world.

Initially the Botha government planned to establish only one university in Cape Town, and an English one at that. After the cabinet had held talks with a delegation from the Victoria College at Stellenbosch, it abandoned its support for the idea of a single university. Cape Town would indeed have its university, but Victoria College could also become a university if it could garner funding to the tune of £100 000.

Just before his death in 1915 Jannie Marais bequeathed £100 000 to Victoria College at Stellenbosch. His prerequisite was that Dutch or Afrikaans would never be placed on a lower footing than English in the institution. Part of Marais's bequest was used to establish lecturing posts and those appointed were expected to give at least half of their lectures in Dutch or Afrikaans. By 1930 there was virtually no tuition given in English. In 1926 work was begun at Stellenbosch on the *Woordeboek van die Afrikaanse Taal*.

In the course of the twentieth century only four languages succeeded in developing from a purely spoken language to one which is used in all spheres of life: Afrikaans, Hebrew, Malay-Indonesian and Hindi.

White and coloured Afrikaans speakers: together or apart?

Afrikaner nationalists could never really find a satisfactory way of including coloured people into their struggle. The major political strife in South Africa at the time was between the two white groups. The reality was that the various white political parties differed very little on the question of race. Virtually all of them wanted better education for white children, the protection of white workers and a solution to the so-called poor-white problem. Coloured people would have to wait until these issues were satisfactorily resolved.

Coloured parents in the Boland placed great emphasis on education and training for their children. Between 1890 and 1905 there was an "enormous increase" of coloured and black schoolchildren in the Cape Colony. In contrast, many Afrikaner parents, especially those on isolated farms, did not immediately realise the great value of good education. In 1905 the Cape government made education for white children compulsory, but not for coloured children. The number of white schoolchildren then rose rapidly.

Between the early 1890s and the early 1920s the situation of the coloured people deteriorated markedly in reaction to circumstances beyond their control. Approximately 400 000 white immigrants settled in the country in the period 1875 to 1904, more than the total white population in South Africa in 1875. Many of these immigrants made their homes in Cape Town and its vicinity. It was primarily these people who exercised pressure on the authorities that white people should be given preference in the training of artisans and in access to employment opportunities.

White workers formed the first trade unions, many of which were under the leadership of British immigrants who were proponents of discrimination in the workplace against coloured and black workers. In 1900 coloured stonemasons in the Cape were barred from working on public buildings; and in the next year the trade union for plasterers instructed its members not to work on the scaffolding together with a coloured person or a Malayan. At the same time employers in the Cape docks began to appoint black workers from the Eastern Cape rather than coloured workers. In other places too, the white trade unions blocked the access of coloured people to certain trades.

In 1922, the government dealt coloured people a heavy blow by passing legislation which opened up apprenticeships for artisans – but only for people who were younger than 26 years and who had passed Standard 6 (Grade 8). The newspaper *APO*, mouthpiece of the coloured group known as the African People's Organisation, wrote that this Act was designed to give preference to the white youth over the coloured youth. Compared to white boys, there were few coloured boys who had passed this standard.

There were two other laws which also impacted negatively on coloured workers' bargaining position. The Industrial Conciliation Act of 1925 empowered industrial councils, comprising employers and trade unions, to negotiate on wages and working conditions. Virtually all the employers and most of the trade union leaders were white; this meant that the interests of the white workers were almost always given preference. For example, many coloured workers were prepared to work for lower wages than white workers, but the law soon put paid to this by laying down compulsory minimum wages.

Between 1915 and 1929 there was a hard-fought struggle in the Western Cape constituencies to win the coloured vote. The coloured people in Cape Town were inclined to be partial towards the English and support the Unionist Party or the SAP. In constituencies such as Paarl and Stellenbosch, where between a quarter and a fifth of the voters were coloured, the NP fared somewhat better, but it seems that the party never won the majority of the coloured votes.

Nevertheless, there were prominent nationalists such as J.H.H. de Waal, who in the 1910s and the 1920s argued that white and coloured Afrikaans speakers should stand together. In 1919 De Waal described the political struggle as one between British imperialists, mine magnates and self-seeking fortune hunters on the one hand; and on the other hand, the "permanent population" of which the white and coloured Afrikaans speakers were the important components. He saw the white Afrikaners and their coloured fellow Afrikaners as people "who speak the same language; have the same love for South Africa; for the most part the same history and interests; and who have been hoodwinked by the same friends". Their mutual enemies were the "imperialists" who encouraged immigration. This would take the bread from the mouths of coloured and white Afrikaners.

The coloured leader, Dr Abdullah Abdurahman of Cape Town, was one of the strongest opponents of the attempt to have the coloured people join the Afrikaner nationalists and the NP. He was born into an esteemed Moslem family and trained as a medical doctor in Britain. In 1905 he became the leader of the first important movement of coloured people, the African Political Organisation (APO). It was formed to strive for equal rights with white people for all people of colour (black, coloured and people of Indian descent). He dominated coloured politics for the first 40 years of the century.

Abdurahman encouraged his supporters to be proficient in English, "the most universal of all languages" and to stop speaking the "barbarous Cape Dutch" (Afrikaans). Nevertheless, his organisation's newsletter, the *APO*, made use of Afrikaans and Dutch on the back page because it was the most widely used language among Cape Town's coloured people. In 1912 the APO adopted a suggestion that "Cape Afrikaners" was a more appropriate term for the community than "coloureds", but nothing came of this.

For several decades after its formation in 1914, the NP remained curiously ambivalent about coloured people. Initially the party toyed with the idea of establishing a multiracial party which could come together to oppose the exploitation of white and coloured workers. In a pamphlet entitled "Die Groot Vlug" (The Great Flight), D.F. Malan, the Cape NP leader, saw the widespread poverty among coloureds and whites as the same problem; both groups had to be protected against black competition. But shortly afterwards Malan began to call for separate voting rolls for whites and coloureds.

Hertzog was not in favour of separate voting rolls. He saw coloureds as people who had been born and bred in the midst of a white civilisation and that language and other interests should be shared with the Afrikaners. However, in the social sphere he wanted coloured people to remain apart. As he put it: "The place for the educated coloured is among his own people. He must serve his own people."

The Rebellion of 1914–1915

In October 1914 the Afrikaner Rebellion broke out after the Botha government decided that South Africa would enter the war against Germany on the side of Britain and its allies. The war was later named the First World War. On its own, the decision to join the war would not have elicited much criticism, but the government went further and agreed to the British request to invade and annex the German colony of German South West Africa (the present-day Namibia).

For the Afrikaner nationalists it was unacceptable that the government was prepared to go so far to meet every British request. Former President Steyn strongly criticised the step and said that he would never have thought that a government run by Afrikaners, "the children of the concentration camps", could contemplate going to war against the German people who had been sympathetic to the Boer republics in their war against the British.

The rebellion was poorly organised and the rebels had very little ammunition and food. Wherever they arrived the rebel forces had to commandeer livestock and in some towns they plundered the local shops. The rebellion was limited to six or seven districts in the northern Free State; a few districts in the north-western Transvaal; and one or two districts in the northern Cape. It was in fact a clash between Afrikaners. In the Union, most of the policemen and soldiers were Afrikaners – and all the rebels were Afrikaners. There were about 11 000 of them, of whom just more than 7000 came from the Free State; just under 3000 from the Transvaal; and slightly more than 1000 from the Cape. Of the rebels, 190 men lost their lives, while 132 government troops were killed.

The government did not want to sentence the rebels to death because it realised that it was already highly unpopular on account of its invasion of German South West Africa and the declaration of martial law. The exception was Jopie Fourie, a citizen force officer who had led a rebel group in attacks against soldiers without resigning his position in the army. Many soldiers had perished and Fourie was sentenced to death. A delegation which included D.F. Malan was unsuccessful in reaching Smuts in time to plead with him to pardon Fourie. He was executed on Sunday, 20 December 1914.

Two rebel leaders were sent to gaol. Jan Kemp was sentenced to a six-year gaol term and fined £1000, and Christiaan de Wet was sentenced to five years and the same fine. Between 4000 and 5000 rebels received fines and gaol sentences but most of the ordinary men were set free at the end of 1915. All the leaders were free by the end of the following year.

The Helpmekaar

The rebellion caused the SAP government to lose a great deal of its support among Afrikaners. In the 1915 election Hertzog's NP won a grand total of 27 seats including, with the exception of one, all the seats in the Free State. The NP grew rapidly on account of its attempts to rescue the rebels from their desperate circumstances.

After the rebellion, many of the rebels were on the brink of bankruptcy as a result of demands for compensation from farmers and shopkeepers they had plundered. In 1916 the Helpmekaar Vereniging (a society to help one another) was established, with branches in all four provinces to collect funds to pay the rebels' fines and the compensation they were required to pay for damages. Contributions were slow in coming until *De Burger* came to the rescue. They approached the wealthier Afrikaners to help. J.E. de Villiers in Paarl promised to contribute £500 if 500 other individuals each gave £100. Before long the Helpmekaar initiative gained momentum with less wealthy people making contributions. Women in many towns also arranged bazaars, concerts and dinners to collect money.

In 1917 it became clear that together the various Helpmekaar branches would be able to pay all the fines and compensation demands, with a balance of £92 000 remaining. This amount was invested and is still today used for study bursaries. In 1918 the great success of the Helpmekaar initiative led to the establishment of the insurance companies Santam and Sanlam.

The Helpmekaar initiative indeed re-created the well-nigh fiasco of the rebellion into a significant achievement for the national movement which was still in its formative years. At the polls the NP took great advantage of this success, because the SAP leaders and supporters had been inclined to distance themselves from the collection of funds.

The 1922 strike

South Africa experienced a dark economic period in the six years after the end of the First World War in 1918; there was also growing unemployment. Most of the miners who did dangerous work underground were Afrikaners and they were highly dissatisfied with their poor working conditions.

The gulf between the white miners and the SAP government widened when the SAP and the Unionist Party, which had always had the mine magnates' support, moved closer to one another. The miners now saw the government and the mine owners as being hand in glove. Shortly after the 1920 election, the Unionist Party was dissolved and its supporters were asked to support the SAP. This was a desperate attempt to prevent the NP from taking power at the next election.

In 1920 the gold price began to drop sharply and many mines could no longer be worked profitably. The Chamber of Mines then acted in a helter-skelter manner – even recklessly. Despite existing contracts more and more workers were dismissed. The white workers were afraid that the mine owners wanted to replace them with black workers who received even lower wages than the white labourers.

In January 1922 white workers on the mines began to strike. Minister Deneys Reitz estimated that 90% of the strikers were Afrikaners. Most of the 2000 policemen and the commandos that were sent to the Witwatersrand (commonly called the Rand) to suppress the strike were also Afrikaners.

Different viewpoints can be identified among the strikers. On the one hand there were the English-speaking socialists and communists. They wanted to overthrow the capitalists. On the other hand, many Afrikaner strikers wanted to revive the Boer republics. Leaders of the strike called the Union Jack a "dirty rag" and promised that the Transvaal Vierkleur (the flag of the former Zuid-Afrikaansche Republiek or ZAR) would once again flutter over the Transvaal.

There were also those who saw the strike as a white-black struggle. At a mass meeting one leader called for Afrikaners to stand together as the Voortrekkers had done in 1838 when they triumphed over Dingane. Similarly the Afrikaners could take a stand to defend themselves against the mine owners and the poorly paid black workers.

Although most of the strikers were Afrikaners, the communists tried to take over the strike for their own purposes. Communist flags and red rosettes were prominent in the marches, and the "Red flag", the communist song, was often sung. Some communist leaders did not hesitate to stir up a brew in which there was a mix of communist and racist propaganda. On one of the banners were the words: "White workers of the world unite" instead of the usual communist slogan: "Workers of the world unite".

The concept "civilised labour" apparently had its origin in the strike. Simply put, it meant that so-called civilised labour should be rewarded with civilised wages. This soon came to mean work that was reserved exclusively for white workers and for which the wage or salary was high enough for a white person to survive on. The Labour Party used this maxim in the run-up to the 1924 election and the NP wasted no time in adopting it.

On 10 March 1922, after the strike had been smouldering for two months, 10 000 white miners attacked police stations, railway lines and mine offices and installations in Johannesburg. The unrest spread to other parts of the Rand in what was in fact a small-scale civil war.

Smuts latched on to the presence of the communists to call the strike a "red revolution" with the aim of establishing a Soviet republic. He declared martial law and deployed soldiers to Johannesburg; they were supported by aircraft, artillery, machine guns and tanks. The strikers' strongholds in Benoni were attacked from the air with machine guns and the buildings were bombarded. The strikers surrendered after heavy artillery destroyed their fortifications. In the skirmishes that lasted five days, 250 people were killed.

The Smuts government's blood-stained suppression of this strike made workers turn against the government. For some years many of them gave their support to the Labour Party and the white trade union movement, but gradually these organisations lost Afrikaner support because they were so strongly pro-British and so unsympathetic of the Afrikaners' efforts to become independent of the British crown.

The Pact's victory

Even before the election of 1924 it was clear that the Smuts government was in trouble. The NP and the Labour Party concluded an alliance, the "Pact", in which the parties promised to rule together after the election if together they won enough seats to take over the government of the country. The NP was reasonably confident that it had the support of most of the Afrikaners.

Nevertheless, a number of eminent Afrikaners were members of the South African Party. There was Jan Smuts himself; the educationists E.G. Malherbe and Leo Marquard; the writers C. Louis Leipoldt and Gustav Preller; and the politicians F.S. Malan, Deneys Reitz and Jan Hofmeyr. Smuts and the SAP's greatest asset was perhaps the brilliant young Hofmeyr, the nephew of J.H. ("Onze Jan") Hofmeyr, who later became Minister of Finance.

However, the Afrikaners in the SAP increasingly realised that the party was lagging behind as far as the promotion of Afrikaans and the Afrikaans culture was concerned. Leipoldt, who was a SAP candidate in 1924, said that the SAP had done nothing to promote Afrikaans while it was in power and that this was the reason for its defeat.

The SAP's blood-soaked suppression of the 1922 strike aroused such antagonism that some black leaders even looked towards the Pact government as a means of fighting the SAP. The ANC leaders sent a telegram to black and coloured voters advising them to cast their votes against the SAP; this can be interpreted as a hint to vote for the Pact. According to *Die Burger*, in 1924 most coloureds voted for the Pact. Among the white community there was also unexpected support: *The Star* reported that even some communists had decided to cast their votes in favour of the Pact.

Unlike those in other provinces, black people who lived in the Cape Province could vote and the leaders of the National Party reached out to them. Hertzog sent a telegram to Clements Kadalie, founder of the Industrial and Commercial Workers' Union (ICU), whose slogan was "Africa for the Africans". He told Kadalie that the cultivation of mutual sympathy between "white and black Afrikaners" was necessary for the prosperity of the South African nation. In a message to black voters, the

Cape NP leader, Malan, called on black nationalists to stand shoulder to shoulder with white nationalists.

The Pact was victorious in the 1924 election. Of the 135 seats, the NP won 63 and the Labour Party 18. The SAP won 52 seats. Smuts was defeated in his own constituency. The NP, under leadership of Hertzog, took the lead in the new government.

A political re-arrangement after 1924

With the National Party's victory in 1924 and the coming to power of the Pact government, the nationalists tasted political power for the first time. For Prime Minister Hertzog it was a priority to bring clarity and redefine the constitutional position of South Africa in the British Empire. Early in the 1920s the South African Party under Smuts absorbed the Unionist Party and also began to gain more support from the Labour Party. The SAP now became the party of the broader white middle class with strong support from the big business sector, professionals and the wealthier farmers.

One of the most marked differences of opinion between Hertzog and Smuts was the nature of South Africa's relationship with Britain. Hertzog wanted to reach the point where South Africa's status was not subordinate in any way to Britain. In contrast, Smuts's view was that South Africa had certain significant advantages and rights as a member of the British Empire, but this also implied having duties to fulfil. For example, not to break away to form a republic and not remaining neutral in a war in which Britain and other members of the empire were involved.

At an Imperial Conference in London in 1926, with the co-operation of the prime minister of Canada, Mackenzie King, Hertzog was instrumental in having a definitive statement issued. Known as the Balfour Declaration, this spelled out that Britain and the dominions (the member states, of which South Africa was one) were equal in status and were in no way subordinate to one another.

The Balfour Declaration was ratified by the Statute of Westminster (1931) and by the Status Act (1934) which verified that South Africa, as was the case with the other dominions, was a sovereign independent state. For Hertzog and his followers these developments dispelled their feelings of subordination and inferiority towards Britain.

In the following almost 25 years Afrikaner nationalism increased dramatically and became more institutionalised. This was clearly apparent in, among other things, the establishment of Afrikaans as an official language; the increase in the number of Afrikaner organisations; and the emergence of economic nationalism.

Afrikaans and Afrikaner organisations

In 1925 Dr D.F. Malan, now a minister in the Pact government, tabled legislation which gave Afrikaans the status of an official language alongside English and Dutch. Afrikaans soon became symbolic of the collective identity of Afrikaners. By the beginning of the 1930s the spelling and structure of the Afrikaans sentence and the largest part of the vocabulary looked virtually the same as it does today. An important breakthrough was the successful translation of the Bible into Afrikaans which appeared in 1933. Malan described it as the most significant event in the life of the *volk* in the sphere of Afrikaner culture and religion.

Various outstanding poets came to the fore, headed by N.P. van Wyk Louw, Dirk Opperman and Elisabeth Eybers; these Afrikaners helped to create a literary treasure trove. An increasing number of good poems, dramas, novels and short stories appeared which demanded respect for Afrikaans as a spoken and a written language.

With his publications *Berigte te velde* and *Lojale verset* (both 1939) and the later *Liberale nasionalisme* (1958), Van Wyk Louw introduced important concepts into Afrikaner political terminology, thereby countering the misuse of the nationalistic idea. One of these was the term "oop gesprek" (open debate); another was "lojale verset" (loyal resistance); yet another was "voortbestaan in geregtigheid" (continued existence without causing injustice to others). The Afrikaner nationalist still had to ask himself whether his party's nationalism did not clash with the Christian moral ethic of existence with justice. If, after penetrating discussion (open debate) it transpired that the national movement was dishonest or caused injustice to other people, the loyal Afrikaner should express sharp criticism, but always from a mindset of identification with the weal and woe of the Afrikaner *volk* (loyal resistance).

By the 1930s the Afrikaner nationalists had become organised people. In the political sphere the most important organisation was the Gesuiwerde (Purified) National Party which was formed in 1934, while in the cultural sphere there were a number of organisations including the Afrikaner Broederbond (AB) (Afrikaner Brotherhood); the Federasie van Afrikaanse Kultuurverenigings (FAK) (Federation of Afrikaans Cultural Associations); and the Afrikaanse Taal- en Kultuurvereniging (ATKV) (Afrikaner Language and Cultural Association).

The AB was formed in 1918 in Johannesburg after soldiers tried to break up an NP meeting in the city. In 1929 it became a secret organisation, while the FAK, which was formed in this same year, acted as its public arm. By 1934 the AB had a thousand members in about 53 branches, most of them in the Transvaal and Free State.

The organisation was determined to fight against the inferior status of Afrikaans in the civil service. It also put pressure on the bilingual university colleges in Pretoria and Bloemfontein to become single-medium (Afrikaans) institutions. Each month the AB head office sent a circular letter to every branch in the country, providing guidance on various matters. The branches then sent back their comments on these issues and also reported on the action taken.

By 1934 the AB was calling for a republic with an "Afrikaner character". A circular made the following statement (translated from Afrikaans): "Brothers, our solution for South Africa's troubles is not that *this* or *that* person, or that *this* or *that* party will gain the upper hand, but that the AB will rule South Africa."

In later years the AB's critics and enemies quoted this statement in trying to prove that in time the organisation prescribed to all institutions in the national movement, and that after 1948 this even included the NP cabinet. However, this is incorrect. The NP leaders used the AB as an instrument to determine how the Afrikaners thought. The organisation was always subject to cabinet decisions.

The FAK took the lead in what they described as handling language matters. As early as 1931 the organisation sent out a letter which explained how people should insist on being addressed in Afrikaans when dealing with officials in the civil service or with staff in shops. The crusaders also tried to modernise the language so that it met all modern requirements. They published lists of words on motor cars, sport and the various trades.

To persuade Afrikaners to go so far as to sing in their own language, in 1937 the FAK published its *Volksangbundel* which included German songs with Afrikaans translations and also some well-loved local songs; a few were of Malayan origin. The FAK also organised Afrikaans book weeks and annual celebrations of cultural days. Furthermore, it sponsored a competition to write a national anthem which could be sung together with "God save the King" on official occasions. In 1938 the government selected a composition by M.L. de Villiers of Langenhoven's "Die Stem van Suid-Afrika" as a national anthem. The FAK and the AB lobbied for an Afrikaans radio service which was introduced in 1938 after the government gained state control over the radio.

The ATKV was formed in 1930 in answer to the call of Afrikaner railway workers for their own organisation. In 1936 it had more than 11 000 members and 46 branches. A campaign was launched with great enthusiasm to promote Afrikaans as the medium of communication in the railway service. It was the ATKV which organised the very successful ox-wagon trek which was part of the commemoration of the Great Trek in 1938.

Economic nationalism

In the economic sphere, as early as the 1880s Afrikaner leaders showed signs of resistance against the free trade policy. This implied that as the mother country, Britain had the right to send its manufactured goods and other produce to South Africa without any restrictive import duties being placed upon them. In the Cape Colony the farmers raised strong objections to this because it meant that wine and wheat were imported at prices that were lower than they could afford to ask.

After Paul Kruger became president in the ZAR, he began to charge import duties so that local industries would develop and the republic could become as economically independent as possible. Kruger's attempt to build up the Transvaal's own industries was unique. None of the colonies in the British Empire followed this policy in the nineteenth century.

With the Union of South Africa in 1910, the government realised that Britain wanted to continue this free-trade policy. This not only suited the "motherland" (Britain) very well, but also the mining houses in South Africa, because financially it was more advantageous for them to import the products they needed for running the mines than to manufacture them locally.

For their part, the Afrikaner nationalists were anxious to help South Africa to develop its own secondary industries; this would ensure greater economic independence. Their aim was South Africa's own iron and steel industry which would make it possible for the development of local industries. Britain was dissatisfied with this because this would be at the expense of its own profitable iron and steel exports. The mine owners and the English newspapers fought against the plan and painted it as a form of socialism.

Despite the opposition, in 1928 the South African Iron and Steel Industrial Corporation Limited (Iscor) was established, in which the government had the controlling interest. Iscor and Escom, the state-controlled electricity provider, served as great encouragement for the development of a manufacturing sector which could cater for most requirements except products such as heavy machinery.

A strong industrial sector developed and by 1945 it made a substantial contribution to the national economy. Indeed, by 1965 this sector contributed more than agriculture and mining together. It was also the sector which provided the highest number of employment opportunities.

The poor white problem

The United Party (UP) government's aim was to develop the economy quickly enough to provide a strongly growing population with food and work. There would also have to be a labour policy which provided enough protection for white labour.

On account of the "civilised labour" policy which was followed by both the SAP government (1910–1924) and the Pact government (1924–1929) wages for work done by white people were higher than those for black people. Smuts, who sat on the opposition benches at the time of the Pact government, wasted no time in criticising the government that whites working on the railways were being paid lower wages than the "suitable" level laid down for whites.

During the 1920s white politicians increasingly expressed great concern about the so-called poor white problem. In point of fact, black and coloured poverty was far more acute but the white politicians did not see this as a major issue. Most of the white politicians advanced two arguments. Firstly, white control could not be sustained if a considerable portion of the white population lived in great poverty. Secondly, what was called "a nucleus of healthy white people" was necessary to tackle poverty among coloured and black people.

In 1929 the Carnegie Corporation in New York agreed to fund a study on the poor white problem. The Nederduitse Gereformeerde Kerk (NG Church) played the dominant role in the local board of control of the Carnegie investigation, and virtually all the researchers appointed were Afrikaans speaking. In 1932 the commission published five comprehensive reports. It was found among other things that there were about 300 000 poor whites. This meant that one out of every six white people were poverty stricken. It was calculated that approximately 250 000 of these poor whites were Afrikaners, which meant that one out of every four Afrikaners was indigent.

For the Cape NG Church a poor white was someone who lacked self-dependence and was not in a position to take care of himself and his family. The church felt that a person who was poor but nevertheless independent was not a poor white. E.G. Malherbe, one of the authors of the Carnegie Report, described a poor white as a white person who had sunk "below the economic standard of living which a white person, because of his white skin, should be able to maintain in comparison to the native, his perceived or actual competitor".

The commission's report paved the way for a new understanding of the crisis that had caused this large-scale poverty. People now realised that poverty was not a problem for which the poor themselves were responsible; it was the outcome of social and economic circumstances over which they had little control.

There were many causes of the widespread poverty among Afrikaners. The most important was that since the 1880s people living on farms had grown progressively poorer. Generally speaking, the farmers had large families and then had to sub-divide their properties so that their children could all inherit a part of the farm. In the modern South African economy there was no longer a place for subsistence farmers who could only take a small portion of their produce to the market. Few farmers had the necessary expertise to use in the town or city once they abandoned their farms.

Another reason was that about a quarter of the white children had left school without being properly taught or trained. The commission's most important recommendation was that the poor white problem had to be addressed by the provision of better instruction at schools, more appropriate education and better technical training.

Between 1933 and 1950 the poor-white problem was largely solved. This was mainly possible thanks to rapid economic growth which was accelerated by a sharp rise in the gold price in 1933. In the next 40 years the South African economy grew at a rate of just under 5% per year, which created new job opportunities on a large scale. The state gave poor white people unskilled work and provided them with the necessary training.

The rise of a radical nationalism

In 1929 the NP won the election again, but this time formed a government without the Labour Party. In the following ten years, under the political leadership of D.F. Malan, a radical national movement developed which was destined to change the political landscape dramatically.

The cause of this was the economic crisis which hit the entire world, including South Africa: the Great Depression, which lasted until 1933. At the same time, South Africa suffered one of the worst droughts ever to hit the country; the impact of this was devastating. By 1933 the production of the manufacturing sector dropped by about a fifth, compared to the figure for 1929, and 22% of all coloured and white men were registered as being unemployed. The income from agriculture dropped by half and many farmers went bankrupt.

The crisis was made even worse by the Hertzog government's refusal to abandon the gold standard. By this is meant the withdrawal of the undertaking which governments of the time gave to pay out the value of any banknote in gold. The crisis became so bad that in 1932 Hertzog and General Smuts decided to merge their parties; the United Party (UP) was formed in 1933. Hertzog was the leader of the party and prime minister, while Smuts was deputy prime minister and deputy leader.

In reaction to the formation of the UP, D.F. Malan, the leader of the NP in the Cape, decided to establish his own party, the gesuiwerde (purified) National Party. The nationalists under Malan were opposed to uniting with Smuts and his followers. They argued that it was ill advised for Afrikaner nationalists to form a party with the English speakers while Afrikaners were strictly speaking not at an equal level socially or economically with the English community.

In the cities, Afrikaners were in much lower posts than their English-speaking counterparts. By the mid-1930s, Afrikaners only comprised 3%

of engineers; 4% of bookkeepers; 11% of attorneys and advocates; 15% of medical doctors; and 21% of journalists. Afrikaners' per capita income was half that of English speakers.

Furthermore, the level of education of Afrikaners was still very low. In a study undertaken in 1933 it was shown that 44 of the children in a class of 100 who began school together had left school without passing Standard 6 (Grade 8). Only 17 of them had passed Standard 8; and only eight of the original 100 pupils had passed matric. Less than three had attended university. In 1939 only a third of all white students at university were Afrikaners although of the total white population 56% were Afrikaners. Many urban Afrikaners had a poor self-image.

Stricter segregation

The fusion to form the UP in 1933 brought a radical change to the country's racial policy. Because it was clear that the United Party would have almost all the coloured support, the NP decided not to expend any more effort on gaining these votes. In contrast there was a great degree of agreement between the white parties on the black vote.

In 1936 the UP passed legislation which disenfranchised the black people in the Cape Province and extended the size of the black reserves from about 7% of the country's total surface area to 13%. In response to the accusation that this Act was unjust and against Christian principles, Hertzog replied that this was not all that counted. He said that other issues, such as self-preservation, were just as important:

> There is a principle of self-preservation for a people; that an individual be prepared to offer up his life in time of war ... this is the only principle, the principle of self-preservation; this is self-defence through which humankind itself, and Christianity itself will be protected.

Smuts and most of the UP members supported the bill, but J.H. Hofmeyr, who was one of the prominent liberal voices in the party, said that all people, regardless of colour, should be permitted to vote. He was of the opinion that the bill took fear as its point of departure; white people could not guarantee their self-preservation in this manner.

> I do not believe that we can ensure the future of white civilisation in South Africa if it does not occur with the permission and goodwill of the non-European population. When I hear that the Christian princi-

ple of self-preservation has been called upon in connection with this bill, then I think of the eternal paradox that the person who wants to protect himself will in the final analysis lose his life.

This was a strong moral call, but very few white voters chose to heed it.

The Great Trek centenary celebration

In 1938, as part of the centenary celebrations of the Great Trek, nine ox-wagons undertook a symbolic trek from Cape Town to the north. One route went to Pretoria, where the foundation stone of the massive new monument in honour of the Voortrekkers was laid on 16 December. The other route went to the site of the Battle of Blood (Ncome) River in northern Natal.

The celebrations unleashed a wave of enthusiasm. Men and women, often dressed in traditional Voortrekker clothes, met the wagons everywhere along the route. The song "Die Stem van Suid-Afrika" (later the national anthem) became familiar countrywide at this time. Many other folksongs from the FAK volume now also became part of the Afrikaners' culture and were subsequently sung on all sorts of occasions. Imitating the Voortrekkers in the veld, people often cooked their meals outside and the "braaivleis" became part of general Afrikaner culture. The high point of the celebration was the huge gathering in Pretoria on 16 December which was attended by more than 100 000 people.

"A people rescues itself"

During the centenary celebration of the Great Trek one speech in particular captured a great deal of attention. It was by the Free State church leader, J.D. ("Vader") Kestell who in February 1938 raised the question of economic empowerment in typically nationalistic language. "Today we bring homage to a previous generation and there are 300 000 of our own flesh and blood who have sunk into hopeless poverty – materially, but also morally. A hand of rescue must be extended to them." Later that same year, addressing a crowd of 20 000 in Bloemfontein, he called for an "ongoing rescue act". The Afrikaners had to help their poor: "A people rescues itself", he said. This call for the Afrikaner to rescue himself became one of the central ideas of Afrikaner nationalism.

The Afrikaner Broederbond (AB) decided against a charitable campaign; instead it had to be a scheme that aimed "to make the buying power and capital capacity of the *volk* productive in the interest of attaining economic independence". In Cape Town, Sanlam's senior members of management came to a similar conclusion. The AB and Sanlam now decided to address the Afrikaners' economic backlog together. The first step was to convince their fellow Afrikaners that capitalism could also be used in the interest of the Afrikaner people. The poor had to be rescued by Afrikaners who could offer them work opportunities.

The AB-Sanlam partnership's first step was to hold a congress of the *volk* in 1939 to discuss the economy. It was attended by politicians, businessmen and academics. The formation of an investment company, Federale Volksbeleggings (FVB) controlled by Sanlam, followed from this. By the end of the Second World War, FVB had significant investment in the fishing, wood, steel, chemical, and agricultural implements industries. One of FVB's first loans was granted to the company of the young Afrikaans entrepreneur, Anton Rupert, who later established the Rembrandt Group.

War: a watershed

The United Party had been formed before the two leaders, Hertzog and Smuts, had ironed out the matter of how South Africa would react if Britain declared war against another power. When the Second World War broke out in Europe in 1939, Hertzog suggested to the cabinet that South Africa should remain neutral.

In any voting on the war the tally would probably be equally divided. Hertzog believed that it would seriously damage the trust between the two white language groups if it was decided by a small majority to support Britain. According to Hertzog, if South Africa took part in the war it would be a "disaster" and create a "distressful situation". In his view it would be "something that affected our mutual relationships for fifty years, if not for a hundred years". In this, Hertzog was fully supported by Malan. His argument was that there was no reason for South Africa to become involved in a conflict in faraway Poland despite its ties with Britain.

Smuts also had strong opinions on the matter. He was convinced that Hitler wanted to dominate the world. According to him, "the destiny of mankind and the future of civilisation" were on the line.

Hertzog's motion was rejected in Parliament by 80 votes to 67. By and large the votes reflected the language differences of the members of Parliament. The governor general refused Hertzog's request to dissolve Parliament and call a general election. *Round Table*, an authoritative periodical, believed it was more than likely that an anti-war party would have won such an election. Instead, the governor general asked Smuts to form a cabinet and he led South Africa into the war.

The decision to enter the war had a radical effect on the nationalists. N.P. van Wyk Louw described the parliamentary vote as "a great defeat" and resolved to make an attempt to build a "non-compromising spiritual Afrikanerdom". The English speakers generally supported the war effort and wanted action taken against South Africans who were opposed to the idea. Although about half of the fighting troops were Afrikaners, the perception remained that Afrikaners as a group were against entering the war on Britain's behalf.

A mutual struggle over democracy

After his defeat, Hertzog was replaced by Smuts as prime minister. Thirteen of Hertzog's followers in Parliament then formed the Afrikaner Party under the leadership of Klasie Havenga. The NP under Malan soon dominated opposition politics.

Two other organisations also emerged at this time: The Ossewabrandwag (OB) (Ox-wagon Sentinel) and the Nuwe Orde (New Order), which was formed under leadership of Oswald Pirow, a member of Hertzog's cabinet before the 1939 split. The Nuwe Orde espoused a form of (Afrikaner) national socialism. The paramilitary OB was the most important anti-war movement, founded to perpetuate the "ox-wagon spirit" of the 1938 celebrations. In 1941 Hans van Rensburg, a previous administrator of the Free State, took over as leader. He was a fiery supporter of Nazi Germany.

As leader of the OB, Van Rensburg began a campaign for "a free Afrikaner republic based on National Socialist foundations". He rejected a parliamentary form of democracy and insisted that the OB as a mass movement represented all Afrikaners. The OB hoped for a German victory and bargained on German assistance in establishing a republic; it had a division of storm troopers called the Stormjaers, who actively resisted the war effort with acts of sabotage and several assassinations.

As a quasi-military organisation, the OB grew strongly, mainly due to Afrikaner disillusionment with the parliamentary form of democracy which had landed South Africa in a war without a clear majority. Some estimations put OB membership as high as 100 000. However, the organisation soon became widely ridiculed for its efforts to inspire enthusiasm by military drills and the spurious award of "military ranks".

The NP regarded parliamentary politics and the ballot box as the only acceptable method for the Afrikaner nationalists to realise its aspirations for a republic. Violent resistance against the war effort was frowned upon, but Malan also expressed the view that South Africa should pull out of the war.

A war measure that outraged the anti-war camp was the order that all white citizens, including farmers, had to surrender their weapons and ammunition. Malan objected strenuously to this. There was also dismay about the government instruction that state officials and teachers had to resign from the OB; and from 1944 this instruction was extended to include the Broederbond. The most hated measure, used on a wide scale, was internment without prior trial. John Vorster, a young lawyer who later became prime minister, was among the internees.

The civil service became politicised and the separation between the ruling party and the civil service became blurred. This was evident in the actions of the director of military intelligence who made his reports on NP leaders available to the UP's secretary.

Early in 1942 Malan and the other NP leaders unequivocally rejected the idea of a dictatorship as an alien import into South Africa from outside; instead they advocated parliamentary democracy. Accordingly, the NP instructed its members to resign from the OB. Thereafter, support for the OB and the Nuwe Orde rapidly declined. Prior to the 1943 election the NP had enough confidence to turn down an election pact with these organisations.

The UP won 89 seats and the NP 43 seats. *Die Burger*, the NP's most influential supporter, summed up the significance of this election, in a single sentence: "There is no other model than the ballot box for our aspirations." The struggle among Afrikaner nationalists during the war had ended in triumph for the NP, which had opted to work towards a parliamentary democracy.

The 1948 election

It was not apartheid, but the controversial declaration of war in 1939 and the turmoil that the war brought, which proved decisive in the Afrikaner nationalists' victory at the polls in 1948. In general, it was felt that the NP would enforce the political authority of white people more assertively.

The NP now had wide support among the various Afrikaner groupings. Some of its strongest supporters were those broadly called the intelligentsia, including academics, teachers, ministers of religion and people involved in cultural activities and the arts. It also had great support among farmers, businessmen and the workers. The intelligentsia clamoured for a republic and equal status for the two languages; among farmers and workers material considerations carried more weight.

The apartheid policy played a relatively small role in the NP's election campaign. In his final call upon the white voting public Malan only made a single, ambiguous comment about apartheid. He said the question was whether apartheid, justice, peace and co-operation between white, black, coloured and Indian could be achieved simultaneously.

In his *Op die vooraand van apartheid* (1994), J.P. Brits analysed the letters which appeared six months prior to the election in *Die Burger* and *Die Transvaler*. He found that issues other than the racial question were important to the letter writers. Of particular significance was the perception that in the previous eight years the UP government had discriminated against Afrikaners. The shortage of food and necessity for rationing, as well as the treatment of ex-servicemen, came under discussion. Although the editorial articles harped on the racial question, only one of every ten letters from the public broached this matter.

On 26 May 1948 the National Party, in alliance with the Afrikaner Party, unexpectedly won the election. The coalition's majority was a slim five seats and together they only won 40% of the votes. Immediately after the election Malan said: "Today South Africa belongs to us again. South Africa is our own for the first time since the Union of South Africa. May God grant that it will always be ours."

With his remark that South Africa "belonged" to the Afrikaners, he did not have the white/black struggle in mind, but the political conflict between Afrikaner nationalists and the English community which had escalated by unknown proportions during the war.

For many years Afrikaner nationalists had dreamt of being completely free. For them this freedom meant that South Africa no longer had to be subordinate to Britain, and that Afrikaners no longer had to occupy an inferior position relative to the English-speaking community. South Africa's participation on the side of Britain in two world wars had caused great resentment among Afrikaners. It is true to say that in 1926, in terms of the Balfour Declaration, South Africa was to all intents and purposes already free.

In the business sphere the progress of Afrikaners was significant. Whereas by 1938 they only had a marginal share in economic undertakings, by 1948 their stake had increased to a tenth of the total, and by 1975, to a fifth. In the Afrikaans business world there was a strong belief that the individual did not merely strive to live for him- or herself, but also for the wider Afrikaner community. Anton Rupert, the most prominent Afrikaner industrialist, said in 1949 that the objective of the Afrikaner business sector was to "advance the freedom of our people and to help the Afrikaner take his/her rightful place in the industrial sector as future employer and employee".

The Afrikaans language developed rapidly. It became the symbol of the Afrikaners' collective identity. However, the manner in which some Afrikaner leaders claimed exclusive Afrikaner "ownership" of the language created a division between Afrikaners and coloured and black people who also spoke the language.

In the first two decades of the twentieth century the nationalists dreamt of Afrikaners taking their place in the country, being true to themselves, and being proud of their language, culture and history. That ideal was largely realised by 1948. The important question was: With the power in their hands how would they fulfil their responsibility to all the people in the country?

14

Black political awakening, 1875-1949

Jackie Grobler

Black political resistance against oppression and white domination goes back in time for some 120 years before it found expression in 1994 in South Africa's first democratic parliamentary election. In this historic general election, black people ("black" in this book takes the Black Consciousness view that includes coloured people and those of Indian descent) were able to participate on an equal footing for the first time. Most historians now agree that this resistance movement began in the Eastern Cape and then spread throughout the country, largely overtaking black ethnic (tribal) clashes which had come to an end by the turn of the nineteenth century.

In the course of these 120 years, the nature of the resistance movement was constantly changing, but three broad phases can be identified. In the first phase the call was for humane treatment; in the second, black people wanted equal political rights; and in the third, they demanded political power. The first two phases are dealt with in this chapter, the third phase in chapter 17.

The call for humane treatment

Over the centuries there were two overarching phases in black South Africans' resistance. In the first of these, black societies such as the Khoekhoen, Xhosa, Zulu, Pedi and Venda societies rebelled against colonial control and white authority. The second phase – true political awakening – followed thereafter.

The political awareness of black South Africans began in the eastern districts of the then Cape Colony, apparently for the following reasons.

Firstly, of all the Bantu-speaking societies in South Africa, those who lived in this region had been in contact with white colonists for the longest time. Secondly, by the second half of the nineteenth century (that is, from 1850 to 1900) a considerable number of black people no longer had close tribal ties. And thirdly, the Cape franchise system encouraged them to become politically involved.

The fundamental contradiction in the Cape political and cultural system made a significant impression on early black political awareness. Although there was no legalised racial differentiation in church, schools or the political system, in practice, racial discrimination was the order of the day. The black political awakening in the Eastern Cape was encouraged by this marked difference between theory and practice. Detribalised black people felt aggrieved and rebelled against it, but at this stage, armed resistance was not an option. The alternative, in which particularly in the last quarter of the nineteenth century black people became increasingly involved, was political resistance.

It was especially those black people who had received education at mission institutions such as Lovedale outside Alice in the Eastern Cape, who took the lead (in contrast with traditional leaders) of the new black elite and began to harbour certain lifestyle changes and expectations. In time these mission-educated people began to take leading positions in their respective societies and some decided to further their education at theological seminaries and overseas universities. Among them were the journalist John Tengu Jabavu; theologian Walter Rubusana; and educationist John Dube, who had studied in the USA. A notable characteristic of these early black leaders and opinion-makers was their versatility. Both Rubusana and Dube, as well as the prominent musician John Knox Bokwe, in addition to all their other activities, published and edited newspapers.

The early black political leaders were not activists in the modern sense of the word. They pointed out blatant injustices and insisted on fair, humane treatment. There were indeed some black churchmen, such as Isaiah Shembe and Mangena Mokone, who made relatively radical statements and insisted on black freedom and the unequivocal end of white minority rule. The most prominent black leaders, however, followed the lead of moderate black American leaders such as Booker T. Washington and merely asked that black people be afforded equal opportunities.

The outbreak of the Anglo-Boer War in October 1899 ushered in a new era of black political resistance. Historians and black politicians agree that at this stage, politically aware blacks overwhelmingly supported the British in their conflict against the Boer republics. One exception was John Tengu Jabavu, publisher and editor of the newspaper *Imvo Zabatsundu*, who instead expressed himself against the war in its entirety in his leading articles, refusing to support either combatant party. Pro-British black people hoped that a British victory would lead to the extension northwards of the colour-blind Cape franchise. However, to their great disillusionment, this issue was placed on the backburner when the terms of the peace agreement were thrashed out between the Boers and the British. Indeed, in the short term, the Anglo-Boer War brought no real change in the political lot of the black majority.

In the first ten years after the signing of the Peace of Vereeniging in 1902, a great many black political organisations were formed in all parts of the country. The most important of these in the Cape Colony was the South African Native Congress which also had branches in the other colonies. Its major concern was to further the interests of black people throughout southern Africa. In the Orange River Colony (the former Orange Free State) the ORC Native Congress was the dominant black organisation, and in Natal, politically aware black people formed the Natal Native Congress. There were a large number of similar organisations in the Transvaal, including the Transvaal Native Organisation. The establishment of all these black political organisations is an indication of a marked increase in the political consciousness of black people on the eve of unification in 1910.

When the Selborne Memorandum, which served as a blueprint for unification, was released in 1906, it did not elicit a significant reaction in black political circles. However, the National Convention, which gathered in 1908 and was comprised exclusively of white delegates, was altogether another matter. Black leaders did not reject the idea of union but there were fears that the political interests of black people outside the Cape Colony would not be taken into consideration in the new dispensation. When the National Convention's draft constitution bill for unification was released in 1909, it appeared that their fears were justified.

Black resistance against the draft constitution bill for the formation of the Union of South Africa in March 1909 led directly to the holding of a conference in Bloemfontein, the South African Native Convention or

Native Convention. This conference was attended by black people from throughout South Africa and many resolutions were adopted, a number of which objected strongly to the terms of the proposed South Africa Act. The most far-reaching resolution taken was that if the National Convention rejected the concerns raised by black South Africans, the Native Convention would send a delegation to Britain in an attempt to persuade the British parliament to amend the Union of South Africa Bill. When the Native Convention's resolutions were simply ignored by the National Convention, a black delegation was duly formed for this purpose.

In Britain the Native Convention's delegation conducted extensive interviews with members of Parliament, newspaper journalists and organisations such as the Aborigines' Protection Society, but were unable to gain any support for their resistance against the proposals. The draft Union of South Africa Bill was passed with a large majority by both houses of the British parliament on 20 September 1909 and the Union of South Africa Act became law in South Africa on 31 May 1910.

Formation and early activities of the SANNC (ANC)

The intention of calling the Native Convention of 1909 was not that it would move forward as an organisation. However, the idea gained support that black people countrywide should work together politically on a more permanent basis and in 1911 plans were made for the formation of an overarching political organisation.

The initiative was driven by Pixley Seme, a lawyer who had trained in the USA and ran a legal practice in Johannesburg. Seme gained support throughout the country from prominent black people, including members of the educated middle class and traditional leaders. Early in 1912 he arranged a meeting in Bloemfontein to form a national organisation. Some sixty delegates gathered in the Free State capital on 8 January and two days later took the decision to form the South African Native National Congress (SANNC). The first president was John L. Dube and the first secretary was Sol T. Plaatje. Seme was to serve as treasurer.

The SANNC's aims were in step with the moderate outlook that characterised black political resistance at the time. Its objectives were to unite black South Africans politically; to inform the general public of the aspirations of black people; to make a call on behalf of black people for equal rights and just treatment; to become the mouthpiece for black people across the board, including traditional leaders; and to gain black South African representation in legislative organs, including Parliament.

One of the first issues in which the SANNC became involved was territorial segregation between white and black. The ownership of land was also one of the questions that the new Union government had to address. The drafting of legislation to give effect to the traditional white policy of territorial segregation had been completed as early as 1911 but had met with fierce criticism from black ranks. In 1913 this bill, despite resistance in Parliament, was passed as the Natives Land Act. The Act had vast implications for black South Africans; among other things it meant that 10 000 blacks in the Orange Free State, most of whom were squatters on white-owned farms, were forced to re-settle elsewhere, leading to great hardship and loss of property.

The SANNC registered its objection against the inhumanity of the law but its representations to the Minister of Native Affairs and the British high commissioner were in vain. An SANNC delegation sent to Britain to inform the king personally of the negative effects of the Act also proved unsuccessful although there was some sympathy in press circles. The delegation was still in Britain when the First World War broke out and the reaction of politically aware black people was to express their loyalty towards the king and to Britain. Thousands of black people joined up as volunteers in the South African armed forces, although they were only used in a non-combatant capacity. This offended them, particularly when they observed that black people from other countries were serving as fully armed soldiers.

At the annual meeting of the SANNC in 1917, delegates expressed vastly different opinions on the principle of territorial segregation. The result was that Sefako Makgatho of Pretoria replaced John Dube as president general.

Although the land question dominated the black political scene for the first ten years after Union, there were also other issues which had a marked effect and led to emotional reactions as well as overt political resistance on the part of black people. In the Orange Free State for example, there was widespread anger at the imposition of the pass system for black women. They refused point blank to carry passes and many women were prosecuted. Several women were also allegedly molested while in detention and these cases were used by the black leadership to encourage further opposition against the pass system. The Minister of Justice was eventually obliged to give the police instructions to stop the prosecution of black women for contravention of the pass laws.

Resistance in the period between the two world wars

At the end of the First World War there was a surge of black political action in the Transvaal and the Cape. In the Transvaal the issues were of a socio-economic nature and Makgatho, the president general of the SANNC, played an important role in voicing these grievances and organising resistance. In April 1919 black municipal workers staged a strike to demand better wages. The fact that this coincided with a campaign against the pass system gave the strike a political hue. Many black people were arrested and prosecuted.

A second and far bigger strike, the mineworkers' strike of February 1920, involving at times as many as 42 000 workers, took place on the Witwatersrand just short of a year later. The call for higher wages was again the reason behind the demonstration; there was unrest and the police used firearms to restore order. After a number of workers had been killed and others wounded, the strikers eventually returned to work. However, the militancy that began to take root among black workers in the first two years after the war aroused a feeling of solidarity among them and this contributed to the eventual radicalisation of the black resistance movement.

The politicisation of the small black population in the Cape Peninsula was led by the charismatic Clements Kadalie. In 1918 he left Nyasaland (now Malawi) and settled in Cape Town where he worked as a clerk in Table Bay harbour. He soon began to organise the dockworkers into a trade union called the Industrial and Commercial Workers' Union (ICU). At the end of 1919 it launched a strike that lasted three weeks, calling for higher wages and objecting to the export of food while there were shortages in the interior.

Once some difficulties in the early 1920s were overcome, the ICU became a countrywide organisation with its own mouthpiece, *The Workers' Herald*. Its membership rose astronomically – by 1928 it had almost 250 000 members – and the head office was moved to Johannesburg where

Kadalie took over as full-time secretary and attended to the interests of his supporters. The ICU was in reality a trade union, but in the South African context black workers' issues are inevitably political issues and the two are difficult to separate. In many respects, then, a black trade union can be seen as a political organisation. This being so, the ICU can lay claim to being the biggest black political organisation in South Africa at least until the 1980s. However, in 1929 when Kadalie resigned from the organisation, the ICU declined rapidly.

In the years between the two world wars the SANNC was in the doldrums and led a precarious existence. The organisation sometimes objected to what it saw as oppressive legislation, but this did not deter the white authority or put it off its stride. At the SANNC's annual congress in 1923 a resolution was accepted alleging that the Union Parliament was planning to permanently enslave black South Africans and that a request should be made to the governor general not to sign the Natives Urban Areas Act of 1923 which made provision for residential segregation in the cities on the basis of race. At the same congress it was decided that the SANNC would henceforth be known as the African National Congress (ANC).

Makgatho, who had been president general of the ANC since 1917, was replaced in 1924 by Rev. Z.R. Mahabane. Like his predecessor, Mahabane was a moderate and set himself the task of asking no more than the recognition of black rights in the existing social order. After a term of office of three years, Mahabane made way for Josiah Gumede. Shortly after his election as president general, thanks to a sponsorship, Gumede travelled to the Soviet Union. He was immediately branded as a communist, but strenuously denied this.

In 1930 he was succeeded by Pixley Seme. Seme was very enterprising and politically driven in the years when he had been the leading personality in the formation of the SANNC, but when he took over the leadership in 1930, he was unable to breathe new life into the ailing organisation. He launched a big project for economic development which involved black people uplifting themselves, but this fell flat. Although he often came under criticism, he was nevertheless re-elected as president general time and again until he was replaced in 1937 by Mahabane.

This experienced politician was also unable to provide positive leadership, with the result that by the end of the 1930s the ANC had virtually no influence.

A claim for equal rights

In the 1930s the ANC all but ceased to exist, but with the help of a group of officials under the leadership of the secretary general, James Calata, the organisation survived the next decade. The election of Alfred Xuma as president general in December 1940 played a big role in this survival. He set himself the goal of making the ANC an effective organisation again. To accomplish this, he put a firm end to the tendency of provincial branches to go their own way. Furthermore, in 1942 he launched a campaign to recruit a million members. Although this ambitious target was not reached, the campaign provided the organisation with a great deal of publicity.

In 1943 the ANC adopted a new constitution in terms of which people of all racial groups were eligible to become members. In practice, however, the ANC remained an organisation exclusively for black people. The new constitution also made provision for efficient control over the organisation's financial matters and a working committee was set up which was the forerunner of the later national executive committee (NEC). This committee, with Xuma as chairperson, met almost weekly in Johannesburg. Thanks to Xuma's reforms, the ANC was able to establish a permanent office in Johannesburg.

During Xuma's term as president general, women were also mobilised to become involved in the organisation and Xuma's wife Madie was elected to head up the ANC Women's League. Xuma, a medical doctor, was a talented organiser with valuable overseas contacts. However, he was not a proponent of displays of power by means of mass action.

The changing socio-economic and political circumstances in South Africa during the Second World War favoured the ANC. Increasing urbanisation of black people led to a massive shortage of housing and the result was seven large squatter movements on the Witwatersrand. James Mpanza, leader of the Sofasonke group, was one of the foremost squatter leaders. Mpanza and his followers demanded houses from the Johannesburg town council, but refused the assistance of the authorities for anything else. The squatter leaders regularly succeeded in getting access to additional ground for black occupation. Mpanza believed that he was leading his followers over the River Jordan into the Promised Land. The ANC only had informal ties with Mpanza and these were strained to say the least. The squatters lived an unsettled lifestyle; when driven out of one area, they simply squatted somewhere else. Understandably, their constant moving from one place to another was often accompanied by bitterness and in 1947 there were riots in Orlando and Moroka, two Soweto suburbs.

During the Second World War, the black working class on the Witwatersrand was exposed to constantly rising prices. Their reaction took the form of resistance campaigns such as bus boycotts. Sky-rocketing bus fares which made commuting by bus unaffordable for many, led to boycotts of short duration in 1940, 1942 and 1943, but in 1944 the residents of Alexandra boycotted buses for a full seven weeks. This meant that they had to walk to and from work every day. The end result was that the Johannesburg town council decided to make a partial subsidy towards their bus fares. In the longer term, the bus boycotts and other expressions of dissatisfaction contributed to the politicisation of black working-class people.

Public statements by prominent world leaders during the Second World War were also reflected in the revival of the ANC. In 1941 Franklin D. Roosevelt, president of the USA, and British prime minister, Winston Churchill, issued the Atlantic Charter declaring their intentions for a changed world order. Xuma appointed a 30-member committee to study the charter and this committee formulated a series of demands in a document called African Claims. It outlined similar freedoms to those expressed in the Atlantic Charter and included a bill of rights demanding universal adult franchise; a reasonable share for black people in the prosperity of the country; and the equal distribution of land. However, it was a statement of objectives and did not suggest a programme on how these goals could be reached.

The establishment of the ANC Youth League

The formation of the African National Congress Youth League (ANCYL) also played a role in the revival of the ANC in the 1940s. At the ANC annual congress of 1942, the idea of a youth wing was approved and the first ANCYL branch was formed in Johannesburg in April 1944. This was followed in September by the establishment of the national youth league.

The founding members of the ANCYL were predominantly young, professional black men. The best known among them were Anton Lembede, Jordan Ngubane, Oliver Tambo, A.P. Mda, Nelson Mandela and

Walter Sisulu. Later they were joined by Robert Sobukwe, Duma Nokwe, Joe Matthews and Congress Mbata. They saw themselves as a pressure group in the ANC and were in favour of working with the black masses to achieve their aims, rather than co-operating with sympathetic white people.

In the early years of its existence, the ANCYL adhered to a radical, Africanist philosophy. Lembede was the architect of this Africanist outlook. Its historical basis was the fact that the heroic deeds of the past were to be the cornerstone of the future. As for its economic base, it was felt that there should be a return to the fundamental socialist structure of the old Bantu-speaking societies where for example there had been no talk of individual landownership. According to the Africanists, socialism was a valuable legacy inherited from the ancestors. The task of the new generation was to strengthen that ancient socialism by infusing it with new, modern socialist interpretations.

The ANC believed that the ideology of Africanism was the only way to rescue black people. Therefore, they were initially anti-communist and against working together with white people. Lembede was outspoken about this: "No outsider can ever be a true, genuine leader of the people of Africa, because no outsider can truly interpret or understand the African spirit which is unique and exclusive to Africans. Some Asians [Indians] and Europeans who profess to be leaders in Africa, must be categorically denounced and rejected."

A.P. Mda added that black people were suffering under nationwide oppression and that they should therefore initiate a national freedom struggle. Until 1947 the ANCYL leaders were extremely dogmatic in their outlook. However, Lembede died in this year and from that time onwards ANCYL and ANC theorists became more amenable to a range of different opinions.

As with the ANCYL, the question of co-operating with sympathetic members of other racial groups was also problematic. After Josiah Gumede's presidency, the ANC leadership was anti-communist and rejected the idea of working with whites. They championed exclusive African nationalism and black unity. However, they were impressed by the boycott tactics of the Non-European Unity Movement (NEUM), which was in reality a Cape-based movement of coloured people; and with the passive resistance campaigns of the South African Indians. In 1948 the ANC accepted a basic policy whereby a co-operative working relationship would be promoted with the national organisations of coloured and Indian South Africans.

Meanwhile the ANCYL leadership was working on a strategy to force the ANC to proceed more pro-actively. The young leaders were convinced that petitions to air grievances and delegations sent to talk to the government would not change the fate of black people in the very least. They drew up a programme of action in which they demanded freedom from white oppression and the right to black self-determination. Boycotts, strikes and non-cooperation campaigns were recommended as the means of achieving these objectives. The programme also suggested setting up a fund to finance the freedom struggle; establishing a national mouthpiece; and forming an action council. Finally, the programme of action envisaged the economic, educational and cultural upliftment of black people.

The ANCYL put forward its programme of action at the ANC's 1948 annual meeting. Xuma was against it because he thought it would prove impossible to implement. The meeting decided to refer it to the youth leaders and the ANC branches for further consideration. However, in 1949 the ANC's annual meeting accepted the programme of action despite Xuma's reservations. Furthermore, in what appeared to be unseemly haste, the meeting elected James Moroka as president general in Xuma's place. Walter Sisulu of the ANCYL became the new ANC secretary-general. In so doing the ANC abandoned its previously moderate stance.

Other black role players in the 1940s

In the 1930s the Communist Party of South Africa (CPSA) which had been formed in 1921 and was initially a white organisation, was a small, ineffectual and divided organisation. At one stage it had only 250 members. Emulating the Union of Soviet Socialist Republics (USSR), it was initially against participation in the Second World War, but after the USSR entered the conflict, the CPSA changed its stance and became more active than before. Indeed, the CPSA prospered in the unstable war years; its membership suddenly began to increase as did the circulation of its newspapers.

In the 1940s the ties between the CPSA and the ANC grew stronger. By 1945 there were three members of the CPSA in the ANC's national executive committee (NEC): Moses Kotane, J.B. Marks and Dan Tloome. At the time, the CPSA believed that the socialist revolution could be accelerated by promoting Africanism. It also believed that black people were being suppressed as a class rather than a racial group. The CPSA took a more active role in the trade unions, gaining greater working class support. It also introduced night schools for black workers which gave it influence in black residential areas. There were even a few Afrikaner members. Indeed at the time the CPSA was the only true non-racial political party in South Africa. It was committed to being a revolutionary party but contested elections. The 1940s was its high point, but scholars agree that it did not make full use of its opportunities.

As far as trade unionism was concerned, leading black trade unionists formed the African Federation of Trade Unions in the 1930s. In 1941 it was absorbed by a new black trade union federation, the Council of Non-European Trade Unions (CNETU). By 1945 as many as 119 trade unions, representing 158 000 workers, belonged to the CNETU. Of these trade unions, 60% were in the Transvaal and many others were active in the Eastern Cape. However, CNETU was unable to protect the interests of black workers in a proactive manner because in 1942 the Smuts government implemented War Measure No. 145 which prohibited strikes. Nevertheless, there were a few strikes, notably in coal mines, the milk industry, the brick industry and in sweet factories.

The government took a conciliatory attitude towards these outbursts because there was such a big demand for labour to produce the necessary war equipment for the South African and the Allied forces. In November 1942 the government decided to freeze wages, which led to a strike by black municipal workers in Johannesburg and riots in Pretoria. There was military intervention to end the strike and deaths occurred.

By 1939 there were more than 400 000 black mineworkers, but they were not well organised. As a result, before the Second World War there was very little activity by the trade unions in the gold-mining industry. This does not mean that black mineworkers were satisfied with their working conditions. They were particularly vocal about their meagre wage of two shillings per shift and restrictions of their rights as workers. The African Mineworkers' Union (AMWU) was formed in 1941 under these circumstances, with the black communist J.B. Marks playing a leading role. AMWU began an active recruitment campaign and by 1944 could claim 25 000 members.

The mineworkers' dissatisfaction reached a high point by 1945, yet because of wartime regulations their right to hold meetings was severely restricted. Furthermore, the end of the war coincided with a shortage of food and a cut in miners' rations. The result of all this was that riots broke out at the Modderfontein East compound. At that stage there was simply no mechanism whereby the grievances of black miners could be relayed to mine management. Neither the mining companies nor the government were prepared to hold discussions with AMWU.

In 1945 Marks was not only appointed as president of AMWU but was also chairperson of the CNETU. The next year AMWU demanded a substantial wage increase and the lifting of war measures. These demands fell on deaf ears because the Chamber of Mines did not recognise AMWU. Strikes then broke out in a few mines but there was still no improvement in the working conditions. Early in August AMWU held a public conference in Johannesburg where more than a thousand delegates unanimously decided to embark on a general strike. At the meeting Marks warned that a strike would be tantamount to an attack on the entire low-cost labour system in South Africa and that the miners would have to be ready to make sacrifices. In response, one of the mineworkers shouted: "We are already dead here in the mines!"

The strike began on 12 August 1946 and more than 70 000 of the total workforce of 308 000 black miners took part. The police became actively involved from the outset with the result that violent clashes occurred; at least twelve strikers died and 1200 were injured. After four days the strike was over, but went on record as the largest industrial strike so far in South Africa.

Jan Smuts, the prime minister at the time, denied that there were valid grievances in the mining industry and maintained that the strike had been instigated by agitators. Communist leaders such as Bill Andrews, Moses Kotane and J.B. Marks were promptly arrested. It was clear that the strike was poorly organised and prematurely staged. For instance no preparations were made to provide food for the strikers. The long-term result of the strike was that it was some time before black miners were prepared to air their grievances in this way again. However, the strike did raise the level of black militancy in the trade unions.

In 1938 radical coloured and Indian leaders established the Non-European United Front (NEUF) with Cissie Gool as national president and Yusuf Dadoo as Transvaal leader. The CPSA also played a prominent role in the formation of the NEUF because it wanted a wider support base. The NEUF was for some years very influential among coloured people in the present Western Cape.

From June 1941, when Germany invaded the USSR, the NEUF was in favour of South Africa's participation in the Second World War with the help of armed black soldiers. In December 1941 the NEUF held a conference in the Transvaal where the Non-European People's Manifesto was accepted. In this document a call was made "for the freedom of the non-European and the sweeping aside of all unjust colour bar laws which prevent the unity of all South Africans on an equal basis ..."

In the 1940s many individuals and institutions made allegations of the intrusion of Indians into areas demarcated for whites. Smuts's reaction was to appoint the Broome Commission to investigate the matter, but in its report of 1940 the commission rejected these rumours. However, three years later it delivered a second report and this time it found that there were grounds for complaint. In reaction, the government tabled restrictive legislation on Indians in the next parliamentary sitting. The press referred to this legislation as the "Pegging Act" and both the Natal Indian Congress and the Indian government reacted sharply. As a result of the widespread criticism, the government decided to withdraw the bill. In turn, the Natal Provincial Council, which represented conservative white interests, reacted negatively to its retraction.

In 1944 the tension between the radicals and the moderates in Indian politics reached breaking point. Militant Indians formed a "nationalist bloc" in the Transvaal Indian Congress (TIC) and an anti-segregation faction in the Natal Indian Congress (NIC). In 1945 the militants took over both the NIC and the TIC; Monty Naicker became president of the NIC and Yusuf Dadoo was president of the TIC. More moderate Indians established the Natal Indian Organisation.

The Smuts government passed legislation in 1946 (the Asiatic Land Tenure and Indian Representation Act) which placed further restrictions on South African Indians, but at the same time offered them limited representation. The Natal Indian Congress rejected this out of hand. Radical Indian leaders then declared a day of mourning (*hartal*) for what they called the "Ghetto Act". On the appointed day, a huge gathering of 15 000 Indians decided to launch a passive resistance campaign similar to the campaign against British control that Mohandas Gandhi launched in the same year in India. The campaign by South African Indians lasted two years and some 2000 Indians were imprisoned for squatting in restricted areas reserved for whites. However, the government persisted and the restrictive legislation stood. A positive outcome as far as Indians were concerned was that the campaign brought increased support for the NIC and its membership rose to 35 000 members.

By this time, Indian leaders were increasingly prepared to play an active part in multiracial co-operation. In 1947, Naicker of the Natal Indian Congress, Dadoo of the Transvaal Indian Congress and Xuma of the ANC – all three medical doctors – issued a joint statement in which they called for the greatest possible collaboration. They also identified certain objectives, including full adult franchise for everyone in South Africa and the expunging of all discriminatory and oppressive measures from the country's statute books. Despite this so-called "Doctors' Pact" the ANC did not support the Indians directly in their passive resistance.

In January 1949 violence broke out between black people and Indians in Durban. This was accompanied by intense bitterness, bloodthirsty attacks and the death of more than 100 people. Despite strong intervention by the government, the riots spread countrywide. When the chaos eventually died down, the ANC and the South African Indian Congress (SAIC) formed a joint committee to improve the relationship between the two groups.

By the middle of the twentieth century the black political resistance movement, after three quarters of a century of sporadic action and somewhat irregular growth, was firmly established throughout the country. Furthermore, in these 75 years the spirit of the resistance movement had become more radical. The demand for humane treatment and a better deal was clearly becoming a demand for political power.

15

The consolidation of the apartheid state, 1948-1966

David M. Scher

Few events in the history of South Africa have been as significant as the takeover of power on 26 May 1948 by the National Party (NP). The new NP government wanted to replace the racial policy of its predecessor and believed that the solution for the country's racial issues lay in the implementation of a policy of apartheid (literally "separateness"). The NP, in co-operation with the Afrikaner Party under N.C. (Klasie) Havenga, set about creating what the author Alan Paton once described as "a new heaven and a new earth, which one day would command the wonder of the world".

After the acrimonious *broedertwis* (fraternal quarrel) in Afrikaner ranks and great political and emotional setbacks of the previous years, the victory at the polls in 1948 was a triumph for Afrikaner nationalism. The political commentator and diplomat Wennie du Plessis declared that the Afrikaners had previously seen themselves as "swamped in a confusion of people". The NP government was determined to rescue the Afrikaners from this unhappy situation which according to them had been created by the unholy alliance between the English, black, coloured and Indian people under the pro-British leader, General Jan Smuts. For this post-1948 government the apartheid policy, the dismantling of coloured people's political rights, and the upliftment of Afrikaans in the following years were therefore to a large extent a process of settling old scores for the losses which Afrikaners had suffered and the humiliation they had endured.

What was apartheid?

The first time that the term apartheid appeared in print appears to have been in a pamphlet issued at a conference on the missionary endeavours of the NG Church in Kroonstad in 1929. It was used in the speech delivered by the Rev. J.C. du Plessis of Bethlehem. In *Die Burger* it was first seen in 1943 in a leading article. At about this time Dr D.F. Malan, leader of the NP, began to use the term in Parliament to differentiate his party's policy from the segregation plan of the ruling United Party (UP).

During the premierships of Generals J.B.M. Hertzog and Jan Smuts, South Africa was a segregated society. Black people had extremely limited political rights, schools and residential areas were segregated, the pass law was enforced to keep black people out of the cities, and there were separate sport and recreation facilities. On the other hand, during Smuts's second term as prime minister (1939–1948) there was an increase in the variety of social services available to black people and the level of these services was improved. Furthermore, virtually every government report, especially the report of the Fagan Commission in 1948, recommended that black people's permanent residence in the cities should be officially recognised. However, the NP was determined to curb this line of reasoning and to extend and enforce the separation between white and black people.

Although the clever use of the apartheid slogan played a role in the NP's victory at the polls in 1948, there was not yet unanimity on its exact meaning and implications. Eventually, in Parliament on 2 September 1948, Malan, now prime minister, explained what this new policy entailed. He said that although complete apartheid, or territorial apartheid, was the ideal, its implementation at that stage was not feasible because many sectors of the South African economy were reliant upon black labour. Nevertheless, separate spheres, not necessarily with absolute territorial divisions, would be established. Within these spheres, each population group would be able to develop fully its own ambitions and unique capabilities.

The NP government was convinced that social apartheid was crucial to the preservation and safeguarding of the white population's identity and wellbeing. The first measure to implement social apartheid was the Prohibition of Mixed Marriages Act of 1949. This made all marriages between white people and those of other races illegal.

In 1950 this law was supplemented by an amendment to the Immorality Act of 1927. The original act had prohibited sexual relations between white and black people; the amendment extended this restriction to all people of colour. C.R. Swart, the Minister of Justice, stated frankly in Parliament that the main purpose of the legislation was not so much to check immorality as to prevent further "admixture of blood" between white people and other races.

To facilitate the administration of social apartheid legislation, the Population Regulation Act of 1950 was passed. It provided for the classification of the population on the basis of racial categories. The racial group of an individual was determined by physical appearance (such as skin colour), general social acceptance and repute. In accordance with this Act racially based identity documents were issued. The NP ignored warnings that this classification system would bring hardship and anguish to coloured, black and Indian South Africans. In its defence the NP said this was a small price to pay in comparison to the advantages a strictly separated society would bring.

> **SANDRA LAING**
>
> Few people personify the suffering that the Population Registration Act caused better than Sandra Laing. Although both her parents were white, at ten years of age Sandra was removed from her school in Piet Retief (today emKhondo) and registered as a coloured person because of her dark complexion and curly hair.
>
> When she married a black man ten years later, her family rejected her. Her father died without ever speaking to her again and her two brothers avoided her. After about thirty years she was eventually re-united with her mother. In 2000 she was quoted in an article in the *Sunday Times* as saying:
>
> "In 1966, when I was 10, the police came to take me away from the school (Deborah Retief boarding school). Mr Van Tonder, the principal, said I was not white and could not stay. I was taken to the hostel and told to pack my things. Two policemen drove me to my father's shop in Panbult. They said I was being expelled because I looked different... My father cried. I stayed at home for two years.
>
> "In 1976 when there were uprisings against apartheid and the education system, I turned 21 and I thought things would change. I applied for an identity document then, but it took six years before I finally got my first ID as a Coloured. Until then I could not prove who I was or find work, or open an account or do whatever a person has to do.
>
> "Through those years I longed for my family, just to hear from them. I wrote several letters but they remained unanswered... Apartheid has ended, and I would like to shake Mr Mandela's hand for that, but it is too late for me."

According to T.E. Dönges, at the time the Minister of Internal Affairs, The Group Areas Act of 1950 was the cornerstone of apartheid. The aim of this Act was to make residential separation compulsory. This meant that the Union of South Africa would be divided into thousands of residential areas so that the different races could live completely separately.

Despite Dönges's assertion that this Act would be administered with justice and without discrimination, in practice this was not the case. It proved to be one of the cruellest Acts ever passed by the South African legislature. The Act cut across all traditional property rights and led to the eviction of thousands of black, coloured and Indian people from their homes, causing deep resentment. An example of this was District Six in Cape Town. From 1966 about 55 000 residents were forced to move from their homes near the city centre to the remote, windswept Cape Flats.

The NP government also wanted separate public facilities for white people and those of other races. The outcome of the Separate Amenities Act of 1953 and its amendments was the implementation of "petty" apartheid (as opposed to "grand" apartheid on a larger scale). Notice boards in public places such as halls, post offices, and restrooms typically read: "Counter for non-whites"; "Entrance for delivery boys"; "Queue for non-white servants"; or "Whites only". In terms of these laws social and cultural apartheid was increasingly imposed in South Africa.

The implementation of apartheid in public theatres regularly led to absurd situations and in most cases exposed the compelling motives of the apartheid ideology. In 1961, when the first drive-in theatre was opened for coloureds in Wetton, near Cape Town, the parking area was divided into two sections: one for coloured theatre-goers and another for white people. This while they were all parked in their cars viewing the very same film.

In 1966 the Minister of Community Development first had to give his permission before the concert pianist Jan Volkwyn, a coloured man who had just returned to South Africa from London, could perform with the Johannesburg Symphony Orchestra in front of a coloured audience in the coloured suburb of Coronationville. The permit stated that Volkwyn could not perform as a member of the orchestra but could merely be accompanied by the orchestra. It was also agreed that he would not be allowed to mix socially with members of the orchestra, nor could he use the same dressing rooms or other facilities as they did.

Another example was when Shakespeare's drama *Othello* was being presented at the Maynardville open-air theatre in Cape Town in 1968. The character in the title role is a black person, but because of apartheid regulations it had to be played by a white actor.

The NP government also advanced apartheid in the field of labour. The Native Building Workers Act of 1951 reaffirmed the "civilised labour" policy of the 1920s. It sought to protect white and coloured workers against the threat of cheap black labour. Certain sections of the Act forbade the employment, unless special exemption had been granted, of black workers by whites at their homes, for bricklaying, carpentry and other skilled work. The Native Labour (Settlement of Disputes) Act of 1953 also prohibited strikes by black workers. Although the Act did not expressly forbid black trade unions, it did not recognise them legally.

The high point of labour apartheid was reached with the passing of the Industrial Conciliation Act of 1956. It reserved several categories of work to safeguard the economic welfare of employees of any race in any undertaking, industry, trade or occupation. This legislation was in fact designed to protect the interests of white labour by preventing competition by black workers in the labour market. Black workers were trapped at the lowest level of the economic scale. One result of this law was that all lift attendants in Johannesburg were dismissed and replaced by white workers.

One of the most controversial measures passed by the NP government was the Bantu Education Act of 1953. Before 1948 most black schooling and virtually all black teachers' training was provided at mission schools. Most NP supporters viewed this as a particularly dangerous situation, believing that liberal anti-government ideas would be pumped into young black minds by malicious outsiders. They were determined to restructure black education in accordance with the new apartheid society.

The Bantu Education Act of 1953 established state control over all black education and the state therefore also took control of existing mission schools. It is notable that the Department of National Education was not given the responsibility for black education; instead it fell under the Department of Native Affairs, headed by Dr H.F. Verwoerd. In the Senate's discussion of the draft bill, Verwoerd declared that the black learner should only be equipped "to meet the demands which the economic life of South Africa will impose on him". According to Verwoerd there was "no place for him in the European community above the level of certain forms of labour". However, in their own communities they would, he said, have plenty of economic opportunities.

Verwoerd also suggested that black people had previously been subjected to a school system that was traditionally European, one which alienated them from their traditional social background. This had misled them by showing them the "green pastures of European society" in which they were "not allowed to graze". According to Verwoerd it served no useful purpose to teach a black child a curriculum that was traditionally European. He went on to say that it would be unnecessary and even absurd to teach a black child mathematics, because he would never use it in practice. Black children should be trained and taught, he said, "in accordance with their opportunities in life".

The Bantu Education Act aroused widespread protest, but Verwoerd was unmoved. The immediate result of the Act was a dramatic decline in the quality of black education. This could be seen in the decline in the number of black teachers in training from 8817 in 1954 to 5908 in 1961. At the same time the pupil/teacher ratio in black schools rose from 40:1 in 1953 to 50:1 in 1960. There was a corresponding deterioration in examination results.

The most telling criticism of Bantu Education was the fact that while the number of black children at school doubled between 1954 and 1965, there was no corresponding increase in government spending. Indeed, in this period the government expenditure on each black learner dropped considerably.

The disenfranchisement of coloured voters

In 1948 the NP government came to power with a minority of the overall popular vote and a small majority of five seats in Parliament. Rural constituencies (the stronghold of Afrikaners) had been loaded with votes since Union and urban constituencies were limited in this regard, so that a rural vote counted more heavily. The new government had a historical fear that English-speaking white South Africans would attempt to negate their minority in numbers by an alliance with black, Indian and coloured South Africans to gain a political majority.

The NP came to power with a mandate from voters to implement apartheid and the government wasted little time in removing coloured voters from the common voters' roll and creating a separate political structure for them. Coloured people's position on the common voters' roll in the Cape Province had since 1910 been entrenched in terms of the constitution of the Union of South Africa. It could only be amended by a two-thirds majority vote in a joint sitting of both houses of Parliament.

The results of the provincial by-elections of 1949 made the NP even more determined to get rid of the common voters' roll in the Cape. In contrast to the general election the previous year, the UP had won the provincial by-elections in Bredasdorp and Paarl. The NP government attributed this setback to the coloured voters who, it alleged, had formed an "unholy alliance" with the pro-British supporters of the opposition UP.

In April 1951 the government introduced the Separate Representation of Voters Bill which removed the coloured voters from the common voters' roll in the Cape. Because the coloured franchise had been entrenched by the South Africa Act of 1909, a two-thirds majority of both houses of Parliament, in joint session, was required in order to remove it. The NP government therefore had to work judiciously. A joint sitting of the two parliamentary houses was initially avoided. Instead, the bill was passed with a majority in the assembly (lower house) and also in the senate (upper house). On 18 June 1951 the bill appeared in the *Government Gazette Extraordinary* as the Separate Representation of Voters Act No. 46 of 1951.

The passing of the Act elicited a huge outcry of unprecedented protest and widespread demonstrations. More than 100 000 voters signed a petition against the government's action. Under the leadership of Sailor Malan, the popular South African pilot and hero of the Battle of Britain in the Second World War, thousands of ex-servicemen and women organised members of the Torch Commando to converge in convoys on Cape Town to present resolutions to Parliament. Malan had formed the Torch Commando earlier in 1951 to oppose, among other things, the misuse of state power, censorship, and the removal of coloured voters from the voters' roll. This outburst of protest was of concern to the government, but it did not alter its stance.

It was no secret that the UP would challenge the validity of the Separate Representation of Voters Act in court. The so-called constitutional controversy that evolved was a long and bitter struggle and led to no less than three high-profile court cases. The Appeal Court in Bloemfontein rejected the validity of the new Act several times. But refusing to accept defeat, the NP reacted by taking three phases of action. Firstly, it increased (by legislation) the number of judges in the appeal court from five to eleven. Secondly, it passed legislation to enlarge the Senate from 44 to 89 members. With the senate "packed" to its advantage, the NP had the required number of votes at a joint sitting to ensure that the entrenched clause in the South Africa Act (specifically the clause on coloured voters in the Cape) be amended. The Appeal Court in Bloemfontein then duly recognised the validity of the Separate Representation of Voters Act in 1956.

This judgement of the Appeal Court was a turning point and moved South Africa into a new political era. The coloured voters of the Cape who had voted with the whites for 103 years, were finally removed from the common roll and given separate representation (by whites) in the House of Assembly, the Senate and the Cape Provincial Council. According to Richard van der Ross, vice-rector of the University of the Western Cape, this was the greatest political setback which the coloured people had thus far experienced.

The NP stood to gain electorally from the removal of 48 000 coloured voters from the common voters' roll. It meant that certain Cape urban seats, where the coloured vote had been concentrated, were moved over to the rural areas where traditionally the NP had a strong base. The political and constitutional struggle for the separate representation of voters was therefore a significant victory for Afrikaner nationalism.

The status of black people as residents of South Africa

The racial policy in South Africa since Union in 1910 was that urban black people were temporary sojourners and that they should be encouraged to "develop along their own lines", preferably in the designated reserves. During the Second World War it became clear that this premise was being doubted.

In the years from 1946 to 1948 the Native Laws Commission (better known as the Fagan Commission) undertook an inquiry into the position of black people. The commission found that the idea of complete segregation between black and white was completely impractical. The stream of black people who were leaving the reserves and moving into the cities could not be stopped, but could be controlled. It had to be accepted that the urban areas would always have a settled, permanent population of black residents.

With the coming to power of the NP in 1948 the more liberal and pragmatic approach of the Fagan Commission was rejected. NP policy was focused on restricting the number of detribalised black people in the urban areas. The ongoing migration of the families of migrant labourers to the cities had to be stopped; and "surplus" black workers (those not required to provide the necessary labour) should be sent back to the reserves.

Initially, there was little change as far as black affairs were concerned. E.G. Jansen, the Minister of Native Affairs, favoured the old school outlook with its moderate segregation policy and hesitated to implement more drastic measures. This state of affairs changed in 1950 with the appointment of Dr Hendrik Verwoerd as Minister of Native Affairs. His appointment and that of Werner Eiselen as Secretary of Native Affairs marks the elevation of the apartheid ideologists in the government over the more pragmatic administrators of previous years.

Verwoerd was emphatic in his belief of total separation. He emphasised that in their own areas, black people could develop to the highest degree of self-government, but added that this only meant local self-government. In a speech in Parliament in 1951 he declared that all the black areas could have self-government which meant that they could decide on their own fate. These black areas would be part of the geographic and economic unit of the Union of South Africa and be dependent on it. According to Verwoerd it went without saying that the central government of the Union would be the trustee and ruler of the entire area. Although white people would always hold governing power, the NP, said Verwoerd, favoured local self-government for the black people in their own areas.

With his relentless energy and determination Verwoerd set about reshaping the whole political structure as it affected the black population. In 1951 he introduced the Bantu Authorities Bill which led to the scrapping of the Natives Representative Council (NRC). According to Verwoerd the NRC had been an absolute failure because it had tried to shape black political development on Western lines. Furthermore, ongoing agitation by the NRC had prevented a sound level of co-operation.

The new Bantu Authorities Act (1951) gave greater recognition to traditional tribal authorities. The chiefs or headmen (installed in terms of the Act) gained greater powers in their areas, but were in the final analysis responsible to the white authority, which could at any time dismiss recalcitrant leaders. An example of this was the dismissal in 1952 of Albert Luthuli, who was stripped of his traditional headmanship of the uMvoti mission reserve in Zululand because he refused to give up his leadership position in the African National Congress (ANC).

In Verwoerd's system of Bantu Authorities there was no place for black people in the Union's white political system. Blacks had to know that their future lay not in the white homeland but in their respective ethnic homelands. Verwoerd never deviated from his stance that black people in the urban areas were merely temporary visitors, even if they had been born in the cities and had lived there for a long time. His policy was strengthened by the strict implementation of influx control in terms of the Natives (Abolition of Passes and Co-ordination of Documents) Act of 1952. This Act introduced a single reference book to consolidate all the information previously kept in various other documents. It also laid down that for the first time, black women also had to carry passes, a measure that led to widespread protest. An amendment to the Urban Areas Act of 1923, passed in 1956, provided that all towns and cities in the Union would now automatically be subject to influx control.

Of all the apartheid measures, the pass law and the curfew restrictions were perhaps the most humiliating for black people. Johan de Wet, at the time editor of *Rapport*, wrote in 2000 about his memories of the curfew regulations (translated):

> Believe it or not, in those days there was a curfew in force in the towns. At 21:15 in the town where I grew up, a siren sounded. You could hear it everywhere in the town. It meant that black people who were still in the streets after 21:15 were committing an offence... People who object to claims that black people had fewer rights in the apartheid years than for example white tramps and layabouts, forget that such circumstances were very real. They are trying to deny our history.

A particular target of Verwoerd's attention was the so-called "black spots" in Johannesburg. The government was determined that these areas should be removed in the interests of apartheid. The black spot that aroused most controversy was known as the western areas, consisting of the black residential townships of Sophiatown, Martindale and Newclare. The ostensible reason for the Natives Resettlement Act of 1954 (also known as the Black Spots Act) was slum clearance. In accordance with this Act black people were forcibly removed and taken to areas beyond the city limits which were for the most part just expanses of open veld. The humiliation was made even more hurtful when the dispossessed western areas townships were converted into a white suburb and renamed Triomf (triumph).

One of the most controversial debates in the 1950s was on the report of the government's commission of inquiry into the socio-economic development of the "Bantu" areas. The commission was headed by F.R. Tomlinson, a leading agricultural economist. The Tomlinson Commission was instructed to conduct an exhaustive inquiry and to report on a comprehensive scheme for the rehabilitation of the designated black areas in the Union. The aim, according to the government, was to develop these areas effectively in accordance with the social structure of each cultural group.

According to Tomlinson's report of 1956, the separate development of the white and black populations was the only way to prevent racial conflict in the future. The report recommended that in the next ten years the state should spend about £104 million to convert the reserves into self-sufficient homelands. This would, according to the report, also check the flow of black migrant workers into the white areas. If the commission's recommended programme was purposefully implemented, it was estimated that the black population in the white section of the country would number some six million by the end of the twentieth century.

Eventually, however, Verwoerd rejected the basic elements of the Tomlinson report. He labelled the suggested expenditure on assistance for black people as extravagant and claimed it would merely destroy the black spirit of self-help. In his view the introduction of private white investment into the homelands was undesirable because it would promote integration of the various races and thereby black people would lose their entire traditional inheritance. The only concession Verwoerd was prepared to make was to agree to border industries built on white land near the black areas. Black workers could then commute to these industries daily, but had to reside permanently in their own homelands.

It must be remembered that at this stage Verwoerd was still a fiery proponent of white dominance or *baasskap* in South Africa. There was apparently no thought yet of eventual independence of the reserves. In March 1959 Eiselen, as Secretary of Native Affairs, still denied that the black areas would be granted full independence. Like his predecessors, Verwoerd still believed in one South Africa in which white people had full control over the economy.

Separate development

When Verwoerd became prime minister in 1958, black nationalism was sweeping across the African continent. In 1957 the British Gold Coast was the first African state since the Second World War to gain sovereign independence and became known as Ghana, its age-old traditional name. Thereafter many other African countries threw off the colonial yoke. The battle cry of "uhuru" (freedom) was heard throughout the continent.

Verwoerd's reaction to this new tide of African nationalism was to emphasise that white domination would have to be replaced by a policy of separate development and that various freedoms would be made available to everyone in South Africa. The Union government undertook to recognise in principle the right of black peoples to self-determination and independence, while ensuring at the same time that there would be no risk of white people being dominated by other races in South Africa.

In May 1959 Verwoerd stunned the country by introducing a master plan for the future division of black and white people in South Africa. The preamble of the Promotion of Bantu Self-Government Bill made it clear that the government did not consider the African a homogenous group but a number of separate national units on the basis of language and culture. Eight homelands would be created in which black people would be able to develop to their full capacity as independent communities. Urban black people were to be linked to their respective territorial authorities through tribal representatives appointed by the new political units. There was no question of these black people being given permanent residence in white areas even if they had been born there and had worked there all their life. It was accepted that these urban black people would eventually return to their respective homelands.

A key element of the bill was the scrapping of the existing system of representation of black people by white representatives in the central Parliament. Verwoerd argued that black people could claim no representation in the white Parliament because the two systems were incompatible. In addition, he believed that the presence of black representatives in Parliament would only strengthen the hand of the pro-integrationists.

In parliamentary debates Verwoerd stressed that the proposed scheme would lead to a permanent white South Africa with separate black national units that would be politically independent but would be bound to white South Africa through economic co-operation. He pointed out that unless the government's plan was accepted, South Africa would become a multiracial country in which the white population, by force of numbers, would be engulfed by black people. Verwoerd went on to say he had no hesitation in choosing a smaller white state rather than a large state which would eventually be controlled by black people.

The eventual independence of the black homelands and the division of South African territory into black and white areas undoubtedly represented a drastic change from the NP's traditional policy. Verwoerd's plan to enforce separate development was widely criticised by local opposition as well as international commentators. Critics emphasised the great disparity in the division of land. The black homelands, which were spread throughout South Africa, comprised only 13,7% of the country's surface area, and the mineral riches, industries and most fertile agricultural land for the most part remained in white possession.

Critics also made reference to the ongoing suppression of black nationalist organisations and the daily humiliation to which black people were exposed in terms of "petty apartheid" regulations. The so-called Bantustan policy, as critics dubbed it, was seen as a device to divide and rule the black majority. It was, said the critics, more in the line of colonial rule than, as Verwoerd claimed, an anti-colonialist measure designed to liberate the black peoples of South Africa.

Nothing identified this difference in outlook between the international community and the Union of South Africa more than the speech delivered in Parliament in Cape Town on 3 February 1960 by the then British prime minister, Harold Macmillan. He rejected the apartheid and separate development approach of the South African government who, he suggested, had not yet appreciated the force of the "winds of change" in the world since the Second World War. These winds, he said, were blowing over simmering nationalisms – especially in Africa.

South Africa's withdrawal from the Commonwealth

Afrikaner nationalists had long cherished the ideal of making the Union of South Africa a republic. In the 1930s and early 1940s they promoted the idea of a republic that would be authoritarian, Christian-National and Afrikaans. However, after the Second World War the NP abandoned the idea of an old authoritarian republic in favour of a democratic republic in which English speakers would also enjoy full rights.

Although various monarchical state symbols were in time replaced by South African ones, little came of the republican ideal before Verwoerd was appointed as prime minister. He was determined to establish a republic during his premiership. He believed that a republic would promote South Africa's independence, foster white unity and provide the framework for a satisfactory solution to the racial question.

On 20 January 1960, Verwoerd announced in Parliament that white voters would be asked to indicate by means of a special referendum if they were in favour of a republic or not. An ordinary majority of voters would decide the issue. The republic, said Verwoerd, would be democratic and Christian, the equality of the two official languages (Afrikaans and English) would be maintained as well as the parliamentary form of government. The post of governor general would be replaced by that of a state president who would be elected by Parliament. The state president would be above politics and be a symbol of national unity. The republic would maintain friendly relations with Britain and the Commonwealth countries, while membership of the Commonwealth would be considered as a separate matter.

Verwoerd's decision to hold a referendum on the question of a republic was a bold political risk. Although the NP had won a large majority of seats in the 1958 general election, together the opposition parties had in fact won more individual votes than the NP.

However, a number of factors counted in Verwoerd's favour, notably the fact that black, Indian and coloured people were excluded from taking part in the referendum, although white people in South West Africa (now Namibia) could vote. Another factor was that not all opposition supporters were necessarily against the idea of a republic. Many English speakers were dismayed by Harold Macmillan's "winds of change" speech. By implication Britain had publicly distanced itself from South African policies and was siding with emerging African nationalism. This perception of Macmillan's so-called "betrayal" undoubtedly won additional votes for the republican cause from opposition ranks.

In 1960 there was serious ongoing unrest in black townships countrywide, particularly in Sharpeville, Langa, Mbekweni, Soweto and KwaMashu. The state of emergency lasted for several months. Although the police shooting in Sharpeville and the government's harsh reaction in general was strongly condemned throughout the world, the criticism did not diminish Verwoerd's standing internally. On the contrary, he was increasingly seen by Afrikaners and English speakers alike as a "pillar of strength" in the face of chaos. Many voters preferred the idea of an ordered republic with Verwoerd at the helm than being part of a monarchy and a Commonwealth that was troubled and divided.

On 9 April 1960 at the Rand Easter Show in Johannesburg an attempt was made on Verwoerd's life. He survived the shooting and received an overwhelming number of messages of goodwill and sympathy. Indeed, the failed attempt on his life brought certain emotional and political rewards.

Verwoerd's personal authority was further strengthened when violence broke out in the Congo after the colony gained its independence on 30 June 1960. The horrific stories of murder and arson in the Congo were fully exploited by the NP government. According to the government, only separate development would prevent similar bloodshed and chaos in South Africa.

Verwoerd's gamble of holding a referendum eventually paid off, but only just. In the referendum of 5 October 1960 there was a small but decisive majority of 74 580 votes in favour of a republic. Of the record number of registered voters (90,5%) who cast their votes, 850 450 were in favour of a republic and 775 870 against.

In one respect Verwoerd's calculations were inaccurate. According to Fred Barnard, his private secretary, Verwoerd had no doubt that South Africa's application to remain a member of the Commonwealth would be approved; he felt the application was a mere formality. He failed to realise the extent of condemnation of South Africa's apartheid policy among other Commonwealth member states and their heads of government. Jawaharlal Nehru of India, Kwame Nkrumah of Ghana and John Diefenbaker of Canada all came out strongly against South Africa's policies. It was clear that continued membership of the Commonwealth would become increasingly intolerable for the South African government.

On 15 March 1961 Verwoerd made a surprise announcement at the Commonwealth conference that he was withdrawing South Africa's application to remain in the Commonwealth. This caused a sensation in South Africa and overseas. What might have been a humiliating rejection became, in the eyes of many, particularly Afrikaners, a national triumph. Large crowds gathered at the airports in Johannesburg and Cape Town to welcome the prime minister home. Despite strong black opposition against the idea of a republic, the planned stay-away of black workers was largely unsuccessful and there were no mass protests.

On 31 May 1961 the Republic of South Africa was officially proclaimed. On Church Square in Pretoria, C.R. Swart was inaugurated as the first state president. A new, but lonely, road lay ahead for the republic.

The struggle against apartheid intensifies

Even before the NP government came to power in 1948 there was growing resistance among black people against discriminatory and oppressive legislation. Their anger was focused to a large extent on the pass law and the Urban Areas Acts.

The African National Congress (ANC) took the lead in the resistance. In January 1952, Dr James S. Moroka and Walter Sisulu of the ANC signed an ultimatum in which they called upon the government to repeal six laws they saw as particularly unjust. These included the Group Areas Act, the Bantu Authorities Act, the Separate Representation of Voters Act and the Suppression of Communism Act. The ultimatum was rejected and the government warned that it would act firmly against those who defied the laws of the land.

This warning did not deter African nationalists and on 26 June 1952 they launched a campaign of resistance which they called the Defiance Campaign. On that day some 250 leaders of the ANC deliberately infringed regulations governing black people and openly courted arrest and jail. By the end of that year more than 8000 black activists had served terms of imprisonment for their participation in the campaign.

After this outburst of resistance the ANC, with its co-operating bodies the Indian National Congress, the Coloured People's Organisation and the Congress of Democrats (a strongly left-wing white group), began to lay plans for a national convention to draft a new constitution. Delegates from throughout the country gathered on 26 June 1955 in Kliptown, near Johannesburg, and within two days they had accepted what they called the Freedom Charter. The charter reaffirmed at the outset that South Africa was a multiracial country that belonged to all its people, both black and white.

A feature of the protests in the 1950s was the prominent role played by black women. The extension of passes to black women in 1952 met with strong resistance. On 9 August 1956 about 20 000 black women marched to the Union Buildings in Pretoria to protest against the pass law.

In December 1956, in a dramatic manner, the government arrested 156 leaders of the ANC and allied organisations and charged them with high treason. Among the accused were Albert Luthuli (president of the ANC at the time), Oliver Tambo, Nelson Mandela, Z.K. Matthews (acting head of Fort Hare College) and Len Lee-Warden (Native Representative for the Western Cape). Most of the accused were known for their stand against violence and it was clear that political considerations played a role in the government's action. The Treason Trial dragged on with many delays and interruptions until March 1961, when all the accused were found not guilty.

The pressure on apartheid increased and a new generation of angry young people demanded radical action. Against this background, a new grouping in the ANC began to question the policy of co-operation with other groups, especially white people. The idea of a multiracial society was rejected and there was a call of "Africa for the Africans". This group eventually broke away from the ANC and formed the Pan Africanist Congress (PAC) under Robert Sobukwe in April 1959.

Both the ANC and PAC were planning action against the pass laws, but the PAC felt the ANC was not proactive enough; they wanted their campaign to be "decisive and final". Their strategy was for all PAC members to leave their passes at home on a certain date and offer themselves at the nearest police station for arrest. On 19 March Sobukwe announced that the PAC would begin its anti-pass campaign on 21 March. However, support for the PAC's call was largely limited to Vereeniging and the Cape Peninsular. It was clear that the police contingent in the township of Sharpeville, near Vereeniging, was surprised by the extent of the restless, milling crowd outside the police station. Some of the policemen were inexperienced and panicky and they fired blindly at the threatening crowd. This led to a massacre in which 69 people were killed, including eight women and ten children, while 180 people were wounded.

The Sharpeville incident brought the campaigns against the pass system in the Transvaal to an end, but in Cape Town the PAC went ahead with new determination with a march in which 30 000 demonstrators from Langa walked to the centre of Cape Town. A state of emergency was declared at the end of March that was only lifted on 31 August 1960. The ANC and PAC were both declared unlawful organisations on 8 April of that same year.

The Sharpeville and Langa incidents and the banning of the ANC and PAC were a turning point in South African history. Driven underground, with headquarters overseas, the two black nationalist movements were now dedicated to winning liberation through military action. With this change of policy, the PAC formed its military wing called Poqo ("pure, alone", in Xhosa). The ANC's armed wing, Umkhonto we Sizwe (MK) ("spear of the nation") was under the leadership of Nelson Mandela and was committed to a programme of sabotaging installations without loss of life. The ANC claimed that a turn to the armed struggle was a result of the proven failure of non-violent methods to achieve change and justice.

The Sharpeville tragedy aroused a great deal of anger and indignation overseas. Foreign investors lost confidence in the country; capital was withdrawn from the country on a huge scale and emigration increased.

The NP tightens its grip

After Macmillan's "winds of change" speech, the Sharpeville crisis, the insurrection in the Congo and the expected withdrawal of colonial powers from Africa, an increasing number of white people regarded the ruling party in South Africa as the only bulwark against rising black nationalism. As a result, the NP's position was strengthened appreciably in the period 1961–1966, the last five years of Verwoerd's term as prime minister.

This period also coincided with one of the greatest economic booms in South Africa's history. Foreign capital flowed into the country once again and a record number of immigrants arrived in South Africa. It appeared that the country could easily ward off attacks from outside and internal unrest was effectively crushed. As was confidently expected, in March 1966 Verwoerd led the NP to its greatest electoral victory at that stage. The results were: National Party 126 seats; United Party 39 seats; and the Progressive Party 1 seat.

After the suppression of black nationalist organisations such as the ANC and PAC, Verwoerd implemented a "carrot and stick" policy towards black people. The "carrot" was the prospect of a bright future in the homelands, which, he said, held unlimited possibilities for black entrepreneurs. In 1976 the Transkei gained so-called independence, although this was not recognised by any other state except South Africa. The "stick" was the continued implementation of influx control, security legislation and other strong-arm measures. Verwoerd made it clear that if urban black people did not accept the homelands policy and abandoned their ideas of a stake in white South Africa, they would end up with nothing.

As far as coloured people were concerned, Verwoerd rejected outright the idea that they should sit in Parliament. As a "nation in the making", the most they could expect was the right to self-government in their own residential areas. Equal treatment with white people was not an option.

Government policy did change as far as the South African Indian community was concerned. Initially, the NP government refused to recognise them as a permanent part of the population and took steps to implement a policy of repatriation to India. Very few Indians took up this offer. Eventually, in 1961, the government granted them permanent citizenship and a Department of Indian Affairs was created. However, as was the case with coloured people, Indian people were also subjected to many apartheid measures such as the Group Areas Act.

Meanwhile, in 1963 the underground movements were dealt a crippling blow when the police raided the Lilliesleaf smallholding in Rivonia, north of Johannesburg, and a large number of ANC leaders were arrested. At the subsequent Rivonia trial, Nelson Mandela, commander of MK, who had been arrested in August 1962, delivered a notable (and much-quoted) address which lasted four and a half hours. After he had explained why MK had turned to armed resistance, he once again declared his willingness to lay down his life for the ideal of a democratic, non-racial South African society, saying:

> During my lifetime I have dedicated myself to the struggle of the African people. I have fought against white domination, and I have fought against black domination. I have cherished the ideal of a democratic society in which all persons live together in harmony and with equal opportunities. It is an ideal which I hope to live for and to achieve. But if needs be, it is an ideal for which I am prepared to die.

On 12 June 1964 Mandela, Sisulu, Govan Mbeki and others were found guilty of the planning and committing acts of sabotage aimed at overthrowing the government. They were sentenced to life imprisonment.

By 1966 the NP government had reached the pinnacle of its power. The campaign of violence against apartheid had been suppressed and virtually all the leaders of the liberation movement were in prison, banned or had gone into exile. In addition the country experienced an unprecedented economic upswing. And of course a strong economy translated into a strong military and security state. Generally speaking, white people enjoyed an exceptionally high standard of living.

However, this was in marked contrast to the fate of the vast majority of black people, who lived a life of poverty and insecurity. The historian Robin Hallett wrote:

> Few communities in the history of urban man have been so bereft of basic human rights as the inhabitants of white South Africa [in the apartheid years]. To live in Soweto or any other black township seems to an outsider like living in a barbed-wire entanglement, so many are the regulations which residents are required to observe.

In this vast labyrinth of bureaucratic controls the lives of millions of people were subject to great pressure. In the years to come the country was destined to taste the bitter fruit of the NP government's obsession with the apartheid ideology and its refusal to make meaningful concessions.

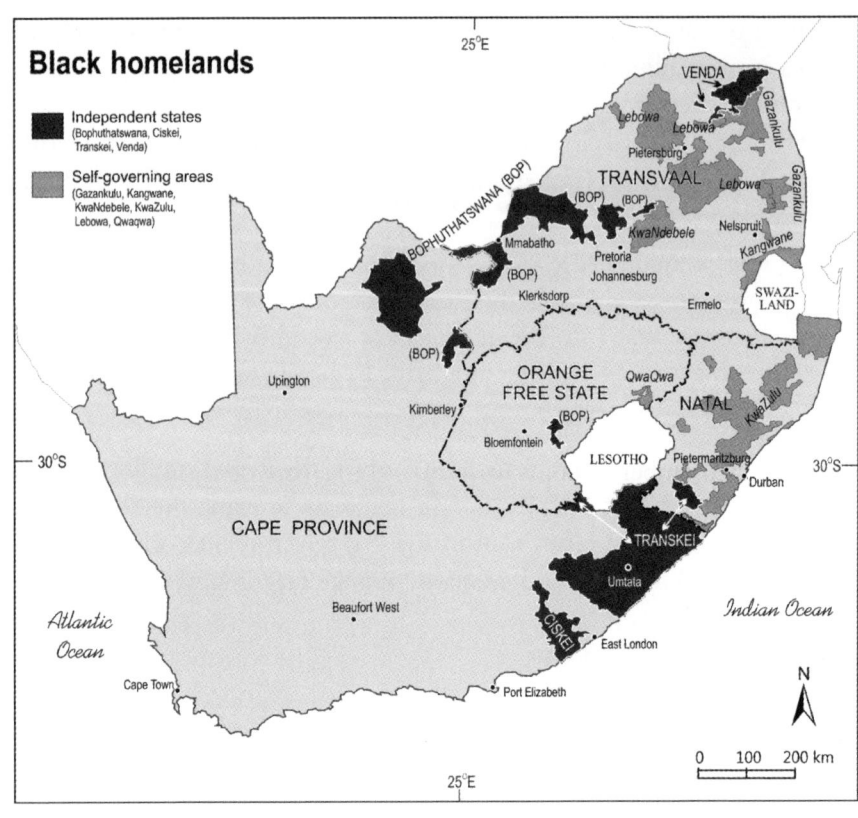

16
B.J. Vorster and separate development
Kobus du Pisani

On 13 September 1966, a week after H.F. Verwoerd was stabbed to death with a dagger in Parliament in Cape Town, the caucus of the ruling National Party (NP) unanimously elected B.J. (John) Vorster as leader of the party and prime minister. As Minister of Justice since 1961, Vorster earned the image of a strong leader who warded off the advances of communists and black nationalists against apartheid South Africa. Vorster undertook to follow in Verwoerd's footsteps and to put the policy of separate development (apartheid) into practice. It was soon clear that as a leader he was far more pragmatic than Verwoerd had been.

As far as internal policy was concerned, one of Vorster's first initiatives was to implement the homeland policy. Verwoerd had initiated the idea that the different black ethnic groups in South Africa – the Xhosa, Zulu, Tswana and others – should each have their own homeland which would eventually become independent states. The Bantu Authorities Act (1951) and the Promotion of Bantu Self-Government Act (1959) were passed to implement the homeland policy. Black authorities were created in the rural areas. When Vorster took over in 1966 the Transkei was the only self-governing homeland with a chief minister, cabinet and legislative assembly.

At the beginning of Vorster's term of office, government committees worked at speeding up the implementation of the homeland policy. More functions were transferred to the homeland authorities; their own government departments were established; and black officials were trained to replace white officials. The other homelands were placed on the same path of self-development as the Transkei. M.C. Botha, the Minister of Bantu Administration and Development, and other policy makers spoke of "multinational development". They argued that the South African population comprised a variety of population groups who were at different levels of development. The ideal was that the various black societies would become independent states in their own territories with their own governments, administrations and amenities.

Black people would eventually gain citizenship of their respective homelands and would thereby lose their South African citizenship and their right to permanent residence in the designated white areas. Every black person would enjoy political rights, such as the franchise and parliamentary representation, in the homeland of his or her own specific group, but would have no political rights in white South Africa.

As far as foreign policy was concerned, Vorster came to power at a time when international pressure against apartheid, which was widely considered racist and inhumane, was mounting in intensity. Anti-apartheid organisations in many countries, the Liberation Committee (LC) of the Organisation of African Unity (OAU) and the United Nations (UN) special committee on apartheid, tried their utmost to isolate South Africa in every sphere.

In 1969 the OAU adopted the Lusaka Manifesto which declared that the dismantling of apartheid and a commitment to majority rule were prerequisites for any negotiations by other African states with South Africa. The OAU recognised both the African National Congress (ANC) and the Pan Africanist Congress (PAC) as representing the legitimate voice of the black majority and endorsed their armed struggle against apartheid.

Against this background of growing pressure Vorster announced that as far as his foreign policy was concerned he envisaged leading South Africa to full international participation. However, he realised that his government would first have to establish cordial relations with black African states to counteract isolation and show that he was prepared to hold mutual discussions with African leaders on an equal footing.

Vorster's initial breakthrough was in September 1967 when he established official relations with Malawi; these were elevated to ambassador level in 1971. His visit to Malawi in 1970 was the first official visit of a South African prime minister to an independent African state. The next year President Hastings Banda of Malawi became the first black head of state to make an official visit to South Africa.

Vorster's first term as prime minister saw the first signs of a dispute between the *verligtes* (Afrikaners who were politically more enlightened) and *verkramptes* (the die-hard conservatives). Among Afrikaners at the time these two opposing factions had different opinions on the nature of their relations with other population groups such as the English speakers and black people. Earlier, the conservative laager mentality – the mindset that Afrikaners' strength lay in their collusion and isolation – had set the tone of Afrikaner society. In the 1960s the voices of less conservative Afrikaans church leaders, academics, writers and journalists became more insistent. They called for greater openness and more interaction with other groups. The tussle between the *verkramptes* and the *verligtes* – names coined by Willem de Klerk, an academic and later newspaper editor – spread to various Afrikaans organisations and the NP.

Initially the quarrel was waged for the most part in the Afrikaans newspapers. The *verkramptes* aired their objections about Vorster's policies on sport, black diplomats, co-operation between Afrikaans and English speakers and immigration. They were afraid that small concessions might prove to be the thin edge of the wedge and eventually lead to a betrayal of the NP's traditional policy. Vorster's reaction was that adaptation to a changing situation was necessary, but he assured his detractors that he would not deviate from NP principles. In 1967 he warned that the "liberal hunters" should stop casting suspicion on their fellow Afrikaners. In 1968 Vorster announced in the NP caucus that Albert Hertzog, a cabinet minister who was regarded as the leader of the *verkramptes* in the NP, was the source of insinuations being made against him. Later that same year he shuffled his cabinet and left Hertzog out. In August, Vorster issued an ultimatum to the *verkramptes* that they either declare their loyalty to him – or look for another political home.

Eventually, in September 1969 at the Transvaal NP congress, the dispute in the party reached crisis point over concessions made in the sport policy. Vorster called an early election, upon which Albert Hertzog, together with three other NP members of Parliament – Jaap Marais, Willie Marais and Louis Stofberg – formed the Reconstituted National Party (Herstigte Nasionale Party or HNP) in October 1969. A bitter fraternal quarrel between the two Afrikaans-oriented parties was the dominant feature of the election campaign.

In the 1970 election the new party was unable to win a single seat but the United Party (UP) opposition took advantage of the dispute in Afrikaner ranks. For the first time since 1948 the NP's total number of seats decreased, while the UP's rose. Vorster was very disappointed about this election outcome; he became almost obsessive to preserve Afrikaner unity and to avoid further ruptures in the NP at all costs. His obsession with NP unity put a definite brake on the policy reforms he was contemplating.

A second term of office, 1970–1974

In his second term as prime minister, Vorster distinguished himself as a skilful party politician. He succeeded in unifying the National Party under his leadership after the breakaway of the HNP. The *verligtes* within the party supported the pragmatic way he made policy adaptations, while the *verkramptes* approved of his decisive stance on state security and the maintenance of law and order.

Vorster's stature as the symbolic leader of the Afrikaner people increased. He prioritised the maintenance of Afrikaner identity and had a keen awareness for the aspirations of most Afrikaners. However, as head of government he also called for co-operation between Afrikaners and English speakers, because addressing Afrikaner interests was not his only concern.

By 1972 the swing towards the UP had been checked. Internal dissent between the so-called Young Turks and the Old Guard put the UP on a downward trajectory. There was also disunity over the UP's race federation policy and over the party's participation in the Schlebusch Commission that was investigating the activities of left-wing organisations. Some English newspapers demanded the resignation of De Villiers Graaff as party leader.

In comparison to the floundering UP, the NP under Vorster with its combination of pragmatism and conservatism went from strength to strength. Its popular support among Afrikaners and conservative English speakers showed a strong upward curve. However, Vorster clashed with liberal-minded English-language newspapers, churches and universities over his strict enforcement of security legislation and his alleged violation of human rights and freedoms by sanctioning arrests, detention without trial and restriction orders.

One of Vorster's policy priorities, despite the worldwide opposition to apartheid, was to consolidate and expand South Africa's foreign relations. In his second term of office he made significant breakthroughs in the area of foreign policy. It was important for Afrikaners to be part of "Christian Western civilisation" and be accepted as a staunch ally against the "communist threat". The apartheid state's most important ties were with the West, particularly Britain, the USA and Western Europe. Britain had strong political and economic links with South Africa and these were maintained despite the tension between the Vorster government and Harold Wilson's Labour government. South Africa also had close ties with the Caetano government in Portugal and the two countries co-operated on development projects in Mozambique and Angola to consolidate white control in southern Africa.

France was the major supplier of military weapons to South Africa and provided nuclear technology and equipment for the construction of the Koeberg nuclear power station in exchange for South African uranium. One of Vorster's top priorities was to maintain cordial relations with the USA super power, the leader of the Western world. In the Cold War, South Africa's mineral wealth and strategic position on the Cape sea route were important for the USA. During Richard Nixon's presidency (1969–1974) it was accepted that white control in South Africa would continue in the foreseeable future and that it was in the USA's best interests to work amicably with the NP government.

Because Vorster realised that South Africa's path to good relations with the rest of the world would be through Africa, he hoped that dialogue with African leaders by way of personal discussions would open doors for him elsewhere in the continent. In 1970, after Vorster had issued a non-aggression pact to African states, President Félix Houphouët-Boigny of the Ivory Coast expressed himself in favour of dialogue with South Africa. However, not all African states supported him in this and the issue sparked a great deal of debate. At the OAU summit of June 1971 in Addis Ababa, the idea of dialogue with South Africa was rejected and the OAU's support for the liberation movements' armed struggle was reconfirmed. However, the Ivory Coast continued its contact with South Africa. For their part, Vorster and his advisers persisted in their endeavours to expand dialogue with African states.

After 1960, the banning of the ANC and PAC and the detention of most of their leaders crippled the black resistance movement inside the country. At the beginning of the 1970s, resistance by the Black Consciousness Movement under leadership of Steve Biko began to gain momentum at black universities. In 1973 there was also a series of strikes by black workers for better wages in the Durban area; these spread to other parts of the country and led to the formation of independent black trade unions. However, the government refused to recognise the trade unions as bodies which could conduct collective bargaining. Popular support among most black people for the Black Consciousness Movement and the strikes forewarned the government that it should prepare for widespread mass resistance.

Vorster brought forward the general election that was due in 1975 to April 1974 because he expected that South Africa's external relations and economy might deteriorate and because he wanted to deal a knock-out blow to the disunited UP opposition. The NP's election campaign was built around Vorster. His pragmatic compliancy and his forcefulness was emphasised to retain the support of the liberal-minded as well as the conservative voters. In his pre-election speeches Vorster was able to exploit the division in opposition ranks. Economic factors also counted in the government's favour because although inflation had begun to rear its head there was still strong economic growth in the country. Salaries and wages were in a rising phase and the unemployment figure was low.

One of the greatest achievements of the Vorster regime in this phase of economic growth was the large-scale establishment of infrastructure in the country. A few examples of strategic infrastructure that were completed while Vorster was in power and were destined to make an impact on the South African economy for a long time are the Verwoerd Dam (now the Gariep Dam) and the Orange–Fish tunnel; the aluminium foundry and the coal export terminal at Richards Bay; the uranium enrichment plant at Pelindaba; the Koeberg nuclear power station; the Atlas Aircraft Corporation; a third Iscor steel plant; a second Sasol fuel plant and Natref refinery; the Saldanha steel factory and the Sishen–Saldanha railway line; the undersea telephone cable (to Europe); the space observation station at Sutherland; and the Hartebeesthoek earth satellite station.

In the 1974 election the NP increased its number of seats from 118 to 123 and the Progressive Party (PP) improved its one seat to five. The UP count went down from 47 to 41. For the shaky UP, which lost seats to both the NP and the PP, the election was a disaster.

In the four years between the general elections of 1970 and 1974, Vorster's stature as leader of the government and the NP grew and he dominated the political scene. While the UP opposition was crumbling, riven by division, Vorster succeeded in halting the NP's backward slide and turning it around. He united the conservative and moderate white people around him; his unquestionable leadership qualities were confirmed in the result of the 1974 election.

The homeland system under pressure

The purpose of the Bantu Homelands Citizenship Act of 1970 was that every black person in South Africa would eventually became a citizen of one of the ten homelands (initially there were only eight). In terms of the Bantu Homelands Constitution Act (1971) the other homelands were placed on the same path to self-government as Transkei by making provision for legislative, executive and judicial powers to be transferred to them. In the years that followed, Bophuthatswana, Venda, Ciskei, Gazankulu, Lebowa, Qwaqwa and KwaZulu all gained self-government.

The chief ministers of some homelands were outspoken in their criticism on aspects of the South African government's policy, which gave a measure of credibility to the homeland system. Vorster's government had more interactive discussions with the homeland leaders than any of his predecessors. From 1973 Vorster held a series of conferences with the chief ministers where black aspirations and grievances were brought to his attention. Thereafter he made certain concessions.

A difficult aspect of the homeland policy was the consolidation of the scattered territories in black possession to form larger geographical entities and make the homelands politically and economically more sustainable. Bophuthatswana for example comprised 19 separate pieces of land, while KwaZulu had 29 large areas and 41 smaller ones. Proposals to consolidate the ten homelands into 24 blocks of land were approved in Parliament. Although much more land was needed to make the homelands sustainable, Vorster refused to abandon the old original land acts of 1913 and 1936 as the basis of land allocation. These two laws had laid down that only 13% of the total area of South Africa could be in the possession of black people. A comprehensive programme for the purchase and transfer of land to the homelands was initiated by Vorster and under his leadership the amount of land owned by black people increased by about 15%, or 2 million hectares.

Certainly the greatest failure of the homeland system was that none of the homelands ever became economically independent. Much was done to stimulate their economic development, but sufficient work opportunities were not created. According to available statistics the homelands remained largely dependent on the central government for their revenue.

The forced removal of entire communities as part of the homeland policy caused a great deal of disruption and suffering. In terms of government policy, all "surplus" black people, that is those who were not involved in productive labour, had to move to the homelands. Pressure was placed upon communities to accept this relocation. While Vorster was in power, an estimated 1,5 to 2 million black people were resettled in the homelands. Despite this, the number of black people living in "white" South Africa was still more than double the number of whites.

These forced removals did not have the desired outcome. Large numbers of economically inactive people were a massive burden on the struggling economies of the homelands; poverty, unemployment and a lack of housing were the order of the day. Opponents of apartheid alleged that the homelands served as reservoirs of cheap black labour for the apartheid economy and a dumping ground for the surplus black population.

The growing number of urban blacks became an increasing obstacle in the path of separate development. According to apartheid thinking, black people were temporary sojourners, visiting labourers in the white areas. As such, they were subjected to strict measures that controlled their movement, employment and period of residence. Thousands of black people were prosecuted for contravention of the pass laws. This led to so much criticism being heaped on the government that it began to devise ways of streamlining influx control.

It was further argued that black people living in urban areas should exercise their political rights in the homelands by voting in the elections held for the legislative organs in these homelands. Blacks therefore had a very marginal role in the local government of black residential areas in "white" South Africa, because local bodies on which they had representation had no real power. There was a growing insistence by black people for a more meaningful input in decision making in the urban areas where they lived. However, with the introduction of Bantu administration boards, the central government took over the control of urban black residential areas that had previously been the responsibility of local government bodies, which meant that the government regulated all aspects of the lives of black people in white areas. Not surprisingly, the administration boards were regarded as agents of government policy and were unacceptable to the majority of urban black people.

They were subjected to so-called "petty apartheid" to limit social integration between white and black to the minimum. Blacks and whites were not allowed to share facilities such as hotels, restaurants, sports fields and beaches. They could not sit on the same park benches or travel in the same train carriages. Black people had to use separate entrances to government buildings and other public places.

Black workers, who made up more than 70% of the total South African workforce, were also strictly regulated. Skilled work was reserved for white workers and black workers could not hold senior positions over white workers. Furthermore, black workers earned lower wages and because their trade unions were not officially recognised, they were reliant upon toothless workers' committees to represent their interests in the workplace.

Minority groups in the Vorster era

The Vorster government was uncertain on how best to make provision for coloured people and those of Indian descent. These groups did not have their own homeland areas and were placed on a trajectory of parallel development living in the same geographical areas, but separate from white people.

In the 1950s coloured people were deliberately separated from the white population in terms of the Prohibition of Mixed Marriages Act, the Separate Amenities Act and the Separate Representation of Voters Act. They had to be satisfied with indirect representation in Parliament, the Cape Provincial Council and an ineffective nominated Coloured Advisory Council. In 1968 the government accepted the recommendations of the Louwrens Muller Commission and scrapped the indirect representation for coloured people in Parliament and the Cape Provincial Council. The Coloured Advisory Council was also dissolved.

Legislation was then passed whereby a Coloured Persons Representative Council (CRC) was formed with limited legislative and executive powers. The first election for the CRC took place in September 1969. When the Labour Party (LP) won the majority of elected seats on the CRC, the government promptly gave all the nominated seats to the pro-government Federal Party (FP) to ensure that the FP had the overall majority. This blatant government manipulation of the system caused great bitterness in LP ranks and seriously undermined the CRC's credibility. The CRC remained an ineffective body because it did not have the support of the majority of coloured people. CRC sittings degenerated into an ongoing spat between the LP and the FP and most coloured people chose not to take part in any CRC elections.

A militant spirit of resistance against apartheid began to grow among the younger generation of coloured people and unrest at the University of the Western Cape in 1972 and 1973 focused attention on their frustration. An increasing number of the coloured elite became more radical in their political outlook; they moved closer to the Black Consciousness Movement.

Prior to 1961 the NP policy towards Indians in South Africa was that they should be repatriated to India. After South Africa became a republic, the government accepted them as permanent residents of South Africa and a Department of Indian Affairs was formed. In terms of the South African Indian Council Act (1968) provision was made for a nominated Indian council. It was envisaged that in time this council would become fully elected and provide Indians with self-government on an increasing range of issues that concerned their wellbeing. However, as had happened among the coloured people, Indians were deeply divided over the best means of gaining meaningful political change: whether to become part of government structures such as the Indian Council, or to boycott it.

The era of détente, 1974–1976

After the 1974 election, circumstances became more difficult for the Vorster government. Demands for internal reform put apartheid under growing pressure. The worldwide economic recession of the mid-1970s impacted negatively on South Africa and led to inflation and balance-of-payments deficits.

The government slowly began to move away from racial discrimination based on skin colour. An interdepartmental cabinet committee gave attention to the elimination of "unnecessary" discrimination and made recommendations to this effect to the cabinet. A move was made to open certain amenities such as hotels, restaurants and theatres to all population groups. Differences of opinion within the NP between conservatives and reformists led to ongoing controversy, for example over the opening of the Nico Malan theatre in Cape Town; the changing policy on sport; and the so-called coloured policy.

In reaction to pressure for change, Vorster once again reiterated that he would continue along the path of separate development. In consultation with the chief ministers of the homelands and the executive committees of the CRC and the South African Indian Council, he emphasised that there would be changes in the framework of separate development. He made it clear that he was not considering sharing of power or direct parliamentary representation for coloured, Indian or black people. However, the government was committed to expanding the homeland system for black people and to effecting parallel development for coloureds and Indians.

By the mid-1970s it was time for the homelands to decide whether they wanted to become independent states. The Mills report, a blueprint for the political development of the homelands, was duly accepted. The chief ministers of some homelands were against being cut off politically from South Africa and instead suggested the formation of a South African federation, but Vorster rejected this idea out of hand. Instead he was in favour of a constellation of southern African states in which politically independent African states could work together for the benefit of the region.

Motions for independence were accepted in the Transkei and Bophuthatswana legislative assemblies and their governments began discussions with the central government on the process of becoming independent. By means of status and constitutional legislation the sovereignty of the two homelands was transferred from the South African government to their respective governments. Official undertakings were signed for future relations between South Africa, Transkei and Bophuthatswana. Elections for members of the national assemblies of the two homelands were also held. Transkei became independent on 26 October 1976 and Bophuthatswana on 6 December 1977; both occasions were lavishly celebrated in Umtata (Mthatha) and Mmabatho respectively.

Homeland independence was meant to be the crowning glory of the policy of separate development, but the majority of South Africans did not support it. This was because it not only fractured the unity of the country into smaller entities; it also denied black people their birthright as South Africans. The biggest blow of all to the homeland policy was that no country other than South Africa was prepared to recognise the homelands as sovereign independent states. In the international arena they were never able to function independently of South Africa. The government had to accept the reality that not all the homelands wanted independence and that the envisaged constellation of states was not to be.

Nor could the Vorster government persuade most of the coloureds and Indians to accept the concept of parallel development. In the second CRC election of 1975 the LP took control of the CRC. This party was in favour of direct parliamentary representation for coloured people and wanted to destroy the CRC from within through a strategy of disruption and boycotts. When Sonny Leon, leader of the Labour Party and chairperson of the CRC's executive authority was dismissed from his position, CRC became a farce. Every year the LP majority rejected the budget and adjourned the sitting before all the matters on the agenda had been handled. The LP held discussions with white opposition parties and black homeland leaders who insisted that a multiparty national convention should be convened to draw up a democratic constitution for the country.

The Erica Theron Commission's report on coloured people was tabled in Parliament in 1976. It recommended direct political representation for coloureds at all levels of government, but the government rejected this. The coloureds who felt aggrieved that they were being oppressed along with black people, found increasing acceptance in the Black Consciousness Movement. They preferred to cultivate links with the black liberation struggle rather than to co-operate with the government. When unrest erupted in Soweto in 1976 and spread countrywide, many coloured people participated in strikes, stayaways and mass campaigns.

Vorster stood firm that he was not planning to disband the CRC or to give the coloured people direct parliamentary representation. He announced that the CRC would become a fully representative body, would be given more powers and a bigger budget. A cabinet council was formed to promote interaction between Parliament, the CRC and the South African Indian Council on the mutual interests of white, coloured and Indian population groups. From September 1976 meetings of the cabinet council were held under chairmanship of the prime minister, but the LP leaders refused to participate.

In November 1974 the first election for the South African Indian Council was held. Similar to the CRC, the Indian Council had no real political power and was unable to gain legitimacy in the Indian community. Vorster had announced that it would become a predominantly elected body and would be given more powers and functions. However, in radical circles it was branded as a mere puppet body manipulated by the apartheid regime. The countrywide unrest since 1976 had also strengthened the politically radical element in Indian ranks and the Natal Indian Congress was revived. Supporters of the strategy of non-cooperation with the government campaigned against participation in the Indian Council.

By the mid-1970s South Africa was a political cauldron. Prior to April 1974, South Africa was surrounded by white-ruled states. South West Africa (now Namibia), a former mandated region of the UN, was administered by South Africa as if it were a fifth province. Rhodesia, a former British colony, at the time under the white minority government of Ian Smith, declared unilateral independence in 1965. The South African government was Smith's greatest ally against international pressure to hand over control of Rhodesia to an elected multiracial black majority government. Mozambique and Angola were under Portuguese colonial control.

In April 1974 the Caetano government in Portugal was overthrown in a military coup and shortly afterwards the Portuguese colonial control over Mozambique and Angola came to an end. With the takeover of majority black governments in both these neighbouring states, the protective cordon of white-ruled states around South Africa crumbled. The so-called frontline states, a new regional grouping was formed, including independent states such as Tanzania, Zambia, Botswana, Mozambique and Angola; their specific aim was to rid southern Africa of white minority rule. The black nationalist liberation struggle had now progressed right up to South Africa's doorstep and presented a very real threat to the country's internal safety.

In an attempt to adapt to the new circumstances, Vorster began his détente initiative, hoping to defuse conflict in southern Africa, particularly in Rhodesia and South West Africa. His aim with détente, or appeasement politics, was on the one hand to form links with moderate African states to create an economic bloc of southern African states, and on the other, to try to gain membership of the OAU. In exchange, Vorster offered to use his influence to facilitate peaceful settlements in Rhodesia and South West Africa.

Vorster and President Kenneth Kaunda of Zambia began a joint détente initiative to solve the Rhodesian impasse. This was the first time that a South African premier and the head of a black independent African state had worked together to solve a southern African conflict. Earlier, negotiations between Smith and the British government had come no closer to finding a solution to the Rhodesian issue, while the military conflict between the Rhodesian security forces and the guerrilla fighters of the black liberation movements grew increasingly heated. Vorster held discussions with Smith and Kaunda spoke to the black nationalist leaders in Rhodesia to bring them to the negotiation table. Although the Vorster government gave both economic and military support to the Smith government, Vorster encouraged Smith to reach an agreement that would lead to a sharing of power between whites and blacks in Rhodesia.

In August 1975 Vorster and Kaunda's intervention led to talks between Smith and the Rhodesian black nationalist leaders on the railway bridge over the Victoria Falls. Although the bridge summit failed and no agreement was reached, they marked a high point in Vorster's rule and he earned great praise for his role in orchestrating the negotiations. The fact that Vorster persuaded Smith to confer with black nationalist leaders improved South Africa's image in the outside world as an honest broker and negotiating partner.

In 1976 Henry Kissinger, the American secretary of state, worked with the Vorster government on a new initiative to solve the Rhodesian question. Vorster's meetings with Kissinger in Europe and South Africa were the first high-level talks between South Africa and the USA since the Second World War. A settlement plan was formulated and Vorster persuaded Smith to accept a majority government, a concession that paved the way, some years later, for the independence of Zimbabwe. Kissinger and Smith agreed on a settlement package but the frontline states refused to sanction it. Vorster remained involved in subsequent Anglo-American settlement initiatives, but a solution was not immediately forthcoming.

Détente contributed internationally to a more positive attitude towards South Africa and Vorster's prestige grew. His talks with eminent USA and British leaders over the Rhodesian dispute were unprecedented in the apartheid struggle; thereby the South African government gained recognition as an important role player in southern African issues.

Vorster also played a key role in the South West African (now Namibia) question. The international dispute over South Africa's refusal to recognise the UN's jurisdiction over the region had dragged on for decades. The UN failed in its efforts to end South Africa's administrative control there and the Vorster government even began to entertain the idea of creating separate homelands for the different ethnic groups in South West Africa. Under the leadership of Sam Nujoma, the South West African People's Organisation (SWAPO) and its People's Liberation Army of Namibia (PLAN) began a guerrilla struggle for independence supported militarily by the Soviet Union.

Kurt Waldheim, secretary general of the UN, and his personal representative, Alfred Escher, visited southern Africa in the early 1970s for discussions with South Africa on South West Africa. A settlement was not on the agenda because the UN's demand for a unitary state with equal voting rights for all was unacceptable to the Vorster government. After Portugal's withdrawal from Angola, Vorster abandoned the idea of incorporating South West Africa into South Africa and instead focused on granting independence to the region – on South Africa's terms. It was hoped that sympathetic black political parties would come to power and that SWAPO's power could be neutralised.

Between 1975 and 1977 a political conference took place in Windhoek with representatives from the different population groups in South West Africa. SWAPO, however, was excluded from this conference, which was known as the Turnhalle conference. A draft constitution for the region was accepted and 31 December 1978 was identified as the target date for independence. However, the UN's council on Namibia, SWAPO, other African states, Britain, the USA and the European Union all rejected the Turnhalle plan.

After Kissinger's seven-point settlement plan for South West Africa had also been rejected by SWAPO, representatives of the UN security council's five Western members began a new diplomatic initiative. Both the South African government and SWAPO were involved in negotiations to find an internationally recognised formula for elections on the basis of one person one vote, to be held under the joint supervision of South Africa and the UN. Vorster agreed that SWAPO could participate in this election. Judge M.T. Steyn was appointed as administrator general of South West Africa. Despite disputes over the supervision of the planned election and the withdrawal of the South African Army from South West Africa, the Vorster government and SWAPO moved towards a compromise. In 1978 a Western settlement plan was formulated and accepted by both Vorster's cabinet and SWAPO.

A Finnish diplomat, Martti Ahtisaari, was appointed as the UN security council's special envoy to oversee the election process in South West Africa. When, in his report to the security council on the implementation of the settlement, Ahtisaari strayed from the approved provisions, the South African cabinet rejected his proposals. The Western-inspired settlement plan was duly scrapped; clearly an internationally acceptable settlement of the South West African issue under Vorster's rule remained a distant dream that was never to be realised.

On the basis of his leading role in southern African détente, Vorster earned the reputation as a true statesman and diplomat; the Afrikaans press sung his praises. He succeeded in keeping the confidence of both the *verligtes* and *verkramptes* within NP ranks; sometimes he accomplished this by delaying decisions on sensitive issues. He successfully combined a degree of flexibility in the implementation of apartheid with an unrelenting attitude on defending the country and internal safety. Although *verligtes* encouraged détente and the softening of racial discrimination in South Africa, Andries Treurnicht and his likeminded rightwingers criticised such policy concessions.

Vorster was an Afrikaner nationalist through and through. For him the maintenance of Afrikaner identity was a priority, but he also stood for co-operation between Afrikaans and English speakers and an inclusive South African patriotism. At the inauguration of the Afrikaanse Taalmonument (Afrikaans Language Monument) in Paarl in October 1975 he said that Afrikaans belonged to the entire nation. He emphasised that the Afrikaners had an inalienable right to be in Africa and that the Afrikaans language had arisen from African soil. He went on to say: "Our map and title deed to be here is written in Afrikaans" (translated from the original Afrikaans). (This is an Afrikaans expression denoting the right to African citizenship underwritten by a legal title deed and a registered plan or diagram.)

By 1975, because of the success of his détente initiative Vorster was at the pinnacle of his popularity among white South Africans. Opinion polls showed that almost 80% of respondents supported détente. Indeed, at this time Vorster was more popular than Verwoerd had been in his prime. It was apparently only J.B.M. Hertzog in the 1930s fusion era (which began with the fusion of the UP and NP in 1933) who had a greater percentage of white voter support.

While the NP was unified under Vorster's leadership, the decline of the UP was ongoing due to the internal feud between the liberal and conservative factions. Weak results in by-elections and suspensions from the UP were a regular occurrence. The NP's dominance in parliamentary sittings caused a feeling of powerlessness in opposition circles and led to calls that all those who were liberal-inclined should re-group and form a unified opposition party.

Setbacks for the apartheid state

The political changes in the two Portuguese colonies in southern Africa brought new challenges for Vorster. In the case of Mozambique his government strictly applied the principle of non-intervention in another state's internal affairs. There was thus no intervention on South Africa's part when the Marxist liberation movement Frelimo took over the Mozambican government in 1975. Despite ideological differences, the two countries continued to co-operate in the economic sphere.

In Angola, circumstances took an entirely different turn. Calls by the OAU for a government of national unity in Angola were ignored and fighting between the three liberation movements – the MPLA, FNLA and UNITA – developed into a full-scale civil war. The Vorster government wanted to prevent the MPLA, which had military support from the Soviet Union and Cuba, from taking political control because an MPLA government would allow SWAPO military bases in Angola. Therefore the South African Defence Force (SADF) launched a military campaign in support of UNITA and the FNLA. As part of Operation Savannah, SADF task forces invaded Angola and progressed towards Luanda, but were unable to take the capital city.

Once Portuguese officials and soldiers had left Angola on 11 November 1975, the military confrontation became more heated. Soviet weapons and Cuban troops streamed into Angola and Operation Carlota – an offensive by FAPLA, the MPLA's military wing – began in full earnest. Vorster's advisers hoped that the USA would be prepared to support the anti-MPLA forces, but the West was ultimately not prepared to provide enough military muscle to counteract the Russian-Cuban assistance to the MPLA.

Once the military situation had swung in favour of the MPLA, the OAU recognised it as the official government of Angola and the South African troops withdrew. However, this was not the end of the Angolan civil war because with South African help UNITA continued a prolonged guerrilla struggle for years against the MPLA forces.

Criticism was heaped on the South African government for its invasion of Angola. Opponents of the regime saw it as a foreign policy fiasco. In reaction to accusations of South African aggression and expansionist designs, Vorster and his colleagues justified the SADF operation in Angola by explaining that South Africa had become involved to counteract the SWAPO threat to South West Africa. According to Vorster, his government wanted to take a stand against the communist threat in the region and ensure that a democratic political agreement be reached in Angola.

The South African intervention in Angola was a mistake. At a military level the SADF operation was a failure and as a diplomatic exercise it served to isolate the country even further. Added to this, Operation Savannah had drastically increased the government's military expenditure at a time when there was an economic recession. Although South Africa's involvement in the war in Angola can be considered an error of judgement on Vorster's part, in the short term it did not detract from Vorster's status or that of the NP in the eyes of the white voters.

In the 1970s the political scene in southern Africa underwent a significant transformation. Angola and Mozambique were now independent states under Marxist-oriented black governments; the white government in Rhodesia was on the brink of handing over power to a black majority government; and possible settlement agreements with an eye to South West Africa's (Namibian) independence were already far advanced. Whereas previously the Vorster government was firmly focused on the maintenance of white control in the subcontinent, it now had to take account of the possibility of growing infiltration and guerrilla attacks from neighbouring states that were being orchestrated by the military wings of the liberation movements.

In the party political context, Vorster benefited from the worsening security situation. To retain the support of the conservatives in the NP he continued to take strong action in the maintenance of law and order and military preparedness. He also took full advantage of the differences of opinion on security matters between the conservative and liberal factions in the UP to widen the wedge between the NP and the UP even further.

The success of the black liberation movements in the former Portuguese colonies brought a new lease of life to the South African liberation struggle. Hopes rose that perhaps, after all, resistance launched inside the country could break down white dominance and apartheid. For more than a decade internal black resistance had to a large extent been stifled by the banning of the ANC, PAC and SACP and by the enforcement of strict internal security legislation; now the Black Consciousness Movement became the internal channel for black protest.

Dissatisfaction with the oppressive apartheid system boiled over in June 1976 when a protest march by Soweto students was met by police violence. Many children, including the 13-year-old Hector Pieterson were shot dead. Thereafter, thousands of young black people ran amok in the streets; they attacked symbols of the apartheid regime such as administration buildings, beer halls, schools, clinics and libraries, many of which were set alight. In the weeks that followed, more than 600 people lost their lives when violent resistance erupted countrywide in the form of demonstrations, unrest, arson, strikes, stayaways and school and rent boycotts. Because the unrest was on such a massive scale, it took the police some time to bring it under control.

Large numbers of young blacks fled the country to join Umkhonto we Sizwe (MK), the ANC's military wing. In September 1977 there was another uproar against the regime when black consciousness leader, Steve Biko, died in police custody; he had been tortured and did not receive adequate medical treatment. The following month a number of black consciousness organisations were banned and a leading black newspaper, *The World*, had to stop publication. It was only after this that the unrest which had engulfed South Africa for a full year began to calm down.

The condemnation of South Africa's apartheid policy had meanwhile sharpened throughout the world. In the UN, where over the years numerous resolutions had been passed against apartheid, the demand for sanctions against South Africa grew more insistent. In 1977 the UN security council imposed a mandatory arms embargo on South Africa; for the first time this was not vetoed by its Western members. As regards the international anti-apartheid campaign, pressure from the UN and the OAU were only the tip of the iceberg. Numerous anti-apartheid groups formed worldwide networks to mobilise public opinion against apartheid and influence decision makers to take action against apartheid.

The range of boycotts against South Africa increased and the country was expelled from many international bodies. Although full-scale disinvestment had not yet begun, banks and corporate investors stopped issuing new loans and approving investments in apartheid institutions. Governments, companies and organisations that had previously been well disposed to South Africa now quietly withdrew their co-operation. The negative outcome of this isolation became palpable in political, economic and social spheres in South Africa.

The Department of External Affairs and the Department of Information tried to counteract the anti-apartheid campaign with propaganda. However, the Angolan invasion; the Soweto shootings and subsequent unrest; Biko's death; and the banning of the black consciousness organisations had caused so much negative publicity that the government could do little to rescue South Africa's international reputation.

Even the stance of South Africa's traditional allies in the West had changed. After Jimmy Carter's inauguration as president of the USA in January 1977, the attitude of America's top officials to apartheid hardened; good relations with independent African states were more important to them than links with South Africa. In discussions between Vorster and Walter Mondale, the American vice-president in May 1977, Mondale insisted that a majority government and a one-person-one-vote system be introduced. Vorster regarded this as unreasonable interference in South Africa's domestic affairs. His reaction was that South Africa would not be prescribed to by the mighty USA – which was applauded by his NP supporters and boosted his popularity.

South Africa had strong ties with Britain, West Germany and France, but because these countries continued to honour these ties, they were targeted by the OAU and UN resolutions. After Harold Wilson's Labour Party came to power again in Britain in 1974, the British arms embargo was reinstated and the Simon's Town Agreement on naval co-operation between Britain and South Africa was terminated. However, despite political differences trade between South Africa and Western Europe went ahead unhindered.

Because South Africa was becoming internationally isolated, the Vorster regime began to seek longer-term allies beyond the circle of the country's traditional Western partners, allies which would hopefully stand it in good stead in time of need. These countries – Paraguay, Israel, Iran and Taiwan – were pro-Western medium-sized powers and were also, like South Africa, isolated and frustrated over the West's attitude towards them. Relations with these countries were of strategic importance. Israel worked with South Africa on the development of arms systems and played an important role in the establishment of the South African arms industry. Iran was South Africa's most important supplier of oil, while trade between South Africa and Taiwan increased tenfold within a decade.

By means of his extensive overseas travels and personal discussions with leaders in various countries, Vorster played a significant role in the maintenance of South Africa's external relations. However, his tireless attempts could not curb the intensifying anti-apartheid campaigns and South Africa's increasing international isolation. Despite the growing pressure on the South African government, or perhaps as a result of it, the support for Vorster and the NP among white voters continued to grow. It was as if the uncertainty over southern Africa's future; fears about the country's security situation; demands for internal reform; the growing momentum of anti-apartheid campaigns; the increasing international isolation of the apartheid state; and the wave of black protest, herded conservative and moderate white people alike into one corral.

After the 1974 election the UP's decline continued. Early in 1975 it split when Harry Schwarz and his supporters left the UP parliamentary caucus and founded the Reform Party (RP). Many UP leaders crossed the floor to join the new party, and hope that the UP might survive as a viable opposition began to fade.

Talks on collaboration between the Progressive Party (PP), the Reform Party and Theo Gerdener's Democratic Party (DP) eventually led to the fusion of the PP and RP to form the Progressive Reform Party (PRP).

The PRP adopted the PP policy of a geographic federation and qualified franchise for all races. It proposed that a multiracial national convention be held to draw up a new constitution for South Africa. The PRP grew at the expense of the UP.

In June 1977 the UP dissolved and former members of the UP and DP formed the New Republic Party (NRP). The liberal faction of the disbanded UP fused with the PRP to form the Progressive Federal Party (PFP). Between 1974 and 1977 the parliamentary opposition parties thus underwent a comprehensive re-grouping.

The end of an era, 1977–1978

Afrikaners who favoured reform were disappointed that Vorster had not used his overwhelming support among white voters to move in a more enlightened direction by making basic changes to apartheid. However, Vorster realised that it was the very conservatism of his policies that had made him so popular among white voters. He was well aware that change was necessary to prevent an even worse flare-up than the Soweto uprisings and took tentative steps in the direction of reform.

Labour was the one area where initiatives by the Vorster government lead to meaningful change. The Industrial Conciliation Act excluded black workers from effective collective bargaining. Their dissatisfaction about this became evident in the wave of strikes in 1972 and 1973. Employers then asked the government to consider the inclusion of black trade unions in the industrial conciliation process. They were fully cognisant that illegal strikes could potentially have a negative effect on productivity and profits. In response, Vorster appointed Nic Wiehahn as chairperson of a commission of inquiry into labour relations. The recommendations of this commission eventually led to an entirely new dispensation for black workers and their trade unions.

Because the CRC and the Indian Council had ended in a cul-de-sac there had to be a re-think on how political provision could be made for coloured people and Indians. In 1976 the cabinet decided that a cabinet committee under the chairpersonship of P.W. Botha should investigate the position of coloureds and Indians in the South African constitutional dispensation. A year later the cabinet approved the committee's recommendations. The 1977 proposals made provision for three separate parliaments, prime ministers and cabinets for whites, coloureds and Indians. Each separate house would handle matters of concern to that particular group. A Cabinet Council, under chairpersonship of the state president, would handle matters of common concern. A multiracial Presidential Advisory Council comprised of experts would advise the state president and Cabinet Council. The three population groups would all have separate provincial and local authorities.

Within the NP there was enthusiastic support for the 1977 proposals which embraced a form of power sharing and yet protected the principle of white self-determination. At all four of the NP provincial congresses the draft constitution was duly accepted. However, coloured, Indian and black people rejected the proposals out of hand, arguing that they were structured to protect white supremacy. They pointed out that coloureds and Indians were simply being co-opted as junior partners in the process of governance and that black people were completely excluded.

Vorster's announcement that an early general election would be held on 30 November 1977 was unexpected although this was the third consecutive time Vorster had done this. He wanted to test the white voters' reaction to the new constitutional proposals; show the outside world that he had overwhelming white support; and also take advantage of the disarray in opposition ranks. As part of its election plan the NP billed the election date as a day of reckoning. White survival and standing together against the onslaught from the outside world was the essence of the ruling party's election campaign. Vorster was depicted as the firm, reliable leader who could be fully trusted.

The hopelessly divided opposition parties faced the prospect of a shattering defeat. Virtually all the English language newspapers threw their weight behind the PFP. In the election the NP captured 18 of the opposition's seats and had a total of 135 seats in the lower house compared to the tally of 30 seats won by all the opposition parties combined. With 17 seats the PFP became the new official opposition. This meant that the NP had won the greatest victory in South Africa's parliamentary history thus far. For Vorster the election was a personal triumph because he gained the most votes ever recorded for a candidate in a parliamentary election, and he won his seat in Nigel with a record majority. He had proved himself as one of the most successful Afrikaner politicians of all time. The election was interpreted as an overwhelming motion of confidence in his government.

However, in the eighteen months after the 1977 election high point, the curtain came down on the Vorster era. The information scandal cast a dark shadow over his political career. As early as the 1960s Vorster considered using an extensive information programme to counteract the ignorance in the outside world about the true situation in South Africa. After Connie Mulder became Minister of Information in 1968 an initiative was begun to expand the Department of Information into a propaganda machine. Mulder appointed the ambitious Eschel Rhoodie as Secretary of Information and together they made a dynamic team. With the approval of the Vorster cabinet they mobilised a secret propaganda war to neutralise the anti-apartheid campaign. In this way Mulder and Rhoodie hoped to influence opinion formers and decision makers in the international community. According to them, unconventional methods were justified because South Africa had to fight for its survival. Almost 200 secret information projects costing millions of rands were undertaken; they were financed from a secret government fund.

In 1977 these secret projects began to come under scrutiny. The auditor general found a confidential report that the Department of Information was squandering state funds. Details of irregularities were leaked to the press. There were disclosures about expensive holidays at the state's expense; irregularities on certain publications; overseas front-organisations; and state funding of an English newspaper, *The Citizen*. Vorster confronted Mulder and Rhoodie, but did not give full details to his cabinet.

At the beginning of 1978 he requested the parliamentary select committee on public accounts to investigate the allegations of unauthorised payments by the Department of Information. The committee found that financial control in the department left a great deal to be desired. In a press statement in May 1978 Rhoodie defended the secret projects and stated that they were monitored by a cabinet committee. Vorster accepted responsibility for the granting of secret funding to the Department of Information, but not for the way it had been utilised. He undertook to act against anyone who misused state funds for personal gain. In June 1978 the Department of Information was disbanded.

Because of the extreme pressure on Vorster, his health deteriorated.

In August 1978 he suffered a light heart attack and on 20 September he announced his resignation at a press conference. Eight days later the NP caucus appointed P.W. Botha as his successor and nominated Vorster as NP candidate for the state presidency. Vorster was elected state president by the parliamentary electoral college and duly inaugurated.

The dust of the information scandal refused to settle. P.W. Botha appointed the Erasmus Commission to investigate the allegations of irregularities and misappropriation of funds in the former Department of Information. In the commission's first report the major blame was heaped on Mulder, Rhoodie and General Hendrik van den Bergh (head of the Bureau for State Security); Vorster was exonerated of all blame. Because the first report had been hurried through in great haste to meet a target date, the government allowed Erasmus to continue his investigation. Meanwhile, an ongoing stream of disclosures about the former Department of Information appeared in the newspapers and doubt was cast on whether Vorster was in fact blameless. In its third and final report the Erasmus Commission found that at an early stage Vorster did indeed have knowledge of the secret propaganda projects and how they were financed. According to the commission, he therefore had to accept responsibility, together with Mulder, for the irregularities.

A disillusioned Vorster took legal advice, but was obliged to resign as state president on 4 June 1979 and withdrew from politics. His reputation was in tatters. He died on 10 September 1983.

Vorster was an outstanding speaker, debater, party politician and negotiator. At the height of his career he was one of the most popular Afrikaner leaders of all times and led his party to great success at the polls. Under him, separate development was expanded dramatically but was already showing signs of its eventual failure.

Vorster ruled in postcolonial Africa; he denied that the Afrikaners were colonialists. He steadfastly clung to the belief held by his forefathers in colonial times that South Africa was a white man's land. It was ironic that he persuaded the white leaders in Rhodesia and South West Africa to accept majority rule and in so doing helped to bring those countries to the verge of political settlements, but was not prepared to sacrifice white control in South Africa. He considered it his calling to win time for white people to retain self-rule on a predominantly black continent.

17
Black resistance against apartheid, 1950s-1980s
Jackie Grobler

In the second half of the twentieth century the black political resistance movement shifted gears and moved forward into a third phase. Black nationalism was awakening and in this phase there was a demand for political power. This occurred at a time when the worldwide anti-colonial movement began; it was also a time when Afrikaner nationalism reached new heights. The apartheid policy would not be implemented without stern opposition.

A multiracial alliance against apartheid

Shortly after coming to power in 1948 the new National Party (NP) government appointed a committee to investigate communism and it was found that it constituted a "national danger" for South Africa. The result was a draft bill for the suppression of communism. Among other things it would legalise action against organisations and individuals that promoted communism. Above all, in terms of this legislation the Communist Party of South Africa (CPSA) could be declared an illegal organisation.

At the time, the bill was criticised in Parliament and the media because it disregarded certain legal principles and basic freedoms. But the government pressed ahead. Just as Parliament was about to vote on the bill for the last time, the CPSA was voluntarily disbanded in June 1950 to prevent action being taken against its members.

The passing of the Suppression of Communism Act was only the beginning of more drastic action on the part of the government. In 1952 the last communists serving as "native representatives" had their parliamentary seats removed. Communist publications, including *New Age*, were banned one by one; and multiracial trade unions were systematically put out of action. In 1957 trade unions were instructed to categorise their membership on the basis of race. Despite these measures there was a stronger communist presence in the ANC and in 1953 white communists secretly re-established an underground South African Communist Party (SACP). The newly formed aboveground wing of the SACP was known as the South African Congress of Democrats.

In 1950 there were various outbursts of unrest and violence, particularly on the Witwatersrand. These usually led to clashes between the police and protestors and were evidence of a simmering anger and growing frustration in black society. The 1950 unrest paved the way for increasing co-operation between the ANC and the communists.

A few months before the CPSA was disbanded, it organised a convention on freedom of speech in Johannesburg on 26 March 1950. James Moroka, the ANC president general, chaired the conference, but both the national and the Transvaal ANC distanced themselves from the proceedings. They were not convinced of the desirability of working with the white communists. The convention decided to celebrate May Day (1 May) as freedom day. On the appointed day thousands of workers took part in strikes which by the evening had become increasingly violent, leading to 18 deaths. The ANC then declared that a national day of protest against the action of police would be held. This day of mourning as it was called, was held on 26 June and was accompanied by a stayaway that was reasonably well-supported in some parts of the country.

Some Africanist-inclined ANC members were still unhappy about the co-operation with communists, and late in 1950 Selope Thema took the lead in the formation of a so-called National-Minded Bloc. This meant that the ANC no longer had access to *Bantu World*, its unofficial mouthpiece, because Thema was the editor of the publication. Thereafter the ANC became increasingly dependent on the SACP for media publicity.

The coloured community's resistance against the government's intention to remove coloured voters from the common voters' roll in the 1950s led to the formation of several protest movements. One of the most important was the Franchise Action Council (FRAC) which was established in Cape Town in February 1951 and organised stayaway strikes and a school boycott. In July 1951 the national executive committees of the

ANC and the South African Indian Council (SAIC) met with FRAC leaders to discuss taking joint action.

They decided to form a planning committee and to begin a campaign against six apartheid measures that were particularly abhorrent to them, namely the pass laws; group areas; the separate representation of voters; the system of Bantu authorities; the suppression of communism; and stock culling, which was part of the government's rehabilitation scheme in the reserves. The planning committee sent a letter to the government in which they asked for the repeal of these measures; they warned that if the government did not comply, they would embark on a passive resistance campaign similar to Gandhi's campaign in India. The government turned down the request. The planning committee reacted by organising a mass gathering for 6 April, the day celebrated as Van Riebeeck day, after which further resistance would follow.

The Defiance Campaign, the countrywide passive resistance initiative, began on 26 June 1952. The idea was that participants – who were called volunteers – would form groups and would deliberately disobey these laws. They were asked to purposely disregard township regulations, curfews, and apartheid laws such as the "whites only" reservation of waiting rooms at railway stations. The idea was to be arrested because the organisers argued that the police stations would not be able to cope with the escalating situation.

In the course of the Defiance Campaign, which lasted until the end of the year, 8326 volunteers were arrested. The most concerted action was in the Eastern Cape which points to the high level of politicisation among the working class in that part of the country. On occasion the campaign led to violence and a total of 26 blacks and six whites were killed in the unrest. The majority of volunteers were black people and Indians. Only a few white people participated.

Those who were arrested and tried in court were initially given light sentences, but as time went by the sentences became heavier and then stricter laws, such as the Public Safety Act and the Criminal Law Amendment Act, were passed to deal more harshly with those who deliberately broke the law. The heavier sentences disheartened the protestors and the campaign gradually began to tail off; it was officially ended early in 1953.

The Defiance Campaign of 1952 did not succeed in its specific goal, because the discriminatory legislation remained in force. However, it had important results in that it became a symbol of resistance against an unrelenting minority government. As such, the campaign strengthened the solidarity among black people; it raised the level of mass politicisation in the interior; and it led to wider support for becoming involved in protest action. In the broader context it promoted international publicity for the anti-apartheid cause and contributed to the strengthening of ties between South African anti-apartheid organisations and those throughout the world. Furthermore, it created a negative image of apartheid in the world at large and focused the attention of the United Nations Organisation (UN) on South Africa. Finally, it led to Moroka's political demise and the election of Albert Luthuli as president general of the ANC.

In the period immediately after the Defiance Campaign, Nelson Mandela devised a plan to centralise the ANC organisationally. This was known as the M-plan and involved dividing residential areas into units. The smallest unit was a cell; a number of cells formed a zone; a number of zones constituted a ward; and wards were grouped to form an ANC branch. The plan received considerable support but was never implemented, largely because of financial constraints, but also because of opposition to renewal within ANC ranks. Furthermore, the government's arrest of many prominent ANC leaders weakened the organisation and curtailed its ability to move ahead as quickly as it would have liked.

The 1955 Congress of the People and the Freedom Charter

In the 1950s rural resistance against apartheid occurred countrywide and was aimed largely at the government's land control measures. In 1950 at Witsieshoek in the Free State, for example, there were uprisings in reaction to a government-driven livestock reduction scheme, and in the Wolkberg Mountains in Northern Transvaal (now Limpopo) in 1956 and 1957 the Mamathola community resisted strenuously against their forced removal. In the Marico (Zeerust) area in Western Transvaal (now North West) there were uprisings in 1957–1959 against both the pass laws and Bantu authorities. And in 1957–1960 in Pondoland, Transkei (now the Eastern Cape) there was resistance against Bantu authorities and the government's agricultural rehabilitation scheme. Rural resistance and unrest generally served to stimulate the politicisation of black people across the board.

When the NP again won the 1953 whites-only election, the opponents of apartheid yearned for an alternative. In August 1953 Z.K. Matthews, president of the Cape branch of the ANC, suggested that a people's congress be held. His proposal was discussed at the ANC's annual national congress that same year and the congress gave the national executive committee (NEC) the instruction to confer with other organisations about the idea. Accordingly, Luthuli raised it at a joint meeting of the ANC, the SAIC, the Coloured People's Organisation (SACPO) and the Congress of Democrats.

At this meeting a national action council was formed to organise the proposed gathering. It was to be called the Congress of the People (COP). To popularise the idea, the action council distributed a regular newsletter, *Speaking Together*, and held local and regional conferences to discuss the coming congress. As part of the call to attend the congress, those who were interested were asked to contribute their ideas for possible inclusion in a charter that was being compiled to articulate the aspirations of the black majority. A sub-committee of the national action council compiled the final document, but the Freedom Charter was not distributed beforehand to branches of the organisations involved. Neither Luthuli nor Matthews saw it prior to the congress. It was already in published form when the ANC's national working committee saw it for the first time, but no changes were made to it either by this committee or at the congress.

The Congress of the People was held on 25 and 26 June 1955 in Kliptown south of Johannesburg. It was attended by almost 3000 delegates and was a multiracial gathering. The Liberal Party was invited but did not participate officially. No representatives of the government attended. Many international messages were sent to the organisers, which was an indication of the worldwide publicity the struggle against apartheid had already gained. At the congress the sections of the Freedom Charter were read out one by one. They were explained in various speeches by prominent leaders and then voting took place. All the clauses were duly accepted; none were amended or rejected. The police, who were present throughout the proceedings, remained in the background until the afternoon of the second day when they moved forward to confiscate documents. By that time, the most important matters had already been handled.

The Congress of the People represents an important phase in the history of the struggle against apartheid. Now, for the first time proactive steps were taken to put forward an alternative to apartheid. The Congress of the People was an early highpoint of the so-called Congress Alliance that was formed between the ANC, the SAIC, SACPO, the Congress of Democrats and the overarching trade union movement, the South African Congress of Trade Unions (SACTU) which was formed in 1955.

The first and most important stipulation of the Freedom Charter is in the first sentence: South Africa belongs to all who live in it, both black and white. It then explains that the country's wealth, which is the heritage of all South Africans, should be restored to the people. This being so, the mineral wealth, banks and monopolistic industries should also be transferred to the ownership of the people as a whole. The charter goes on to demand a non-racist, democratic system of government; equal status of all before the law; and equal work and education opportunities for all South Africans. It also calls for the repeal of restrictions on home and family life.

The Freedom Charter contains no class-struggle terminology and is not a Marxist master plan. The demands for nationalisation and redivision of resources can at most be considered socialistic. Furthermore, the charter is clearly anti-racist and makes no reference to divisive ethnic groups. Nevertheless, there is some mention of minority national groups and the promise that they will be protected from any disparagement of their race and national pride.

An important question that is often asked with regard to the Freedom Charter is whether or not it is a revolutionary document. There are divergent interpretations on this and a great deal of rhetoric, which makes a balanced opinion difficult. Suffice it to say that the simultaneous attainment of all the demands and objectives that the charter envisaged would lead to a large-scale – even revolutionary – change of the existing dispensation in South Africa. The Freedom Charter soon became the cornerstone of ANC policy.

Many women attended the Congress of the People. In 1954 a multiracial women's organisation – the Federation of South African Women (FSAW) – was formed that played a co-ordinating role in the Congress Alliance with regard to women's concerns. In 1955 the government announced that from the next year onwards black women would also be subject to the pass law. Women were enraged by this and in August 1955 staged a protest march to the Union Buildings in Pretoria. The march was repeated the following year on 9 August 1956 when thousands of women took part. Tens of thousands of women in other parts of the country were politicised by this show of solidarity and pass-burning ceremonies were held at various places, notably in the Free State. Since 1994, Women's Day has been commemorated as a public holiday in South Africa on 9 August each year.

In the 1950s the ANC was also involved in campaigns against the government's imposition of the "Bantu" education system and the use of convict labour on farms. The government were perturbed about these outbursts of unrest and acted strongly to quell them. In December 1956 there were 156 people arrested and accused of high treason, including most of the leaders of the Congress Alliance. The treason trial dragged on until March 1961, but all the accused were eventually acquitted.

The armed struggle

The Sharpeville tragedy

Throughout the 1950s the Africanists in the ANC were dissatisfied with the way the organisation had conducted the 1949 programme of action. They were against working with white organisations and were strongly anti-communist. In addition the Africanists were sceptical about the SAIC's passive resistance campaigns and against co-operation with Indians. They maintained that during the Defiance Campaign of 1952 the interests of African people had been jeopardised by those of other groups.

It was especially the Africanists in Orlando under the leadership of P.K. Leballo who expressed such views. They distributed a duplicated newsletter, *The Africanist*, in which they disputed the Freedom Charter's opening statement – that South Africa belongs to all its people, both black and white. In their opinion all white people were thieves who had dispossessed the Africans of their land. They also criticised the Congress Alliance because according to them whites and Indians were not to be trusted. They blamed the whites for the hopeless situation of black people and their aversion to whites was frequently evident in their pronouncements.

The Africanists' criticism of the ANC leadership came to a head in November at the organisation's annual Transvaal congress and lead to a split in ANC ranks. In April 1959 the Africanists broke away and formed their own organisation, the Pan Africanist Congress (PAC) in Johannesburg, with Robert Sobukwe as president. The major difference between the ANC and PAC was that the PAC was exclusively black, while the ANC was multiracial. The PAC's target was to recruit 100 000 members as quickly as possible, but by August 1959 there were only 25 000 registered members. Nevertheless, it began a campaign to make black people aware that they deserved a higher status in society. Indeed, this was an early expression of black consciousness in South Africa.

At the end of 1959 the PAC decided to launch a countrywide campaign against having to carry passbooks. It announced that this was to be the organisation's first step to free black people from all forms of white oppression by the year 1963. Black people across the board condemned the pass system because the police enforced it in a heavy-handed manner which was experienced as extremely degrading. Because the PAC knew the ANC was planning a similar campaign, it was determined to claim the limelight as the first organisation to launch a pass campaign. However, the PAC was too hasty. The announcement that the campaign would begin on 21 March 1960 was only made on 18 March so arrangements had to be made in an impossibly short time. The campaign was to take the form of a stayaway strike. Participants had to leave their passbooks at home and present themselves for arrest at police stations.

The PAC's campaign was only well supported in some places. In the Vaal Triangle, participation was at its best in Bophelong and Sharpeville. There were about 10 000 people in Sharpeville who were milling around the police station demanding that they be arrested and asking for the pass system to be scrapped. By midday the tension began to build. It reached breaking point when the police, some of them with automatic weapons, fired on the crowd. In the bloodbath that followed, 69 people died and about 180 were wounded. In a later commission of inquiry it was found that the majority of victims were shot in the back; it appeared that the police had panicked. On that same day in the Cape Peninsula police fired on black crowds and two people were killed in Langa township. In Soweto, Sobukwe and other PAC leaders insisted that they be taken into custody at the Orlando police station because they had contravened the pass law.

At first there was a stunned silence following the shocking events of 21 March. On Monday 28 March, a mass funeral was held in Sharpeville for the victims of the tragedy. In response to a request by Albert Luthuli, president general of the ANC, many black people observed the day as one of mourning. There were also strikes and pass-burning ceremonies elsewhere in the country – Luthuli also burnt his pass – and many people stayed away from work.

Two days later, on 30 March, a spontaneous protest march of about 30 000 black people moved from Langa to the Caledon Square police station in the Cape Town city centre. Philip Kgosana, a young PAC member, led the march. The crowd only dispersed when Kgosana was promised that he could meet the Minister of Justice later that afternoon to discuss the people's grievances. However, when Kgosana arrived at the Caledon Square police station for his appointment with the minister, he was taken into custody.

The general state of unrest became so serious that on 30 March the government declared a state of emergency; in time this was extended to almost the entire country. On 8 April 1960 Parliament hurriedly passed the Unlawful Organisations Act and enforced it immediately by banning both the ANC and PAC.

The South African government was heavily criticised worldwide for the Sharpeville bloodbath. A false image was created that the country was on the brink of collapse and as a result many international investors withdrew from South Africa. Although this so-called flight of capital was only temporary, the Sharpeville massacre undoubtedly played a significant role in South Africa's growing isolation. However, Prime Minister Hendrik Verwoerd refused to be cowed and made no concessions to his critics. In fact the incident strengthened his position of power.

The ANC and PAC, now banned within the country, had to operate underground. In December 1960 the two organisations were represented unofficially at a conference in Orlando south of Johannesburg which had been organised by black members of the Liberal Party and members of the two banned organisations. The conference declared itself in favour of a non-racial democracy and non-violent action against the apartheid government. On 25 and 26 March 1961 a similar conference took place in Pietermaritzburg. Among other things it focused on the envisaged republican status of South Africa, due to be implemented on 31 May 1961, and on the poor state of race relations countrywide. Nelson Mandela was one of the main speakers. The conference called for a new constitution for the country and demanded that a fully representative national convention be held to reconsider the whole idea of a republican dispensation. The demand was that this convention should take place before 31 May, failing which there would be countrywide protests and stayaways. The conference even appointed a national action council under the leadership of Mandela to make the necessary arrangements and to compile a letter to the government informing it of the council's decisions.

The government ignored these demands and the national action council went ahead to organise a strike. The protest action had considerable support in some parts but South Africa nevertheless became a republic under white minority control.

The formation of Umkhonto we Sizwe

After the tragedy of Sharpeville and South Africa's new republican status, many opponents of apartheid began to feel that violent and armed resistance was the only way out of the impasse. In 1961 the ANC formed its armed wing, Umkhonto we Sizwe (MK), with Mandela as commander. The MK base was set up on a peri-urban estate called Lilliesleaf in Rivonia on the northern outskirts of Johannesburg. MK immediately began to plan a sabotage campaign that was to be launched on 16 December 1961, the date on which MK was to announce its manifesto. These initial plans were implemented successfully.

MK envisaged embarking upon a guerrilla war against the government, but to do so with success, some form of military training was necessary. Early in 1962 Mandela therefore left on a secret mission to find allies in other African states. He attended a conference of African leaders in Ethiopia and then among other stopovers received some military instruction in Algeria and visited Britain before slipping back secretly into South Africa.

By mid-1962 the police were conducting an intensive search for Mandela. He was eventually arrested, tried in court and sentenced to five years' imprisonment for engaging in unlawful activities. Meanwhile the ANC had enlisted recruits for military training. In October 1962 at an ANC conference held in Lobatse, Bechuanaland (the present Botswana), MK was duly recognised as the "army of the freedom movement"; despite Mandela's imprisonment, MK's sabotage campaign went ahead. In May 1963 MK claimed that its members had already been responsible for more than 70 acts of sabotage. The apartheid government's reaction was to clamp down with ever more restrictive legislation. For example, Parliament passed the General Laws Amendment Act in terms of which people could be held for 90 days without being charged before a court of law. At about the same time MK began to plan a full-scale guerrilla campaign known as Operation Mayibuye (an operation to restore, or give back).

On 11 July 1963 the police swooped on the MK headquarters in Rivonia in a surprise attack and arrested a group of leaders including Walter Sisulu and Govan Mbeki. Together with Mandela and several other MK leaders, they were then charged with high treason in the widely publicised Rivonia trial. The state called for the death sentence and submitted various pieces of documentary evidence in an attempt to prove that the accused were guilty of high treason. Amongst these was a written document headed "How to be a good communist", in Mandela's handwriting. On 12 June 1964 eight of the accused, including Mandela, Sisulu and Mbeki were sentenced to life imprisonment. Albert Luthuli expressed his shock at the severity of the sentences; they were also greeted by widespread international condemnation. MK members who had so far evaded the police tried to continue the sabotage campaign, but they met with little success and many of them were arrested. Thereafter, the ANC's fate rested largely in the hands of the external mission, the ANC in exile.

The PAC and Poqo

Like the ANC, the PAC was initially crippled by its banning in 1960 and the fact that its leader Robert Sobukwe had been arrested. In August 1962 the situation improved when the PAC secretary general, P.K. Leballo, was released; he crossed the border into Basotholand (now Lesotho) and settled in the capital, Maseru, from where he was able to co-ordinate PAC activities. At that stage there was already a PAC underground military wing with the name Poqo, apparently formed without Sobukwe's approval or even his knowledge. Poqo's aim was to overthrow white domination by a reign of terror.

The organisation had a fair amount of support, particularly among Xhosa-speaking migrant workers in the Western Cape. In November 1962 Poqo leaders in the Mbekweni township near Paarl decided to carry out an attack on the white community. About 250 Poqo members, some of whom were armed with pangas and axes, entered the town in the dead of night with the intention of attacking and occupying the gaol and the police station. The police were able to foil the attackers before they could achieve their aim, but by this time two white civilians and five Poqo members were already dead and 19 people were wounded.

Despite their failure in Mbekweni, Poqo (and the PAC) still felt that 1963 was the year of the final showdown. In the former homeland of the Transkei Poqo murdered three headmen and tried, without success, to launch an attack on Chief Matanzima. In February 1963 they attacked a road-workers' camp near Bashee Bridge and murdered a group of unsuspecting civilians. In the aftermath of these attacks, the government declared a state of emergency and arrested numerous Poqo and PAC members.

Leballo tried to activate Poqo in the Pretoria-Witwatersrand-Vereeniging area, but because of his amateurish attempts at organisation, the police intercepted thousands of PAC circulars which led to the arrest of hundreds of PAC cell leaders. As a result, the PAC's planned attacks on Pretoria and Johannesburg did not materialise.

In May 1963 Sobukwe had served his sentence handed down in 1960, but the Minister of Justice, John Vorster, would not allow his release. Sobukwe was held for another extended period in terms of a clause in the General Laws Amendment Act. As for Leballo, in 1964 he moved from Maseru to Tanzania, which meant that he was too far away from South Africa to organise any campaigns. By this time the underground PAC within the country was a spent force and the fate of the organisation rested with the external mission.

Anti-apartheid resistance inside the country was meanwhile pursued by the extremist African Resistance Movement (ARM). In July 1964 John Harris, an ARM member, was responsible for a bomb explosion on Park Station in Johannesburg which killed one person and injured about 20 others. Harris was later sentenced to death and hanged. In the aftermath of this attack, the ARM faded into oblivion.

The NP government also stepped up its campaign against the underground SACP and this led to the arrest and trial of the advocate and activist, Bram Fischer, who was eventually sentenced to life imprisonment. Hereafter, the SACP's future was in the hands of its exiled leaders and supporters. Fischer was released in 1975 shortly before he died of cancer.

The Black Consciousness Movement

After the banning of the ANC and PAC, black South Africans were without an official mouthpiece for their grievances. The homeland politicians could not fill the void because they were seen as being hand in glove with the apartheid regime and were branded as collaborators. By 1970 a new ideology of black awareness known as the Black Consciousness Movement (BCM) came to the fore. Its roots can be traced back to the USA and Algeria (the works of Franz Fanon). The tenets of Black Theology and the Black Power movement played a role in the rise of black awareness in South Africa.

Steve Biko, a medical student at the University of Natal, was a key figure in the rise of the BCM in South Africa. He believed that black people should be freed psychologically of a mindset of inferiority and from white liberal paternalism that had suppressed black people culturally. In his terminology all black people in South Africa were victims of racial oppression. He denounced the homeland system as a creation of the suppressor.

Under Biko's leadership black students broke away from the white-oriented National Union of South African Students (NUSAS) and the following year he founded the South African Student Organisation (SASO). In 1972, when he was no longer a student, he was involved in the establishment of the Black People's Convention (BPC), a political front to promote black consciousness.

Several commentators in government circles initially welcomed the breakaway of black students from NUSAS. They saw it as an acceptance by black students that they should develop separately along their own path. But in March 1973 the government detained some of their leaders, including Biko. In September 1974 the regime condemned SASO and the BPC when they openly celebrated Frelimo's political takeover in Mozambique. Nine of the black consciousness leaders were detained and charged under the Terrorism Act for the incitement of students. They were found guilty and sentenced to imprisonment on Robben Island.

As a restricted person, Biko was placed under house arrest in King William's Town. When he defied his restriction orders and visited Cape Town he was arrested. While in police custody in September 1977, he was subjected to torture and died a few days later.

The Black Consciousness Movement survived the flurry of restrictions in 1977 as seen for example in the formation of the Azanian People's Organisation (AZAPO), a strongly Africanist organisation, in 1978. In 1983 AZAPO tried to unite all those who aspired to the black consciousness ideology and were sceptical of Marxism, under an umbrella organisation called the National Forum formed in 1984.

The banned organisations outside the country

A few days before the ANC was banned in April 1960, Albert Luthuli sent his vice-president, Oliver Tambo, out of South Africa with a dual mission. First, he was to raise international support for the ANC; second, he was charged with encouraging worldwide condemnation and isolation of the apartheid regime. At the time, international sentiment was strongly against racism and colonialism. Furthermore, by 1960 there was already a decade-old tradition of international censure against apartheid. In the light of the Cold War, the ANC was also able to gain allies from among the opponents of capitalism.

In time the ANC opened a number of offices such as in London in Britain, Washington in the USA, Paris in France and in African states such as Tanzania and Zambia. They then began propaganda campaigns and other initiatives. The ANC hoped that South Africa's growing isolation would turn white voters against apartheid. They wanted to win over the entire international community for a total onslaught against South Africa. Examples of early successes were the support the ANC gained from the Africa Bureau, the Anti-Apartheid Movement and the International Defence and Aid Fund. They also warned multinational companies that they would be reviled and marginalised if they persisted in supporting apartheid.

In 1960 the ANC, PAC, SAIC and the South West Africa National Union formed an alliance of freedom movements in Britain: the Southern African United Front (SAUF). Early in 1961 the SAUF agitated against South Africa's continued membership of the Commonwealth after becoming a republic. It enjoyed a fair amount of support in Britain and other Commonwealth countries. When South Africa decided to leave the Commonwealth voluntarily, the SAUF saw it as a triumph. However, the alliance broke down eighteen months later due to clashes between the ANC and PAC.

By the mid-1960s the ANC had trained guerrilla cadres in MK ranks and had to find a route to infiltrate them from Zambia into South Africa. The most suitable route would clearly be through South Africa's northern neighbour Rhodesia (now Zimbabwe). At the time, Rhodesia was under white minority rule that was threatened by, among others, the Zimbabwe African People's Union (ZAPU) led by Joshua Nkomo. In 1967 the ANC concluded the Freedom Alliance with Nkomo and shortly afterwards guerrillas were sent through western Rhodesia to South Africa. However, the guerrillas were dispersed by Rhodesian government forces and only a few reached Botswana; none reached South Africa. The next year ANC cadres were again involved in clashes in eastern Rhodesia, but were still unable to infiltrate into South Africa. The ANC considered alliances such as this, and with other freedom movements elsewhere in Africa, as very valuable.

The ANC and PAC soon gained the United Nations (UN) as a stalwart ally. The UN even set up a Special Committee Against Apartheid and the South African government regularly came under criticism in the UN general assembly. Other allies of refugee South African organisations included the World Council of Churches, the Organisation of African Unity (OAU) and the World Peace Council. These allies offered the ANC the necessary support by distributing ANC mouthpieces such as *Sechaba*, *Mayibuye* and *Voice of Women* and broadcasting propaganda over the ANC's radio transmitter, Radio Freedom.

In 1969 the ANC held a consultative conference in Morogoro in Tanzania. It was a multiracial conference but all the members of the newly elected national executive committee (NEC) were Africans, with Oliver Tambo as president general. At the same conference a new multiracial body called the Revolutionary Council was formed; among its members were Joe Slovo, Reginald September and Yusuf Dadoo.

While the ANC was in exile it strengthened its ties with the SACP and the Soviet Union. The SACP was also involved in the formation of MK. In 1962 the ANC held its sixth conference and a programme with the name "Road to South African Freedom" was announced. Joe Slovo, a prominent SACP member, left the country in 1963 and established the SACP in exile. The close ties between the SACP (and the ANC) with the Soviet Union were probably largely due to his efforts. These co-operative links led to something of an ideological split within the ANC when Tennyson Makiwane and the so-called "Gang of 8" broke away in protest against what they labelled communist domination of the ANC.

The exiled ANC was taken by surprise by the Soweto uprising in 1976 because it had played no part in organising it. However, the student uprising proved advantageous because the intensity and long duration of the unrest guaranteed a permanent stream of young, eager recruits who left South Africa and contacted the ANC at its various offices outside the country. This, together with the fall of the Portuguese colonial empire, positioned the ANC to re-group and resume its assault on the apartheid government. The result was that many new military training camps were set up in countries such as Angola and Mozambique and an increasing number of trained cadres could be infiltrated into South Africa. Indeed, the ANC's next external conference, held in 1985 at Kabwe in Zambia, took the form of a council of war.

The PAC's first official representatives outside the country were appointed in 1960. They were Nana Mahomo and Peter Molotsi. Shortly after Leballo moved his PAC base to Dar es Salaam in Tanzania he announced himself as the foremost PAC leader and president of the organisation. But his term of office was anything but successful and he periodically expelled other leading members from the PAC. The Revolutionary Command which was directly under his control, was virtually powerless despite generous financial support from the OAU. The morale of his guerrillas was poor and many drifted away from the organisation. The biggest setback was when the PAC office and its representative were kicked out of Zambia.

Leballo succeeded in holding his own, but even after the Soweto uprising he failed in his attempts to launch any meaningful action against the apartheid government. After his expulsion from the PAC in 1979, there was little improvement and the PAC rapidly became a fringe organisation.

The Soweto uprising

On 16 June 1976 violent riots broke out in Soweto when the police opened fire on thousands of unarmed black students who were taking part in a protest march. The unrest, in which many people died, soon spread throughout the country.

The causes of the unrest were many and varied, but at the root of the trouble was the government's decision to make Afrikaans compulsory as the medium of instruction in some subjects in black high schools. There was great frustration over this and as one newspaper put it, "it was unrest looking for a place to break out". However, the march was about more than just Afrikaans as a teaching medium. It was an uprising of the black youth against the government's Bantu education system which was of an inferior standard. The growing housing shortage due to the development of the homelands was another grievance among urban blacks, as was the unsympathetic treatment they received at the hands of the Bantu administration boards; all this had made them desperate.

Those student leaders who had organised the march on 16 June 1976 and had not been arrested, quickly dispersed to avoid being tracked down. Thereafter a "nameless" group of leaders saw to it that the unrest spread countrywide. They drew in the working class in August and September 1976 and asked them to arrange strikes. The riots often went hand in hand with violence that usually targeted government buildings and other structures such as the Bantu administration offices, but the students also attacked bottle stores and shebeens because these were places where their parents wasted their wages. In Soweto an organisation of community leaders, the Group of Ten under Nthato Motlana, came to the fore to exercise a measure of control over the unrest. Meanwhile the chaos spread throughout the country, notably to the campuses of black, coloured and Indian universities. At this time many schools and other buildings, including the library at the University of Zululand, were set on fire. In some areas the unrest only died down after a year.

Prime Minister John Vorster believed that the police should put a stop to the unrest with whatever force was necessary. Virtually all meetings in the black townships were forbidden and the police did not hesitate to end illegal gatherings with heavy-handed tactics. This often resulted in casualties and deaths among the protesters and the funerals of victims frequently developed into political meetings. Later the police even began to fire on riotous funeralgoers, which in turn led to even more funerals.

The death toll in the unrest that followed in the wake of the Soweto uprising eventually rose to 600. A large percentage of these died as a result of police action. Many young people and other protesters were taken into custody and in some cases they were tried. On 19 October 1977 the government adopted an even more aggressive stance by banning all black consciousness organisations, including SASO and the BPC. At the same time the newspaper *The World*, which had a largely black readership, and the Christian Institute were both banned.

The troubled 1980s

Following the wave of unrest that began in Soweto in 1976, the ANC was able to draw thousands of young people into its ranks as they fled the country. This gave the organisation a new lease of life and until 1979 the ANC carried out thorough preparations to resume the guerrilla struggle against the apartheid regime. From 1980 onwards strategic targets such as Sasol and Koeberg were attacked and from 1983 "soft targets" involving civilians became more frequent. Attacks on civilians included the explosions in Church Street, Pretoria, and at Ellis Park in Johannesburg where bombs were planted by MK cadres that had been infiltrated into the country; both attacks led to loss of life.

However, the P.W. Botha government's Nkomati Accord signed with the Mozambican government and the New York Accord concluded with Cuba and the Soviet Union, both represented setbacks for the ANC. The former agreement meant that the ANC bases in Mozambique had to be closed down and cadres could no longer be infiltrated into South Africa through that country. In terms of the New York agreement Cuba and the Soviet Union had to withhold support of the ANC in Angola. As a result, the ANC became increasingly dependent on mass politicisation of the black majority inside South Africa.

In August 1983 the United Democratic Front (UDF), the brainchild of the Rev. Allan Boesak, was established. It was a countrywide federation of anti-apartheid community organisations and proved to be an important milestone in the struggle against apartheid. The UDF adopted the 1955 Freedom Charter as its directive and rejected all apartheid structures. Despite its efforts the organisation did not succeed in disrupting the white referendum in November 1983 on the proposed tricameral parliament to give (limited) parliamentary representation to coloured people and Indians. However, the UDF did in large measure manage to undermine the election process for coloured and Indian representatives in the tricameral parliament.

By the mid-1980s the UDF began to focus on making South Africa ungovernable for P.W. Botha's NP government. Street and ward committees were set up everywhere in black townships. Entire communities were persuaded, sometimes coerced, to participate in politically motivated action such as consumer, bus and rent boycotts. Black councillors were intimidated to resign and large-scale stayaways were arranged from time to time.

The fact that the UDF was able to persuade millions of South Africans, particularly African, coloured and Indian communities, to take part in these various forms of protest action was evidence of the profound antagonism against apartheid in black societies countrywide. Although the UDF could not make the country completely ungovernable, it was so successful with its campaigns that in an attempt to keep control, the government declared a nationwide state of emergency.

In the late 1970s and early 1980s four of the biggest homelands – Transkei in 1976; Bophuthatswana in 1977; Venda in 1979; and Ciskei in 1981 – officially gained their "independence" from the South African government. The residents of these homelands also lost their South African citizenship and became "citizens" of their respective homelands. However, the homeland governments were not recognised internationally. In all four "independent" homelands there was political instability and high levels of internal corruption; they were also heavily dependent on huge subsidies from the South African government.

In the KwaZulu homeland in the then province of Natal there was a unique progression of events. Mangosuthu Buthelezi was the chief minister and turned down the Pretoria regime's offer of "independence". In 1975 he was also the founder of Inkatha (the forerunner of the Inkatha Freedom Party). In 1980, together with a number of white politicians, he explored the possibility of joint self-government for Natal and KwaZulu. In 1982 the Buthelezi commission's report recommended this option, but the South African government rejected the proposal. Nevertheless, the government of the KwaZulu homeland and Natal white politicians continued their discussions in an official indaba in April 1986. But the Pretoria government was not to be persuaded; it turned down the indaba's proposals on self-government for KwaZulu-Natal. This was the end of the homeland policy in that province.

Inkatha was initially to all appearances a Zulu cultural movement, but over time it played a strong political role. In practice, Inkatha was in direct opposition to a number of organisations which supported the ANC and Buthelezi became an outspoken critic of the ANC; in turn the ANC rejected his credentials as a liberation leader and branded him as a collaborator.

Black communities throughout South Africa, particularly in the present Gauteng and KwaZulu-Natal, became intensely involved in the political competition between the ANC and Inkatha. This led to large-scale black-on-black violence which led to even greater loss of life than that caused by the struggle against apartheid. It is alleged by some historians that there was government collusion with the IFP in this escalating violence. In some townships street committees virtually took over and exercised their own extreme form of rule, making use of people's courts. Those who were suspected of being in cahoots with political opponents were simply "tried" in these makeshift courts and often sentenced to death. In several hundred cases people found "guilty" were killed by the horrific so-called necklace method which involved placing a motor-car tyre around the victim's neck and setting it alight.

Needless to say, the attempt by the UDF-aligned street committees and people's courts to take over control of the townships prompted resistance in these communities. Here the vigilantes led the way. Their cruel reprisal tactics often exacerbated the black-on-black violence. The police often supported the vigilantes to help undermine the UDF's alternative power structures.

Although the government introduced several reforms in the education system, from 1980 there was another surge of resistance in black schools. It began as a protest against the government's use of national servicemen as teachers, but other grievances were also taken up such as the poor facilities in schools. The unrest continued for almost the entire year.

In 1984 another wave of school boycotts followed. In the Vaal Triangle these boycotts were linked with wider community issues. In Cradock in the Eastern Cape it was the dismissal of a popular local teacher, Matthew Goniwe, who was also the chairperson of the Cradock Youth Association (CRADOYA), a front organisation for the UDF. Goniwe and three other leaders of CRADOYA, the so-called "Cradock four", were murdered shortly afterwards. In the 1990s the Truth and Reconciliation Commission (TRC) found that the security forces were responsible for the murders. The emotionally charged funeral of the Cradock four was the first of a series of politicised mass funerals which were even attended by overseas diplomats in South Africa and where the flags of the ANC and the SACP, which were still banned organisations, were openly on display.

The Cradock four were not the only victims of the political suppression by the government security forces. Leaders of political resistance, or sometimes simply participants in resistance action, were on many occasions shot or taken into custody. Numerous monuments have been erected in residential areas such as Guguletu and Athlone in Cape Town, Mamelodi in Pretoria, and even small towns such as Sterkstroom, Molteno, Barkly East and Middelburg in the Eastern Cape, to remind the public of the anti-apartheid activists who lost their lives in the 1980s.

By 1985 school boycotts had become almost ongoing in South Africa. They were often organised by COSAS, a front organisation for the UDF co-ordinated under the motto "No education before liberation". On black university campuses libraries and administrative buildings were burnt down in protest against the exclusion of black students from traditionally white universities.

The government's relaxation of the strong restrictions on black trade unionism at the end of the 1970s soon gave rise to politicised black trade unions, and in 1979 an umbrella organisation of black trade unions, the Federation of South African Trade Unions (FOSATU), was formed. The black trade unions organised many strikes, some of which became violent, to protest against poor working conditions especially in the motor, transport and food industries. Of great significance was the rapid growth of the National Union of Mineworkers (NUM) under leadership of Cyril Ramaphosa, because the mining sector was one of the main pillars of the South African economy and the disruption of this industry by strike action could potentially cripple the economy.

Another important development was the establishment of the Congress of South African Trade Unions (COSATU) in 1985. Grouped together under this organisation were some of the most numerous and powerful trade unions such as the NUM and other UDF-aligned trade unions. COSATU often acted as an ally of the UDF in confrontations with the apartheid regime. In this way the foundation was laid for the tripartite alliance of the ANC, the SACP and COSATU which has dominated the South African political scene since 1994.

From the mid-1980s the exiled ANC repeatedly called upon the UDF and other organisations sympathetic to the ANC cause to make the country ungovernable. In black townships great success was achieved in this aim. The government reacted by declaring a state of emergency and restricting the activities of anti-apartheid organisations where it could, but it was unable to contain the wave of resistance to its oppressive policies. One after another, black local authorities became dysfunctional; they were also crippled financially by rent boycotts. Informal street committees took over de facto control and although the government continued to exercise power through its security forces, these efforts were by no means always effective.

Commentators predicted that the situation in South Africa was fast becoming a ticking time bomb that could explode at any moment. For many South Africans a devastating bloodbath seemed increasingly inevitable; the opinion was even aired that only a miracle could rescue the country.

18
"Adapt or die", 1978-1984

Hermann Giliomee

On 28 September 1978 Pieter Willem (P.W.) Botha became the eighth prime minister of South Africa. In the last years of his predecessor B.J. Vorster's term, the emphasis had been largely one of clinging to the old apartheid model and there was intensified pressure from the outside world that the government should abandon apartheid. After the Soweto uprisings of 1976, several thousand young black people left the country to join the liberation movements.

The years 1977–1978 were dominated by the so-called "Information Scandal". The former Department of Information not only conducted a secret propaganda campaign in an unlawful manner to improve the government's international image; they also used secret funding. Among their tactics was to use state funds to launch a local newspaper, *The Citizen*, which supported the National Party (NP). Vorster initially denied any knowledge of these propaganda projects and the misuse of state funds, but after the Erasmus Commission's investigation, it became clear that he was indeed informed about them. After the scandal had been exposed in the press, Vorster resigned as prime minister.

The challenge of reform

Shortly after he became prime minister, Botha said: "We are part of Africa and we must play that role or we will die." The press adapted these words slightly and came up with the catch-phrase "adapt or die" to describe Botha's political approach. This is a very apt summary of the first phase of Botha's term. There was an urgency and dynamism about his leadership which was in sharp contrast with Vorster's hesitant last years.

Botha was a determined, energetic and purposeful leader but was also impetuous, impatient and rash. He was a leader who was prepared to adapt, but was also more than ready for a fight. He could intimidate people and make them toe the line like few other leaders could. After a visit to South Africa in 1983, Dr Javier Perez de Cuellar, at the time secretary general of the United Nations, said: "Two leaders in the world made a great impression on me: China's Deng Xiaoping and South Africa's P.W. Botha. They understand power."

In Botha's first year in office it seemed that the idea of reform took precedence and that far-reaching changes were on the way. He called black people "fellow South Africans", visited Soweto with a "message of hope" and toured through all the homelands. He asked Afrikaners to read their own history and to realise that everyone should have political rights. He went on to say: "If people are oppressed, they fight back. We must respect the rights of other people and free ourselves by giving to others in the spirit of justice, what we Afrikaners asked for ourselves."

After his first year as prime minister the most influential American newspaper *The Washington Post* wrote that black people were astonished by such statements by Botha and his ministers; they kindled hopes among them that an alternative could be found for violence and despair.

By the end of the 1970s the most senior positions in the central government, the security forces, provincial administrations (with the exception of Natal) and public corporations, were filled by Afrikaners. However, there was never an exclusively Afrikaner or white civil service. Even in the 1950s there were more black people than white people appointed in the civil service, because services to the black population were provided by black people – such as policemen, teachers, nurses, etc. A large number of unskilled workers were also employed in the civil service. By the early 1980s approximately 2 million people worked in the public sector, including the homeland administrations, and only a third of these were white.

One can almost say that there were two states side by side. There was the "inner state" which was under the control of Afrikaner politicians and senior government officials. Here, Afrikaner pressure groups such as the NP caucus; the Afrikaner Broederbond (Afrikaner Brotherhood); the Afrikaans churches; and the Afrikaanse Handelsinstituut (Afrikaans Trade Institute) exerted the most influence. Alongside this core state there was also a multiracial "outer state", in which the heads of the security forces, business leaders and the homeland leaders with their leading officials, played an important role.

Since the mid-1970s the NP had declared that the reform of the apartheid state was its most important aim. This was, however, not entirely accurate. Although Botha spoke out strongly against offending or belittling coloured or black people on the basis of their colour, he wanted to retain the cornerstones of apartheid such as population registration and group areas. The core of his political outlook was that South Africa did not have a race problem; instead it had a problem with "minorities". According to this view there are white people, coloured people, Indians and black people who are minorities, and also "minorities within minorities" (for example Moslems in the coloured group) all of whom are concerned about their political future and the survival of their culture.

The problem with this argument was that birth determined the membership of race groups which Botha regarded as so-called minorities. For the majority of people in the country, reform was only possible if people had the freedom to become a member of a group of their choice, or could elect to renounce their birth membership of a "minority". This Botha would not allow. Nor would he abolish group areas, because in his view each minority had its own residential area and the right to have its own government or local authority in that region (for example Transkei) or residential area (for example Mamelodi).

Botha was keen to draw the coloured people and Indians into the government and the parliament but as separate groups and without affecting the position of power enjoyed by the whites. He was against any plans to give black people representation in the central government and this brought him into confrontation with Gatsha (later called Mangosuthu) Buthelezi.

Buthelezi, as leader of the Inkatha movement and chief minister of the KwaZulu homeland, was at that time the only black leader in South Africa who had mass support. In 1979 he broke his ties with the leaders of the African National Congress (ANC) in exile because he rejected the ANC's sanction campaign and their decision to turn to armed struggle. According to him, such tactics would jeopardise all hope of peaceful change. Thereafter the ANC-Inkatha relationship quickly deteriorated into bitter enmity.

The Botha government did not trust Buthelezi. He spoke out strongly against the independence of the Zulu people, who comprised more than 20% of the total population. It was him, more than any other grouping, including the ANC, who frustrated the government's hopes of making all black people citizens of homelands – with an eye to a confederation or constellation of states comprising the republic's government and a number of homeland governments. In 1981 a commission appointed by the KwaZulu government suggested that the province of Natal and KwaZulu be integrated. It proposed that a legislative assembly be elected on the basis of universal franchise and a multiracial executive committee formed to take decisions along power-sharing lines.

Buthelezi believed that if such a system succeeded, other regions could replicate it and in this way strong and credible leaders could come to the fore. Eventually this would lead to the formation of a federal system in which power could be spread rather than concentrated in the central government. He argued that this would relieve the international pressure on the South African government and would also mean that the large majority of black people would not give their support to the ANC.

Botha's reaction to this was in the old apartheid idiom. He replied that although Buthelezi was welcome to investigate issues which concerned KwaZulu, he had no right to meddle in matters which were the prerogative of the central government.

The ANC's new challenge

By the end of the 1970s the ANC had persuaded the governments of various countries to discontinue their normal diplomatic relations and sporting contacts with South Africa and to introduce limited sanctions. Many large international companies began to withdraw their investments from South Africa.

At this time the ANC also intensified its armed struggle against the government and public institutions. In 1979 an ANC delegation visited North Vietnam to consult with the Viet Cong guerrillas about their tactics and strategy against the American forces. The delegation returned with the conviction that the best way to wage the liberation struggle was a so-called civil war aimed specifically at making the black residential areas ungovernable. Accordingly, armed attacks by trained military units were alternated with mass protests over payment for services, inadequate service delivery and public transport. School boycotts increased dramatically.

Between 1976 and 1983 the ANC was also responsible for 362 sabotage and other violent incidents. Prominent targets included a Sasol installation in 1980; the Voortrekkerhoogte military base in Pretoria in 1981; the Koeberg nuclear power station near Cape Town in 1982; and a car bomb outside the headquarters of the South African Air Force in Church Street Pretoria which exploded, killing 19 civilians in 1983.

White dominance under pressure

One of the main reasons why Botha was anxious to introduce reform was the declining number of white people in relation to the population as a whole. Between 1910 and 1960 white people comprised about 20% of the population, but after 1960 this percentage dropped to 17% in 1976; and to 12% in 2000. This declining number of whites was eventually one of the major reasons why the government relinquished power in the mid-1990s.

From the 1930s onwards the urban workforce comprised a growing proportion of black people. They also played a role in the manufacturing sector where a higher level of competence was required than in the mines and on farms. In 1935 there were about 100 000 white and 100 000 black workers in the manufacturing sector; by 1975 the number of black workers had escalated to 726 000 and there were twice as many black as white people employed in the sector.

It was not the numbers as such, but the level of competence that was so significant. The white trade unions tried to reserve the skilled work for white workers, but later there were not enough white workers to fill all the posts. As a result, in the 1970s only a quarter of skilled workers were white. The transformation of the labour market went even further than this. Between 1965 and 1980 the white workers' contribution in posts at the middle level of the labour hierarchy dropped from four-fifths to two-thirds, and it was destined to fall even further.

The economy began to rely increasingly on the skills of coloured and black people in the mines, factories, shops and in the public service. They were soldiers, policemen, nurses and teachers who wanted proper homes and schools for their children. They also wanted to be treated as fully fledged citizens of the country and to have the right to vote.

From the beginning of the 1970s black and coloured workers participated in more and more strikes. In 1973 the government allowed black people – with the permission of the white trade unions – to be employed as skilled workers. Shortly afterwards, this requirement was set aside, as were various regulations that had previously reserved certain work for white people. In 1979 the government permitted black workers to form official trade unions and to bargain, along with white or multiracial trade unions, for higher wages. Black people now had workers' rights, but they were still without political rights.

From 1970 onwards the state also spent far more on black education. The number of black children who passed through to the higher standards (these days called grades) increased exponentially in the next 20 years. This had a decided political outcome. There was a realisation of how much further black children had progressed at school; how more politically aware they had become; and how intolerant they had grown of accepting apartheid.

Black people in higher education institutions

Year	Secondary school	Reached highest standard	University
1960	54 598	717	1871
1970	122 489	2938	4578
1985	1 192 932	34 733	49 164

From the mid-1970s there was a large and growing group of job seekers who were unable to get permanent or acceptable work. Black children now progressed to standards of which their parents could only dream, and yet they had a much slimmer chance than their parents of finding fixed work. In the Soweto uprisings of 1976 the majority of participants were school children and the unemployed youth.

To create a stable middle class, in 1977 the government allowed black people to take out a 99-year lease on their houses. They and their descendants could now live permanently in the towns and cities. However, the government refused to abolish the pass system which the black majority saw as a symbol of white suppression. The state felt that this law was necessary to control black people and to curb urbanisation. The pass law was only scrapped in 1986. The previous year the Mixed Marriages Act was abolished.

The economic decline

In the first 50 years of the Union of South Africa's existence, segregation and apartheid did not have a negative effect on the economy. Employers were inclined to use a great many poorly paid, unskilled or semi-skilled workers in a lavish manner, and to give little attention to their productivity. The pass law and other restrictions on black political organisations and trade unions meant that black people's ability to bargain for higher wages was severely hampered. The government spent very little on the development of black reserves or the upliftment of the poorest of the poor communities.

This situation changed dramatically in the 1960s. The most important reason for this was the unexpectedly high economic growth rate. There no longer were enough white people to do all the work at the middle and higher level of the labour hierarchy and the shortage of skilled workers began to pinch the economy. The poorer basic education that coloured and black workers had received often made it impossible to become adequately skilled. In addition, legislation excluded black and coloured workers from some skilled jobs. The cost of segregation and apartheid was becoming ever more evident. The poorest workers often had to travel a long way to their workplaces because in terms of the Group Areas Act black and coloured townships were usually on the outskirts of towns and cities. Furthermore, most black and coloured people were poor and had no significant buying power.

From 1973 the growth rate began to slow down. It dropped from an average of 4,5% between 1948 and 1976, to an average of only 1,65% between 1976 and 1994. This latter growth rate was far below the 3% annual population increase and caused unemployment to escalate. The reasons for the economic decline were complicated and some factors were beyond the control of the state, such as the sharp rise in the petrol price after 1974; the lower price for exported South African minerals; and the deceleration of growth that South Africa's foremost trading partners were experiencing. One of the most important reasons for the lower growth rate was the manufacturing sector's inability to export enough to make up for the drop in the value of mineral exports. However, it was not only South Africa that was hit by this weakening of the economy; the growth rate of other countries with economies of comparable size also declined.

Local and foreign investors had in addition become reluctant to invest in South Africa by for example opening new mines or factories. The ending of Portuguese colonial rule in Angola and Mozambique; the guerrilla war in Rhodesia; the wave of strikes in 1973 in Durban; and the Soweto uprisings of 1976 made investors wonder about South Africa's stability.

From the mid-1970s onwards the government began to make the salary gaps smaller between white and black people and between white and coloured people. Employers in the private sector also narrowed the wage gap. In the 1970s and 1980s the proportion of white to black wages in the mining industry fell from 21:1 to 6:1, and in the manufacturing sector from 6:1 to 4:1. To remain profitable, employers reduced their workforce and demanded higher productivity from the remaining workers.

White workers still had a considerable head start because the state spent far more on white education. One of the major reasons for this was that white children attended school for far longer than black learners and progressed to higher standards. In 1970, 79% of urban black people and 93% of those in the rural areas had not reached Standard 6 (Grade 8), in comparison with only 4% of white people in the labour force.

After 1979, when the government allowed all workers to join trade unions, it became more difficult for employers to dismiss workers. They were also under more pressure to pay higher wages. They reacted by employing fewer workers or resorted to mechanising their factories, both of which made the unemployment problem even worse. By the end of the 1970s South Africa's labour costs were higher than those of its competitors and it struggled to compete in the manufactured goods export market. The economy declined and only lifted its head again when the prices of export metals and minerals rose.

Divided Afrikaners

The NP government which came to power in 1948 was a party of Afrikaners of whom the large majority could be classified as lower middle-class people (including farmers and state officials) and manual labourers. By the end of the 1970s the Afrikaners, from a class perspective, were no longer such a homogenous group. They had begun to differ politically because the various categories of Afrikaners – businessmen, workers, professional people and farmers – had different interests and concerns.

As can be seen in the table below, the proportion of Afrikaners who were farmers declined sharply after the mid-1930s; most people had moved to the towns and cities. The proportion of office workers (government officials, clerks, businessmen, and professional people such as attorneys) doubled between 1936 and 1980. This represents a sharp increase in what is usually described as the middle class.

With the rapidly growing economy it was possible for the NP to keep all the different Afrikaner interest groups satisfied and at the same time to increase the expenditure on education, healthcare and pensions for black and coloured people. In the 1970s the high economic growth rate of the previous 40 years came to an end. To balance its budget, the government began to withdraw its support to farmers and alienated white workers by also allowing black and coloured people to do skilled work. Furthermore, the NP government also began to narrow the gap between the salaries and pensions of white people and those of the other racial groups. The great measure of unanimity among Afrikaners was beginning to disappear.

The composition of the Afrikaner labour force

	1936	1946	1960	1980	1990
Farmers	41%	30%	16%	7%	5%
Manual workers	31%	41%	40%	32%	29%
Office workers	28%	29%	44%	62%	66%

Many conservative NP supporters felt that the government had left them in the lurch. Among them were workers who still insisted on white privilege; less prosperous farmers who opposed the government's curtailment of subsidies; and government officials on the lower levels whose salary increases were not keeping pace with the rising cost of living. All three of these groups were experiencing hardship because of high inflation and taxes.

Those in the NP who favoured reform included business people, professionals and academics, all of whom were identifying themselves increasingly with universal values such as freedom and equality regardless of colour. They were aware that a coloured and black middle class was emerging that would no longer tolerate discrimination. For those who wanted reform, economic and social apartheid had become an embarrassment.

Only one factor still held the Afrikaners together: the conviction that political power was a prerequisite for their survival as a people and for Afrikaans to remain a widely used publicly recognised language.

Botha was less reliant on Afrikaner support than his predecessors. A new fluidity had emerged in white politics after the United Party, which had been led for more than 20 years by Sir De Villiers Graaff, crumbled in 1977. Many English-speaking voters sympathised with the NP's carefully paced reform process. The old Afrikaner-English friction had largely disappeared in the face of growing political pressure from black people and the antagonism of the outside world. In the 1980s between a quarter and a third of white English speakers voted for the NP.

Constitutional reform

In the John Vorster era the last forms of political representation for black, coloured and Indian people were scrapped. Thereafter only white people sat in Parliament, the provincial councils and local councils. At the same time, many black and coloured people moved up from the level of unskilled work to semi-skilled and skilled labour, where they worked shoulder to shoulder with white people. Increasing economic integration began to clash more and more with the policy of apartheid.

Botha insisted that the entire process of constitutional reform was to take place under the NP government's direction and control. As Buthelezi put it, Botha was the man who managed the reform process and also the one who settled differences. He wanted, in other words, to be both player and referee. The important question was whether the constitutional changes would initially include only the coloured and Indian communities, or whether they should include black people from the outset.

In 1977 the government accepted a plan to include coloured people and Indians along with white people into a collective system of representation. At first the idea was to have separate parliaments, but later it was decided to have one parliament with three chambers. The NP made vague promises that black people would also be involved. However, this was not to be by means of representation in Parliament.

To those who were more inclined to accept reform, the party leaders explained that the symbolism of white supremacy and exclusivity in Parliament first had to be negated and that the inclusion of black people would have to wait until the voters became accustomed to the idea. To its more conservative followers the party said that white, coloured and Indian people had to stand together against black people and should therefore sit together in Parliament. Dr Andries Treurnicht, leader of the conservative wing in the party, was against this. He was intolerant of the fact that coloured and Indian ministers would co-rule over "me and all other whites". However, Botha persisted that there should be only one government in one country.

Early in 1982 the tension between Botha and Treurnicht's supporters in the NP reached breaking point. On 24 February 1982 Treurnicht and 21 other NP members of Parliament walked out of the NP caucus and formed the Conservative Party (CP). This was the end of Afrikaner unity that for so many decades had been championed, cherished and protected.

In 1983 a referendum for white voters was held on the proposed new constitution. Both the Progressive Federal Party, which was against apartheid, and the CP, which wanted to retain apartheid, asked people to say "no" to a new constitution. However, eventually two-thirds of those who voted expressed themselves in favour of the proposed changes. Chris Heunis, the experienced and intelligent but domineering Minister of Constitutional Development, persuaded the Labour Party, the strongest coloured party which worked within the apartheid system, to agree to the proposals. Thereupon, plans went ahead to establish the new tricameral parliament. Small Indian parties also agreed to co-operate.

The tricameral parliament

The tricameral parliament came into being in September 1984. It comprised a white chamber, a coloured chamber and an Indian chamber, elected on separate voters' rolls according to a 4:2:1 ratio that corresponded with relative population size of the three groups. The majority party in the white chamber could not be voted out (and thus lose power) because the opposition parties in the white house could not team up with parties in the coloured and Indian houses.

Each chamber had its own cabinet and budget to deal with "own affairs" in its particular community, such as education, housing and social services. There were also "general affairs" which included defence, law and order, and economic policy. Bills were discussed separately by each house and were duly passed or rejected. The only power sharing element was in the requirement that all three chambers had to approve a bill and the fact that coloured and Indian representatives could serve in the general affairs cabinet. Botha appointed the leaders of the coloured and Indian chambers in his cabinet.

The post of prime minister was scrapped and there would now be a state president who was both the symbolic head of state and the head of the executive authority. He also chaired cabinet meetings. An electoral college comprising all three chambers elected the state president who had executive powers. Here too, the majority party in the white house had the deciding vote.

The state president could make use of the President's Council, a multiracial advisory body of experts who were virtually all supportive of the NP, to break any constitutional deadlock if one of the chambers refused to approve a bill. It was, as the saying of the time went, a form of "sharing power without losing control".

Black reaction to the tricameral parliament

Black people saw their exclusion from the tricameral parliament as a rejection of their demand for full citizenship of the country together with the white and coloured people and the Indians. They were alienated even further when government spokespersons insisted that the black homelands, together with the new system of black local governments, were the justification for the exclusion of black people from the new constitutional dispensation.

Although the government pumped huge amounts of money into the homelands from the mid-1970s onwards, it became increasingly clear that they did not have the potential to become economically sustainable. The migrant labour system had led to the deterioration of agriculture in the homelands and the residents were poverty stricken. From the early 1970s onwards there was a stream of people moving from the homelands into the towns and cities, where they settled on the outskirts of white areas. The government could do nothing to check this influx of job hunters. The pass law system collapsed and was abolished in 1986.

In 1976 the South African government granted independence to the Transkei, but it was the only government in the world which recognised Transkei as an independent state. Bophuthatswana became independent in the same manner in 1977 and Ciskei (1979) and Venda (1980) followed. After gaining their independence, the citizens of these "states" lost their South African citizenship, despite the fact that they lived virtually permanently in Soweto or other towns and cities in South Africa.

Connie Mulder, who in 1978 became Minister of Plural Relations and Development (previously Bantu Administration and Development), declared that once all the homelands had gained their independence there would no longer be any black South Africans. In 1981 Xhosas who were living in informal settlements (squatter camps) in Cape Town were "deported" to the Transkei in terms of legislation which controlled the influx of "foreign" citizens into South Africa. The government even classified money provided for the homelands as "foreign assistance".

The various homeland governments, each with its own chief minister, cabinet, legislative assembly and civil service, gave black people who lived in the homelands a form of self-government which did not threaten whites. These governments concerned themselves mainly with their own domestic affairs and did not endeavour to gain meaningful concessions from the South African government.

Power in the balance

In 1984 – six years after Botha took over the political leadership – it was difficult to assess whether the reforms had succeeded in preventing a more serious uprising or whether South Africa had declined into an even greater political crisis.

In certain respects the picture appeared bleak. The economy had grown slowly. The number of unemployed black and coloured people and poverty-stricken people from the homelands who were streaming into the urban areas, had become far larger. The black trade unions were beginning to flex their muscles; not only were they calling for higher wages, they were also making political demands. They wanted the gap between white and black wages to close more rapidly and were insistent that white racism against them in the workplace had to stop. The number of white people as a proportion of the total population had dropped from just under 20% in the mid-1950s to under 15% by the mid-1980s. White people urgently needed allies, but few black and coloured leaders were prepared to side with the government.

On the other hand, the Botha government had gained notable support from foreign leaders after the introduction of the tricameral parliament. These heads of state believed that a parliament in which white, coloured and Indian people sat together was the beginning of a process of abolishing apartheid and that the government would soon give significant rights to black people.

Furthermore, it appeared that the state had managed to withstand the security challenge presented by the ANC. With its operations across the country's borders, the army had prevented a large-scale infiltration of ANC fighters. In March 1984 the ANC had to close its bases in Mozambique after South Africa signed the Nkomati Accord with the Mozambique government. In terms of this agreement the two countries would not allow attacks to be made on the other alliance partner from within their own borders.

To show their support for Botha as a leader and reformer, the heads of governments in Britain, Germany, Switzerland and Portugal invited him to travel to their capitals to engage in diplomatic talks, and in July 1984 Botha undertook official visits to all these countries. For a moment it looked as if South Africa was about to make an important diplomatic breakthrough.

Under Treurnicht the CP attempted to whip up enthusiasm for the Afrikaner nationalist movement by turning the clock back to the mid-1960s when it had looked as if the Afrikaners would rule for ever. But it was no longer possible to revive the driving force and conviction of the people's movement (*volksbeweging*) of old. The solutions that the CP put forward were already discredited. The NP had tried to implement them and had failed. It was impossible to create a white homeland and the black homelands were clearly not a viable solution.

White people who favoured reform increasingly accepted that there would have to be black people in the government. They wanted a stable government, efficient state officials, an independent judiciary and a strong economy. Rather than a majority government they wanted a system which would create a balance between the black majority on the one side and a combination of minority groups on the other. Very few white people were in favour of a government in which the black majority had the whip hand, wielding full control. Afrikaners in particular were pessimistic about a black government. More than four-fifths of the Afrikaners who took part in an opinion poll in the mid-1980s believed that reverse discrimination would take place under a black majority government and that the Afrikaans language and culture would be threatened. Furthermore, more than 80% believed that the physical safety of white people would be threatened and that their possessions and property would not be safe.

Since the mid-1980s the government's own secret opinion polls show that the ANC would secure more than 60% of the votes in a free election and the NP 19% to 23%. The ANC insisted on what it called "an ordinary democracy". By this it meant majority government in a unitary state. "The majority takes all" is the term usually used in describing this system. In such a dispensation, mechanisms which protect minorities such as a government of national unity, group rights, federalism and the decentralisation of power to the provinces, are largely absent.

For Botha and his voting corps this was completely unacceptable. In a survey in 1987 it was found that only 3% of Afrikaners would accept a political dispensation in which the majority party exercised complete power, while 11% of English speakers would be prepared to do so. Only 1% of Afrikaners and 3% of English speakers wanted Nelson Mandela as state president compared to 12% and 39% respectively who wanted Buthelezi in this post. White people were worried that there were many communists in the ANC leadership structures and that they might well place certain large companies under state control. A political agreement between the NP and the ANC looked extremely unlikely.

19
Uprising, war and transition, 1984-1994

Hermann Giliomee

After the tricameral parliament was introduced the questions arose: What about black people's political rights? The apartheid system's greatest weak spot was indeed the lack of representation, especially as regards urban black people, for whom there were not even efficient black local authorities.

In the early 1980s the government brought in its most catastrophic model of all. For the first time in history black local authorities received some measure of self-sufficiency, with virtually the same powers as white city councils. However, they did not have an adequate revenue base and this meant that they had too little money to provide proper services. Very few residents in black townships owned property, with the result that the income from rates was very limited.

Previously, municipal beer halls were a big source of income, but most of these had been burnt down in the uprisings of 1976/1977 and the unrest that followed. Furthermore, there was no formula to channel funds from white city councils to black local governments.

The government tried in vain to promote the new form of black local authorities as justification for the exclusion of black people from the tricameral parliament in which whites, coloureds and Indians were represented. Meanwhile, black town councils were elected throughout the country, but with low percentage polls.

Many residents stopped paying rent and their water and electricity accounts. To make matters worse, some of the new councils pushed up rates and taxes somewhat recklessly.

"Make South Africa ungovernable"

In September 1984 the tricameral parliament assembled for the first time. The same month unrest, accompanied by a higher level of violence, broke out in the black townships of the Vaal Triangle, south-east of Johannesburg. The local mayor and his deputy were among the first people to be killed in Sebokeng. With this, the final phase of the struggle against apartheid began.

In the last quarter of 1984 and the first few months of 1985, the protest in the Vaal Triangle townships spread to other parts of the Transvaal, Natal and the eastern Cape. In Natal and KwaZulu a small-scale civil war broke out between Inkatha, which had a strong support base in the rural areas, and the United Democratic Front (UDF) which ruled the roost in the larger towns and cities.

There were countless stayaways, strikes, consumer boycotts and protest marches, and black urban residents refused to pay their rent and service charges. In many cases the protest marches were led by prominent churchmen and were supported largely by students and the youth; they often led to violence. In many black townships riotous crowds attacked the homes of black town councillors and forced them to resign their posts. The aim was to cause the entire system of local government to disintegrate. Crowds also burnt down government buildings and bottle stores.

Another target was the homes of black policemen and many of them had no alternative other than to live outside the towns. Those who were suspected of being collaborators and spies for the state were killed, some by the notorious necklace method. These horrendous killings soon dried up the police's sources of information. Emotions ran high at the funerals of people who had been killed in clashes with the police; the coffins were often draped with the ANC flag.

In March 1985, after the police had fired on a peaceful crowd in Uitenhage, protest action spread from the eastern Cape to Cape Town and other parts of the province. On 16 June 1985, the day that the Soweto uprising was commemorated, bombs exploded in Durban and Johannesburg. On 20 July 1985 the government declared a state of emergency that was limited to certain magisterial districts.

Two days later the ANC responded by way of a call from its leader, Oliver Tambo. Speaking in a radio broadcast he appealed to his followers to make South Africa ungovernable. It seemed that South Africa was teetering either on the brink of a full-scale civil war or a dramatic step that might lead to a negotiation process with the liberation movements. However, it was generally accepted that Nelson Mandela's release from prison was a prerequisite before negotiations could begin.

The Rubicon speech

By mid-1985 it was clear that only radical reform would be able to counter the wave of international sanctions and possibly pave the way for negotiations. There were expectations of important new developments ahead of President Botha's speech that was planned for 15 August 1985. In cabinet meetings Chris Heunis, the Minister of Constitutional Development, had suggested that black leaders should be included in the cabinet. He was under the impression that the president had agreed with him, but Botha had no intention of giving any meaningful power in the central government to black people. He was only prepared to agree to the formation of a federation of states in which the governments of the homelands and the Republic of South Africa would confer together from time to time.

When he began his speech on the appointed evening, millions of people, locally and abroad, followed him on television; expectations were high. But Botha was unyielding. He came across as a hard-core proponent of white dominance. He said in no uncertain terms that he was not prepared to lead white South Africans on the "road to abdication and suicide". According to him, without white South Africans and their influence the country would decline into strife, chaos and poverty. He added that he had no respect for revolutionaries who had changed Africa into a "dying continent" and that "Mandela and his friends" were in gaol because they had planned a revolution; they would only be released if they agreed to renounce violence.

Although Botha announced that his government had crossed the proverbial Rubicon, the speech in no way lived up to expectations. (The Rubicon is a small river in Italy which Julius Caesar crossed more than 2000 years ago, signalling the beginning of his rise against the state.) There was a great deal of dissatisfaction, especially in the outside world, about Botha's Rubicon speech. Shortly afterwards a new wave of sanctions was imposed on South Africa and more investments were withdrawn.

The speech was so unfavourably received that few observers noticed that Botha had in fact scrapped an important part of apartheid's "master plan". He had announced that residents of the six homelands which did not want to accept independence would be recognised as South African citizens; they would be given representation in a common political system. This put an end to the idea that all black people in a "white South Africa" had to give up their right to a political voice.

More unrest and a national state of emergency

By November 1985 there were about 8000 office-bearers of the United Democratic Front (UDF) in police custody. Many leaders were imprisoned; others had fled the country. In March 1986 Botha lifted the partial state of emergency for a short while, but on 12 June 1986 he announced a national state of emergency which was destined to remain in place until 1990.

Government forces tried to suppress the countrywide unrest using firm and heavy-handed tactics. By the end of 1986 more than 20 000 people were in detention. The State Security Council, an elite group which included certain ministers and senior generals from the police and the army, met regularly to discuss security matters. However, many members of the cabinet had no input at all in major decisions.

The government went ahead with reform in the hope of reviving the confidence of investors. "Petty apartheid" was scrapped but the pillars of apartheid such as the Population Registration Act were retained because the NP leadership saw this as necessary to keep white control. Urban black people throughout the country now had full rights to residence in white towns and cities and the ban on mixed race marriages and sexual relations between whites and people of colour was abolished. The pass law disappeared and black people were allowed to own property in "white" South Africa. In addition, public facilities were opened to all races and official discrimination in the labour market was now something of the past. There was still a large gap in government spending per head for learners of different races, but this dropped from 10:1 in the 1960s to 1:3,5 in the 1990s.

However, these reforms did not lighten the burden of international sanctions. Foreign banks called in South Africa's loans and refused all new loan applications. The US also clamped down on new investments in

South Africa and banned all loans to the government. In Britain, Margaret Thatcher's Tory government tried to maintain its links with Pretoria, but the Commonwealth dug in its heels and placed a ban on the import of all agricultural products and manufactured goods from South Africa, as well as a banning of all new loans and investments. Thatcher informed Botha that she would not be able to support him any longer unless he released Nelson Mandela. About a fifth of the British companies based in South Africa withdrew and direct British investment decreased by half in the course of the 1980s.

Sanctions could not bring the government down and they did not really hurt the middle class financially. Often it was a case of overseas companies who had withdrawn selling their local interests cheaply to South African companies. Trade links with the West did indeed weaken as a result of sanctions, but at the same time those with Asia improved. Overall, total overseas trade grew. By the end of 1986 the country had a trade surplus of R15 billion. However, the prohibition on new overseas loans and investments did do serious damage to business confidence. South Africa's economic growth declined even further, which in turn caused higher levels of unemployment.

Destabilisation

In the early 1980s South Africa's neighbouring states wanted to reduce their economic dependency on South Africa and increase their support to ANC guerrillas. The idea was that these guerrillas could infiltrate South Africa through neighbouring countries, particularly Mozambique, Lesotho, Swaziland and Botswana. In 1982 William Casey, head of the US Central Intelligence Agency (CIA) met with Botha and his security advisors in Pretoria. Together they agreed that it was possible to create a security zone by forcing South Africa's neighbour states to stop harbouring ANC guerrillas.

South Africa's disruptive attacks on hostile border states, or destabilisation as it came to be known, were particularly severe in Mozambique which had become the major route for ANC guerrillas to infiltrate South Africa. The Frelimo government under Samora Machel was an easy target. The South African security forces used the resistance movement Renamo as an instrument against the Mozambican government. Unlike UNITA (an Angolan liberation movement) Renamo was not primarily an ethnic group and in addition did not have a charismatic leader. Furthermore, it was opposed to the Frelimo government's Marxist policy and was prepared to sow destruction in Mozambique with weapons supplied by South Africa. Its guerrillas blew up railway lines, planted landmines on roads and blew up petrol depots and grain silos.

By 1984 the pressure on the Machel government was so great that the Frelimo government signed the Nkomati Accord with South Africa. Both sides agreed that they would not support guerrilla forces. The Machel government expelled 800 ANC activists and in turn, South Africa sent 1000 Renamo guerrillas back to Mozambique. However, both governments secretly continued their support of the relevant parties.

On South Africa's borders there were a number of states that, because of the destabilisation policy, were reluctant to help the ANC. The Nkomati Accord was certainly a setback for the ANC, but was by no means devastating. For many black people in South Africa any sign of the ANC's armed action was a source of hope. The knowledge that the ANC had a military organisation that could hit back was enough to encourage many young people to fight back, even if only with stones.

The NP moves in a new direction

In the last years of the 1980s most leaders in government ranks lost their will to use violence to enforce white supremacy and to rule the country on an apartheid basis. In wider society and the private sector there was a similar change in mindset.

The Afrikaans churches, which had long adhered to apartheid, now decided to reject it. In 1986 the Nederduitse Gereformeerde Kerk (Dutch Reformed Church) declared that its doors were open to everyone, regardless of colour. The church officially decided to base its racial policy on the New Testament, in which the concept of race plays no role. The church also declared that the majority of the population experienced apartheid as an oppressive system and that discrimination violated their human dignity. Such a system was therefore sinful and was a mistake.

Business leaders felt that the cost of apartheid had become too high. They suggested that the policy be scrapped and that negotiations which included the banned organisations take place. In addition, a group of

English-speaking captains of industry visited the ANC headquarters in Lusaka and held talks with Oliver Tambo, the ANC leader.

Anton Rupert, doyen of the Afrikaans businessmen, wrote an outspoken letter to P.W. Botha in which he posed the following question (translated): "Is apartheid the cornerstone of our survival? Certainly not. The notion that apartheid guarantees the survival of the whites is a myth. Indeed, it threatens their survival. Too many people see apartheid as a sin against humankind – the neo-Nazism of a *Herrenvolk* (master race)." He closed with a solemn warning that "one day we will surely end up with a Nuremberg" if the government did not scrap apartheid. With this remark he was referring to the trial and sentencing after the Second World War of certain leaders of Nazi Germany.

Whereas division in black ranks had for long made it easier to rule the country, black leaders across a broad spectrum now began to stand together. They refused to hold talks with the government before Mandela and his comrades had been released and until the government had declared that apartheid would be abolished.

Senior members of the National Intelligence Service (NIS) came to the conclusion that without a negotiated settlement the state would weaken even further. Looking back, Mike Louw, second in command of the NIS, described the situation in the late 1980s as follows: "Nowhere was the situation out of hand, but it was clear that politically and morally we were losing our grip. Everywhere in the townships we encountered intimidation and a strong political consciousness. The political system had become obsolete and a long, bloody struggle lay ahead. It had become clear that the sooner we negotiated a new system, the better."

Chester Crocker, the US assistant secretary of state for African affairs, summed up the situation as follows: "The government and its opposition placed one another in a stalemate position. Neither could move ahead. The black resistance movement did not have the means to force the government to surrender, but the government could not regain its former prestige."

The border war

When Botha came to power in 1978 there were 13 000 Cuban soldiers in Angola and this number soon doubled. The South African government saw their presence as a threat to its control of South West Africa (the present-day Namibia). The South West African People's Organisation (SWAPO) under the leadership of Sam Nujoma was ready to take power in South West Africa with the support of the United Nations (UN). The opinion in government circles was that SWAPO would not hesitate to make use of Cuban support. However, the commanders of the South African Defence Force (SADF) were keen to enforce South Africa's military might far beyond its borders and thereby prevent guerrillas from infiltrating across the boundary.

In February 1978 the Vorster government committed South Africa by the end of that year to lead South West Africa, with the UN's co-operation, to internationally recognised independence. However, the Botha government withdrew from this undertaking and instead announced that in December 1978 an election would be held under the supervision of the South African government. As was expected, SWAPO refused to participate in this election. The government's plan was to build up an internal bloc that would be able to oppose SWAPO.

In the election, the Democratic Turnhalle Alliance, a multiracial, moderate alliance, emerged victorious. But as had happened in the Rhodesian election in 1979, the international community refused to recognise the election; in this case because SWAPO had not participated.

The US administration under President Ronald Reagan agreed with South Africa that it would be impossible to hold an election in South West Africa while there were so many foreign troops in Angola. As part of the plan to weaken SWAPO and to place pressure on the Cubans in Angola to leave the area, South Africa decided to give large-scale support to UNITA, an anti-communist movement based in southern Angola. With South African assistance, UNITA became a significant force and was able to control large areas in the south of the country.

Although the combined forces of South Africa and UNITA were heavily outnumbered, in September 1987 at the Lomba River, they inflicted a heavy defeat on the Cuban-Angolan force that was under the direction of Russian military advisers. The Cuban-Angolan force retreated to Cuito Cuanavale. Although the South African and UNITA forces wanted to drive them further back, the resistance they offered was strong and the SADF/UNITA force eventually withdrew. The Cubans and SWAPO tried to create the impression that this was a South African defeat but senior officials in the Reagan administration rejected this view out of hand.

CUITO CUANAVALE

Seldom in the annals of South African history has a historical event been used so extensively in the present to serve opposing political interests as the so-called Battle of Cuito Cuanavale.

On the one hand the ANC/South African Communist Party (SACP), SWAPO, Cuba and Angola (together with certain academics) claim not only that the forces of the SADF suffered a shattering defeat but that it was this military setback that forced the South African government to the negotiating table where it had to try to reach a compromise from a position of weakness. Proponents of this view argue that this was the first blow that rocked the apartheid government back on its heels and paved the way for its defeat in 1990-1994.

On the other hand, politicians of the then South African government and a number of former SADF generals are adamant that they achieved a resounding victory and that it was indeed the Cubans and Angolans who were later forced to make concessions at the negotiation table.

For the historian who aims to let the past speak for itself, the truth lies somewhere between these two extremes.

The Battle of Cuito Cuanavale was in fact a series of military encounters which lasted from August 1987 to April 1988 (or, depending on how one views it, until June 1988).

These battles began on the Lomba River, spread northwards as far as the Chambinga and finally ended at Tumpo along the Cuito, a stone's throw away from Cuito Cuanavale on the other side of the river. There was also a final episode to the west in the vicinity of Techipa and Calueque. In this last phase the SADF leadership changed its mobile warfare approach for a war of attrition which led to three failed attacks at Tumpo.

This sequence of events eventually led to a deadlock which is reflected in the outcome of the negotiations. Cuba had to pull out from Angola. SWAPO could not take sole authority of Namibia through the barrel of a gun; and South Africa had to accept that SWAPO would rule an independent Namibia.

The outcome was facilitated by the collapse of communism as a factor in global politics, which meant that a SWAPO government in Windhoek no longer held an existential threat for South Africa as was previously feared. A strong case can thus be made for the conclusion that all those involved "won" this particular war.

Leopold Scholtz

Early in 1988 the Reagan administration learnt from the Soviet Union that it wanted to withdraw from southern Africa. South Africa and Cuba were now also keen to end the war. The war not only had huge financial implications and significant loss of life for South Africa; the fruits of the conflict were also questioned. From the Botha government's point of view, an independent Namibia could now be born without the South African government being accused of selling out the white people in the region.

The Cubans were forced to withdraw. In 1989 the election for a constituent assembly took place peacefully in Namibia and SWAPO emerged victorious.

The discussions begin

In 1988 President Botha allowed Niel Barnard and Mike Louw, the two most senior officials in National Intelligence, together with other officials, to hold secret talks with the imprisoned Nelson Mandela. They were immediately aware of his stature as a leader, his integrity and his lack of bitterness despite his imprisonment for more than 25 years.

According to Mandela a majority government was non-negotiable, but a system would have to be created which would ensure that white dominance was not replaced by black dominance. The aim with the armed struggle, he said, was not to overthrow the state but to force white people to give a hearing to the justifiable demands of black South Africans.

By 1989 conditions for negotiation with the ANC were a great deal more favourable than in 1985 or 1986. The war in Angola was over; South West Africa was due to hold an internationally recognised election shortly; the Soviet Union wanted to withdraw from Africa; and the African states in the region were looking forward to a settlement in South Africa so that stability and peace could reign. In South Africa there was a checkmate situation between the security forces and the resistance movement. In the ANC leadership in exile, there was a faction under Thabo Mbeki which could clearly see that victory via the "armed struggle" was still a long way off. He exercised a great deal of influence on the ANC leader, Oliver Tambo.

In January 1989 Botha suffered a stroke. The next month he resigned as NP leader but remained on as state president. F.W. de Klerk was elected as NP leader by a narrow margin.

As was expected, friction soon arose between Botha and De Klerk, both of whom had their supporters. Botha resigned as president on 14

August 1989 and after a general election, De Klerk was elected as state president.

Botha is widely criticised as a politician who began his career well but eventually could not manage to cross the Rubicon. He wanted to include coloured and Indian people into the government but rejected black majority rule out of hand. After 1984 his priority was to suppress the widespread unrest of 1984–1986 in the country. Some commentators suggest that negotiations are impossible unless there is stability.

Under Botha there was also a significant redistribution of wealth from white to black. To do this, taxes had to rise. And yet the NP under Botha's leadership easily won the 1987 election. When he resigned in 1989, stability had to a large extent been restored. This was accomplished without the high death toll that tends to result when there is conflict in countries comprised of various races or ethnic groups. It is true to say that Botha laid the table in preparation for negotiations with the black liberation movements.

The fall of the Berlin Wall in November 1989 signalled the beginning of the end for communism. This was for President F.W. de Klerk what he was later to describe as a "God-given" opportunity. The NP could now tell its critics that the ANC and its ally the South African Communist Party, now without Soviet backing, was no longer a real threat to stability and property rights in South Africa.

At the end of 1989 De Klerk took his great leap forward. In December 1989 he persuaded his cabinet to lift the banning orders on the ANC, Pan Africanist Congress (PAC) and other liberation movements; to release political prisoners; and without any preconditions, to begin multiparty negotiations on a new constitution. On 2 February 1990 De Klerk announced this decision in Parliament. Just before beginning his speech De Klerk said to his wife: "South Africa will never be the same again."

Mandela: a legend in his own time

Nelson Mandela was released from gaol on 11 February 1990 after 27 years in prison. He immediately re-entered political life.

Mandela left the Transkei as a young man and went to Johannesburg where he qualified as an attorney. He was one of the prominent ANC leaders in the protest politics of the 1950s. The police and court cases seriously disrupted his life but thanks to his strong will and his convictions, he continued the struggle at a time when the chances of success seemed slim.

Mandela possessed exceptional characteristics which were well suited to the circumstances. He had a great deal of personal presence and was able to combine seriousness towards life and charisma with a sense of humour and humility. Even before he was sent to gaol he was a remarkable figure. While in gaol, he refused to make any compromises to secure his release and this increased his stature immeasurably. He had an autocratic streak – a combination of the styles of a tribal chief and a democratic leader – but his actions were always accompanied by courtesy and good manners.

In his attempt to persuade Afrikaners to surrender their power, he acknowledged their history and showed it respect. He condemned apartheid as a serious crime against humanity, but he regarded Afrikaner nationalism as a legitimate indigenous movement. Afrikaner nationalists, in the same vein as black South Africans, had fought against British imperialism. In 1961, when the ANC decided to move from civil disobedience to the armed struggle, it was Mandela who established Umkhonto we Sizwe (MK), the ANC's armed wing, and became its first commander.

To emphasise the similarities between Afrikaner and African nationalism, Mandela decided that the ANC's first acts of sabotage would take place on 16 December 1961, the day of the Voortrekker victory over Dingane in 1838. In the late 1970s when a cabinet minister promised to release him from prison on condition that he retire in the Transkei, Mandela referred to the example of General Christiaan de Wet, who in the 1914–1915 rebellion took up arms against the state, but was soon set free unconditionally. ANC leaders who were in gaol, he argued, were entitled to the same treatment. On Robben Island he learnt to speak Afrikaans so that he could understand the spirit and outlook of the leader on the other side of the negotiating table. This was also a tangible demonstration of the Freedom Charter's recognition of cultural diversity.

While still in gaol, Mandela began talks with the authorities without consulting his fellow ANC leaders in gaol or Oliver Tambo, leader of the ANC in exile. Some of the exiled ANC leaders wanted the armed struggle to continue until the NP government was forced to hand over power. However, Mandela knew that negotiations were the only option and that the time for this process had arrived.

The ANC was initially caught unawares by De Klerk's announcement but soon began to make the necessary arrangements. In alliance with

COSATU, mass marches, strikes, stayaways and consumer boycotts were organised. The ANC suspended the armed struggle, but as yet refused to foreswear violence completely.

A bloody conflict for control broke out between the ANC and Inkatha in KwaZulu and Natal. By August 1990 this ongoing battle had also flared up in the Witwatersrand area. The death toll increased rapidly as the violence grew fiercer. Between September 1984 and December 1993 as many as 20 500 black people perished in political violence. The majority of these deaths were caused by the struggle between the ANC and Inkatha.

"A feat that resounded throughout the world"

De Klerk wanted to reach an agreement that would keep the black majority party in check. The NP's election manifesto of 1989 had promised to introduce an inclusive democracy in which groups would be recognised as the basic components of the system. There would be power sharing and no race group would be able to dominate the other. Each group would have self-determination over its "own affairs". De Klerk put forward the idea of a rotating presidency similar to that in Switzerland.

In contrast, the ANC wanted what Mandela called an "ordinary majority government" in which the party with the most votes had the overriding voice. Nor would the ANC entertain the idea of a federal system; it insisted on a strongly centralised government.

The NP's negotiators were led by Dr Gerrit Viljoen and NP teams took part in the various workgroups of the negotiating process. On the basis of opinion polls, of which the results were kept secret, the NP knew that the ANC would gain at least 60% of the votes in the first election. The NP pinned its hopes on gaining a collaborative government in which the cabinet would be made up of three or four of the parties which gained the most support in the election, rather than insisting on a white veto or comprehensive group rights. The cabinet would then try to make decisions on a consensus basis. The NP also wanted to make the constitution, which would include a Bill of Rights, the highest authority. People or organisations had to be able to use it against the violation of individual and minority rights.

De Klerk had one important card which he could play in his efforts for a system based on power sharing: He could say to the ANC and Western leaders that he could not lead white people into a system which they opposed. There was at that stage strong opposition from the right wing against the political changes. The Conservative Party (CP) with Dr Andries Treurnicht as leader, and other right-wing groups, labelled De Klerk's speech of 2 February 1990 as the beginning of the Afrikaners' "Third War of Independence". Paramilitary organisations such as the Afrikaner Weerstandsbeweging (AWB) were openly making threats of insurgence and terror.

The CP used by-elections to cast suspicion on the negotiations and in these elections the NP suffered a series of losses. Early in 1992 the CP gained an impressive win in the "safe" NP seat of Potchefstroom. The government had two options if it wanted to show that it still had the majority of white support: a general election or a referendum. In the 1989 election the NP leadership had promised that any agreement that differed substantially from the NP's election mandate would be put to a referendum. De Klerk repeated this promise on 30 March 1990 and in January 1992.

The big question was: At what stage of the negotiating process should the referendum be held? If it was held too early, it would leave him without any real leverage to resist the ANC's demands. If it was held when the details of the constitution were already known, it would no doubt alarm the ANC a great deal because it would look as if he was giving the white voters a chance to exercise a veto. However, De Klerk had made a specific promise to his voters to hold a referendum at the end of the process.

The setback in Potchefstroom made De Klerk decide to use the referendum to test the idea of a negotiated constitution. He also wanted to defeat the CP which had rejected the negotiations. The promise of a second referendum soon disappeared into oblivion. The ANC would probably have opposed it with mass action.

More than 87% of white voters took part in the referendum in March 1992 and 69% of them registered a "yes" vote. However, for Afrikaners in particular, this "yes" vote was somewhat ambiguous. Some took it that they were being asked to endorse the transfer of power to the black majority. Others believed that the NP would accept nothing other than power sharing. One NP placard read: "Oppose majority rule: Vote Yes". There were also those who believed that the NP had a hidden agenda and was trying to undermine the ANC and make it powerless.

Nevertheless, almost all those who voted "yes" accepted that it would mean the end of apartheid and the end of exclusive white power. Among the middle class there were perhaps less illusions. In an opinion poll held late in 1991 it was found that only 15% of whites believed that they would fare better in the new South Africa. Nevertheless, the result of the referendum meant, as Mandela noted, that white people now understood that the days of white privilege were over.

The international reaction was highly favourable. Afrikaners had handed over power with a measure of grace. They had relinquished sole dominance before they were defeated. What they did not know was whether power sharing in South Africa could work. It was on power sharing that the De Klerk government now placed all its hope.

De Klerk played a crucial role in assuring the "yes" majority. In his victory speech after the referendum he declared that few people get the opportunity to rise above themselves and that most of the white voters had done exactly that. He referred to the poem "O wye en droewe land" (Oh wide and sad land) of Afrikaans poet N.P. van Wyk Louw, and said in the poet's idiom: "Today a feat occurred in South Africa which now resounds throughout the world; it holds a message of reconciliation; it is a powerful reaching-out to create true justice."

From referendum to constitution

In the referendum of 1992 the question was posed whether the government should move ahead with the reform process and the negotiations for a new constitution. In the 1994 election the NP made an unconvincing attempt to show that the constitution complied with the promises which it had made to the voters in 1989. Without the possibility of another referendum or another white election, the close ties that had endured for so long between Afrikaner voters and their political leaders were now broken.

In the negotiations that were resumed after the referendum, the ANC tackled the following aims: ANC supporters were to remain united; plans had to be laid to break ties between the NP and any black allies; the security forces, the most important pillar of the government's power, had to be discredited; and any constitutional limitations on the majority party's power had to be prevented.

What made the government's position more difficult was the political violence which characterised the transition period. Between 1984 and

1994 there were 20 500 people killed in political violence, 9500 of them between the beginning of 1990 and April 1994. The large majority of these perished in violence between black factions. The ANC and ANC-allied journalists claimed that a so-called third force that was linked to the government, instigated this violence, but this was never proved. The Truth and Reconciliation Commission (TRC) later established that there was little evidence of a centrally orchestrated third force; it claimed instead that it was an informal network with its own command structure that was involved in illegal action of this nature.

In an attempt to defuse the situation, De Klerk appointed Judge Richard Goldstone to investigate the wave of political violence that dominated this period. At no time did De Klerk ever interfere in post-mortem investigations or hearings in which policemen stood trial.

The scale tips

On 15 May 1992 the negotiating process reached a checkmate position on the matter of what percentage support was necessary to take decisions in the constituent assembly. The NP wanted to fix this at 75% and the ANC at 66%.

The ANC tackled the negotiations under the leadership of Cyril Ramaphosa, an experienced trade union leader. He knew that it was of prime importance to find a particular issue around which pressure could be exerted in the negotiations. Such an opportunity soon presented itself when 38 residents of Boipatong, a black township 150 km south-east of Johannesburg, were murdered on 17 July 1992. The murders were perpetrated by residents of a hostel on the outskirts of a township that supported Inkatha. The people living in Boipatong were virtually all ANC supporters.

The ANC immediately alleged that the police were heavily involved in the killings and halted the negotiations indefinitely. As was shown later, there was no conclusive evidence that implicated the police. However, shortly after the killings the ANC laid down the framework on which the press based their reports of the events in such strong terms that it was widely believed that the police, the state and possibly even De Klerk, were to blame.

The ANC's withdrawal from the negotiations and its subsequent programme of rolling mass action presented an extremely dangerous moment for the country. It was possible that the economy could be irreparably damaged if investors lost all hope that the situation could be rescued. The government wanted to avoid a long drawn-out power struggle between the state and the liberation movements. The negotiations had to be handled as quickly as possible so that the economy could lift its head again and work be created.

The longer the negotiations lasted, the more the government's hope faded of reaching an agreement in which the power and interests of the majority were satisfactorily balanced against those of minorities. Viljoen, who as the leading NP negotiator was now well versed in the intricacies of the negotiations, had to resign for health reasons. He was replaced as chief negotiator by Roelf Meyer (accompanied by Leon Wessels and Dawie de Villiers) but Meyer did not have the same prestige and stature. However, the government reached an important goal when it persuaded Derek Keys, Minister of Finance and a key figure in the economic division of the ANC, to continue the government's conservative economic policy, putting a premium on growth and a balanced budget.

To get the negotiations back on track, the government had to make certain concessions to the ANC in the Minutes of Understanding document that the parties released on 26 September 1992. Among other things, amnesty was granted to various ANC leaders who had committed less serious offences regardless of the principles that the government had laid down previously; and certain hostels where Inkatha supporters were housed would now be fenced.

Public opinion was that the government had suffered a reverse. This impression was not prompted by any specific concession but the perception was confirmed that the ANC now had the whip hand; the scale had tipped in the ANC's favour. It was clear that fairly soon all power would be handed over to the majority.

Shortly afterwards, when the ANC made the offer of a government of national unity for a five-year period after the first election, De Klerk immediately accepted it as the basis for an agreement. Thereafter, the coalition of white and black parties under the NP which took part in the negotiations was disbanded. An angry Mangosuthu Buthelezi, leader of Inkatha, withdrew all support for the De Klerk government.

In terms of the interim constitution every party which had more than 80 seats in the national assembly of 400 members was eligible to nominate one of the two executive deputy presidents. Furthermore, a party was entitled to a cabinet post for each 20 elected members. Mandela made it clear that the majority would take the decisions at cabinet level.

The constitution also made provision for elected governments for the nine provinces that had been delineated. "Federalism with fig leaves" was how this weak form of federalism was described. There was to be no decentralisation of power to the racial or ethnic communities; nor was there any self-determination for the white people on matters such as education or residential areas.

A system of proportional representation with a closed list was adopted. This meant that voters did not vote for individual candidates but for a party list compiled by party leaders.

Miracles and ambiguous compromises

That the different parties could agree on a constitution was widely praised as a miracle, but the truth was far more humdrum. The ANC and the NP reached "full consensus" with one another by accepting clashing demands in the provisional constitution and leaving the settlement of these conflicts for a future government.

The question of the labour market was for example handled in the interim constitution by accepting two different principles in the same clause. On the one hand there was the principle of affirmative action, which was to correct the imbalances of the past, and on the other, the recognition of merit. After 1994 the government spoke little of merit and focused only on affirmative action. By 1998 the ANC made an even more radical demand than affirmative action, namely that at all levels the labour market had to reflect the composition of the population (demographic profile).

The same happened with language rights, which can be regarded as the key to Afrikaners' cultural survival under a black government. In the constitution both the right to be taught in one of the official languages (where practically possible) and the obligation to correct the discrimination of the past were accepted as principles. Later, this latter principle was reformulated as the "right of access to education", which implied access to education in English. The compilers of the constitution made no attempt to define what should happen if these two principles came up against one another in a particular school. After 1994 the government placed emphasis on access to education in the medium of instruction that learners happened to choose – which is usually English.

The new government also put pressure on Afrikaans schools, where numbers made it possible, to offer a stream of English-medium classes that ran parallel with the Afrikaans stream. Most of the universities that previously only offered lectures in Afrikaans voluntarily introduced English streams. This is sufficient evidence for concern that parallel-medium institutions are at great risk and that in time English will replace Afrikaans.

In the final round of the negotiations a clause was hurriedly included in the agreement to the effect that people who had infringed human rights in the apartheid years were forced to apply for amnesty in order to avoid prosecution. The ANC, as the future majority party, would presumably have the most say in the composition of the commission that was charged with the amnesty issue and the way it would function. The NP's security forces felt that they had been thrown to the wolves.

The NP's black support soon disappeared when it became clear that the government was no longer in control of proceedings. Early in 1992 approximately 9% of black people indicated in an opinion poll that they supported the NP, while 14% said that they would support De Klerk as leader. But as soon as the government was seen as having to play second fiddle in the negotiation process, the party's black support base shrunk. Just before the election it had dropped to as low as 3% to 4%.

With the exception of Buthelezi, who formed the Inkatha Freedom Party (IFP), none of the homeland leaders succeeded in building up a strong party. Mandela assured the traditional leaders in the homelands that they would retain their rights and powers. The black residents of the former homelands became the ANC's strongest support base.

A last fight

From the middle of 1992 onwards the balance of power had turned against the government. It now devoted much of its energy to avoid the symbolism of an utter defeat. They insisted that there should be no victory marches by ANC cadres in the streets or statues knocked off their pedestals. The security forces were to remain under the NP government's orders until and during the election. The constitution that had been negotiated would furthermore not come into effect until passed into law by the tricameral parliament. The chief justice would invest the new president and all the white judges would retain their posts.

The ANC was prepared to meet the NP on the question of the symbolism and rituals of power while it concentrated on the takeover of power per se. Most white people and about half of the Afrikaners were in favour of reform. Mandela soon won their respect and even their goodwill. They were prepared to suspend their judgement on the interim constitution until such time as the new government took over power and was able to prove itself.

An uprising by the white right wing with the support of elements in the army and the active citizen force presented a very real danger. A million white people and about half the Afrikaners had voted "no" in the 1992 referendum. They rejected the constitution which had now taken shape. However, they had no alternative plan in place and had not even been represented in the last stage of the negotiations.

In many countries the army would be expected to play an important role in a situation similar to that in South Africa at the beginning of 1994. However, the SADF was fairly small. There were fewer than 70 000 full-time soldiers, of whom only half were white. They had a tradition of respect for and obedience to the political leadership. The active citizen force comprised a large number of members but was decentralised and reflected the political and ethnic differences of white society.

The most significant unknown factor was General Constand Viljoen who had retired as head of the army in 1985 and then went to farm in the Northern Transvaal. Viljoen joined the Afrikaner Volksfront (Freedom Front), a coalition of right-wing parties, organisations and movements. They demanded an Afrikaner *volkstaat*. The Volksfront formed a Freedom Alliance with Buthelezi of the IFP, as well as Lucas Mangope and Oupa Gqozo, the chief ministers of Bophuthatswana and the Ciskei respectively.

De Klerk rejected the idea of a *volkstaat* because he argued that it would undermine the position of Afrikaners in the rest of the country. Viljoen and his followers had no fixed plan on the future of South Africa. He later admitted: "We would never have been able to get consensus among our people on where our *volkstaat* would be established." Most of them wanted a state which included parts of Western Transvaal, Eastern Transvaal and the northern Free State, with Pretoria as capital. But although about two-thirds of the Afrikaners lived in these areas, the majority of people who lived there were not Afrikaners. An opinion poll in 1993 showed that only a fifth of the Afrikaners felt strongly enough about a *volkstaat* that they were prepared to move there; more than half either rejected the idea or were uncertain about it.

With such divided opinions on the *volkstaat* issue, Viljoen decided to focus instead on disrupting the first democratic election. He hoped to replace De Klerk as leader and begin anew with negotiations. Estimates on the troops he would be able to muster varied form 50 000 to 100 000. There was also talk that units in the citizen force and the armed forces would join him. General Georg Meiring, head of the armed forces, warned the government and the ANC that there could be shedding of blood if Viljoen went ahead with his plan to oppose the election.

Viljoen's greatest dilemma was certain elements in the right wing, particularly the Afrikaner Weerstandsbeweging (AWB), a poorly disciplined paramilitary organisation under the leadership of Eugène Terre'Blanche. As a professional soldier, Viljoen did not want to fight with Terre'Blanche and his suspect "troops". Viljoen's moment of truth arrived when the ANC stirred up a rebellion in Bophuthatswana which threatened to oust Mangope and his government in Mafikeng (now Mahikeng). Mangope asked urgently for Viljoen's assistance, but when Viljoen arrived, he realised he was in an impossible situation. He had not chosen the battlefield (to defend a homeland government) nor had he selected his allies (bloodthirsty AWB members who had rushed to Mafikeng with the aim of shooting black people). On 9 March 1994 shots rang out and dramatic images were flashed around the world of a black soldier's "execution" of four AWB members.

This was not a conflict for disciplined soldiers and Viljoen and his men left Mafikeng. Shortly afterwards he announced that he was going to participate in the coming election. The ANC promised him that the new government would appoint a council of his followers to examine the future prospects for an Afrikaner *volkstaat*. Viljoen was the first candidate on the party list drawn up by the Vryheidsfront, the party he had established. At the very last minute, the IFP under Buthelezi, which during the negotiations had argued strenuously for an independent Zulu state, also decided to take part in the election.

A free election

The election took place on 27 and 28 April 1994. In large parts of the country there was no talk of the usual election campaigns. It was difficult for the ANC and other black parties to canvass for votes among farm workers, while the NP and the Democratic Party (DP) struggled to reach voters in the black townships and those in the homelands. There were evidently many irregularities in the manner in which the votes were cast and counted. There was, for example, a strong suspicion that the result was determined on the basis of the pre-election opinion polls rather than the number of votes that were counted.

Western observers enthusiastically declared the election process to be free and fair. The South African David Welsh, a respected liberal analyst, labelled this as rank hypocrisy. In his view, in their own countries the same observers would certainly not have declared elections free and fair if there had been so many shortfalls in the process. The truth was that it was impossible to declare the election defective and to insist that the voting begin again. This would more than likely have unleashed widespread violence.

The election proceeded peacefully. The supervisory officials declared that the ANC gained 62,7% of the votes; the NP 20,4%; Buthelezi's IFP 10,5%; Viljoen's Vryheidsfront 2,2%; the DP 1,7%; and the Pan Africanist Congress 1,2%. More than 94% of the ANC's votes were cast by black people. The NP gained half its votes from people who were not white.

NP and ANC quota of the ethnic vote in 1994

	Black (%)	Coloured (%)	Asian (%)	White (%)
ANC	81	27	25	3
NP	3	67	50	60

The Afrikaners who voted were more or less split down the middle between the NP and the conservatives. Against expectations the NP won control of the new Western Cape Province where 60% of the population was coloured; 22% Xhosa; and 24% white; and where 60% of the voters spoke Afrikaans in their homes. The press put the coloured and Indian support for the NP down to the fear of a black government. The considerable progress made in the tricameral parliament period by the coloured people and Indians in the spheres of education and welfare services is another factor which had been completely underestimated or perhaps even suppressed.

Mandela and De Klerk were the two leaders who united the South Africans behind the process. But the election could easily have turned into a fiasco without the participation of Buthelezi and Viljoen and their followers and the professional action of the armed forces and the police under the command of Generals Meiring and Johan van der Merwe respectively.

The new dispensation in South Africa began officially on 10 May 1994 when Mandela was inaugurated as president of the Republic of South Africa. The ANC dominated the government of national unity with 18 ministers. The NP had six ministers and De Klerk was one of the two deputy presidents. Buthelezi and two other IFP members were also in the cabinet.

A spirit of reconciliation characterised the first years of the new era, with Mandela as an outstanding symbol of the new democracy and white-black reconciliation. He did not spend much time on cabinet meetings; the growing rate of unemployment; or the decline in the criminal justice system. His leadership was that of a wise statesman, worthy peacemaker, accomplished politician and imaginative reconciler of people across the racial divide. Among other examples, he drank tea with Mrs Betsie Verwoerd and other widows of NP leaders. He showed no evidence of harbouring bitterness despite his 27 years in gaol.

From the early 1990s onwards the world began to open for South Africans and after the 1994 election it was fully open. The boycotts stopped and normal academic, cultural and sporting ties were re-established with many overseas countries. South African passports were now acceptable worldwide. South Africa re-joined the Commonwealth, which made young South Africans eligible to work in countries such as Britain. Tourism to South Africa experienced an upsurge, but very few fixed investments flowed into South Africa.

The younger generation in particular were overjoyed that they were free of apartheid. In general, people in all communities were proud to live in an inclusive democracy and they embraced the country's new flag and national anthem.

20
Apartheid: a different angle
Hermann Giliomee

These days apartheid is regarded by some politicians and commentators as an ideology that was uniquely evil and far more oppressive than the segregation policy of the pre-1948 period. The impression is incorrectly created that race relations were previously harmonious and that the implementation of apartheid was a major turning point. According to this view, after 1948 the country, politically, economically and socially, was on a slippery downward slope and this retrogression was only halted in 1990.

This chapter does not in any way refute or underestimate the suffering, hardship and hurt, as outlined in other chapters, that apartheid caused to black, coloured and Indian people. However, the point of departure is different. It makes the point how unique apartheid was and emphasises the close interaction between politics and the economy. Experience in other countries has shown that it is only after a country has reached a specific level of development that mass democracy can be introduced. The chapter aims to provide overarching answers to two questions: Firstly, in what ways did apartheid differ from the segregation policy that was implemented before 1948? Secondly, how different would the country be now if a more liberal policy had been in place between 1948 and 1994?

To understand apartheid it must be weighed up in the light of how people viewed it in the years 1948 to 1958 when the policy was in place. The British historian Herbert Butterfield rightly warns that if we try to pass judgement on history in accordance with present-day moral convictions we create nothing other than a huge optical illusion. It is entirely incorrect to take events out of their historical context and to judge them in isolation of their time period.

However, this is not what most political leaders and commentators have done since 1994. Instead, after the ANC government came to power in 1994, they began to judge apartheid according to the liberal values which only began to find acceptance on a wide basis in the 1990s. These values – individual freedom, rights and the correction of the wrongs of the past – are reflected in the 1996 Constitution.

In extreme cases apartheid is described these days as a policy that was unique and vicious by comparing it to the elimination of Jewish societies in Europe by Nazi Germany in the Second World War. The model which politicians of the National Party (NP) used was however not based on that of Nazi Germany as is sometimes alleged, but on the policy of southern American federal states such as Virginia and Alabama, where segregation was still strictly applied in the 1950s. According to a survey done in 1956, only a quarter of the white people in the southern states were in favour of white and black children attending the same school; and only 14% consented to multiracial schooling.

In 1961 when the mother of Barack Obama, later to become American president, wanted to marry a black man from Kenya, there were 30 of the USA's 52 states which still forbade such "mixed marriages". As late as 1971 the state of Louisiana passed a law which laid down that a person with just one black ancestor out of 32 had to be classified as black.

Others point out that in 1973 apartheid was declared a "crime against humanity" by the United Nations (UN). However, one should take the framing of this UN resolution into consideration. The 20 countries who submitted the proposal were all dictatorships in the bloc of countries which regularly voted with the Soviet Union. None of the major Western powers supported the resolution. The American representative said that a charge of a crime against humanity should be restricted to highly serious cases of inhumanity and that apartheid could not be regarded in this light.

Whereas critics of apartheid erred in comparing it with the race policy of Nazi Germany, the leaders of the NP made a different error. They tried to show that black residents of South Africa fared better than black people in many other African countries, but this argument does not hold water. It is possible to look at material or physical pointers such as life expectancy and the death statistics of infants, and to suggest that black South Africans are better off than elsewhere in Africa. But black South Africans always compare their position to that of white people in the country, never with people elsewhere on the continent. In addition, nobody can ever measure the suffering, hardship, humiliation and injustice which a policy like apartheid meant to its victims. In South Africa, black, coloured and Asian people were kept in a state of oppression for far longer than any other country.

It is crucial to understand apartheid because it forms an important part of our recent history. We can approach the subject in terms of the following questions:

- Was apartheid different from the segregation policy that was followed from 1902 to 1948?
- Could South Africa have fared better without apartheid?
- Would South Africa have been more politically stable without apartheid?
- Can a post-apartheid South Africa grow to become a successful state?

Apartheid and segregation

This chapter takes the standpoint that apartheid was an offshoot of segregation rather than a radical new policy. If he were alive today, Alfred Hoernlé, an outstanding liberal thinker of the 1930s and early 1940s, would have been amazed that people could think that race relations were so much better before the 1948 election than thereafter. As early as 1936 – in the era of the segregation policy – he wrote that a visitor from Mars would be immediately struck by the comprehensive way in which black people were excluded and were discriminated against. Such a visitor, he wrote, could only come to one conclusion: "[There] was a dominant urge towards segregation, which has moulded the structure of South African society and made it what it now is."

Yet the myth developed that in the years prior to 1948 race relations were far better than afterwards. Piet Cillié, editor of *Die Burger* from 1954 to 1977, published an article in 1985 in which he ridiculed this false opinion (translated):

> From a period of good and relaxed race relations before 1948, South Africa was suddenly by virtue of a change of government dumped into almost four senseless decades of growing tension and racial hatred. An evil ethnic ideology was systematically enforced upon an often un-

suspecting country. The once easy-going togetherness of a multiracial society was now divided, fragmented and uprooted by a sectional, dictatorial authority. Because of this fragmentation and oppression the country was prevented from developing the friendly relations that were previously in the making.

In writing this, Cillié wanted to show how a distorted image of race relations before 1948 had become the vogue by the 1980s. This sort of image is still being used regularly in newspapers and on television.

Today people are trying to make peace with the past by persuading themselves that race relations in the country, except in the apartheid era, were reasonably good. Then they blame apartheid for everything that is wrong or less than perfect. For example a film reviewer in the *Cape Times* of 14 June 2001 wrote that apartheid had shattered the dream that South Africa could become a country free of race discrimination and racial hatred. This while there has never been any question of such a reality at any time in our past – or in the history of other multiracial societies.

The apartheid policy did indeed differ from the segregation policy in certain aspects. In the first place the governments before 1948 regarded the black "reserves" as part of the administration of the country. Black people also had the right to a (very limited) form of representation. However, for the NP government which came to power in 1948, the granting of political rights to black people in the "homelands" served as some form of compensation for the fact that their rights and representation in the so-called "white" South Africa, which comprised 87% of the area of the country, was taken away.

In the second place, after 1948 the NP government implemented certain forms of separation and discrimination, which were already in place between white and black, making them applicable to the social interaction between white, coloured, Asian and black. The most important were the scrapping of the coloured vote; the enforcement of separate residential areas (group areas); and the classification by the state of people into specified racial groups. Before the apartheid years, coloured people in the Cape Province could buy land; there were no laws against their having sexual relations with white people; and there was no racial classification.

The pass law, which was applicable to black people, was also implemented far more rigidly after 1948. Education for black people was extended considerably, but initially this was for the most part limited to primary education. As was the case before 1948, the state spent far more on educating a white child than a black, coloured or Indian child. Before 1948 the black leaders, including people such as Z.K. Matthews and the young Nelson Mandela and Oliver Tambo, were already alienated from the political system. They not only resisted apartheid; they rejected all forms of white domination.

Under NP rule the domination over other population groups was therefore harsher and more systematic, but it was not fundamentally different from state rule prior to 1948. In a country such as Brazil white domination was far more subtle after slavery had been abolished in 1888. These days white people comprise half the Brazilian population while black and coloured people together make up the other half. Although there have never been any laws of a racial nature in Brazil, the income of white people is twice that of black and coloured people. Only 7% of the residents of the upmarket suburbs in cities are black and only 6% of the black people between the ages of 18 and 24 have attended college or university. Whereas in the USA, where 12% of the population is black, a black president was elected in 2012, in the Brazilian cabinet in that same year there was only one black member. Nevertheless, this country's official policy is that there is no racial discrimination.

In an article entitled "Race in Brazil" in its issue of 28 January 2012, the British periodical *The Economist* quotes the words of a black Brazilian activist on the "invisible enemy" that confronts black people in his country. White people in Brazil, he says, do not regard themselves as racist, "but when a black man begins to go out with a white woman, there is trouble". It is increasingly acknowledged that racism is a complicated phenomenon. On the one hand there is blatant racism (of which apartheid is an example), but on the other hand there is hidden racism, of which the case in Brazil is an example. In this regard, segregation is nearer to apartheid than the "saintly" form of racism in Brazil.

Could South Africa have fared better without apartheid?

Between 1948 and 1981 the South African economy grew at a rate of 4,5%. This was about the average growth of a group of 20 comparable mid-level developing economies in those years, including countries such as Austria, Venezuela, Argentina, Spain and Chile.

The claim is sometimes made that a South Africa without apartheid would have grown even faster, possibly like Japan or South Korea, and that this would have brought significant poverty alleviation. This view cannot simply be dismissed out of hand. Theoretically, South Africa could have grown faster, but growth in developing countries such as South Africa is only possible if there are investors, both within the country and foreign investors, who are confident that the country will remain stable; that labour costs are low; that its economic policy is consistent and predictable; its judicial system reliable; that private property is inalienable; and that corruption is under control.

In the apartheid years many investors felt that the NP's policy framework was advantageous for sustainable growth. They believed the same when a country such as Botswana became independent under a government with a conservative economic and social policy.

It is therefore doubtful whether after the Second World War South Africa would have attracted many investors if there had been a government that was sympathetic towards socialism. In his autobiography that appeared in 1994, Nelson Mandela wrote that the Freedom Charter was one of the ANC's key documents; that it was a "revolutionary document" which could not be implemented without first making "radical changes to economic and political structures". To do so without these "radical changes" would presumably have caused a great withdrawal of investments from the country.

Apartheid kept the lid on the pressure cooker until about the mid-1970s. Until the early 1970s an average growth rate of just below 5% was maintained. Then, as far as investors were concerned, the costs of apartheid became greater than the benefits. Workers lacked skills, their buying power was limited and their homes were often far from the workplace.

It is important to realise that a high economic growth rate is not necessarily the destiny of all countries. In those with weak and corrupt governments the growth rate can even be negative; in other words the country is going downhill. In Argentina, for example, the income per head until the 1950s was comparable to the average of a group of eight West European countries. However, thereafter it experienced a period of political instability, large-scale corruption and inconsistency in its economic policy. By 2001 the income per head was only half the average of the same group of eight West European countries. The same could have happened in South Africa had there been political instability and an unstable economic policy.

A country's political system and economic policy go hand in hand to promote prosperity or cause decline. Two well-known authors, Samuel Huntington and Joan Nelson, in the book *No Easy Choice: Political Participation in Developing Countries* (1976) put forward three models to illustrate the links between politics and the economy. They differentiate between the technocratic model, the populist model and the liberal model.

Although these writers did not have South Africa in mind when the book was written, the first model in particular is relevant for our country. The technocratic model provides a good explanation of what happened in South Africa in the years between 1948 and 1976. In this model, those who are best trained and have the most experience exercise control. According to Huntington and Nelson, "the vicious circle of the technocratic model" consists of:

- less political participation (the limitation of the franchise, the restriction of opposition leaders and the press, and a ban on protests);
- [which leads to] greater socio-economic development as a result of the repression of the working class (restrictions on or the oppression of trade unions resulting in lower wages);
- less socio-economic equality (unskilled and semi-skilled workers in particular are heavily affected);
- less political stability (resistance builds up against the repression and unrest breaks out from time to time);
- [which again ends in] a "participation explosion" (mass protest in which radical democratic demands are made).

The participation explosion in South Africa's case took the form of the urban black people's resistance of 1976 to 1977. The government then tried to reform apartheid by bringing in a greater level of socio-economic equality. The discrepancies in government spending on education, pensions and salaries of civil servants for the various racial groups were made smaller. By the early 1990s South Africa spent a greater percentage of its gross domestic product (GDP) on social support in the form of non-contributory schemes than many developing countries, and more than any other country in the developing South. In 1993 the gap between the races as far as old-age pensions are concerned was evened out. These reforms did not, however, prevent the NP from having to hand over power.

Huntington and Nelson call their second model "the vicious circle of populism". In this model the government tries to satisfy the masses and the rich are heavily taxed. The model comprises:

- more political participation (the extension of the franchise, politicians who represent the "masses" and make irresponsible promises in elections, and an increase in demands for the redistribution of wealth);
- [which leads to] greater socio-economic equality (achieved by heavy taxation of the more well-off classes and the enforcement of affirmative action in the labour market);
- less socio-economic development (companies are increasingly unwilling to invest because high wages force profits down);
- less political stability and the outflow of capital (a higher rate of inflation and the lowering of the currency's value against that of other countries); and
- a "participation implosion" (a state of emergency is declared which temporarily suspends the democracy).

This model could possibly have been applicable to South Africa if universal franchise had been introduced in 1948. The government would presumably have first brought in a qualified franchise and before long this would have led to the rapid extension of the franchise. To continue the conjecture, this would then have given rise to the acceptance of a policy document such as the Freedom Charter; the resultant nationalisation of certain sectors; and the inevitable outflow of investment capital. This would imply low levels of socio-economic development, followed by less political stability (white resistance and urban unrest) which would end in a "participation implosion" (the suspension of Parliament and the rule of law).

Huntington and Nelson call their third model the supposedly "benign liberal model". Most of the conventional liberals in South Africa adhere to this model. They believe that strong economic growth after 1948 would have led to greater socio-economic equality which in turn would have meant political stability and that this, with time, would ensure the development of a liberal democracy. In more detail, the model looks as follows:

- The more people, irrespective of their colour or origin, who were brought on an equal basis into the market and into schools (initially

a qualified franchise which would rapidly become universal franchise);
- the more the economy would blossom and the more free the market would become;
- the more the economy would grow;
- the more political freedoms would increase;
- the more stable the political system would become;
- the more racial and ethnic tension would ease; and
- the more all the people would experience wellbeing and happiness.

The opinion that South Africa could have fared far better arises from the view that "all good things work together" which is sometimes propounded in liberal circles. This rests on the idea that a free labour market (where no one's promotion is influenced by race, colour or gender) and a free political system (where all adults may vote) mutually strengthen and work together to achieve a higher economic growth rate, political freedom and the resolution of conflicts.

A comparative study shows that in the twentieth century this model worked in developed countries such as the USA and Western European states. Here liberal capitalism (equal opportunity for all in a free labour market) and liberal democracy (universal franchise, individual rights and a definitive separation between the ruling party and the state) go hand in hand. However, this model seldom works in developing countries where the average income is far lower than that of developed countries and where there is a history of conflict between racial or "ethnic" groups. (Usually the most prosperous group originated in the colonial period.)

The major problem is that people in these countries and also in other countries that are divided along racial and colour lines do not compete and vote as individuals, but as members of a particular grouping. The previously disadvantaged or excluded group usually demands affirmation and compensation when it takes power.

In Amy Chua's book *World on Fire: How Exporting Free Market Democracy Breeds Ethnic Hatred and Global Instability* (2004) she uses examples in Africa and Southeast Asia to show how the free market, which tends to favour certain ethnic minorities, increases tension between races and ethnic groups. The minority uses its power to dominate the economy and generally fares well. The government also makes the needs of the minority its major concern (as in South Africa until the early 1970s).

However, when the poor majority comes to power, the new government begins to favour the majority and to curb the minorities by means of legislation. They nationalise industries and lay claim to, or expropriate the minorities' possessions. Affirmative action takes place to accomplish "transformation". Over the last 75 years this pattern has played itself out in one country after another. However, in Western countries liberals continue to believe that equal opportunities in the labour market (where there is no affirmative action) and a liberal democracy (universal adult franchise) go hand in hand.

But, as Chua explains, there is generally great tension when those who belong to the majority party are obliged to compete with people from minority parties who have better skills or more money. The conflict is particularly acrimonious when the minority group is of another race or ethnic group. Governments often intervene to correct inequalities and favour their voters. Sometimes this leads to disastrous policies, including the nationalisation of land, banks, mines and industries, and the expulsion of minorities. This often brings a marked decline in economic growth while the democracy disintegrates or becomes a mere empty shell.

Would South Africa have been more politically stable without apartheid?

The big question is what would the outcome have been if the United Party (UP) had remained in power? The fact is that by 1948 the UP government had reached a political dead end with its policy. The urban black elite's patience had run out, but the body of white voters was by no means prepared to extend the franchise.

By 1948 when the NP came to power, liberal academics in South Africa were not calling for universal adult franchise. Two promising young liberal historians of that time, Arthur Keppel-Jones and Leonard Thompson, were of the opinion that a policy of universal franchise would not work in a multiracial South Africa. The liberal politician Jan Hofmeyr realised that the white voter corps would not accept the kind of reforms which the leaders of urban black people were demanding.

Liberals hoped that the introduction of a non-racial, qualified vote (for example those who had reached a certain standard at school, and owned or rented property of a certain value) would mean that black voters would become more moderate and in time, in exercising their vote, be led more by their interests than by their race or ethnic identity. However, this has never happened in any multiracial country.

In South Africa a qualified franchise would probably not have brought stability. The level at which people qualified to vote would more than likely have been extremely controversial and also have caused tension between the white communities. If the level to vote was set low too quickly, it would probably not have been long before a government came to power which would try to implement "state capitalism" or socialism.

Experimenting with the socialist model would potentially have dealt South Africa a death blow. Even the implementation of the Congress of the People's Freedom Charter could possibly have caused serious economic disruption because the Charter calls for the nationalisation of mines, heavy industries and banks; and for the redistribution of land. It is worth repeating that in his autobiography Mandela recognises that the Freedom Charter is a "revolutionary document" and that putting it into practice would "radically change the economic and political structure" of the country.

What South Africa had after 1948 was not socialism or a liberal democracy, but apartheid. After its victory in the 1948 election, the NP government retained a conservative economic policy which laid the basis for consistent economic growth. It used budget surpluses to pay back debt and rejected excessive wage demands from white workers. Although Verwoerd's Bantu education system was justifiably criticised because state spending for white and black had remained unequal for so long, it did nevertheless improve the literacy of the masses considerably.

In the first half of the 1960s the South African economy grew at a rate of 6% per year, with an inflation rate of only 2%. Large investments flowed into the country: there was stability, labour was cheap and companies made substantial profits. Production, consumer levels and the demand for labour went sky high. In its leading article of August 1966 the periodical *Time* wrote: "South Africa is in the middle of a massive boom." The article labelled Verwoerd as "one of the ablest white leaders Africa has ever produced".

The liberal *Rand Daily Mail* wrote that the country was experiencing an "excess of prosperity". In 1967 the *Financial Mail*, the leading financial periodical, published a special supplement on the period 1961 to 1966, which it called the "Fabulous Years". In this period South Africa's gross domestic product grew 30% in real terms.

Apartheid cost the country dearly, especially in the form of poor quality education for black, coloured and Indian children; an unproductive labour force; a lack of skills; and a large turnover of workers as a result of the enormous scope of migrant labour. However, in the 1950s and 1960s this did not harm the economy too much because the manufacturing sector was still relatively small and uncomplicated. The price the country paid for apartheid would only begin to become conspicuous in the early 1970s with the strong growth of the manufacturing sector.

These days Verwoerd is branded as a "wicked genius" who, it is alleged, single-handedly devised and implemented apartheid. Stephen Mulholland, former editor of the *Financial Mail*, called him "one of history's monsters" and placed him together with Saddam Hussein in the same category as the mass murderers Josef Stalin, Adolf Hitler, Mao Zedong and Pol Pot. But while he was still alive, prominent historians who were not supporters of apartheid, judged him differently. In 1963 while on a visit to South Africa, C.W. de Kiewiet, a respected liberal historian, made the following remark: "Verwoerd is addressing the country's grave problems with boldness, shrewdness and even imagination. It is by no means absurd to suggest a comparison between Verwoerd and Charles de Gaulle, the stern, headstrong but deeply imaginative leader of France."

There are people who suggest that the economic growth in the apartheid years put nothing in the pockets of black people. Although the gap in the income and prosperity of white and black remained very large and black people were subject to comprehensive restrictions which hampered their progress, the expendable income of black, coloured and Indian people in the 1960s and 1970s grew faster than that of white people, although it began from a very low base.

The business magnate Harry Oppenheimer wrote in the annual report of the Anglo-American Corporation in 1964 that the average wages of the "non-white" workers in the secondary sector (manufacturing and construction) in the previous five years had risen by 5,4% per year as compared to a 3,7% rise for white workers. Based on these statistics, Oppenheimer suggested that the country was far more stable than many people thought.

This was of course little comfort for poverty-stricken people in the reserves. However, for them, there was hope of finding work, even if it was for a very low wage. J.L. Sadie calculated that 73,6% of the new workers who joined the labour market in 1965 found work in the formal sector. This was a rate that had not been reached before. It would rise in 1970 to 76,6%, but thereafter it fell to 43,4% in 1998. It is now even lower.

Expendable personal income (1990 prices)

	1960 (Rand)	1970 (Rand)	1980 (Rand)
White people	12 114	17 260	17 878
Indians	2171	3674	5655
Coloured people	2000	3033	3933
Black people	1033	1439	1903

Can a post-apartheid South Africa grow to become a successful state?
There is a perception among today's political leaders that South Africa must first overcome the legacy of colonialism and apartheid and must put right decades of poor administration before the country can be seen as successful. Although colonialism was cruel and unjust, it did however establish the potential for a successful state. By 1976 South Africa was well on the way to becoming a successful state. On the world ratings it had the 18th largest economy and was the world's 15th largest trading country. By 2010, however, South Africa had slipped to 28th and 37th respectively on this same list. One can argue long and hard about what has gone wrong, but that is a debate for another day.

To think the unthinkable

People who study history are obliged to "think the unthinkable", as Yale University put it in a statement made some time ago. If the unthinkable must be thought about apartheid, some of these statements should perhaps be considered:

- After the Second World War South Africa could have become a liberal democracy, or for 25 years the country could have had an annual economic growth rate of almost 5% per year. There is no way, however, that both these two things could have happened.
- Rapid racial integration could have taken place, or the country could, for the greatest part of 25 years, have experienced a reasonable measure of stability. There is no way, however, that both these two things could have happened.
- After 1945, the country could have continued to exploit the low-grade gold mines with cheap black labour; and by way of taxes have

made significant contributions to the state treasury and paid dividends to shareholders; or black trade unions could have been allowed. There is no way, however, that both these two things could have happened.

Not one of the "unthinkable" or controversial statements in this chapter can be proved. But they must certainly be considered in any impartial analysis of apartheid.

21
The South African economy in the twentieth century
Grietjie Verhoef

South Africa's economic development is the outcome of interaction on the one side between the people of the country and on the other, between the local and the international economy.

In the nineteenth century the international flow of goods, services, capital and labour was facilitated by the British free-trade policy of the 1840s. Although protectionism (the shielding of a country's markets against cheaper imported products) reared its head again in the 1880s, international trade and the flow of capital occurred more freely in the twentieth century. Through British colonial control South Africa was integrated into the world economy. International developments therefore had a direct impact on the domestic economy.

The two world wars of the twentieth century divided the international world into two power blocs: the so-called communist (eastern) bloc and the free-market capitalist (western) bloc. This had a significant impact on the development of the international economy and thereby also on South Africa's economy.

South Africa's surface area is 1 121 942 km^2, similar in size to the total land mass of Germany, France and the Netherlands. By 1910 the official population was 5,878 million and by 1950 this had doubled to 12,671 million. The size and increase of the population is an indication of the availability of labour in this period. In the first half of the twentieth century the white population comprised about 20% of the total population, black people 68%, Indians 8% and coloured people about 3%. At the time the population increased by an average of 3% per annum.

Between 1870 and 1913 – after the discovery of diamonds and gold and shortly before the outbreak of the First World War – the economy expanded and changed dramatically. From 1860 to 1865 exports comprised mainly wool, fruit and raw materials. However, the value of South Africa's exports was only £4,3 million, far less than that of other British Commonwealth countries such as Canada with exports averaging £8 million per annum. By 1870 about a million immigrants had voluntarily left Britain to settle in Australia and approximately 500 000 went to Canada, whereas only about 100 000 came to South Africa.

By 1913 South Africa's per capita gross domestic product (GDP) was in the twelfth position in a comparable group of 28 countries. "Per capita GDP" is the total production of a country (the gross domestic product) divided by the total population, which then gives the total production per person in that country. From this particular group of countries with comparable market economies Australia had the highest per capita GDP followed by New Zealand and Canada.

The world economy expanded rapidly between 1870 and 1913. This was the first period of globalisation following the expansion of international communication in terms of railways, shipping and international telegraph technology. Because of the discovery of diamonds and gold, South Africa was integrated into the international globalisation dynamics. The economy benefited from strong growth, higher trade volumes, the inflow of capital and the population growth stimulated by immigration.

Composition of South Africa's gross domestic product, 1912–1951

	GDP £ m.	Agriculture	Mining	Manufacturing	Trade
1912	£132,9	17,4%	27,1%	6,7%	13,5%
1951	£1248,4	16,3%	10,1%	21,4%	15,7%

By the first decade of the twentieth century the South African economy had developed from a purely agricultural economy to an industrial economy in which agriculture and mining contributed the bulk of the GDP. In 1912 the GDP was £132,9 million and the per capita GDP £21,8. By 1951 the GDP had risen to £1248,4 million and the per capita GDP to £98,2. This represents an average increase of 1,3% in per capita GDP per annum.

From the land, 1900–1949

Agriculture

After the destruction of the Anglo-Boer War, agricultural production in the Transvaal and Orange Free State slowly recovered, while agriculture resumed without much disruption in the Cape and Natal. The total value of agricultural production increased from 1911 to 1951 by an average of 18,4% per annum. In what is today the Western Cape, fruit and wheat were grown while in the summer rainfall region further east the farmers concentrated mainly on keeping livestock, and growing mealies and fruit. Sugar and subtropical fruit was cultivated in Natal and there were also those who farmed with cattle. The so-called maize triangle was in the central part of the country and fruit and sugar were cultivated in the Lowveld.

This part of the agricultural sector is generally known as the commercial agriculture sector, which was largely, but not exclusively, built up by white farmers, most of them Afrikaans-speaking farmers. The other segment of the farming population was the traditional black subsistence farmers. However, there was a growing number of black farmers who, like farmers in the commercial agriculture sector, delivered their surplus products to the flourishing urban markets – sometimes to the great consternation of white farmers. Once reserves and trust lands were designated for black people in terms of legislation passed in 1913 and 1936, black farmers were increasingly confined to black reserves.

The agricultural sector is vital for economic development. Agriculture contributes in various ways to modernisation. Its most important function is the provision of food, but by 1880 the country already had to import food. It is safe to concur that food production was inadequate and that farming methods were outdated and inefficient. Subsequently, farmers developed a dependency on state assistance, something which remained characteristic of South African agriculture until late in the twentieth century. This dependency on state subsidisation was unheard of in Britain, but was characteristic of state policies in the USA and Western Europe.

There were different kinds of state assistance available to farmers, namely in the form of education and research, legal protection, financial subsidies and support with prices and marketing. In 1898 the Elsenburg Agricultural College was established in the Cape and in 1926 it was placed under the supervision of the University of Stellenbosch. In 1908 the Veterinary Research Institute was opened at Onderstepoort outside Pretoria.

From 1920 the University of Pretoria's Faculty of Veterinary Sciences was accommodated at the Institute at Onderstepoort. Both were administered by the Department of Agriculture. Various other agricultural colleges were opened throughout the country to promote scientific agriculture.

In 1912 the Land Bank was established to provide loans for (white) farmers and various agricultural co-operatives were then formed to assist farmers with planning, capital equipment, financing and information. By 1950 there were about 300 agricultural co-operatives with more than 280 000 members and a turnover of more than £580 million. In 1918 the Koöperatiewe Wijnbouers Vereniging (Co-operative Winegrowers' Association, KWV) was established. Particularly after the Pact government came to power in 1924, control boards were established to help specific sectors in agriculture with marketing and price control. In 1925 the Fruit Export Board and the following year the Perishable Products Export Board (for diary products) were established. By 1933 this latter board was replaced by the Diary Products Control Board which fixed prices and laid down production and import quotas to protect the domestic industry against foreign competition.

The large number of white farmers who were members of the National Party protected this symbiotic anti-market relationship. State protection of agriculture was accomplished more specifically by the Marketing Act of 1937. In terms of this Act the marketing of all agricultural products was centralised in boards such as the Dairy Board, the Egg Board and the Meat Board. In this way domestic agricultural products were protected by duties and state subsidies ensured the modernisation of agriculture. (A duty is an "impost" or charge on a product which has to be paid to the government. Domestic products were "protected" by duties because imported products were more expensive – over and above the selling price, imported products had to include the cost of the duty.) These agricultural boards fixed the price and thus exercised a monopoly on the marketing of agricultural produce. By 1960 there were already 17 such boards, and by 1939 state subsidies to agriculture already exceeded £15 million.

The collapse of the American stock exchange in Wall Street, New York, on 29 October 1929 ushered in one of the most devastating world depressions in history. The depression played a major role in the South African government's decision to continue its protection of the agricultural sector. By 1925 the government appointed a commission of inquiry into the

Economy and Wages (UG14/25), which found that the per capita agricultural production in South Africa was only £80, compared to £420 in Australia and £320 in Canada. This was put down to unscientific farming methods. The government was convinced that improved agricultural production had to be the foundation of future industrial development.

The depression caused a worldwide collapse in agricultural prices. This occurred because the value of all currencies linked to the gold standard, collapsed. In the South African agricultural sector the value of farm produce tumbled from £31,8 million in 1928 to £12,8 million in 1931, despite the fact that the volume of produce had increased by 20%. Britain decided in September 1931 to leave the gold standard and most other Commonwealth countries followed suit.

Being linked to the gold standard meant that the value of a particular currency had a fixed value that was linked to the price of one ounce of fine gold held by that country. Countries with a large holding of gold could place more of their money into circulation and because their currency was therefore not "scarce" (supply was high) it was not "expensive". On the other hand, countries with limited gold reserves had "expensive" money. When money was "expensive", commodities from those countries were also expensive and less was imported from such countries.

The South African government wanted to display its "independence" from Britain, and its "faith in gold", so it initially remained on the gold standard. In the long run this had a very negative effect on the economy. While the currency of countries that had left the gold standard depreciated (the value of these currencies decreased and the price of goods traded in those currencies dropped), the South African pound remained an expensive currency. This meant that South African produce was more expensive than similar produce from countries that had already left the gold standard. On 28 December 1932 South Africa also abandoned the gold standard and the demand for locally produced goods immediately recovered.

By 1950 the extensive state assistance for the agriculture sector in the form of price regulation, marketing boards and financial assistance for modernisation laid the foundation for the transformation of the agricultural sector. In 1946 the first Land Conservation Act forced farmers to adhere to certain basic guidelines to the conservation of agricultural land. The Second World War provided a powerful incentive for increasing agricultural produce throughout the English-speaking world. In South Africa, mechanisation of farming improved rapidly and between 1933 and 1960 production under irrigation increased six-fold.

The provision of water to farmers was another important initiative and to this end the state began implementing its dam-building programme. Between 1920 and 1956 at least eleven large dams were built to provide irrigation for agricultural development. One of the most important was the Hartebeespoort Dam in the Crocodile River which was completed in 1925. Another was the Vaal Dam, built in the Vaal River and completed in 1938. Water from the Vaal Dam was circumvented into the Vaalharts barrage to provide irrigation for the poor white farmers in the area as part of the Vaalharts settlement scheme. In 1938 the Loskop Dam in the Great Olifants River was completed, while the Boegoeberg Dam in the Orange River, halfway between Prieska and Upington; and the Clanwilliam Dam in the Olifants River just outside Clanwilliam, were also built in the 1930s.

South Africa's largest dam is the Gariep Dam, previously known as the Hendrik Verwoerd Dam, which has a total capacity of 5,5 million m³ of water and was constructed in the Orange River in the 1970s. It forms part of the integrated Orange River system which provides water to parts of the Vaal, Fish and Sundays River catchment areas through the Orange-Fish River tunnel. This tunnel is 82 km long and is the longest continuous water conveyance tunnel in the world. The last of the irrigation dams constructed in this period was the Pongolapoort Dam (also called the Jozini Dam) which was built in 1970 in north-eastern Natal in the Pongola River. This extensive dam-building programme is evidence of the government's long-term planning for a successful commercial agricultural sector.

In its attempt to prove that the country was independent, the National Party government followed an economic policy to protect and strengthen the domestic economy. This protectionism slowly but surely stimulated internal growth, but in the long run protection promoted non-competitiveness and unproductive labour practices. The negative outcome of this would become clear towards the end of the twentieth century when the country began to compete freely on international markets.

Mining

The development of the mining sector in South Africa played a stabilising role in the economy. When droughts, disease, pests or war disrupted agriculture, diamonds, gold, coal and other minerals could still be mined and exported. Diamonds were initially discovered in Kimberley but after 1903 were also mined at Cullinan near Pretoria and after 1908 in South West Africa (now Namibia). After the First World War, De Beers Consolidated Mines acquired a share in South West Africa's diamonds. Other alluvial diamond deposits in the Orange and Vaal rivers (1860s), Lichtenburg (1926) and Namaqualand (Alexander Bay, 1928), meant that the market was well supplied with diamonds but prices were low and unstable.

The depression of 1929 caused a further sharp drop in prices, but in the late 1930s De Beers secured an international monopoly by establishing a central marketing agency. By buying up all available diamonds De Beers was able to smother free competition and by the 1950s made substantial profits on its diamond stockpile.

The gold-mining industry was the largest contributor to the economy. Gold production increased from £32 million in 1910 to £144,8 million in 1950. The volume of ore mined rose from 19,7 metric tons in 1910 to 56,5 tons in 1950. By 1910 gold comprised 60,9% of total exports but by 1950 it had dropped to 42,5%. The depth of the ore and its low grade put the profitability of the South African gold mines under pressure. By the early 1930s the Low Grade Ore Commission came to the conclusion that the high costs involved in mining gold would make future deep-level mining unsustainable. In addition, since 1917 the gold price had remained fixed at 84 shillings (£4.4.0) per fine ounce.

After Britain left the gold standard in 1931, the value of the British pound declined, which made products from Britain and other Commonwealth countries considerably cheaper than South African products. As indicated above, the following year circumstances forced South Africa to leave the gold standard, after which the British sterling price of gold immediately rose. The price of gold continued to rise until it was fixed in January 1934 at $35 (142 shillings, or £7.2.0) per fine ounce. Thanks to this rise in the gold price, South Africa earned welcome foreign exchange, which mitigated the adverse effects of the depression. The depression therefore had a less destructive effect on the South African economy than in other Commonwealth countries. This illustrated the deep integration of the South African economy in the international economy.

Gold production between 1932 and 1941 virtually doubled, but thereafter the Second World War disrupted production as a result of labour and equipment shortages. During the war the gold price was again suppressed and it was only in September 1949, when the British pound sterling and the South African pound were devalued, that the gold price rose again to 248 shillings (£12.8.0) per fine ounce. In the late 1950s new life was breathed into the gold-mining industry when new rich gold deposits were discovered on the far West Rand and in the Orange Free State.

The mining of coal received a boost with the expansion of the railway network after 1900. Coal was mined in northern Natal and the Transvaal (in the present-day Gauteng, Limpopo and Mpumalanga) and was used largely for the generation of electricity and the production of iron and steel. Coal production increased from 7,6 metric tons in 1910 to 29,3 tons in 1950. South African coal was fairly cheap and contributed to the profitability of gold-mining and the development of the local industrial sector.

By the 1950s coal had overtaken diamonds in importance as far as mined minerals were concerned. In 1950 coal production brought in £14,79 million compared to the value of diamond sales which was £14,3 million in the same year. The government controlled the coal price, keeping it low to stimulate domestic development, but this resulted in a great deal of wastage.

Early industries

Apart from gold, coal and diamonds, platinum and many other base metals were also mined, including iron, manganese, asbestos, chromium and copper. For the most part these minerals and metals were processed in local industries and therefore did not make a significant contribution to earning foreign exchange in the first half of the twentieth century.

The most important aspect of South Africa's economic development was the diversification of economic activity from primary production (agriculture and mining) to secondary production (industries). The first small manufacturing concerns of the nineteenth century were linked to agriculture – such as wagon making, furniture factories, brick-works and factories to process fish. In the Cape Colony import duties were introduced which benefited local production. Britain had a free trade policy which allowed the Cape to engage freely in trade with any country in the world. Mutual preferential treatment with other British colonies in fact linked Cape industries to the British market. However, the manufacturing sector was very elementary and small.

With the mineral revolution, the same happened in the vicinity of the mines: manufacturing concerns developed to service the mining industry, factories appeared to provide food, clothes, tools and building materials. After the formation of the Customs Union in 1889 between the Cape Colony and the Orange Free State, duties were lowered on goods traffic between these two regions. In 1908 the Customs Union was expanded and reviewed. Domestic duties were aligned, which stimulated trade and also encouraged factory production.

After 1910 all duties on domestic goods distribution in South Africa were abolished, which resulted in further stimuli for manufacturing production. In 1910 the Cullinan Commission was appointed to investigate the viability of the development of local industries. According to the commission's report which was tabled in Parliament in 1912, the protection of deserving domestic industries could lead to the diversification of manufacturing and greater self-sufficiency in the South African economy. However, by 1912 industrial production still only contributed 6,7% to the GDP. The government then systematically introduced a policy of tariff protection and import substitution as a strategy to stimulate domestic industrial development. (Import substitution means that products that are imported are replaced by similar products manufactured by local industries. To implement a policy of import substitution, higher duties are often charged on imported products. This then discourages consumers from buying the more expensive, imported products and they are more inclined to buy locally produced goods.)

The systematic protection of South African industries began with the Customs Tariff Act of 1914. Exactly two months after the Minister of Finance tabled the proposals on tariff protection in Parliament, the First World War broke out. This in itself stimulated South African industries because of the greater demand for wartime goods (food, clothes and ammunition) and South Africa being outside the area of conflict, could supply in the war demand. Between 1915 and 1919 (the period of the war) industrial production increased by 65%. After the war local industries once again began to meet domestic consumer demand and by the late 1920s production had risen by more than 200% since 1919.

The depression and the gold standard crisis again caused a levelling out of the growth rate, but after 1924 the government provided further legal protection for industries, leading to another massive revival in production.

The Second World War again boosted domestic industrial production to the extent that by 1950 manufacturing was the major contributor to the GDP.

The government stimulated local industrial development by means of legislation and at the same time developed strategies to ensure that white people were employed in these industries. These two aims received government attention in various ways.

In 1921 the Board of Trade and Industries was formed to investigate how industrial development could be promoted. In 1924 a new, permanent Board of Trade and Industries was established to advise the Pact government on the progress of local industries. On the recommendation of this board, increased duties were announced in terms of the Customs Tariff Act of 1925. The Act, for example, made provision for a levy of between 20% and 25% on the value of imported motor cars, which encouraged the local assembly of motor vehicles. In 1926 General Motors opened the first vehicle assembly plant in Port Elizabeth.

In 1924 the Industrial Conciliation Act was passed which reserved certain categories of work for skilled white people. The Act also prohibited the formation of trade unions for black workers. In 1925 the Wage Act made provision for setting up a Wage Board. This board determined the wages for certain types of work where workers were not organised into trade unions. This ensured that unskilled white workers in particular were paid higher (and protected) wages. The Mines and Works Act of 1926, the so-called Colour Bar Act, stipulated that competency certificates for skilled tradesmen could only be issued to white and coloured employees. This form of job reservation gave white and coloured people preferential access to certain categories of work by barring black people from holding such jobs. This was flagrant interference in the labour market which in the longer term disrupted the transfer of skills, gave undue protection to white people, and undermined productivity. It did, however, ensure that in a time of rapid industrial development there was sufficient skilled labour.

In 1928 the government established the Iron and Steel Industrial Corporation (Iscor) which eventually began production in 1934. The state was the majority shareholder in Iscor and the price of iron and steel was strictly controlled until Iscor was privatised in 1989. By providing reasonably cheap iron and steel to local industries, domestic industrial production was encouraged. By 1950 Iscor had already manufactured 600 000 tons of steel and was providing half of the country's steel requirements.

The government established the Electricity Supply Commission (Escom) in 1923 to regulate the supply of electricity from a central organisation. Some years later, in 1940, the Industrial Development Corporation (IDC) was formed through which expert advice, assistance with managerial skills and financial aid were provided for new industries. The IDC focused particularly on giving technical and financial assistance to industries with the objective of making South Africa more self-sufficient with regard to consumer goods, food and clothing. Although the IDC enabled local industries to establish themselves and expand, this in practice constituted preference to local manufacturers and offered them protection in the local market. Less attention was given to domestic processing and benefication of locally mined minerals and metals. It was only in early 2000 that the government introduced incentives to promote the local processing of minerals and metals.

In 1950 the South African Coal, Oil and Gas Corporation (Sasol) was established to produce fuel from coal and production commenced in 1955. Sasol eventually became the world leader in the manufacture of fuel from coal and second to African Explosives and Chemical Industries (AECI), grew to become the largest chemical corporation in the country. The establishment of the petrochemical industry by Sasol made an immense contribution towards making South Africa one of the leading states on the African continent.

By 1950 the South African government was a dominant role player in the economy. Transport (the South African Railways and Harbours, or SAR&H), electricity, and iron and steel production were all controlled by the government. Labour and wages were strictly regulated and segregated to the short-term benefit of poor white people in particular, but in the longer term this had very detrimental consequences for labour productivity and the quality of industrial production. The policy of tariff protection and import substitution helped to create and expand new industrial sectors. There was particularly good growth in engineering industries, automobile manufacturing, the chemical industry and metallurgical enterprises. The protection of the domestic market made it more advantageous for multinational companies to establish subsidiaries in South Africa and manufacture their products here. Examples include the pharmaceutical products manufactured by Imperial Chemical Industries (ICI) based in Britain, electrical accessories by AEG (West Germany), Philips (the Netherlands), and GEC (United States), as well as Stewarts & Lloyds

(Britain) that manufactured steel piping, and the local assembly of automobiles (Ford, Chevrolet, Volkswagen, etc.).

The major problem of industrial protectionism in South Africa was that production was shielded from international competition. Because of tariff protection more raw materials were imported for processing in domestic industries than was earned in foreign exchange by the exportation of industrial products. It was the export of agricultural and mining products which financed the bulk of industrial imports. Because South African industrial production was meant to meet the demand within South Africa and to make the country more self-sufficient, production remained uncompetitive – reasonably high priced and of somewhat poor quality. It was only in the late 1980s that the government acknowledged that globalisation made continued trade protectionism counter-productive.

Afrikaners in the economy

In the first half of the twentieth century, Afrikaners as a segment of the white population purposely developed strategies to facilitate access into the mainstream of the economy. After the destruction of the Boer republics, the white Afrikaans speakers in the north were impoverished. In the Cape influential Afrikaners such as J.H. Hofmeyr and W.A. Hofmeyr were successfully involved in agriculture and business circles. They and other leading Afrikaners sought to improve the economic and educational progress of their fellow Afrikaners.

After the success with the establishment of *De Burger* in 1915 and the fund-raising initiative of the national Helpmekaar Vereniging (an initiative to assist fellow Afrikaners in need) in 1916, Afrikaner leaders established the Suid-Afrikaanse Nasionale Trust- en Lewensassuransiemaatskappy (Santam) (South African National Trust and Life Assurance Company). Barely two months afterwards, in June 1918, a separate life insurance company, known as the Suid-Afrikaanse Nasionale Lewensassuransiemaatskappy (Sanlam), was formed. The objective was to establish a South African insurance company, and in particular to mobilise Afrikaners' savings. Between 1918 and 1935 Sanlam and Santam struggled to survive but thereafter, in the context of the growth of the South African economy, these companies developed a strong position in the local market.

Thanks to the leadership of the Sanlam directors, the company made a significant contribution in uplifting Afrikaners. People such as W.A. Hofmeyr (the first chairman and managing director), and Dr M.S. Louw (the first Afrikaans actuary), saw Sanlam's role in greater perspective. The company emerged as a vehicle for ensuring that Afrikaners acquire a meaningful share in the mainstream economy. This could only be accomplished by investing Afrikaners' money and by promoting entrepreneurship amongst Afrikaners.

Sanlam collected savings money paid in lieu of insurance premiums and invested this money in new enterprises. As a prominent role player in the Ekonomiese Volkskongres (the economic congress of the Afrikaner people) in 1939, M.S. Louw proposed the establishment of a finance house in 1942, particularly aimed at supporting Afrikaner enterprises. The result was the establishment of Federale Volksbeleggings (FVB). Sanlam used part of its capital and for the rest used the capital from ordinary shareholders. In addition to its investments in industries, FVB eventually also invested in the mining sector.

In 1948, with a loan from FVB, Dr Anton Rupert formed the Voortrekker Tabakmaatskappy (Voortrekker Tobacco Company) in Paarl. Within 15 years it had grown into the Rembrandt Tobacco Company group with representatives in 16 countries worldwide and a turnover of more than £250 million per annum. Through FVB and Rembrandt, Afrikaners could begin to participate in the mainstream economy. In 1951 FVB and Bonuskor established Federale Mynbou Beperk (Fedmyn). Bonuskor was an investment company which invested policy holders' bonuses on their behalf in equity. Federale Mynbou was seen as one such company in which these funds could be profitably invested. Sanlam later also bought shares in Fedmyn. By 1963 Fedmyn gained control over the third-largest gold-mining house in South Africa, the General Mining Corporation, and in this way ensured Afrikaner interests in the mining industry. FVB developed into a widely diversified industrial conglomerate with investments in virtually every industrial sector.

In the banking sector the British imperial banks, namely Standard Bank and Barclays Bank DCO, completely dominated the scene. In 1934 Volkskas was formed on the initiative of the Afrikaner Broederbond and the personal enthusiasm of J.D. ("Oom Bossie") Bosman. Volkskas grew slowly because not all Afrikaners severed ties with their existing banks immediately. In 1956 Dr Jan Marais founded Trust Bank, also with the help of FVB. Trust Bank introduced the American banking practice to South Africa by supporting new entrepreneurs with short-term personal loans as start-up capital. In the 1920s the Saambou Building Society was established and by the end of the Second World War Afrikaners already had a substantial foothold in the economy.

The role played by Afrikaners in the economy was increased exponentially by the leading role they held in parastatal enterprises. Examples are Dr H.J. van der Bijl in Iscor, Dr H.J. van Eck in the IDC, Dr J.H. Laubser in the SAR&H and Dr P.E. Rousseau in Sasol. Although these positions were not representative of Afrikaner entrepreneurship and capital, Afrikaners were beginning to feature prominently in the business world. If the business activities of the agricultural co-operatives are also taken into consideration, Afrikaners had acquired a significant stake in the economy by 1950.

In 1951 a second economic congress of the Afrikaner people was held and a survey was conducted on the progress made since 1939 in the efforts to empower Afrikaners economically. Progress had indeed been made, although this was not necessarily dramatic in all instances. Between 1939 and 1950 the stakeholding of Afrikaners in the mining industry had risen from none at all to 1%, in the financial sector from 5% to 6%, in the manufacturing and construction industry from 3% to 5%, and in trade and business undertakings from 8% to 25%. After 1950 an economic upswing led to a strengthening of this position.

Positive and negative effects of state intervention in the economy, 1950–2000

When most of the countries on the British sterling monetary exchange devalued their currencies in 1949, South Africa followed suit and the South African pound was devalued. This immediately brought balance of payments relief after a sharp rise in the cost of imports during the immediate post-war growth phase. (A balance of payments is the difference between total payments due to foreign countries, and total revenue from exchanges with foreign countries. When a currency is devalued, the value of this currency decreases and the products from that country become cheaper. Devaluation therefore means that other countries will probably begin to import more from the country which devalues its currency. This increases the flow of money into that country and improves its balance of payments.)

Between 1950 and 1970 there was unprecedented economic growth in South Africa. The increase in the GDP in constant prices (prices that account for inflation) between 1950 and 2000 are shown below.

Gross domestic product (in constant prices)

	GDP (R million)	% Growth	
1950	119 857		
1960	186 174	4,5	(1951–1960)
1970	324 466	5,7	(1961–1970)
1980	451 983	3,4	(1971–1980)
1990	525 066	1,6	(1981–1990)
2000	618 666	1,7	(1991–2000)

From the table above it is clear that the 1960s was a decade of remarkable growth. In 1963 there was growth of 7,4% and in 1964 this rose to 7,9%, but thereafter it dropped to 4,2% in 1968. This impressive growth of the South African economy in the 1960s compared very favourably with other Commonwealth countries (Australia, New Zealand and Canada) but was nowhere near the levels reached by Japan, South Korea or Taiwan. Furthermore, although South Africa compared well with other Commonwealth countries in the 1960s, since the 1970s it performed progressively weaker. There are two main reasons for this: Very rapid population growth and excessive state intervention in the economy.

In the 1960s the South African population grew at a rate of 3% per annum (compared to 1,2% in developed countries). Then between 1980 and 1996 growth declined to a rate of 2,4% per annum, while the GDP in the same period increased at less than 2%. The per capita GDP did indeed decrease throughout the world in the 1970s and 1980s, but South Africa's performance was weaker than those countries with which it had compared favourably in the 1960s.

Composition of GDP, 1960–2000

	% Agriculture	% Mining	% Manufacturing	% Trade	% Finance
1960	12,4	13,4	19,3	12,7	3,8
1970	8,3	10,3	25,2	15,1	11,1
1980	6,4	13,9	24,4	13,3	12,3
1990	5,9	12,7	24,5	12,7	13,2
2000	2,9	6,5	21,9	22,7	22,7

When the structure of the South African economy is examined, it is clear that industrial production (the manufacturing sector) performed poorly in relation to the growth in other sectors. Between 1960 and 1970 the manufacturing sector grew by 14,7%, but thereafter this expansion dropped to only 2,2% in the 1980s and 4,5% in the 1990s. To explain the course of events, for practical reasons the development in each of the various sectors is discussed separately below.

Agriculture

The dramatic improvement of agricultural activity was limited to white farming, but by the middle of the 1980s this situation deteriorated. The production of mealies rose from 5,2 metric tons in 1961 to 8,7 tons in 1982, but then it dropped. Wheat production increased from 1,4 tons to 1,98 tons by the end of the 1980s and as far as mealie production was concerned there was virtually a doubling of output per hectare. Wheat production between 1960 and 1990 increased four-fold and the output per hectare was three times as much. The production of other grain crops, such as rye and barley, gradually decreased from the 1960s. The growing demand for beer from the mid-1970s meant that by 1990 eleven times as much barley was cultivated than in 1960.

During the 1970s cotton production increased significantly, but the production of wool peaked and then declined. The production of sugar between 1960 and 1990 increased three-fold as did that of sunflower seeds and fruit. The growth of fruit production was largely thanks to exports. With most other foodstuffs, production was able to keep up with domestic demand. However, by the 1970s South Africa's output of wine compared poorly to the strong growth of the industry in California (USA) and Australia. Apart from poultry production, which was stimulated by mechanisation in the form of battery-bred chickens, the production of animal products did not match population growth.

The impressive performance of agricultural production can generally be ascribed to government subsidies and the regulation of prices, marketing, and intervention through marketing boards. It is estimated that up to 20% of farming revenue (*revenue* is earnings in the macro-economic sphere, as opposed to *income* which refers to personal earnings) in the 1960s came directly from the government. Locally, to keep the large farming community content (there was strong support for the National Party government in this community), prices were kept artificially high. However, this meant that surplus production which was exported often had to be sold at lower prices on the international market. This was particularly the case with sugar and mealies, where local producers could not compete with producers in the USA or the West Indies because of high levels of state subsidies in South Africa. In 1960, 36,8% of the goods that South Africa exported was agricultural produce, but in the mid-1980s this dropped to 20%. The most important agricultural exports were sugar, mealies, wool and fruit.

In the black homelands agricultural production was primarily in subsistence farming. Whereas mechanisation advanced the levels of commercial agriculture for white farmers, black farmers did not receive the same subsidies. To them, therefore, similar achievements were beyond reach. Although homeland development corporations undertook large development projects in the black homelands to address the "lack of entrepreneurship and managerial ability" among black farmers, these initiatives met with little success. The explanation for this failure was a lack of consultation with the communities and the reluctance of black farmers to participate in these initiatives.

By the mid-1980s the international trend was towards reduced government intervention and free open markets and this manifested in South African agriculture as well. In its report on monetary policy (1985) the De Kock Commission recommended that financial markets, rather than the Reserve Bank, should determine the cost of money. This meant that interest rates and exchange rates were to be determined on open financial markets. The value of the South African Rand immediately started to fall while interest rates rose. The Land Bank could not continue to subsidise the interest rates on farmers' loans.

In the context of open free markets, labour was also allowed to move more freely and a large number of black people migrated from the homelands to settle in and around urban areas. An enormous informal sector soon emerged through which agricultural production and marketing developed outside of existing regulated markets. In 1982 there was a record mealie harvest and it cost the government R500 million to export surplus production at prices lower than domestic prices. A devastating drought followed in 1982–1983 and the writing was on the wall for the subsidisation of agriculture. From 1987 inflated government subsidies were abolished and the market for agricultural products was gradually de-regulated. Production quotas were scrapped, as was the regulation of marketing. In 1992 a commission of inquiry into the Marketing Act recommended that agriculture should be de-regulated. In 1996 the Marketing of Agricultural Products Act was passed which gave the Agricultural Marketing Board the authority to phase out market regulation. Legislation was also passed to re-distribute land and to improve access to water.

A stronger market-oriented approach to the economy was therefore also introduced into agriculture. By 2000 the results of the restructuring of the agricultural policy, control and markets were still unstable. It seemed that new provincial departments of agriculture could not give adequate support to new farmers. Crop production became more extensive and as a result there were fewer employment opportunities for farm workers. (Because of the less intensive production there was a reduced demand for labour.) Less food was therefore produced, and food security was in jeopardy. The abolition of tariff protection on agricultural products since the mid-1990s, except for sugar, gave rise to a strong export market for fruit in particular. South Africa earned far more from the export of farming products, but agricultural production fell short compared to international standards. Much of South Africa's best agricultural land is currently not being used optimally.

Mining

The mining industry's relative contribution to the GDP has systematically shrunk since 1950. Until about 1990 gold played a dominant role. Gold was always the major stabiliser in the South African economy and gave the country a bigger role in the international economy than was perhaps deserved. Since the 1990s gold has no longer been the engine of growth in the economy. Other minerals have begun to play a more prominent role. By 1990 the production and export of platinum rose in relative importance. The mining industry nevertheless remains an important earner of foreign exchange and helps to maintain equilibrium in the balance of payments.

HARRY FREDERICK OPPENHEIMER (1908-2000)

Harry Oppenheimer is regarded as South Africa's foremost industrial titan in the twentieth century. He was the son of mining magnate, Sir Ernest Oppenheimer (1880-1957), and was chairman of Anglo-American Corporation – the South African mining, industrial and finance company – and its sister company, De Beers Consolidated Mining, for close on three decades.

Born in Kimberley to an assimilated Jewish family of German origin, Oppenheimer completed his primary schooling in Johannesburg and then attended Charterhouse School in England. Upon completing his studies in philosophy, politics and economics at Oxford University in 1931, he returned to Johannesburg to join Anglo-American Corporation which was founded by his father in 1917. After service in the Second World War, Harry Oppenheimer became managing director of the Corporation in 1945.

During the 1950s Oppenheimer was deeply involved in the expansion of Anglo-American's gold-mining operations on the Witwatersrand and copper mining interests in present-day Zambia. Particularly from the 1960s onwards, he was pivotal in overseeing the expansion of the diamond industry internationally, building up De Beers and Anglo-American as major global players.

Apart from his business enterprises, Oppenheimer played a crucial role in politics. A political moderate, he remarked in 1984 that "in a South African context I may seem to be a liberal, but at heart I'm just an old-fashioned conservative". Oppenheimer served as the United Party member for Kimberley from 1948 to 1957, being well-respected for his knowledge of economics, finance and constitutional affairs.

A political pragmatist, Oppenheimer saw the impracticality and unsustainability of the apartheid policy. In 1959 he joined the new anti-apartheid Progressive Party, which he largely financed. In the 1970s and 1980s, he financed the Progressive Reform Party and the Progressive Federal Party, the forerunners of the Democratic Alliance.

Oppenheimer was one of the few South African business titans to realise in the early 1980s that dialogue with the then-banned African National Congress was an unavoidable and historical necessity for the future of the country. Some commentators attribute the ANC's departure from any thought of nationalising the country's mining industry to his sage and considered intervention.

THE SOUTH AFRICAN ECONOMY IN THE TWENTIETH CENTURY 467

> Oppenheimer was a cautious reformer who recognised that black people had legitimate political claims and the right to participate fully in the economic growth of the country. In his restrained and gentlemanly manner, he negotiated with a wide range of leaders in the economy ranging from Wim de Villiers of Federale Mynbou to Cyril Ramaphosa of the National Union of Mineworkers to ameliorate the migrant labour system, promote welfare and housing schemes for urban black people and secure labour peace in South Africa. His standing as the "grand old man of South African mining" ensured that he was always listened to with the greatest respect.
>
> David M. Scher

In 1971 the price of gold began to rise after the USA suspended the fixed exchange rate agreement entered into in 1945 at Bretton Woods. (After the Second World War the Allies decided at the Bretton Woods conference how the international monetary and financial system would be regulated.) In 1971 the price of gold was R28,64 per fine ounce. In 1973, with the first rise in the oil price, the price of gold rose to more than R100 per fine ounce. In January 1980 the international price of gold reached a record high of $850 (a phenomenal rise of 2217% between 1970 and 1980), after which by 1990 the price dropped again by more than 40%. In 1987 another 16 gold mines were opened and six platinum mines were put into operation, which meant a capital investment of more than R6 billion.

Although by the end of the twentieth century the role of mining was reduced significantly, it had a much greater impact indirectly in terms of the multiplier effect of the mining industry in general. When mineworkers go down a shaft to mine the ore, sophisticated machinery is required to lower them safely down the mine shaft. There is a demand for protective clothing, for special equipment, for fuel to drive trucks and other machines, and so forth. This means that the demand for one commodity also creates a demand for related commodities. There is also an additional social gain through the development of human resources and infrastructure such as housing, schools and clinics. Furthermore, there is a primary income multiplier because wages earned are spent by households. There is the employment multiplier, which refers to employment opportunities created by other demands in the mining industry itself. There is also the income foreign exchange multiplier, which is the impact of foreign exchange earnings (when gold or other raw materials are exported) on the balance of payments, monetary policy and general business activities in the country. Finally, the capital formation multiplier is important because the mining industry attracts foreign capital through investments on the Johannesburg Stock Exchange and through domestic capital formation. (Capital formation is the expenditure on machinery and equipment which is a prerequisite for the physical production of the particular goods concerned.) The discovery in the 1970s of valuable iron ore deposits on the Orex line near Sishen (in the present-day Northern Cape) led to the construction of the world-class iron exporting harbour at Saldanha Bay. The state installed the latest technology at both the Saldanha and Richards Bay harbours to facilitate the huge iron ore and coal exports. This development of freight rate infrastructure placed the users of these facilities on the cutting edge of raw material export technology. This momentum in infrastructure development was not continued after 1994. Since the 1990s the decline of harbour freight handling in all South African harbours is evidence of the gradual stagnation in the maintenance and modernisation of infrastructure.

> Infrastructure is the oil that turns the wheels of manufacturing, agriculture and mining. Roads, railway lines and harbours, together with dams and water reservoirs, are the responsibility of the state. Since the 1920s dams, roads, railways and airports have been built to facilitate goods traffic and the movement of people. The construction of the Richards Bay and Saldanha Bay harbours, for example, led to the building of rail links and roads to support the goods traffic. South African engineers displayed international leadership in the design and construction of these facilities. In 1976 the annual spending on infrastructure as a percentage of GDP was 8,1%. Thereafter the state neglected this responsibility and by 2002 this percentage had dropped to a mere 2,6%.

In the twentieth century the mining industry played a different role than it had in the nineteenth century. In particular this became apparent with the depreciation of the Rand in the first decade. In 1985 South Africa was unable to repay its foreign debt and a "debt standstill" was declared. This means that debt repayment was re-negotiated and new, longer-term repayment agreements were entered upon. Between the "debt standstill" of 1985 and 1997, the South African Rand depreciated by 67%.

The depreciation of the South African currency benefited South African exports (exports were reasonably cheap) which resulted in a strong rise in the value of gold and other mineral exports. The value of gold production rose because of the higher gold price and weaker Rand but the physical volume of gold produced declined. The higher international gold price encouraged exploration in other parts of the world. Gold mining increased to such an extent in the USA, Brazil, Canada and Australia that the South African gold production of 70% of the world production in 1980 fell to 40% in 1990 and a mere 18% in 2000.

The high costs of gold production, and especially the cost of labour, resulted in the drastically reduced volumes of gold production. Coal production rose in prominence in the mining industry in the 1980s and platinum in the 1990s. Coal production received an enormous boost in 1969 when Japan concluded a contract to purchase 25 million tons of coking coal over a period of ten years. This was after researchers in the coal section of the Anglo-American Corporation (AAC) developed a new method of washing coal which delivered coking coal of a higher quality. The contract with Japan and the expectation of new markets in Europe led to the construction of the new harbour facility at Richards Bay with a terminal for the bulk export of coal.

By 1976 the first coal was exported from this harbour facility. In 1985 the value of coal exports was already exceeding the value of domestic production. New technology was developed to transport bulk coal over long distances and this increased the demand for coal in Europe and Southeast Asia. It was easier to transport coal over long distances than iron ore, so heavy iron and steel industries in Europe and eastern Asia began to import more coal. However, coal from west Canada and Australia was nearer to eastern Asia and therefore enjoyed preference. Since the 1980s most of South Africa's coal has been exported to Europe. General deregulation in the 1980s also led to the scrapping of price control in the coal industry. Furthermore, the massive price hike of oil in 1973 and 1979 provided an even greater stimulus to the export of coal. The oil price shocks led to an international turn to coal as a source of electricity instead of oil. By 2000, 55,3% of coal sales in South Africa was exported, mainly to Europe. The harbour at Richards Bay was also expanded to increase the coal handling capacity for export to 84 million tons.

The development of the automobile catalytic converter, a device fitted to the exhaust system of a motor vehicle by which pollutant gases such as carbon dioxide are rendered less harmful; as well as a greater demand for platinum in the jewellery industry and electronics, stimulated the importance of platinum just when gold came under pressure. The year 2000 was of historic significance for the South African mining industry when the value of the sale of metal in the platinum group exceeded R27 million. For the first time platinum sales exceeded the value of gold sales of R25,2 million. The market-driven demand for platinum therefore changed the structure of the mining industry in South Africa for the first time since the discovery of gold.

Although South Africa had a reputation for the size and clarity of its diamonds, diamond mining between 1950 and 2000 comprised only between 3% and 5% of the total mining production. The importance of South Africa in the diamond-mining industry went beyond production: De Beers Consolidated Mines controlled the central marketing agency and in this way exercised control over the international price of diamonds. In 1973 De Beers geologists discovered an important diamond pipe at Jwaneng in Botswana. This made Botswana, in terms of the value of the deposits, the world's largest producer of diamonds. By 2000 South Africa's diamond production was only about 10% of the value of world production.

South Africa also mined and exported a variety of other minerals and metals by 2000 – silver, chrome ore, copper, iron ore, lead concentrate, manganese ore, nickel, asbestos and granite.

By the end of the twentieth century the most notable feature of the mining sector was the sharp decline in employment. Employment at gold mines declined more rapidly than in the more mechanised coal and platinum mines because of rising wages and marginal gold deposits. By 2000 the cost of labour as a portion of sales in gold mining exceeded the cost structure in other sectors of the mining industry – 38,7% for gold mines, 21,6% for coal mines, 16,1% for platinum mines, and 11,3% for iron ore. These excessively high costs, together with the freer movement of workers, led to a declining non-South African labour force and a rising South African mining labour force.

Growth and stagnation in the manufacturing sector

Thanks to the foundation that had been laid since 1920 with the protection of local industries, between 1950 and 1970 the manufacturing sector grew impressively. The 1950s and 1960 are generally regarded as decades of exceptional industrial achievement. However, this also caused serious structural problems in the economy at a later stage.

The policy of import substitution and the protection of local industries behind high tariff walls had served its purpose by 1970. The lack of export-oriented production was a serious mistake. For strategic considerations the government wanted to prevent a potentially crippling situation of insufficient imported inputs into South African industries in the wake of sanctions. However, government intervention resulted in the misallocation of resources and inappropriate utilisation. Restrictions on the free movement of labour, control over the movement of capital, and stunted competition provided little incentive to improve labour productivity by better training. The oil crises of 1973 and 1979 led to even higher levels of government intervention which stifled the phasing out of protectionism.

Between 1946 and 1971 the industrialisation of the South African economy was impressive. The value added to the manufacturing sector increased in real terms by an average of 7,1% per annum, while the GDP rose by 5%. This performance can be attributed in particular to the growth in the motor industry, iron and steel production, engineering industries and especially the chemical industry.

In the motor assembly industry, by 1960 the local content was only about 18%, which caused the Board of Trade and Industries to recommend that tariff protection, customs duties and legislative prescriptions ensuring a higher local content be implemented gradually. In successive phases increased ratios of locally manufactured components were made compulsory in locally assembled vehicles. Local content had to be 75% for locally produced components in the manufacture of motor vehicles by 1997. The IDC also provided assistance with the construction of the Atlantis Diesel Engine factory on the Cape west coast to stimulate the production of local content. The local content programme met with significant success: employment more than doubled and manufacturing technology improved – but it was an expensive initiative. The cost of duties blocked imports. By 1973 there were 420 motor-car models on the South African market. In the 1980s Austin, Fiat, Renault, Peugeot and Chrysler closed their plants in support of the international sanction campaign against the South African domestic policy of separate development. Others, including Ford and Mazda, consolidated their industrial operations. The successes with motor manufacturing were mixed: highly technologically advanced components still had to be imported and the export of South African manufactured vehicles only began in the late 1990s. Vehicle manufacturing therefore still placed pressure on the balance of payments.

The iron and steel manufacturing sector benefited largely from the development of the vehicle assembly sector and vice versa. Cheap iron and steel was readily available. The great demand for steel led to the construction of Highveld Steel and Vanadium by AAC at Witbank (now eMalahleni) in 1968. By the end of the 1980s the plant had already produced more than one million tons of steel and had become the world's largest manufacturer of vanadium (which is used to harden steel). As for Iscor, it increased production at its plants in Pretoria and Vanderbijlpark exponentially – to four million tons per annum by 1973. A new harbour facility was built at Saldanha Bay to export iron ore from the opencast mine at Sishen, some 860 km away. Exporting began in 1976. Iscor also expanded its operations to Newcastle.

The metal and engineering industries naturally benefited from the readily available locally produced iron and steel and by the end of 1979 this sector's production exceeded a value of R11 billion per annum. The manufacturing of weapons and ammunition was one of the industries in this sector and proved so successful that it was decided in 1967 to establish the Krygstuigkorporasie van Suid-Afrika (South African Armaments Corporation), abbreviated as Krygkor. The manufacturing of armaments also stimulated the electronic engineering industry to the extent that Altron was established by Bill Venter in 1965 to initiate electrical and electronic engineering production.

The most impressive growth was in the chemical industry, centred on Sasol. From 1961 onwards, Sasol gradually began to show a profit and was soon manufacturing rubber, plastic, paint, soaps, fertiliser and other chemical by-products. AECI concentrated particularly on chemicals and paint, while Sentrachem's focus was on fertiliser and pharmaceutical products. The oil crises of 1973 and 1979 spurred on Sasol to develop new technology to manufacture fuel from gas as well. Sasol expanded so rapidly that Sasol 2 and Sasol 3 went into production at Secunda in 1983 and 1985 respectively. Between 1960 and 1985 Sasol's turnover rose from R1,4 million to more than R5000 million. However, Sasol received large government subsidies and in 1979 the company was listed on the Johannesburg Stock Exchange. The last government subsidies to Sasol were only discontinued in 2005. Sasol brought great prestige to South Africa as an international chemical company leading in the development of technology to transform natural gas into fuel; and by providing more than 25% of the local fuel demand.

The growth of manufacturing began to level out by the 1970s. Various factors were responsible for this, including labour and trade union activity and militancy, the oil price hikes, domestic unrest, sanctions and debt. These factors are discussed below.

Labour and trade unions

In the period of strong economic growth there was a huge demand for labour. White labour increased in the 1960s by a mere 2% per annum, while the economy grew by an average of 5%. There was clearly a shortage of labour, particularly skilled labour. The result was that job reservation in terms of section 77 of the Industrial Conciliation Act of 1956 was increasingly ignored. Industrialists and businessmen simply appointed black, coloured and Indian workers in positions that had in fact been reserved for white people, because the demand for white labour could not be met.

The South African Employers' Consultative Committee on Labour Affairs (Saccola) – the representative body of ten large employers – had as early as 1977 undertaken to work towards the removal of all racial discrimination in employment practices. Ongoing racial discrimination in the workplace came under growing public criticism because it led to a sub-optimal allocation of resources. As a matter of fact, the pressure on apartheid by economic realities had reached breaking point. The oil crises plunged the entire world economy into recession and South Africa was equally hard hit.

In reaction, the government appointed two commissions of inquiry in 1977. The Wiehahn Commission investigated labour legislation with particular emphasis on the organisation of labour in trade unions, and the Riekert Commission's inquiry was directed at the utilisation of the labour force. The Wiehahn Commission recommended that the definition of an "employee" should be changed to include black people, in this manner paving the way towards the recognition of black workers' right to organise themselves into trade unions. Although the government initially attempted to keep white and black trade unions separate, all such restrictions were scrapped in 1984 when all workers, regardless of race, were free to join the trade unions of their choice. Many new trade unions, especially those with a largely black membership, were soon formed. The attitude and conduct of these trade unions was militant but this can be ascribed to the fact that black people had no political parties in South Africa to represent their opinions directly. The Riekert Commission found that there was no coherent government strategy on labour supply and therefore the labour market was seriously unstable and dysfunctional. The commission also recommended that black urbanisation should be permitted in order to improve the supply and demand of labour.

The proposals put forward by these two commissions implied that government intervention in the economy, in this case with regard to the labour market, had to be terminated. Black trade unions were legalised in 1979 and influx control was abolished in 1986. Between 1979 and 1982 virtually all job reservation was scrapped. Because these trade unions also emerged as the vehicles of domestic expression of political aspirations, black trade unions became highly militant and caused massive economic industrial production disruption.

The world recession and domestic unrest

The rise in the oil price in 1973 and 1979 caused massive inflationary pressures throughout the world and led to a worldwide recession. South Africa could not escape either. The crisis came just at the time when the South African government was beginning to move away from import substitution, import quotas and tariff protection.

In 1972 the Reynders Commission of Inquiry into exports recommended that industrialisation should rather be promoted by export promotion than by import substitution. When South Africa embarked on an export promotion strategy, the world was in a serious recession. In 1994 the World Bank identified two major problems in a study of the South African economy. Firstly, too much emphasis had been placed on capital intensive manufacturing (for example Krygkor and defence production, as well as Sasol and fuel production). Secondly, there was an undue focus on consumer production for the domestic market rather than producing for international markets.

In 1976 massive unrest flared up in Soweto and spread throughout the country. By 1986 the level of black resistance had escalated and a state of emergency was declared. There was also severe international pressure on the South African government in the form of trade sanctions, disinvestment and boycotts. In 1985 Chase Manhattan Bank and other American banks refused to "roll over" (extend the term of repayment) of loans to South African banks; and in 1986 a comprehensive agreement for the repayment of total outstanding foreign debt of South African banks of $13,6 billion was negotiated. Although the president of the USA, Ronald Reagan, and Margaret Thatcher, the prime minister of Britain, had persistently pleaded against sanctions, the United Nations approved the adoption of trade sanctions against apartheid South Africa. Foreign investment had declined since 1980 and from 1985 was negative. A number of large international companies withdrew from the South African market (for example IBM, Kodak and General Motors).

This international reaction gave the country's industrial strategy – which was to focus on exports – little chance of success. The political changes of 1994 and the signing of international trade agreements in 1995 at last gradually began to stimulate the export of manufactured goods.

The financial services sector

Since the second half of the nineteenth century there was a reasonably well-developed banking and financial services sector in South Africa. This was largely due to the stabilising role played by the imperial banks, namely Standard Bank and the African Banking Corporation (ABC). After 1926 the ABC was taken over by Barclays Bank and this bank, together with Standard Bank, dominated the banking scene with their strongly capitalist British shareholders and conservative approach to banking.

As already mentioned, Volkskas (in 1934) and Trust Bank (1956) were established with Afrikaner capital as South African banks. The Netherlands Bank of South Africa (NBSA) (later Nedbank) was also on the scene from 1888. All these banks opened branches throughout South Africa to offer banking services to both private individuals as well as companies.

In 1923 the South African Reserve Bank (SARB) was formed which kept a careful watch over the operations of domestic banks and determined general monetary policy. The first banking legislation of 1942 prescribed the functions of banks and made it mandatory for them to report at regular intervals to the SARB. With the impressive economic growth of the 1950s and 1960s new types of banks entered the market, for example investment banks and building societies. In 1964 the Bank Act was amended to regulate the activities of various types of banks differently.

By the late 1960s an active money market had also developed and there was a growing demand for finance capital. The big commercial banks gradually consolidated a variety of financial services under one roof, offering a wider variety of services than were traditionally offered by commercial banks. Therefore, Standard Bank, Barclays Bank, Volkskas and Nedbank each formed bank holding companies which combined (in addition to ordinary commercial banks) their own investment banks and industrial banks. Technological development, especially computerisation, placed banks in a position to offer a wider variety of products. By the 1970s banks also began to grant mortgages on property and to accommodate insurance agents.

By 1973 the government decided that foreign shareholders could no longer hold a majority share in South African banks. This being so, Barclays shareholders in Britain sold their interests in 1985 to the Southern Life insurance company. By the 1990s the three big insurance companies, namely Old Mutual (Nedbank), Liberty (Standard Bank) and Sanlam (Volkskas) each had a controlling share in one of the large bank groups.

In 1985 the president of the SARB, Dr Gerhard de Kock, in his report on monetary policy in South Africa, recommended that the current strict and direct control over banking should be modified to comply with the international tendency of market deregulation. The Bank Act was therefore changed in 1992 so that building societies could offer bank functions and vice versa. In other words, the free-market principle would be applied and under the supervision of the SARB all banks and financial institutions were permitted to offer the full range of services. This soon led to the big banking groups taking over the smaller building societies. Nedbank took over the Permanent Building Society, and the United Building Society together with Volkskas, Trust Bank and the Allied Building Society formed a new large banking group, Amalgamated Banks of South Africa (Absa). These developments in banking brought a significant saving of costs.

These banking groups which were controlled by the big South African insurance companies, operated mainly in the domestic market, because exchange control and SARB supervision monitored international transactions very strictly. (Exchange control refers to restrictive measures introduced by the government which forbid citizens from taking more than a certain amount of money out of the country without permission from the

SARB.) For the government, control over the banks was of strategic importance – therefore the banks had to be South African companies under South African control.

After Barclays sold its controlling share to Southern Life, the bank changed its name in South Africa to First National Bank (FNB). In 1997 Rand Aksep Bank (Rand Merchant Bank) which had been formed by the Afrikaners Laurie Dippenaar, G.T. Ferreira and Johann Rupert, bought a controlling share in FNB to establish the First Rand Group. As a result, by 2000 Afrikaner interests played a fairly strong role in the financial sector. Although shareholding was not exclusively in Afrikaner hands, Absa and the First Rand Group comprised insurance companies and banks with an unmistakeable Afrikaner origin. It was largely thanks to Afrikaners in the financial sector that the contribution of Afrikaners to private sector economic activity had exceeded 25% by 1975. This is particularly notable if one considers that in 1948–1949 this figure was only 9,6%.

Along with the enormous expansion of the financial sector there was also the development of computer companies, telecommunication companies and professional auditors' groups in the services sector. South African banks, with their extensive functions, sophisticated money market and merchant bank operations, compared very favourably with those of other Commonwealth countries. It was only after 1994 that they gradually entered the international banking arena on a reasonably wide scale. After 1993 the SARB allowed South African banks to open new offices in other parts of the world and permitted foreign banks to establish branches in South Africa. After 1994 South African companies gradually established foreign companies as subsidiaries or merged them with their own operations.

The globalisation of the South African economy really only began in 2000. The country still had a remarkably open economy because of the fairly large role of foreign trade in the GDP. However, South Africa lost its international attractiveness because gold was demonetarised (when a currency is no longer linked to gold and its value does not depend on how much gold a country has). This meant that other countries surpassed South Africa in general economic performance and the mining of gold and other minerals. The full advantage of the free-market economic system is also currently restricted by a policy which focuses on economic empowerment of certain historically disadvantaged groups.

22
The development of trade unions and organised labour
Wessel Visser

Trade unions arose in reaction to the desperately bad labour conditions, particularly in Britain, that were prevalent at the time of the Industrial Revolution. The emergence of capitalism – an economic system whereby a few wealthy individuals finance the development of industries – created a small private ownership class. They owned and controlled all means of production such as mines and factories. During the Industrial Revolution the development of steam-driven machines largely replaced manual labour and the resultant oversupply of labour in the saturated labour market meant that those who were able to secure jobs had to work long hours, often in dreadful, unhealthy conditions and for extremely low wages. Initially there was no legislation to protect workers and they were widely exploited.

Workers began to realise that they could negotiate for better working conditions and wages if they grouped together to form trade unions. Joint action strengthened their bargaining power considerably. Trade unions ensured that competition to secure employment was kept to a minimum so that wage levels could be maintained and increased; and that undercutting of wages could be prevented. (In the South African context it meant that skilled white workers were often replaced by black workers who did the same work for lower wages). If collective bargaining failed, workers were able to withhold their labour by means of strike action. To operate effectively, trade unions had to be in a position to control the demand for labour.

The earliest trade unions were craft unions. Workers were usually taken on as apprentices and trained in particular crafts or trades such as carpentry, ironworking, printing, bricklaying or mechanical drilling. When they were fully qualified in their craft or trade they were permitted to join the relevant artisans' trade union.

The first trade unions in South Africa

In South Africa the first trade unions were those in the printing industry established in Cape Town. The Cape of Good Hope Printers' Protection Society was formed as early as 1841, while the Cape of Good Hope Printers' and Bookbinders' Society was established in 1857. By the early 1880s there were various printing trade unions in the bigger cities. They were eventually amalgamated with the South African Typographical Union which at the time was the most effective and best organised trade union in South Africa. In 1881 carpenters formed the Amalgamated Society of Carpenters and Joiners in Cape Town.

However, the greatest impetus for the development of trade unions and organised labour took place after the discovery of minerals in the last quarter of the nineteenth century. For the mining of these minerals, particularly gold, which was of low-percentage quality per ton of ore mined, highly mechanised and industrialised technology was required. Engineers, technicians, scientists and a range of artisans had to be employed in the mining industry.

At first South Africa itself simply could not provide enough skilled workers and technical experts for the diamond and gold industries. Thousands of technicians and skilled workers were therefore brought into South Africa, especially from other countries in the British Empire, the USA and Europe. Eventually, it was these immigrants who initiated trade unionism in South Africa. The first generation of gold-mine workers were mainly from Cornwall, Northumberland and South Wales in Britain, Western Australia, California in the USA, Canada, Italy and Greece. There were also Portuguese, Germans, Russians, Jews, Poles, Frenchmen and Dutchmen. The Witwatersrand became a vibrant cosmopolitan mining community, with British workers in the majority.

The Witwatersrand Mine Employees' and Mechanics' Union, better known as the Labour Union, was established as an umbrella labour organisation for British mineworkers and artisans among others. The aim was to unite all white workers on the Witwatersrand. Between 1866 and 1893 branches of the British trade union, the Amalgamated Society of

Engineers (ASE) – a trade union for the engineering industry – were formed in Cape Town, Durban, Kimberley and Johannesburg. Another early prominent trade union was the South African Engine Drivers' and Firemen's Association that was formed for engine drivers on the Witwatersrand.

After the Anglo-Boer War of 1899–1902 the ranks of the South African labour force were swelled by demobilised soldiers from the British army, including men from Britain, Australia, New Zealand and Canada. In 1902 the Transvaal Miners' Association was formed for mineworkers and in 1913 it was re-named the South African Mineworkers' Union, commonly known as the MWU. The MWU became one of the most influential and successful labour organisations in the history of South African trade unionism.

> **J.T. BAIN**
>
> James Thompson Bain was one of the most prominent figures of the early South African labour movement. He was born in 1860 in Dundee, Scotland, where at the time workers were being exploited by capitalists. During the Anglo-Zulu War of 1879 in Zululand he was a soldier in the British army.
>
> In 1888 he immigrated permanently to South Africa and as an artisan he was soon heavily involved in trade union activity on the Witwatersrand. He became a naturalised burgher of the ZAR and during the Anglo-Boer War he was an agent for the ZAR's secret service under Jan Smuts. This made him the only British-born South African labour leader who fought on the side of the Boers.
>
> Bain was at the forefront of a wide range of labour disputes. In the miners' strike of 1913 he was a member of the strikers' committee with whom Louis Botha and Smuts were obliged to negotiate about a ceasefire. With the general strike of 1914, he was one of nine strike-leaders who were deported to Britain for a while. During a municipal strike in Johannesburg in 1919 the strikers' committee under Bain's leadership took over the functions of the city council for a short time by forming the so-called Provisional Joint Board of Control, which was nicknamed the "Johannesburg Soviet".
>
> Bain was a self-taught, dedicated socialist and a well-known labour activist; he had an intense dislike of the capitalist system which dominated the Rand gold-mining industry. He died in Johannesburg in 1919.

The early South African labour movement had a number of distinguishing characteristics. Firstly, the labour force on the mines had an overwhelming British character because it was particularly the British who had the necessary technological skills and expertise for deep-level and hard-rock mining. The British workshop and trade union traditions were therefore inculcated on the Witwatersrand and immigrant workers cast the first trade unions in South Africa in the same mould as similar movements in Britain. Some of these trade unions were indeed branches of the British mother organisations.

A second characteristic of the early trade unions and labour movement was the presence of considerable division. To attract and retain (white) artisans who had the necessary scarce skills to work on the Witwatersrand mines, they were paid higher wages and they enjoyed a privileged labour status. In South Africa they formed craft unions to control the provision of labour for a specific trade by a system of closed membership. This gave them a great deal of power and influence; they could keep wages high and monitor the kind of work that their members were required to do.

This meant that unskilled and semi-skilled Afrikaner workers were initially excluded from trade unions and therefore from better-paid positions on the mines and in associated industries. Because deep-level mining was so expensive and the ore was of such low gold content, it could only be profitably mined by a large, unskilled black workforce that was paid very low wages. These mine labourers were heavily controlled by discriminatory legislation such as the colour bar and the pass system and were housed in mine compounds. They were barred from organising themselves into trade unions. (The term "colour bar" refers to a series of regulations and other legislation which entrenched job reservation for whites in certain trades and barred black and coloured workers from holding jobs in these categories). When the number of unskilled black workers on the mines increased, the role of white supervisors became more important. It was in this way that Afrikaner workers eventually gained access to trade unions such as the MWU.

The nagging fear that they might be replaced by lower-paid unskilled black workers encouraged the development of trade unions by white workers. The unions in this manner played a significant role in entrenching certain industrial job opportunities for white workers and protecting their higher wages from being undercut by cheaper black wage levels. The early South African labour movement was therefore notable for its race-based structure – a smaller white labour force which was largely organised into trade unions and a massive poorly paid and unorganised black proletariat (the lowest class of society which made a livelihood by selling their labour).

A third characteristic of early trade unionism and organised labour in South Africa was the confrontational nature of workers' attitudes towards their employers – as was the case in Britain. Issues such as mine regulations and safety matters; occupational illnesses such as miner's phthisis; workers' compensation in the case of mining accidents; an eight-hour working day; a ban on Sunday work; white job reservation; and minimum wage levels, were typical controversial issues in negotiations between trade unions and employers' associations such as the Chamber of Mines. In the prelude to unification in 1910 efforts were also made to gain more political power so that white labour could be protected by labour legislation. With this in mind certain trade unions and other labour organisations established the South African Labour Party (SALP) in Johannesburg in October 1909 under the leadership of F.H.P. Creswell.

In the first quarter of the twentieth century particularly, the confrontational nature of the relationship between trade unions and employers' associations led to industrial unrest between labour and capital. This unrest culminated in four large and militant strikes – in 1907, 1913, 1914 and 1922. The government was drawn into the confrontation by stepping in to end the strikes by force. Trade unions such as the MWU and the ASE were actively involved in the strikes.

The first trade union established for black workers was apparently the Industrial Workers of Africa (IWA). The IWA was formed in 1917 with the assistance of left-wing white revolutionary socialists such as S.P. Bunting and D.I. Jones who broke away from the more conservative SALP in 1915.

In contrast to artisans' trade unions, the IWA was a general industrial trade union for black workers. It was expected that it would soon develop into a massive trade union for unskilled black workers but due to police infiltration among other things, it was disbanded in 1918. In 1917 and 1918 skilled Indian workers in Natal formed trade unions in the printing, clothing, furniture, tobacco, leather, liquor and catering industries.

With the establishment of the Industrial and Commercial Workers' Union of South Africa (ICU) in 1919 for black and coloured dockworkers in Cape Town, the black trade union movement took a new turn. The ICU which was formed by Clements Kadalie (originally from Malawi) and the white socialist A.F. Batty, was the first nationally organised mass trade union and political movement for black workers in South Africa. It eventually included black workers across a wide spectrum – unemployed rural farm workers, domestic workers, factory workers, dockworkers, teachers and retailers.

However, the impenetrable compound and migrant labour systems ensured that black mine workers were unable to form themselves into a trade union. The ICU unleashed a tradition of militancy among black workers and in the 1920s it was even more popular than the African National Congress (ANC). It soon spread countrywide to the Free State, Transvaal and Natal and in 1925 its headquarters was moved to Johannesburg.

Before long, communist influences also began to filter into the ICU. James la Guma, the trade union's assistant general secretary joined the Communist Party of South Africa (CPSA) which was established in July 1921. Other ICU leaders followed his example. By 1926 there were six CPSA members in the national council of the ICU. However, this co-operation did not survive for long. When the communists accused the trade union leadership of internal corruption, a lack of discipline and financial mismanagement, they were served with an ultimatum in December 1926 – they had to choose between the ICU and the CPSA. Those who did not resign from the CPSA of their own free will were expelled from the ICU.

By the end of 1927 the ICU reached the high point of its popularity with a membership of about 100 000. In this same year, while Kadalie was in Europe, the ICU's hub of influence shifted to the Natal branch headed by A.W.G. Champion. Leadership disputes between Kadalie and Champion deepened and the trade union began to decline. In May 1928 Champion broke away from the ICU and formed his own organisation, the ICU yase Natal. This was the death knell of the original ICU because Natal members were an important source of income for the trade union.

In July 1928 W.G. Ballinger, a Scottish trade unionist, was appointed as financial adviser to the ICU but before long he also clashed with Kadalie over the necessity for a major overhaul of the trade union's chaotic administration. In 1929 Kadalie established an independent ICU with its headquarters in East London, but due to financial straits and a marked lack of nationwide support, it struggled to survive. By 1934, for all practical purposes the ICU as a trade union organisation had disappeared from the scene and dozens of Kadalie's disillusioned black members turned to the ANC.

The rise of the trade union federations

In 1922 the largest and most violent strike in the history of the white labour movement, the so-called Rand Revolt, broke out. In essence the strike was about the concerns of the mining industry (represented by the Chamber of Mines) that the economic affordability of white workers (who earned higher wages and held a privileged, entrenched position in the mining industry and associated industries on the Witwatersrand) was becoming impossible to sustain. Furthermore, and closely interlinked, white workers objected to the ration between black workers and white supervisors on the mines; they also complained that the negotiating power of the white trade unions was significantly less than that wielded by the Chamber of Mines. About 22 000 white workers took part in the strike and it escalated out of control so rapidly that the state had to intervene with force to restore order.

Many workers lost their jobs after the strike and the authority and influence of the trade unions took a severe knock. However, it was in the political terrain and on trade union organisation that the 1922 strike had its most far-reaching implications. White workers held the Smuts government responsible for the blood that was shed in the ruthless suppression of the strike and the large-scale unemployment that followed. Aware of this, the National Party (NP) of J.B.M. Hertzog and the SALP under Creswell came to an election agreement and managed to defeat Smuts in the 1924 election. Before the election the Smuts government passed the Industrial Conciliation Act of 1924, which on the one hand secured the jobs held by members of white trade unions against wage undercutting, but at the same time also supported employers in that legal restrictions were placed in the path of trade unions from calling unauthorised "wild cat" strikes. Furthermore, black workers were forbidden from becoming members of recognised trade unions because in terms of the Act they were not classified as "workers".

The new coalition government, which became known as the Pact government, deepened the racial divide in the trade union and labour movement even further with its pro-white labour policy. The new Mines and Works Amendment Act of 1926 – the so-called Colour Bar Act – ensured that militant action by white workers became a thing of the past. The law promoted white job reservation and protected skilled and semi-skilled white workers by reserving certificates of competency in certain skilled trades exclusively for white and coloured workers. Black people and Asians were not issued with these certificates and were therefore barred from holding down these jobs. Furthermore, organised white labour was drawn into state structures on a large scale. Henceforth trade unions had to follow bureaucratic negotiation processes before they could call a strike; this effectively ended militant white opposition.

When its attempts at conciliation with the SALP in the 1924 election campaign failed, the CPSA concentrated its efforts on organising the black proletariat with the aim of eventually effecting a black majority government in South Africa.

The Colour Bar Act not only regulated the development of trade unions, it also stimulated them to move in a new trajectory. From 1924 onwards, the development of trade unions was characterised especially by the formation of industrial trade unions and the establishment of trade union federations. Other than in the earlier era when craft unions dominated the labour scene, the new trade union structures offered wider access to organised labour for far more workers. It was also partly in reaction to the Pact government's "civilised labour" policy that employers embarked on a deliberate "de-skilling" process to create more job opportunities for unskilled white workers. In this way, unskilled odd-jobbers were categorised as "competent workers" and more unskilled and semi-skilled white workers came into the labour market. These two groups of unskilled whites systematically replaced skilled artisans and were paid lower wages in industries such as the railways.

The Spoorbond was established in 1934 as a trade union for unskilled and semi-skilled railway workers. In 1936 the Suid-Afrikaanse Yster-en-Staalbedryfsvereniging (South African Iron and Steel Trade Union) was formed for metal workers; by 1976 it had more than 38 000 members. In 1949 the Blankewerkersbeskermingsbond (an association to protect the interests of white workers) was formed under the leadership of Gert Beetge, and in 1953 a trade union was set up for leather workers. The Blankewerkersbeskermingsbond organised industrial trade unions for white workers in the clothing and leather industries and in the commercial sphere. There was also the Suid-Afrikaanse Vereniging vir Munisipale Werkers (for local government employees).

A characteristic of these exclusively white trade unions was that almost all were in the state sector such as the railways and municipalities, or were closely linked to parastatals, as were the iron and steel industries. The members of these trade unions could easily have been replaced by cheaper black workers. The state therefore played an important role in the protection of white labour. For their part, the white trade unions were in favour of job reservation, the suppression of black trade unions, and the banning of "communist" trade union leaders.

Trade union federations began to gather momentum when the South African Trade Union Congress (SATUC) was formed in 1924 with 30 000 members. With the communist Bill Andrews as secretary, SATUC was left-wing-oriented and black trade unions could become affiliated to it. With the support of SATUC the first black industrial trade unions, such as those in the dry-cleaning, furniture, sweets and automobile industries, were established under the leadership of, among others, the communists who had been pushed out of the ICU.

In 1928 these trade unions, together with others in the dairy products, meat, canvas, transport and engineering industries, amalgamated in the Federation of Non-European Trade Unions (FNETU) with La Guma of the CPSA as national secretary. In 1928 FNETU had a membership of 10 000. However, factors such as the Great Depression of 1929 to 1934, its close ties with the CPSA, and internal disputes led to the demise of the FNETU.

SATUC prepared the way for the establishment of the South African Trades and Labour Council (SAT&LC) in 1930, which at that stage was the biggest and most influential federation of trade unions in the country. Black trade unions could also join. By 1946 the SAT&LC comprised 115 trade unions and had a membership of 93 337 workers. Fifty of these trade unions were multiracial. The federation thus stood for the abolition of race-based labour legislation. In 1941, during the Second World War, the African Mineworkers' Union (AMWU) was formed as a counter against low wages and harsh treatment of black mineworkers in the gold mines. J.B. Marks, a communist, was AMWU's president.

In November 1942 delegates from 29 black trade unions met in Johannesburg to form the Council of Non-European Trade Unions (CNETU). This co-ordinated body comprised 29 trade unions with 150 000 members and set itself the task of gaining full legal recognition, i.e. registration of black trade unions. The federation dominated the black labour movement for the next decade. In 1946, in the tough post-war conditions of food shortages and low wages, AMWU with the support of CNETU called a general strike in which about 70 000 black mineworkers from twelve gold mines participated. However, the police put down the strike and CNETU was seriously weakened.

By 1948 the SAT&LC had crumbled due to the withdrawal of six trade unions the previous year, including the MWU, the metal workers and railway workers, all of which objected to the inclusion of black trade unions in the SAT&LC. This led to the formation of two new white trade union federations, namely the Suid-Afrikaanse Federasie van Vakbonde (South African Federation of Trade Unions) with 100 000 members in 23 trade unions; and the Koördinerende Raad van Arbeid (Co-ordination of Labour Council) with 13 000 members in seven trade unions. In 1957 these two bodies fused to form the conservative Suid-Afrikaanse Konfederasie van Arbeid (SAKVA) (South African Confederation of Labour) with 30 trade unions and 155 000 members.

The Suppression of Communism Act of 1950 was the death knell for the SAT&LC. Thereafter this trade union federation was dissolved because virtually all its experienced black leaders were listed as communists and had to resign from their trade union posts. In 1954 the South African Trade Union Council was established with 61 trade unions and 147 000 workers. In 1962 it changed its name to the Trade Union Council of South Africa (TUCSA) but was somewhat ambivalent about the affiliation of black trade unions and this led to the withdrawal of a significant number of founding trade unions from TUCSA. In 1986 it was finally dissolved.

Trade unions that had formerly been affiliated to the SAT&LC and the CNETU (which closed down in 1953) and disagreed with TUCSA's race-based policy, formed the South African Congress of Trade Unions (SACTU) in March 1955. The new federation comprised 19 trade unions (with largely black membership) in the manufacturing, provision of services and food processing sectors and had a membership of 30 000. SACTU had close ties with liberation movements such as the ANC and the leadership of the two organisations overlapped to some extent. However, in terms of the Suppression of Communism Act and the General Laws Amendment Act (the so-called Sabotage Act) of 1962, all SACTU's leaders were banned. By the mid-1960s the federation had largely lost its influence in the South African trade unionism sector.

The Wiehahn Commission and trade unionism

The early 1970s were marked by violent struggles against the NP government's policy on black labour. From January to March 1973 about 61 000 black workers took part in massive strikes in the Durban area. The strikes were an indication of the failure of the Native Labour (Settlement of Disputes) Act of 1953 which had attempted to regulate black labour by providing workers with an alternative to trade union membership.

It was against this background that in 1977 the government appointed the Commission of Inquiry into Labour Legislation, also known as the Wiehahn Commission. Its task was to examine existing labour legislation and make recommendations in an attempt to ensure peace on the labour front in the future. Among the most significant recommendations, which the government duly accepted and implemented, was that black trade unions should be legally recognised and that (white) job reservation should be scrapped in terms of the law.

The momentum which the Wiehahn recommendations gave to the formation of new (legally registered) black trade unions also coincided with the increase in black support for anti-apartheid liberation movements. In this way the black trade union and labour movement became a legal channel for black political resistance against apartheid in the absence of the banned liberation movements such as the ANC and the PAC; the labour movement therefore gained great influence among the black masses.

In 1979 the Federation of South African Trade Unions (FOSATU) was formed. It was the first multiracial trade union federation since SACTU, although it was largely representative of black trade unions. FOSATU had nine affiliated trade unions in the automobile, metal, food, transport, textile, chemicals, and paper industries. In 1980 the Council of Unions of South Africa (CUSA) was established; it had close ties with the Black Consciousness Movement. In 1986 CUSA fused with other black federations to form the National Council of Trade Unions (NACTU). The influential National Union of Mineworkers (NUM) for black mine workers was established in 1982 with Cyril Ramaphosa as national secretary.

FOSATU paved the way for the biggest and most powerful trade union federation ever formed in South Africa – one that is still in existence. After four years of planning the Congress of South African Trade Unions (COSATU) was established in Durban in November 1985 at a time when political unrest was ravaging the country. The founding of COSATU introduced a new dynamic in the politicisation of trade unionism. Initially, it comprised 33 trade unions, old FOSATU affiliates and independent trade unions such as the NUM, and could boast some 450 000 members.

Within the black labour movement COSATU became a leading antiapartheid organisation. It stood for disinvestment and sanctions against the NP government; the lifting of the state of emergency; the unconditional release of all political prisoners; and a pro-socialist economic policy. COSATU was also highly prominent in mass demonstrations and strikes in the 1980s and early 1990s.

After the unbanning of the liberation movements in 1990, COSATU held negotiations with the ANC and the communists who had regrouped underground in the 1950s as the South African Communist Party (SACP). This led to the formation of a formal three-part alliance between the ANC, COSATU and the SACP. The organisational support of COSATU in the general election of 1994 was a key factor in the ANC's election victory.

Since then, COSATU has exercised significant influence on the ANC government's labour, economic and social policies and some COSATU members have been elected as ANC members of Parliament. In 2009 there were 21 trade unions affiliated to COSATU with a total membership of 1,8 million members.

Trade union organisations after 1994

After the first democratic election, the passing of the Labour Relations Act of 1995, and the new South African constitution, there was no longer any future for racially exclusive trade unions. The conservative trade union federation SAKVA which still represented a few exclusively white trade unions, eventually faded away.

As already mentioned, in 1924 in terms of the Industrial Conciliation Act white trade unions were co-opted into state structures, effectively neutralising all forms of militant resistance by white workers. Yet there is a saying: "When the lion has lost his teeth, he continues to roar fiercely to disguise his other shortcomings." Similarly, some white trade unions such as the MWU still stubbornly tried in the late 1970s and the 1980s to resist the scrapping of job reservation for white workers as recommended by the Wiehahn Commission.

However, by 1997 even this trade union realised that it would have to transform its strategy, vision and objectives in order to survive in a world where the labour market has shrunk and the labour scene has changed completely. The diminishing labour market was due among other things to the revolution in information technology and to greater mechanisation, automation and technological specialisation in manufacturing. These tendencies stimulated trade union federations rather than independent trade unions.

Even as early as 1978 the MWU expanded its reach by recruiting members from outside the mining industry. Workers were systematically brought into the MWU from among others the steel, chemical and petrochemical, wood, food and communications industries as well as from the ranks of state and semi-state officials. Under the dynamic leadership of Flip Buys as chief executive officer, the MWU was re-conceptualised in 2002 as Solidariteit (Solidarity), a wide-ranging labour service organisation with federal characteristics. By 2009 Solidariteit's membership of 130 000 represented virtually all sectors of the South African economy and even individuals are permitted to join. More than 20% of the members were women and 15% were black, coloured or Indian.

In April 1997 the Federation of Unions of South Africa (FEDUSA) came into being with 556 000 members in 23 trade unions. FEDUSA represents workers such as those in the aviation, health, catering, automobile and hospitality industries, as well as municipal and state officials and workers in the education, medical services and banking sectors. The United Association of South Africa (UASA) with 75 000 members was formed in 1998 and was also affiliated to FEDUSA. UASA represents an amalgamation of trade unions in sectors such as mining, forestry, chemical, jewellery, automobile, transport, aviation, railways, media, pharmaceutical, metal, engineering, security, sugar, atomic energy, post and telecommunications, as well as civil service, semi-state service, municipal and health workers.

A noteworthy feature of the labour scene is how quickly the power and influence, particularly of government service trade unions, has increased in twenty-first-century South African society. Whereas in the twentieth century both white and black trade unions often had to engage in concerted efforts to gain recognition, improved working conditions and better remuneration, it appears that circumstances for workers have turned around in the twenty-first century. This can be attributed to the wave of worker-friendly labour legislation that has been passed since 1994.

Civil service trade unions are currently among the most influential interest groups in South African society. In this respect South Africa has followed international trends. Large and influential civil service trade unions under the COSATU umbrella that are often involved in disruptive strike action, include among others the South African Democratic Teachers' Union (SADTU); the National Health and Allied Workers' Union (NEHAWU); and the South African Municipal Workers' Union (SAMWU).

The members' wages, pensions and fringe benefits of civil service trade unions tend to be higher than those of members of trade unions in the private sector and their positions are more secure. Because of their large membership, municipal trade unions for example are able to cripple a city with a strike. Members of civil service trade unions are often better educated and are comparatively fearless in hard bargaining for more resources. Furthermore, due to inflexible labour laws it is very difficult to get rid of employees who are performing poorly.

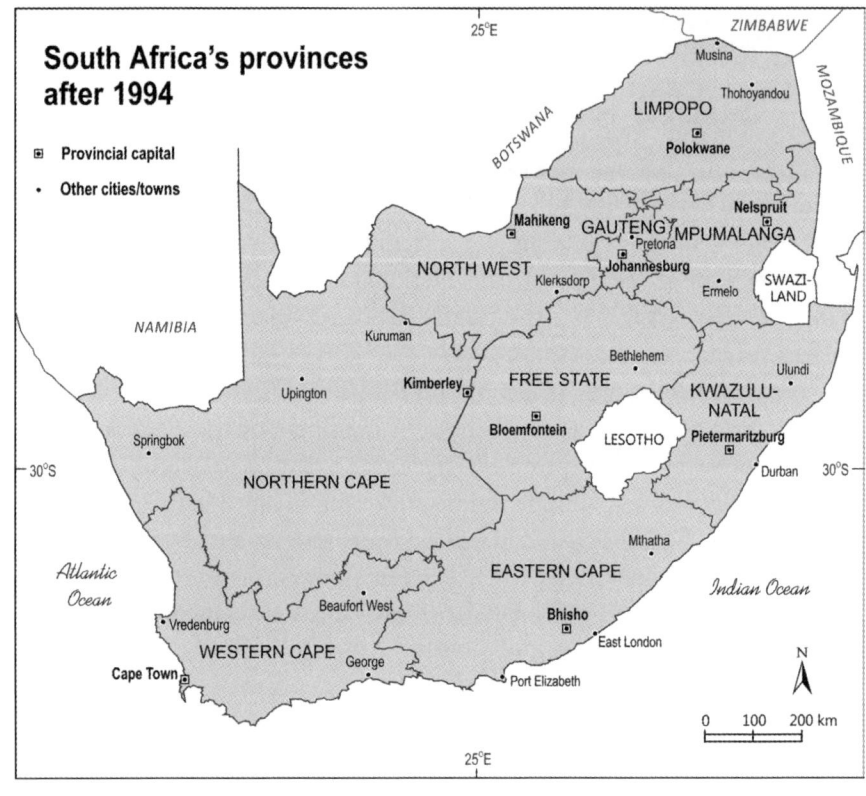

23
South Africa after apartheid, 1994-2004

Japie Brits

The South Africa that took shape in 1994 would never again be the same country as the one that for almost four and a half decades was run on a racial basis. The African National Congress (ANC) won the first democratic election in April 1994 by gaining 62,7% (12,2 million) of the votes cast. Thereby, apartheid rule of almost 46 years came to an end.

In terms of the interim constitution, a government of national unity (GNU) would rule for the next five years. Accordingly, any party with twenty or more seats in the National Assembly was entitled to make claim to one or more cabinet portfolios. Although the ANC had the majority of seats in the National Assembly and could therefore form a government on its own, the National Party (NP) and the Inkatha Freedom Party (IFP) made use of the stipulations for the GNU.

The minority parties that fared the best in the election could also name candidates for minister and deputy minister positions as well as for the position of deputy president. The same formula applied at provincial government level. F.W. de Klerk, leader of the New National Party or NNP (as the NP was re-named after 1994) became one of the two deputy presidents together with Thabo Mbeki of the ANC. The NNP also had five additional national cabinet posts and the IFP three.

South Africa's interim constitution that was accepted on 27 April 1994 was one of the most liberal constitutions in the world. Among other things it made provision for a Bill of Rights, a Human Rights Commission, and a Commission for Gender Equality. The final constitution that was accepted in 1996 virtually confirmed the interim version. The most important difference between the interim and the final constitutions was the creation of a National Council of Provinces which replaced the Senate. Furthermore, after the 1999 election it was no longer necessary for the government to give members of other parties representation in the cabinet or provincial legislatures. This meant the end of power sharing at central government level.

The leadership of Nelson Mandela

A great many challenges awaited the new government under President Nelson Mandela – and specifically the ruling ANC component. In its role as government, this party, which had virtually no experience in running a country, had to simultaneously tackle the inequalities of the past and strive for national unity in a highly divided country. The ANC had to work on the highest level with its traditional "enemy" the National Party and with a fierce rival in recent black politics, the IFP. In addition, the party also had to take into account the interests of its election allies, the South African Communist Party (SACP) and the Congress of South African Trade Unions (COSATU).

To transform itself from a freedom movement to a national government was in itself a potentially difficult process. Much would depend on the abilities and disposition of the new president. Mandela had spent nearly 27 years in gaol and had become a national and international symbol of the struggle against apartheid. During these years he had shown remarkable leadership and forbearance. Furthermore, his extraordinary political acumen became very evident after 1990 in the negotiations with the De Klerk government for a new dispensation.

Former president De Klerk remarked that Mandela had the ability to make whomever he met feel special. The new president had indeed become a symbol of national reconciliation and the embodiment of the "rainbow nation" (so-named by Archbishop Desmond Tutu). Mandela reached out to white South Africans, who appreciated this gesture. He was also very sensitive about the Afrikaners' cultural heritage and was reluctant to change Afrikaans place names. For many South African sports lovers he became an icon; they all remembered how he appeared in Springbok captain Francois Pienaar's rugby jersey after the Springboks won the 1995 Rugby World Cup.

Mandela was indeed committed to national unity, but this did not necessarily mean that he was prepared to work with De Klerk and his NNP colleagues at any price. By the end of 1996 De Klerk withdrew the NNP from the government of national unity because he felt that the ANC was not serious about power sharing and was simply disregarding smaller parties when it came to important matters. In addition, De Klerk did not like the way Mandela reprimanded him when he defended his right to criticise the government. He argued that it was the ANC who compiled the agenda in the cabinet and complained that Mandela and other members of the cabinet did not give him due recognition for his attempts to attract overseas investments to South Africa by supporting the new dispensation. When Mandela publicly attacked the NNP in September 1995 and the ANC expressed its unwillingness to include the principle of power sharing in the final constitution, De Klerk decided that further participation in the GNU was futile. Some of his colleagues had misgivings about his standpoint, but the majority supported his recommendation to withdraw from the government.

Mandela was in many ways a realistic and rational leader. Even before he came to power he was aware that some of the ANC's socialist objectives were no longer attainable and he was prepared to use the expertise of white people who were not members of the ANC. Examples of this are the inclusion of Derek Keys and Chris Liebenberg in his cabinet and the use in government departments of officials from the previous regime. The international community increasingly called upon him as a peace mediator, which elevated his international status even higher.

On the home front he saw it as his main task to build a new nation and often left practical managerial matters to his adjutant, Mbeki. Possibly he was not involved enough in the daily management of the country and this was the reason behind the inability of some government departments to function properly. It can also be argued that the Reconstruction and Development Programme (RDP) which was directed at providing basic social services to disadvantaged communities was abandoned too soon.

Mandela's period of rule represented a decided break with the past and the beginning of a new era. Important changes, including land reform, affirmative action and black economic empowerment were introduced. Considerable progress was also made to promote national unity.

MANDELA: THE NATION BUILDER

Nelson Rolihlahla Mandela was born on 18 July 1918 in Mvezo near the present Mthatha in the Transkei, as the son of the head advisor to the paramount chief. He studied at the Methodist College of Healdtown and the University of Fort Hare before settling in Johannesburg. He worked as a clerk in a law firm while studying at the University of South Africa and later at the University of the Witwatersrand, and was awarded a law degree.

During the 1950s he and Oliver Tambo – who later became president of the ANC – were partners in a law firm in Johannesburg. Both were involved in resistance politics as members of the Congress Youth League (CYL) of the ANC. The CYL became a vigorous political movement, particularly in the 1940s. Initially Mandela adhered to the Africanist ideals of the CYL which had the credo that Africa belonged exclusively to the Africans (the indigenous black people); that a pride in African traditions should be cultivated; and that the Africans themselves should be responsible for realising their liberation without the support of non-Africans.

From 1947 Mandela served as a member of the executive committee of the Transvaal ANC. In the 1950s he revised his Africanist stance and now saw multiracialism as basis of the political system for which South Africa should strive. This implied that a political alliance with white liberals, coloured people and Indians would form a more effective bulwark against apartheid. Because of his activities in resistance politics he was banned and in December 1956 was arrested and charged with high treason. But after a marathon trial that only ended in 1961, he and his co-accused were set free.

After the Sharpeville tragedy in 1960 both the ANC and PAC were banned. Mandela went underground and then left the country to seek overseas support for the liberation struggle. He also received military training in Algeria and began to consider the establishment of an underground organisation. While still operating underground, he formed a military wing of the ANC which was called Umkhonto we Sizwe (Spear of the Nation). MK, as it became popularly known, launched sabotage attacks against targets that were apartheid government structures. Violence against civilians was initially forbidden, although in time "soft targets" unavoidably also became victims of the liberation struggle.

Mandela's movements remained a secret until he was arrested in August 1962. Together with other MK leaders he stood trial in the so-called Rivonia Trial of 1963. In his defence plea he stated that he had fought his entire life against domination of any kind – both white and black domination. He was subsequently sentenced to life imprisonment and while he was a prisoner on Robben Island, he did a great deal to improve the circumstances of other prisoners. As time passed his incarceration became a matter of international

concern and in the troubled 1980s there were growing demands that he be set free. In 1982 he was transferred to the Pollsmoor Prison.
In 1985 President P.W. Botha offered to set him free on condition that he renounced violence but Mandela was not prepared to compromise; he refused to sacrifice the freedom of black people for his own release. In the late 1980s there were talks between Mandela and representatives of the government (especially with Kobie Coetsee) to pave the way for his release. Nine days after De Klerk's speech on 2 February 1990, in which the ban on the ANC and other liberation organisations was lifted, Mandela walked out of the Victor Verster Prison in Paarl.
During the early 1990s talks were held on drafting a new constitution and after a lengthy negotiation process there was agreement on an interim constitution. In 1993 Mandela and De Klerk were jointly awarded the Nobel Peace Prize. After the election in 1994, Mandela, as leader of the victorious ANC, became the first president of a democratic South Africa.
He died at the age of 95 on 5 December 2013.

Thabo Mbeki at the helm, 1999-2004

As representative of the ANC in exile, established outside the country after its banning in South Africa, Mbeki played an important role in forging ties with white South Africans, including business leaders who wanted to talk to the ANC. During the constitutional negotiations with the De Klerk government Mbeki was part of the ANC negotiation team. Although by the early 1990s at times his influence appeared to have waned, he made his influence felt again before the first democratic election. As Mandela's deputy president, Mbeki was earmarked as the next president.

His managerial skills became of increasing importance after the acceptance of the final constitution in 1996. His "I am an African" speech which he delivered on that occasion made a wide impression and is still quoted today. He was praised for his far-sightedness in influencing financial policy making and for recommending competent individuals like Trevor Manuel for key positions in the Department of Finance.

After Mbeki took over the presidency, transformation was high on the agenda and affirmative action was speeded up considerably. Under his rule concerted efforts were made to ensure fiscal discipline; to cut back state expenditure; and to curb corruption. Despite criticism from communist circles, the new president had good relations with the business sector. Foreign relations enjoyed high priority and Mbeki himself devoted a considerable part of his time to overseas visits. (Indeed, in the last years of his rule he was criticised for the extended periods that he spent out of the country.)

In one respect Mbeki diverged significantly from Mandela's approach. He was less inclined to engage with white South Africans and under him the transformation of South African society enjoyed very high priority. This did not mean that he sought confrontation. On the contrary, he retained firm ties with Afrikaner academics such as Professor Willie Esterhuyse and on occasion referred to the need for the government to win the support of the white middle class. He also met with different Afrikaans groups on several occasions (after he had taken over as president) to discuss issues concerning the Afrikaans language and culture.

However, Mbeki's inclination to regard race as a defining factor on many social issues was conspicuous. His public statement in May 1998 in which he made reference to there being two nations in South Africa – one black and poor, the other white and wealthy – was widely criticised by white economists and political commentators. In comparison to the broader South Africanism which Mandela propounded, Mbeki was more disposed to Africanism.

The contrast between Mandela and Mbeki was striking. Mbeki was by no means a charismatic leader figure; his leadership style, which was often described as autocratic, also aroused far more criticism than Mandela's. Political analyst James Myburgh attributes Mbeki's rise to his creation of a network of personal supporters in influential positions, while independent thinkers within the ANC were completely pushed aside. All important decisions were made within the inner circle of Mbeki's confidants, often at the expense of effective administration. In areas where the president had no input at all, indecisiveness reigned supreme.

A further point of criticism was Mbeki's intolerance towards difference of opinion. Precisely because of the growing centralisation of power under his rule, Parliament began to lose its status as a forum for debate. Mbeki, the master negotiator, displayed a staggering sensitivity to criticism, particularly when it came from the liberal white opposition and the press.

Although his "silent diplomacy" towards Zimbabwe and an unbending opinion on the connection between the HI virus and AIDS brought sustained criticism in South Africa and the outside world, few people denied his ability to propel Africa in a new direction. Most international governments and business leaders held him in high regard. Mbeki was a progressive leader who believed in the advantages of the technological revolution and apparently did not doubt the ability of the new political elite after 1994 to rule the country successfully.

However, he was an extremely competent political manager, negotiator and strategic thinker who preferred to work behind the scenes rather than on the political platform. In the context of nation building he may well not have been as successful as Mandela, partly because he was inclined to overemphasise the inequalities of South African society. Nevertheless, his experience and pragmatism often balanced his shortcomings when important national issues were on the line.

MBEKI: THE NEGOTIATOR

Thabo Mvuyelwa Mbeki was born on 18 June 1942 in Mbewuleni near Idutywa in rural Transkei. He matriculated at St John's College in Mthatha and then studied by correspondence for his degree, followed by a master's degree in economics at the University of Sussex in England.

As the son of two prominent ANC activists, Govan and Epainette Mbeki, he worked underground for the banned ANC in South Africa and also received military and political training in the Soviet Union. Mbeki then worked in the London office of the ANC as political secretary to the president of the ANC, Oliver Tambo, and at the same time served as the ANC's director of information and publicity. As a senior diplomat he worked in various other African countries and in 1975 he became a member of the ANC's national executive committee (NEC).

Despite his links with the Soviet Union Mbeki was neither an ardent communist nor a military leader, but his historical consciousness was shaped by a Marxist interpretation of South African society. According to Mbeki the enslavement of black people was the outcome of an agreement between white Afrikaners and English speakers to ensure that there was a steady flow of cheap black labour. Black people therefore became the "exploited producers". For Mbeki this explanation formed the central theme of South African history.

A specific dualism in Mbeki's political philosophy was part of his enigmatic personality: He was expected to embrace non-racialism as stipulated in the ANC's Freedom Charter, but he was also an Africanist who felt strongly about the promotion of the continent's interests. However, he also showed that he was a practical thinker and was among the ANC leaders who believed that the South African Defence Force (SADF) was far too powerful to be defeated militarily and that diplomatic contacts with influential white people could be to the advantage of the ANC in the long run. Tambo agreed with this analysis and in the early 1980s he instructed Mbeki to co-ordinate the ANC's diplomatic campaign.

One of the party's new strategies was to draw more white South Africans into anti-apartheid campaigns. A meeting of particular importance took place on 13 September 1985 when the ANC met prominent South African businessmen in Zambia. This delegation mainly represented the interests of the organised business world. Very encouraging was the ANC's assurance that it sought peace and was not aiming to nationalise industries. Knowing that Mbeki had never preached Soviet socialism or its Eastern European equivalent apparently put businessmen at ease and made it possible for them to talk to him. Tambo felt that such talks were absolutely necessary and was able to win over sceptics in the party such as Chris Hani.

For the rest of the 1980s Mbeki's secret talks in Britain with influential Afrikaners largely contributed to paving the way for official constitutional discussions that led to the acceptance of a new constitution. During the negotiations between the government and other parties at the Convention for a Democratic South Africa (CODESA), concern arose in the ranks of the ANC over rightwing Afrikaners who did not want to accept the changes. Mbeki allayed these fears by making an agreement with General Constand Viljoen, former head of the SADF, that a future ANC government would recognise the Afrikaners' aspirations for self-determination. In exchange for this, Viljoen undertook to use his influence to see to it that the elections were held peacefully. Although Mbeki had sympathy for the Afrikaners' sentiments, he rejected the idea of an ethnic Afrikaner state (a *volkstaat*) as envisaged by rightwing Afrikaners.

In his discussions with a variety of organised Afrikaner groups after 1994 Mbeki impressed with his intellect and his preparedness to listen to Afrikaners' concerns. He showed understanding of their fears and ideals and Afrikaners accepted the fact that he would give them the necessary space to exercise their ideals, particularly as far as the Afrikaans language and Afrikaans educational institutions were concerned.

Mbeki was appointed as the first deputy president in the government of national unity. After the final constitution was accepted he was the only deputy president. In this capacity he played an increasingly important role in the day-to-day administration of the government. His influence within the party increased markedly and at the end of Mandela's term, Mbeki was the obvious choice as the new president.

The three-party alliance

The three-party alliance was an informal partnership between the ANC, the SACP and the trade union federation COSATU. This implies that SACP and COSATU members can also be members of the ANC and that they both undertake to support the ANC, particularly in elections. The three-party alliance was not formally established at a conference or meeting, but flowed from a series of discussions in 1990. Despite this working relationship each of these three organisations remains essentially autonomous.

In the first ten years after the 1994 election mutual tensions within the alliance often simmered just below the surface. The Growth, Employment and Redistribution (GEAR) programme that replaced the RDP in 1996 evinced great discord between the ANC and its alliance partners. The RDP was aimed at poverty alleviation and was an important ANC election rallying call in the 1994 election. GEAR targeted greater economic growth and the programme was drawn up secretly without proper consultation within the alliance.

The SACP and COSATU argued that the ANC had sacrificed the socialist ideal; that GEAR would be to the detriment of workers' interests; and that it was focused purely on local and international capital. In the light of the country's new and growing middle class, these allegations had an element of truth. Prominent ANC and trade union members such as Cyril Ramaphosa, Mathews Phosa, Tokyo Sexwale and Nthato Motlana soon joined the business world. Some trade union leaders also aspired to managerial positions outside the trade union environment.

Trade union federations increasingly began to accuse the government of being too well disposed towards capitalism in South Africa. In 1998 both Mandela and Mbeki openly confronted left-wing elements of the alliance (the more radical socialists) and demanded that they abide by government policy. Although the muttering about the government's neo-capitalist policy did not cease, there were more than enough members to counteract them and the alliance still appeared solid in the 1999 election.

By 2002 the ANC announced a shift in its economic policy, which would now place the emphasis on the generation of South African capital so that the country was less reliant on foreign investments. The interests of the alliance were once again confirmed when the ANC outlined the important role of the alliance in improving employment opportunities.

A second bone of contention between the partners was the perception that the ANC dominated the alliance. Political analysts differ on this. According to one view the ANC leadership elite concentrated the power in its own hands to control not only the party but the government as well; and that this leadership was also involved in the election of political leaders so that there was no devolution of power to provincial authorities with regard to matters such as health and education. The result was that debate was smothered within the ANC and the wider alliance. Another view is that the ANC leadership was not as powerful as this suggests and that for example it did not enforce its will on the election of provincial premiers.

However, tensions within the alliance remained on important national questions such as the government's policy on HIV/AIDS and the policy towards Zimbabwe. In 2002 Jeremy Cronin, the SACP's deputy head secretary, was on the receiving end of heavy criticism from the government when he suggested that the liberation movements had tended to become bureaucratic after assuming power. When he went even further and drew a comparison between the ANC and the autocratic ZANU-PF party of Zimbabwe, leaders in the ANC called him to order and he had to extend an appropriate apology. However, this was by no means the end of the disagreements.

Later in 2002, shortly before a strike against privatisation organised by COSATU was due to take place, Mbeki expressed sharp criticism of the proposed action. He accused the ultra-left wingers of misusing the democratic order to further their own ends. The small number of workers who eventually took part in the strike indicated something of a defeat for COSATU and the SACP. This incident possibly also discouraged any plans to form a left-wing labour party. Hence, with the general election of 2004, the three-party alliance was still intact.

Minority politics

By 2004 the ANC completely dominated the political scene. In the 1994 election it had already gained what was almost a two-thirds majority and this was pushed up to 66,35% in the 1999 election and 69,6(9)% in 2004. Political commentators regularly expressed criticism over this state of affairs and more generally the unbridled growth of the ANC's political power aroused concern. One study declared categorically that since 1994

South Africans voted according to race, which has made the ANC so powerful that it pays little attention to the interests of minority groups. The dividing line between party and state has become increasingly blurred. There is also another point of view. This claims that South Africa has such a diverse population make-up with, for example, sharp ethnic divisions and an overwhelming number of black people, that a strong opposition could possibly upset political stability.

The opposition virtually disappeared from the political scene. Whereas in 1994 a fifth of the voters cast their votes in favour of the National Party, its support faded to 6,87% in 1999 and 1,65% in 2004. The NNP declined considerably when De Klerk and other prominent leaders withdrew from mainstream politics. Afrikanerdom was divided and the national movement almost ceased to exist. Parties that represented far-rightwing Afrikaners gained less than 1% of the national vote in 1999 and 2004.

Poor leadership was the main reason for the NNP's decline. Marthinus van Schalkwyk, De Klerk's successor, was simply unable to inspire confidence in Afrikaner voters. Shortly before the NNP fused with the Democratic Party (DP) to form the Democratic Alliance (DA), Van Schalkwyk withdrew from the alliance citing his dissatisfaction with the political situation. Crossing the floor by NNP backbenchers to the DA dealt the already weakened party another blow. The writing was on the wall for the NNP when Van Schalkwyk, in an attempt to keep a foot in the Western Cape door, made an election agreement with the ANC prior to the 2004 election. This decision alienated the NNP even further from white voters and the party was virtually wiped out in the election. In 2005, in a small meeting in a hotel in Kempton Park, it officially came to an end.

The DP, which gained less than 10% of the votes in 1994, became the official opposition after 1999. The DA – as the DP became known after its fusion with the NNP – claimed that it could bring more to the table than the NNP, particularly as far as its anti-apartheid record was concerned. Its class base included the wealthy white English-speaking business community; the traditional "liberal" white middle class; and the wealthier urban Indians and coloured people. Tony Leon, the DA leader, was never afraid to lash out at the ANC on a variety of issues. He reached out to Afrikaners and urban black people, but although the DA gained more Afrikaner support than ever before, he did not succeed in gaining meaningful black support.

Mangosuthu Buthelezi's IFP lost ground in every election since 1994. In 1994 the IFP gained 10,5% of the votes, but this support dwindled to 8,58% in 1999 and 6,97% in 2004. The IFP was indeed relegated to an ethnic regional party, centred in KwaZulu-Natal. This means that the chronic violence that arose from the IFP-ANC confrontations of the 1980s and early 1990s decreased appreciably.

The parties that represented a more exclusive African nationalism – the Pan Africanist Congress (PAC) and the Azanian People's Organisation (AZAPO) – fared even worse and could not even manage 1% of the national votes in 1999 and 2004. Poor organisation and leadership as well as the international community's condemnation of racial exclusivity tended to marginalise extremism. Furthermore, the ANC's "broad church" could easily accommodate both supporters of the Freedom Charter (the so-called Charterists) and the Africanists. Supporters of the black consciousness movement apparently also chose to come under the sway of the ANC rather than to support losers at the polls.

Further attempts to form a truly non-racial party included the establishment of the United Democratic Movement (UDM). This party was formed in September 1999 by Bantu Holomisa, former military ruler of the Transkei, and Roelf Meyer who headed the NP's negotiating team at CODESA and subsequently became a member of the ANC. However, this party only gained 3,42% of the national vote in 1999 and 2,28% in 2004.

Another turn of events involved Patricia de Lille, an outspoken member of the declining PAC; in 2003 she broke away to form her own party, the Independent Democrats (ID). In the 2004 election this young party attracted more votes than the NNP. This convinced De Lille that she had to develop a more comprehensive national policy. Her party (in reality an anti-corruption party) began to build an infrastructure in 2004 and received financial support from traditional "white" circles. This gave the ID an advantage over many other minority parties.

Organised labour

With COSATU (in the 1980s an important UDF ally in the struggle to end apartheid) as part of the three-party alliance, one would expect that after 1994 the labour movement, generally speaking, would be in a far more favourable position. The Labour Relations Act of 1995 gave the trade unions enough power to become part of future labour legislation. Organised labour also now had access to parliamentary structures which implied its increased bargaining power. It also took part in the National Economic Development and Labour Council (NEDLAC), which ensured its influence on government policy.

After 1994 most trade unions were represented in the three trade union federations: COSATU; the National Confederation of Trade Unions (NACTU); and the Federation of Unions of South Africa (FEDUSA). Of the three COSATU was by far the most influential, with a membership of 1,8 million. NACTU, with 200 000 members, was more racially exclusive and its membership was comprised largely of black factory workers and manual workers. NACTU was in opposition to COSATU. For the most part, FEDUSA comprised white members, many of whom were white-collar workers.

Despite the apparently favourable conditions, the labour movement did not really flourish in the years after 1994. COSATU, for example, began to lose influence after the ANC government increasingly introduced free-market principles. During the strikes in the early 2000s it even seemed that COSATU had alienated itself from other trade union federations and its disputes with the government over a range of matters did not improve relations.

There were also other reasons for the decline of the labour movement. Financial problems, fraud and corruption played a role but globalisation also took its toll. Free-market institutions benefited more from the impact of globalisation and the ANC government moved increasingly in the direction of this worldwide trend.

Apart from these external factors there were also basic internal reasons that cannot be ignored. After 1994 the labour movement in general began to lose its vitality. According to the sociologist Sakhela Buhlungu this can be put down to the fact that organised workers' initiatives were replaced by a full-time bureaucracy and a national leadership for trade unions. More positions, specifically for black professional people, became available after apartheid and trade union leaders tried to become part of this new corporate culture.

The politics of transformation

In the decade after 1994 the government had mixed success with its efforts to handle the urgent day-to-day issues. The challenges were formidable: The socio-economic position of black people had to be drastically improved, but at the same time economic growth had to be maintained. To remove more than five decades of inequality in the public and private sector was no small task. The government's promise to provide houses, electricity and clean water to poor communities was to a large extent accomplished. During the first five years of its rule it built 40% more houses, while the provision of electricity was increased by 69% and that of water by 47%. And yet population growth and poverty in the years that followed delayed further headway.

Transformation of the civil service

In time, affirmative action in the civil service became one of the government's most controversial and economically disruptive decisions. Its injudicious implementation caused the country untold harm.

Large amounts of money were spent on financing (mainly white) employers to pay retirement packages. By 2002 about 117 000 packages were offered for early retirement. While in 1994 some 44% of civil service positions were held by white people, this dropped to a mere 18% by 1999. Managerial positions were likewise filled by people from previously disadvantaged backgrounds. Transformation applied in this manner led ultimately to a loss of valuable expertise because newly appointed employees often lacked experience.

Restructuring of the judicial system was also introduced because the ANC alleged that the incumbent judges were out of touch with the sentiments of those who had been involved in the liberation struggle. Pressure therefore increased to appoint judges from previously disadvantaged groups.

Economic policy

The ANC's Freedom Charter of 1955 made provision for nationalisation and state ownership of industries. For more than two decades this ideological direction formed the basis of the ANC's economic thinking until it became clear in the late 1980s that communism had failed. Consecutive

ANC policy statements now involved the private sector to work together with government to improve social wellbeing, although nationalisation still remained an option. This aroused bitter opposition from the business sector and other mainstream political parties.

At the important ANC policy congress of 2002, COSATU and the SACP insisted that a policy of radical redistribution of wealth be adopted. However, Mbeki, supported by an influential faction within the ANC (including Trevor Manuel, Alec Erwin and Joel Netshitenzhe), took the viewpoint that the promotion of macro-economic development and the growth of company earnings had to take precedence over redistribution. This economic alignment remained official policy, but not without sustained protest from the left wing.

RDP and GEAR

The Reconstruction and Development Programme (RDP) which was launched by the ANC shortly before the 1994 election was one of the pillars on which the party rested. It was an ambitious, comprehensive national project which made provision for housing, electrification, a public works programme and the extension of health services. However, the RDP was abandoned after two years because the economy had not grown sufficiently to finance the programme. Furthermore, inefficient administration hampered development.

The RDP was replaced by the Growth, Employment and Redistribution (GEAR) programme, which was based on free-market principles with a focus on growth. It projected a growth rate of 3,5% per year and the creation of more than 800 000 new work opportunities in the future. These goals were to be attained by fiscal discipline, new investment initiatives and lowering of rates. However, in the political arena the new initiative heightened the tensions within the three-party alliance considerably because COSATU and the SACP were vehemently opposed to the scrapping of the RDP.

In the beginning of 1997 the signs were there that GEAR was not going to meet expectations. South Africa was in the grip of a recession and could not compete with other developing countries as far as overseas investments were concerned. As had been the case with the RDP, inadequate administrative competence was a limiting factor. In the early 2000s the international climate began to improve and was helped along by the government's sensible macro-economic policy, better growth was achieved. GEAR began to look more viable.

Financial administration

An area in which the ANC government excelled in the period from 1994 to 2004 was that of macro-economic development. The minister concerned, Trevor Manuel, assisted by the accomplished director general of finances, Maria Ramos, developed the ministry into one of the most successful portfolios in the history of modern South Africa.

The budget deficit was reduced from more than 9% in 1993 to 1% in 2002/2003. While the country had a negative per capita income growth under the NP government, this was turned around to an average growth of 2,8%. Debt in the public sector was reduced by more than 10% in the ten-year period. Inflation and interest rates were lowered and the country was highly praised as an upcoming power with a healthy fiscal and monetary policy plus an efficient and proven banking system. Purposeful restructuring of the tax system added to the economic successes achieved since 1994.

The economic progress of black people

The rise of a black middle class after 1994 gave the economy a big boost. In the ten years after apartheid this class grew by about 25% per year. By 2004 black people comprised 11% of the South African middle class, although this figure represented less than 1% of all black people in the country.

For the ANC government it was a priority to empower black people economically and particularly to establish a black capitalist class. At the ANC congress of December 1997 it was decided to embark on a policy of Black Economic Empowerment (BEE) which among other things laid down that traditionally white companies had to make provision for black candidates in their middle and top management. The Employment Equity Act (1998) which determined racial quotas for positions in the public sector, was promulgated almost simultaneously and these requirements were soon extended to the private sector.

BEE was heavily criticised by black and white political and economic analysts as a policy that was only of advantage to a small black elite. They alleged that it was of no benefit at all to the small business sector and did not create more job opportunities. A small number of black politicians who gained access to the business sector were able to pick the fruits of highly advantageous deals.

Defence and the police force

To correct the inequalities of the past became the ANC government's main objective. It was determined that the government and civil service should reflect the racial composition of the country. This was no easy task considering the inexperience of the newly appointed officials. The first cabinet was truly non-racial, but Mandela inherited a civil service in which white men were in the overwhelming majority. To re-organise this body (by affirmative action for example) was high on the list of the new administration's priorities.

Transformation of the armed forces and police presented unique problems. In the case of the army, the interim constitution laid down that there had to be integration of the apartheid era's South African Defence Force (SADF); members of Umkhonto we Sizwe (MK); and those of the PAC's military wing, the Azanian People's Liberation Army (APLA). However, this meant that forces who had been bitter enemies, who had fought one another for decades and differed fundamentally from one another on military matters now had to work together at national level. Initial problems such as dissatisfaction among cadres of the former liberation movements over their treatment soon came to the fore. The new South African National Defence Force was also seriously restrained by budget cuts, while incidents of racism also flared up from time to time.

The South African Police Service (SAPS) became a civil portfolio when the new government took over, and a secretariat for safety and security was introduced in 1996 to manage the day-to-day duties of the police. George Fivaz, an Afrikaner from the former dispensation with an impeccable record, became the first national commissioner. A new innovation was the independent complaints directorate which was to handle complaints from the public about the police service. As in the armed forces, incidents of racism also caused division in the SAPS. Racial inequality persisted for a considerable time. Although two thirds of the force was black, the large majority of officers were white, and the pace of transformation was slow. However, as time passed, this situation began to change. Another nagging problem was the low morale among members of the force.

Local government

Better provision of services at the local level to wipe out the inequalities of the past was another priority for the ANC government. During the apartheid era only white local governments benefited from taxes paid by the business sector. Business undertakings that moved from the central business district into the suburbs lightened the tax load of white urban residents in those areas considerably, to the extent that they were undertaxed. As a result, the government put in place a new tax structure which translated into higher taxes in wealthier suburbs. These people resisted the new measures strenuously and even embarked on rate boycotts.

At the same time the government introduced the Masakhane Project, a public information programme to encourage black communities to pay for municipal services. In the Johannesburg metropolitan area alone, residents' debt for unpaid municipal accounts and taxes had reached about R900 million by the mid-1990s. A system was introduced whereby poorer communities paid a "flat rate" corresponding to their usage. The problem was that coloured people who lived in poor communities – and in some cases comprised the majority there – were excluded. Naturally they protested vehemently about this.

Restructuring at local government level had mixed success. In large cities such as Johannesburg, revenue increased dramatically and healthy financial management made progress possible. Smaller town councils elsewhere in the country could not match this success. There was large-scale deterioration of service delivery and bankruptcy was often the fate of these local authorities. A reassessment of the future of local authorities led to the decision to re-demarcate municipal boundaries. After the 2000 municipal elections, 843 municipal councils were replaced by six metropolitan councils, 241 local councils and 52 district councils.

Redistribution of land

The unequal possession of land in South Africa has deep historical roots. In the past only a very small minority of black people had access to land and land dispossession often occurred. Prior to 1994 white people still owned 84% of the land, while agricultural activity in the homelands was in a pitiful state.

The foundation of the government's land policy after 1994 was land restitution (giving back that which had been taken); the redistribution of land; and the safeguarding of property rights. Legislation placed official focus on all three of these elements. Derek Hanekom, Minister of Land Affairs in the Mandela cabinet, followed a two-part approach. He planned to give land to poor landless people and to assist existing farmers. His aim was to re-divide 30% of the land by 1999, which would mean resettlement of 600 000 peasant farmers. His scheme to pay grants for the acquisition of land for settlement (Settlement Land Acquisition Grant Scheme, or SLAG) soon appeared far too ambitious. Among the obstacles he had to overcome were staff shortages and internal differences on how best to implement transformation. Added to this, land prices rose appreciably after the introduction of the scheme, which meant that restitution became a very cumbersome process. Unused funds began to accumulate.

After the 1999 election Hanekom was left out of the cabinet and the new minister, Thoko Didiza, diverged markedly from Hanekom's directives. In place of the "welfare approach" the emphasis shifted to developing the capacity of existing black farmers. In the face of criticism for the reduced assistance to the poor, Didiza foresaw that within the next 15 years as many as 70 000 commercial farmers would be fully operative. By 2004 it was still too early to pass judgement on the success of this new scheme.

THE ANC GOVERNMENT AND TRADITIONAL LEADERS

After the 1994 election 10 000 traditional chieftains in South Africa exercised a significant influence over communal tribal land. In the 1996 Constitution provision was made for a house of traditional leaders in the different provinces which would have advisory functions.

Although the ANC did not want to accommodate ethnicity and undemocratically chosen leaders within the party, it was careful not to alienate traditional leaders, particularly those who belonged to the Congress of Traditional Leaders of South Africa (CONTRALESA). The influence of these traditional leaders, particularly in the rural areas, could have a bearing on ANC support in elections. For example, the government was not prepared to react to pressure from the IFP to control remuneration to chieftains.

However, by no means all the problems on the powers of traditional leaders were addressed. The complex issues concerning administration and land were still there and many chieftains were dissatisfied with the principles and processes of land distribution. In many cases the boundaries laid down by the new local and district councils cut across those of traditional authorities and many chieftains felt that this was undermining their powers.

Education

The ANC government inherited a school system which reflected ethnicity and racial inequality. Shortly after the 1994 election schools were desegregated and a single school system came into being. This changed the profile of education, but the previously disadvantaged black majority did not derive much advantage from all the changes.

A high percentage of teachers were not fully qualified and the morale in schools was generally low. A culture of learning was absent in many traditionally black schools, which can in part be ascribed to the consequences of the Soweto uprising; the 1976 slogan "freedom before education" was re-echoed. Because many parents saw English as the passport to a proper education and access to good careers, indigenous languages were neglected. This led to a situation whereby many children were unable to fully grasp the necessary skills required for specific subjects.

Funding to schools did indeed improve under the new government, but many schools were still poorly equipped as far as textbooks and other educational aids were concerned. Although more teachers were appointed, the matriculation pass rate and percentage of learners who completed their full school curriculum was still shockingly low. The mathematics pass rate was particularly worrisome.

Sibusiso Bengu, the first Minister of Education after 1994, showed no great initiative in trying to breathe new life into the portfolio, but when Kader Asmal succeeded him, expectations rose. Asmal promised a drastic improvement in the matric pass rate as well as a lowering of illiteracy. He attained a measure of success in both these endeavours and also expanded the educational infrastructure. However, there were still significant shortcomings including a shortage of teachers, particularly in science and mathematics; there was also poor discipline in schools.

Ongoing curriculum changes were characteristic of the new education administration. Curriculum 2005, with outcomes-based education as its basis, was introduced. This approach was aimed at the stimulation of critical thought and purported to be a countermove against mechanical rote learning, which was considered an educational principle derived in the apartheid era. However, many teachers and lecturers could not master the extensive technical vocabulary of the new system and Curriculum 2005 eventually had to be revised.

After 1994, universities, technicons, technical colleges and teacher training colleges were stripped of all racial identification. However, this did not address the imbalances as far as patterns of personnel provision, resources, research output and pass marks were concerned. For example, traditional black universities were still lagging behind and their financial crises were exacerbated by the backlog of students' debt.

The ANC believed that tertiary education should not merely be a privilege accorded to a select few, but at the beginning of the 1990s black students did not yet on a large scale have the admission requirements to attend tertiary institutions. From the late 1990s onwards it became a priority to merge higher-education institutions. According to the government the rationale behind this was to encourage national development in order to enhance the country's global competitiveness. In terms of the National Plan for Higher Education of March 2001 the 36 higher education institutions were reduced to 21 and the 120 colleges to 25.

Health

Weak leadership and various errors of judgement meant that between 1994 and 2004 health was one of the most controversial portfolios. Nkosazana Zuma (later Dlamini-Zuma), Minister of Health in the Mandela government, began well with fresh ideas such as the expansion of primary health care and the restructuring of professional councils. However, the department's programme of building clinics in the rural areas exhausted financial resources to the extent that big hospitals in the cities eventually began to suffer under serious financial cutbacks.

The Minister also made herself unpopular by introducing a compulsory community-service year for medical students in an effort to relieve the shortage of doctors. When this did not have the desired effect Cuban doctors were brought in, but their competence and lack of communication skills were often questioned.

Zuma's handling of the HIV/AIDS crisis was even more controversial. In 1995 she gave approval for the production of a musical comedy *Sarafina II* for which the department granted more than R14 million without the correct tender procedures being followed. Furthermore, with the support of Deputy President Mbeki, Zuma backed the efforts of two Pretoria scientists who claimed that their remedy, Virodene, could treat HIV/AIDS effectively. Although this remedy had not at that stage been tested on humans, Zuma was unwilling to agree that a proven remedy, AZT, be administered to infected pregnant women.

By 1999 this viral disease was spiralling out of control. More than 3,6 million South Africans were HIV positive and HIV/AIDS action groups actively opposed the government's policy. To make matters worse, Mbeki (now president) became involved in the dispute. Under the influence of a revisionist "alternative" scientist, David Rasnick, Mbeki made the claim that it was not only the HI virus that caused AIDS. He referred to the relationship between AIDS and other African illnesses that were linked to poverty. Nor did Zuma's successor, Manto Tshabalala-Msimang, take issue with Mbeki on this controversial opinion, which delayed the effective combating of the sickness even further.

In October 2000 Tshabalala-Msimang gave permission for some hospitals to use a new remedy, Nevirapine. However, by that time South Africa's status as far as health matters were concerned had already taken a serious knock because of its AIDS policy.

The cancer of corruption and crime

As a young democracy South Africa's image had suffered a decided setback because of corruption in all spheres of society and an unacceptably high crime rate. From the outset the new government had committed itself to clamping down on these evils, but by 2004 it did not have much to show by way of results. In 1998 alone, fraud and inefficient management cost the government more than R10 billion. Poor financial control was often the biggest cause of corruption.

The office of the auditor general and the public protector were given powers to curb irregularities. A special unit under the chairmanship of Judge Willem Heath was formed in 1995 to investigate the mismanagement of money. In 1999 a national anti-corruption conference was held and this led to the establishment of a National Anti-Corruption Forum and an appropriate educational programme. As was the case with many other necessary and promising projects, this one was also largely unsuccessful because of a lack of money and staff. Looking at the period until 2004, the Scorpions, a hand-picked investigative unit, apparently had the most success in combating white-collar crime.

One of the most unsettling trends after 1994 was the spiralling incidence of crime which labelled South Africa one of the "crime meccas" of the world. The reasons for the high crime statistics after 1994 are complicated to unravel. Urbanisation and poverty probably contributed, as did ineffective policing. The SAPS was under-financed for a long time and many members of the force were targeted by criminals; low morale made matters even worse. The culture of violence that had arisen during the apartheid years also contributed to the creation of a criminal class of young people. International crime syndicates then used the 1994 to 2004 period to establish themselves in the country, leading to a rapid escalation of crime.

For a long time in the early 2000s crime statistics were withheld from the public, but the figures that were indeed made available told a shocking story. In 1994 approximately 27 000 people were murdered and in 1997 the number of victims dropped only slightly to 25 000. Between 1994 and 1999 more than 500 farmers were murdered on their farms; and in the mid-1990s about 12 000 vehicles were hijacked. In 1998 alone, 49 280 women – according to the number of reported cases – were raped. All this had a significant impact on society. Ordinary citizens had to take a variety of measures to protect their property; emigration increased; and many business concerns vacated the central business areas of big cities such as Johannesburg and Pretoria that had become increasingly derelict. Crime also became a convenient political weapon for opposition parties.

The government set up a variety of programmes to combat crime and there was also co-operation between the government, the business sector and local communities. Despite requests that the police force be managed at provincial level, the government insisted that the system be centralised under national government control.

The inadequate prosecution system was also to blame for the increasing crime rate. The resignation of about a third of the experienced prosecutors after 1994 left the system in the hands of a large number of inexperienced people. In the 20 years after 1980 the number of crimes per every 100 000 people increased by a third and the number of transgressors who were sentenced decreased by a third.

Truth and reconciliation

The Truth and Reconciliation Commission (TRC) gave those who since 1960 had been guilty of human rights violations the opportunity to apply for amnesty. They could have their prosecution waived if they made a full confession of all the incidents in which they were involved. This was part of an attempt to heal the wounds of the past.

Archbishop Desmond Tutu was the chairperson of the TRC and Alex Boraine was his deputy. The TRC held public hearings and the victims were encouraged to share their painful experiences with the audience. These hearings differed from court proceedings in that the cross-examination of witnesses was not permitted, but hearsay evidence was allowed. Three committees, of which the human rights and amnesty committees were the most important, led the proceedings.

The TRC committees were faced with a multitude of challenges. For example, the amnesty committee struggled to differentiate between politically motivated deeds and ordinary criminal offences. In addition, institutional bodies were reluctant to give evidence. For example, no member of the former National Intelligence Service (NIS) applied for amnesty. As far as this was concerned, policemen from the old dispensation were more helpful. Apart from Adriaan Vlok, former Minister of Law and Order, members of the apartheid cabinet did not give evidence to the TRC. Almost half of the ANC members that were involved in human rights violations, applied for amnesty.

On the other hand there were cases where offenders admitted their guilt and registered a public apology. Examples include Brian Mitchell, commanding officer of a police unit which committed offences in KwaZulu-Natal; and Aboobaker Ismael, the ANC head of special operations, who was responsible for the Church Street bomb explosions in Pretoria.

De Klerk registered an apology on behalf of the NP (P.W. Botha refused to give evidence), but the TRC felt that he could have offered more evidence on the bomb explosion that damaged the headquarters of the South African Council of Churches. Furthermore, the State Security Council, which included senior NP politicians, was held responsible for the murders of political activists. However, no evidence of alleged third-force activities came to the fore. Mangosuthu Buthelezi, the IFP leader, was also held responsible for violations of human rights.

The TRC received more than 21 000 statements from victims and amnesty was granted to more than 1000 people. These figures must be seen against the background of estimates that almost two thirds of the murders were not investigated and that important findings were based on untested or unverified evidence. The final report brought to light the activities of the state's security machinery and provided insight into the methods of the former Bureau of State Security (which was widely known as BOSS). Atrocities by not only the agents of the state but also by Inkatha members, white rightwingers, the ANC and other liberation movements, were made public. The latter soured the relations between the TRC and the ANC and at one stage the ANC accused the TRC of trying to "criminalise" the liberation struggle.

Doubts were also expressed about the methodology and the findings of the TRC. One point of criticism was that the TRC was heavily loaded with ANC sympathisers and that other parties were under-represented. Another argument was that there were not enough scientific contributions from academics in the proceedings of the commission. One researcher, Anthea Jeffery of the South African Institute of Race Relations, alleged that the TRC had overlooked incidents in which Inkatha followers were killed on a large scale because the researchers had followed a specific chronology which had excluded these mass deaths.

The historian Hermann Giliomee has questioned the TRC's pronouncement that apartheid was the only causative factor behind the violence. According to him apartheid should be grouped together with other social phenomena such as colonialism and segregation, and should be seen against the background of the Cold War. He also pointed out that the United Nations' description of apartheid as a "crime against humanity" was never qualified by the TRC and that any association with genocide in this definition would be highly inappropriate.

In general, Afrikaners disapproved of the TRC process and many felt that its final report singled out Afrikaners unfairly. The Afrikaans press was particularly critical of the commission's findings. A group of 127 journalists of Nasionale Pers submitted a document to the TRC in which they said, among other things, that the group's newspapers had been an integral part of apartheid's machinery and that morally they felt jointly responsible for what had happened in the name of apartheid. The Afrikaanse Handelsinstituut (AHI) was the only Afrikaans body that acknowledged its support for racial discrimination in the past; and the Nederduitse Gereformeerde Kerk (NG Church) confessed that it was a mistake to approve of apartheid.

Despite the criticism directed at the TRC, it fulfilled an important role. In various ways it served as a cleansing of the nation's morale. According to some commentators the TRC achieved more success in reconciling South Africans than similar commissions in other countries. It is said that the TRC exposed the relentlessness of the apartheid regime in dealing with those who opposed apartheid. In this way public attention was brought to the atrocities that would otherwise have remained hidden.

External relations

South Africa's new role in world politics

The end of apartheid coincided with the collapse of communism and the end of the Cold War. There were great expectations for world peace and progress but the euphoria did not last long. Conflict, especially in the Middle East and in Third World countries, was still by no means resolved.

Whereas the apartheid government had been increasingly marginalised, the new ANC rule was welcomed with open arms throughout the world. South Africa was seen as an intermediate or upcoming power which could play a meaningful role in a wider context. As a celebrated international politician Mandela acted as a political mediator in various conflict-ridden countries, which meant that South Africa on occasion played a key role in peace negotiations. Sometimes the country had to wrestle with tricky decisions such as whether to maintain relations with the People's Republic of China (Beijing) or the Republic of China (Taiwan).

A commitment to human rights was a serious consideration for the ANC as far as its foreign policy was concerned. It felt that South Africa should not belong to any military power bloc and should strive to negotiate for amicable solutions. Nevertheless, Pretoria decided to negotiate with Beijing, which cast something of a shadow on its neutrality. The government's commitment to human rights also brought problems such as the millions of Mozambican refugees who have lived and worked in South Africa for years. They have put pressure on the country's natural resources and compete with local black people to find work. Repatriation and deportation were possible solutions, but this placed the ANC government in a difficult position: Could it act against the residents of a country that had stood by South Africans in the struggle against apartheid?

Another example is that in 1994 the new government expressed its opposition to the export of weapons to countries with undemocratic governments. And yet the weapons industry was such a lucrative source of income for South Africa that the government began to promote such exports with the stipulation that it would "monitor" the process.

As time passed, two groups emerged within the ANC with divergent opinions on foreign policy. The "internationalists" saw human rights as an integral part of external relations, while the "pragmatists" placed the immediate political and economic interests of the country in the foreground. A policy document in 1999 re-emphasised the government's commitment to human rights, but also referred to matters such as security; improvement of living standards; better communication with the outside world; and a more global focus as necessary components of foreign policy.

A new focus: Africa

In 1995 the ANC government announced that in the future Africa would become South Africa's first priority. Accordingly, it began to play a prominent role in trying to bring peace to the continent. South Africa was involved in various capacities in conflicts in Lesotho, Mozambique, Rwanda and the Democratic Republic of the Congo. It also supported Tanzania in the floods of 1998 and neighbouring Mozambique when it was hit by floods in 2000. The South African business sector was keen to support this Africa policy in order to find new markets and trade did indeed increase by about R10,9 billion in 1994 to R25,3 billion in 1998.

Initially, the new government acted cautiously in its role as a leading state in Africa, but gradually it began to gain more confidence and on several occasions acted on behalf of African interests, for example in requesting that it be given a permanent seat in the UN security council. However, South Africa's leading role did not go unchallenged. In the mid-1990s relations between South Africa and Nigeria were tense when the Nigerian head of state, General Sani Abacha, violated human rights and democracy in that country. South Africa exercised great pressure on Nigeria, but with little success. However, relations improved again when General Olusegun Obasanjo introduced democratic government.

Mandela also experienced opposition from some of the countries of the Southern African Development Community (SADC) when he suggested certain restructuring of the organisation and punitive measures against member states that were not ruled according to democratic principles.

Limited resources and inadequate infrastructure in other countries made South Africa's leadership role difficult, but in terms of a 1998 white paper the country nevertheless remained committed to providing help elsewhere in Africa. South Africa was also determined to continue playing its role as peacemaker. Its leading position was also apparent in its role in the establishment of the African Union (AU), the successor of the Organisation for African Unity in 2002. Mbeki was elected as chairperson of the AU and South Africa has since housed the Pan-African Parliament in Midrand.

When South Africa became part of the SADC in 1994 its role in the development of the security and infrastructure of the region became even more important. The country was involved in eleven protocols including those on water resources, transport, trade and communication. At the SADC summit conference in 1996 the development of a free-trade area within the next ten years was envisaged. Trade with southern Africa comprised about 90% of the trade with the entire continent. Regional resources would be combined and developed as an entity, for example the Highland water scheme in the mountains of Lesotho. In addition, South Africa also had trade agreements with individual countries in the region.

Regional security appeared to be a more testing matter than expected when South Africa, in accordance with SADC goals, became involved in the Lesotho conflict of September 1998. Although peace was eventually restored, South African troops had to remain in Lesotho for seven months.

The situation in Zimbabwe tested South Africa's diplomatic ingenuity to the full. The violation of human rights by the government of President Robert Mugabe was widely criticised and the results of the parliamentary election of June 2000 were questioned – especially by Western countries. Instead of criticising the Mugabe government openly, Mbeki and his cabinet followed a policy of so-called "silent diplomacy" and chose to work behind the scenes. This policy brought little in the way of tangible results and the West, the white opposition in South Africa, and a number of high-profile South Africans (including some black leaders) often criticised the president and the government.

The ambivalence of the country's position must perhaps be understood in the context of its complex diplomatic ties with Africa and the West. Some African states are inclined to show solidarity towards fellow Africans even if their leaders are corrupt, rather than subject themselves to Western pressure. In a bid to show that it was not pro-Western, the South African government felt obliged to avoid openly criticising a respected African leader such as Mugabe, a vigorous critic of Britain and the USA.

THE AFRICAN RENAISSANCE

When Thabo Mbeki became president, South Africa had already established itself as an economic power in Africa and a facilitator in regional disputes. Mbeki, with his wide experience of international diplomacy, saw a more comprehensive role for his country in Africa. In Parliament in June 1997 he outlined the concept of an African renaissance – and since then various interpretations and definitions of this have been forthcoming. Some interpretations, mainly those by black academics, take a more exclusively Afrocentric stance. Mbeki's ideas, in contrast, were more inclusive Africanistic, with a broader field of vision so that they were acceptable in international circles.

The African renaissance is rooted in African tradition and the legacy of pre-colonial times. Some intellectuals have also linked it to the *ubuntu* philosophy which emphasises common humanity and interdependence between people. However, Mbeki's idea goes even further than this and incorporates modern statesmanship as well as technological and economic development. Against the background of underdevelopment in many parts of Africa, South Africa's role becomes even more significant. A sponsorship from Engen Oil provided great assistance in initiating upliftment projects, and companies such as Anglo-American, Gencor and Shoprite Checkers extended their activities to other African countries.

An integral part of the African renaissance is the New Partnership for Africa's Development (NEPAD), a development plan in which Mbeki also played a key role. NEPAD is based on the view that if Africa wants to benefit from the growth of the world economy it must create better infrastructure and it needs stable leadership. Accordingly, African countries need liberal constitutions to spread a culture of democracy. The South African government is strongly linked to NEPAD despite misgivings in some circles about whether there is the necessary political will to give momentum to the project. It is often said that Mbeki's trepidation to criticise the Mugabe government openly was detrimental to the development of NEPAD. One political analyst noted in August 2003 that Africa's debt crisis has in fact grown worse since NEPAD's introduction.

South Africa's relations with the West

After 1994 South Africa was still dependent on trade relations with the USA and Europe. Western ties therefore remained in place despite the country's focus on Africa. The USA saw South Africa as the major player in Africa even though the country's strategic value after the end of the Cold War was no longer of cardinal importance. Financial assistance to the value of $212 million in 1994 and a promise of a further $500 million per year for the next four years thereafter was an indication of South Africa's importance for the USA. Through an initiative promoted by Al Gore and Thabo Mbeki in 1995, the American congress passed legislation that it would reward democratic African states with market-oriented economies by, for example, giving them special trade preferences.

Trade with the European Community (EC) made up more than 40% of South Africa's trade, while in contrast the EC's trade with South Africa was less than 2%. Therefore, the country's bargaining power was not strong enough at all times to broker favourable agreements with the European Union (EU). Nor could South Africa succeed in becoming a full member of the Lomé convention which granted certain trade and development partnerships to some countries in Africa, the Pacific Ocean and the Caribbean. Nevertheless, in March 2009 it was able to secure a free-trade agreement which led to the Trade and Development Co-operation Agreement (TDCA) between the EU and South Africa.

A young democracy under review

After ten years of democracy the critical question posed in 2004 was: Is the country a better place than it was in 1994? Such a comparison will of course reflect the political standing of people before and after the dramatic surrender of power.

In an attempt to rid South African society of racial inequality and the legacy of apartheid, the ANC government's point of departure was to create a unified country. True democracy brought equality, opportunities and freedom for all South Africans. Also included were freedom of the press, freedom of expression and a constitution that guaranteed the individual's basic rights.

As far as service delivery is concerned, the state expanded access to social services to a great many South Africans. In the aftermath of 1994, more than 1,4 million subsidised houses were either built or were in the process of being built. Furthermore, 8,4 million poor South Africans received access to running water and 3,8 million were given access to electricity. And yet it was precisely service delivery at local level, which was supposed to correct the inequalities of the past, which remained inadequate and became the government's Achilles heel as far as the running of the country was concerned.

On the other hand, with regard to economic growth, financial and monetary policy, in its first ten years the new government was nothing less than impressive. However, macro-economic achievements did not make up for structural shortcomings; the reality is that unemployment remained a problem and a large percentage of rural black people still lived in poverty.

While the country's economic growth encouraged investments, South Africa still could not compete with other developing countries. One of the important reasons for this was the lack of skills. The education system was apparently unable to equip people with the necessary basis on which they could be trained in specific career paths.

Added to this, the ANC followed a transformation policy that was inflexible and appeared to be applied without any discretion. To observers, the implementation of this policy across the board in civil service positions looked like a simple replacement of white people by black people. This also spilled over into sports teams for which quotas were introduced, and into the private sector, where certain requirements were laid down. The lack of expertise and specific skills due to the replacement of experienced personnel with those who were often poorly qualified and/or inexperienced people from disadvantaged communities, led to poor service delivery.

Black empowerment and affirmative action made it possible for black professional people to move into top positions. A large number of qualified (mostly white) people, including many Afrikaans speakers, began to leave the country because they could see no future for themselves in South Africa. There was talk of the Afrikaner diaspora.

The concerted effort to achieve national unity began to lose momentum after Mandela left the political scene. The "Mandela magic" disappeared and his successor's priorities were different. It can perhaps be said that Mbeki was as distant as Jan Smuts had been more than 50 years earlier; he too gave the impression that South Africa's problems had become too small for him. Mbeki's leadership ability is sometimes questioned and so is his government's capacity to deal with burning issues such as HIV/AIDS, crime and corruption. Without question Mbeki played an important role in the country's progressive economic policy; he also had a vision to elevate the entire continent through the African renaissance and NEPAD. But was he in a position to motivate the people of the country to strive towards a common national goal? By 2004 it appeared that South Africa was still a divided society.

By 2004 it was clear that the ANC had not yet transformed itself from a liberation movement to a national government. The dividing line between the governing party and the state was in reality beginning to fade with the ANC increasingly attempting to centralise its power. Corruption, agreements with countries with poor human rights records and a culture of self-enrichment increasingly placed the ANC government in a poor light.

These and other issues concerned some South Africans. Was the Mbeki era only a teething period after the euphoria of the Mandela years? The "rainbow nation" moved forward to meet the second decade of democracy with expectation, but this was tinged with uncertainty.

24
The troubled teens: South African democracy, 2004-2013

Jan-Jan Joubert

The years 2004 to 2013 can be compared with an adolescent's rebellious stage – this was the tenth to the nineteenth year of the democratic dispensation in South Africa. Growth, growing pains and uncertainty were the order of the day. With the security of a parental home deprived of a back-up state, there was a great deal of uncertainty over whether the country would eventually be successful, with various scenarios that might develop – some positive, others negative.

The period was characterised by a reasonably stable economy despite the worldwide depression after 2007. At a political level there was the most serious infighting yet in the country's history within government circles, and growing questions on social inequality. The rise of two populist leaders, Jacob Zuma and Julius Malema, did not help to curb the governing ANC's decline. Unrest orchestrated by the poor who could see how the fruits of democracy were benefiting only a select few, gave rise to the term "service delivery protest".

As far as opposition politics was concerned, the National Party, which had been the political home of most Afrikaners, came to an ignominious end; a new party arose from the "struggle" ANC; and most opposition voters found refuge in the liberal values of the Democratic Alliance (DA) under leadership of Helen Zille.

Political upheavals in government circles

The result of the 2004 election did little to prepare South Africans for the power game that was to follow. For the first time the ANC gained more than two thirds of the votes and with 69,69% won no less than 279 seats in the National Assembly. The DA was second with 50 seats. This meant that if it saw fit to do so, the ANC was free to make changes to the constitution, although President Thabo Mbeki gave the undertaking (and kept his word) that there would not be large-scale constitutional change.

Furthermore, the ANC gained a clear majority in seven of the nine provinces, and ruled the other two by means of coalition agreements (in KwaZulu-Natal with the Minority Front and in the Western Cape with the New National Party). For the first time all nine provinces had ANC premiers.

Time would show that the ruling ANC functioned like a duck on a pond. While the election results made it seem that the duck was cleaving tranquilly through the water, the internal dissent meant that its feet were kicking frantically beneath the surface. The catalyst that exposed the disunity was an investigation carried out by the special crime prevention unit, the Scorpions, into the activities of a controversial Durban businessman, Schabir Shaik. Shaik persuaded people to do business with him on account of what he called his "political connections" – a term he coined to show that his friendship with leaders of the liberation struggle would ensure that business associates who worked with him would win tenders, particularly in view of the regulations on black economic empowerment.

The key to Shaik's connectivity, as he put it, was his close friendship with Jacob Zuma, who had been the country's deputy president since 1999. On 2 June 2005, following a year-long investigation, Judge Hilary Squires found Shaik guilty on two charges of corruption and three of fraud. He appealed, but was finally found guilty and sentenced to a gaol term of 15 years. Nothing of the kind occurred. Within two years Shaik was released on the pretext that he was terminally ill and virtually on his deathbed. His extravagant lifestyle, ongoing excursions and regular participation in sport made a mockery of his so-called terminal sickness and was widely put down to his "connectivity". This did not, however, lead to any attempt on the part of the South African government to show that the combating of corruption was a matter of serious concern.

The Shaik judgment potentially held grave repercussions for Zuma. South African legislation to combat corruption is among the strictest in the world. It lays down that anyone who is involved in corrupt acts, or who can reasonably be expected to know of such acts but does not report them, is liable to prosecution. The judge's pronouncement made it clear that Zuma and Shaik's relationship played a big role in Shaik's conviction.

To a significant extent Shaik had supported Zuma financially and used his alleged hold over the deputy president to persuade entrepreneurs to invest their money in his projects.

This provided Mbeki with an opportunity to take action. On 14 June 2005, in a sensational speech in Parliament, he dismissed Zuma as deputy president. However, what was intended to lead to Zuma's downfall led instead to Mbeki's demise. Mbeki made three fatal political errors with Zuma's dismissal. In the first place, more than a week passed between Mbeki's first indication that he planned to fire Zuma and the day on which he actually put his plan into action. His hesitation gave Zuma and his supporters the opportunity to plan and regroup to launch their counter-attack against Mbeki.

Secondly, the ANC's major internal challenge since 1994 was that it was impossible to suddenly provide a better life for all its people. Realistically speaking, given the gap in the standard of living in the country and the limited resources available to the government, nobody could do this. The ANC had created the expectation of greater improvements than were possible in practice. This led to a large number of disillusioned people. Zuma could now express their frustrations in a populist manner because as someone who had been dismissed from his post he was no longer co-responsible for the government's failures. He was thus a standard bearer and a gathering place for those who were dissatisfied.

In the third place, although Zuma was fired as deputy president, he remained a member of the ANC. He could therefore take Mbeki on within the structures of the party, rather than having to build up his own party.

The result was a political street fight in the ANC. For the next two years, until the election of party leaders at Polokwane in December 2007, the ANC's internal unity was torn asunder by quarrels the like of which were unprecedented in the history of South African party politics. There were now two main groupings in the ANC which confronted one another. The division was more or less as follows: Mbeki could rely on the support of the elected top leaders; the business sector; the black middle class; the cabinet; the majority of ANC branches where Xhosa speakers predominated; and the branches in parts of the country where white people predominated; and those who believed that Zuma had too little academic training to lead the country.

Zuma could rely on the support of those who wanted leadership positions but had not yet made the grade; the trade unions and communists;

the majority of ANC branches in predominantly Zulu-speaking and Indian parts of the country (ANC branches in predominantly coloured areas were divided between him and Mbeki); and those who thought Mbeki was too refined and "distant" to lead the country.

For two years, between 2005 and 2007, ANC-supporting branches, families and neighbourhoods were torn apart by this conflict. Eventually at the ANC leadership elections in December 2007, Zuma drew 61% of the votes and Mbeki 39%. There were a number of reasons why Zuma won:

- Because of his non-involvement in the government he could exploit the shortcomings of the state at every opportunity, and the idea took root that he would manage things better despite the fact that he was not actively proposing any alternatives.
- Because he had no government duties to perform he had enough free time at his disposal to travel throughout the country and run an efficient election campaign.
- Because COSATU and the South African Communist Party (SACP) opposed Mbeki's macro-economic policy (known as GEAR, see chapter 23) they made their structures available to Zuma and at their meetings created a stage for him from which he could launch his campaign.
- Zuma used his many court appearances (see the box on Zuma on p. 530) exceptionally well to drum up mass support. Excitable crowds held night vigils outside the court buildings and he often addressed them after his hearings.
- Zuma conducted a populist campaign, for which his relaxed, easy-going personality prepared him perfectly. His talent for singing meant that he made the controversial song "Awuleth' umshini wami" (Bring my machine gun) his own. It was recorded on CD and became a hit – a dynamo which unleashed great energy for his campaign.
- His very effective use of ethnic politics (he marketed himself as "100% Zulu Boy") ensured that he enjoyed overwhelming support in Zulu-speaking parts of the country such as KwaZulu-Natal and Mpumalanga. At the Polokwane leadership elections no less than 99% of the ANC delegates from KwaZulu-Natal had the mandate of their branches to support Zuma.

- His supporters were hungry for success and worked hard from branch to branch to run an excellent campaign.

There are also various reasons why Mbeki lost:
- Because of his position as head of state, all the shortcomings of the government and public service were attributed to him personally – to Zuma's advantage.
- Because he was overseas so often, he lost pace with trends inside the country and was unable to launch an efficient campaign against Zuma. He was destined to learn the same political lesson as General Jan Smuts learnt some 60 years previously: absentee landlords gather no crops.
- His supporters were so out of touch with the spirit of the times in the country that right up until the end they were convinced that Mbeki would win.
- His detached attitude towards the SACP and COSATU aggravated leaders such as Dr Blade Nzimande (SACP) and Zwelinzima Vavi (COSATU); they turned against him personally and criticised his GEAR policy.
- Mbeki's more reserved personality meant that he had no counter against Zuma's populism. People experienced him as being detached and haughty.
- Mbeki did not have blocs of supporters like Zuma's Zulu voters, the communist voting bloc and trade union votes. This proved damaging at Polokwane.
- Many of Mbeki's supporters were in comfortable positions of power and were not as hungry for victory as Zuma's supporters were. As a result, they did not actively canvass for support, going from ANC branch to branch like Zuma's supporters did.
- Mbeki could not escape the image of the villain in the piece. For example, Zuma's supporters firmly believed that his many court appearances were part of a plot hatched by Mbeki and other powerful politicians to oust Zuma from a possible presidency.

The Polokwane result placed the ANC in an impossible situation – there were two power blocs within the party. Mbeki was the head of the government and Zuma the head of the ruling party, but between them there were serious differences.

After a decidedly troubled few months, the ANC's national executive committee announced in September 2008 that Mbeki no longer enjoyed the ANC's confidence and on Heritage Day, 24 September 2008, Mbeki resigned. Kgalema Motlanthe succeeded him as president.

A year later, Mbeki's resignation led to the most serious split in the ANC in about 50 years – indeed the worst split since the establishment of the PAC in 1959. A new party, the Congress of the People (COPE) was born. COPE won 7% of the votes in the 2009 election. As for the ANC, in this election its percentage of the votes dropped from 69% to 65% and it lost control of the Western Cape, which nipped ANC plans to devise new provincial borders in the bud.

After the election, Zuma was elected as president with Motlanthe as his deputy. There was frequent uncertainty about government policy, with Zuma trying to keep his diffuse group of supporters together. The glue that had held them together was their opposition to Mbeki. With Mbeki out of the picture, they were no longer working in unison and it was difficult for Zuma to maintain unanimity.

PRESIDENT JACOB ZUMA

Jacob Gedleyihlekisa Zuma was born on 12 April 1942 in Nkandla, Zululand, and was inaugurated as the fourth president of a democratic South Africa in 2009. His second given name, Gedleyihlekisa, can be translated from Zulu as "he that will mislead you with a smile". According to his supporters this was merely coincidental; those who oppose him say it was prophetic.

Zuma had a rural education and his family's dire poverty demanded that he herd the cattle rather than attend school. He enjoyed very little formal education and as a youth went to Durban to make his own way in life. In the city his eagerness to learn and friendly nature enabled him to improve his level of literacy. He worked during the day, studied at night, and became involved in the trade union movement.

In 1959, at the age of 17 he joined the ANC. In 1962 he became a member of the ANC's armed wing, Umkhonto we Sizwe (MK) – translated as the Spear of the Nation – and in 1963 a member of the SACP. He was taken into custody at Zeerust in 1963 on a charge that he had collaborated with others in an attempt to overthrow the government. He served a ten-year gaol term on Robben Island until 1973. While in prison he formed close ties with the later head of state, Nelson Mandela.

After his release, Zuma was again busy with trade union matters and he joined the banned ANC. In 1975 he left South Africa and became involved in the armed struggle from outside the country. This involvement and his leading role in the ANC's intelligence and espionage sections later stood him in good stead in his political career.

In 1990 the ANC was unbanned and Zuma rose quickly through the ranks in the party's KwaZulu-Natal structures. At the time of the 1994 elections he was the provincial leader of the ANC and the party's candidate for the premiership. In the 1994 elections in KwaZulu-Natal the ANC lost to the Inkatha Freedom Party (IFP), but Zuma became a member of the provincial council (MPC) and was included in the provincial cabinet as Minister of Economic Development. From 1994 to 1999 Zuma and Dr Frank Mdlalose of the IFP earned high praise for the way they defused the long-standing violence between the IFP and the ANC in the province.

In 1999 President Thabo Mbeki appointed Zuma as deputy president of the country. However, by about 2002 the two had begun to clash. When Zuma's friend and financial advisor Schabir Shaik was found guilty of fraud and corruption, it became clear that the national prosecuting authority would charge Zuma with the same crimes Shaik had been guilty of. Mbeki therefore dismissed Zuma.

From 2005 to 2009 Zuma was regularly involved in court cases. Not only was he charged with fraud and corruption, but in a separate court case he was accused of raping a considerably younger HIV-positive daughter of a former friend. Although he was found not guilty of rape, in his evidence he said that he had showered thoroughly to avoid the risk of infection with the virus, which many people felt was proof that he was ignorant. This did his reputation a great deal of harm.

In 2007 Zuma was elected as leader of the ANC. In 2009, in a highly controversial manner, the national prosecuting authority decided to drop the charges of fraud and corruption against him, and after the 2009 election he was appointed president of the country.

As president, Zuma's controversial behaviour continued and this was the direction which his government was destined to follow – generally unpredictable because of the absence of a coherent ideology and ideal on the part of the leader.

Zuma's often ethnic-driven worldview found expression in regular assertions such as that it was not customary for black people to own dogs; that imprisonment was not the African way; and his negative references to "clever black people" (educated black people). He was also continually involved in court cases over policy decisions, his personal life, and cartoons which he did not take kindly to.

Nevertheless, at the Mangaung national conference in Bloemfontein in December 2012 he was re-elected as ANC leader with a majority of 75%.

In the relative policy hiatus that resulted, a new voice was raised, that of Julius Malema, leader of the ANC Youth League (ANCYL). With his inflammatory rhetoric to crowds of cheering supporters, he made a number of demands, including the nationalisation of mines and that agricultural land be taken from farmers and redistributed to subsistence farmers. Malema, a resident of Limpopo, joined the ANC at the early age of nine years and wrote his matric at 21 years old. In 2001 he was elected as national leader of the ANC-affiliated Congress of South African Students (COSAS) and in 2008 as leader of the ANCYL.

Malema's fiery outspokenness on explosive issues made him highly popular among some, and feared by others. His insulting remarks about opposition leaders and racially based speeches against white South Africans heightened his prominence. When the internal structure of the 2009 Zuma government became increasingly divided and directionless, Malema was gradually regarded as a potential future ANC leader and president of the country, although some critics felt that his fiery and sometimes ill-considered outspokenness would eventually bring him down.

Poor communities, who were disappointed that their living circumstances had not improved more rapidly, increasingly blamed the badly managed ANC-controlled municipalities for poor service delivery, and public resistance escalated countrywide. Violence, vandalism and loss of life characterised these protests. The ANC therefore lost more support and in the municipal elections of 2011 it dropped back to 63%.

By 2012 Malema had become too great an embarrassment for the ANC and he was expelled from the party. Charges of fraud and gangsterism stared him in the face and because of tax evasion his property was put up for sale. In 2013 he announced plans for the formation of his own political party, the Economic Freedom Fighters – a typically populist next step in a colourful political career.

Political opposition

The 2004 election was the death knell for the once powerful National Party and in 2005, after ninety years, the party disbanded. The party leaders went to the ANC and their voters turned to the DA. Under the leadership of Helen Zille the DA's support grew from 12% in 2004, to 16% in 2009, and 23% in 2011.

HELEN ZILLE

Helen Zille was born in Johannesburg on 9 March 1951. Her parents were refugees from Nazi Germany who settled in South Africa.

From early in her life, Zille was involved in the liberal opposition to the apartheid system and helped the legendary stalwart, Helen Suzman, and the Progressive Party to campaign for votes in the Houghton constituency.

From 1974 she was political reporter for the newspaper *The Rand Daily Mail*, and proved an outspoken critic of the apartheid government. Zille was the journalist who revealed that the black consciousness leader Steve Biko had died as a result of injuries inflicted by the security police, and not because of a hunger strike as the government claimed. This and other political disclosures made her well known.

In the 1980s she continued to fight against apartheid and was an active member of the Black Sash (which came to the assistance of uprooted black people) and the End Conscription Campaign (which was vehemently against compulsory national service).

In 1996, as chairperson of the management committee of The Grove Primary School in Cape Town, she gained prominence yet again when the school won a protracted and extremely important court case against the government, and as a result ensured that schools retained the right to have an input in the appointment of staff.

In 1999 Zille, a member of the Democratic Party (DP) which in 2000 became the Democratic Alliance (DA) was elected to the Western Cape legislature, where she served from 1999 to 2001 as an MEC (a provincial minister) for education. In this post she gained high praise and her popularity increased.

In 2006 Zille was elected as mayor of Cape Town. With the DA's victory, for the first time since democratisation, the ANC was voted out of a municipal constituency. As mayor, Zille consolidated her image as a fearless campaigner for a clean government, free of corruption; in this she was in sharp contrast to the ANC.

In 2009 Zille became premier of the Western Cape. This was the first time that the ANC was unseated in a provincial constituency.

In the municipal election of 2006 the Independent Democrats (ID) came to power in several rural Western Cape municipalities. In Cape Town the ID initially worked together with the ANC, but later switched its allegiance to the ruling DA. After the parliamentary election of 2009, in which the ID lost ground from seven seats to four, negotiations were started to fuse the party with the DA. The negotiations were concluded in

2010 and virtually all the ID members joined the DA. Patricia de Lille, ID leader, was then nominated as the DA candidate for Cape mayor and in the municipal election of 2011 was elected with a large majority of more than 60% as Cape Town mayor.

In 2011 COPE drew a mere 3% of the votes. It seemed as if a promising opposition project was on the point of unravelling. This was a great disappointment for COPE supporters, who thought this party could perhaps present a stable opposition under black leadership. Two established ANC leaders, Mosiuoa Lekota and Mbhazima Shilowa were the initial leaders. However, they clashed, which weakened the party.

In 2013 the widely respected black consciousness leader and former rector of the University of Cape Town, Mamphela Ramphele, also established a new party, Agang (which means "we build"). The party wants to strive for a more active citizenry and has made much hue and cry about the ANC's high level of corruption.

There were strong indications that the South African political scene might develop into one in which two parties were dominant, but those who attempt to predict the South African political future usually burn their fingers.

The economy

From 2004 to 2007 the South African economy enjoyed the fruits of a careful economic policy, with a growth rate that increased to 6,5% in 2007. The country's policy to live within its means and avoid falling into a debt trap, was the basis of its success. The state's increased revenue from taxes was largely used for poor relief by the payment of various grants to the most vulnerable part of the population.

This well-considered policy was continued after 2007, but any country is to a certain degree also subject to world trends. With its fairly open economy South Africa could not remain unscathed by the worldwide recession in the wake of particularly the USA's ill-advised macro-economic policy which from 2007 cast a shadow over the world. South Africa's growth rate dropped to −1,7% in 2009, although by 2011 it had recovered to 4,5%.

A number of factors contributed to the stronger than expected performance of the economy:

- A careful economic policy with reasonably low state spending; decreased state debt; and a fairly small budget deficit.
- A strictly regulated banking sector.
- A strong gold price.
- A growing black middle class with new expendable income and a large need for consumer goods.
- A fairly stable currency.
- Exceptionally good agricultural conditions.
- Relative isolation from world markets; Africa was, relatively speaking, affected less by the recession than the rest of the world.

However, there were also danger signs for the South African economy:

- The country's unemployment figure in 2010 of between 24% and 42% (depending on which definition of unemployment is used) was indeed lower than the few years previously, but was still frighteningly high and the better economic growth rate did not mean that enough work opportunities were being created. A rigid wage structure and employment restrictions contributed to this.
- South Africa was still one of the countries with the greatest inequality between rich and poor in the world as measured by the Gini coefficient. Between 1994 and 2011 this inequality grew worse because enterprising people grasped the opportunity of open markets while less endowed people lost the protection of closed markets: South Africans now had to compete with the entire world. The strong ones flourished while the weak grew more wretched.
- With more people receiving grants than taxes being paid, there was concern over whether the payment of grants and allowances would eventually be impossible to sustain.
- One of the reasons for low state spending was a neglect of the upkeep of infrastructure. Particularly as far as roads and power stations were concerned, the situation grew so bad that more toll roads became necessary and the cost of electricity increased dramatically – with significant implications for consumers.
- There was concern about the continued availability of highly trained and experienced managers because of the government's racially based implementation of affirmative action; and the resultant exodus of highly skilled people to other parts of the world began to take its toll.

- International companies were worried about the possibility of nationalisation and the potential impact of black economic empowerment on the share-holding in their South African affiliates. This had a negative effect on overseas investment in South Africa.
- The perception that corruption, poor management and tender fraud were becoming the order of the day was not adequately addressed by strong action on the part of government. In this respect the ANC's policy of cadre deployment as a sub-division of the National Democratic Revolution (NDR) (see below) played a significant role.

The worldwide depression placed the economic pressure cooker in South Africa under ever increasing strain. Unemployment increased, in part because of the rigid labour legislation mentioned above. The crux of the matter was that the South African underclass is not to be found among the poorly paid working class. The true South African underclass is the unemployed, outside the remit of the trade unions, and thus often in direct opposition to the basic core of any trade union mandate, which is to protect the interests of its paid-up membership.

In addition, the trade union COSATU'S close relationship with the government gave the general impression that COSATU no longer opposed governmental authority; instead it had itself become the most powerful authority in the land. Furthermore, COSATU has begun to invest trade union money in companies and in this way has gained an interest in companies' profitability – inherently incompatible with the basic focus which trade unions are supposed to espouse, which is to work towards higher wages and better (but more costly) fringe benefits.

This situation is specifically identifiable in the mining sector. Mineworkers realised this and started to search for an alternative to the COSATU-affiliated National Union of Mineworkers (NUM). An increasing number of mine workers began to join a new populist trade union, the Association of Mineworkers and Construction Union (AMCU) which demands far higher wage increases. This caused the political temperature in the mining industry to rise.

In August 2012 on Lonmin's Marikana platinum mine near Rustenburg the situation began to escalate out of control; by the middle of the month there were already ten deaths including mine workers and members of the police force who were at the scene. On 16 August 2012 AMCU-supporting mine workers gathered on a nearby *koppie*. According to the police, whose version is seriously questioned by other observers, some of the workers were armed and threatened to attack the police, who then fired on the workers, killing 34 of them. This was the greatest number of deaths due to a single police intervention in South Africa since the Sharpeville shooting in 1961.

Although the extent of the deaths jolted the country back to its senses and the parties involved in the mining dispute reined themselves in, the South African Revenue Services (SARS) estimated that because of the tension on the mines, the country had lost R11 milliard in taxable revenue. The mining industry stared a tension-filled, uncertain future in the face.

As if the uncertainty on the mines was not enough, a second important sector, namely agriculture, was rocked by unprecedented unrest at the end of 2012. The Western Cape wine farmers were in the eye of the storm which began at De Doorns near Worcester. For many years wine farmers have employed temporary labour at harvest time; these workers arrived from all parts of the country to take advantage of the opportunity to earn a daily wage. With time, fewer returned to their original homes and instead squatted in poverty-stricken informal settlements near small towns – such as those on the outskirts of De Doorns. When the 2012 harvest time came around, these squatters used the temporary indispensable nature of their labour to demand wage increases of more than 100%, which the local farmers refused to pay.

The Western Cape ANC which sensed an opportunity to undermine the DA-controlled provincial government, spurred workers on. Violence, arson, intimidation and vandalism became the order of the day and only subsided in February 2013 when the minimum wage in the agricultural sector countrywide was increased from R69 per day to R105 per day. Organised agriculture reacted by saying that farmers would have to dismiss workers to be able to pay the higher wages, and it was clear that farming had entered a dangerous and unknown terrain.

By 2010 South Africa had joined the already established economic bloc known as BRIC to extend it to what is now BRICS, comprising Brazil, Russia, India, China and South Africa. This was an attempt by South Africa to find new import and export markets outside the country's traditional trading partners like the USA and the European Union. More emphasis was also placed on breaking new ground in Africa as a market for South African products. These developments meant that in 2012, despite being in the midst of a worldwide depression, South Africa was able to maintain an economic growth rate of 2,6%.

Black economic empowerment

After 2004 the government moved ahead forcefully with its policy of black economic empowerment (BEE) in its efforts to empower black people economically, and more specifically, to create a black capitalist class. The South African constitution includes an interesting faux pas which in the period after 2004 was destined to have an enormous impact on the everyday life of South Africans. Although non-racialism and equality form the moral basis of the 1996 Constitution, recognition is also given to more than three centuries of inequality and unequal opportunities. The constitution compels the government to set this matter right by implementing a structured system to the express benefit of South Africans of colour, specifically black people.

The Mbeki government made a determined foray into affirmative action by trying to ensure that the composition of, among others, as many occupations, sports teams and student numbers at universities were representative of the racial composition of the population, with less emphasis on expertise. At the level of the economy, this endeavour found expression in the policy of BEE.

It was Mbeki's often repeated and strongly expressed belief that in practice South Africa comprised two separate economic entities: a developed, formal, prosperous economy which he typified as being largely white; and an underdeveloped, informal economy of poor people which he typified as black. According to Mbeki, there was "no escalator" between the two economies and the state therefore had to empower poor black people to advance into the white economy.

This race-based policy demanded that staff in the civil service and private companies and even the shareholding in listed companies had to be more representative of the general population's racial composition. In practice, the manner in which the policy was implemented means that coloured, white and Indian voters were alienated from the ANC because colour quotas in the workplace, in training and on the sports fields gave preference to black people and was to the detriment of these three minority groups.

Companies had to transfer about 26% of their shareholding to black people. Overseas companies, in particular, protested vehemently because it meant that they had to give up their control over about a quarter of their South African subsidiaries without necessarily getting any quid pro quo in the form of expertise from their black partners. Naturally, South Africans who for reasons of race could not benefit from this empowerment, raised strong objections to the policy. However, it was eventually class rather than race which made the government reconsider.

Because the policy was based purely on race, in practice it meant that only a small group in the black elite benefited from the empowerment agreements – and they were enriched by billions of rands. The trade unions, the black workers' class and unemployed blacks objected so vehemently about this that by 2011 the government was busy revising its policy and making income a factor in empowerment. The new policy would rest on wider black economic empowerment in an attempt to give more poor people a share in the economy.

The National Democratic Revolution

One of the most controversial concepts in the South African political vocabulary after 1994 was the so-called National Democratic Revolution (NDR). For ANC supporters it was synonymous with the full realisation of liberation from the legacy of apartheid. For those who opposed the ANC, it was synonymous with jobs for pals, corruption and an obsession for power.

The concept of the NDR has been nurtured within the ANC for a long time. Different people understand it differently. There has always been one school of thought in the ANC which associates it purely with the creation of a non-racial, non-sexist South Africa, as foreseen in the 1996 Constitution.

Another school of thought that has come to the fore particularly since the ANC's national conference in Mafikeng (now known as Mahikeng) in 1998, and is now being expressed more widely, is that the NDR should lead to the total transformation of South Africa. This school of thought believes that although the ANC came to power in 1994 it has never really been in control of South Africa. Political control must be transposed into economic power by ANC supporters in the civil service.

From 1999, during the presidencies of Mbeki, Motlanthe and Zuma, this vision of the NDR was put into practice by a policy known as cadre deployment in the public service; and by black economic empowerment which was implemented through the adjustment of tender regulations and prescriptions regarding shareholding in private companies.

The most controversial of these measures was cadre deployment – the undisguised ANC policy of appointing ANC supporters in top positions. Particularly in the civil service; municipal management; the security forces; the highest posts in the judiciary; the country's secret service; the SABC; state-controlled companies such as Eskom and Transnet; semi-state institutions such as the Land Bank; and constitutionally entrenched institutions such as the public protector and the national director of public prosecutions, a history of loyalty to the ANC became important when appointments had to be made.

Those who oppose cadre deployment and the NDR argue that it leads to a situation that the best-equipped, most suitable individual is not necessarily appointed in a post, with negative consequences for service delivery to the wider population and the vital division between the government and the ruling party. Advocates of the policy defend it by arguing that it levels the playing field for all South Africans and transforms the country by erasing the inequalities of the past. They allege that criticism of cadre deployment is racially based and is an attempt to protect the privileges enjoyed in the past.

Land reform: an opportunity becomes a nightmare

In the period from 2004 to 2013 the land question moved remorselessly into the spotlight and became a major public debate in South Africa. Few issues have aroused more emotion; and on few issues has the government been in a more difficult situation than it found itself in 2011.

The objective of having 30% of cultivable agricultural land in black possession by 2014 was unrealistic and was furthermore hampered by corruption. By 2011, the Minister of Rural Development and Land Reform, Gugile Nkwinti, admitted frankly that the land reform policy had failed. New ideas were necessary. Among the causes of the failure were:

- There was no audit of the racial division of land. The government therefore had no idea of how much land was in possession of which race group, which made it impossible to measure the success of land reform with any degree of accuracy.
- There was no reliable register of the land which the state owned.

- Some farmers were demanding too much money for their land.
- There was large-scale mismanagement and corruption had hampered the process.
- When a privileged society acquired a piece of land, the state did not always do the necessary follow-up by providing training, seed, livestock, implements and bridging finance. This meant that most of the newly privileged farmers failed.

Nevertheless, the government remained committed to the process of correcting the imbalance of landownership which had evolved from the apartheid system and had indeed been its cornerstone. But by 2013 the realisation had begun to dawn within the government and among the rural poor (such as those represented in the Landless People's Movement) that agriculture in South Africa was not necessarily profitable in the short term; that farmers, farm workers, newly privileged landowners and the state would have to work together if the policy was to succeed. By the end of 2013 negotiations were still underway to devise a workable model for land reform; there was a great deal of goodwill but few feasible ideas. The time bomb is still ticking.

Foreign policy

South Africa persisted in its efforts to enjoy access to the highest international council chambers and from January 2011 served a second term in the United Nations (UN) Security Council. Officially, the country still honoured the premise espoused by the Mandela era – that the upholding of human rights would provide the moral compass for its foreign policy.

In practice, however, these noble intentions were not often transposed into deeds. Zimbabwe continued to stumble from one crisis to another, but the South African government did not speak out against the transgressions of President Robert Mugabe's government. Nor did South Africa support the UN's strong actions against the oppressive military rule in Myanmar (Burma). South Africa is often criticised because it seems to be led by solidarity with other African countries rather than by UN principles.

Foreign policy focused on Africa. On the positive side, South Africa played a leading role in the quest for peace in the Great Lakes region in central Africa (including Burundi, Rwanda and the Democratic Republic of the Congo) and after his resignation as president, Mbeki had a lion's share in the orderly attainment of independence in South Sudan. On the negative side, South Africa often remained sitting on the fence when corrupt African countries came under pressure, only to choose a side at the very last moment when the blow had already been delivered. Examples in 2011 include the change in government in the Ivory Coast and the African coup d'états in Tunisia, Egypt and Libya as part of the Arab Spring.

The growing influence of China worldwide is not leaving South Africa untouched. Chinese government delegations and businessmen regularly visit the country. Many South Africans are disturbed that Chinese investors make so little use of local labour. Nevertheless, official ties with China continue to flourish. At times this causes embarrassment such as when the South African government repeatedly yielded to Chinese pressure and refused to issue a visa for the Dalai Lama (spiritual leader of Tibet, whose country is occupied by China) to deliver an address in South Africa.

South Africa's decision to join the trade bloc now known as BRICS, along with Brazil, Russia, India and China, has also had a strong influence on the country's foreign policy. South Africa has begun to position itself nearer to its BRICS partners (two of which, Russia and China, have veto rights in the UN) in the event of international disputes. This implies that South Africa is slowly moving away from the influence of the Western powers.

THE CHINESE IN SOUTH AFRICA

The first Chinese to arrive in South Africa came to the Cape in the latter half of the seventeenth century. They came as small-scale hawkers selling fish, fresh produce, confectionery and hand-crafted items, while others ran small restaurants. There were also those who arrived as exiles, having been banished to the Cape settlement by the Dutch East India Company authorities in Batavia to serve out limited sentences. In this period (1652-1795) there were never more than 350 Chinese in total and no more than 50 present at any one time. However, a few were so prosperous that they became slave owners, while the success of others led to the Dutch burghers submitting numerous petitions against their competition, resulting in regulations being introduced to curb their activities.

The next identifiable wave of Chinese to arrive in South Africa comprised those who were part of the mid-nineteenth century international diaspora of over 200 million Chinese. They settled in the coastal towns of the colonies and after the discovery of minerals also migrated to Kimberley and Johannesburg. They were primarily involved in the service industries and small-scale trade and by the turn of the twentieth century the number of these free individuals had risen to just over 1000 in the Johannesburg region. With the devastation of the gold mining industry after the Anglo-Boer War (1899-1902), the British colonial government agreed to the Transvaal Labour Importation Ordinance to introduce Chinese indentured mine labourers to the gold mines. Over a period of six years (1904-1910) as many as 63 659 Chinese unskilled workers were imported to work on three-year contracts after which they returned to China. While they were heralded as having saved the goldmining industry with production rising to an all-time high, their presence had widespread repercussions.

Politically, the termination of the Chinese indentured labourer scheme played a key role in the electoral victories of both the Liberal Party in England and Het Volk Party in the Transvaal. Of greater significance was that it also precipitated the first overtly racist piece of exclusionist legislation hitherto promulgated in South Africa, the Cape Chinese Exclusion Act of 1904. This legislation made the Chinese the first people in South Africa to be singled out and discriminated against in such a blatant manner. In addition, in 1906 the Transvaal Colony introduced the so-called "Black Act" whereby all "Asiatics" had to re-register. This led to the Chinese embarking on a passive resistance movement under the leadership of Leung Quinn, similar but separate to that of Mahatma Gandhi.

After the formation of the Union in 1910 the Chinese became classified as "prohibited immigrants" according to immigration legislation passed in 1913 and therefore their numbers were reliant on natural increase and gradually dwindled. By the mid-twentieth century they numbered a mere 7000 and according to the 1950 Population Registration Act were classified as a sub-group of the coloured population. Under apartheid legislation they were treated as "non-white" and one group area, Kabega Park, was identified for them in the eastern Cape. As the apartheid government's trade relations with the Republic of China on Taiwan increased, the South African Chinese were gradually subjected to permits for certain concessions, making them one of the first "non-white" groups to straddle the apartheid divide. For example, with official permission their children could attend white schools and they could make application to live in certain residential suburbs, but they still remained without the vote until after the new South African dispensation was introduced in 1994.

> Yet even in the new South Africa, the South African Chinese community continued to be discriminated against when they were excluded from the Employment Equity Act of 1998 and subsequent related legislation. This meant that the Chinese as a group did not qualify for the benefits of affirmative action. After a nine-year court battle - and a century of discrimination since the arrival of their ancestors - the Chinese were eventually vindicated in the Pretoria High Court in June 2008, winning their case against four ministerial departments. Yet, this small culturally identifiable community still remain on the periphery of South African society in the interstitial spaces between black and white.
>
> Karen L. Harris

Social questions

In the period from 2004 to 2013 South Africa has faced significant social challenges. In addressing some of these issues significant progress has been made, but others continue to falter. Health, the combating of crime, xenophobia and nation building are among the matters that require urgent attention.

On the health front, there was no greater crisis than HIV/AIDS. Mbeki and the Minister of Health, Dr Manto Tshabalala-Msimang, gained worldwide notoriety for their reaction to this deadly pandemic. Mbeki claimed that there was no incontrovertible evidence that HIV causes AIDS and went on to say that people's views on sex, HIV/AIDS and the fact that the illness occurred on such a wide scale in Africa, meant that they looked down on black people as primitive, sexually driven animals. For her part, Tshabalala-Msimang said that a diet of garlic, beetroot, lemons and African potato worked better than antiretroviral medication for treating HIV/AIDS. The international community reacted to Mbeki and Tshabalala-Msimang's statements with utter horror and disbelief, but some ANC supporters, notably the poor, believed them and the death toll rose.

Mbeki made the biggest mistake of his political career by making this serious health issue a political football. His government's policy to conceal the truth, his denial that the HI virus causes AIDS, and the refusal to distribute antiretroviral medication to critically ill people, is widely blamed for the exceedingly high HIV/AIDS death toll in South Africa.

After Mbeki was outvoted as ANC leader in 2007 a turnabout took place. In the presidencies of Kgalema Motlanthe and Jacob Zuma, under the purposeful guidance of ministers of health Barbara Hogan and Dr Aaron Motsoaledi the world's most comprehensive programme in the fight against HIV/AIDS was launched – with immediate results. By 2013 there is still no cure for the illness, although the use of antiretroviral medication can now delay death by up to forty years.

After Zuma came to power in 2009, concerted efforts were made in this and other health-related matters such as tuberculosis and other preventable contagious diseases. Motsoaledi has placed greater emphasis on the improvement of primary health care and both the conditions and services provided at state hospitals. When strikers have threatened health services, Motsoaledi, a qualified medical practitioner, has been known to jump in himself to provide medical care.

Crime statistics remain high. Highly skilled emigrants mentioned crime and the results of affirmative action as the main reasons why they wanted to leave the country. By appointing more police officers the government gave the appearance of having stabilised violent crime in particular by 2013, but South Africa's crime rate remains one of the highest in the world.

Xenophobia (dislike or fear of people from other countries) has increasingly raised its head in South Africa since 2008. The root cause of the trouble is that South Africa is not strict with its border security policy and large numbers of people, especially from other African countries, find shelter in South Africa when circumstances in their home countries run amok. These immigrants come mainly from Zimbabwe, the Democratic Republic of the Congo, Somalia, Nigeria, Rwanda and Burundi. Many of them provide unskilled labour which gives the perception to South African workers that the immigrants are taking their jobs. With South Africa's high unemployment level this is tantamount to a match in a powder keg. Violence against the immigrants soon became a regular occurrence despite the outspoken opposition on the part of the government.

Given the country's divided past, nation building and reconciliation remain a priority and a challenge in South Africa. Especially on great sporting occasions, South Africans were able to focus on the things that united them rather than those that divided them. This was the case with the Springboks' victory in the Rugby World Cup in France in 2007. Similarly, the hosting of the Soccer World Cup tournament in 2010 was a triumph for countrywide reconciliation, and for South Africa's image overseas. Although for most people integration gradually became a more comfortable everyday reality, inflammatory politicians like Malema put a spoke in the wheel, especially with racially-based utterances against the country's white residents.

The period 2004 to 2013 was therefore one in which the country's political development crystallised out into a two-party system, with the ANC and the DA taking a position against one another. In the economic sphere South Africa flourished in 2007 and thereafter handled the bite of the worldwide depression better than most other countries. As far as social issues were concerned, grants were paid out to more people, which held the danger of creating too great a tax burden. HIV/AIDS was tackled strongly from 2009 onwards. Afrikaners continued to function as a group and there was a blossoming of the arts, but the use of Afrikaans at official level was discontinued.

At the end of a turbulent, formative adolescence of fret and fury, South Africa stood on the brink of adulthood in which its precise nature would be formed by its people; and the precise nature would only become clear in the fullness of time.

25
Coloureds: a complex history
Cornelius Thomas*

Coloureds are constituted of a mix of genes, cultures and classes. They carry genes from Europe, Asia, and Africa. From the mid-seventeenth century, slaves and free people of colour and Europeans, the latter either as owners of "the other" or as ordinary folk who sought answers to life in southern Africa, mixed in the vital melee of life, especially in and around Cape Town. As a result, Coloureds have the most diverse genetic make-up of all discernible groups.

Many have a demonstrable European ancestry. Cape Malays (Muslim Coloureds) are of partial Asian descent. Then there are the predominantly Khoisan Coloureds and the Griqua sort. There are also many people who carry a predominance of ethnic African genes. Given the impossibility of defining this group on the basis of ethnic make-up or physical appearance, it may be best to approach its history from a cultural perspective.

At the "moment" of coming into being, Coloureds adopted the main tenets of European culture. Thereafter, they assimilated cultural snippets and so fashioned a uniquely stylised version of European culture. Comedian Trevor Noah puts it that he is Coloured, but not "Coloured Coloured", meaning he is the result of ethnic mixing but did not grow up, culturally, as Coloured. Educationist Richard van der Ross puts it that Coloureds

> ... knew the culture of the Hottentots and, to a lesser extent, the Bushmen; they had come to know the Bantu culture in the Eastern areas and in the North; they must have gained some familiarity with the

---

*The author of this chapter prefers to capitalise the term "Coloured" in accordance with its historical and, more importantly, its current resurgent and assertive usage. The editor has opted to respect his wish.

customs which African slaves had brought mainly from Madagascar and Mozambique; they were acquainted with the cultural patterns of Malay slaves, and they knew the culture of the white man [the European]. They knew and experienced, albeit from the vantage point of the slaves or the domestic servant, the whole cultural gamut from skin karos to fine silk, from reed hut to stately houses of brick, bow and arrow to musket; from paganism to Christianity.

Al J. Venter shows that sub-groups lived throughout South Africa. However, a majority of Western-cultured Coloured folk lived in greater Cape Town, and they unfolded most of this group's history.

This group existed by the early to mid-nineteenth century, and the missions looked upon them as "gekleurd" (coloured). Three-quarters into that century, they identified themselves as Afrikaner or Coloured. Over time they stratified into classes. Van der Ross correctly puts it that one of the markers of this group is a sub-culture (underclass) of poverty.

Therefore, Coloureds – those who proclaim themselves capital C Coloureds or, at least, "*bruin mense*" – emerged from ethno-genetic mixing, imitatively embraced European and other cultures, practised Christianity, and pursued life, liberty and happiness with the tools of pragmatic inclusivity, manly resistance, cultural constructionism, and intelligent contributions. An account of real history-making, not a theatre of theories, is what this chapter attempts.

Genesis

Coloureds are the newest identifiable group in the world. How did this cultural group come into being, how did it evolve, and how did it play out in South Africa's drama the past 150 years? This new cultural group assumed vague form in the first half of the nineteenth century, at the latest shortly after the emancipation of the slaves; and certainly after the liberal Cape laws of the 1850s. This new group referred to itself as "Afrikanders" in the 1850s and as Coloureds by the 1880s. By the 1860s there existed a mass of brown people in Cape Town. They formed a servant class and worked in the city's commercial enterprise sector. On the Cape Flats, people in the process of becoming Coloured owned smallholdings or worked as farm hands from as early as the earthquake of 1809. Of course, slaves, in as far as they could be considered of this group, worked on farms throughout the Cape Colony since 1658.

Strengthening the imprint of being "Coloured" can also be ascribed to theories of race kicked up by the eugenics and Social Darwinist orientations of the 1870s. Difference and "the other" began to matter, and groups made "racial" separations – in the United States of America and the colonial Cape. Here "brown" people began to see themselves as significantly different; they were also seen, albeit pejoratively, as half-breeds or offspring of some undesirable mix. Seeing themselves as Coloureds, however, did not mean historic and immutable racial compartmentalisation. The self-interested come and go of life allows for permutations and adjustments.

By the beginning of the nineteenth century, they began to embrace Christianity, which became the basis of their culture. And the mission societies in the Cape made great strides converting "the heathen" to Christianity. Rhenish mission registers show the term "gekleurd" in the 1830s; the term "Kleurling" suggested itself. The apartheid government did not impose the term; the missions' head counted the conversion of "the other" this way. The misnomer Cape Malays, built on Islam, nudged this subgroup into a self-segregating Muslim ethos. The brown people of Christian persuasion, however, felt a close affinity to European society.

The cultural embrace

The "emergence" of Coloureds splashed new and unique paint on the South African canvas. This newness placed them close to the Europeans. As slaves or servants or artisans, they adopted Christianity and found themselves swept into a hegemonic European cultural garment. Christianity anchored "gekleurdes" from the time of the missions to the present. The church had spin-offs that spiced Sundays: Sunday school; the pomp of confirmation; boys' brigade; choirs; hospital visits; youth organisations; the cooked lunch; the promenade, etc. All pursuits brown people undertook flowed and ebbed, but the church remained a constant that anchored them.

Coloureds developed or created unique sub-cultural styles and ways of expressing European culture. Cuisine, clothing, song and dance became distinctive features of their culture. These expressions emanated from inherited and creative processes that continue.

They spoke Dutch in 1900 – "kitchen" Dutch daily and "high" Dutch when necessary. Dutch or remnants of it remained part of daily expression into the 1960s. The table prayer, "*Segen Vader gijwe eten; laat ons nimmer u vergeten*", for instance, survived into the 1970s. Meanwhile, they had, with people of European descent, co-crafted from Dutch, Malay-Portuguese and some indigenous words, a new language – Afrikaans. The Afrikaners held on to Dutch, but J.B.M. Hertzog made Afrikaans an official language in 1925. Coloureds lived in Afrikaans throughout the country.

Throughout the nineteenth century, brown folk did not have the luxury of leisure. What time they had for leisure may have been spent in music, song, drink and dance. Towards the end of that century, they had made *Nederlandse liedjies* (Dutch songs) and the Cape coon carnival their own – the latter a dynamic sub-cultural expression. They sang *moppies* and *ghoema-liedjies* (comic songs). The visit of the *Alabama*, an American schooner that docked in Cape Town in 1863, inspired the folk song "*Daar kom die Alibama*", which shows an example of cultural assimilation.

The coon carnival annually culminated in *Tweede Nuwe Jaar* (Second New Year, 2 January), later dubbed "the festival of the oppressed". The "coon" carnival later came to be known as the Cape Town Minstrel Carnival. The origin of the carnival stretches back to the nineteenth century in the time of slavery. Over time Coloureds also imbibed the spirit of the Rio de Janeiro Carnavale and the Mardi Gras of New Orleans, and made these echoes across the Atlantic their own. The event, which has developed a distinct Cape flavour, is also supposed to have "hereditary" ties to the minstrel entertainers on American ocean liners who stopped off in Cape Town over 100 years ago. The evolution of this carnival can be said to be part of the cultural syncretism that osmosed into culture.

When time permitted for leisure, Coloureds also played and watched the Victorian games of cricket, rugby and association football (soccer), making these their own. And in the period 1870 to 1910 there was "brown" Victorianism for the elite – they liked to be gentlemen or ladies in the style of the dominant culture – and muscular Christianity emerged.

Being born into or close to European culture, both as elite and as an underclass, "brown people" found themselves a sub-cultural group expressing themselves in unique style.

Early "political" formations

As Coloureds began to identify themselves as a group in the second half of the nineteenth century, and in as far as they saw and accepted the social separations brought about by the power of the dominant group, the need to advance or protect group and self-interest pressed them into various forms of organisation. The earliest included vigilance and temperance bodies and civic groups, including the Coloured People's Vigilance Society; and the Coloured Men's Protectorate and Political Association. These organisations, and also sports clubs, were led by the "better sort" of men.

Already in 1883, Coloureds led by Pieter Johannes Daniels formed the Afrikaner League in Kimberley, suggesting they were part of Africa. The organisation remained local, but showed a consciousness of group identity and politics. Scarcely a decade on, the elite in Kimberley founded the South African Coloured People's Association in 1892. This organisation intended stretching its reach nationally with a political agenda. After protest meetings in Kimberley and Cape Town, it forwarded a petition to Parliament opposing the Franchise and Ballot Bill. Although the bill would raise voter qualifications, excluding more Africans, overtures to John Tengo Jabavu to support the campaign failed.

The bill raised the property requirement from £25 to £75 and replaced the salary qualification (£25) with an education test. This would have excluded more Africans than Coloureds, but Jabavu felt his opposition to it would alienate liberal white politicians. This early instance of "race" politics shows that brown people wanted to include Africans in their campaigns.

Soon to emerge (as of 1896) were the "B" branches of Cecil John Rhodes's South African League, an imperial political organisation. Coloureds accepted the "B" branch status because the League adjusted its position from "equal rights for all white men south of the Zambezi" to "equal rights for all civilised men". Here we see inclusivity (of ethnic Africans) and deferential pragmatism (to the dominant group) on the part of the politicians.

In 1894 Ahmed Effendi stood for election to the Cape parliament. He campaigned as a "working man's candidate" and, according to Van der Ross, "he claimed to be concerned about the welfare of all groups". The Cape parliament changed the electoral law and thwarted Effendi's chances of being elected. Afterwards, significantly, he said: "It is the first time in the history of South Africa that a non-European candidate has stood for Parliament. I have had the moral courage to do so – I bear my defeat like a man."

A white man's war

When the Anglo-Boer War broke out in October 1899, loyalty to the Crown, the Cape liberal tradition, and defence of person and property mattered to Coloureds. They therefore pressed for "armed units", formed vigilance committees; they even held "war councils". In one instance, Coloureds marched on a magistrate's office demanding to be armed. They formed units of what they called "town guards". These drew on "an intelligent class of Cape boy". As the war progressed, *agterryers* (literally, after-riders, those riding behind, military servants) became involved on the English side of the military divide. They also served on the Boer side. This indicated their place in society – sub-cultural (servant) presence. In 1901 a young man wrote:

> I hope you will not mind, I am a coloured boy of 18. My skin is coloured but my heart is bold … my master is very good to me but I am going to leave him for the sake of our Empire and Queen. I will take the rifle in my hand and the bandolier round my body.

Many "brown" Calvinians concurred. As the war approached, Coloured associations consolidated ranks behind the British, spewing rhetoric against the Afrikaners. During the war, cultural association with the Dutch gave way to political solidarity with the English. Over the next two years, they fully supported the British war effort.

In Calvinia, Abraham Esau supported the British war effort. An Afrikaner who communicated with a Free State commando fingered "the English Coloured Esau" as the main troublemaker in the area. Esau commanded significant support among young men. When a Boer commando took the town in January 1901, they arrested Esau. He did not cower or recant. They dragged Esau through the town and shot him. This marked the first instance of manly resistance; Esau became one of the first martyrs of the twentieth century and support for the British grew.

Early sport in the community

Sport featured prominently in Coloured culture. Men of means started playing cricket, rugby and association football (soccer) when these sports arrived on the Cape shores. In the 1850s whites and Afrikanders (Coloureds) played a cricket match; the latter won. Rugby took off with the formation of Roslyns and Arabian College in Cape Town in the early 1880s and the Universal Rugby Club in Kimberley in 1886. Association football followed suit.

In 1894 fast bowler Krom Hendricks earned a spot in the national team. The selectors decided it would be "impolitic" to include him. Those who had the advantage of "our game" excluded the identifiable "other".

In 1896 rugby leaders formed the South African Coloured Rugby Football Board in Kimberley. By that time "brown" men had been playing rugby for more than a decade in the Cape, Griqualand West, and Eastern Province. In 1898 Transvaal joined the board. That year, Western Province won the first inter-provincial tournament, the Rhodes Cup competition. Although EP was nominally a Coloured union, a majority of Africans played for EP in this tournament, which shows the trend toward inclusivity. As informal segregation hardened, rugby maintained its segregated organisations.

Greater sophistication entered the sports arena. The years 1929 to 1945 saw the emergence of a host of sports clubs, especially in association football. Administration was solid, the outcomes community theatre and social discipline. Football levelled middle- and working-class elements and gave young men with nothing to do a social purpose. Middle-class leadership and working-class players forged unions from Salt River via Kuils River to Stellenbosch.

By the 1930s, young men also embraced "physical culture". It built on late nineteenth-century "muscular Christianity", which preached the gospel of the body as a temple, and sportsmanship (taking victory with grace and defeat "like a man"). The activist and itinerant poet Dennis Brutus read *Tom Brown's School Days* in the late 1930s and it mightily impressed him. It inspired him to embark on his mission to obtain fairness and justice in society and sport.

By the late 1930s, the Health and Spiritual Club and the Hyman Liberman Institute held wrestling tournaments in the Railway Institute, Salt River. When the Wesley Physical Culture Club showcased their talents in the hamlet of Genadendal, ministers of religion attended and "gave their support and expressed their appreciation" of physical culture. In 1940 Charles Swanson from Glenlily did wrestling, bodybuilding and weightlifting under Matt October in the Wesley Club. October coached Swanson into a glorious advertisement for physical culture. Physical culture endured until the 1970s, adding beauty pageants in 1956. Weightlifter Precious McKenzie, bodybuilder David Isaacs, and beauty queen Lydia Johnson became role models.

John Tobin and the stone meetings

Coloureds who qualified voted in Cape elections from 1853. They saw their destiny entwined with that of European society. They considered themselves loyal subjects of Queen Victoria; they offered the mission churches homage and labour; they slotted into the market economy. Many made a living as workers, servants, shopkeepers, hawkers, cabinet-makers, masons, and small-scale farmers. A majority of them, however, formed a working class and an underclass of urban and farm labourers. The tiny propertied elite took the lead in public affairs. Historian Gavin Lewis calls one of them, W.A. Roberts, "a shopkeeper and the epitome of the Cape Town Coloured elite".

Lewis asserts that around 1901 another shopkeeper (and manager of the Cape Town Minstrels), John Tobin, started "stone meetings" among the boulders at the top of Clifton Street, District Six, to discuss rights and grievances. "Tobin stressed ... the themes of black self-help and uplift, probity and race pride, all on the principle of equal rights for civilised men." Discussions also revolved around jobs and fair treatment in the workplace. People flocked to Tobin's Sunday morning gatherings. The venue also served as a springboard for socialising and networking.

Tobin supported John X. Merriman's South African Party; a party that seemed to have an inclusive South African vision. Tobin's motto was "Africa for the Africans, black or white". Accordingly, he encouraged the formation of "multiracial" unions, albeit with no effect. Despite the bubonic scare of 1901, Tobin opposed residential segregation. By the end of 1902 he had decided, with one W. Collins, to form "a permanent organisation to protect the liberties of the Coloured people". On 30 September 1902, Tobin and Collins played a leading role in establishing the African Political Organisation (later African People's Organisation). One of the inclusive aims was to "promote unity between the coloured races". In 1905 Dr Abdullah Abdurahman became president of the African People's Organisation (APO). Despite its inclusive intentions, this was a brown people's organisation.

Van der Ross said that Daniels, Tobin and Collins, "in the tradition of fighters for freedom the world over, sensed a threat to their people, and called on them to unite with one another in the struggle to protect their interests and to obtain the universal values of freedom and justice."

In January 1901, leaders who purportedly represented 100 000 Coloureds pledged their loyalty to the British crown and asserted that only within the British Empire would they enjoy constitutional justice and equality as subjects. However, between 1902 and 1905, Sir Milner, British high commissioner in South Africa, made no effort to broaden rights. Lord Selborne's memorandum of 1907 also envisaged a union with differentiated rights.

In 1909 the Daniels-Effendi-Tobin-Collins-Abdurahman initiatives culminated in a series of protest meetings. These leaders had hoped that in the wake of the war the Cape franchise would be extended to the northern "crown colonies" (the former Boer republics of Transvaal and Orange Free State). At the time Coloureds constituted 10,1% of the electorate and Africans 4,7%. In mid-1909 Abdurahman, Matt Fredericks, D.J. Lenders and a number of Africans, led by W.P. Schreiner (a member of the Cape parliament), took their case – equal rights for all civilised men – to London. The British government declined to intervene and the franchise status quo remained intact.

Still, this group had found political voice and vehicles. They remained a cultural and political sub-group, powerlessly yet assertively close to European society. As they retained the vote in the Cape, they believed they held value and affinity in the Euro-dominant society.

Teens and twenties

Smarting from the rebuffs between 1901 and 1910, especially the rejection of an appeal for an inclusive union and the decision not to extend the qualified franchise to the conquered ex-Boer republics, Coloured leaders turned inward. In 1913 they founded the Teachers' League of South Africa (TLSA) whose motto was (and still is) "Let us live for our children". The vision of the TLSA was to uplift people from generational poverty through education. It saw itself as a Coloured teacher's body, but included African teachers teaching in its schools.

Harold Cressy (1889–1916) towered as a TLSA leader. In the teens of the twentieth century, he agitated for increased access to education. Children attended church primary schools from the last quarter of the nineteenth century to the 1960s. Pressure on the Cape school board resulted in the founding of the first secondary school for Coloured pupils, Trafalgar High in central Cape Town, in 1912. Sixty pupils enrolled the first year, 32 of them girls.

The year 1919 saw labour upheavals and a post-war depression. Poverty worsened. Jan Smuts, prime minister from 1919 to 1924, maintained the conciliation between "Boer and Briton" and adopted a laissez-faire stance toward domestic policies and social mores, allowing matters of race to go their natural way.

His successor, J.B.M. Hertzog, took whites living in cheek-by-jowl squalor with browns seriously and embarked on social engineering by the mid-1920s. The Mines and Works Act as amended in 1926, swept whites and browns into a number of protected jobs. They benefited economically because certificates of competence were issued to them. This was the Colour Bar Act. The Cape became a Coloured labour preferential area. Coloureds were now preferred as dock workers over Africans, as had previously been the case. Artisans benefited and became adjuncts to construction companies. Coloureds, especially of the Cape Malay sub-group, found a niche in the hawking business. With the emergence of secondary industries, Coloured girls wafted in droves into "sleep-in" and day domestic work. Summarising a circular of the pro-Hertzog Afrikaans Nasionale Bond (a Coloured organisation), Van der Ross lists twenty benefits alleviating the lot of Coloureds in the period 1924 to 1929.

In 1926, the second high school, Livingstone, opened its doors in the Cape Town suburb of Claremont – an indicator of the growth of the elite.

The previous year Afrikaans had become – together with English and Dutch – one of the official languages. At last, the Afrikaners made official what "the help" had co-created from the kitchens and fields. At that time they did not see this as an achievement, but it was: a new people had co-created a new language.

Coloured leaders joined whites and Africans in "joint councils" – founded by American missionaries and local liberals to promote good relations between Europeans and non-Europeans. These councils exuded a Christian social ethos. They highlighted the social malaise suffered by brown communities. They lived into the 1950s but hardly made an impression on the political landscape. At least, through them, Coloured leaders continued their penchant for inclusivity.

In 1927 Abdurahman organised a non-European conference. This suggested an adversarial attitude, a movement toward a trans-Coloured approach to politics, and it implied radicalism. Addressing the issues of segregation and opportunity, further non-European conferences took place in 1930 and 1931.

In 1929 Hertzog won the general election on a "*swart gevaar*" ticket. The Coloured elite probably voted for Hertzog. Working men probably sighed relief when he won.

Radical shifts

By 1933, the political clouds darkened over Coloureds and Africans when the NP and SAP entered into a coalition. This co-operation between Hertzog and Smuts conjured up fears among people of colour who saw the united white front as a threat to their rights. After all, for two decades political talk had been thick with the need to settle the questions of native representation and segregation.

In 1933, Professor D.D.T. Jabavu, calling for the fourth non-European conference, urged the "three non-white races" to unite and fight the imminent erosion of their rights:

> We can best do that by showing a good example among ourselves, by mutual respect and helping each other. The Indians have money and business ability, the Coloureds have culture and leading intelligence, and the Bantu have the brawn and numbers.

Addressing the fourth conference in January 1934, Abdurahman called on the non-white groups to unite in matters of common political interest, but emphasised that the conference did not seek to "break down group consciousness". To ignore group identity or culture would be fatal, he said. He in effect implied there would be inclusivity of "the other" for political purposes, but there would not be surrender to any other group. He considered "the true spirit of loyalty to God and country" ahead of race, he said. He pursued a national analysis in the broad sense but a racial or cultural approach in the micro-political sense to the governance challenges of the

Union. Abdurahman kept his politics within constitutional parameters; implied radicalism came to naught.

In the mid-1930s then, the white power structure and the non-European opposition stood at the cusp of what to do next. How were they to disfranchise the Africans and keep Coloured people close but segregated, government asked. The African question was settled in 1936 with the Native Representative Council which removed Africans from the common voters' roll. The Coloureds had to labour on.

Meanwhile, teaching remained the main vehicle for upward social mobility. The "*meester*" (teacher) strode as king of the community. In education Coloureds saw opportunity for improved material production and prestige. By the end of the 1930s, classes at Glenlily Primary School (in Parow) averaged over 40 pupils.

In 1935 Zainunissa "Cissie" Gool broke with the reformist APO politics of her father, Abdurahman, and spearheaded the formation of the National Liberation League (NLL) which sought to win "complete social, economic and political equality" for the oppressed. The League advocated socialism, and through John Gomas and James la Guma, helped form a number of unions – which did not last. Gool also plunged the NLL into a mix of non-collaboration and electoral politics, the latter with little success. It had a spin-off in the New Era Fellowship, a debating society for the sorting of ideas by leftists.

Benjamin Kies, 20, joined the New Era Fellowship in 1937. As a teenager he had been excluded from participating in the Woodstock Anglican Church choir because he was not fair enough. He steeled his resolve against discrimination. He earned a Master's degree at the University of Cape Town that year. Kies leaned left, both on the basis of a critique of race and an analysis of class. He rejected conciliation, joint councils, non-European conferences, and deference to the empire. Gool and Kies also rejected Hertzog's political machinations. They brought a world view to politics. Linking to the (Trotskyist) Fourth International, they dedicated themselves to trans-racial and indeed international working-class solidarity and socialism.

The left radicals called for a united front among non-Europeans in 1938. The time had come to set aside notions of "higher or lower levels of culture" and to stand together in tackling political problems. As many as 45 organisations sent delegates to the conference and formed the Non-

European United Front (NEUF). This front would embark on political and industrial action, its founding document promised.

The Wilcocks Commission (1938) revealed horrendous poverty. In response the APO asserted that it was "entirely a Coloured People's Organisation" and in the best position to discuss their interests. It called a national convention to discuss concerns and grievances. The convention accepted the need for social reform and rejected segregation.

Despite its radical rhetoric, the NLL, NEF and NEUF too found themselves fighting segregation in the years 1938 to 1940. Yet, a greater differentiation and sophistication had clearly entered politics in the 1930s. Both reformists and radicals followed an inclusive approach to politics.

In 1940 the elder statesman Dr Abdurahman died. A swell of change was already under way before his passing. The years from 1930 to 1940 could be seen as the wane of deferential politics and the rise of the leftist critique.

Apartheid ascendant and challenged

The working class grew during the Second World War. Young men and women flocked into the factories that supplied the war effort. South Africa participated in the war because Smuts's argument that South Africa as part of the British Commonwealth was automatically at war with Germany, held sway.

On the domestic front Afrikaner nationalism had been growing since the centenary of the Great Trek in 1938. But when Smuts ousted Hertzog in 1939 they felt vulnerable. Afrikaner formations, including the Ossewabrandwag, supported Germany in the world war. Coloureds, however, signed up to serve on the front; their loyalty remained with the British crown.

In the middle of the war, Smuts created a Coloured Affairs Department (CAD). Kies and the leftists saw this as a step to replace natural segregation with statutory segregation. In 1943 Kies and company formed the Anti-CAD. It opposed segregation and wanted to force the government to undo this nascent apartheid structure. In 1944 the Anti-CAD and several other formations established the Non-European Unity Movement (NEUM). The NEUM, a multiracial instrumentalist movement, sought to counteract the politics of divide and rule. Political leaders now marched in the vanguard of a non-European dialectical movement – of "us, the oppressed" against "them, the oppressor". Kies advocated the positive state, one of fairness for all and interventions favouring the poor. In addition, the NEUM mooted the political concepts of non-collaboration and boycott. Yet, despite this movement's left leanings, it still searched for an ideology that would transcend race in the 1950s.

The National Party won the general election of 1948 and shortly afterwards started implementing its policy of apartheid. Coloureds had always been loyal to the British Empire, now a group either averse or hostile to the empire held political power. They were always close to Afrikaners (despite their support for the English in three wars) because of language, religion and culture. Their "mid-field" position had sheltered them and they lived relatively better than Africans. They feared this would change.

With bickering and schisms being the order of the year, the NEUM wilted in the 1950s. It was also cast into the shadows by ANC initiatives – the Defiance Campaign, Congress of the People, and the Freedom Charter. The NEUM with its socialist policy therefore failed to unite the oppressed. Still, while the Unity Movement made no headway in 1943 through 1960, members who were sports organisers and activists saw a niche and an opportunity.

In the immediate post-war period on the rugby front, for instance, Parow and District Rugby Football Union, a tiny area north of Cape Town, boasted 14 rugby clubs. The 1950 Rhodes Cup tournament was splendid. At the end of it, Coloured "Springboks" played the first test against Bantu "Springboks". Cricket clubs popped up in urban and semi-urban areas. The national Coloured cricket team led by all-rounder Basil D'Oliveira toured Kenya where they played the Kenya Asians. Association football clubs flowered, and skills reached such a level that footballer Albert Johanneson departed to play professional soccer abroad as of 1961, the first Coloured to break into the English league.

Sports gathered players and spectators in a manner that suggested social power. Sports showed excellence and unfair discrimination more plainly than other fields of social endeavour. For instance, weightlifting allowed no leeway to cheat the best. In 1936 top weightlifter Milo Pillay was kept off the Olympic team; in 1948 the ignominy repeated itself when Ron Eland was denied the right to represent his country in the London Olympic Games.

Dennis Brutus (1924–2009) entered sports activism in the mid-1950s. In his private capacity Brutus opposed world chess champion Max Euwe's visit in 1955. Despite Brutus's appeal for him not to give apartheid South Africa chessic comfort, the former world champion still played in the Johannesburg Open. This setback hardly deterred Brutus. His next project concerned South Africa's application for membership to the soon-to-be-founded International Table Tennis Board. He asked Ivor Montague in the United Kingdom to block the application. Montague, a socialist, and his allies turned South Africa's application down. This "small victory" showed Brutus "what was possible". The anti-apartheid sports struggle had begun – at a time when the *"bruin mense"* still played segregated sports without challenging it. In 1958, Brutus, G.K. Rangasamy and Arthur Lutchman, a triumvirate of Port Elizabeth sports administrators, led the formation of the SA Sports Association (SASA) in East London. Sports leaders now stood clearly on the frontline against sports apartheid. In quick succession Brutus and company weakened the white Football Association of South Africa's position in FIFA; thwarted the intended visit of a Brazilian football outfit Portuguesa Santista; and prevented an all-black West Indian cricket team from touring here.

After the formation of the SA Non-Racial Olympic Committee (SANROC) in 1963, Brutus continued to lead "the sports and liberation movement". Putting alliances together in the late 1960s and early 1970s, he managed to have South Africa expelled from the Olympic movement.

His anti-apartheid sports campaign was greatly helped by the D'Oliveira affair in 1968. Basil D'Oliveira was a late inclusion in the English test squad to tour South Africa in 1968–69. John Vorster, prime minister at the time, made it plain that the team would not be welcome in South Africa because it was the team of the anti-apartheid movement. The tour was cancelled and the world's sporting floodlights washed over South Africa.

In 1969–1970, South African-born British citizen Peter Hain raised a massive protest against the Springbok rugby tour in the United Kingdom. Despite the posters, paint, weedkiller, nails and denunciations by Hain, Brutus and Chris de Broglio, the Springboks played all the tour matches. But the activists had served notice, and the action carried into other realms.

Uncommon voters' roll

By the mid-1950s, Coloureds had been voting for a century. This vote occasionally constituted a swing vote. In 1951 the government introduced the Separate Representation of Voters Bill to remove them from the common voters' roll and place them on a separate roll to vote for four members of the House of Assembly. Although the franchise enjoyed entrenched status in the constitution, the ruling National Party ignored the clause and passed the bill with a simple majority in each chamber of Parliament (House of Assembly and Senate) sitting separately. The result was the Separate Representation of Voters Act. This political stunt was unconstitutional, and four Coloured voters challenged the act in the Supreme Court. The United Party initiated and funded the lawsuit. In Harris *vs* Minister of the Interior, the Supreme Court dismissed the case stating that it could not question the validity of an Act of Parliament. Harris and friends escalated the case to the Appellate Division. The state responded to the applicants' grievance with complex constitutional and theoretical arguments. On 20 March 1952, the Appeal Court ruled the new law "invalid, null and void and of no legal force and effect". Harris and company had won; judicial activism had triumphed. Next, Parliament passed an Act constituting itself as the High Court, whose authority, the Act said, even the courts could not challenge. Again the court knocked down the political ploy.

After the 1953 election, which the NP comfortably won, government pushed again to disfranchise the Coloureds. This time the NP passed the Senate Act (1955) which allowed them to pack the Senate so as to have a two-thirds majority in a joint session of Parliament. This they duly did and in 1956 a joint session passed the Separate Representation of Voters Act. More dark clouds rolled in.

However, at a visual-aural level, brown folk fashioned public culture around street life, the cinema and sport in the 1950s. A body of non-fiction literature shows that in areas such as North End, South End and District Six, they engaged in street games, corner crooning, women borrowing and gossiping, and sports.

"Free bioscope" – bare-knuckle fights and, occasionally, knifing duels – formed an odious part of street culture. Worse, people slept outdoors and gangs stirred. Journalist and criminologist Don Pinnock found that in District Six, during the Second World War, "the street corners seemed to fill up overnight and the sight of people and even whole families sleeping on stair-landings and in doorways became common". Gangs kept watch.

While these constituted normative reality, Coloured people derived joy from the corner, the café, and the cinema. Halt Road in Elsies River boasted three movie houses – Astra, Panorama and Monaco. Films glamorised violence, which became part of the cult of working men's machismo. They also transported viewers into elegance and excellence, and vicarious living. "Brown" life turned technicolor.

The roof and the street

Social engineering or "urban planning", later called "forced removals" by its victims, began in the mid-1950s. At first, Coloureds moved voluntarily. When it came to the politics of the roof, people panicked.

Wholesale eviction from District Six from 1966 to 1982 constituted the most traumatic part of Coloured history. Forced removals ripped home and heart and community out of District Six, and scattered 40 000 onto the Cape Flats, the sandy flatland east of the city of Cape Town. Coloured people, Malays, Indians and a few whites were also removed from South End (Port Elizabeth), North End (East London), and a hundred other residential pockets. District Six stole the headlines, but the North End removals lasted longest, from 1966 to 1991.

Forced removals affected a long-settled community of whites also. In 1958, Parow passed an ordinance giving effect to the Group Areas Act. The Coloured people of Glenlily had to move to the other side of the Cape Town-Stellenbosch railway. When Charles Swanson of Glenlily saw the writing on the wall, he viewed properties in white Bellville South. In less than two years, he had secured one. The Bellville South-Oakdale exchange then unfolded. Coloured people had to leave Oakdale and settle in Bellville South; whites in Bellville South were forced to leave and set up residence in Oakdale.

The library on District Six suggests that when people were dumped on the Cape Flats, community cohesion disintegrated and social problems followed. Indeed, they failed to reconstitute the old community. They were pressed into "matchbox" houses, in townships: Bonteheuwel, Manenberg, Hanover Park. Gangsterism reared its violent head, as Pinnock and Jonny Steinberg have shown.

Colourful characters like Puffy Botha and Lallam Richardson in East London; Eier in Port Elizabeth; and Motjie Jesus in Cape Town, explored alternate sources of income. Some 3000 shebeens dotted greater Cape Town by 1980, many of them amid the skin-and-bone poverty of squatter camps. These illegal liquor outlets spawned a new subterranean sub-culture and economy. Often a gang adhered itself to, or ran, a shebeen. While the "better sort" shied from it, shebeens and gangs became endemic to a certain class and the general experience.

While the period 1965 to 1970 enjoyed urban economic growth, the years 1970–1975 suffered rural depression and the latter unleashed about 40 000 farm labourers onto the Cape Flats. The townships also offered living space for *bo jongens* – migrants from upcountry. Most of them were unskilled; they could not get work, and many of them joined the gangs. So the social problems on the Cape Flats did not necessarily emanate from District Six people.

District Six had the Globe Gang, a protective family outfit. Warlock in North End, and later the Bungalows in Bellville South, were accepted as positive social institutions. There existed a benign nexus between gangs and the domestic economy, which they served as agents of acquisition, social control and protection. With the great migration to the Flats, however, a new form of gangsterism emerged. These gangs operated on quick-money imperatives and drugs; they often turned to violence to claim territory and to assert power. The *Cape Herald* routinely reported the rape of young women. In the 1970s the gangsters from upcountry were certainly of the Khoisan-Coloured sort. They were vicious and self-destructive – especially as of the late 1970s, when the Cape Town Scorpions owned the crooked crevices of the Cape Flats.

At the same time, positive forces emerged. The first public protests post-Rivonia came from the "brown" community: the protests at Arcadia High School in Bonteheuwel (1969); the Desmond Demas "tie affair" at UWC (1970); and the Gelvandale bus protest (1971). The Gelvandale action turned violent, with boycotters attacking the Gail Road police station to have their leader, Abraham Rhode, released. This action echoed the courage of Calvinia. Buses were stoned and Katie Jasson died during the protest. These protests took place independent of any ethnic African initiative, before black thinking took root in brown soil.

With leading intelligence, the activists took to the frontline. Three strands could be discerned: mass consumption of music (1965–); student activism (1972–); and sports activism (1973–).

From Cape jazz to pop

The 1863 Alabama sailors left a minstrel imprint. Then Orpheus Mac-Adoo's (African-American) Jubilee Singers thrice visited Cape Town between 1890 and 1898. The crush on American music continued with an embrace of ragtime, swing, bebop, and later folk, rock and pop, all of which Coloured people assimilated into an inclusive musical culture over the period from 1863 to 1963.

The late-1950s saw the emergence of Cape jazz – an American cultural creation enriched by local idiom. Cape jazzists – Dollar Brand (Abdullah Ibrahim), Beattie Benjamin, and Cecil Barnard – added *marabi*, *kwela* and *mbaqanga*. As producers and consumers of popular music, "brown" folk enriched their cultural hybridity in this way. Cape jazz grew spectacularly from 1959 to 1965, but the best practitioners hurried into exile. Still, this music added a unique dimension, asserts aficionado Lars Rasmussen, to the world's jazz catalogue. In 1975 Dollar Brand came home a while and released the quintessential Cape jazz album, *Mannenberg – 'Is where it's Happening'*.

Cliff Richard from the United Kingdom toured here in 1961 and 1963. He sang youngsters into dance with the lyrics of love, and into strumming the guitar. In 1965 Coloureds bopped on the wave of "She's a Yum-Yum" by the Lunar 5. This band consisted of local Cape boys who had made it big – they got onto the radio. Their lead singer Bernie Brown brought joy to youngsters. Also in 1965–66, the Invaders recorded several numbers. In 1967 they released their debut album, *Two Sides of the Invaders*. Later that year their signature LP, *Shock Wave*, aired, and the eponymous single rocketed into the Top 20 hit parade.

African-American soul singer Percy Sledge visited Cape Town in 1970. From 29 May to 21 June he performed to Coloured audiences, packing the Luxurama theatre in Wynberg. Never before and never since had any singer or band performed for so long in a venue for Coloureds. And they made soul and its manifestations – music style, clothing and hairdo, body language – part of their culture.

Next, Motown Records flew in from Detroit. Marvin Gaye, Diana Ross, and Michael Jackson became household names. Gaye's critically acclaimed album *What's Going On?* (1971) caused a commotion. "I pray every single day FOR A REVOLUTION! ... And I scream from the top of my lungs, WHAT'S GOIN' ON?!" It became young activists' research question in the early 1970s.

The 1970s saw a flourishing of pop music. Richard Jon Smith, Jonathan Butler, Colin Ricketts and the Prumes, and the Rockets, burst on to the scene. They enjoyed a ready niche, playing to capacity crowds in the Dolly-Doo (Elsies River), Black Coffin (North End), and Hustler's (in Port Elizabeth).

The standard bearer remained the Invaders. They best understood their sub-culture. Speaking in 1968, Invader Johnny Burke described the pertinence of the group:

> We are really bringing happiness to our friends. We make people forget their cares and worries. To most of our people life is a burden. When they come into the hall they are wrapped up in our music and forget all about debts and where tomorrow's food is coming from. They can let out all their pent-up feelings and, for an hour or two, just forget about life.

This held true for the next five decades. The Invaders are still going strong.

In the mid-1970s, however, a revolutionary music, reggae, contended for space with Motown and pop. It started with Peter Tosh's *Equal Rights* album. Soon after, University of the Western Cape students adopted Bob Marley's "Redemption Song" as their anthem – "Emancipate yourselves *from mental slavery*, none but ourselves can free our minds!" – stepping up from Gaye's question and Tosh's lament, and reaching to what Ngugi waThiongo called "the decolonisation of the mind". As they creatively assimilated this music, it became one of the bases of their revolution.

Coloured sport: into the straight

Like music, sport carried more weight in Coloured circles than party politics. In the 1960s and 1970s, political parties were of little consequence; and the NEUM and an off-shoot, APDUSA, languished in a near-dead slumber.

The "relative" prosperity nudged youngsters into competitiveness and allowed the joy of playing and watching sport. In 1970 football clubs had one, maybe two, teams, drawing mainly on the middle class. By 1975, clubs throughout the country boasted three senior teams and under-18, -16, -14 and -12 teams. In greater Cape Town at least 60 clubs played soccer. Rugby held its own, and cricket and hockey grew. For the first time, juniors played cricket.

In 1973 activists formed the SA Council on Sport (SACOS) and youngsters flocked into its clubs, unions and federations. Here they found a platform for recreation; here they heard unfairness in sport and society addressed. SACOS taught non-racialism, sports management, and democracy.

Drawing on the working class, this council massified sport. Significantly, it expanded the multi-coded SA Primary Schools' Sports Association and SA Secondary Schools' Sports Association into truly national outfits. Inter-provincial multi-code winter and summer tournaments took place annually. It helped SACOS that at its birth, the government had had no choice, given the population growth, but to massify education. In the 1970s Coloured children attended school for longer than their parents and even attended university. They had leisure time, and places where they organised sport. SACOS seized the moment.

Protest assumed the form of support for the All Black rugby team also. The 1970 All Blacks touring South Africa drew near unanimous Coloured support because of the presence of Samoan winger Bryan Williams and Maori scrumhalf Sid Going – even if the tour itself was opposed. In 1976, Maoris Billy Bush, Kent Lambert, Bill Osborne and Tane Norton toured here, and Coloured support for the All Blacks grew exponentially. At a political level they wanted the tour cancelled and the Springboks expelled from test rugby; from a personal plane they wanted to see the All Blacks humiliate the men in green and gold. When, after the killings of 1976 and 1980, the 1981 Springbok tour to New Zealand proceeded, SACOS campaigned to have it cancelled. They found comrades in Halt All Racist Tours' Trevor Richards and John Minto who put their bodies on the bloody lines of protest. Thirty-odd years on, the link endured, as evidenced by film-maker Mark Fredericks's 2011 tour to New Zealand and his documentary "MzaNZi Black: All Black Support in South Africa". Springbok rugby suffered as it teetered, in the 1980s, on the precipice of international isolation.

At the same time, SACOS connected Coloured and African townships, forcing inclusivity. In Port Elizabeth, activists Allan Zinn, Harold

Wilson and Cornelius Thomas respectively brought African athletics, rugby and chess into the non-racial sports movement.

In 1982 SACOS organised the multi-code SACOS Sports Festival in Cape Town, dubbing it the "Olympics of the Oppressed". This grand success showed athletic prowess, organising expertise and social commitment.

For the next six years SACOS set the pace. Excellent sportsmen and sportswomen stepped forward. Debates raged. One asked: Whom to pick, Alistair Coetzee or Divan Serfontein? No objective answers came forth, but an empowering belief suffused the Coloured community. Looking at the textures of post-apartheid sports teams, it seems that belief is now vindicated. The names of the denied – Precious McKenzie (weightlifting), Derrick Orderson (swimming), Terence Smith (100 m track), Lyndon Bouah (chess), Kulu Maclons (cricket) and many others – therefore resurface. By 2013, with many Coloureds representing South Africa in sport, one could allow those who recall the greats of before the slack of history-as-therapy. "We were always good enough," they would say. And who could contradict them?

In this process, Coloureds and Indians (and some Africans) embraced non-racialism. This did not negate the comfort the majority of Coloured people had with Euro-culture, and the pragmatism with which they approached politics.

From 1973 to 1988, SACOS refused to play normal sport in an abnormal society; they asked the world not to play with apartheid. They politicised sport and rallied the sports bodies everywhere against apartheid sports. By 1988, through sports activism, Coloureds had made a vital contribution to forcing the apartheid government toward the rendezvous of negotiations.

Starting in 1988, however, the ANC sports body, the National Sports Congress (NSC), outmanoeuvred SACOS and negotiated South Africa's return to the Barcelona Olympic Games in 1992, and found a nation-building moment in the Springbok victory in the 1995 Rugby World Cup tournament. School and community sports collapsed though. SACOS blamed the NSC's emphasis on Model C schools and sports academies which neglected township children. In 2006 New Unity Movement president Basil Brown lamented this "betrayal". But who betrayed Coloured sports people? The NSC who worked for change, or the SACOS politicos who slipped into bourgeois privacy?

Over and above music, sports and politics, the 1970s and 1980s also saw Coloureds participating in service clubs, and the finer arts of drama, opera and dancing. As the working class gate-crashed into the pop music scene, the middle class gracefully glided into *langarm* (long-arm) and ballroom dancing, the latter at a competitive level. Ballroom clubs started up all over. *Langarm* bands tightened up and played in "strict time" for these events. In 1978, the South African (Coloured) Ballroom and Latin Dancing championship took place in Bellville. World ballroom champions Chu and Susie Tanaka from Japan served as judges. All and sundry glowed to see their children impressing the Tanakas. Coloured "society" found pride and joy in being part of the finer world.

Activism

From 1972 to 1978 students at the University of the Western Cape (UWC) and a minority of community-based activists adopted black consciousness (BC) as an ideological instrument – to achieve liberation from psychological deference to white supremacy and to overthrow apartheid. UWC students Peter Lamoela and Henry Isaacs led the BC torchbearer, the South African Students' Organisation, in 1972–73.

Did this instrumentalism detract from the cultural constructionism of "brown" people? This cannot be asserted. After all, they lived their lives as "*bruin mense*". BC did not negate difference. In fact, the students' position aside, many Coloureds quietly and gratefully accepted racial separations.

The UWC philosophy lecturer and poet Adam Small perhaps offered a bridge between Coloured culture and black consciousness. In the 1960s Small produced plays and poetry anthologies in Coloured Afrikaans. This way he brought Coloureds home to themselves and indeed to the community (one of the main tenets of BC). Not surprisingly, then, much of black consciousness at UWC and in Cape Town was expressed through Afrikaans. Because of Small's literary oeuvre, Coloureds held on to a newfound pride. At the level of culture, Small gave a new form of Afrikaans (as it spilled out authentically) acceptance, even legitimacy. Small was belatedly (in 2012) awarded the Hertzog Prize for drama – poetic justice for *Kanna Hy Kô Hystoe* (Kanna, he came home).

However, even as the mostly Afrikaans-speaking UWC students entered BC, they sang songs from the American folk canon for inspiration –

"We shall Overcome", "Little Houses", and an adaptation of Woody Guthrie's "This Land is your Land" – this cultural connection continued.

UWC students therefore drove many of the protests of 1973 through 1980. In 1973 they tried to close down their university as a "tribal" institution, an apartheid instrument. They failed. But they fuelled a new conversation about being inclusively "black" for political purposes. They rejected Colouredism as a divide-and-rule instrument, but not as culture.

In 1976 they sparked the uprising in the Western Cape and made it part of the national liberation project. They attacked the apartheid dispensation in violent rhetoric and in deed. More than a hundred people, mostly children, died on Cape Flats streets in 1976, including Christopher Truter, Sandra Peters and Christie Swart.

The "classes" of '76 and '73 laid the basis for the uprising of the 1980s. The 1980 school boycotts began in February 1980. At Mountview and Crystal high schools the children refused "gutter education", insisted on equal education, and demanded salary parity (with white teachers) for their teachers. They called for "people's education". "Another Brick in the Wall" from Pink Floyd's *The Wall* album became their anthem. Within two months, schools from across the Western Cape had joined the action. The boycott spread to Johannesburg, and in one incident there, police detained hundreds of Coloured pupils on 29 April 1980.

This protracted boycott resulted in sophistication in protest organisation. The high schoolers, including pupils from African schools, formed the Committee of 61, which grew to the Committee of 81. This body openly orchestrated the boycott. Yet, neither the security police nor their uniformed peers could quash it because each member had a lieutenant, an alternate, to attend the next meeting in case the police detained the previous member.

Police shot dead Bernard Fortuin (15) and William Lubbe (19). Street protests resulted in 42 shot dead. The list of martyrs grew but, like Abraham Esau, Truter and Peters, Fortuin and Lubbe were soon forgotten.

Concurrently, a number of boycotts – the red meat, bus and Fattis and Monis boycotts – raged in the mother city, children and parents all involved. Reflecting on 1980, one of its leaders, 30 years later to become Minister of Economic Affairs, Ebrahim Patel said:

> Hundreds of thousands of young people got their first taste for organisation, from a young 13-year-old Ashley Kriel who organised ... at

Central Park Primary School in Bonteheuwel ... to Galiema Pieterson, who was to become a garment worker a year or two later. Student organisation was firmly entrenched after the boycott. SRCs were maintained at most schools and [one] was re-established at UWC in 1981 ... The young people of 1980 were special. They took on a big task; they changed our world.

The activists of 1980 worked with their African peers; they reached for an inclusive solution. Anti-apartheid cleric Allan Boesak stirred liberation and black theology into this mix. In January 1983, he proposed the idea of a United Democratic Front (UDF) to oppose implementation of the tricameral parliamentary system. This apartheid initiative offered Coloureds and Indians side-rooms in Parliament to address their own affairs. Except for a minority of "collaborators", these groups rejected this ploy. In August 1983, civic, labour, church and activist bodies formed the UDF in the township of Mitchell's Plain. Leaders present at the formation included Trevor Manuel, Cheryl Carolus and Feroza Adam.

The headline-grabbing Labour Party and Coloured Management Committee politics distracted attention from the leadership role Coloureds played in the liberation movement. Despite the formation of the UDF, Allan Hendrickse and cohort entered the tricameral parliament in 1984.

In the wake of 1973, 1976 and 1980, young men slipped into exile, some for military training. From 1976 to the mid-1980s, youngsters formed underground cells. For them one solution existed: destroy apartheid.

In April 1984, MK soldier Clifford Brown from East London died in a shoot-out with police in Durban. It was one of the few frontal combats involving an MK soldier. While other MK soldiers may have been victims of assassinations or of one-way attacks, the Brown incident constituted manly resistance to a "military" force. He stood his ground; he fired back until he died.

Despite proscriptions, Brown's burial became a funeral-cum-political rally, over which the Rev. Eddie "Klein Boesak" Leeuw presided. Although unstated, it revealed a "brown" presence in the ANC-MK. Brown's martyrdom served as a turning point in Coloured politics in East London, a shift toward the ANC. The subsequent assassination (in Maseru in 1985) of Leon Meyer and his partner Jackie Quinn further steeled brown East London to support the ANC.

Boycotts and unrest flooded the Cape Flats in 1985. On 15 October, police officers hiding in wooden boxes on the back of a truck opened fire on a group of protesting school children, adults going about their business, and inquisitives. Michael Miranda (11), Jonathan Claasen (21) and Shaun Magmoed (16) collapsed, dead, on the frontline of the struggle. "*Julle's moordenaars*" (You are murderers), an eyewitness said. Given the visual footage of the incident, this assertion is correct.

This Trojan Horse-like incident turned the people of the Cape Flats away from whites, especially Afrikaners, and toward the ANC. Many young men joined MK. The Bonteheuwel Military Wing (1984–1987) associated itself with MK and increased its nocturnal activities, erecting blockades and launching petrol bomb attacks. Cadres fell on the frontline: Coline Williams, Robert Waterwich, Anton Fransch, Ashley Kriel. Policeman Jeffrey Benzien shot a handcuffed Kriel, killing him on 9 July 1987.

From 1969 to 1989, Coloureds engaged in the struggle, mustering cultural materials and manly resistance to achieve freedom. This period constituted a revolution in their thinking and action.

Ungrand finale

On 30 December 1993, with South Africa on the verge of a new, negotiated dispensation, six Azanian People's Liberation Army "soldiers" raked a civilian crowd in the Heidelberg Tavern in Observatory (Cape Town) with bullets. Young people across the "racial" spectrum frequented "Obs" clubs and bars. Two Coloured girls, among others, died in the spray of bullets.

Five months later, 67% of Coloureds who voted in the first democratic election in South Africa gave their vote to the National Party; 50% of Indians and 60% of whites did so too. The ANC pulled 27% of the Coloured vote. What made brown people change their minds about the ANC? Despite having had some of their boys on the struggle frontline, the more cautious parents never supported or trusted the African majority. The numbers tell other stories also. The practice of inclusive and pragmatic politics remained alive. This time, Coloureds sided with cultural kin – from John Tobin to Peter Marais – they had come the full circle. They refused to make a pact with cowardly behaviours – attacks on civilians, necklacing and the "burning down the house" trend. Finally, they probably feared the loom of (reverse) racism. As a powerless minority, they had to make pragmatic choices.

In the new South Africa, the Coloured elite hurried into white suburbs and schools. "Let us live for our children" was the TLSA resonant. Parents thought: "We fought for opportunity and freedom of choice so we're going to send our children to the best schools."

The talented 10% of Coloured children as a result disappeared into better schools, sports academies, and, eventually, good jobs. Those left behind in township schools suffered lack of resources, role models, coaches, and sports administrators. However, most Coloured people still knew themselves and continued to practise their language, religion, and culture.

Economic empowerment and equity policies favour(ed) Africans over Coloureds. The latter have consequently become poorer in the new South Africa. They also became disaffected and found political homes outside the ANC.

The majority of Coloureds suffered colonialism, segregation, apartheid and exploitation. Yet, at various times in the twentieth century they were let down by those who commanded power, if by their cultural kin (Afrikaners and English), political comrades (ethnic Africans), or by the "better sort" of "browns". They will remember history with a blend of bitterness and joy.

26
The Indians in South Africa
Goolam Vahed

The first Indians to arrive in what is today South Africa were slaves imported by the Dutch East India Company in the seventeenth century from Bengal and South India. They were few in number and over time became absorbed into the Cape Malay population. The majority of the Indians in present-day South Africa are descendants of the 152 184 indentured labourers who came to the British colony of Natal between 1860 and 1911 to work mainly on the coastal sugar plantations that were established by British settlers. The need for labour arose because the indigenous Zulu people had access to land in reserves and on Christian missions, and resisted absorption into the colonial economy.

The first group of 342 indentured Indians arrived aboard the *Truro* on 16 November 1860. Indentured migrants were highly stratified. Of these, 62% were men, 25% women, and 13% children. Two-thirds were Tamil and Telegu speakers from Tamil Nadu and Andhra Pradesh in south India; the rest were from Bihar and Uttar Pradesh in the north. Over 80% were Hindu, around 15% Muslim, and there were a small number of Christians. Indentured migrants were from several hundred castes, ranging from upper-caste Brahmins to the outcaste Pariahs. Madras was the point of departure from the south and Calcutta from the north. Migrants from southern India mainly spoke Tamil and Telegu; northerners spoke various dialects of Hindi which came to form a South African Hindi.

In terms of the contract that the indentured people signed, they agreed to work for five years for the employer to whom they were assigned. They were to perform all tasks given to them and were free, at the end of five years, to either re-indenture or seek work elsewhere in Natal. Although they were entitled to a free return passage after 10 years, the majority remained in the colony after indenture. The terrible working conditions on plantations have been well documented. Hard work, long hours, inadequate medical facilities, and appalling living conditions were the norm. Indentured Indians had few ways of resisting their exploitation. Formal control included draconian laws which viewed all contractual offences as criminal acts and sanctioned legal action against the indentured for "laziness" and "desertion". Workers could not venture more than 3 km from the estate without the employer's written permission, even if the purpose was to lay a charge against that employer. They could not live off the estate; refuse any work assigned to them; demand higher wages; or leave the employer. Most protest was consequently individualistic, and comprised acts like absenteeism, desertion, suicide, feigning illness, and destruction of property.

Traders from Gujarat on the west coast of India followed from the early 1870s. They were termed "passengers" because they came at their own expense and were subject to the ordinary laws of the colony. Passenger Indians settled mainly in Natal and the Transvaal (ZAR), although there were small numbers in the Cape as well. According to the 1911 census, there were 149 791 Indians in South Africa, with just over 130 000 living in Natal. Around 30 000, or 20%, were of passenger origin.

Religion and culture were the strongest bases around which the first Indian migrants organised their lives. From their very arrival, Indians erected tiny wattle, daub, and thatch shrines and temples on sugar estates. The first wood and iron temple was built in Rossburgh in 1869. Temples dotted the Natal coastline and it was here that communal worship was experienced; birth, marriage and death ceremonies observed; and festivals carried out.

Numerous festivals were observed: Thaipusam (Kavady), Diwali (Dipavali), Purattasi, Holi, and Krishnasthmi (or Krishna Jayanti) marking the births of Rama and Krishna. They also read about them in the two great Hindu scriptures, the *Ramayana* and the *Bhagavad Gita*. Visiting Indian missionaries helped to establish bodies to unite Hindus, establish vernacular education, and provide religious training. Swami Shankeranand convened a national conference in 1912 where the South African Hindu Maha Sabha was formed. The mosque was the heart of Muslim community. The first mosque was built in Grey Street in 1881 by passenger Indians Aboobaker Amod and Hajee Mahomed. It remains the largest mosque in the southern hemisphere. Most Muslims observed the festivals of Muharram and Eid. Anglican and Catholic organisations were also active. They used the networks of relations with Chennai (Madras) to import educated Christian Indians from the southern parts of India to teach in state and church schools.

Constructing a racial order, 1890–1910

Economic competition from Indians was a major cause of white hostility, particularly from around 1894 when Natal's Indian population of 46 000 exceeded the then white population of 45 000 for the first time. While indentured migrants were entitled to a free return passage to India after ten years in the colony, more than half remained in Natal. They earned a living primarily as market gardeners and farmers but as the 1904 census showed, Indians were involved in a variety of occupations – there were accountants, clerks, cooks, domestic workers, laundry workers, plumbers, fishermen and tailors. Growing Indian economic competition was, according to the Wragg Commission of 1885, the cause of "much of the irritation existing in the minds of European colonists". Once Natal achieved self-government in 1893, laws were promulgated to limit Indian franchise, curb immigration, restrict trade, and impose burdensome taxation. Laws also limited the entry of Indians, and those who were already in the colony had to re-indenture or return to India after completing their indentures.

Anti-Indian legislation was introduced throughout southern Africa. In the Transvaal, Law 3 of 1885 provided for separate residential and trading areas for Indians and "Arabs"; the Free State prohibited Indian settlement from 1891; and the Cape introduced immigration restrictions from 1903. In 1906 a law was passed in the Transvaal, now a British colony, requiring Indians to register. As South Africa moved towards Union in 1910, Indians made representation to the imperial authorities in Britain for protection, but to no avail. Indians, coloured people and black people were made to suffer in the interests of reconciliation between the Afrikaners and the English.

Mohandas K. Gandhi and the Natal Indian Congress

Mass-organised political activity began in 1894 with the founding of the Natal Indian Congress (NIC). Mohandas K. Gandhi, a London-educated lawyer who had been brought to Natal in 1893 by a trader to assist in a legal case, was its first secretary. The NIC's strategy was primarily constitutional and comprised petitions and memoranda to private persons and government officials, and, when these failed, passive resistance. Gandhi fought for Indian rights on the basis that they were citizens of the British Empire and he tried to demonstrate Indian loyalty to the empire by volunteering to serve as ambulance corps during the Anglo-Boer War (1899–1902) and the 1906 Zulu Rebellion in Natal.

The aftermath of the Anglo-Boer War saw more anti-Indian legislation being introduced in the Transvaal, which was now under British rule. This resulted in Gandhi changing his politics and tactics. He started a newspaper, *Indian Opinion*, in 1903 to publicise the grievances of Indians and put across his own ideas about life, religion, economics, and politics. He opened his first ashram (place of community retreat) in Phoenix where the newspaper was housed, and another at Tolstoy Farm outside Johannesburg in 1910, where he attempted to put his ideals into practice. While Indians in Natal laboured under the burden of the poll tax, between 1906 and 1910 Gandhi was preoccupied with passive resistance against racial legislation in the Transvaal. By 1909 only a few loyal supporters remained engaged in Gandhi's "movement".

Gandhi's philosophy and political ideology underwent an important transformation between 1906 and 1909. He was deeply influenced by the works of John Ruskin, Leo Tolstoy and William McIntyre, and in 1909 wrote *Hind Swaraj*, in which he argued that "Home Rule is Self-Rule", that is, Indians should not adopt a British-styled society when the British left. He also rejected Western civilisation itself and called on Indians to adopt Swadeshi (self-reliance), which implied giving up all trade with the British. He also argued passionately that Indian independence would only be possible through passive resistance. This meant forsaking violence in favour of the "force of love and pity".

The Act of Union in 1910 confirmed existing anti-Indian legislation. When G.K. Gokhale, member of the Imperial Legislative Council of India, visited South Africa in 1912, the tax was in the forefront of Indian grievances. Gokhale discussed the tax issues with the Union government which gave the impression that it would be repealed. When the government denied this, Gandhi considered it ethically proper to pursue its repeal. The tax was one of several demands listed by Gandhi – others included the right to inter-provincial migration; equitable licensing laws; and recognition of Indian marriages. The government rejected these demands and Gandhi initiated a strike by 4000 Indians on 16 October 1913 at the coal mines in northern Natal. The success of the strike was assured when 15 000 Indians on coastal sugar estates joined at the end of October.

Violence associated with the strike, police brutality, and the use of mine compounds as prisons led to widespread negative media coverage in India and England. The Indian government pressured the South African government to appoint a commission of inquiry and to release Gandhi. Shortly after his release Gandhi met with General Jan Smuts, the Minister of the Interior at the time, and their agreement and the findings of the Solomon Commission led to the passing of the Indian Relief Act of 1914, which abolished the tax; facilitated the entry of wives and children of Indians domiciled in South Africa; and recognised marriages contracted according to Indian religions.

However, Indians were still banned from the Free State and only Indians born in South Africa before August 1913 were allowed to enter the Cape. Furthermore, the restrictions against Indian immigration remained in place. Gandhi left South Africa in July 1914 and the Indians themselves continued the struggle to resolve outstanding grievances.

The era of segregation, 1914–1948

Indians became transformed into an urban-based proletariat in the three decades that followed the First World War. The percentage of economically active Indian workers in agriculture fell from 26% to 3% between 1921 and 1950, while the number in industrial employment increased from 14% to 33%. Indians were loyal to the British Empire and when the First World War broke out, more than 700 Indians served as stretcher-bearers in East Africa. The expectation that this would result in more equitable treatment was shattered with the revival of anti-Indian agitation and legislation after the war. A 1922 law restricted Indian trade and land-ownership in Durban, while Indians were deprived of the municipal franchise in 1924. Laws were also passed in the Transvaal to close loopholes that allowed Indians to purchase property outside township areas.

The Areas Reservation Bill of 1925, which provided for compulsory segregation, struck directly at the material interests of traders who suggested a round-table conference with the imperial and Indian governments. The conference, held in Cape Town in December 1926, resulted in the Cape Town Agreement, in terms of which the bill was scrapped. India agreed to a scheme for the voluntary repatriation of Indians, and South Africa pledged to "uplift" the living standards of Indians through education and welfare. An Indian agent was appointed to monitor the agreement and facilitate relations between Indians and the Union government.

Indians became firmly rooted in South African during these decades. This is reflected in developments in education, welfare, and sport. Government neglect resulted in welfare work being carried out by private Indian organisations. One of the earliest was the Aryan Benevolent Home (ABH), opened in 1921 by the Arya Yuvuk Sabha (AYS), a religious group established in 1914 to preserve Vedic culture. Muslims led by A.I. Kajee formed the Muslim Darul Yatama Wal Masakeen (Muslim Home for Orphans and Destitutes) in 1934 to feed and educate orphans. The R.K. Khan Hospital and Dispensary Trust, founded by Gandhi's contemporary, Advocate R.K. Khan, started clinics at Somtseu Road, Clairwood, and Sea Cow Lake from the mid-1930s that provided free medical treatment to the poor. The Durban Indian Child Welfare Society was formed in 1927 by middle-class women to deal with poverty, neglect and mental deficiencies among children. By 1950, 44 Indian organisations were registered under the Welfare Organisations Act. Racist policies compelled Indians to look after themselves.

Early education was provided by Christian missions rather than the government. The 1909 Education Commission noted that the government was seriously lagging in providing schools for Indians. Another commission in 1926 reported that existing facilities only accommodated 30% of Indian children of school-going age.

The pride of Indians was Sastri College in Durban, the first high school for Indians in South Africa, which was opened in October 1929. It was named after the Indian agent general, Sir Srinivas Sastri, who had procured funds from Indian merchants throughout South Africa for the school. In the field of technical education, major progress was made when M.L. Sultan, who arrived in Natal as an indentured labourer in 1890, donated the sum of £50 000 for Indian higher education in January 1942. His contribution led to the establishment of the M.L. Sultan Technical College, which evolved into one of the largest providers of technical education in South Africa.

Desperate urban economic conditions in the 1930s led to the emergence of dynamic young leaders such as H.A. Naidoo and George Ponnen who challenged the political hegemony of Indian traders. The majority of Indians lived in extreme poverty during these decades. C.S. Smith of London, who had been working for two years for Hulett's Sugar in Rossburgh, wrote to the town clerk in February 1940:

> As a stranger to Durban from overseas, one of the first things that struck me was the appalling conditions of the majority of Indians here, malnourished and housed in hovels, without any sanitation... Just before Xmas I had to give out the meagre Xmas boxes to the Indians. I have never seen such hopeless, emaciated specimens of humanity. Some had the apathetical look of the half-starved.

G.H. Gunn, Durban's medical officer of health, reported in 1935 that tuberculosis, bronchial asthma, rheumatism, arthritis, dysentery, diarrhoea and pneumonia were widespread among the Indian working classes. The main causes were listed as poor diet, defective sanitation, overcrowding, and the fact that many homes had poor ventilation with clay soil and cement floors.

Many of the new Indian leaders had experienced the harshness of working class life, and were members of the Communist Party. They took up worker issues and tried to forge cross-race partnership with black people. Between 1934 and 1945, as many as 43 unions (16 617 workers) with Indian membership were registered in Durban and they were involved in 46 strikes in Durban between 1937 and 1942. During strikes employers deliberately replaced Indians with black scab labour, resulting in many Indians becoming disenchanted with unions and strike action and more concerned about protecting their jobs.

A radical professional class emerged in the early 1940s. It included Dr G.M. "Monty" Naicker and Dr Goonam, whose grandparents had come as indentured workers, and Dr Yusuf Dadoo of Johannesburg. All three qualified as medical doctors in Edinburgh in the 1930s and became involved in politics when they returned to South Africa. Dadoo, for example, was elected to the National Council of the Non-European Unity Front (NEUF) in April 1939. This was the first attempt by Indians to join forces with other "Non-Europeans", something that the moderate Indian agents had opposed.

These developments took place in a context of increasing anti-Indianism on the issue of residential and business segregation. Older Indian politicians were seen as very moderate and younger politicians, led by Monty Naicker, and with the support of trade unions, ousted the old leadership of the NIC in October 1945. The same thing happened in the Transvaal where Dadoo became president of the Transvaal Indian Congress (TIC).

The NIC launched a passive resistance campaign against the Ghetto Act of June 1946, which limited Indian property ownership. The campaign began on 13 June 1946. By the time it was halted in June 1948, over 2000 arrests had been made. Factory workers, housewives, laundry workers, municipal workers, shopkeepers, tailors, waiters, and bus conductors volunteered for arrest.

The NIC then turned to India for support. Dadoo and Naicker visited India in March 1947, where they met with Gandhi. The Indian government also raised the question at the United Nations (UN). In December 1946 the UN called upon the South African government to treat Indians in conformity with the provisions of the UN Charter. Passive resistance ended suddenly in June 1948. When the National Party (NP) came to power that same year, the Indian congresses congratulated Dr D.F. Malan and announced that the campaign was being suspended until the new government pronounced on the future of Indians.

The age of apartheid

In March 1947 Dr Dadoo of the TIC and Dr Naicker of the NIC signed a declaration of co-operation with Dr A.B. Xuma, president general of the ANC, pledging "the fullest co-operation between the African and Indian peoples". This so-called "Doctors' Pact" was intended to herald joint political campaigns. Yet, less than two years later, the spectre of racial tension reared its ugly head when the Afro-Indian riots of 1949 brought the relationship between Indians and black people into sharp focus. Simmering tension between them gave way to four days of violence in January 1949 between these two groups, resulting in 142 deaths, 1087 injuries, and the destruction of many shops and homes. Thousands of refugees remained in emergency camps months after the riots.

The roots of the riots are to be found in the competition for jobs, social space, and services between Indians and black South Africans as they moved into the city in large numbers. Durban's population had in fact more than doubled between 1936 and 1951. The number of Indians increased from 15 631 to 123 165 and that of black people from 18 929 to 109 543 between 1904 and 1949. In addition to competing for the same jobs, black people had to travel on Indian-owned buses; rent shacks from Indian landowners in Cato Manor; and buy from Indian traders. As inflation cut the level of real wage levels and increased levels of joblessness among black people in the 1940s, competition became racialised and exploded into violence.

The violence shocked the Indian and African Congresses, who tried to build on the "Doctors' Pact" by carrying out joint campaigns in the 1950s, starting with the Defiance Campaign of 1952. Around 8000 people were arrested during this protest against apartheid laws. In June 1955 the Congress of Democrats, which included the South African Indian Congress, adopted the Freedom Charter, which embraced a non-racial identity. The Treason Trial (1956–1961) that followed included many Indians, such as Dr Dadoo, Dr Naicker, Ayesha Dawood, and M.P. Naicker, and helped to strengthen unity. The year 1960 saw the banning of the ANC, the South African Communist Party (SACP), and the Pan Africanist Congress (PAC), following the killing of 67 protesters against passes at Sharpeville on 21 March 1960.

Although the NIC was not banned, its leaders were served restriction orders and the organisation was effectively silenced. This ended an important link between Indians and black people, albeit a tenuous one, since the alliance between the NIC and ANC had failed to effect a transition to non-racial politics at the level of the masses. Ahmed Kathrada, Billy Nair and many other Indians were incarcerated on Robben Island, while others like Mac Maharaj, Sam Ramsamy, and M.P. Naicker carried on the struggle in exile. Many of those who remained in South Africa suffered imprisonment and torture. Some even paid the ultimate price – Suliman Saloojee (1964), Ahmed Timol (1971), and Dr Hoosen Mia Haffejee (1977) for example, were political prisoners allegedly murdered by the security forces while in detention.

As apartheid became entrenched, racial boundaries were more fixed. Apartheid had ambiguous consequences for Indians. Many suffered emotionally, psychologically, and materially as over 140 000 Indians were forcibly relocated from their original homes in Durban to two new major townships, Chatsworth and Phoenix. They were moved far from their places of work, resulting in higher transportation costs, and extended families were torn apart because township life encouraged nuclear living. This disruption of family and community life increased alcoholism, crime, and divorce rates. Areas like Reservoir Hills, La Mercy and Westville were made available for segregated Indian middle-class housing.

While apartheid caused a great deal of suffering, some Indians benefited from the establishment of "own" institutions and the period from the mid-1960s to the early 1990s witnessed economic mobility. The legal position of Indians changed in 1961 when they were granted the status of permanent residents. A Department of Indian Affairs was established and Indian advisory bodies were created. The South African Indian Council, which comprised nominated members, was inaugurated in 1968. Local Affairs Committees (LACs) were also established to advise local authorities on matters affecting Indians. Conservative elements who had been displaced from the NIC in the 1940s found a home in these bodies.

Economic mobility among Indians after 1960 was due in large measure to the expansion in education, which came under the control of the Department of Indian Affairs in 1965. The 2001 census showed that among Indians over the age of 20, only 13% had not been to secondary school. The enlargement of the M.L. Sultan Technical College and establishment of the Springfield College of Education for teacher training, and the University of Durban-Westville, which was an apartheid era institution established in 1961 for Indians, increased the number of Indian professionals and artisans. Working classes benefited from the growth of industry in Durban, particularly women who found work in clothing and textile factories.

From the late nineteenth century Indians were actively involved in a host of organised sports – soccer (football), cricket, cycling, boxing, and wrestling, to name a few. In soccer, an indentured migrant named Sam China sponsored the Sam China Cup and between 1903 and 1971 provincial Indian soccer teams competed against one another every two years for this trophy. Until the 1950s sport was played along racially divided lines. The first tentative steps towards non-racialism were taken in the 1950s when Indian, black and coloured "national" teams competed against each other. This, however, was seen to reinforce racial identities and from the 1960s soccer and cricket was played under non-racial bodies, the South African Soccer League and the South African Cricket Board of Control. Indian sports officials were involved in the formation of the South African

Council of Sport (SACOS) in 1973 which led the drive to isolate South African sport internationally.

The most famous Indian sportsman of this era was undoubtedly self-taught golfer Papwa Sewgolum, a caddie at the Beachwood Country Club, who was spotted by a local benefactor who took him to the Netherlands to compete in the 1960 Dutch Open. Sewgolum won the tournament, won again in 1961 and 1963 and was runner-up in 1964. Allowed to compete in South Africa for the first time in 1963, Sewgolum won the Natal Open, defeating Harold Henning, a player with more than 50 tournament wins in his professional career. In 1965 Sewgolum defeated South Africa's greatest-ever golfer and a legend of the game, Gary Player, at the Natal Open. Due to apartheid laws, Sewgolum was not allowed to enter the Country Club and had to collect his prize outside in pouring rain. There was an international outcry when photos of Sewgolum receiving his trophy in the rain while white players, officials, and spectators sat inside, were shown all over the world. Sewgolum was the runner-up in the South African Open in 1965. The apartheid government responded to Sewgolum's success by banning him from local tournaments and withdrawing his passport, which meant that he could not play overseas. Not even 50 years of age, he died a pauper in 1978.

The politics of moderation was challenged from the early 1970s by extra-parliamentary opposition bodies on several fronts. Steve Biko's Black Consciousness Movement (BCM) sought to construct a proud new political identity of being black. Young Indians like Saths Cooper and Strini Moodley found this philosophy appealing and challenged the racialised politics of older leaders. This was accompanied by a resurgence of worker action which was stimulated by the Durban strikes of 1973. Political resurgence made mass confrontation inevitable. Starting in Soweto on 16 June 1976, the sustained turbulence of the black youth forced the government to institute reforms. In 1983 the tricameral parliament gave ineffective representation to Indians and coloured people, while ignoring black South Africans. The TIC and NIC's vigorous anti-election programme, which included mass rallies and house-to-house visits, resulted in voter turnout of around 10% as Indians emphatically rejected the "reforms".

The revived Indian Congresses formed strong components of the United Democratic Front, which was launched on 20 August 1983 to protest against the tricameral dispensation. It included trade unions, religious bodies, student organisations and civic associations. Another worker's organisation, the Congress of South African Trade Unions (COSATU), became a powerful player in South African politics in the mid-1980s. An Indian, Jay Naidoo, was one of its highest-ranking officials. Mass campaigns heralded a cycle of protest in townships, schools, and factories. Internal unrest, coupled with international sanctions which induced an economic crisis as a result of the shortage of skills and capital, forced the government into reform.

President F.W. de Klerk released Nelson Mandela in February 1990, unbanned political organisations, and initiated multi-party negotiations which ultimately led to South Africa's first democratically elected government in April 1994. As the April 1994 elections loomed, some Indians, like other minority groups, were concerned about looming majority rule given the memories of the 1949 riots and concerns about the impact of possible affirmative policies, and many voted for the National Party in the April 1994 elections. Support for the ANC came mainly from professionals and students.

The post-apartheid era

Indians faced new challenges in post-apartheid South Africa, challenges that reshaped their identities in fundamental ways. South Africa's first democratic election of April 1994 gave birth to the "rainbow children of God". Indians participated in drawing up the constitution and became fully fledged citizens of the country. But apartheid had cast a long shadow by legally separating people on the basis of skin colour, and skin colour ("race") continued to have salience in post-apartheid South Africa where citizens are classified according to race for official purposes. While government considered this essential to achieve affirmative action objectives, this practice perpetuated identity politics. The situation was compounded by South Africa's neo-liberal economic transition. The ANC government is a left-wing alliance but a right-of-centre government whose support comes from white capital and an aspirant black elite. Capital benefited from downsizing, tax concessions, lower inflation, privatisation, and exchange control liberalisation, while Black Economic Empowerment (BEE) policies allow elite black groups to achieve upward mobility. The burden of the poor, meanwhile, increased though a shift from subsidised to commodified services. This resulted in price increases in basic services such as water, electricity, and transport, and the imposition of cost-recovery mechanisms such as disconnecting services and repossessing property when the poor were unable to pay. Unemployment hovered around 40% (unofficially) and 25% (officially), while there was a growing casualisation of labour, and widening gulf between unionised and non-unionised workers.

Periodic anti-Indian outbursts magnified Indian fears in the post-apartheid period. Mbongeni Ngema's 2002 song "AmaNdiya", meaning "Indian" in Zulu, attacked Indians for their alleged unwillingness to accept black people as equals; resisting change; being interested only in making money; and remaining exploitative. Ngema urged "strong men" of the Zulu nation to stand up to Indians. Lyrics such as "we are faced with hardship and poverty because everything was taken by the Indians, but they turn around and exploit us" and "Indians are abusive to black people, being more racist than whites", stirred criticism from many Indians. The song pandered to the aspiring black middle classes, who felt sidelined by Indian retailers who serviced a predominantly black clientele. Though this was a historical grievance, the dynamics were new. Since the late 1980s predominantly white-owned businesses in the major cities have drifted to suburban malls, with immigrants from Bangladesh, India, and Pakistan replacing them. In May 2013, when some government officials allowed the mega-rich Gupta family of India, which had close links with the family of South African president Jacob Zuma, to land a private jet at the Waterkloof Air Force Base, there was widespread anti-Indian sentiment in South Africa.

Many Indians in the post-apartheid period also sought to link with the diaspora. This emergent diasporic identification was not a remnant of dormant apartheid racial identities but the result of new historical circumstances. It was facilitated by the formation of the Global Organisation of People of Indian Origin (GOPIO) in 1989, which successfully fought for dual nationality for overseas Indians. Much of the image of India is a romantic one forged through satellite television catering for both northern (Sony, B4U and Zee TV) and southern Indians (Sun TV and KTV), Bollywood movies, and a knowledge of the "homeland" acquired through websites. Many Indians visit India on pilgrimage, as tourists, or in search of their "roots". There has been negligible secondary migration of Indians to Canada, Australia, and the United States, mainly among professionals.

Despite exciting opportunities on the sporting front, few Indians feature in professional soccer, rugby, and cricket. One exception is batsman Hashim Amla, who became the first South African to score a Test match triple century with his 311 not out against England in 2012.

The South African constitution respects difference and many Indians have been turning inwards in defining themselves. The sense of "Indian" community was always a loose one, and Indian identities have been revolving around religious revival (Hindu, Muslim, Christian); ethnic and language consciousness (Hindi, Telegu, Gujarati, Tamil); and identification with region of origin in India (north, south). One notable feature has been the high level of Hindu conversion to Pentecostalism. In 1996, 18% of Indians were Christian; by 2001 this had increased to 24,4%. The 2011 census did not take account of the category "religion" but the percentage would have increased significantly. Class divisions among Indians have become starker, as reflected in the movement of middle-class Indians from the old neighbourhoods of Chatsworth and Phoenix in KwaZulu-Natal and Lenasia in Gauteng and into the formerly white areas such as Queensburgh in KwaZulu-Natal (KZN) and Robertsham in Gauteng, while more affluent Indians have migrated to Houghton in Gauteng and Umhlanga in KZN. The formerly Jewish stronghold of Houghton now boasts two large mosques.

South Africa's Indians have featured strongly in representative institutions since 1994. Members of Parliament included Kader Asmal, Valli Moosa and Dullah Omar; Essop Pahad was a key member of President Thabo Mbeki's office; Dr R.A.M. Saloojee and the late Ismail Meer featured at provincial levels; and the late Justice Ismail Mahomed occupied the most senior legal position in the country.

Despite a strong Indian presence in government, support for the ANC amongst Indians fluctuated in the post-apartheid period, peaking in 2004 as a result of political stability; a perception that crime was decreasing; and the middle and upper strata enjoying economic prosperity. In a context of rising xenophobia, African nationalism, and increasingly violent service delivery protests, some Indians have expressed concern about their place in a future South Africa. On the other hand, in townships like Chatsworth, the Indian and black residents joined forces from the late 1990s to jointly confront local municipalities over commodified services. While there have been mixed signals, it has been clear from the time that indentured Indians began arriving in South Africa from 1860 that most regard South Africa as their home.

27
English-speaking South Africans: uncertain of their identity
John Lambert

While many South African historians have written about Afrikaners, Zulu or other groups, the history and experiences of English-speaking white South Africans remain largely neglected. One of the reasons for this is that it is difficult to say exactly who English-speaking white South Africans are. Until the mid-twentieth century, the great majority were British; today they include all white South Africans who accept English as their home language. Among this diverse group, who often have little other than their language in common, there is a distinct uncertainty about their identity.

The history of English-speaking South Africans began with the British occupations of the Cape Colony in 1795 and 1806. Few Britons settled permanently in the Cape until 1820 when the British government brought in about 4500 settlers and established them mainly in the Eastern Cape frontier region. There were also a number of smaller immigration schemes in the nineteenth century, for example the Byrne scheme of 1849, which introduced about 4800 settlers to Natal. After the discovery of minerals in the 1870s, an increased number of British immigrants flocked to the colonies and the two interior republics. Finally, after the Anglo-Boer War, British immigrants were encouraged to settle in the newly annexed Transvaal Colony.

The British settlers' sense of identity was shaped by local South African conditions. Without adequate roads and postal services, early communities were isolated from one another and developed their own characteristics. Particularly in the early days, many formed close links with Afrikaners and in some cases intermarried. Prominent Afrikaner families such as the Murrays are descended from Scottish settlers who came out to the Cape Colony as teachers in British service or as church ministers. Indeed, had the Great Trek not taken place, it is possible that an Anglo-Afrikaner white group may have emerged.

Within the Cape Colony there were considerable differences between the British who settled in the Eastern Cape and developed a frontier way of life and those of Cape Town with their metropolitan and more liberal traditions. The British settlers in Natal identified so strongly with their region that they adopted a distinctive name for themselves, the Natalians, and developed an aggressively British identity. In the Free State republic, particularly during the presidency of J.H. Brand, they became part of an Anglo-Afrikaner elite group. Most British settlers identified themselves as middle class but after the discovery of gold on the Witwatersrand in 1886, a largely British mining community consisting mainly of miners and artisans settled in the Transvaal, adding a working-class dimension to the community.

Compared to the Canadian and Australasian colonies, relatively few Britons came to settle in southern Africa in the nineteenth century. By 1910, there were less than 500 000 British inhabitants compared to over seven million in Canada, Australia and New Zealand. The British who arrived in South Africa were part of the four main groups who made up the United Kingdom: English, Scottish, Welsh and Irish. Relatively few Welsh or Irish came. The English were the largest group, followed by the Scots whose contribution to the development of white South Africa was also significant.

The great majority of settlers, whether English, Scottish, Welsh or Irish, wherever they settled in South Africa and whether middle class or working class, were staunchly British. They came to South Africa at a time when Britain was the world's main industrial, naval and commercial power. This encouraged a sense of pride in British achievements among the settlers, which they shared with British settlers elsewhere in the British Empire.

The term English-speaking South Africans only came into general use in South Africa from the early twentieth century. Until then the settlers and their descendants referred to themselves as British or as English, because most of them were from England. Their Afrikaner neighbours seldom made a distinction, referring to all as either "*die Engelse*" or "*die*

Britte", arguing that they were all English because the language they spoke was English. This chapter will also refer to the "English" to distinguish the British in South Africa from those in the United Kingdom.

> **STILL BRITISH**
>
> The English in South Africa maintained their British identity by continuing their links with their families in Britain through letters and by visits to the United Kingdom which succeeding generations still referred to as "home". The English language obviously linked them to the British in the United Kingdom and elsewhere in the British Empire. Most of the English speakers belonged to churches such as the Anglican, Presbyterian or Methodist which also retained close links with their mother churches in Britain.
>
> Their whole way of life, their habits and traditions in southern Africa continued to be predominantly British. Because the settlers found conditions in South Africa strange and alien, they did their best to make their new home as similar to Britain as possible. They planted British plants and trees and built homes which they filled with furniture, pictures, books and flowers from home. The first settlers renamed the Zuurveld "Albany" and they and their descendants gave British place names to farms, towns, streets and suburbs.
>
> Although some of the settlers remained on the land as farmers in the Eastern Cape and Natal, most moved into the towns and villages, dominating urban life even in the Transvaal and Orange Free State until the 1930s. Many South African towns owed their vitality to their English inhabitants. Through close links with the United Kingdom, they developed southern Africa economically and commercially and introduced agrarian, industrial and mining capitalism to the region. They also opened schools, libraries, museums, and cultural and philanthropic societies in southern Africa and established branches of British or imperial charitable associations, such as the Freemasons, various Caledonian societies and the Sons of England. These served as important agents in maintaining British cultural identity and values as well as providing congenial meeting places where men could make important business as well as social contacts.

Institutions that shaped British identity

From the 1820s prominent Scottish settlers such as John Fairbairn and Thomas Pringle led the campaign for a free press which, once established, became an important influence in shaping English identity in South Africa. The press reflected English political and cultural dominance in South

Africa and provided a useful picture of the way in which the English developed and changed over the decades. With many of their editors drawn from the United Kingdom, newspapers modelled themselves on British newspapers. They upheld a belief in the British Empire and in the excellence of British institutions, particularly the monarchy (which they referred to as the Crown). By providing constant news on the royal family they ensured that the English retained their support for the monarchy. Indeed, the monarchy was to become one of the most important symbols binding the English together in South Africa and in maintaining their links with Britain. Until 1961 they enthusiastically celebrated royal occasions and visits and displayed a personal loyalty to Queen Victoria and her heirs, seeing the monarch, whose authority was symbolised by the presence of the Royal Navy and by the singing of "God Save the Queen/King" and the flying of the Union Jack, as guaranteeing their position in South Africa.

The press led the early campaign for parliamentary government in the Cape and Natal and were strong critics of the powers exercised by British governors and nominated officials in the colonies. Largely through their agitation, representative government was introduced in the Cape in 1853 and Natal in 1856, followed by responsible government in the Cape in 1872 and Natal in 1893. Until the 1930s, the London-based Reuters controlled news entering and distributed within South Africa and kept the English aware of developments in Britain and the empire, particularly the political reforms taking place in Britain and the Canadian and Australasian colonies. The press accepted that the English colonists would control the parliamentary institutions and that they would use their powers to ensure the supremacy of whites in South Africa.

Newspapers also enthusiastically encouraged education. The English established private and government schools that were based on the British school system. They imported principals and senior teachers from the United Kingdom who maintained British syllabi and standards. These teachers believed that character building was as important as formal education and they aimed at turning out not merely educated but also respected members of society – adults who could provide leadership in their own communities and also be well-equipped to rule over the black population. This profoundly shaped the way of life of generations of English-speaking boys and girls and also influenced many Afrikaans-medium schools and those established for black people and coloureds by the missionaries.

The English-oriented schools established cadet corps to train future leaders by instilling obedience and respect for authority. These corps were linked to the volunteer regimental system, the urban English equivalent of the Afrikaner commando system, but were based on British army traditions. Sport was also important both in training future leaders and in shaping English South African identity, both at school and among adults. Boxing was seen as essential in instilling manliness while team sports such as cricket, soccer and rugby were believed to instil leadership qualities.

British team sports and the introduction from the 1880s of competitions between the colonies and republics strengthened British identity at a regional and South African level. The Currie Cup competitions for rugby and cricket as well as test matches played between teams from South Africa, England, Australia and New Zealand were a positive influence. Sporting rivalry often created friction between English and Afrikaans players but playing together in test matches as rugby Springboks was a unifying factor.

Like Afrikaners, most English took racial differences and white superiority over black, coloured and Indian people for granted. This was part of an awareness of their shared white identity with Afrikaners. Clashes between the 1820 settlers and the Xhosa set the pattern for English attitudes. The black population was seen as being a threat to settler life and security and to their economic prosperity. From 1820 onwards, steps were taken to dispossess black people of their lands, either by force or through legislation. They were also socially segregated from whites and were reduced to being suppliers of labour.

Although the Cape had a "colour-blind" franchise, in Natal the English-dominated authority raised the franchise qualifications so much that black people (and in 1896 Indians too) were effectively excluded from voting. The Natal secretary for native affairs, Sir Theophilus Shepstone, introduced a "native" policy that profoundly influenced the development of segregation in twentieth-century South Africa. There were, however, a number of English humanitarians and liberals who advocated non-racialism and rights for blacks. Most were in the Western Cape and included prominent individuals such as John X. Merriman and William Schreiner.

A change in English attitude towards Afrikaners

English attitudes to Afrikaners were initially ambivalent. There was an acceptance that as whites they had more in common with Afrikaners than with black or coloured people. On the other hand, the fact that (as far as white society was concerned, except in Natal) they were outnumbered by Afrikaners, created tension. In the Cape Colony and Free State the English established good relations with the educated Afrikaner upper class. Elsewhere, although at first there was little anti-Afrikaner feeling, there was a general attitude that as British, they were superior to Afrikaners.

By the 1870s, English attitudes to Afrikaners were beginning to change. The formation of the Afrikaner Bond in the Cape in 1879 was followed by the re-establishment of Transvaal independence after the Battle of Majuba in 1881. Afrikaner self-confidence and assertiveness increased and made the English aware of their precarious position as a minority in the white community, leading to an increase in anti-Afrikaner feeling.

Relations between the two groups further deteriorated after the discovery of gold on the Witwatersrand in 1886, which shifted the economic balance of power from the Cape Colony to the Zuid-Afrikaansche Republiek (ZAR). The English in the Cape feared this would undermine their position. The arrival in the Transvaal of working-class British miners and urban dwellers, who were dubbed the Uitlanders (foreigners) further undermined relations between the two groups in the ZAR. The newcomers, especially their leaders, the mine magnates who wanted higher profits in the mining industry, were far more chauvinist, arrogant and contemptuous of Afrikaners than the earlier settlers had been. The Uitlanders resented the taxes the republican government levied on them and its refusal to enfranchise them. Many distrusted Britain's ability or will to protect them and were considering the desirability of establishing an anglicised and reformed republic on the Witwatersrand which they would dominate.

Other Uitlanders wanted British intervention, including the prominent mining group, the Corner House, which gained a monopoly of news when it acquired the Argus Company with newspapers in the Cape and Transvaal. This established a link between mining capital and the press which lasted until the second half of the 20th century and which used its influence to promote British interests. The Johannesburg Reform League was established with Lionel Phillips of the Corner House as its president and Percy Fitzpatrick, also of Corner House, as its secretary. In 1895 the League and another Uitlander body, the National Union, demanded reforms.

In the Cape Colony meanwhile, concerned that the Uitlanders could establish a reformed republic that would be detrimental to Cape interests, the premier, Cecil Rhodes, tried to influence the direction the Uitlanders were taking; in doing so he set in process events that culminated in the abortive Jameson Raid of December 1895. The failure of the Raid polarised English and Afrikaner opinion in southern Africa and led to great bitterness. It also destroyed Rhodes's power base in the Cape that rested on an alliance with the Afrikaner Bond and he had to resign.

While English South Africans like Merriman and Schreiner and the Natal premier, Sir John Robinson, condemned Rhodes and vigorously opposed the direction British policy was taking in the ZAR, many English were convinced that Britain had to become more involved in South Africa if their own position was to be secured. In March 1896 they founded the South African League to work for British supremacy. Throughout southern Africa petitions demanded the redress of Uitlander grievances and called for British intervention. The appointment of Sir Alfred Milner as British high commissioner in 1897 and his forceful assertion of British interests, particularly his 1899 reference to the Uitlanders as "helots" (slaves), convinced the English that the British government would act to protect its paramountcy in South Africa, and their demands for British intervention became louder. When Milner linked the Uitlander franchise question to that of imperial supremacy in South Africa, war was difficult to avoid and the English press stepped up its campaign for intervention. By the time the Anglo-Boer War broke out in October, the Uitlanders were leaving the Transvaal in droves, with many either joining colonial volunteer regiments or forming regiments such as the Imperial Light Horse to fight against the republics.

On the whole, English South Africans, led by their press, staunchly supported British actions during the war. They condemned colonial Afrikaner support for the republics and clamoured for the annexation of the two Boer republics. They also did not condemn the British army's scorched-earth policy nor the establishment of the concentration camps. In the Cape many supported Milner's attempts, ultimately unsuccessful, to suppress the constitution, and supported the disfranchisement of colonial rebels after the Anglo-Boer War. The English community's jingoism and anti-Afrikaner attitudes did much to destroy any chance of a lasting Anglo-Afrikaner understanding after the war.

English identity and political developments after the Anglo-Boer War

By the end of May 1902, with the war over and the mines on the Witwatersrand reopened, the Uitlanders returned to what was now the Transvaal Colony. Imperial rule was established throughout the entire subcontinent and conditions provided the English with the opportunity of re-establishing themselves as the dominant white group in South Africa. Crown colony administrations with British officials governed in the new colonies; they encouraged British immigration and rebuilt the mining industry.

In the Cape Colony, the South African League, now called the Progressive Party, was committed to maintaining British predominance. In 1904 Leander Starr Jameson (of Jameson Raid notoriety) became the party leader. In the 1904 election, largely because of the disfranchisement of Afrikaner rebels, the Progressives obtained a narrow victory of five seats over the (Cape) South African Party (not to be confused with the SAP formed in 1910, see below). This latter party had been formed by an alliance between the Afrikaner Bond and a handful of anti-imperialist British under Merriman. Jameson formed an exclusively English ministry which remained in office until 1908.

Milner realised that to secure British domination a broad imperial South Africanism should be encouraged, bringing the two white groups together as partners in a united South Africa which could take its place as a dominion alongside Canada, Australia and New Zealand. Milner's efficient young officials in the Transvaal, known as the Kindergarten, including Patrick Duncan as colonial secretary, worked towards establishing a united South Africa. This ideal was supported by the two defeated Boer generals, Louis Botha and Jan Smuts, both of whom were prepared to accept the sovereignty of the Crown and South Africa's place within the British Empire. Symbolic of this new South Africanist attitude was the growing tendency for the English to describe themselves as English-speaking South Africans.

Yet, divisions within English society meant they could not capitalise on the imperial triumph. In the Transvaal the English were divided into three political parties: The first was the Transvaal Progressive Association under Sir George Farrar and Sir Percy Fitzpatrick, which supported Milner's policies. The second was the National Association under E.P. Solomon which allied itself with the Het Volk Party established by Botha and Smuts, and supported the call for responsible government for the Transvaal. The third was the Labour Party which was formed to protect the interests of skilled workers.

Responsible government was granted to the Transvaal in 1906 and Orange River Colony in 1907 by the new Liberal Party government in London. In the subsequent elections in the Transvaal, the Het Volk Party gained 37 seats; the Progressives 21 seats; the National Association six; and the Labour Party three. In the Orange River Colony, the Orangia Unie under J.B.M. Hertzog won an overwhelming victory. This meant that Afrikaner governments came to power in both colonies with Botha as prime minister of the Transvaal and Abraham Fischer in the Orange River Colony.

In the Cape election in 1908, after the rebel disfranchisement had been lifted, the (Cape) South African Party swept to power with 69 members compared to the Progressives' 33. Merriman became prime minister but real power was wielded by his Afrikaner Bond allies. In other words, Afrikaner-led or dominated parties were now in power in three of the four British colonies. English-speaking South Africans were disappointed with this post-war situation. To them it seemed that all that had been achieved by Britain in the Anglo-Boer War had been lost and their position undermined. They blamed the Liberal Party government in Britain for this; few of them accepted that it was largely their own folly and the divisions within their ranks that were responsible.

Afrikaners were convinced that the primary allegiance of the English was to Britain and not to South Africa. They felt that this was evident in the support they gave to Rhodes and his ambitions and for Milner's aggressive imperialism; their demands for the disfranchisement of Afrikaner rebels; and their support for the suspension of the Cape constitution (responsible government).

Because of the divisions among the English it was impossible for them to take part as a united group in the National Convention (1908–1909) which met to discuss the future constitutional status of South Africa. Because of this, Afrikaners gained political dominance of the new Union of South Africa which came into being on 31 May 1910. The South African Party (SAP) was formed in 1910, thereby uniting the old South African Party of the Cape Colony; the Afrikaner Bond; and Het Volk of the Transvaal. The Afrikaners were in the majority in this new South African Party. The first governor general of the Union of South Africa, Lord Gladstone, decided to appoint Botha rather than Merriman as the Union's first prime minister. This was the final death-blow for English political aspirations.

Under the leadership of Botha and Smuts, the SAP advocated a South Africanist policy based on equality and co-operation between the two races in South Africa as part of the British Empire. In the 1910 general election of 15 September, a minority of English voters supported the party. Natalians voted overwhelmingly for independent candidates in order to protect their distinctive identity under the *Natal Witness* slogan "We are British". In the rest of the country most English speakers voted for the Unionist Party under Jameson's leadership. This was an overwhelmingly middle-class, urban party which incorporated the Cape and Transvaal Progressives. Under the slogan "Vote British", it campaigned for the strengthening of British influence in the Union. Because it was supported by most of the mining magnates, particularly those of the Corner House group, and by the English-language press, the Unionists represented British capitalism in the Union.

For their part, English workers found their political home in the Labour Party under the leadership of F.H.P. Creswell which was essentially a British party. As early as the 1890s, miners had formed branches of their United Kingdom trade unions and these were given political expression in the new party. Despite their rejection of the middle-class and capitalist values of the Unionist Party, they remained closer in sentiment to the English middle class than to their fellow Afrikaner workers.

The political exclusiveness of most English speakers reflected the fact that few had become South African in culture, habits or outlook; they also made a point of retaining their social exclusiveness. Socially, the English tended to mix with only anglicised Afrikaners and this was reflected in the British atmosphere of their clubs, associations, schools, churches and regiments in which few Afrikaners were welcome. Anti-Semitism was rife after large numbers of East European Jews entered the country. The English excluded Jews other than those who came from Britain or who had become anglicised.

Although there were a number of English-speaking ministers in Botha's cabinet, the English had little political power in the Union of South Africa. They were numerically outvoted, divided, and essentially urban in an electorate that was loaded in favour of rural constituencies. The English were also deeply concerned when in 1914 the Afrikaners formed the National Party (NP) under J.B.M. Hertzog. Hertzog's slogan "South Africa First!" and the adoption of secession from the British Empire and republicanism as official policy by the National Party in 1919, threatened everything that the English stood for.

The NP's policy made the English aware of how much they depended on the support of moderate Afrikaners like Botha and Smuts and an increasing number of English speakers transferred their allegiance to the SAP. Jameson had retired in 1912 leaving the Unionist Party with no charismatic leader who could match Botha. The fact that the Unionist Party identified strongly with mining interests made it impossible for it to broaden its base. Furthermore, Smuts's firm handling of the general strike of 1913 encouraged many Unionists to join the ruling party (the SAP). Although the strike was crushed, organised labour had made its strength felt; the Labour Party benefited from this and gained control of the Transvaal Provincial Council in the 1914 election.

The First World War

Political developments in the Union were overshadowed in August 1914 when Great Britain and Germany went to war. The declaration involved the British Empire and English-speaking South Africans responded overwhelmingly. Botha had the support of the Labour Party and the Unionists when he committed South Africa to give Britain military support. Although a small section of the Labour Party broke away, English workers in South Africa proved as committed to Britain's cause as did the British middle class.

On the other hand, Botha realised that he needed English support for his political survival, especially after the National Party began to agitate against the war and a rebellion broke out in October 1914. In the general election of 1915 the SAP won 50 seats and the Unionists 40. Together they therefore had the majority of seats in the newly elected parliament. The NP progressed to 27 seats but uncertainty about where the Labour Party's allegiance lay, saw only four of the party's candidates returned.

With their relatively small numbers in the Union of South Africa and with most of the 8551 white men killed being English, many English-speaking families were directly affected by the war. English troops took part in crushing the rebellion in the Union; fought in South West Africa; and from 1915, served in the 1st and 2nd Infantry Brigades in Flanders and East Africa respectively.

Over 100 000 white men served in South African regiments during the war (official figures of 146 000 are based on a miscalculation) while an estimated 12 000 officers enlisted in imperial units, the Royal Navy and Royal Flying Corps. Of the approximately 160 000 Englishmen of military age in the Union, about 43% served in the Union or British forces.

Churches, sporting and charitable associations urged English South Africans to volunteer. Schoolboys, exposed to military service as cadets, rushed to join their affiliated regiments and many schools ended the war with proud records and the names of old boys inscribed on rolls of honour and memorials. There were many reasons for men volunteering. Patriotic enthusiasm and a sense of duty, of fighting for "King and Country", were important. Other reasons included a desire for excitement and adventure and the need to escape from poverty and unemployment. Comradeship and the need to prove one's masculinity to one's peers was also important in the close-knit world of old boys' associations and patriotic societies.

On 15 July 1916, the 1st Infantry Brigade was ordered to capture and hold Delville Wood in France as part of the British Somme offensive. Driven from most of the wood, the Germans retaliated. Raked by artillery and machine-gun fire from the surrounding hills, the South Africans were pushed into the south-western corner of the wood. They maintained their position until relieved by other Allied forces on 20 July. Of the 121 officers and 3032 other soldiers who went into battle, only 29 officers and 751 other ranks were present at roll call on 21 July. The South Africans had withstood one of the most intense counter-attacks of the Somme and prevented the Germans from re-taking the strategic south-western corner of Delville Wood.

The Battle of Delville Wood was a defining moment in the formation of English-speaking South African identity. Soldiers and civilians alike believed they had upheld British traditions and had fought as valiantly in the war as had soldiers from the other dominions. The camaraderie and danger they had shared with Afrikaner soldiers strengthened their view of themselves as South Africans fighting for the future of their own country, for Britain and for the British Empire. The legend of the "Springboks on the Somme" became an important South Africanist rallying call in the following years.

The English saw the support given by Botha and Smuts to the imperial cause, the co-operation between the SAP, Unionists and the Labour Party, and the number of Afrikaners who fought alongside them, as evidence of growing unity between English and Afrikaner. But English admiration for Afrikaner loyalists was counter-balanced by hostility towards the NP. They blamed the NP for encouraging the rebels and for being so against the Union's participation in the war. Most Afrikaners, by contrast, found English pro-British enthusiasm and their attitude to the rebels deeply offensive.

The inter-war years

Although the war had strengthened their South Africanism, most English continued to regard themselves first and foremost as British subjects, part of the wider British world of which the Union was a part. Yet, as a political minority they remained aware of the dangers that Afrikaner nationalism posed to their position and to the imperial connection.

In the 1920 general election, the National Party won more seats (44) than the SAP (41). Smuts, prime minister since Botha's death, could govern only with the support of the 25 Unionist MPs and in November the SAP and Unionists amalgamated.

In 1923 there was a further significant shift in the political scene. The Labour Party had enjoyed a remarkable recovery since the war and had 21 MPs and now entered into a political "pact" with the National Party. Before the war, for a predominantly British party (the Labour Party) to enter into a pact with the NP (that was in favour of secession from the British Empire) would have been unthinkable. But the leaders of the Labour Party had been angered by Smuts's ruthless suppression of the Witwatersrand miners' rebellion in 1922. The Labour Party also believed that the Pact could strengthen its support among the rapidly growing Afrikaner urban working class.

The victory of the Pact in the 1924 general election established a government overwhelmingly dominated by Afrikaners of the NP, but did have two English Labour Party members in the cabinet, namely Creswell and Walter Madeley. Many SAP Afrikaner supporters had deserted to the NP with the result that the SAP was now largely made up of ex-Unionists.

As part of the Pact government, the NP had agreed not to advocate secession from the British Empire, but the English, including many Labour Party supporters, doubted Hertzog's sincerity. In 1926, their fears were assuaged when Hertzog returned from the Imperial Conference in London, claiming the Balfour Declaration (establishing the equality of the dominions and Britain within what was now becoming known as the British Commonwealth) as a triumph for his diplomacy. This, he argued, made the call for secession unnecessary.

Much of the goodwill towards Hertzog disappeared, however, as a result of the government's introduction of a Flag Bill which threatened the position of the Union Jack. The English in the SAP and the Labour Party rallied to the Jack and in 1927 the government was forced to concede a compromise whereby the Union Jack continued to fly as a national flag alongside a new Union flag.

The worldwide depression of the early 1930s saw a weakening of the government's position and in 1933 Hertzog began negotiations with Smuts which culminated in a coalition between the NP and SAP, with Hertzog as prime minister and Smuts as his deputy. This was followed the next year by the fusion of these two parties as the United South African National Party (UP).

Despite coalition and fusion, Hertzog was determined to stress the independence of the Union. In 1931 the British Statute of Westminster had given legal enforcement to the Balfour Declaration and Hertzog now insisted that the SAP accept the NP's Status Acts which proclaimed the sovereign independence of the Union. The Status Acts provided the English with their first test of loyalty since the Flag Bill. Although uncomfortable with the constitutional change, most English MPs and newspapers accepted the new legislation.

In Natal and the Eastern Province, however, where the English retained a far more British outlook than elsewhere in the Union, eight SAP MPs under Colonel Charles Stallard broke away to form the openly anti-Afrikaner Dominion Party committed to repeal the Status Acts and maintain British interests. However, the new party enjoyed little support and in the 1938 general election won only seven seats in Natal and one in East London. The Labour Party, too, had not recovered from its Pact alliance with the NP and although it retained control of a number of municipalities, the party was reduced to four MPs.

The failure of the Dominion Party to attract much support shows how English-speaking South Africa was changing, even in Natal. Few now saw the Union as a British colony or believed they had the right to impose their views on Afrikaners. Although they, together with Jewish South Africans, continued to dominate economic life in the Union, most were politically apathetic or realised that their numerical inferiority (less than 800 000 in 1936 in a white population of over 2 million) made them dependent on Afrikaner UP leaders like Smuts, trusting them to continue protecting English interests and South Africa's position within the Commonwealth.

English-speaking South Africans' acceptance of the changes taking place was made easier by the fact that they lived in a country which remained outwardly British. The Royal Navy maintained its presence in Simon's Town; English regiments were often designated "Royal" and had royal colonels-in-chief; the governors general (Sir Patrick Duncan was the first South African to hold the office from 1937) continued to represent the Crown in the Union government; and Empire Day and the king's birthday were still public holidays. Commonwealth kinship was also maintained by the Empire Games and test matches with Britain and the dominions; "God Save the King" continued to be sung; and the Union Jack to wave. Parliamentary government remained essentially British, while the English saw the Crown as the ultimate guarantee of their position in the Union.

The arrival of Union Castle Mail ships every week with British imports, including books and magazines, was an important event cementing cultural ties with Britain. Children grew up reading British comics and books which gave them a firmly British view of the world while British journals and books were far more widely available for adults than were American publications. English ties with Britain were cemented by the fact that English-language newspapers continued to reflect British cultural values and followed a pro-British line while the new South African Broadcasting Corporation relayed daily BBC news bulletins and British programmes.

English-speaking South Africans' continuing attachment to Britain and the Commonwealth was strengthened by developments taking place within Afrikaner society. They were concerned by Hertzog's stress on the Union's right to neutrality if Britain was involved in war. They were even more concerned by the formation of D.F. Malan's Gesuiwerde (Purified) National Party and its increasing support among Afrikaner cultural organisations, schools and universities which played an important role in encouraging a separatist Afrikaner identity.

During the centenary commemoration of the Great Trek in 1938 it was obvious that the English were not welcome which did much to alienate them and to encourage their own jingoist attitudes. The situation was reached by the late 1930s where growing intolerance for each others' views made it extremely unlikely that there could be any future in the Union for any form of South Africanism let alone for one based on the acceptance by white South Africans of loyalty to Crown and Commonwealth.

British identity and the Second World War

By the late 1930s, Commonwealth membership seemed increasingly necessary as Nazi Germany became more aggressive and Fascist Italy flexed its muscles in Africa. The English saw Commonwealth membership as incompatible with neutrality and when war broke out in September 1939, the overwhelming majority of English, including the Union's Jewish population, which was now largely middle-class, was profoundly shocked when Hertzog supported neutrality in Parliament.

For Hertzog, participation was incompatible with South African independence. The English-language press spearheaded a vigorous attack and protest meetings were held in the major cities. In Parliament 54 English-speaking members of the UP, Dominion Party and Labour Party and 26 Afrikaner MPs supported Smuts's successful amendment rejecting neutrality. Only one English MP, S.C. Quinlan, who later became a Smuts supporter, and 66 Afrikaner MPs, supported Hertzog.

Patrick Duncan, the governor general, rejected Hertzog's advice that he dissolve Parliament and hold an election. He asked Smuts to form a new government, after which, on 6 September 1939, the Union declared war on Germany. Now with only minority Afrikaner support, Smuts had to rely heavily on English MPs. Eight Dominion Party and four Labour

Party MPs agreed to form a coalition with Smuts and Stallard and Madeley were included in Smuts's cabinet. For the first time since Union, English and Afrikaners had an equal number of cabinet posts.

Volunteering was brisk; by late 1939 most regiments were at full strength and in February 1940, Parliament authorised volunteers to take the Red Oath (or Africa Oath) committing themselves to wear the Orange Flash on their uniforms showing their preparedness to serve anywhere in Africa. By 1945 about 9,3% of the Union's white population had enlisted in the army – 186 218 white men and 24 975 white women – while a further 15 000 men served in the Royal Air Force (RAF) and 2944 served in the Royal Navy (RN).

Information on the number of English who served is based on a general estimate of about 40%. This is conveniently based on the ratio of English to Afrikaners in the country. If this is correct, just over 41% of the approximately 180 000 English speakers between the ages of 18 and 44 years volunteered. This was about 2% less than during the First World War.

Far more contributed in other ways. Many older men or those in the new munitions industry became National Reserve volunteers to maintain internal security. Women served in the Union but some went to North Africa. There they worked in the English Red Cross, St John's Ambulance Service, the South African Military Nursing Service, and the South African Women's Auxiliary Defence Corps.

About 65 000 women, most of whom were English speaking, served in the South African Women's Auxiliary Services. They collected funds and provided comforts and hospitality for the Allied troops stationed in the Union as well as to the crews of the 49 241 ships passing through South African ports. The two ex-servicemen's organisations formed in the 1920s – the British Empire Service League (known from 1941 as the South African Legion of the BESL) and the MOTHS (Memorable Order of Tin Hats) – were active in encouraging volunteering and supporting servicemen's families.

As in the First World War, there were many reasons for volunteering, ranging from the need for employment, particularly among working-class men, to those influenced by a sense of duty. To many, as in the other dominions, the threat of a Nazi invasion of Britain in mid-1940 was a turning point, arousing an instinctive emotional reaction among many English. The decision to volunteer would seldom have been easy, often causing disruption to families, careers and studies.

Serving in North Africa in the Eighth Army (made up of British, dominion and colonial regiments) made the war very much a Commonwealth war, generating enthusiasm for the Commonwealth. There was great admiration for the way the British were enduring the Blitz and the hardships of war and this increased English attachment for Britain. The RAF received particular praise for defending the United Kingdom. Although it was difficult for the English to maintain their illusion that Britain remained a great power, the British connection still shaped the ways the English identified themselves. The generosity with which English-speaking South Africans raised funds for Britain during and after the war bears witness to these sentiments.

Even more than the First World War, English awareness of their South African identity was stimulated by the Second World War. Fighting side by side with Afrikaner soldiers in North Africa built up a spirit of camaraderie between English and Afrikaner soldiers who wore the Orange Flash.

As after the Anglo-Boer War, however, the English squandered the opportunities the war offered. The 1943 general election saw the Smuts coalition government increase its seats to 105 while the opposition's number dropped to 43. This gave the English the opportunity both of consolidating their position in government and of strengthening South Africanism through their alliance with moderate Afrikaners. But they failed to take these opportunities. English MPs, including new cabinet ministers, Harry Lawrence and Sidney Waterson, proved ineffectual, prepared to leave political leadership to their Afrikaner colleagues. Although the Dominion Party had gained nine seats and the Labour Party seven, these were largely through agreements with the United Party; their support among the electorate had in fact plummeted.

After the war, the Labour Party lost control of its municipal strongholds in Johannesburg and Durban and the Dominion Party eventually disbanded and formed a new South African Party (SAP). This latter party became increasingly racist and anti-Indian and in fact had far more in common with Malan's Herenigde (Reunited) National Party (HNP) than with the UP.

To returning soldiers, the war had changed little for the better. Many believed that the UP and English South Africa generally were insensitive to their needs and to those of black ex-servicemen. The English generally were not prepared to accept that the new radicalism reflected in the Springbok Legion could be used to establish a truly South Africanist identity which could embrace all races in the Union. In addition, the spirit of togetherness experienced by English speakers and Afrikaners in North Africa was not reflected at home where at the time, strict segregation between the two groups remained the norm. The post-war years were a time of wellbeing, security and complacency for most English who remained incapable of visualising a changing South Africa. They were remarkably unaware of the threat posed in the short term by Afrikaner nationalism or in the long term by black aspirations.

The visit of King George VI and his family in 1947 gave English-speaking South Africans their final opportunity to celebrate their links with Britain and, as such, its symbolic importance was immense. At a time of growing Afrikaner support for nationalism and for a republic outside the Commonwealth, it reaffirmed their loyalty to the Crown and reinforced their pride in being British.

English speakers and politics from 1948 to the present

The English reaped the reward of their complacency and detachment from politics in the general election of May 1948 which returned an Afrikaner nationalist government to power. The UP polled 47,9 % of the votes compared to the NP's 37,2 %. It also won most urban constituencies and 11 of Natal's 16 constituencies. However, the UP was overwhelmingly defeated in the predominantly Afrikaner constituencies. In total the NP won 70 seats, while its coalition party, the Afrikaner Party, won nine. The UP won 65 seats and the Labour Party six.

Although the great majority of English voted for Smuts, many had been sufficiently alienated from the UP either to abstain or to support the NP. These included English who had more in common with the NP's racial policy or those who were angered by the UP's failure to address the issues that concerned them. Realising the extent of this antipathy, the NP played down their republican policies before the election, concentrating instead on publicising their racial policies.

The new South African Party won no seats while Labour was now supported by only a handful of urban English voters. The UP retained a small core of Afrikaner support (commonly called "*Sappe*") but became essentially an English-speaking, urban party whose only significant rural support was in the English farming heartland of the Eastern Cape and Natal and which maintained provincial control only of Natal.

The defeat of the UP with its commitment to Crown, Commonwealth and South Africanism, profoundly altered English-speaking South Africa's world. From 1948 South Africa was governed by Afrikaners for the benefit of Afrikaners. In the 1950s republicans were appointed as governors general, and the position of the Crown and the obligations of Commonwealth membership were effectively ignored. All things British in South Africa were downgraded. In 1957 for example, "God Save the Queen" and the Union Jack lost their official status.

White South Africa's official memory was manipulated to ensure that Afrikaner history and traditions were privileged. BBC news bulletins were ended and nationalist control of government schools meant that the British contribution to South Africa was ignored or presented as negative. English allegiance to their British traditions and lineage was presented as being "un-South African". The NP ideology effectively alienated many young English speakers from their heritage. Many became, in the South African writer Christopher Hope's words, a "generation who went into exile before they left home".

The changes taking place were not unchallenged. The coronation of Queen Elizabeth II in 1953 saw an upsurge in royalist and Commonwealth sentiment and in the 1960 republican referendum, the English voted overwhelmingly against the republic. The advent of the republic in 1961 marked a traumatic end to their relationship with Britain, forcing the English to confront a future in which more than just political conditions were changing.

They firstly had to accept that they were changing as a group. Although they now numbered over a million, the percentage of British-born among them was steadily dropping because fewer British emigrants came to South Africa. The composition of the group was also changing. As mentioned, while retaining their strong group and religious identity, many Jews were integrated into English-speaking life, as were other whites who were adopting English as a home language. English-speaking South Africa was now more than a British community.

Secondly, they had to accept that the British government was no longer prepared to support white minorities in Africa. The British Labour Party government's response to Rhodesian UDI (Unilateral Declaration of Independence) in 1965 did even more than South Africa's republican status to encourage the English community to rethink their ties with Britain.

The Commonwealth had now become an association dominated by black members and the English were angered by the way in which Commonwealth countries ostracised South Africans and excluded them from international sporting and cultural events. The British cultural boycott of South Africa ensured that young English speakers grew up with an American, not British, cultural worldview.

The English were uncertain of their identity and what their role should be in a republican South Africa. This uncertainty was reflected in the UP (by the 1970s called the New Republic Party) and the newly formed Progressive Party, as well as in the English press. They retained their language rights and continued to dominate South Africa economically and financially, despite NP control of the political structures of the state and Afrikaners beginning to advance in the economy. In addition, the English realised that African nationalism was beginning to threaten their way of life; they now identified with Afrikaners so that they could stand together against black Africans.

Not all did so, however. English speakers in the universities, churches, press, ex-soldiers' organisations and women's organisations such as the Black Sash, and the Progressive Party and Liberal Party were in the forefront of attempts to improve race relations in South Africa and vigorously opposed the NP government. They were relatively few in number, however, and most English speakers reluctantly accepted the disappearance of civil liberties and of British traditions such as free speech, justice and democracy that had underpinned their identity. This was primarily because there was little they could do about it.

Some English remained nostalgic about the past, retaining the symbols of their lost identity. Until the 1990s Union Jacks flew on days of royal and British South African significance on municipal buildings in cities like Durban, Pietermaritzburg and Port Elizabeth. Royal portraits retained their places in city halls, clubs and associations. The Natalians advertised their province as the "last outpost of the Empire". But even nostalgia was declining; by the 1990s ex-servicemen's and other associations such as the Freemasons, Caledonians and the Sons of England were finding it difficult to attract members; many branches were closing.

Despite the general euphoria that accompanied the birth of the new South Africa in 1994 and a greater understanding between whites and blacks arising particularly out of growing social integration at school and in the workplace, both conservative and liberal English-speaking South Africans seemed wary of accepting the new dispensation. Just as Afrikaners accused them in the past, so now do Africans, of being un-South African with roots in what is now a foreign land. Many English-speaking white South Africans who have been alienated by crime, corruption and affirmative action and by what has happened to their kith and kin in Zimbabwe since the late 1990s, have opted out and emigrated to other English-speaking countries. Others have taken refuge in a cynical Afro-pessimism. As an ever-shrinking community uncertain of its identity it is difficult to foresee what the future holds for white English-speaking South Africans.

28

The South African churches and apartheid

J.W. (Hoffie) Hofmeyr and
J.A. (Joan) Millard

Christianity is the largest faith community in South Africa with almost 80% of South Africans calling themselves "Christian". This does not mean that they necessarily belong to one of the main-line denominations or even that they go to church. It just sets them apart from the other faith communities like Islam, Hinduism, Buddhism, Judaism, African Traditional Religion, Atheists and Undisclosed.

Which are the most important Christian churches in South Africa? Firstly, there are the Afrikaans-speaking churches which use Afrikaans as their main language. The most important churches in this group are the Nederduitse Gereformeerde Kerk (Dutch Reformed Church, DRC), the Gereformeerde Kerk (Reformed Church) and the Nederduitsch Hervormde Kerk (NHK, also known as the Nederdutch Reformed Church of Africa). However, a number of the Pentecostal churches like the Apostolic Faith Mission and the Full Gospel Church also use Afrikaans as one of their languages for worship.

Secondly, there are the English-speaking churches which have derived from Britain and who use English as their principle language of worship. There are also other churches like the Roman Catholic, the Pentecostal and Charismatic churches that use English as their language for worship.

Black churches of British origin primarily use languages like Zulu, Xhosa, Tswana and Sotho as their languages of worship, rather than English. The leaders of these English-speaking churches are now mostly black and they are decision makers in their denominations.

Laws that entrenched white privilege in the early twentieth century included the Natives Land Act of 1913, with its purpose of confining black people to certain proscribed limits, and the Urban Act of 1923 which made provision for segregated locations for urban black people. This was further entrenched in 1936 with the passing of another Land Act. Black churches had to apply to the government for recognition and provide evidence of their support before they were allowed to build churches in urban areas. However, mission work continued, especially in the rural areas and mission schools like Lovedale (Presbyterian), Healdtown (Methodist) and Tiger Kloof (Congregational) trained many of the future African leaders, both for South Africa and other parts of Africa. Ex-president Nelson Mandela is an "old boy" of Healdtown.

The constitution of the Union of South Africa in 1910 ignored the voices of African leaders like the Rev. John Dube and J. Tengo Jabavu. It was small wonder that when the South African Native National Congress – the precursor of the African National Congress – was formed in 1912, there were many clergymen, trained in mission schools, among their numbers. The first president of the SANC was the Rev. John Dube, a Congregationalist, while the Women's League was formed a year later by Charlotte Manye Maxeke, a leading member of the African Methodist Episcopal Church.

Pre-1948 the English-speaking churches had separate churches for black and white members although some like the Methodists and Anglicans had one Conference, Assembly or Convocation that encompassed all their members. The Baptist Church had separate organisations with the Assembly for white and the Convention for black members. Although the churches were separate, there was no legal objection to mixed services. Theological training was also separate. Training for Anglican, Presbyterian, Congregational and Methodist African probationer ministers took place at Fort Hare University where each denomination had its own hostel but academic classes were shared. Theological training for white ministers took place at Rhodes University and denominational seminaries like the Roman Catholic St John Vianney Seminary. African education in the mission schools was of a high standard, with Kilnerton (Methodist) being one of the few schools in South Africa that wrote the Joint Matriculation Board Examinations. Leadership in the churches was invariably white even though there were capable black ministers who had been trained in mission schools. During these years there were some voices like Senator Rheinalt Jones of the Institute of Race Relations who spoke out against the lack of rights for black people, but on the whole the white population accepted the status quo. Everything to do with mission and mission education would change after 1948.

One cannot fully understand the Afrikaans churches and their position on apartheid without taking cognisance of their theological and socio-cultural background. Firstly, the three major Afrikaans-speaking churches had a common reformed theological root as from the 1650s onwards before they split into three different branches in the 1850s. The DRC remained a reformed church but with a specific evangelical and missionary-conversion strand to it. The Gereformeerde Kerk was more orthodox reformed in its position, while the Nederduitsch Hervormde Kerk largely split off because of a strong anti-liberal political position, basically aimed at the DRC of the 1850s. Calvinism played an important role in the theological thinking of all three the Afrikaans churches. Eventually this developed into a neo-Calvinism or Afrikaner Calvinism which implied a combination of Calvinism with Afrikaner nationalism. This was to lead to a scriptural foundation for apartheid or separate development.

Secondly, the socio-cultural background of the Afrikaans churches was strongly influenced by the major clash in the late nineteenth century between Afrikaner nationalism and British imperialism. After especially the Anglo-Boer War of 1899–1902 and the scorched-earth policy pursued by the British military, the Afrikaners experienced themselves as a downtrodden nation. The upliftment of the Afrikaners in the decades to come had many economic, political and social dimensions to it. This eventually found a certain culmination point with the taking over of political power in 1948 by the National Party.

The North American historian Richard Elphick argues that apartheid in South Africa must be understood in the context of the Christian message being preached to the coloured, Indian and black members of the DRC. He states that in South African historical studies the role of religion is largely neglected and he therefore pleads for a sufficient account of the religious sphere in South African historical writing and interpretation.

Since the 1960s it has often rightly been stated that the church did not learn about apartheid from the National Party but rather vice versa. In 1929 already, the term apartheid was for instance for the first time used in a publication by the Free State Synod of the DRC on missionary work. With the formulation of a new Mission Policy for the DRC in 1935 it actually preceded what would eventually develop into the political policy of apartheid. All of this would have had a very specific effect in the decades to come on the thoughts of the Afrikaans-speaking churches in the development of the apartheid ideology, but also eventually in the specific role of the Afrikaans-speaking churches in the demise of apartheid.

Post-1948: a new government takes over

The year 1948 was a watershed year in South African history. In May that year the National Party was voted into power which brought an end to the rule of the essentially English-speaking United Party and the colonialism of the past.

From the beginning there were warning voices and in 1948 the Fagan Commission, appointed by the United Party, declared that "total segregation is utterly impracticable". From 1948 new laws built on existing legislation ensured that the regulations were adhered to. "Petty apartheid" became part of South African life and many more draconian laws were promulgated. What made post-1948 apartheid different was the way in which the policy of segregation permeated every area of South African life, to the extent that even park benches were designated either "white" or "black". In an era when the rest of the world was loosening the shackles of colonialism, the government of South Africa was taking away the few political rights that had been afforded black South Africans.

Unlike most of the English-speaking churches, at this time the African and coloured churches of the DRC were not part of the congregations of the "Mother" or white Church, although many of them used Afrikaans as their language for worship. Those linked to the DRC were referred to as "daughter" churches. They were the Nederduitse Gereformeerde Sendingkerk (Dutch Reformed Mission Church) for coloured people, the Reformed Church in Africa for Indians and the Nederduitse Gereformeerde Kerk in Afrika (Dutch Reformed Church in Africa) for black people. Although similar doctrinally, they were run autonomously and had their own synods. The Dutch Reformed Mission Church and part of the Dutch Reformed Church in Africa would later join to form the Uniting Reformed Church. The Gereformeerde Kerk had a mission branch linked to the white church while from 1951 the Nederduitsch Hervormde Kerk became an all-white church.

It was only with the demolition of District Six in Cape Town and the visible suffering of the forced removals in the 1950s that concerned people in all the churches began to question the actions of the Nationalist government. From this time voices like that of Father Trevor Huddleston, condemning the harsh enforcement of the new laws, began to be heard. From this time, too, dissident voices began to be heard not only in the English-speaking and non-white churches, but also, in spite of opposition from their church leaders and the government, a few voices from the Afrikaans churches like Professors Bennie Keet and Ben Marais who voiced their rejection of policies that caused suffering to black Christians.

New legislation ensures white privilege

In 1948 the first glimmers of what was to come began to show. The National Party proposed legislation which would deprive black people of their already limited parliamentary representation. The English-speaking churches reacted immediately in an effort to stop the proposed legislation from becoming law. The General Assembly of the Presbyterian Church of South Africa said: "Our earnest prayer is that white South Africa may be saved from the contempt in the eyes of the world which such an action is bound to produce." The Assembly of the Congregational Church stated: "It is our sincere conviction that the government's policy of apartheid has no sanction in the New Testament scriptures." Other denominations added their voices too. In spite of such wide-spread opposition the government continued with their policy of separate development or apartheid and several new laws were promulgated in the next few years.

In 1949 the South African Citizenship Bill was intended to loosen the ties with the Commonwealth and Britain, while the Prohibition of Mixed Marriages Act prohibited all future marriages between whites and members of other race groups. Many "mixed" couples were forced to leave the country and the churches were no longer to marry people from different race groups.

With the Population Registration Act of 1950 every person was registered according to race. Where there was doubt, the matter was decided by officials in Pretoria. The churches were called on to help people who found themselves "reclassified".

The Group Areas Act of 1950 provided for the proclamation of segregated areas for the various race groups where only they were allowed to live and conduct business. This led to the gradual separation of races, making it difficult for members of any denomination to meet members of the same denomination from a different race group. It also set the scene for what would become the "Homelands Policy" with different "homelands" for the various tribal groups.

The Suppression of Communism Act was passed in 1950. More and more the rejection of apartheid legislation came to be seen by church members and structures as communist and therefore anti-Christian.

In 1951 the Native Representative Council was abolished. This was an all-white body, but liberals like Margaret Ballinger and Dr Gordon Mears were able to contest repressive legislation. By this time repressive measures were also entering the church and in 1951 the Nederduitsch Hervormde Kerk published Section 3 of their Canon Law which proclaimed the NHK a "whites only" church.

1951 also saw the beginning of the constitutional struggle to remove coloured voters from the common voters' roll. This affected coloured members of the churches, especially in the Cape, as it took away one of their basic rights as citizens of South Africa.

The Abolition of Passes and Coordination of Documents Act of 1952 provided for the issuing of reference books to all black people – the hated "dompass". These had to be carried at all times by both men and women and were important in the implementation of influx control. It set black people apart from the other people of South Africa who, at the time, did not have to carry identity documents. The Native Laws Amendment Bill effectively prevented black and white Christians from worshipping together. The implementation of this law was one of the factors leading to the Defiance Campaign of 1952.

In the light of the increasing hardships experienced by South Africa's non-white peoples, the African National Congress and the South African Indian Congress declared war on Pass Laws and planned a mass campaign against oppressive measures. They called on the government to repeal the oppressive laws or face mass action on 6 April 1952, the tercentenary of the arrival of Jan van Riebeeck at the Cape. This became known as the Defiance Campaign.

In 1953 white voters returned the National Party to power for another five years. They now had the mandate for introducing more and harsher apartheid legislation.

The Bantu Education Act of 1953 impacted greatly on the churches. The mission schools had been responsible for a large part of African education in South Africa. Now the government took over all church schools, both black and white, and introduced their National Christian Education syllabus in white schools and "Bantu Education" in black schools. Many church schools closed, but others remained within the system feeling that any education was better than none at all.

The government take-over of mission schools affected even tertiary education. The main-line English-speaking churches – Anglican, Methodist, Congregational and Presbyterian – had separate hostels at Fort Hare although the students were together for lectures at the university. These were taken over by the University of Fort Hare and became ordinary university hostels. The churches moved their educational facilities and eventually established Federal Seminary (Fedsem) near Pietermaritzburg. Fedsem was an ecumenical venture in theological education for African students between the Anglicans, Congregationalists, Methodists and Presbyterians. Once again they joined for academic work, but there were separate hostels for each denomination.

That year also saw the Reservation of Separate Amenities Act (1953) which provided for separate premises for the different race groups and entrance was restricted to the designated group. This involved everything from churches, doors into government buildings and ordinary things like buses. The government also took over mission hospitals that had been successfully run by the churches for many years.

The Tomlinson Commission was set up by the government in 1954 to determine the socio-economic development of the areas occupied by black people within the Union of South Africa. Large numbers of people were interviewed, among them the leaders of several Christian denominations as well as leaders from the black churches. The commissioners examined the activities of a number of denominations as well as the "separatist" or African Independent Churches. The government believed that the Tomlinson Commission, which explored far more than just church life in South Africa, provided them with a mandate to continue implementing their policy of separate development, and the Homelands Policy of separate Bantustans was initiated. The Bantu Self-governing Act was promulgated in 1959 and the Transkei became the first of the "homelands" to be established.

The Dutch Reformed Church, in the meantime, not only accepted the scriptural foundation of apartheid as first drafted by Professor J.D. du Toit (Totius) of the Reformed Church, but even went so far as to propagate it in different ways in the years to come, both in church and in society. Some of the church leaders in this process were Professor A.B. du Preez, Dr A.P. Treurnicht and Dr J.D. Vorster, the brother of Prime Minister B.J. Vorster.

In 1955 the Freedom Charter was accepted by a multiracial meeting of the Congress of the People in Kliptown, Soweto, which embodied the equal rights of all South Africans. Father Huddleston of the Anglican Church was a signatory. He had seen how the forced removals brought misery to his own congregation in Sophiatown, Johannesburg, which had been recognised as a black suburb for decades. In 1955 they were moved to Meadowlands in Soweto. During the years 1960–1983 as many as 3,5 million people were moved from their traditional homes.

Amidst the political turmoil the people turned to God for answers and guidance. New mission groups like Africa Enterprise (1962) were established. However, for some the religion of the 1950s and 1960s seemed rigid and did not seem to provide answers. The University Christian Movement was started at Rhodes University by the Rev. Basil Moore to address this and also to answer the question: What is our Christian duty in the light of the current political situation in South Africa?

The World Council of Churches

The year 1948 saw the formation of the World Council of Churches (WCC), a platform for discussion and dialogue between the different member denominations worldwide. The seeds for the new Council were sown as far back as 1910 when the biggest ecumenical gathering of church leaders to date was held at the International Missionary Conference in Edinburgh. Out of this grew two further movements, "Faith and Order" and "Life and Work". The WCC was formed by the amalgamation of Faith and Order and Life and Work. The International Missionary Conference did not join the WCC until 1961. The membership of WCC included most of the main-line denominations and South African churches were among the members, including the DRC synods of the Cape and Transvaal and the Nederduitsch Hervormde Kerk.

Delegates were sent to the Conference held in Amsterdam in 1948 and again in 1954 at Evanston, Illinois, USA. One of the delegates was Alan Paton, an Anglican who supported the Archbishop of Cape Town in his opposition to apartheid legislation. Another prophetic South African who attended the WCC meetings was Professor Ben Marais, a Dutch Reformed minister. Even before 1948 he had warned the DRC not to accept apartheid as being scripturally justifiable and after 1948 he continued to reject the entrenchment of apartheid. He was in turn rejected by a number of his fellow ministers.

Although a large number of South African denominations joined the WCC in 1948, there was no real South African ecumenical platform. The earliest such ecumenical meeting was the General Missionary Conference in 1904 where mission work and reconstruction after the Anglo-Boer War (1899–1902) were discussed. In 1936 the Christian Council of South Africa was formed. In 1949, as the first effects of the new apartheid legislation were being felt, the Council met at Rosettenville, Johannesburg, to discuss the implications of being a Christian in a multiracial society. They reaffirmed that God created all people in His own image and said that what South Africa needed was not apartheid but unity. Every child had the right to the best education that the community could offer and every person had the right to work in the sphere where they could make the best use of their abilities for the common good. These affirmations did little to stem the tide of legislation which separated the race groups. The Christian Council of South Africa became increasingly ineffective as the voice of the voiceless and of its member churches, and in 1969 it was disbanded when the South African Council of Churches (SACC) was formed.

Sharpeville and the 1960s

In 1959 another black political party was formed – the Pan African Congress (PAC) – with the Methodist lay preacher, Robert Sobukwe, as its leader. The PAC called for a peaceful mass demonstration against the Pass Laws for 21 March 1960. Passes were to be burnt and Sobukwe led the demonstration in Soweto. On the whole the demonstrations passed peacefully, but at Sharpeville in the Vaal Triangle things went horribly wrong. The police fired on the crowd as they marched unarmed to the police station and 69 people were killed and 189 injured.

The massacre ushered in a new era in anti-apartheid demonstrations and even more stringent laws. It also led to criticism from the churches overseas. *The British Weekly* of 18 July 1963, in an unprecedented step, published a statement by the leadership of the British churches on the situation in South Africa which read: "Recent events in South Africa, including the recent legislation such as the General Laws Amendment Act, impel us to make this statement. This Act provides, among other things, as was stated in *The Times* on 2 May, for 90 days' detention incommunicado (except for magistrates' visits for those accused of contravening previous Acts passed by the Nationalist government)." They begged the leaders to take heed before it was too late. The statement was signed, among others, by the Archbishop of Canterbury, the Archbishop of York, the President of the Methodist Conference and the Moderator of the General Assembly of the Church of Scotland.

The Sharpeville massacre also presented a major crisis for the churches in South Africa with regard to racism. According to De Gruchy, thousands of black people were arrested and many were banned in the post-Sharpeville state of emergency. The leadership of the ANC and PAC, including Albert Luthuli, Nelson Mandela and Robert Sobukwe, was arrested and the organisations declared illegal. Many black people fled the country and became part of the anti-apartheid organisation in exile. Archbishop De Blank of the Anglican Church demanded that the World Council of Churches become involved. He even demanded the expulsion of the Dutch Reformed Church from the WCC. In December 1960 the WCC facilitated a Consultation at Cottesloe in Johannesburg under the chairmanship of their general secretary, Dr W.A. Visser 't Hooft. The Declaration or report that emerged from the Consultation read: "We make bold to address this appeal to our churches and to all Christians calling on them to consider a spirit of equity. All racial groups have the right to make their contribution towards the enrichment of the life of their country and to share in the responsibilities, rewards and privileges. The church has a duty to bear witness to both white South Africans in their uncertainty and black South Africans in their frustration."

The members drew attention to the evils of migrant labour, of low wages for people of colour and of job reservation, while they criticised the law which denied non-white people the right to own land wherever they were living and to participate in the government of the country.

This document could have had a far-reaching effect, but there was strong opposition especially from the Afrikaans-speaking churches, which resigned from the WCC because of political pressure. In 1963 the Rev. Beyers Naudé, moderator of the Southern Transvaal Synod of the DRC, and some of the Cottesloe delegates from the English-speaking churches formed the Christian Institute (CI). The aim was to provide an ecumenical platform for those who opposed apartheid. The CI was an attempt to establish a confessing movement in South Africa. Naudé was the director of the CI. He had to face fierce pro-apartheid attacks from within his Dutch Reformed Church and was forced to leave their ministry. The CI kept alive the struggle against apartheid from 1963 until 1977 when it was banned by the Vorster government.

The CI provided Bible studies and theological training for the African Independent Churches, and was in continuous consultation with the Black Consciousness Movement and Black Theology in South Africa. A newspaper, *Pro Veritate*, was published from 1963 to 1976. The CI also joined the SACC in its efforts, like the End Conscription Campaign in 1974. The government tried to stop their work by cutting off funding from overseas. Then, on 19 October 1977, 17 organisations such as the Black Consciousness Movement; three newspapers, among them *Pro Veritate*; and one religious organisation, the CI, were banned. Naudé and others who worked for the CI were issued with banning orders restricting their movements.

Two major ecumenical events of the 1960s influenced the churches in South Africa. The first was the Second Vatican Council of the Roman Catholic Church that convened in 1962. The Roman Catholic Church has numerous members, both black and white, and at the Vatican Council far-reaching decisions were made that affected the church worldwide as it encouraged ecumenical contact between the Catholic Church and other churches. The Catholic Bishops Conference was to become a strong opponent of apartheid.

The second was the Geneva Conference on Church and Society held in 1966 which called on Christians to participate in the struggle for justice for oppressed peoples. This led to the WCC's Programme to Combat Racism (PCR) in 1974, the impact of which would also affect South Africa.

The next action by the churches that elicited public comment was the publication of the "Message to the People of South Africa". The Message was formulated by members of the Christian Council and the CI. It emerged from the Geneva Conference of the WCC in 1966. The theme of the conference was "Church and Society" and inspired the South African delegates to look at their own society, especially at the ways that apartheid was incompatible with the Christian message. It appealed to the obedience of Christians in South Africa and to their loyalty to Jesus Christ. The Message quoted scripture to show that racial segregation was incompatible with the gospel. A thorough policy of racial segregation must ultimately require that the Church should cease to be the Church. This message was sent to all the member churches of the WCC and Christian Council.

In 1969 the Christian Council of South Africa reinvented itself and became the South African Council of Churches (SACC). This was to be a fellowship of churches and most of the English-speaking churches became members. The principle objectives of the SACC were:

- To foster that unity which is both God's will and his gift to the church;
- To co-ordinate the work and witness of churches and missionary societies and other Christian organisations and institutions in South Africa in order to carry out more effectively the church's mission in the world;
- To undertake joint action and service and to encourage such things as may be calculated best to reduce in scope the divisive factors, whether doctrinal or otherwise, presently existing among Christian churches.

Membership was for all churches that confessed Jesus Christ as Lord and Saviour according to the scriptures and who sought to fulfil their common calling to the glory of God. John Rees, a Methodist, became the first director. The SACC became very active in helping those who were suffering under the injustice of apartheid.

The turbulent 1970s, Soweto and the 1980s

In spite of the continuing repressive legislation, the English-speaking churches began to assert themselves from the 1970s. After the election by the Methodist Church of the Rev. Seth Mokitimi as president of Conference in 1964, a black Anglican bishop, Desmond Tutu, was appointed general secretary of the SACC in 1978. More and more of the English-speaking churches began electing black leaders.

In 1970 the general secretary of the WCC, Dr Eugene Carson Blake, visited South Africa. On his return to Geneva, the executive meeting of the WCC resolved to give financial aid to liberation movements fighting in southern Africa against white minority governments. The church leaders in South Africa were totally unprepared for this step and the ordinary person in the pew, whether he had previously been anti-racism or not, began to view the WCC with suspicion. Prime Minister John Vorster demanded that the member churches leave the WCC. He now considered the WCC a "communist organisation" although their grants were mostly for humanitarian purposes supporting those in exile and their families. In answer the SACC rejected violence in any form, whether in support of the status quo or those fighting to change it. The member churches issued a statement saying they would retain their membership of the WCC but rejected the WCC's implicit support of violence by making grants to liberation movements. The government then made it illegal to send any money to the WCC.

In 1974 the annual National Conference of the SACC took place at the St Peter's Roman Catholic Seminary in Hammanskraal, a black township outside Pretoria. It afforded an opportunity for white and black delegates to live and meet together. In view of the wars taking place in southern Africa the question of conscientious objection was raised. Some of the English-speaking churches that had military chaplains for the armed forces, decided to appoint chaplains to those fighting apartheid as well. The CI also joined the SACC in its efforts such as the End Conscription Campaign in 1974.

The 1970s also saw the establishment of the Black Consciousness Movement with Steve Biko as its leader. The Rev. Allan Boesak described black consciousness as "the awareness of black people that their humanity is constituted by their blackness. It means that black people are no longer ashamed that they are black, that they have a black history and a black culture distinct from the history and culture of white people. It is an attitude, a way of life." At the same time a black theology was emerging which was a liberation theology, but unlike the liberation theologies of South and North America, it had a distinctly African focus.

The year 1974 saw the Declaration of the Church Unity Commission (CUC). For six years, since 1968, there had been discussions between the Anglican Church, the Methodist Church, the Uniting Presbyterian Church of Southern Africa, the Evangelical Presbyterian Church, the United Congregational Church and the Reformed Presbyterian Church.

Two of these were black churches while the others may be considered multi-racial. A draft plan of union was drawn up in 1972. By 1974 all these churches had accepted the Declaration to seek union, in which they undertook:

- To seek agreement on a common form of Word and Sacrament with due regard to the pattern of ministry and oversight;
- To admit to the Lord's table communicants from all the member churches;
- To work for increasing co-operation in all areas of church life.

This covenant of the CUC was accepted by the member churches in 1982. This allowed communicants from member churches to attend services and take communion in CUC churches.

Following the Soweto riots of 1976 there was renewed clamping down on dissidents. In 1977 a small group of black church ministers staged a protest march in Johannesburg. They were arrested and the march declared unlawful. When they appeared in court they read out a statement of what was causing great unhappiness in the country. They stated that detentions without trial, banning orders, the enforcement of Bantu education, mass removals, job reservation, the muzzling of the black press and a disproportionate military budget caused great distress. All these were perpetrated by a white government that called itself Christian and so black Christian ministers and priests had great difficulty explaining the gospel to young black people in their congregations.

However, there were also black Christians who believed that the gospel could bring liberation to both blacks and whites in South Africa. Some of the white church ministers recognised this dilemma. In September 1976, after the Soweto riots, Archbishop Bill Burnett of the Anglican Church wrote to Prime Minister Vorster and said: "Unless white Christians in particular admit the wrongs they have done to black people, and take action to redress them, there can be no possibility of healing in our land."

Afrikaans voices against apartheid

In 1970 the DRC appointed a commission to examine racial and ecumenical issues within the South African context. They published their findings in a document called "Ras, Volk en Nasie" (Human Relations in the Light of Scripture) in 1974. It was presented at the General Synod in 1974 and signed by the members of the Moderature. It stressed the good mission work done by the DRC and said that the church voiced its disquiet about the Christian implications of apartheid and separate development.

Another attempt at bringing reconciliation and helping to foster cross-cultural understanding was the Koinonia Declaration from within reformed circles. The Koinonia movement originated in Cape Town where three ministers of the DRC led by Professor Nico Smith reacted against the government ruling that made public agitation against detention without trial an offence. The 1977 declaration called upon all functionaries of the state – inter alia the state president, cabinet ministers, members of Parliament, all government officials including both members of the police force and men serving in the Defence Force, all judges and judicial officers – to submit themselves, in all their decisions, formulation and carrying out of policy, all their judgments, and in their actions in general, to the demands of the Word of God so it will not be necessary for anyone to disobey their authority. Christians from both the English- and Afrikaans-speaking communities joined the movement which brought together black and white Christians to meet on an equal footing and come to a greater understanding of each other's cultures and way of life.

The Kiononia Declaration was a demonstration of a reaction by members and clergy of the Afrikaans churches against the repressive apartheid legislation. It was a strong statement of fellowship between the different races coming as it did after the death of Steve Biko while in detention. Koinonia was followed by more statements by the Afrikaans churches. In 1978 the Synod of the Nederduitse Gereformeerde Sendingkerk published a statement condemning detention without trial. Ministers, lecturers and laymen from the four Dutch Reformed Sister Churches established the Broederkring. This was originally formed to try to effect unity between the mother DRC and the so-called daughter churches. This unity was partially realised with the formation of the Uniting Reformed Church which comprised parts of two of the non-white churches.

In contrast to these moves by the DRC community, the Nederduitsch Hervormde Kerk General Assembly expressed their support for equal but separate opportunities, i.e. apartheid.

On 31 October 1980, Reformation Day, eight academics who were all ministers of the DRC published the Reformation Day Witness in which they stated that existing group differences between people need not be a source of friction because of prejudice, self-interest and defensiveness, but can, through the power of God's renewing grace, be developed into something that provides mutual enrichment. Other statements followed, like Storm Compass in 1981 which looked at the relationship between the church and the state. This statement was called that way so as to provide a compass to the church in those stormy days. It was in 1982 that 123 ministers and theologians from the DRC family wrote an open letter in which they pledged themselves to work for justice and openly criticised apartheid. This was in direct opposition to the recognised policy of the DRC which supported the Nationalist government.

The Reformed Churches in South Africa belonged to the World Alliance of Reformed Churches (WARC) and at the 1982 meeting in Ottawa, Canada, a South African, the Rev. Allan Boesak, as chairperson declared racism a sin and apartheid a heresy. The membership of the DRC was suspended. Subsequently, in 1986 the Synod of the Nederduitse Gereformeerde Sendingkerk issued a confession of faith which has become known as the Belhar Confession. In the confession apartheid was declared a heresy. In this they were supported by various English-speaking churches like the United Congregational Church, a reformed denomination, the Methodists and the Anglicans.

In 1986 the DRC published a document named Church and Society which discussed socio-political concerns and the need to focus on scripture and the kingdom of God. The DRC was declared an open church and racism was declared a sin. This document was signed by the chairman of the General Synodical Commission, Professor J.A. Heyns. This was a very well-considered document, and in many ways it represented indeed a change of heart in the DRC, and it is widely accepted that it helped to pave the way for the political changes of the 1990s.

The English-speaking churches speak out against apartheid

In 1977 the South African Catholic Bishops' Conference published a statement entitled Social Justice and Race Relations in which they expressed concern that while 80% of their laity were black, 80% of their clergy were white. They encouraged all Catholic schools to open their doors to all races. Ways were sought to involve lay people, especially black people, in determining non-doctrinal or canonical matters affecting church life.

The new decade started with a multi-racial Methodist Conference on Obedience in Johannesburg which published a Message of Obedience in 1981. The Message stated, among others, that God wanted His people to demonstrate His grace in visible social action and to be a pattern of His way of love.

The Presbyterians, too, made a commitment to work for justice, peace and equality for all peoples when they revised their Declaration of Faith. They rejected the ideological heresy that insisted on the separate identity of racial groups as a supreme value and therefore divided and segregated them geographically, socially and politically. The following year the Anglican Synod also denounced apartheid as totally un-Christian.

These were the years of detention without trial and escalating violence against anti-apartheid dissenters. Peaceful protest marches were led by clergy like Bishop Michael Nuttall (Anglican), the Rev. Peter Storey (Methodist) and the Rev. John Thorne (Congregational). A number of the clergy were imprisoned for their beliefs as were many of the marchers. The ANC activists also took a more militant stance and electrical pylons were blown up and a number of bombs exploded, injuring innocent civilians. These events led to the formulating of the Kairos Document in 1985 which presented a challenge to action. The Kairos Document was formulated mainly by theologians belonging to the Institute for Contextual Theology which was established in Johannesburg that year, but was supported by clergy from many denominations.

The Kairos Document spoke of three theologies – state theology which was preached by the state in South Africa; church theology, a critique of the theology preached by the churches; and prophetic theology, a way forward with a message of hope for South Africa. This document provoked heated debate, support from some Christians and harsh rejection from others. It looked at the role of the church in South Africa and said that it was time that the church took sides with the poor. It called for Christians to work and plan for a change of government and challenged the church to renewal and action.

This was followed by declarations and further statements from other churches, like those from the DRC early in the 1980s. Some of the Roman Catholic clergy like Father Smangaliso Mkhatshwa from Regina Mundi

Church in Soweto had been imprisoned and tortured. A year later the Roman Catholic Church addressed social injustice and the conditions leading to the crisis. The bishops declared: "Our unity is about being one in Christ." In response Prime Minister P.W. Botha proclaimed a state of emergency which led to even more restrictions, especially for black people.

These were turbulent years with unrest in the townships and fighting between the ANC and the IFP (Inkatha Freedom Party) in the streets of Soweto. There was "necklacing" of people who were considered to be on the side of the government. A second "state of emergency" followed the first. The government deployed the army in the townships to the dismay of many church leaders. However, it was widely believed that it was not the army that brought peace to the townships, but a group of Christian church leaders under the Rev. Mvume Dandala, the Presiding Bishop of the Methodist Church, who visited the hostels to meet with the workers and help them find a solution to their problems.

The compilers of the Evangelical Witness acknowledged in 1986 that there was a socio-political crisis in South Africa and confessed that as evangelicals they had been too conservative and so had supported the status quo. They saw that black Christians, especially in the townships, were experiencing a crisis of faith. They identified all the areas of church life where change was needed and called upon evangelical Christians to be more critical of their own witness.

In 1989 a group of Pentecostal pastors produced the Relevant Pentecostal Witness. This traditionally conservative group of churches now saw their conservatism as unfortunate and felt that they had to make a stand against the injustice in the country. Many of these pastors were from the Indian community in Natal and had experienced discrimination themselves. They saw that there was an unchristian separation between black and white churches. They agreed to inform the clergy and laity about the Witness and encourage them to get involved with the community in a practical way.

The same year the Institute for Contextual Theology (ICT) published a document called The Road to Damascus. In spite of the government's ban on mixed gatherings, the ICT was a multi-national group of Christians who saw that the Church had become a site of struggle and they looked at the roots of the conflict calling all Christians to stand together.

The African Independent Churches traditionally took an a-political stance when it came to the government although their members lived under the same discriminatory laws as anyone else. They had become the largest church grouping in South Africa, made up of numerous independent churches. Many of their members had links with the SACC and the Institute for Contextual Theology.

An anomaly was the Zion Christian Church with its headquarters at Moria near Pietersburg (now Polokwane), in what was then the Northern Transvaal (now Limpopo). The ZCC was established in 1910 and is one of the largest African Independent Churches with thousands of members. During the 1980s several cabinet ministers were invited to attend their Easter gatherings and in 1985 P.W. Botha, then the state president, attended the Easter services.

All the documents above were written against a background of increasing violence. Even though the government was beginning to talk to the ANC there was still violence against anti-apartheid activists. An example of this is the letter bomb that was sent to the Anglican priest, Father Michael Lapsley in Harare, Zimbabwe, in August 1990. It was meant to kill him but caused him the loss of his hands and one eye. He was in exile at the time and with him were other South African clergymen, the Methodist Cedric Mason, and the Rev. Frank Chikane of the Apostolic Faith Mission. Chikane himself had been tortured by the security police.

The Rubicon of the 1990s

The decade of conflict ended on a note of confession and penitence. For a number of years the different churches had been questioning their role in the climate of violence and injustice. In February 1990 the ANC, the PAC and the South African Communist Party were all unbanned. A number of political prisoners were released and Nelson Mandela himself was freed. Following these events, a very significant church conference took place at Rustenburg in the North West Province in November 1990.

In many ways the Rustenburg Conference of Church Leaders paved the way and set the tone for the vision and the role of the churches in South Africa in the coming period of transition and democratisation. About 230 church leaders from 80 denominations and 40 para-church organisations met in an attempt to work towards a united Christian witness in a changing South Africa. This meeting was extraordinary in that it brought together a cross section of all the traditions and confessions of churches in South Africa. It unified Catholics, Anglicans, Methodists, Lutherans, Reformed Churches, Pentecostals, Evangelicals and African Independent Churches. In spite of differences with some aspects of the Rustenburg Declaration, there remained a consensus among most churches represented at the conference. For the first time the sins of the past were confessed together, and together the system of apartheid was condemned as well. For the first time those represented in the SACC and those representing evangelical and other traditions got together in a formal declaration in which consensus was reflected almost across the board.

Possibly the most significant and touching moment was between the Dutch Reformed Professor Willie Jonker and the Anglican Archbishop Desmond Tutu. The watershed event was when Jonker came with the following confession in his address: "I confess before you and before the Lord, not only my own sins and guilt, and my personal responsibility for the political, social, economical and structural wrongs that have been done to many of you and the result of which you and our whole country are still suffering from, but vicariously I dare also to do that in the name of the Dutch Reformed Church of which I am a member, and for the Afrikaner people as a whole. I have the liberty to do just that, because the DRC at its latest synod has declared apartheid a sin and confessed its own guilt of negligence in not warning against it and distancing itself from it long ago."

Following Jonker's address, Tutu spontaneously rose to receive the confession and offer forgiveness in the following words: "I believe that I certainly stand under pressure of God's Holy Spirit to say that ... when confession is made, those of us who have been wronged must say 'we forgive you'. And that together we may move to the reconstruction of our land. It is not cheaply made and the response is not cheaply made." The entire conference rose to its feet in applause, as if to express that this was a moment when the grace of God had broken through into the affairs of the church and nation.

The Declaration of the Rustenburg Consultation was a comprehensive document confessing the wrongs of the past, remembering with sorrow the victims of apartheid and appealing to political leaders to negotiate a new and just order for the country. It looked at the role of the church and ended with a call for restitution and a commitment to action. Apartheid was a sin, and forgiveness and practical restitution were necessary if reconciliation were to take place.

After 1990 the cultural, socio-economic and political situation in South Africa changed radically. People reacted differently to the change which took place. For some it was the long-anticipated outcome of many years of political struggle. For others it brought uncertainty and despair. The secularisation of everyday life and the phenomenon of the postmodern paradigm were also escalating forces. The churches in South Africa stood within the sphere of influence of these phenomena. The scene was however set in 1990 for the sometimes very difficult process of multi-party negotiations known as CODESA in the years to come, and the eventual first democratic elections in 1994 in which all of South Africa's peoples took part.

The aftermath of apartheid

With the change to a new democratic government the churches in South Africa found themselves facing new challenges. With the new constitution, which was acclaimed worldwide, all religions were given equal opportunities and privileges and Christianity lost its privileged position. Religious education ended in government schools and was replaced with "life skills". In private schools run by various religious groups, religious studies could still be taught. Religious non-governmental organisations (NGOs) no longer received subsidies from the government and church welfare organisations suffered. This affected Christian old age homes and orphanages as well as organisations helping the poor and needy. A positive aspect was the growth of inter-faith dialogue and co-operation between the different religions, especially in times of crisis. Ironically, in times of crisis the government regularly called on the churches to pray and for church leaders to intervene.

Many prominent representatives from different churches and cultures not only earlier on campaigned against apartheid but also worked for peace, transformation and reconciliation. Only a few are mentioned here. Among the Dutch Reformed representatives one can find David Bosch, and Johan Heyns who was assassinated in 1995. Others from the Dutch Reformed and Reformed tradition who worked for peace and reconciliation were the Reverends Willie Jonker, Allan Boesak and Amie van Wyk.

Archbishop Desmond Mpilo Tutu was another prominent figure in this process: a highly respected Anglican priest and bishop. Central to his thinking was the way he described the transition to the new democracy: "Our God was the God of surprises... The God of surprises was at work. He worked to inspire the state president (F.W. de Klerk) to act in an unexpectedly courageous way." Tutu called South Africa the "Rainbow Nation" to express the potential for all the races to work together in harmony. Many other black theologians and ministers also worked for transformation and reconciliation, among them Frank Chikane, Stanley Mogoba and Caesar Molebatse.

In many ways the South African population was greatly fragmented before 1994. One of the efforts to bring about reconciliation and unity was the Truth and Reconciliation Commission (TRC) which was established in 1997 to lead South Africa to some form of hope and reconciliation. Tutu, the chairperson of the TRC, said that its task was to encourage reconciliation and not to attain it completely. Even the Dutch Reformed Church eventually showed its willingness to participate before this commission. This proved to be an important opportunity for the DRC which was deeply involved in the old South African system, for introspection and to co-operate in discovering some level of truth and reconciliation. The TRC made a major contribution to reconciliation although it may not have made a lasting impression. Poverty, corruption, racism and crime are among some of the greatest challenges confronting the churches in South Africa today.

The 1994 General Synod of the DRC for instance became known as the "Synod of Reconciliation". It did not only attend to external reconciliation towards fellow South Africans who were marginalised in the old South Africa, but also towards those within the DRC such as Ben Marais and Beyers Naudé who had been rejected because they stood up as prophets against an inhuman system and theology supported by the DRC.

However, racial issues still remained, especially in some Afrikaans-speaking churches. The English-speaking churches largely became integrated with relatively little resistance. On the other hand a traditional Afrikaans-speaking Pentecostal church like the Apostolic Faith Mission was also integrated with a multi-racial leadership. The Gereformeerde Kerk, although embracing integration in the 1970s, still has different ecclesiastical meetings and synods. At the beginning of the twenty-first century the Dutch Reformed Church of Africa (NHKA) decided that it is not any longer only a church for the Afrikaner population. Although the DRC decided in 1986 that they are an open church, the re-unification with the rest of the DRC-family remained an outstanding issue.

It was after 1994 that a greater ecumenical awareness and involvement resurged in the South African context. The South African Council of Churches retained its position as a representative and interdenominational ecumenical body in the South African context. Its mission remained to work for "moral reconstruction in South Africa, focusing on issues of justice, reconciliation, integrity of creation and the eradication of poverty and contributing towards the empowerment of all who are spiritually, socially and economically marginalised."

Although many of the English-speaking churches remained deeply involved in the SACC and other ecumenical bodies before 1990, the Afrikaans-speaking churches for obvious reasons became more and more isolated. In July 1995, however, the DRC was granted observer membership of the SACC and in 2004 it was granted full membership.

After having been suspended as a member church of the World Alliance of Reformed Churches in 1982, the DRC was once again invited as a provisional member of this global reformed ecumenical body in 1997, and after having complied to the proviso of confessing its guilt in apartheid as a sin at the General Synod of 1998, it once again became a full member. In 2007 the DRC also once again became a full member of the World Council of Churches after having resigned from this body in 1960 after the Cottesloe Consultation.

Conclusion

The churches in South Africa have played an impressive positive and negative role since 1948. Their historical role in spreading the Bible message in South Africa and beyond its borders has been immense. Sadly, the churches were far too deeply involved in the policy of apartheid, and their voices have in the course of time been too silent.

The words of hope by Desmond Tutu in 2004 reminded South Africans that they needed to be a nation where all belonged and knew they belonged, where all were insiders, none was an outsider, and where all were members of a remarkable, crazy country.

29
An environmental history of South Africa

Elize S. van Eeden*

Environmental history is the study of the influence that humankind and nature exercise on one another over time. Sometimes this process is referred to as part of ecology (the study of organisms in their interaction with the environment and with one another).

Environmental research in the discipline of History received a boost when socio-political movements in the United States of America (USA) and Europe reacted to the frustrations of ecological and animal rights pressure groups. Gradually the growing awareness of a worldwide environmental crisis and the resultant "green revolution" approach began to make an impression on the thought processes of historians. In the USA and Europe they began paying attention to environmental issues and included the "landscapes of the past" in their historiography.

However, environment-oriented research on South Africa's past is still a recent field of endeavour. Due to the country's intellectual and political isolation in the apartheid era, the worldwide green revolution received rather limited attention from local historians. Instead they mostly focused their attention on opposing or defending apartheid. However, in the last few decades historians have begun to approach their studies differently. Amongst others they started exploring issues on humankind's interaction with the environment.

Environmental history covers various aspects of our natural surroundings, including the lithosphere (the rigid part of the earth's crust); the

---

*The author extends a vote of thanks to the following historians for supplying information and insight used in the compilation of this chapter: Professors William Beinart; Fransjohan Pretorius; Phia Steyn; Kobus du Pisani; Alan Kirkaldy; and the late Prof W.S. Barnard, an expert in geography.

pedosphere (concerning soil and soil types); the atmosphere (air); hydrosphere (the various waters of the earth's surface); and the biosphere (regions occupied by living organisms, such as forests). In this chapter a broad multidisciplinary outline is provided on the environment from a historian's perspective. The chapter begins by placing the environment in a broad context with geography as the point of departure. The landscape and its different ecosystems are first discussed. Thereafter we travel back in time with a discussion on how indigenous groups such as the Khoekhoen, black societies and other powerful centralised African groupings adapted themselves to an ever-changing environment – and how they in turn changed the environment.

An analysis of the impact of white settlement and expansion on the environment follows, noting that from the mid-eighteenth century to the mid-twentieth century the major reason for environmental transformation was the development of the agricultural sector.

The rise of "environmental awareness" (although initially it was highly politicised) and the simultaneous growth of national parks is then investigated.

The focus then shifts to the apartheid government's management of the natural surroundings, seen within the context of the international environment – particularly against the backdrop of the growing international environmental crisis from the 1960s. The chapter closes with a brief look at environmental initiatives since 1994 and the challenge of continued development in the midst of ongoing environmental crises.

> **THE WORLD BECOMES ENVIRONMENTALLY AWARE**
>
> In the outside world the environment-oriented behaviour of individuals or groups ensured that policies on sound environmental management were gradually introduced. However, formal environmental consciousness only became a reality from the nineteenth century onwards. It was in the twentieth century, after the Second World War (1939-1945), that progressive movements which focused on conservation of the environment took these issues further. This coincided with the contributions of environmental scholars.
>
> It was mainly in the 1970s that internationally driven environmental measures were implemented. Concerted public action and reactions to negative or irresponsible environmental conservation have therefore only just reached the 50-year mark. However, long before this, individuals often took govern-

ment departments to court over environmental questions which troubled them in their residential areas or workplaces. A co-ordinated system of regulations and policies on the environment was laid down from the 1960s. In many ways this milestone spontaneously led to political debates and public campaigns on environmental issues, and these directed the way to international agreements on the conservation of the environment.

The United Nations' Bruntland Report of 1987, for example, which dealt with the relationship between the economy and the environment, made recommendations to governments on environmental planning and sustainable development. In the same year the Montreal Protocol followed which emphasised the contributions of scientific findings and diplomacy to the growing awareness of conservation. It was especially the wealthy countries which benefited from this, but many other governments simply ignored the agreements in general – and the Montreal Protocol in particular. Examples are Japan and Norway who were unwilling to place restrictions on their whaling activities. Others include Saudi Arabia who reacted negatively to the request to restrict its carbon emissions; and Brazil's insistence on its right to develop the Amazon River as it pleased, regardless of the negative implications of their actions for humankind in general.

Another stumbling block by 2011 was India, Brazil and China refusing to become signatories to the Montreal Protocol. Though this strategy may discourage the use of ozone destructive substances, these countries have installed several precautionary measurements to reduce ozone destructive activities. Countries differ on how strictly their legislation on environmental awareness and control are applied. With its new regulations and laws at the beginning of the twenty-first century, South Africa is held up as a model as far as environmental legislation is concerned.

However, in the past few years the ineffective (sometimes purposely so) lack of control on the part of the government with regards to the implementation of environmental regulations has led to many public awareness campaigns by non-governmental organisations (NGOs). In 2007 these led to the formation of the Federation for a Sustainable Environment (FSE). Within government circles – as the policy makers and executive authority – there has been an upswing of serious concern about the environment since 2005. The indispensable economic role played by primary industries such as the mining industry to ensure the prosperity of South Africa has for decades been the main reason why environmental policy has not been applied strictly by the government – and is the reason why the government apparently is prepared to endure criticism.

Tough, changeable and vulnerable

South Africa has a surface area of about 1 219 090 km² and stretches to the furthest remote corner of the Old World's land mass on a latitude of between 22° and 34° south. The country is bordered by both the Atlantic and the Indian Ocean.

In general, South Africa is geologically old and stable. One of the best-known rock formations on earth – 3500 million years old – is an outcrop on the border between Mpumalanga and Swaziland, while small stretches of plains on the edge of the plateau in Bushmanland are perhaps 60 million years old. This age-old exposure translates into millions of years of erosion; rocky outcrops that have been scraped clean; and shallow soil. We live, literally, in a demanding and tough country.

Further, all continents situated on the 30º line of latitude are arid and southern Africa (the region in which South Africa falls) is no exception. South Africa's average annual rainfall is 464 mm, while the world average is 857 mm. Five-sevenths of the country receives summer rainfall coming in from across the Indian Ocean. The east coast receives more than 1000 mm per year, the central part of the interior (where the Vaal River and the Orange or Gariep River join) 400 mm, and the west coast less than 50 mm.

In contrast the winters are dry. However, in the far south-west and south there are small, scattered areas that show a different pattern and have a very high rainfall (above 2000 mm). This southern "mosaic" is a result of the winter rainfall from the Atlantic Ocean which comes in from west to east. Between the summer and winter rainfall regions lies a small strip – more or less from George on the Garden Route to Naminüs (Lüderitz) in Namibia – which receives rain throughout the year.

In general, South Africa is a drought-afflicted country. At greatest risk are the regions with summer rain from between 200 mm and 600 mm, namely the central and eastern Karoo; the western Highveld; the Bushveld; and the Northern Cape Kalahari. These regions constitute four-sevenths of the country's surface area.

Regions with a rainfall of above 600 mm per annum, even in below-average years, receive a little more rain. However, if there is less than 200 mm per annum the farming system usually makes provision for the risk of drought. Droughts also occur in the winter rainfall area, but winter rain is generally more reliable.

Droughts, however catastrophic they might be for a farming community, are generally a short-term occurrence. Southern Africa finds itself uncomfortably situated between two climatic zones. As far as temperature is concerned the country lies in the transition between the tropical and moderate zones, and as for rainfall, on the transition between arid (dry) and humid (wet) regions.

A simpler way to unravel South Africa's ecology is to study the spread of biomes across the country. A biome is a region that is host to a particular variety of plant and animal life that is characteristic of a specific combination of climate, relief (geographic character such as elevations and depressions) and soil type. This combination of physical elements creates the habitat for the region's flora and fauna and sets the limitations on their survival there. Seven biomes or plant life regions are spread across southern Africa.

Characteristics of South Africa's biomes

Biomes	Surface area (% of RSA)	Average rainfall p.a. (mm)	Type/structure of plant life*	Max. productivity ton/ha/year
Fynbos (shrub land)	7	250–2000	Closed evergreen shrubs	4
Succulent Karoo	10	100–200	Open dwarf shrubs, annuals	2
Nama Karoo	28	100–500	Open dwarf and low shrubs, grass	3
Desert[†]		10–70	Annuals, river oases	<0,35
Grassland	20	400–1000	Closed perennial grasses	6
Savannah	35	400–1000	Grass with scattered trees	7
Forest	<1	>1200	Closed evergreen trees	15

*A closed plant life structure means that the leaves of the shrubs or trees or the sods of grass are close together. An open plant life structure means that they are so far from one another that there is open space/ground between them.

[†] Although the Namib Desert, strictly speaking, does not fall within South Africa's borders, it is included so that the desert biome is also represented.

As far as wealth of species is concerned – 8500 in an area of only 71 000 km² – *fynbos* is only topped on a world scale by the equatorial forests. The Fynbos Biome houses 1320 of the subcontinent's 2351 scarce and endangered species. Flowering plants from this biome such as arum lilies, gladioli, nerines and pelargoniums make this vegetation unsuitable for grazing, and the sandy mountain soil is leached and sour. The most suitable area for farming is the loamy soil at the foot of the western folded mountains, but even this is barely moderate.

Succulents (colloquially in Afrikaans known as *vetplante*, and inclusive of cacti) are adapted to store water in the leaves, stems or roots of the plant. Perennial succulents vary widely from the 4–5 m high Namaqualand quiver tree (*kokerboom*) to the small flat *bokkloutjies* (literally goats' hoofs) which hide between the quartz stones of the Richtersveld.

More typical are the masses of brightly coloured daisy-like succulents often called *vygies* (*Mesembryanthemum*) in the Knersvlakte (literally "gnashing plain", an area in Namaqualand) and the Little Karoo where there are extended areas covered with these 50–70 cm high succulent bushes. Although in this region there are few species, nevertheless per hectare it has double the number of species to be found in the North American succulent deserts, making this South African biome (as in the case of fynbos) one of the world's 16 most important biodiversity areas. Productivity, however, remains low and centuries of grazing have led to the deterioration of the plant growth.

Characteristic of the Nama Karoo are the open *peperkorrelbossies* – *ankerbos*, *perdebos* (so-called "Christmas berry"), *driedoring* (wild pomegranate) and *gannabos* (lye-bush or psilocaulon) – with their stunted growth and hard yet dainty, pale green leaves and thorns. Karoo bushes provide useful grazing for sheep and goats and in good years are interspersed with grass, but in arid years this grass becomes scorched and worsens the effects of the drought. Over the years edible plants have made way for those that are unpalatable and soil erosion has taken over where grasses have disappeared permanently.

The Karoo environment is also exposed to ecological explosions – an enormous increase in the numbers of any species can temporarily upset the ecological balance and spells disaster for the farmers. Some major culprits are swarms of locusts, but in the nineteenth century the massive springbok herds in their spectacular migration towards the west (Namaqualand) were feared even more.

True desert conditions are limited to the sea of dunes and gravel plains of the Namibian coast and strictly speaking lie outside South Africa. The plant life consists either of annual plants which react quickly to the infrequent episodes of rain, or super adaptive perennials such as the *Welwitschia mirabilis* which is in fact a tree with branches deep under the ground. Alongside the few rivers there are also trees and shrubs which survive on surface water.

Most indigenous trees in Africa are sensitive to frost with the result that South Africa's eastern interior above 1500 m is virtually true grassland. This covers some 20% of the country's surface area. In the wetter terraced regions and foothills east of the Drakensberg, the grass is lush (40 to 100 cm in height), but it loses its nutritional value once the rainy season is over. The local farmers call it *suurveld* (literally "sour veld").

Over the plains west of Gauteng the rainfall dips below the 600 mm per annum level and the short grass known as *soetveld* (sweet veld) remains nutritious throughout the year. The roots of grasses are shallow and compact; they form sods and enrich the organic content of the underlying soil. This biome has the country's largest surface area of arable land and 10 000 hectares of the Highveld are currently under summer crops. It is also especially in this area that mining and other industrial activities are pursued, which not only puts great pressure on the quality of the country's water sources but also causes other forms of environmental pollution.

Savannah curves in a semi-circle around the grasslands. Savannah regions have two characteristics in common: subtropical summer rain and plant growth of interspersed high grass and scattered trees, typically with sturdy trunks and umbrella-shaped branching. Certain areas have their own variations: In the wet valleys that cut through the mountains of the east coast the trees are twisted into undergrowth, while the camel-thorn trees of the semi-arid Kalahari stand far apart and patches of red soil are visible between the tufts of grass.

Savannah regions were very "user friendly" for precolonial societies. In areas with more than 600 mm of rain summer crops could be planted. The long grass provided good grazing for livestock. Trees were an ample source of building material and firewood and some trees, such as the marula, even provided edible fruit. Then too, of all the South African biomes the savannahs have retained most of their animal wealth, from herds of herbivorous buck to large predators.

Natural forests are only found in the southern Cape apart from a few along the Eastern Cape and KwaZulu-Natal mountainsides. As in any forest, the biological productivity is high and the forest structure comprises several layers: 50 m high yellowwood trees are the skyscrapers; somewhat smaller trees of 20–25 m in height form a forest ceiling and twining plants and ferns flourish in their shade. Tree varieties such as yellowwood, stinkwood, ironwood, and assegai-wood are excellent for construction purposes and making furniture, but are slow growers. In the nineteenth century they were over-exploited and the Cape government's measures to control the situation marked the beginning of nature conservation in South Africa. In a tree-scarce country such as South Africa they are now a tourist attraction and as such are sustainably utilised.

Our discussion of biomes shows that the South African environment possesses a rich diversity and is highly changeable in both the short and the long term. For this reason it is also vulnerable, as the following examples show.

Firstly, fynbos is being increasingly threatened by urbanisation and agriculture. The plant life adapts itself well to runaway fires and after 15 years has fully recovered. However, as the population of the Western Cape increases, mountain fires now follow one another in quicker succession and scarce species – some with a habitat (natural home) of only a few hectares – are in danger of simply disappearing.

Secondly, the boundaries of some biomes are inherently unstable. The border between the Nama Karoo and grassland, for example, shifts according to the condition of the grass – westwards in good years and eastwards during droughts. There are ecologists who claim that over the past 200 years the Nama Karoo has moved into the grassland by as much as 250 km due to overgrazing.

In conclusion, southern Africa has been populated for some 120 000 years by modern man, *Homo sapiens* – longer than any other part of the world except perhaps East Africa. Over all this time communities must of necessity have had an impact on the environment. Hunters of the Middle Stone Age, according to some ecologists, regularly burnt down subtropical bush. The result was a plant life of scattered trees and grass – the savannah of today.

In southern Africa grazing and cultivation is 2000 years old and permanent landownership began more than 350 years ago. In these three and a half centuries all open plant life formations – fynbos, succulent Karoo,

Nama Karoo and grassland – lost their animal diversity. With all sorts of activities, humankind alters the environment, but a changing environment can, over time, also transform human societies.

The environment and indigenous residents before and during the period 1652–1795

Hunter-gatherers

The first residents in the country known today as South Africa were the Bushmen, also known as the San. They were hunter-gatherers and did not keep livestock or plant crops. The largest part of their diet was plant food collected in the veld by the women – fruit, seeds, leaves and roots of edible plants. They also ate locusts and other kinds of insects. To supplement this diet, the men hunted a variety of wild animals and small rodents, reptiles such as tortoises and also large species of buck, including eland.

Over many centuries their hunting methods improved and were adapted to the environment. Initially, they had to track or run down their prey and kill the animal by beating it with stones or sticks. Later they learnt to work together in groups – one group drove the game in the direction of another group, or towards a hole they had dug in the ground to catch the animals. Their hunting technology took a decided leap forward when the Bushmen learnt to make bows and arrows with tips that were coated with poison. This meant that they could hit their prey from a distance but it still demanded great effort, ingenuity and fieldcraft to follow the tracks of a wounded animal to where it had died. Because this whole process took so much effort, the Bushmen only hunted just enough game to meet their basic food requirements.

It is generally accepted that hunter-gatherers, because of their way of life, only had a marginal impact on the environment. Their numbers were limited and they moved around in small groups. They lived in caves or temporary shelters of branches, grass and animal skins but generally their lifestyle was nomadic – they moved to where they could find enough food to survive. When their source of food in a particular area became scarce they went to another where more food was available.

Because such a wide variety of plant and animal species was used as food, we can assume that the hunter-gatherers did not completely wipe out any specific species in certain areas. Although each Bushman group in southern Africa controlled its own territory, these were expansive and the group sometimes moved around over distances of more than 100 km. Then too, because they did not exhaust one area entirely before they moved to another, the vacated terrain had time to recover from any damage the environment had suffered. If there was an extended drought, the older and weaker members of the hunter-gatherer clan died of starvation along with the animal life in the area.

Although the number of hunter-gatherers and their technological level was too low to have a dramatic effect on the environment, one should not lose sight of the fact that when all is said and done, the Bushmen were probably the only members of *Homo sapiens* who were able to adapt to virtually any environment on earth.

They gradually settled in even better with the support of technological developments. With stone tools, for example, they could use a wider variety of food sources, make clothes and erect shelters, all of which placed them in a position to survive in terrains which would otherwise have been unsuitable for human habitation. In this way people influenced the environment far more than animals.

Although their technological development was primitive, the Bushmen devised ways of gaining power over nature. From the rituals that are depicted in their rock art it can be inferred that prior to a hunt, under the direction of their traditional healers, they carried out certain rites, which actions they believed would give them power over the game they were about to hunt.

Some researchers claim that the impact on the environment by these hunter-gatherers was perhaps greater than was previously thought. They argue that particularly because of their ability to make fire, the Bushmen – like hunter-gatherers elsewhere in the world – contributed to ecological change. The occurrence of fires in southern Africa, as in other parts of the world, was an important factor in the shrinking of forests and the increasing of grasslands. These fires were often caused by humans.

By the patterns of their hunting expeditions the Bushmen exercised some influence on the wildlife. Although unlike their counterparts in the western hemisphere they did not wipe out certain big game species, their hunting methods may have disrupted the balance between different types of wild game to some extent. It is also true that the Bushmen's preference for certain types of edible plants might have altered the composition of plant life in some southern African biomes.

Although the Bushmen did have an impact on the natural environment, their fairly limited numbers and sparse settlement ensured that their influence was limited to certain areas. In comparison to later farming communities, their environmental impact was minimal.

Cultivators and livestock farmers

The Khoekhoen and the various Bantu-speaking black societies who migrated into South Africa from the north both kept livestock. Although they also had small stock (sheep and goats) their socio-economic livelihood revolved around their cattle. The search for suitable grazing, free of hazards such as the tsetse fly, was one of the reasons for the spread of Bantu-speaking groups across the grasslands of the Highveld in the interior of South Africa.

By the time that the foremost groups of Bantu speakers had reached southern Africa they had already learnt how best to cultivate grain crops such as sorghum, but like the hunter-gatherers they still collected edible plants from the veld and hunted game.

Increased food production by cattle herders and cultivators meant they now enjoyed an improved diet and this led to a quicker population growth. The Khoekhoen settled on a much more permanent basis in areas where there was water, grass for grazing and good soil available for cultivation. Because they lived in more permanent and bigger homes, they accumulated more personal possessions and social equality between members of the community disappeared.

Greater material wealth led to enhanced status and therefore cultivators – in contrast to hunter-gatherers – produced more than was necessary to meet their basic daily requirements. This meant that they also used more natural resources per head and their impact on the physical environment was appreciably more than that of the hunter-gatherers.

With time, the cultivation of land for agricultural purposes and the grazing of the veld by a growing number of cattle inevitably changed these components of their environment dramatically. Soil erosion, for example, was accelerated by the cultivation of the land and overgrazing, while nutrients in the soil were depleted by constant crop production. Where lands were irrigated from the rivers, there was salinisation of the soil.

When lands were being prepared for planting crops the soil was cleared of all other plant species prior to ploughing. Then too, the same grain crop was usually sown or planted repeatedly which means that the ecosystem on that cultivated land was reduced to a monoculture (only one plant in one cultivated field). In this way other plant species were systematically reduced as the cultivation of grain increased. This process is referred to as the reduction of biodiversity (the variety of life) in agricultural areas. Large parts of South Africa that were too dry for grain crops were, however, not affected in this way.

Animals tamed for domestic use and kept by humans, including cattle, sheep, goats, pigs and horses, also evolved over the centuries and underwent evolutionary changes. Of greater significance in the southern African context is that the destruction of the natural habitats of wild animals as a result of agriculture and cattle breeding led to the migration of wild animals to areas where very few or no people lived. The wiping out of "vermin" such as animals of prey which posed a danger to people and their livestock also had a marked influence on the fauna (animal life) of southern Africa.

Metalworking changed the natural environment in southern Africa still further. Iron smelting was apparently carried out a long time ago – possibly as early as 300 AD – by black communities in the eastern parts of the subcontinent. This influenced the environment in two major ways. Firstly, a great deal of firewood was used in the smelting ovens, and secondly, iron smelting produced smoke pollution and other waste products.

In conclusion, it can be reiterated that the migration to southern Africa and the increase in population of the Bantu-speaking societies in this region caused greater pressure on the environment. Historians maintain that the depletion of the environment began to play an increasing role in the settlement and migration of human societies in this region, for example the evacuation of Great Zimbabwe. We do not know for certain why large settlements such as these were established and then later vacated, but environmental factors in the Iron Age must have played a role.

The eastern frontier zone

Interpretations through an environmental history lens

For the major part of the eighteenth century – the last phase of VOC rule – the Cape settler frontier expanded as hunting areas became larger and it was necessary to open up new grazing areas. By and large the trekboers (nomadic white livestock farmers) avoided the areas with rainfall of less than 250 mm per year. This meant that most of the expansion was to the wetter Eastern Cape rather than north or north-west of Cape Town.

For the most part, earlier settler and Afrikaner nationalist historians depicted the wars that were to follow between the settlers and Bantu-speaking groups as a conflict between Western civilisation and the so-called "barbarism" of Africa. To force black people to work on settlers' farms, it was considered necessary to take away their independence and their right to gain access to land.

However, modern historians are in agreement that the conflict in the eastern frontier zone in the eighteenth century was instead largely due to competition for access to land for grazing, suitable water sources and hunting.

The following excerpts from some recent studies on environmental history in the eastern frontier zone provide us with significant insight.

In 2007 Kylie van Zyl investigated the role of drought and other causes of environmental stress in furthering violence on the eastern frontier between 1828 and 1857. She argues that many of the victories achieved by colonial governors were not due to their superior military prowess; their opponents were unable to keep fighting because of diminishing resources. She also claims that indigenous people began these frontier wars in an effort to protect their remaining resources. This then led to the tragic contradiction of wars that were fought to conserve resources, but were lost because of the lack thereof.

As far as the impact of the settlers on the environment is concerned, Jill Payne conducted research on the way the British outlooks on life at the end of the eighteenth century caused human-made environmental changes. Attempts to create a "home away from home" became linked to the colonists' desire to exercise control over what they regarded as an "untamed wilderness". They undertook a large-scale clean-up operation and applied new methods of land usage. Wild species which were seen as a threat to productivity were removed.

Loss of their habitat forced many species to move to areas outside the occupied regions which meant that indigenous flora and fauna were replaced by exotic species. Bigger demands were made on the carrying capacity of the soil with the rise of a capitalist economy where the pursuit of profit dominated. Conservation legislation which was gradually introduced to limit the deterioration of the environment and protect commercial undertakings, also increasingly limited black people's access to land and its resources. Control of land was of necessity linked to control over black people and the use of black labour to cultivate the land also contributed towards subjugating them.

Recent research by environmental historians has also had a significant impact on interpretations of the Xhosa cattle killing in 1856–1857. This catastrophe involved wiping out virtually everything the Xhosa owned, including cattle and crops, and was triggered by a Xhosa prophetess, Nongqawuse. She was convinced that the Xhosa ancestors had appeared to her at the Gxarha River (near today's Wild Coast, Eastern Cape), given her the order to destroy everything and instructed her to pass on the message to the rest of the Xhosa. She insisted that this "sacrificial offering" would prompt the ancestral spirits to drive the British settlers into the sea.

Early settler historiography is inclined to depict this incident as proof of the disastrous outcome of African superstitions. However, on a more positive note, revisionist historians such as Jeff Peires interpret it as a "millenarian movement" which was attempting to re-build a society that had been crushed not only by the failure of its military resistance in eight frontier wars but also by the assault of Christian missionaries, settler domination and settler culture in general.

For his part, Julian Cobbing argues from a more cultural-materialist and environmentally based perspective. He claims that the origin of the cattle killing should be traced to the spread of lung sickness among cattle in Mossel Bay after 1853, the scorched-earth policy which the British troops applied in the wars of dispossession, and the loss of the Xhosa's most productive grazing in these wars which was exacerbated by drought and the exploitation of their labour.

C.B. Andreas and Adam Ashforth researched similar themes and although they come to similar conclusions, they differ somewhat from Cobbing as regards the motivation for the Xhosa's actions and the role of European slave traders and settlers in the "Nguni reaction" of the time. From a feminist perspective Helen Bradford argues that an explanation of the extent of the disaster should be sought in the refusal of the women to work in the lands, rather than in the destruction of male prestige items (cattle).

Regardless of how these various interpretations differ or concur, all the historians referred to above emphasise that it is vital to take note of the role of the environment in the history of humankind in order to gain a more comprehensive understanding of the course of events over time.

The Zulu kingdom

Input from environmental history has also totally re-shaped our understanding of the rise of the Zulu kingdom. In a pioneering study, historian Jeff Guy investigated the underlying ecological causes of state formation rather than focusing on prominent leaders such as Dingiswayo, Zwide and Shaka. Guy argues that oral traditions and the stories of shipwrecked soldiers indicate that in the seventeenth and eighteenth centuries the population increased in the region that later became known as KwaZulu-Natal.

Studies in the fields of dendroclimatology (determining the historical climate using the annual rings of trees) and archaeology suggest that the rapid growth of the population might have been due to an extended period of plentiful rain. High rainfall led to the cultivation of what might otherwise have been marginal land and the increased production of mealies (maize) rather than the drought-resistant sorghum. In the aftermath of floods, the human population and their livestock grew exponentially.

MEALIES AS A RESOURCE: HISTORICAL ORIGIN AND SIGNIFICANCE

Mealies, a maize crop (also known as Indian corn), is indigenous to the central parts of the American continent. As long ago as 1500 BC, hunter-gatherers in today's Mexico and Peru were growing mealies. At the time the societies in these areas were the Olmecs and the Chavín.

The Maya society (the indigenous population of Central America from about 683 AD) was well known for their cultivation of mealies. Apparently, a number of ferocious rituals were regularly performed to appease the gods so that they would bless the mealie crops, the basis of Mayan agriculture.

The production of mealies also became known in Europe shortly after the Americas were explored by the Spanish navigators. In accordance with American tradition, cornbread (mealie bread) is still served today as part of the annual Thanksgiving meal.

It was the Portuguese navigators who brought mealies to the Gold Coast (present-day Ghana) and in South Africa from 1652 the small group of Dutch East India Company employees seemingly popularised the growing of mealies (which came from the western parts of Africa). The Hollanders knew the crop as *turchse tarwe* and for the Spaniards it was *maise*. Maize and sorghum cultivars in the Gold Coast were known by the general Portuguese term *mihlo*. It is accepted that the Afrikaans word *mielie* and the English word maize or mealie, developed from the wide use of *milho* and *maise*.

> The first migrations ("treks") from the later Cape Colony and the migrations of a number of black societies to the northern parts of South Africa shifted the boundaries of the cultivation of mealies. It was particularly the black communities who expanded the growing of maize.
> Through the centuries, the cultivation of mealies has improved a great deal. They were even used as a popular element of decoration in the ancient settlements of America. In the 1920s second only to potatoes, mealies were the world's leading agricultural product; and by 1930, of South Africa's total cultivated area under agriculture, approximately 40% was mealies.

As the human population spread and occupied more land, the balance between the residents and the available resources was disturbed. The amount of land available for the seasonal migration of cattle became increasingly restricted and there were more signs of overgrazing and the exhaustion of agricultural land. However, as long as the plentiful rainfall continued, the situation did not escalate out of control.

However, at the end of the eighteenth century the rainfall fell dramatically, which led to extreme drought conditions and the Madlathule famine of 1801–1802 among the northern Nguni groups in the present KwaZulu-Natal. This caused a crisis situation. There was increased competition to gain access to the remaining water sources, grazing and agricultural land and there was a drastic escalation of tension between the various communities. Sharing gradually became an unrealistic option and intervention by the state became necessary to maintain the ideal combination of water and land resources.

At about the same time, the formation of age regiments led to the strengthening of the military power of growing black societies. They were now able to protect the seizure of their land, water and cattle by others. In this way age regiments not only led to the restriction of marriages and curbed the establishment of new domestic units, but also provided an opportunity for leaders to regulate the exploitation of the environment.

The Great Trek

Another well-known migration that led to the formation of new states in the interior in the nineteenth century is the Great Trek. It is one of the aspects of South African history that environmental historians first focused upon. A contribution in which specific attention is given to the role of environmental factors in the Great Trek is a short essay on the influence of the tsetse fly on South African history written by B.H. Dicke in 1932.

What is of interest is that his comments have specific reference to the fate of the Voortrekker group under the leadership of Hans Janse van Rensburg. His was one of the first groups that left the Cape Colony in 1835 – as was the Louis Tregardt group – and he then moved northwards to the later Transvaal in search of a route to Delagoa Bay (now Maputo). This meant that they broke away from the majority of their countrymen, whose initial migration from the Cape to the Transgariep (the present Free State) was followed by a movement into Natal.

By mid-1936 the entire Van Rensburg party had been wiped out by the Tsonga Shangaan people of the Makuleka and Mahlangwe communities. According to Dicke, historians have overemphasised the role of the Tsonga Shangaan in the obliteration of the Van Rensburg group and that they merely delivered the "death-blow" to Van Rensburg's party who were virtually on their knees already. Dicke believes that the tsetse fly was the primary reason why the group was so debilitated. They had lost their draught animals and had been forced to leave their wagons behind because of exposure to the dreaded tsetse fly. This meant that they could not form a laager for protection when danger threatened. Without wagons and with only ten rifles to defend themselves, they stood no chance of survival in the event of attack. However, Dicke's conclusion that the tsetse fly "killed" the Van Rensburg party long before the Tsonga arrived was a controversial one in 1932 given the Afrikaner sentiment on the Great Trek at the time.

In 1959 the historical geographer F.J. Potgieter became one of the first environmental history academics when he investigated the environmental factors that influenced the settlement patterns of the Voortrekkers in the then Transvaal (an observation by the historian Phia Steyn). Potgieter not only focused on the exploitation of natural resources such as indigenous forests, game, minerals, water sources and land, but also on the environmental factors that motivated the seasonal migrations of farmers between their winter and summer farms.

His observation was that the Transvaal government (the ZAR) was in no position to choose when they became involved in wars against the indigenous black groups. The government first had to consider environmental factors such as the tsetse fly (that carried the protozoan sickness trypanosomiasis and caused sleeping sickness in humans and nagana among draught animals); horse sickness and malaria; as well as the movement of the farmers and hunting expeditions during the winter seasons. With the majority of burghers out of action for at least three months of the year the ability of the former Transvaal to protect itself during certain periods was extremely tenuous.

For her part, Isabel Hofmeyr argues strenuously that the portrayal of the Voortrekkers as agriculturists and the black people as hunters in much of the "frontier literature" is flawed and is used to justify the right of white farmers to land. This, she claims, is especially evident in the portrayals of Schoemansdal, the Voortrekker settlement which was established in the northern region in 1848.

In sharp contrast are the opinions of other environmental historians such as Johann Tempelhoff who feel that it was not agriculture but the hunting industry which was the main source of income for the Soutpansbergers. For about 19 years Schoemansdal was the most important trading centre in the old Northern Transvaal. Thousands of tons of venison, horns, whips and salt were taken to Mozambique, the Cape Colony and Natal.

White employers also armed local black people with firearms to hunt elephants for them. This region became one of the main centres for ivory trading in the South African interior. Ivory was the old Transvaal's single largest export commodity prior to the discovery of gold and the Soutpansberg settlement dominated this trade. In the 1850s an estimated 45 000 kg of ivory per year was exported from Schoemansdal.

Two local warlords of Schoemansdal, João Albasini and Michael Buys, enjoyed a considerable following among black groups and had a large number of black hunters in their employ. It is alleged that Albasini's hunters possessed as many as a hundred elephant rifles. By special permission he was allowed armed guards for the protection of his hunting groups although no more than five per party. Furthermore, in terms of the hunting law of 1858, Buys and his marksmen hunted on behalf of the ZAR government. Some of the participating men were therefore also legally armed.

Space constraints prevent the inclusion of similar studies of other regions settled by the Voortrekkers, but it can be argued that such trends were also seen in other parts of the then Orange Free State and Transvaal.

> **MICHAEL BUYS AND HIS PIONEER FATHER**
>
> Michael Buys's exceptional bond with the black people who were part of his hunting parties is by no means strange because he virtually grew up among them. His father was the well-known Coenraad de Buys who in the years 1761 to 1821 led an active life as a nomadic trekker and environmentalist. He has been described as a pioneer, adventurer and wanderer.
>
> Of Coenraad it is said that he was a well-spoken person in his years as a town-dweller in the Eastern Cape and was a proactive republican. But he clashed constantly with the Cape authorities over his wilful actions and refusal to pay taxes. In addition he was an alleged agitator, rousing black people to agitate against the authority of the state. De Buys was also, among other things, an advisor to chieftains such as Ngqika (the Xhosa leader), Dingiswayo (the Zulu king) and Mahura (leader of the Batlhaping) and on occasion acted as commander of their troops. In the period 1813–1821 he was associated with various black leaders.
>
> Coenraad de Buys is known as one of the first white pioneers north of the Vaal River long before the Voortrekkers arrived in this area. One of the oldest farms in the former Transvaal, Buisfontein, is associated with him.

The environment in the period 1750–1948

The agricultural environment

The expansion of cattle farming and agriculture was arguably for two centuries – from 1750 to about 1948 – the activity that caused the greatest environmental transformation in South Africa.

It was in the hands of the Khoekhoen and other indigenous groups that livestock farming became widespread in southern Africa before the arrival of the settlers. Initially, the settlers' income from livestock farming was sparse and economic growth was generally slow due to a lack of internal and external markets. Growth was also hampered because there was little by way of political and environmental control.

Available statistics indicate that by the beginning of the nineteenth century there were less than 2 million head of livestock in the hands of the settlers. During the next 130 years the situation had completely changed. The number of cattle in the country reached its peak in about the early 1930s at which stage the census indicated that there were about 12 million, of which more than half were in the possession of whites, and there were in addition almost 60 million head of small livestock, of which about 90% belonged to white farmers.

The number of merino sheep for wool production expanded most rapidly and South Africa took second place worldwide behind Australia as a wool exporter. Livestock, particularly sheep, were abundant in the South African interior. They not only survived but flourished in the semi-desert regions which made up 55–60% of South Africa. This meant that the Karoo and the southern and western Free State specialised in the production of livestock. The provision of water was important and the use of natural fountains; the control of rivers and marshy hollows; the construction of earth dams and the sinking of boreholes, which took off from the late nineteenth century onwards, improved the capacity to control the available water supplies. These developments were particularly important for white farmers of livestock on privately owned land.

Both white and black South African owners of livestock were hit by a destructive series of animal sicknesses which attacked cattle in particular. There was lung sickness in the 1850s; scab and heartwater among sheep, and rinderpest in the 1890s; followed by east coast fever in the early twentieth century, all of which temporarily diminished the number of livestock. However, from that time onwards veterinary services were available and measures to control the movement of livestock and compulsory dipping were gradually introduced.

The increase in the number of livestock in white and black possession undoubtedly changed the South African environment. Grasses and edible bushes were heavily grazed, which exposed the soil to erosion. Water sources dried up. Exotic plants such as the burweed (*Xanthium spinosium*) and prickly pears became major invaders. During the interwar years the Drought Commission (1922) and the Natives Economic Commission (1932) perceived rapid environmental degradation – a wind-blown dust region was beginning to develop – and drastic measures were recommended.

The worst deterioration of the environment was noted for example in old, established vineyards and wheat lands which had spread considerably in the twentieth century and were encroaching on the sensitive fynbos plant life of the valleys in what is now the Western Cape. Regular burning to encourage new growth for grazing had destroyed indigenous plant life in the high-lying regions. Australian gum trees (eucalyptus) and acacias, as well as European fir trees (conifers) were widely imported as a source of wood and for establishing plantations to avoid deforestation. These species are still widely found in the Western Cape.

Along the east coast of South Africa – the most valuable region where there is high rainfall – sub-tropical crops began to encroach on the relatively small areas of indigenous forest. In addition, sugar plantations had increasingly shored up the agricultural economy of the former Natal since the late nineteenth century and this singly grown crop was widely replacing the natural sub-tropical bush. Ironically, trees were also responsible for the deforestation because the wetter parts in the north of the Natal Colony were suitable for wattle and other plantation trees.

After the establishment of cities in the interior; the agricultural revolution in the early twentieth century; and the importation of tractors after the Second World War, mealie production on the Highveld was transformed.

Rapid population growth occurred, especially in the twentieth century. In the first few decades both white and black population groups increased dramatically in number and South Africa's segregation policy significantly influenced the social and environmental outcome. Poor white people moved to the cities and in a white controlled state enjoyed protected employment. The white population in the rural areas, living for the most part on private farms, had stabilised by the mid-twentieth century.

Many black people also went to the cities, but their freedom was restricted by pass laws. They were also denied other opportunities due to the severity of race-based legislation. The rural black population, especially those in the reserves or so-called homelands, increased exponentially in the twentieth century. This was in the light of the fact that by the 1940s the black population percentage growth rate had already overtaken that of the whites.

Many rural people tried to maintain a level of income from the soil. As a result, fields for planting were even developed on hillsides vulnerable to erosion, while the reserves were teeming with livestock. However, segregation and apartheid also prevented black people from accessing land in the white farming districts. Growing populations were therefore trapped in the homelands. By the mid-twentieth century there was evidence in parts of the black reserves of the worst soil erosion in the country. Soil erosion was also fostered by communal forms of property ownership.

Shortly after the Second World War the South African government increasingly began to intervene in an effort to curb environmental deterioration in rural areas. The Soil Conservation Act of 1946 and subsequent legislation put in place an institutional framework to regulate land use, livestock numbers and landholding by whites. More and more farms were fenced off and were alternately grazed.

In the black homelands the government followed a more forceful policy of rehabilitation, including establishing towns on a large scale in an attempt to rationalise black land use and make it comply with conservative farming strategies. Included here were the officials' objectives to arrest soil erosion by encouraging contour ploughing, and to enforce the sale of livestock so as to relieve the debilitating overgrazing of the land. The compulsory fencing of grazing land was also enforced. These interventions were among the most far-reaching in the lives of black people in the twentieth century and evinced a number of small rural rebellions. Settlement patterns in black areas were also changed, although the outcome of this on conservation was less effective.

At the same time a number of protected areas were created throughout the country, including national, provincial, and municipal parks as well as small nature reserves in private possession, carved out of farmland. This meant that some of the most sensitive areas were saved from the impact of heavy agriculture and grazing. In a national survey of land degradation in 1999 the conclusion was reached that government control measures and changing farming methods and attitudes had led to the stabilisation – and even improvement – of the environment in some of the rural districts which had been the worst affected.

Although at the beginning of the twenty-first century the government professed to be inclined to implement environmental management, it was precisely the lack, the deliberate delay or ignoring thereof by 1948 that placed some parts of the country under great pressure.

A century earlier, during the Anglo-Boer War of 1899 to 1902, certain parts of the environment in present-day South Africa were also exposed to extreme stress. An interesting aspect that ties in with this is how the environment was used by the strategists of both sides to the benefit or detriment of the combatants.

The influence of environments on the course of the Anglo-Boer War

All environments inevitably have a crucial influence on the strategy employed in a war and on the tactics used in each battle. Add to this the British use of the scorched-earth policy in the war of 1899–1902 and its dreadful results, and it becomes clear that the landscape indeed exercised a significant influence on the Anglo-Boer War.

Early in June 1899 the British high command devised an attacking military campaign. However, by the end of July 1899 it is striking that the Boer high command still had no military plan of action in place. When the war broke out in October 1899, the Boer high command made the error of not immediately occupying the railway lines in the British colonies at strategic places. The British breakthrough in Natal and the massive attack over the plains of the Free State completely changed the character of the war. When Bloemfontein was occupied on 13 March and Pretoria on 5 June 1900, the period of conventional trench warfare was of necessity over.

This signified a new direction; a change of strategy by the Boers and the beginning of the guerrilla phase of the war. As far as was feasible, Generals Christiaan de Wet and Louis Botha sent the various commandos to their home districts. There they were instructed only to come to blows with the enemy when the opportunity arose. If a British column was too strong, a commando simply stood aside and allowed it to pass.

On the wide plains of the Free State and in the mountains of the Eastern Free State and Eastern Transvaal, as well as behind the thorn trees of the Western and Northern Transvaal, the commandos simply disappeared. They divided into small groups to hide more easily. When an isolated British column was spotted, the commandos were assembled with lightning speed, ready for a surprise attack. Mobility was the all-important password. This emphasised the vital role of horses.

The expansive Free State and the Eastern Transvaal Highveld offered excellent grazing for horses and in this climate these animals flourished. However, it became more difficult in the summer months in the Eastern Transvaal Lowveld with the danger of horse sickness, which meant that those commandos were inactive. The drives Lord Kitchener launched in January 1901 using a large force to carry out sweeping attacks in an effort to contain the enemy, backed up by the construction of a network of blockhouse lines throughout the theatre of war, succeeded to some extent in curtailing the Boers' military initiatives. But it was the relentless implementation of Lord Roberts's scorched-earth policy that eventually led to a British victory.

During the war the environment also determined the diet of the Boer fighters. On the Transvaal Highveld for example, mealies were grown and livestock comprised mainly cattle and sheep, while in the Free State sheep were abundant and the eastern Free State was well known for its wheat. These products became the most important source of sustenance for the Boers on commando. The staple food in the first months of the war was meat and either bread or rusks.

But even in this phase there were periodic shortages, primarily because the government commissariat was poorly administered. Commandos that were encamped nearest to food depots tended to receive the most generous supplies, while those who were coping with difficult conditions in the furthest outposts were often neglected. Inaccessible terrain, as on the Tugela line, meant that there was often a highly disproportionate spread of supplies.

In the guerrilla phase meat came strongly to the fore as a staple food. The Free State largely met the requirements not only for its own commandos but also those of the Eastern and Western Transvaal. At the same time in both the Free State and the Eastern and Western Transvaal *mieliepap* (a stiff porridge made from maize meal) took the place of bread or rusks as a staple ingredient of the diet for those on commando. Although hunting for wild game was forbidden in the first phase of the war, when small groups were in action during the guerrilla phase, hunting was often the solution to the scarcity of slaughter stock.

In the first six months of the war salt was still freely available. However, by the beginning of May 1900 the commissariat in Pretoria had only a small supply left. As was the case with other food supplies, with the occupation of Pretoria and the closing down of ZAR's military commissariat in September 1900, salt became extremely scarce. According to General Ben Viljoen, after March 1901 the Boer commandos virtually had to manage without it. From time to time the environment with its salt pans at Bloemhof, Wolmaransstad, the western Free State and in the Soutpansberg Mountains, brought some relief in this respect but because of the presence of British columns or black groups who supported the British, these sources were not always accessible.

The environment was one of the main reasons why the Boer delegates at the peace negotiations in 1902 accepted the British peace conditions, in terms of which the Boers lost their independence. Kitchener's scorched earth policy meant that with the winter of 1902 close at hand the burghers were enduring an acute shortage of food. Kitchener's troops had wiped out all the livestock they could lay their hands on and destroyed the grain crops. The women and children had been taken to concentration camps. Apart from this, a network of blockhouses had been built to restrict the movement of commandos.

In the Heilbron district of the Free State and in about eleven other districts in the then Eastern and south-eastern Transvaal (in other words about half of the old Transvaal Republic) the shortage of foodstuff had become a very serious crisis indeed. Whereas other regions could still obtain food supplies from better-endowed areas, these worst-hit districts were unable to do so because of more effectively controlled blockhouse lines.

Environmental management under apartheid

Proper environmental control was apparently not a priority for the National Party government which came to power in 1948 and ruled until 1994. In the late 1940's this government inherited an environmental agenda which in many ways in the context of Africa could be categorised as typically colonial. In an international context this category is called a first-generation agenda. (In the USA a first-generation environmental agenda refers to a system where central control over environmental issues is exercised by the state.)

In these years the focus was largely on the protection of natural resources – particularly soil conservation – and the protection of flora and fauna species (plant and animal species). However, until the late 1960s the government gave little attention to the exploitation of the environment by external factors (such as foreign companies) and domestic activities in various parts of the country. Quite apart from the fact that many industries brought in far more revenue than environmental conservation could, the country's leaders were also politically swamped with the implementation of discriminatory legislation and the suppression of anti-apartheid movements.

Other priorities were extensive industrialisation initiatives with the aim of strengthening the country's economy. Ironically enough the promotion of economic and industrial development forced the government to pay attention to environmental matters. Water-related issues in particular were addressed with the passing of the Water Act, No. 54 of 1956 and in the 1960s it was the turn of pollution, with the Atmospheric Pollution Act, No. 45 of 1965. Although these were important laws, their aim was not environmental protection as such, but rather the regulation of water use and competition between the various water-user sectors.

At this stage, on the instructions of the government, the Council for Scientific and Industrial Research (CSIR) had already been active for a few years on environment research in various regions. Their closed reports were used if and when it suited the government or the particular industry. Today we know that as far back as the 1950s there were valuable research reports that made reference to the degradation of the environment and the possibility of future environmental crises. These were ignored or downplayed in favour of economic growth.

In the absence of television to make people aware of environmental crises in the industrial countries, and as a result of increasing isolation from the 1960s as far as most citizens were concerned, environmental crises in South Africa tended to simply pass unnoticed. However, in countries such as the USA, Germany and Britain, environmental activism was stimulated and led to the formation of non-governmental organisations (NGOs) such as Greenpeace and Friends of the Earth, which had far-reaching environmental agendas in which the natural environment became a political issue. However, at that time no comparative NGOs came to the fore in South Africa.

Greater awareness on the condition of the environment gradually filtered through to South Africa. More involvement was also apparent among environment-related NGOs such as the Association for the Protection of the Environment, the National Association for Clean Air and an old favourite, the Wildlife Society. However, by the early twenty-first century all environments became a priority for some state departments, environmental researchers, and a number of NGOs (for example the Federation for a Sustainable Environment, formed in 2007).

Despite increasing international isolation as far back as the 1970s in reaction to its apartheid policy, the South African government was unable to ignore the new developments in environmental management by the state. The country took part in the UN's high-profile Conference on the Human Environment held in Stockholm in 1972, which ensured that the environment gained a place on international and national political agendas.

The newly appointed secretary of planning and the environment, Dr P.S. Rautenbach, was passionate about the country's participation in the international environmental management arena and was actively involved in all UN-sponsored environmental campaigns until 1974 when the UN General Assembly expelled South Africa from the UN because of its apartheid policy. This step also excluded South Africa from many international initiatives.

Specifically as regards environment-oriented discussions, South Africa was after that only invited to take part if matters that impacted directly on the country were under discussion, such as the conservation of wildlife and the protection of Antarctica. On the other hand, the South African government reacted to its increasing isolation by withdrawing from many of the international environmental initiatives that were still open to the country, particularly those that placed restrictions on economic growth.

Between 1972 and 1994 the South African government maintained a somewhat ambivalent stance on environmental questions. On the one hand, as early as 1972 it established a "home" for environmental matters within government structures, although it only made provision for the formation of an independent Department of Environmental Affairs in 1984. A number of environment-related laws were passed and in 1982 the government also issued a wide-ranging declaration on the environment and actively began to promote nature conservation in the country.

On the other hand, the government refused to introduce environment impact assessments – even for developments in ecologically sensitive areas. After 1910 there was a tendency to allow development in ecologically sensitive regions (such as road development along the Garden Route; in the Kruger National Park and many other parks) and to give industries free rein to pollute the air, water and soil resources. After 1973 international sanctions and boycotts began to bite and created further troublesome circumstances from which the country increasingly struggled to survive economically.

Apartheid also played a role in the degradation of the environment in the black homelands and black residential areas. Overpopulation as well as a lack of adequate housing, sanitation and water held untold danger for people as well as the environment. It also created a perception among black South Africans that white people, lions and rhinos were more important than black people.

On close examination, the calibre of the natural and human-made environments in South Africa declined during the apartheid era because the government neglected to address the profusion of environmental problems that arose as a result of ill-advised industrialisation processes and its controversial policy of separate development. Accordingly, the dubious environmental legacy of the apartheid era continues – long after apartheid has been scrapped.

South Africa after 1994

As in many other spheres, the political changes in South Africa in 1994 also had a marked influence on the country's handling of environmental issues. The lifting of apartheid and the transformation to democracy made South Africa acceptable once more as a member of the international community. The UN restored South Africa's full membership of the world body.

It also meant that the new ANC government had the opportunity to participate fully in decision making on international initiatives to manage and protect the environment, as well as their implementation. For example, South Africa became a signatory to the important environmental conventions on climate change, desertation and biodiversity which were introduced early in the twenty-first century.

After 1994 the ANC was therefore theoretically obliged to protect and conserve the physical environment. In clause 24 of the new (1996) South African constitution, which is part of the Bill of Rights (chapter 2), the right of every citizen of the country to a clean and healthy environment is entrenched. Various government departments – particularly the departments of environmental affairs, tourism, water affairs, mineral resources, agriculture, and forestry and fisheries – should play an important role on behalf of the government to ensure the implementation of these constitutional rights.

In the Government of National Unity which was formed after the 1994 election, a member of the National Party, Dr Dawie de Villiers, was initially named as the Minister of the then Department of Environmental Affairs and Tourism. He was followed in this portfolio by Dr Pallo Jordan (1996–1999); Valli Moosa (1999–2004); and Marthinus van Schalkwyk (from 2004). The urgency to be environmentally more accountable, especially with regards to the country's water resources, led to President Jacob Zuma's reshuffling of these departments in 2009 and the establishing of connections with others. Therefore, the original department was divided to be known as the Department of Tourism and the Department of Water and Environmental Affairs. The inclusion of the water sector (originally under the Ministry of Water Affairs and Forestry) provided for a stronger emphasis on crucial environmental matters. In 2009 Ms Buyelwa Sonjica, followed by Ms Edna Molewa in 2010, became Minister of Water and Environmental Affairs.

The former Department of Environmental Affairs and Tourism did not summarily wipe from the table the apartheid government's adherence to a system of integrated environmental management that was embodied in the Environmental Conservation Act of 1989, but did indeed begin to effect the internal transformation of this department. An advisory national environmental conservation policy process (widely known as CONNCEPP) was initiated to develop a new environmental policy. In 1996 a discussion document and in 1998 a white paper on a national environmental management policy were compiled.

Among the most important laws with the implementation of the new policy was the National Environmental Management Act, No. 107 of 1998. A stricter system of environmental impact assessment was brought in, which meant that a large development project (for example a building project) could not be started before it was established that it would not perhaps be detrimental to the environment.

Another very important piece of legislation was the National Water Act, No. 36 of 1998. It laid down that the state, and not individuals, was the owner of all the water sources in the country and that private persons or institutions of any kind had to apply for licences for various forms of water usage. Furthermore, the management of the country's water supplies was assigned to various management authorities, comprising a variety of role players in the different catchment areas.

The vision of the Department of Environmental Affairs at the time was to create a society of prosperity and equality in South Africa which is in harmony with its natural resources. To realise this vision it is the mission of that department to become a frontrunner in the terrain of sustainable development; to promote the conservation and sustainable use of the natural resources for economic growth; to protect and improve the quality and safety of the environment; and to help with the global promotion of sustainable development.

On the government's side, since the implementation of comprehensive legislation in 1998, progress has been made in the handling of a number of environmental issues in South Africa. Conservation areas, including national parks, have been extended and cross-border parks which stretch across national borders have also become a reality. A number of sites in South Africa – for the most part natural heritage sites – have already been declared world heritage sites or are in the process of being so named.

And yet there are still many questions that must be handled by the various departments, including a more efficient management and restriction of acid mine drainage which reached drastic proportions by 2010–2013, particularly in the vicinity of Gauteng's gold mines. In the long term it will have a highly negative effect on town and industrial environments.

Other causes for concern are the poaching of wildlife for ivory and rhino horn; the so-called "canned" hunting of lions; the destruction of maritime resources (such as abalone); water and atmospheric pollution; and participation in international programmes to work against global warming, climate change and desertification. Then there is also the administrative handling of thousands of environmental impact studies every year.

It is a huge challenge for the government to give adequate attention to all these matters with its available human resources.

The private sector also has an impact on the environment. Many privately owned farms are becoming involved in game farming for the purposes of hunting and ecotourism and this means that the number of game on farms has increased. However, the erecting of game fences can also have certain negative environmental results. A major problem is the perception among some decision makers that environmental conservation stands in the path of socio-economic development and does not deserve to enjoy the highest priority. There is not yet full realisation that economic, social and ecological factors must be considered together to accomplish sustainable development.

Within government ranks the various departments that are involved in environmental matters do not always have enough status, power or expertise to support one another in issues that involve society at large as well as the environment. Furthermore, it is often local governments who are the greatest sinners as far as pollution is concerned because in some cases they do not possess the necessary skills and capacity to keep the sewerage purification works in good working order in the environments for which they are responsible. In many instances they are guilty of allowing large volumes of raw sewage to flow into South Africa's river systems and filter into the ground water.

The environmental education of schoolchildren in particular is of great importance to promote environmental conservation in the longer term. South Africa must also create a proper environmentally friendly structure for reclaiming waste products and in this way place less pressure on available resources. One of the high points on South Africa's agenda in the twenty-first century was to act as host country for the World Council of Sustainable Development in 2002. In this way the country received recognition for taking the leading role in environmental conservation on the African continent.

30

From state capture to Covid: the decline of the ANC, 2014–2020

Jan-Jan Joubert

The 2014 election

The year 2014 dawned with President Zuma's stature very much diminished by growing evidence of malfeasance and an increasing credibility gap between Zuma as ANC leader and head of state on the one hand, and the citizenry on the other.

Zuma's credibility was seriously dented in March 2014, a mere two months before the election, when Public Protector Adv. Thuli Madonsela made damning findings against Zuma pertaining to the construction of his homestead at Nkandla, KwaZulu-Natal. Wholesale abuse of tender processes at the taxpayers' expense caused her to order Zuma personally liable for much of the costs. The finding significantly diminished Zuma's already damaged moral and political standing. The election took place in an atmosphere of growing resentment against the ANC government and the results indicated a disparate search for alternatives, with parties to the government's left and right showing solid growth and the ANC losing its hold in eight provinces – all but KwaZulu-Natal, the ethnic heartland of its leader, Jacob Zuma.

The ANC ended up with 62,15% of the vote, down from 65,9% in 2009, which left the party 15 seats weaker in the National Assembly. The DA grew from 16,66% to 22,23%, gaining 22 seats for its best showing yet. The new kid on the block, the EFF, did much better than pundits expected, polling 6,25% for 25 seats, whilst the IFP continued its decline by falling from 16 seats to 10 (just 2,5% of the national vote). The Freedom Front Plus remained stagnant, retaining their four seats. More interesting results were registered in the provinces. The ANC retained control of eight of the nine provinces, but its majorities were slashed everywhere except in KwaZulu-Natal. The DA retained the Western Cape by a heavily increased majority. In KwaZulu-Natal, the DA overtook the IFP for the first time to become the official opposition in the province. As a sign of things to come, the EFF obtained more than 10% of the vote in Gauteng, North West and Limpopo, becoming the official opposition in the latter two provinces.

United against the ANC

When Parliament met after the 2014 elections, it was in a changed atmosphere, exemplifying the electorate's yearning for an alternative to the ANC. Opposition to the ANC had increased on the back of growing indications of mass corruption, which added the unwelcome term "state capture", as coined by the United Nations, to the South African political lexicon. Further impetus to growing dissatisfaction with the ANC was added by very poor levels of service in ANC-led municipalities, leading to widespread protest actions which were often brutally suppressed. These suppressions often invoked images of times past, with the ANC turning into the type of oppressor it had previously opposed. The ANC's dictatorial streak was clear in its legislative agenda, typified by the draconian Protection of State Information Act, aimed at limiting the very press freedom the ANC had espoused for so many years.

The new element in a radicalised parliament was the EFF, whose opposition to the ANC was on a level not previously seen in local parliament. They encapsulated South Africans' anger at the extent of state capture and the ANC's cover-up thereof when they disrupted Zuma's speech in the budget vote on the presidency with chants of "Pay back the money!", causing the sitting to adjourn. Later in 2014, the police were summoned to the National Assembly chamber after the EFF resisted efforts to eject one of their MPs, Reneiloe Mashabela, for calling Zuma a liar and a thief. Violence erupted as members of the DA and IFP wrestled side by side with the EFF to physically eject the police from the chamber.

In 2015, the DA made history by finally electing a black leader, Mmusi Maimane, a former pastor from Johannesburg. His election went a long way to allay the apprehension of many black voters to vote for the DA. However, warnings to the DA establishment on his lack of political gravitas fell on deaf ears. His easy-going manner cemented ties between the DA and other parties opposing the ANC.

Governments all over the world are masters at oppressing and delaying details of state corruption, but after 2014, the eye-watering extent of state capture by ANC flunkies like the Gupta family became increasingly apparent. The Guptas were a family who had settled in South Africa from their native India and had developed close personal relationships with Zuma and others in his inner circle. Although details were sketchy at first, it became increasingly clear that they were calling the shots in government, to the point of allegedly influencing and even determining key cabinet appointments and then using their growing list of ANC dependants to score lucrative state contracts illegally, growing fabulously rich at the country's expense. They were hardly the only ones. Countrywide, ANC politicians, their families and cronies had their hands in the cookie jar, with billions of rands siphoned off in every imaginable and unimaginable way from municipalities, government departments and state-owned entities like Eskom, SAA, Transnet, PetroSA, Denel and many more.

Gradually, through excellent investigative journalism, strong parliamentary opposition by parties united against ANC malfeasance and damning reports by the auditor general and independent forensic auditors, the public began to guess at the extent of the rot. As the 2016 local government (municipal) elections drew near, informal contact between opposition parties of differing ideological hue continued. Though many believed the ANC to be unbeatable, options were kept open just in case.

On local government election day, 3 August 2016, the ANC was shaken to its core. It held on to many municipalities, especially rural ones with limited tax bases. But the party lost its majority in numerous large towns and in three major cities, namely Port Elizabeth (later renamed Gqeberha) in its Eastern Cape heartland, Johannesburg in the country's economic hub, and Tshwane, which includes the national capital of Pretoria, the centre of government. It had already lost Cape Town to an ever-strengthening DA in 2006. Desperately clinging to power, the ANC was suddenly looking for coalition partners and was sure that it could cajole the EFF into working with it. But the party's woes had caught up with it and the EFF chose to co-operate across the ideological divide with the DA, IFP and Freedom Front Plus, hence denying the ANC power in dozens of municipalities in all provinces except Mpumalanga where the party still had control. Overall, ANC support nationally had dipped to an all-time low of 53%, and change was in the air.

The 2016 local government election results provided a further platform for opposition co-operation towards a future post-ideological good governance coalition against the ANC, which struggled to deal with the pincer movement unleashed by opposition parties. The growing evidence of ANC corruption and self-enrichment provided endless fodder to these parties, who were co-operating in joint marches and tabling ever more successful motions of no confidence in Zuma.

And then a strange thing happened. After a DA caucus breakaway in late 2017, the party started acting without consulting its fellow opposition parties. The DA argued that they were much stronger and larger than the other parties and did not have to consult with them. This was factually true and strategically stupid. The other opposition parties were completely blind-sided and surprised by the DA's change in tack, which strained and eventually destroyed the trust between the DA and other opposition parties. For this, the DA blamed all other opposition parties, and all other opposition parties blamed the DA.

The ANC and state capture

In the meantime, allegations surfaced about state capture by the Gupta family and other commercial interests, aided and abetted by Zuma as president of the country, and assisted by numerous senior ANC leadership figures as well as senior ANC-supporting cadres deployed to the civil service and state-owned enterprises. Public Protector Thuli Madonsela investigated the issue, and on 14 October 2016, the last day of her seven-year tenure, she issued an explosive report of 355 pages entitled "State of Capture" which made major accusations against several important figures, Zuma included. Her main finding was that Chief Justice Mogoeng Mogoeng had to appoint a Commission of Inquiry into state capture, headed by a judge of his choosing. Mogoeng chose Deputy Chief Justice Raymond Zondo, and the Zondo Commission of Inquiry was duly established in August 2017.

The hearings proved to be as crucial for its time as the Truth and Reconciliation Commission's hearings had been back in the nineties. Because the Zondo Commission's hearings were televised live, it had a massive impact on the thinking and perceptions of those who watched – a viewership that included the elderly and the unemployed, both groups fertile sources of ANC support. Citizens watched the alleged perpetrators attempt to answer or dodge allegations put to them by evidence leaders and by Zondo himself. It allowed members of the general public to watch history being made and make up their own minds. Judge Zondo set himself a deadline to hand in his final report by the end of 2021. Decisions on possible prosecutions would, as ever, reside with the national director of public prosecutions.

The ANC chooses Ramaphosa

With its national support down to 53% in the local government elections, the ANC was staring down the barrel of defeat. Such a possibility strikes dread into the heart of every politician, and fear of exposure and arrest into the hearts of the corrupt. With the ANC having plenty of both, its elective conference taking place at Nasrec, south of Johannesburg, was bound to be a tense, dirty and tightly contested affair. Having served two successive five-year terms as ANC president, Zuma could not stand for re-election.

For months leading up to the Nasrec conference, the race was building up between those who wanted to perpetuate Zuma's policies, crony networks, behaviour and legacy (including state capture) on the one hand, and those who did not on the other. The pro-Zuma grouping had Zuma's former wife, Dr Nkosazana Dlamini-Zuma, as their candidate, and the anti-Zuma faction put forward the deputy president, Cyril Ramaphosa. It later transpired that each candidate spent millions of rands trying to capture the presidency, which is a kind way of saying the branch delegates' votes were up for auction, and both contestants were buying. It was a clear and horrifying indication of the heart of darkness the ANC had become.

Ramaphosa triumphed, narrowly beating Dlamini-Zuma by 179 votes out of about 4500 cast. It was an inconclusive victory to say the least. It was achieved on the back of court orders nullifying the election of delegates from Zuma-supporting branches in the Free State and North West, but included the votes of many delegates from recently recognised ANC branches in Mpumalanga, which had the mercurial and deeply feared David Mabuza as ANC provincial chairperson.

In an evenly matched race, it was the Mpumalanga vote that proved to be the deciding factor, and Mabuza manipulated it masterfully to his own advantage. In the months leading up to the conference, Mabuza made two things clear: he did not mind much who became ANC president as long as he became deputy president; and "unity" in the ANC was the only way of staving off ANC defeat in the 2019 general election, given its setbacks in the 2016 local government elections.

The pro-Zuma grouping believed they had Mabuza in the bag, but at the last moment he and the delegates he controlled switched sides to back Ramaphosa. That sealed Ramaphosa's victory, and Mabuza was indeed elected ANC deputy president. The Mpumalanga faction's tightly controlled votes saw to it that the other four positions were filled by two pro-Zuma and two anti-Zuma candidates, at first glance fulfilling Mabuza's goal and promise of ANC "unity".

That it was less a matter of unity than balance between irreconcilable groupings was evidenced by the contradictions in the policy proposals the conference accepted as resolutions, many of which were anathema to the Ramaphosa vision. These included expropriation without compensation, the nationalisation of the Reserve Bank and an instruction not to privatise or sell the mismanaged and corrupt state-owned entities, which were sucking state tax revenue into a seemingly bottomless pit to the benefit of a deeply tainted elite whose interests were well represented at the Nasrec elective conference.

Hence, Ramaphosa inherited a house divided and a dream deferred. He also faced the rather more prosaic reality that Zuma was still president of the country. Following a messy and unseemly struggle, an angry and hurt Zuma was forced to resign as the country's president on 14 February 2018. Parliament duly elected Ramaphosa as South Africa's fifth democratic president, and he undertook to restore the "nine lost years" which, the ANC now claimed, the Zuma presidency had caused. In due course, dubious Zuma allies like the Gupta family fled the country, becoming fugitives from South African justice.

How precarious and flaccid Ramaphosa's position was, was evidenced by his retention of some of the worst Zuma cronies in his cabinet. It set the tone for a presidency which was as much an improvement as it was a disappointment.

CYRIL RAMAPHOSA

Matamela Cyril Ramaphosa was born in Johannesburg on 17 November 1952. He became South Africa's fifth democratic president in February 2018, after his predecessor, Jacob Zuma, was forced out of office.

Ramaphosa was born of Venda parents. His father was a policeman during the apartheid era. After matriculating, Ramaphosa, who was actively involved with Christian students' organisations, enrolled at the University of the North (also known as Turfloop, currently called the University of Limpopo), where he studied law. As a student, he joined Black Consciousness organisations such as the South African Students' Organisation (SASO) and the Black People's Convention (BPC). His political activities saw him serve two stints in jail, both of which he spent in solitary confinement – once for eleven months after his arrest in 1974, and once for six months after an arrest in 1976. After being released from jail the second time, Ramaphosa started working as a clerk at a Johannesburg legal firm. He finally graduated from Unisa with a BProc degree in 1981.

After graduation, he immediately joined the trade union movement as a legal adviser to the Council of Unions of South Africa (CUSA), before becoming the first general secretary of the National Union of Mineworkers (NUM) in December 1982.

When the Congress of South African Trade Unions (COSATU) was founded in 1985, Ramaphosa played a leading role and delivered a keynote address at the trade union federation's launch rally in Durban. When NUM staged a massive strike crippling the mine industry, the eloquent Ramaphosa's national profile increased hand over fist.

Throughout the 1980s, he acted as liaison between those battling apartheid locally – including the trade union movement – and the ANC leadership in exile based in Lusaka. Therefore, it came as no surprise when Ramaphosa was appointed to head the committee co-ordinating struggle icon Nelson Mandela's immediate actions and movements after his release from prison on 11 February 1990.

At the ANC's first elective conference after its unbanning in Durban in 1991, Ramaphosa was elected secretary general.

The run-up to the 1994 elections was punctuated by much talk about who Mandela would appoint as his deputy after the inevitable ANC victory – Ramaphosa or Thabo Mbeki. In the end, Mandela – under pressure from ANC leaders who had been in exile – opted for Mbeki. Ramaphosa was instead appointed to chair the Constitutional Assembly, which drafted the Constitution. After the Constitution was adopted in 1996, Ramaphosa left Parliament. He did not avail himself for re-election to the ANC leadership at the ANC's elective conference in Mahikeng in 1997, although he was unfailingly re-elected to the national executive committee (NEC) of the ANC from 1997 to 2012.

Instead of active politics, from 1996 to 2012 Ramaphosa opted for a career in business. He became one of South Africa's wealthiest people. His positions included chairing the Shanduka Group, with its varied interests in banking, telecommunications, resources, real estate, energy and insurance, and leadership roles in MTN, Bidvest, Macsteel, Standard Bank, Alexander Forbes, Mondi, McDonald's, SABMiller and Lonmin, among others. In 2018, his wealth was estimated at R6,4 billion. His image as a beneficiary of capitalism, his own financial prowess, and Black Economic Empowerment (BEE) was cemented by his success in buffalo farming.

In 2012, Ramaphosa was embroiled in controversy after it was claimed that he was the catalyst for the police action at a Lonmin mine near Rustenburg in North West during which more than thirty striking mineworkers were killed, and which became infamous as the Marikana Massacre. The Farlam Commission of Inquiry later found Ramaphosa's call for "concomitant" action to be taken by the police after the loss of life preceding the massacre did not in fact trigger the police action. However, the events at Marikana, and his perceived role in it, would taint Ramaphosa's political career from that day onwards.

Nevertheless, when the serving deputy president of the ANC and the country, Kgalema Motlanthe, announced that he would challenge President Jacob Zuma for the leadership of the ANC at the organisation's 2012 elective conference in Bloemfontein, Zuma was in dire need of a running mate with gravitas, as the clouds of corruption and state capture claims were gathering above the presidential head. He asked, Ramaphosa agreed, and the businessman was duly elected ANC deputy president.

After the 2014 general election, Ramaphosa earned an ambivalent reputation as the man at Zuma's side while state capture became evident but was denied, while at the same time becoming the primary focus to end state capture. Ramaphosa was sometimes rumoured to be resisting Zuma and his cronies' worst excesses, but he remained at Zuma's side at all times, not distancing himself from what was going on.

In the run-up to the 2017 ANC elective conference at Nasrec, south of Johannesburg, Zuma was not a candidate for re-election. His supporters flocked to the cause of his former wife, Dr Nkosazana Dlamini-Zuma. Ramaphosa declared his candidacy and beat her by the narrow margin of 179 votes.

After becoming president of the country in February 2018, Ramaphosa steered a precarious course to combat state capture but not hold those ANC members implicated in the rot politically accountable. This led to his presidency being described as being stuck between caution and hesitancy. With the advent of the Covid pandemic in South Africa in March 2020, it was clear that the calamitous circumstances would put strain on Ramaphosa, his vision and his leadership style.

The 2019 general election and its aftermath

Just when the ANC was at its weakest, opposition co-operation started to unravel. As indicated, from late 2018 onwards, the DA had created clear blue water between itself and those opposition parties who wanted to co-operate to unseat the ANC. It required skills and tenacity – which the DA lacked – to keep the disparate groupings teaming up against the ANC together. Many of the more reactionary DA leadership figures, of which former party leader Helen Zille was most outspoken, distrusted the other opposition parties and resented working with them, especially the EFF. Opposition co-operation at municipal level began floundering, and one by one these municipal councils fell back into the waiting arms of the ANC crony networks.

In the run-up to the 2019 general election, a weakened ANC gained some traction from having a less odious leader, but most of the larger opposition parties were also growing. The exception was the DA, whose leadership made some poorly judged interventions on hot-button issues like racial discrimination and mother-tongue instruction, thereby alienating many of the more conservative white Afrikaans voters who had flocked to the party when Zille was leader.

When the results were announced, it became clear that the opposition had jointly come within one seat of toppling the ANC in South Africa's economic hub, Gauteng. That result proved decisive and proved Mabuza's calculations, however morally questionable, to be correct: had Ramaphosa not been their candidate, the ANC would have lost Gauteng. The fact that they held it, made all the difference.

Nationally, the ANC's support declined from 62,15% to 57,5%, reducing its seats in the National Assembly from 249 to 230. The DA lost parliamentary seats for the first time in its existence, ending up with 84 seats, five fewer than in the 2014 election. It reflected the loss of about 250 000 conservative white Afrikaans votes to the Freedom Front Plus, resurgent under the firmer leadership of Dr Pieter Groenewald. Equally it indicated the failure of the DA to make up the votes lost with black votes gained under Maimane's leadership. The EFF grew spectacularly, gaining 19 seats to climb from 25 seats to 44 (11% of the vote) in the National Assembly. The IFP grew for the first time in 25 years, adding three National Assembly seats to end up on 13, and the Freedom Front Plus broke the stagnation of the Pieter Mulder years to return the best result of its existence, growing by six seats and ending up on ten.

In the DA the results caused tension, tumult and chaos quite out of kilter with the loss of five seats. An internal inquiry paved the way for Maimane's demise and the return of Zille, who had drifted into obscurity having been prevented by term limits to run again for the premiership of the Western Cape. From the sidelines, Zille had been making hay out of the loss of the 250 000 votes and her sentiments were echoed by the findings of the inquiry. One of the findings was that Maimane had to resign, which he did, complaining bitterly about the actions of Zille and her ilk. Herman Mashaba, the prominent and widely admired DA mayor of Johannesburg, resigned in protest. The DA had, by then, long forced out its other strong black leader, Cape Town mayor Patricia de Lille. John Steenhuisen was elected interim leader and Zille made a comeback into the powerful position of chairperson of the DA's federal executive. These and other power shifts prompted allegations of efforts to "make the DA white again" under Zille as the power behind the throne – claims which the DA's actions, beyond blunt denials, did precious little to dispel. It was losing support hand over fist in by-elections where minority racial groupings were in the majority, and for all intents and purposes the party stopped contesting by-elections in black-majority wards. The effects of these trends did not augur well for its performance in the next round of local government elections scheduled for 2021.

The EFF faced troubles of its own. Its leader, Julius Malema, and his deputy, Floyd Shivambu, were implicated in the so-called VBS Mutual Bank scandal, which saw the savings of the poor looted and the EFF leaders benefiting. Other controversies hounded Malema – from racially inflammatory behaviour to alleged assault and illegally discharging a firearm in a public space, to name a few.

The ANC-in-government had to deal with its own conundrums, many rooted in the decisions of ANC national conferences past, including but not limited to the 2017 Nasrec conference. The decision by the 2017 ANC conference in favour of expropriation of property without compensation, as well as an earlier decision to introduce national health insurance, sent shivers down the spines of investors and many opposition voters (but not the EFF) alike, as it seemed to represent a shift to the left in ANC policy, towards a more socialist future. The fact that Ramaphosa himself, as well as ANC economic policy chief Enoch Godongwana, actively opposed expropriation without compensation did little to allay such fears, although the practical outcomes of such policy debates remained very much in the balance, to be decided at the ANC policy conference scheduled for mid-2022.

On the eve of the unexpected and profound effect the Covid-19 pandemic would have on the world, South Africa was with its back to the wall. Years of state mismanagement had gutted the fiscus and debilitated state-owned enterprises. In many ANC-controlled provinces and municipalities, road networks and other infrastructure were crumbling because the money allocated for its upkeep was misappropriated or stolen, and the expertise base had been hollowed out by the ANC's policy of cadre deployment which favoured party loyalty over the qualifications or skills needed to get the job done properly, leading to the entirely predictable effect that the job was done poorly. Such inadequacies conspired with policy uncertainty and socialist policies which had failed everywhere in the world but had been resuscitated by resolutions of the 2017 ANC elective conference to undermine domestic and international investor confidence in South Africa and resulted in a sovereign investment downgrade to junk status by all major players in the market.

Ramaphosa attempted to remedy some of these ills by appointing stronger leaders to the failing state-owned enterprises and the national prosecuting authority. He also prevented the potentially most damaging and populist decisions of the ANC elective conference from being enacted, thereby buying himself some probable trouble if he wanted to be re-elected at the ANC's next elective conference. But the precarious ANC power balance which Mabuza had engineered meant the president seemed powerless to act decisively against the corruption in his own party – a weak position to be in with the advent of Covid-19 in South Africa.

The first case of Covid-19 in South Africa was identified by the Pretoria-based Centre for Disease Control on 5 March 2020. Covid cases increased rapidly and on 23 March 2020, Ramaphosa announced a nationwide hard lockdown with effect from 26 March 2020. It ushered in a response to the unexpected calamity which was bound to have a profound effect on South African history.

Bibliography

Chapter 1
Bergh, J.S. (ed.), *Geskiedenisatlas van Suid-Afrika: Die vier noordelike provinsies*. Pretoria, 1999.
Boonzaier, E., et al., *The Cape herders: A history of the Khoikhoi of Southern Africa*. Cape Town, 1996.
Clutton-Brock, J., "The legacy of Iron Age dogs and livestock in Southern Africa", in Sutton, J.E.G. (ed.), *The growth of farming communities in Africa from the equator southwards*. Special Volume XXIX–XXX. The British Institute in Eastern Africa, Nairobi, 1996.
Coertze, P.J. (ed.), *Suid-Afrika binne Afrika-verband*. Cape Town, 1973.
Deacon, H.J. and Deacon, J., *Human beginnings in South Africa*. Cape Town, 1999.
Giliomee, H. and Mbenga, B. (eds), *New history of South Africa*. Cape Town, 2007.
Harlan, J.R., "The tropical African cereals", in Shaw, T., et al. (eds), *The archaeology of Africa: Food, metals and towns*. London, 1995.
Junod, H.A., *The life of a South African tribe, Vol. II*. Second edition, London, 1927.
Manyanga, M., *Resilient landscapes: Socio-environmental dynamics in the Shashi-Limpopo Basin, Southern Zimbabwe c. AD 800 to the present*. Studies in Global Archaeology 11. Uppsala, 2007.
McCarthy, T. and Rubidge, B., *The story of earth and life*. Cape Town, 2005.
Murdock, G.P., *Africa: Its peoples and their culture history*. New York, 1959.
Summers, R., *Ancient mining in Rhodesia: Museum memoir no. 3*. Salisbury, 1969.
Van Warmelo, N.J., *A preliminary survey of the Bantu tribes of South Africa*. Ethnological Publications, *Vol. V*. Pretoria, 1935.
Van Aswegen, H.J., *History of South Africa to 1854*. Pretoria, 1993.
Walton, J., *African village*. Pretoria, 1956.
Wentzel, P.J., *A History of the Kalanga, Vols. I–III*. Pretoria, 1983.

Chapter 2
Beyers, Coenraad, *Die Kaapse patriotte*. Pretoria, 1967.
Böeseken, Anna, *Die Nuusbode*. Cape Town, 1966.

Böeseken, Anna, *Jan van Riebeeck en sy gesin*. Cape Town, 1974.
Böeseken, Anna, *Simon van der Stel en sy kinders*. Cape Town, 1964.
Coertzen, Pieter, *Die Hugenote van Suid-Afrika*. Cape Town, 1988.
De Kock, W.J., *Portugese ontdekkers om die Kaap*. Cape Town, 1957.
De Villiers, Anna, *Vrouegalery*. Cape Town, 1962.
Elphick, Richard and Giliomee, Hermann (eds), *The shaping of South African society, 1652-1840*. Cape Town, 2nd edition, 1989.
Giliomee, H., *Die Kaap tydens die eerste Britse bewind*. Cape Town, 1975.
Giliomee, H., *The Afrikaners: Biography of a people*. Cape Town, 2003.
Heese, Hans F., *Groep sonder grense*. Pretoria, 2005.
Hofmeyr, George (ed.), *NG Kerk 350*. Wellington, 2002.
Krynauw, D.W., *Beslissing by Blouberg*. Cape Town, 1999.
Sleigh, Dan, *Die buiteposte*. Pretoria, 2004.

Chapter 3

Elphick, Richard and Giliomee, Hermann (eds), *The shaping of South African society, 1652-1840*. Cape Town, 2nd edition, 1989.
Shell, Robert, *Children of bondage: A social history of the slave society at the Cape of Good Hope, 1652–1813*. Hanover, 1994.
Shell, Robert, *Slavery at the Cape of Good Hope, 1680–1731*. New Haven, 1986.

Chapter 4

Balie, Isaac, *Die geskiedenis van Genadendal*. Johannesburg, 1988.
Bergh, Johan and Bergh, Annemarie, *Tribes and kingdoms*. Cape Town, 1984.
Böeseken, Anna, *Van oorloë en vrede*. Cape Town, 1983.
Bryer, Lynne and Hunt, Keith, *The 1820 Settlers*. Cape Town, 1984.
Campbell, John, *Travels in South Africa*. Reprint, Cape Town, 1974.
Elphick, Richard and Giliomee, Hermann (eds), *The shaping of South African society, 1652-1840*. Cape Town, 2nd edition, 1989.
Giliomee, H. and Mbenga, B. (eds), *New history of South Africa*. Cape Town, 2007.
Heese, Johan A., *Slagtersnek en sy mense*. Cape Town, 1973.
Marais, J.S., *The Cape Coloured people, 1652–1937*. Johannesburg, 1968.
Metrowich, Frederick C., *Frontier flames*. Cape Town, 1968.
Milton, John, *The edges of war*. Cape Town, 1983.
Rivett-Carnac, Dorothy E., *Hawk's eye*. Cape Town, 1966.
Van Aswegen, H.J., *A history of South Africa to 1854*. Pretoria, 1993.

Chapters 5 and 6

Du Bruyn, J.T., "The Great Trek", in Cameron, T. and Spies, S.B. (eds), *Illustrated history of South Africa*. Cape Town, 1986.
Duly, L.C., *British land policy at the Cape, 1795–1844: A study of administrative procedures in the Empire*. Durham, 1968.

Duvenage, G.D.J., *Die Groot Trek: Die eerste drie jaar, deel 2 (Die manifes)*. Pretoria, 1987.
Duvenage, G.D.J., *Van die Tarka na die Transgariep*. Pretoria, 1981.
Giliomee, H. and Mbenga, B. (eds), *New history of South Africa*. Cape Town, 2007.
Hamilton, Carolyn (ed.), *The Mfecane aftermath: Reconstructive debates in Southern African history*. Johannesburg, 1995.
Liebenberg, B.J., *Andries Pretorius in Natal*. Pretoria, 1977.
Muller, C.F.J., *Die oorsprong van die Groot Trek*. Cape Town, 1974.
Oberholster, J.J., "A.H. Potgieter", in *Dictionary of South African biography, Vol. l*. Cape Town, 1968.
Thom, H.B., *Die lewe van Gert Maritz*. Cape Town, 1965.
Tromp, A.H., "J.J. Janse van Rensburg", in *Dictionary of South African biography, Vol. I*. Cape Town, 1968.
Van Aswegen, H.J., *A history of South Africa to 1854*. Pretoria, 1988.
Van der Merwe, P.J., "Die Matebeles en die Voortrekkers", in *Archives Yearbook, 1986, Vol. II*. Pretoria, 1968.
Visagie, Jan C., *Voortrekkerstamouers 1835–1845*. Second edition, Pretoria, 2011.

Chapter 7
Bergh, J.S. (ed.), *Geskiedenisatlas van Suid-Afrika: Die vier noordelike provinsies*. Pretoria, 1999.
Davenport, T.R.H. and Saunders, C., *South Africa: A modern history*. London, 2000.
Delius, P., *The land belongs to us: The Pedi polity, the Boers and the British in the nineteenth century*. Johannesburg, 1983.
Grobler, J., *Uitdaging en antwoord: 'n Vars perspektief op die evolusie van die Afrikaners*. Pretoria, 2007.
Giliomee, H., *The Afrikaners: Biography of a people*. Cape Town, 2003.
Giliomee, H. and Mbenga, B. (eds), *New history of South Africa*. Cape Town, 2007.
Laband, J., *Rope of sand: The rise and fall of the Zulu kingdom in the nineteenth century*. London, 1995.
Shillington, K., *The colonisation of the Southern Tswana, 1870–1900*. Johannesburg, 1985.

Chapter 8
Callinicos, L., *Gold and workers 1886–1924, Vol. I*. Johannesburg, 1985.
Callinicos, L., *Working life 1886–1940: Factories, townships and popular culture on the Rand, Vol. II*. Johannesburg, 1987.
Coleman, F.L. (ed.), *Economic history of South Africa*. Pretoria, 1983.
Keegan, T.J., *Rural transformation in industrializing South Africa: The southern Highveld to 1914*. Johannesburg, 1986.
Trebilcock, C., *The industrialization of the continental powers 1780–1914*. London, 1981.

Turrell, R.V., *Capital and labour on the Kimberley diamond fields, 1871–90*. Cambridge, 1987.
Van Onselen, C., *New Babylon New Nineveh: Everyday life on the Witwatersrand 1886–1914*. Johannesburg, 1982.
Van Zyl, D., *The discovery of wealth*. Cape Town, 1986.

Chapter 9
Coleman, F.L. (ed.), *Economic history of South Africa*. Pretoria, 1983.
De Kiewiet, C.W., *A history of South Africa, social and economic*. London, 1941.
Feinstein, C., *An economic history of South Africa: Conquest, discrimination and development*. Cambridge, 2005.
Jones, F.S., *The great imperial banks in South Africa: A study of the business of Standard Bank and Barclays Bank, 1861–1961*. Pretoria, 1992.
Jones, S. and Müller, A., *The South African economy, 1910–1990*. Basingstoke, 1992.
Keegan, T.J., *Rural transformation in industrializing South Africa: The southern Highveld to 1914*. Johannesburg, 1986.
Marks, S. and Atmore, A., *Economy and society in pre-industrial South Africa*. London, 1980.
Marks, S. and Rathbone, R., *Industrialisation and social change in South Africa: African class formation, culture and consciousness, 1870–1930*. London, 1982.
Schumann, C.G.W., *Structural changes and business cycles in South Africa, 1806–1936*. London, 1938.
Wilson, M. and Thompson, L. (eds), *The Oxford history of South Africa, Vol.1*. Oxford, 1969.

Chapter 10
D'Assonville, V.E., *S.J. du Toit*. Weltevredenpark, 1999.
Davenport, Rodney, *The Afrikaner Bond, 1880–1911*. Cape Town, 1966.
Tamarkin, Mordechai, *Cecil Rhodes and the Cape Afrikaners*. London, 1996.
Zietsman, P.H., *Die taal is gans die volk*. Pretoria, 1992.

Chapter 11
Nasson, Bill, *The war for South Africa: The Anglo-Boer War 1899–1902*. Cape Town, 2010.
Pakenham, Thomas, *The Boer War*. London, 1979.
Pretorius, Fransjohan, *The Anglo-Boer War 1899–1902*. Cape Town, 1985, 1998 and 2013.
Pretorius, Fransjohan, *The A to Z of the Anglo-Boer War*. Lanham, 2010.
Warwick, Peter and Spies, S.B. (eds), *The South African War: The Anglo-Boer War 1899–1902*. London, 1980.

Chapter 12
Brits, Jacob P., *Op die vooraand van apartheid: Die rassevraagstuk en die blanke politiek in Suid-Afrika, 1939–1948*. Pretoria, 1994.

Liebenberg, Ben J. and Spies, S.B. (eds), *South Africa in the twentieth century*. Pretoria, 1993.
Odendaal, André, *Vukani Bantu! The beginnings of black protest politics in South Africa to 1912*. Cape Town, 1984.
Paton, Alan, *Hofmeyr*. Cape Town, 1964.
Scholtz, G.D., *Generaals Hertzog en Smuts en die Britse Ryk*. Johannesburg, 1975.
Thompson, Leonard, *The unification of South Africa, 1902–1910*. Oxford, 1960.

Chapter 13
Booyens, Bun, *Die lewe van D.F Malan: Die eerste veertig jaar*. Cape Town, 1969.
Giliomee, H., *The Afrikaners: Biography of a people*. Cape Town, 2003.
Kannemeyer, J.C., *Langenhoven: 'n Lewe*. Cape Town, 1995.
Geyser, O. and Marais, A.H., *Die Nasionale Party*, Vol. 1. Pretoria, 1975.
Muller, C.F.J., *Sonop in die suide: Geboorte en groei van Nasionale Pers*. Cape Town, 1990.
Muller, Tobie, *'n Inspirasie vir jong Suid-Afrika*. Cape Town, 1925.
O'Meara, Dan, *Volkskapitalisme: Class, capital and ideology in the development of Afrikaner nationalism, 1934–1948*. Cambridge, 1983.
Sadie, J.L. *The economic demography of South Africa*. Doctoral thesis: University of Stellenbosch, 2000.
Thom, H.B., *Dr. D.F Malan*. Cape Town, 1980.

Chapter 14
Grobler, J., *A decisive clash? A short history of black protest politics in South Africa 1875–1976*. Pretoria, 1988.
Karis, T., Carter, G.M. and Gerhart, G. (eds), *From protest to challenge*, 5 Vols. Stanford, 1972–1997.
Lodge, T., *Black politics in South Africa since 1945*. Johannesburg, 1983.
Odendaal, A., *Vukani Bantu! The beginnings of black protest politics in South Africa to 1912*. Cape Town, 1984.
Roux, E., *Time longer than rope: A history of the black man's struggle for freedom in South Africa*. Madison, 1966.
Walshe, P., *The rise of African nationalism in South Africa: The African National Congress 1912–1952*. Berkeley, 1971.

Chapter 15
Botha, J., *Verwoerd is dead*. Cape Town, 1967.
Hallett, R., *The burden of black grievances: Soweto and Cape Town, 1976*. Cape Town, 1977.
McLennan, B., *Apartheid: The lighter side*. Cape Town, 1950.
Munger, E. (ed.), *The Afrikaners*. Cape Town, 1979.
Sampson, N., *Mandela: The authorised biography*. London, 1999.
Suttner, R. and Cronin, J., *30 Years of the Freedom Charter*. Johannesburg, 1985.

Chapter 16
Botha, M.C., *Die swart vryheidspaaie*. Johannesburg, 1981.
Cockram, Gail-Maryse, *Vorster's foreign policy*. Pretoria, 1970.
Dawie and Ries, Alf, *John Vorster: 10 jaar*. Cape Town, 1976.
D'Oliveira, John, *Vorster: The man*. Johannesburg, 1977.
Du Pisani, J.A., *John Vorster en die verlig/verkrampstryd: 'n Studie van die politieke verdeeldheid in Afrikanergeledere, 1966–1970*. Bloemfontein, 1988.
Geyser, O. (ed.), *B.J. Vorster: Selected speeches*. Bloemfontein, 1977.
Rhoodie, Eschel, *Die ware Inligtingskandaal*. Pretoria, 1984.
Schoeman, B.M., *Vorster se 1000 dae*. Cape Town, 1974.
Serfontein, J.H.P., *Die verkrampte aanslag*. Cape Town, 1970.
Terblanche, H.O., *John Vorster: OB-generaal en Afrikanervegter*. Roodepoort, 1983.

Chapter 17
Gerhart, G.M., *Black power in South Africa*. Berkeley, 1977.
Grobler, J., *A decisive clash? A short history of black protest politics in South Africa 1875–1976*. Pretoria, 1988.
Karis, T., Carter, G.M. and Gerhart, G. (eds), *From protest to challenge*, 5 Vols. Stanford, 1972–1997.
Liebenberg, I. (et al., eds), *The long march: The story of the struggle for liberation in South Africa*. Pretoria, 1994.
Lodge, T., *Black politics in South Africa since 1945*. Johannesburg, 1983.
Mandela, N., *Long walk to freedom*. London, 1994.
Ministry of Education, *Every step of the way: The journey to freedom in South Africa*. Cape Town, 2004.
Seekings, J., *The UDF: The United Democratic Front in South Africa, 1983–1991*. Cape Town, 2000.
South African Democracy Education Trust, *The road to democracy in South Africa, Vol. 1* (1960–1970). Cape Town, 2004.

Chapter 18
De Villiers, Dirk and Johanna, *PW*. Cape Town, 1984.
O'Meara, Dan, *Forty lost years: The apartheid state and the politics of the National Party*. Johannesburg, 1996.
Pottinger, Brian, *The imperial presidency*. Johannesburg, 1988.
Ries, Alf and Dommisse, Ebbe, *Broedertwis*. Cape Town, 1982.
Sadie, J.L. *The fall and rise of the Afrikaner in the South African economy*. Stellenbosch, 2002.
Slabbert, F. van Zyl, *The last white parliament*. Johannesburg, 1985.
Welsh, David, *The rise and fall of apartheid*. Johannesburg, 2009.

Chapter 19

Butler, Anthony, *Cyril Ramaphosa*. Johannesburg, 2008.
De Klerk, F.W., *The last trek – A new beginning: The autobiography*. London, 1998.
Friedman, Steven, *The long journey*. Johannesburg, 1993.
Giliomee, H., *The best-laid schemes: Afrikaner leaders and the annihilation of distance*. Cape Town, 2012.
Mandela, Nelson, *No easy walk to freedom*. Johannesburg, 1994.
Papenfus, Theresa, *Pik Botha and his times*. Pretoria, 2010.
Temkin, Ben, *Buthelezi: A biography*. London, 2003.
Wessels, Leon, *Die einde van 'n era*. Cape Town, 1994.

Chapter 20

Giliomee, H., *The Afrikaners: Biography of a people*. Cape Town, 2003.
Kinghorn, Johann (ed.), *Die NG Kerk en apartheid*. Johannesburg, 1986.
Lipton, Merle, *Capitalism and apartheid*. Aldershot, 1986.
Moodie, Dunbar, *The rise of Afrikanerdom*. Berkeley, 1975.

Chapter 21

Coleman, F.L. (ed.), *Economic history of South Africa*. Pretoria, 1983.
Feinstein, C., *An economic history of South Africa: Conquest, discrimination and development*. Cambridge, 2005.
Houghton, H., *The South African economy*. Cape Town, 1976.
Jones, S., *The decline of the South African economy*. Cheltenham, 2002.
Jones, S. and Müller, A., *The South African economy, 1910–1990*. Basingstoke, 1992.
Kenwood, A.G. and Lougheed, A.L., *The growth of the international economy*. Fourth edition, London, 1999.
Nattrass, J., *The South African economy: Its growth and change*. Cape Town, 1982.
"The South African economy in the 1980s". Special edition: *The South African Journal of Economic History*, 9(2), 1994.
"The South African economy in the 1990s". Special edition: *The South African Journal of Economic History*, 18(1&2), 2003.

Chapter 22

Baskin, J., *Striking back: A history of Cosatu*. Johannesburg, 1991.
Callinicos, L., *Working life 1886-1940: Factories, townships and popular culture on the Rand, Vol. II*. Johannesburg, 1987.
Du Toit, M.A., *South African trade unions: History, legislation, policy*. Johannesburg, 1976.
Greenberg, S.B., *Race and state in capitalist development: Comparative perspectives*. New Haven, 1980.
Hepple, A., *South Africa: A political and economic history*. London, 1966.

Katz, E.N., *A trade union aristocracy: A history of white workers in the Transvaal and the general strike of 1913*. Johannesburg, 1976.
Lewis, J., *Industrialisation and trade union organisation in South Africa, 1924–55: The rise and fall of the South African Trades and Labour Council*. Cambridge, 1984.
Luckhardt, K. and Wall, B., *Organise or starve! The history of the South African Congress of Trade Unions*. London, 1980.
Visser, W.P., *Van MWU tot Solidariteit: Geskiedenis van die Mynwerkersunie, 1902–2002*. Pretoria, 2008.

Chapter 23

Adam, H., Slabbert, F. van Zyl and Moodley, K., *Comrades in business: Post-liberation politics in South Africa*. Cape Town, 1997.
Beinart, W., *Twentieth-century South Africa*. Second edition, Oxford, 2001.
Brits, J.P., *Modern South Africa: From Soweto to democracy*. Pretoria, 2005.
Daniel, J., Habib, A. and Southall, R. (eds), *State of the nation: South Africa 2003–2004*. Cape Town, 2003.
De Klerk, F.W., *The last trek – A new beginning: The autobiography*. London, 1998.
Fourie, L., Landman, J.P. and Schoombee, P. (eds), *South Africa, how are you?*. Paarl, 2002.
Gevisser, Mark, *Thabo Mbeki: The dream deferred*. Johannesburg, 2007.
Giliomee, H., *The Afrikaners: Biography of a people*. Cape Town, 2003.
Giliomee, H. and Mbenga, B. (eds), *New history of South Africa*. Cape Town, 2007.
Giliomee, H. and Simkins, C. (eds), *The awkward embrace: One-party domination and democracy*. Cape Town, 1999.
Gumede, W.M., *Thabo Mbeki and the battle for the soul of the ANC*. Cape Town, 2005.
Harber, A. and Ludman, B. (eds), *Weekly Mail & Guardian A–Z of South African politics: The essential handbook, 1995*. London, 1995.
Jeffery, A., *Chasing the rainbow: South Africa's move from Mandela to Zuma*. Johannesburg, 2010.
Johnson, R.W., *South Africa's brave new world: The beloved country since the end of apartheid*. London, 2009.
Landsberg, C. and Mackay, A. (eds), *Southern Africa post-apartheid? The search for democratic governance*. Cape Town, 2004.
Lodge, T., *Mandela: A critical life*. Oxford, 2006.
Lodge, T., *Politics in South Africa: From Mandela to Mbeki*. Cape Town, 2002.
Southall, R. (ed.), *Opposition and democracy in South Africa*. London, 2002.
Sparks, A., *Beyond the miracle: Inside the new South Africa*. Johannesburg, 2003.
Thompson, L., *A history of South Africa*. Third edition, New Haven, 2001.
Venter, A. (ed.), *Government and politics in the new South Africa: An introductory reader to its institutions, processes and policies*. Second edition, Pretoria, 2001.

Internet sources:
www.anc.org.za
www.sahistory.org.za
paul.bulllen.com/BullenEthnicism.html
www.labourhistory.org.za
www.ananzi.co.za

Chapter 24
Accone, Darcyl and Harris, Karen L., "A century of not belonging: The Chinese in South Africa", in Kuah Pearce, K.E. and Davidson, A. (eds), *Power of memories: Negotiating belongingness in the Chinese diaspora*. Hong Kong, 2008.
Basson, A., *Finish & klaar: Selebi's fall from Interpol to the underworld*. Cape Town, 2010.
Calland, R., *Anatomy of South Africa: Who holds the power?* Cape Town, 2006.
Du Toit, F. and Doxtader, E. (eds), *In the balance: South Africans debate reconciliation*. Johannesburg, 2010.
Du Preez, M. and Rossouw, M., *The world according to Julius Malema*. Cape Town, 2009.
Feinstein, A., *After the party: A personal and political journey inside the ANC*. Cape Town, 2007.
Forde, F., *An inconvenient youth: Julius Malema and the "new" ANC*. Johannesburg, 2011.
Gevisser, Mark, *Thabo Mbeki: The dream deferred*. Johannesburg, 2007.
Gordin, J., *Zuma: A biography*. Cape Town, 2008.
Green, P., *Choice not fate: The life and times of Trevor Manuel*. Cape Town, 2012.
Gumede, W.M., *Thabo Mbeki and the battle for the soul of the ANC*. Second edition, Cape Town, 2007.
Gumede, W.M. and Dikeni, L., *The poverty of ideas: South African democracy and the retreat of intellectuals*. Johannesburg, 2009.
Harris, Karen L., "Accepting the group, but not the area: The South African Chinese and the Group Areas Act", in *South African Historical Journal*, Vol. 40, 1999, pp. 179–201.
Harris, Karen L., "Sugar and gold: Indentured Indian and Chinese labour in South Africa", in *Journal of Social Studies*, Nov. 2010, pp. 147–158.
Harris, Karen L., "'Whiteness', 'Blackness', 'Neitherness': The South African Chinese: A study in identity politics", in *Historia*, 47(1), May 2002, pp. 105–124.
Hermann, Dirk, *Die keiser is kaal: Waarom regstellende aksie misluk het*. Pretoria, 2007.
Holden, P., *The arms deal in your pocket*. Cape Town, 2008.
Johnson, R.W., *South Africa's brave new world: The beloved country since the end of apartheid*. London, 2009.
Le Roux, M., *Misadventures of a Cope volunteer: My crash course in politics*. Cape Town, 2010.

Leon, Tony, *On the contrary*. Cape Town, 2009.
Misra-Dexter, N. and February, J. (eds), *Testing democracy: Which way is South Africa going?* Cape Town, 2010.
Pottinger, Brian, *The Mbeki legacy*. Cape Town, 2008.
Ramphele, M., *Laying ghosts to rest: Dilemmas of the transformation in South Africa*. Cape Town, 2008.
Russell, A., *After Mandela: The battle for the soul of South Africa*. Cape Town, 2010.
Southall, R. and Daniel, J., *Zunami! The 2009 South African elections*. Johannesburg, 2009.
Yap, M. and Man, D., *Colour, confusion and concessions: The history of the Chinese in South Africa*. Hong Kong, 1996.

Chapter 25
Adhikari, Mohamed, *Not white enough, not black enough: Racial identity in the South African Coloured community*. Athens, Ohio, 2005.
Booley, Abdurahman, *Forgotten heroes: History of black rugby 1882-1992*. Cape Town, 1998.
Brown, Cliffie, File – "Soldier", in author's possession.
Burke, Johnny, quoted on http://theinvaders.co.za/bio.html.
Hommel, Maurice, *Capricorn blues: The struggle for human rights in South Africa*. Culturama, 1987.
Krog, Antjie, *Country of my skull: Guilt, sorrow, and the limits of forgiveness in the New South Africa*. Cape Town, 2000.
Lewis, Gavin, *Between the wire and the wall*. Cape Town, 1987.
Nasson, Bill, *Abraham Esau's War: A black South African War in the Cape. 1899-1902*, Cambridge, 2002.
Pinnock, Don, *The Brotherhoods: Street gangs and state control in Cape Town*. Cape Town, 1984.
Rasmussen, Lars (ed.), *Cape Town Jazz, 1959-1963*. Cape Town, 2001.
Rasmussen, Lars (ed.), *Jazz people of Cape Town*. Cape Town, 2003.
Steinberg, Jonny, *The number – one man's search for identity in the Cape underworld and prison gangs*, Johannesburg, 2004.
Thomas, Cornelius, Family Papers – Private Collection, Boxes 1-32.
Thomas, Cornelius (ed.), *Finding freedom in the bush of books: The UWC experience and spirit*. Grahamstown, 2010.
Thomas, Cornelius (ed.), *Sport and liberation in South Africa*. Alice, 2006.
Thomas, Cornelius (ed.), *Time with Dennis Brutus*. Grahamstown, 2012.
Truth and Reconciliation Reports, various.
Van der Ross, Richard, *The rise and decline of apartheid*. Cape Town, 1986.
Venter, Al J., *Coloured: A profile of two million South Africans*. Cape Town, 1974.
Western, John, *Outcast Cape Town*. Cape Town, 1981.

Chapter 26
Bhana, Surendra and Vahed, G., *The making of a political reformer: Gandhi in South Africa, 1893-1914.* New Delhi, 2005.
Bhana, S., *Gandhi's legacy: The Natal Indian Congress 1894-1994.* Pietermaritzburg, 1997.
Bhana. S. and Brain, Joy, *Setting down roots: Indian migrants in South Africa 1860-1911.* Johannesburg, 1990.
Brain, J., *Christian Indians in Natal, 1860-1911.* Cape Town, 1983.
Desai, Ashwin and Vahed, Goolam, *Inside Indian indenture: A South African story, 1860-1914.* Cape Town, 2010.
Freund, Bill, *Insiders and outsiders: The Indian working class of Durban, 1910-1990.* Portsmouth, 1995.
Swan, Maureen, *Gandhi: The South African experience.* Johannesburg, 1985.
Vally, R., *Kala Pani: Caste and colour in South Africa.* Cape Town, 2001.

Chapter 27
Bond, John, *They were South Africans.* Cape Town, 1956.
De Villiers, André, *English-speaking South Africa today.* Cape Town, 1976.
Lambert, John, "Britishness, South Africanness and the First World War", in Buckner, Phillip and Francis, R. Douglas (eds), *Rediscovering the British world.* Calgary, 2005.
Lambert, John, "The thinking is done in London: South Africa's English-language press and imperialism", in Kaul, Chandrika (ed.), *Media and the British Empire,* London, 2006.
Lambert, John, "'An unknown people': Reconstructing British South African identity", in *The Journal of Imperial and Commonwealth History,* 37(4), Des. 2009, pp. 599–617.
Thompson, Paul S., *Natalians first: Separatism in South Africa, 1909–1961.* Johannesburg, 1990.

Chapter 28
Adonis, J.C., *Die afgebreekte skeidsmuur weer opgebou.* Amsterdam, 1982.
Alberts, L. and Chikane, F., *The road to Rustenburg: The church looking forward to a new South Africa.* Cape Town, 1991.
De Gruchy, J.W. *The church struggle in South Africa.* Cape Town, 1979.
De Gruchy, J.W. and Villa-Vicencio, C., *Apartheid is a heresy.* Cape Town, 1983.
Elphick, R. and Davenport, R., *Christianity in South Africa: A political, social and cultural history.* Cape Town, 1997.
Elphick, R., *The equality of believers: Protestant missionaries and the racial politics of South Africa.* Pietermaritzburg, 2012.
Hofmeyr, J.W., Millard, J.A. and Froneman, C.J.J., *History of the church in South Africa: A document and source book.* Pretoria, 1994.

Hofmeyr, J.W. and Pillay, G.J., *A history of Christianity in South Africa*. Pretoria, 1994.
Millard, J.A., *Malihambe – Let the Word spread*. Pretoria, 1999.
Villa-Vicencio, C. and De Gruchy, J.W. (eds), *Resistance and hope: South African essays in honour of Beyers Naudé*. Cape Town, 1985.
Van Vught, W.E. and Cloete, G.D. (eds), *Race and reconciliation in South Africa: Multicultural dialogue in comparative perspective*. New York, 2000.

Chapter 29
Beinart, William and McGregor, JoAnn (eds), *Social history and African environments*. Oxford, 2003.
Dovers, Stephen, Edgecombe, Ruth and Guest, Bill (eds), *South Africa's environmental history: Cases and comparisons*. Cape Town, 2003.
Du Pisani, J.A., "Storie van die natuur: Omgewingsgeskiedenis as groeiende navorsingsveld", in *Historia*, 49(2), November 2004, pp. 3–21.
McNeill, J.R., *Something new under the sun: An environmental history of the twentieth-century world*. London, 2000.
Pretorius, Fransjohan, "Die invloed van landskap op die Anglo-Boereoorlog", in Le Roux, Schalk and De Villiers, André (eds), *Essays oor die Suid-Afrikaanse landskap*, pp. 35–47. Pretoria, 2003.
Steyn, Phia, "Industry, pollution and the apartheid state in South Africa", in *History Teaching Review Year Book*, Vol. 22, 2008.
Steyn, Phia, "Popular environmental struggles in South Africa, 1972–1992", in *Historia*, 47(1), May 2002, pp. 125–158.
Steyn, Phia. "Environmental management in South Africa: Twenty years of governmental response to the global challenge, 1972–1992", in *Historia*, 46(1), May 2001, pp. 25–53.

Chapter 30
Basson, A., *Blessed by Bosasa*. Cape Town, 2019.
Maseko, T., *For my country: Why I blew the whistle on Zuma and the Guptas*. Cape Town, 2021.
Myburgh, P., *The Republic of Gupta: A story of state capture*. Cape Town, 2017.
Myburgh, P., *Gangster state: Ace Magashule's web of capture*. Cape Town, 2019.
Pauw, J., *The President's Keepers: Those keeping Zuma in power and out of prison*. Cape Town, 2017.
Williams, A., *Deep collusion: Bain and the capture of South Africa*. Cape Town, 2022.

Authors' biographies

FRANSJOHAN PRETORIUS (editor) is professor of history at the University of Pretoria. He has written six books on the Anglo-Boer War and has served as editor for three others, of which most have appeared in both English and Afrikaans. His most recent book is *The A to Z of the Anglo-Boer War*. He has received a number of awards for his work, including the Stals Prize for Cultural History from the Suid-Afrikaanse Akademie vir Wetenskap en Kuns; and the Recht Malan Prize for *Kommandolewe tydens die Anglo-Boereoorlog 1899–1902*. For the English translation, *Life on Commando during the Anglo-Boer War 1899–1902*, he was runner-up for the *Sunday Times* Alan Paton Award. He is chairperson of the history commission of the Suid-Afrikaanse Akademie vir Wetenskap en Kuns.

JAPIE BRITS was emeritus professor of history at the University of South Africa. His study field is South African history of the twentieth and twenty-first centuries. From his pen six books have appeared, including *Tielman Roos: Political prophet or opportunist?* and *Op die vooraand van apartheid: Die rassevraagstuk en die blanke politiek in Suid-Afrika, 1939–1948*. He passed away in 2020.

JOHAN DE VILLIERS is emeritus professor and research associate at the University of Zululand, where he was head of the department of history. He was previously on the staff of the Rand Afrikaans University and the University of the Western Cape. His research covers the field of military and socio-cultural South African history.

KOBUS DU PISANI has held posts as researcher and lecturer at four universities in South Africa and South Korea and is at present professor of history at the Potchefstroom campus of North-West University. He holds post-graduate degrees in history and environmental sciences and has undertaken research projects on political, gender and environmental history. He is currently working on a biography of B.J. Vorster.

HERMANN GILIOMEE lectured at the University of Stellenbosch and the University of Cape Town where he was professor of political studies. His publications include *The Afrikaners: Biography of a people* (translated into Afrikaans as *Die Afrikaners: 'n Biografie*); *Nog altyd hier gewees: Die verhaal van 'n Stellenbosse gemeenskap*; and *Kruispad vir Afrikaans, 'n Vaste plek vir Afrikaans: Taaluitdagings op kampus*. He is co-editor of *New history of South Africa/Nuwe geskiedenis van Suid-Afrika*.

JACKIE GROBLER is a senior lecturer in history at the University of Pretoria. He was awarded his doctorate for a thesis on the First War of Independence (1880–1881). He is the author of seven books on a wide range of topics. In the cultural sphere he is an active member of Die Voortrekkers and serves on the board of directors of the Voortrekker Monument Group as well as the Erfenisstigting.

KAREN L. HARRIS is professor in the department of historical and heritage studies at the University of Pretoria. She is also director of the university's archive. She is the president of the Historical Association of South Africa and an executive council member of the International Society for the Study of Chinese Overseas (ISSCO). Her research field is Chinese studies.

JOHANNES W. (HOFFIE) HOFMEYR is emeritus professor in church history at the University of Pretoria. He is currently extraordinary professor in theology at the University of the Free State; the evangelic theology faculty of Leuven (Belgium); and the Liverpool Hope University (England). His research field is the post-Reformation period in the history of the Netherlands, and contemporary South African church history. Among his most important publications are *Die Nederlandse Nadere Reformasie en sy invloed op twee kontinente*; and *A history of Christianity in South Africa*. He is co-chief editor of *NG Kerk 350* and *African Christianity: An African story*.

JAN-JAN JOUBERT is an experienced political journalist and writer who has authored three books on South African politics and politicians. He was political editor of *Beeld* and *Sunday Times*. Since 2001 he has reported from the parliamentary press gallery in Cape Town. He has an honours degree in history (cum laude) from the University of the Free State.

JOHN LAMBERT is emeritus professor and research associate in history at the University of South Africa. He has published extensively on the socio-economic and political history of colonial Natal as well as on the identity and history of white English-speaking South Africans. He is particularly involved in studies of "Britishness" and the relation between Britishness and South Africanism in the English-speaking community.

AUTHORS' BIOGRAPHIES 689

ANDRIE MEYER has been associated with the University of Pretoria since 1966, where he was awarded the degrees BA (Library Science), BA Hons, MA and DPhil. During his career as a researcher, senior lecturer, professor and chair of the department of archaeology, he specialised in research on the cultural heritage of Africa.

JOAN MILLARD (JACKSON) has a doctorate in church history from the University of South Africa where she taught for more than 20 years. She is a member and was secretary of the Church History Society of Southern Africa. In 2011 she retired after ten years as a vice-president of the World Methodist Historical Society. She has written various articles and chapters for a number of books. Her major publications are *Malihambe – Let the Word spread* (1999), and *Open Doors Methodism in South Africa 1883-1933* (2013), the latter co-authored with Donald Cragg.

DAVID SCHER is a senior lecturer in history at the University of the Western Cape. He specialises in political and constitutional history and has published extensively on South African politics before and after 1948. His doctoral thesis was on the disenfranchisement of the coloured voters in the period 1948–1956. His MA dissertation was published in 1979 under the title *Donald Molteno: Dilizintaba: He who removes mountains*.

LEOPOLD SCHOLTZ studied at the University of Stellenbosch, the Rand Afrikaans University and the University of Leiden where he obtained a PhD in history in 1978. He served as deputy editor of *Die Burger* (1997 to 2007). Between 1998 and his retirement in 2013, he was Media24's correspondent in Europe. He still contributes political commentaries to *Die Burger*. Scholtz was professor extraordinaire at Stellenbosch University (2007 to 2010) and continues as research fellow. He authored or co-authored five books and 50 academic articles and chapters in various books.

ROBERT SHELL was extraordinary professor in historical demography at the University of the Western Cape. For six months in 2003 he occupied the Nelson Mandela chair of Africa studies at the Jawaharlal Nehru University in New Delhi, India. He has written extensively on slavery, Islam and HIV/Aids in Africa. His published works include *Children of bondage: A social history of slavery at the Cape of Good Hope*. He passed away in 2015.

CORNELIUS THOMAS is Head of Cory Library for Humanities Research at Rhodes University. He holds a PhD in history from the University of Notre Dame. His current research focus is on student activism and community histories. He wrote or contributed to several books, including *Dust in my coffee* (2008), *Cocktails of liberty: Contours of the 1976 Western Cape student uprising* (2009), *Finding freedom in the bush of books* (2010), and *Time with Dennis Brutus* (2012).

GOOLAM VAHED is an associate professor in the department of historical studies, University of KwaZulu-Natal. He completed his undergraduate studies at the University of Durban-Westville and received his PhD from Indiana University, Bloomington. His research focuses mostly on Indians/Muslims and the role of sport and culture in South African society. He has co-published such books as *Blacks in Whites: A century of sporting struggles in KwaZulu-Natal, 1880-2002* (2002) and *Inside Indian indenture. A South African Story, 1860-1914*.

ELIZE S. VAN EEDEN is professor of history attached to the Vaal Triangle campus of North-West University. She is the author of many academic articles and books. She is currently doing research on regional multidisciplinary environmental projects. She is chairperson of the South African Association for History Teaching and is editor of the scientific journals *Yesterday & Today* and *New Contree*. She also serves on other national and international management committees.

GRIETJIE VERHOEF is professor of accountancy and economic history, as well as director of the South African Centre for Accounting at the University of Johannesburg. Her area of speciality is the company history of large business concerns in South Africa, Afrikaner company conglomerates, and the history of the insurance and banking sector in South Africa. She has published a number of articles and chapters in books. She is deputy president of the International Economic History Association.

JAN VISAGIE is a retired history lecturer and a research associate of the department of history at the University of Stellenbosch. He is the author of five books and has also contributed many chapters in various books. One of his recent publications is *Voortrekkerstamouers 1835–1845*.

WESSEL VISSER is an associate professor in history at the University of Stellenbosch. His research field is South African labour and trade union history in the twentieth century. His book *Van MWU tot Solidariteit: Geskiedenis van die Mynwerkersunie, 1902–2002* appeared in 2008.

Index

Abacha, Sani, 519
Abdurahman, Abdullah, 272, 275, 293, 554–555, 557–559
Aborigines' Protection Society, 316
Abraham, slave, 90
Absa, 476–477
Acheul industry, 32, 35
Adam, Feroza, 571
Adderley Street, 83
Addis Ababa, 353
affirmative action, 544
Africa, 10, 25–26, 28, 30, 32, 33, 37, 41, 68, 76, 77, 84, 116, 154–155, 159, 189, 203, 205, 224, 229, 230, 239, 298, 322, 338–340, 344–345, 350, 353, 359, 362, 364–365, 368, 373, 380, 383, 387–388, 396, 413, 417, 420, 435, 442, 458, 496–497, 499, 514, 519, 521–523, 531, 535, 537, 541–542, 544–545, 547, 551, 554, 603, 637, 639, 645, 647, 651, 663
Africa Bureau, 387
Africa for the Africans (Africanists), 298, 322, 344, 380, 504, 554
African Banking Corporation (ABC), 475
African Explosives and Chemical Industries (AECI), 458, 472
African Federation of Trade Unions, 324
Africanist, The, 380
African Mineworkers' Union (Amwu), 324, 480
African National Congress (ANC), 258–259, 273, 298, 316–323, 327, 336, 343–346, 354, 367, 375–389, 391, 394–395, 398–400, 409–410, 412, 415–433, 435, 443, 466, 483, 487–489, 493–503, 505–509, 511–512, 516–519, 522–523, 525–534, 536–540, 544–545, 560, 568, 571–573, 581–582, 585, 587, 611, 619, 626–628, 660, 664–674
African People's Organisation, 272, 275, 292–293, 554, 558–559
African Political Organisation (APO), 293, 554
African Resistance Movement, 385
Afrikaans, 84, 104, 136, 170, 223–225, 228–231, 235, 237, 281–286, 289–291, 293, 298, 300–302, 304, 328, 340–341, 364, 390, 405, 410, 416, 422, 425, 429, 432, 450, 459, 464, 494, 498, 500, 523, 546, 550, 556, 569, 592, 610, 613, 623–624, 631–632, 638, 647
Afrikaanse Christelike Vrouevereniging, (ACVV, Association of Afrikaans Christian Women), 282
Afrikaanse Handelsinstituut (Afrikaans Trade Institute), 397
Afrikaanse Nasionale Bond, 275
Afrikaanse Patriot, Die, 170, 229
Afrikaanse Taal- en Kultuurvereniging (ATKV), 223, 301
Afrikaner(s), 9–13, 49, 74, 84, 125–126, 128, 131–135, 140, 148–149, 153–154, 169–170, 172, 174, 175–176, 179–180, 183, 185, 193–196, 204, 223–224, 226–237, 239–240, 250–253, 259–263, 267, 273, 276–278, 280–287, 289–291, 293–298, 300–312, 324, 328, 333, 335, 340–342, 351–353, 364, 370, 372–374, 397, 403–406, 409–410, 422, 424–425, 428, 430–432, 459–461, 475, 477, 481, 494, 498–500, 503, 509, 517, 523, 525, 546, 548, 550–552, 556, 559–560, 572, 576, 588–589, 592–598, 600–609, 612, 629, 631, 645, 649
Afrikanerbond, 170, 230–231, 234, 236–237, 261, 284, 593–597
Afrikaner Broederbond, 308, 397, 460
Afrikaner, Jager, 64–65, 224
Afrikaner, Jonker, 65, 224
Afrikaner League (Coloured), 224, 551
Afrikaner nationalism, 11–13, 169, 176, 179, 204, 223, 236–237, 239–240, 251, 259, 281, 300, 307, 328, 335, 374, 422, 559, 600, 606, 612
Afrikaner Party, 280, 309, 311, 328, 606
Afrikaner Volksfront, 430
Afrikaner *volkstaat*, 430–431
Afrikaner Weerstandsbeweging (AWB), 424, 431
Africanism, 322, 324
African Renaissance, 521, 523
African Union (AU), 520
agriculture, 11, 46–48, 61, 66, 80–81, 84, 87, 89, 102, 171, 180–181, 184, 188, 195, 197, 199, 205, 207–210, 213–221, 281, 303, 305, 308, 338, 340, 377, 407, 415, 449–453, 455, 459, 461, 463–465, 468, 510, 532, 535, 537, 540–541, 578, 634, 643–644, 647–648, 650–651, 653–654, 660
Ahtisaari, Martti, 364
Alabama, 435
Alabama, The (schooner), 550, 565
Albany, 95, 107, 127, 131, 135, 140, 590
Albasini, João, 650
Alexander Bay, 454
Algeria, 383, 386, 496
Algoa Bay, 102
Alice, 314
Allied Forces, 324, 599, 604
Aliwal North, 140–141
Aliwal North, Treaty of, 163–164
Altron, 472
amabutho, 122, 160
Amalgamated Society of Carpenters and Joiners (ASCJ), 479
Amalgamated Society of Engineers (ASE), 479–480
Amalinde flats, 95
AmaWasha, 196
Amazon River, 635
Amersfoort, 46
Amiens, Treaty of, 66, 79
Amla, Hashim, 587
amnesty (post-1994), 427, 429, 515–516
Amod, Aboobaker, 575
Amsterdam, 42, 58, 83, 617
ANC (see African National Congress)
ANC Women's League, 320, 611
ANC Youth League, 421–423, 496, 532
Anderson, Albrecht, 88
Anderson, William, 88, 111
Andreas, C.B., 646

Andrews, Bill, 325, 486
Andrews, Caesar, 99
Angela (Ansiela) from Bengal, 57
Anglican Church, 558, 576, 590, 611, 616–617, 619, 621–623, 626, 628–630
anglicisation, 81, 103–104, 169, 225, 259, 284, 593, 597–598
Anglo American Corporation, 289, 362, 445, 466, 469, 521
Anglo-Boer War, 9–11, 145, 170, 177–178, 183, 186, 195, 201, 204, 212–213, 220–221, 228, 234, 239–260, 264–265, 281, 314–315, 450, 480, 543, 552, 577, 588, 594–596, 605, 612, 618, 654–655
Anglo Boer War, First, 177, 204, 212–213, 228, 234, 239
Anglo-French Company, 194
Anglo-Zulu War, 161, 213, 215
Angola, 46–47, 353, 361–363, 365, 368, 389, 391, 403, 416–420
Ankaisoa, 44
Antarctica, 20, 25, 28, 659
Anthonie from Angola, 47
Anti-Apartheid Movement, 387, 561, 657
antimatter, 20
apartheid, 9–10, 12–13, 154, 259, 311, 328–347, 349–350, 353, 356–358, 361, 363–365, 366–370, 372, 374, 376–379, 382–383, 385–389, 391–396, 394–395, 398–399, 402, 404, 405–406, 409, 411–412, 414–417, 419, 422, 424, 429, 433–440, 443–446, 466, 475, 488–489, 493–494, 496, 500, 503–505, 508–510, 512, 515–518, 522, 533, 539, 543, 549, 558–561, 568–571, 581–587, 610, 612–626, 628–630, 632–634, 653, 657–661
apartheid, petty, 331, 340, 357, 414, 613
Apies River, 120, 172
APO, 292–293
Apostolic Faith Mission, 610, 628, 631
Arab (traders, script, Spring), 37, 189, 229, 542
Arbousset, Thomas, 124
Archbell, James, 124, 138–139
Ardipithecus ramidus, 31, 34
Argentina, 438–439
Argus Company, 593
Arktika, 22, 24, 27, 29
Arnot, David, 182
Arya Yuvuk Sabha (AYS), 579
asbestos, 455, 470
Ashforth, Adam, 646
Asia, 32–33, 36, 46, 74, 80, 415, 442, 469, 547
Asmal, Kader, 512, 587
Asquith, Herbert H., 267
Association for the Protection of the Environment, 658
asteroid, 15, 20–21, 24, 26, 30
Athenaeum, 225
Athlone, 394
Atlantica, 22, 24, 27, 29
Atlantic Charter, 321
Atlantic Ocean, 41, 75, 550, 636
Atlantis, 471
Atlas Aircraft Corporation, 354
Atmospheric Pollution Act, 658
Auckland Park, 196
Australia, 22, 25, 28, 33, 181, 189, 193–194, 220, 242, 244, 449, 452, 462, 464, 469, 479–480, 586, 589, 592, 595, 652
Australopithecus afarensis, 35
Australopithecus africanus, 32, 35
Australopithecus anamensis, 35
Australopithecus robustus, 32, 35
Australopithecus sediba, 32, 35
australopithecenae, 15, 31–32
Autshumao, 44
Awuleth' umshini wami, 528
Azanian People's Liberation Army (Apla), 509, 572
Azanian People's Organisation (Azapo), 386–387, 504
AZT, 513

Back, Ernestus, 59
Baden-Powell, Robert, 244
Baía da Lagoa, 39
Bailie, John, 102
Bain, James Thompson, 480
Baird, David, 67, 81
Bakenlaagte, Battle of, 248
Bakgatla, 166
Bakwena, 166
bacteria, 18, 22–23
Balfour, Alfred, 268
Balfour Declaration, 268, 270, 299, 312, 601
Ballinger, Margaret, 615
Ballinger, W.G., 483
Banda, Hastings Kamuzu, 350
banking, 82, 460–461, 475–477, 490, 508, 535, 679
Bank Act, 475–476
Bantjes, Jan, 193
Bantu Education Act, 332–333, 615
Bantu Authorities Act, 336–337, 343, 349
Bantu Homelands Citizenship Act, 355
Bantu Homelands Constitution Act, 355
Bantustan policy, 340, 616
Bantu speakers (education, administration), 15, 34, 36–38, 106, 113, 116, 314, 322, 357, 376–377, 380, 390, 444, 623, 643–645
Bantu World, 375
baptism, 55–56, 58, 65, 70, 73–74, 87, 89
Barberton (rock formations), 15, 22, 24, 26, 29, 184, 192–193
Barclays Bank, 460, 475–477
Barends, Barend, 110, 112
Barkly, Henry, 182–183, 190
Barkly East, 394
Barkly West, 189
Barnard, Anne, 57, 72
Barnard, Cecil, 565
Barnard, Fred, 342
Barnard, Niel, 420
Barnard, W.S., 633
Barolong, 166, 182, 190, 232
Barnard, Fred, 338
Barnato, Barney, 192, 194, 212
Barrow, John, 57, 80
Bashee Bridge, 385
Basotho, 106, 112, 116–117, 151–153, 162–164, 180, 191, 196, 199–200, 218, 384
Basotholand (see also Lesotho), 164, 196, 384
Basson, Willem, 57

INDEX 693

Bastard Poster, 277
Basters, 55, 63, 81, 109-110, 255
Batavian rule, 66-67, 81, 148, 209
Batavia, 43, 56, 542
Bathurst, Lord, 100, 103-104
Batty, A.F., 483
Baviaanskloof, 51, 59
Baviaans River, 98, 100, 102
BBC, 602, 607
Beaufort West, 107
Bechuanaland Protectorate, 167, 179, 240, 254, 383
Beersheba, 123
Beetge, Gert, 485
Beinart, William, 633
Beit, Alfred, 193-194
Bela-Bela (Warmbaths), 215
Belgium, 205, 677
Belhar Confession, 625
Bengal, 47, 55, 57, 68, 574
Bengu, Sibisisu, 512
Benin, 76
Benjamin, Beattie, 565
Benoni, 193, 297
Benzien, Jeffrey, 572
Berea, 202
Bereaberg, 153
Bergendal (Dalmanutha), 246
Bergh, Hendrik van den, 373
Bergh, Olof, 57
Berg River, 47
Bergville, 119
Berigte te velde, 300
Berlin Stock Exchange, 197
Berlin Wall, 421
Berlin Missionary Society, 87, 258
Bermuda, 248, 253
Bethelsdorp, 85, 87
Beutler, August, 60
Beyers, Christiaan, 185
Bezuidenhout, Cornelis Frederik, 98-101
Bezuidenhout, Gerrit, 99, 101
Bezuidenhout, Hans (Johannes), 98-101
Bezuidenhout, Martha, 99, 101
Bhaca, 149
Bhagavad Gita, 575
Bible, 59, 85, 89, 133, 229, 300, 620, 632
Biebouw, Hendrik, 49
Big Bang theory, 18-19, 23
Biggar, Alexander, 146
Biko, Steve, 354, 367-368, 386, 533, 584, 622, 624
Bill of Rights, 321, 423, 493
biodiversity, 648, 653, 660
biome, 15, 29, 31, 637-640, 642
biosphere, 634
bittereinders, 247, 252, 261, 282, 286
Black Act, 543
Black Circuit, 87
Black Consciousness Movement, 313, 354, 358, 360, 367-368, 381, 386-387, 391, 488, 504, 533-534, 569, 584, 620, 622
Black Economic Empowerment (BEE), 495, 508, 526, 536, 538-540, 585, 671

Black People's Convention (BPC), 386, 391, 670
blacks, 9, 11-12, 46-47, 51, 55, 57, 59-60, 69, 75-76, 100, 105, 107-109, 112, 115-116, 118, 121-125, 128, 133, 138, 141, 145, 149, 152, 155-156, 163, 166, 168, 170-171, 174, 178, 180-181, 188-189, 191, 195-197, 199-204, 207-209, 213, 217-219, 231, 239, 242, 247-249, 252-267, 271-280, 290-294, 296-299, 303-304, 306, 311-333, 335-343, 345-347, 349-351, 354-363, 366-371, 373-414, 417, 420-429, 431-438, 443-448, 450, 457, 464-465, 467, 473-474, 478, 481-490, 495-499, 503-506, 508-513, 518, 520-523, 526-527, 531, 533-536, 538-540, 543-544, 554, 561, 564, 569-571, 576, 580-587, 591-593, 605-606, 608-627, 631, 634, 643-646, 648, 650-654, 656, 659
Black Sash, 533, 608
black theology, 571, 622
Blankewerkersbeskermingsbond, 485
Blesberg, 137
Blitzkrieg, 605
Bloemfontein, 33, 137, 151-152, 163, 172, 187, 199, 211, 217, 227, 232-233, 245, 252, 257, 262, 265-266, 277, 282, 285-286, 288, 290, 301, 307, 315-316, 334-335, 531, 655
Bloemfontein Bank, 218
Bloemfontein Convention, 151, 153, 217
Bloemhof, 216, 656
Bloem, Jan, 108, 112
blockhouses, 248, 255, 655, 657
Blombos, 33
Blommaert, W., 145
Blood River (Ncome River), 147, 227
Blouberg, 39
Bloukrans River, 144
Boegoeberg Dam, 453
Boers, 9, 145, 154, 157, 160-161, 163, 165-168, 172, 174, 176, 178-180, 183, 185-187, 226, 228-229, 239-259, 260-261, 277, 281-283, 285-286, 315, 480, 552, 556, 595, 655-656
Boer Republics, 11-12, 154-155, 172, 174, 179, 180, 182-183, 186, 188, 203-204, 210, 215, 220, 230, 237, 240, 242, 260-261, 264, 267, 294, 296, 315, 459, 555, 594
Boerevrou, Die, 286
Boers, Willem, 61
Boesak, Allan, 391, 571, 622, 625, 630
Boesak (Khoekhoe leader), 96
Boesmanspoort, 137
Boipatong, 426
Bokkeveld, 52
Boksburg, 185, 193
Bokwe, John Knox, 314
Boland, 291
Bonteheuwel Military Wing, 572
Bonuskor, 460
Booda, Christlief, 85
Boom, Annetje (Annetje de Boerin), 56
Boom, Hendrik, 56
Boomplaats, 150
Booy, 98
Booysens, Ingrid, 14
Booysens, 196, 202

Bophelong, 381
Bophuthatswana, 355, 359, 392, 407, 430–431
Boraine, Alex, 516
Borcherds, Meent, 85
Borckenhagen, C.L.F., 232
Border War, 417–418
Bosch, David, 630
Boshof, 245
Boshof, Jacobus, 163
Bos indicus, 36
Bosman, J.D., 460
Bos primigenius, 36
Bos taurus, 36
Botha, Louis, 243–246, 248, 252, 261, 263, 266–267, 270, 272, 282–283, 287–288, 290, 294, 480, 595–598, 600, 655
Botha, M.C., 349
Botha, Puffy, 564
Botha, P.W., 370, 373, 390–392, 396–400, 405–408, 410, 413–415, 417–418, 420–421, 497, 516, 627–628
Bothma, Abraham, 99
Bothma, Stephanus, 99
Botswana, 34, 38–40, 113, 117, 181, 188, 240, 254, 361, 383, 388, 415, 439, 470
Bouah, Lyndon, 568
Bourke, Richard, 45, 86, 97
Bowker, Miles, 102
Bowker, Thomas, 136
Boy Scouts, 289
Braamfontein, 194–196
Bradford, Helen, 646
Brakpan, 201
Brakrivier, 134
Brand, Christoffel, 81, 85
Brand, Dollar (Abdullah Ibrahim), 565
Brand, Jan (J.H.), 175, 182–183, 232–233, 589
Brandwag, Die, 285
Brandwater Basin, 246, 248
Brazil, 75–77, 189, 438, 469, 537, 542, 561, 635
Brebner, John, 232
Bredasdorp, 334
Brereton, Thomas, 95
Bretton Woods Conference, 467
Brickfields, 195, 202
Brink, Linda, 14
British Empire, 103, 131, 170, 182, 225, 227–228, 230–231, 236, 241, 248, 260–261, 275, 277, 282, 287, 289, 302, 479, 555, 560, 577–578, 589–591, 595, 597–598, 600–601, 604
British Empire Service League, 604
British Settlers, 101–103, 127, 207–208, 574, 588–589, 646
Brits, Japie (J.P.), 12, 493, 676
Bronkhorstspruit, 177
Broome Commission, 326
Brown, Basil, 568
Brown, Bernie, 565
Brown, Clifford, 571
Bruintjeshoogte, 94, 100
Bruntland Report (UN), 635
Brutus, Dennis, 553, 561

Bryce, James, 233
Buffels River, 107
Buhlungu, Sakhela, 505
Buisfontein, 651
Buisset, Maria, 57
Buller, Redvers, 178, 243–244
Bultfontein, 189–190
Bunting, S.P., 482
Burchell, William, 89
Burger, Die (De), 298, 310–311, 329, 436, 678
Burger, J.J. (Kootjie), 150
Burgersdorp, 202
Burgher Council, 140, 150, 152
Burghersdorp, 195, 202
Burgher Senate, 66, 81, 104
Burgers, T.F., 175–176
Burgerwachthuis, 83
Bureau of State Security (BOSS), 517
Burundi, 542, 545
Bushmanland, 108, 156, 636
Bushmen (see also San, Khoikhoi, Khoekhoen and Khoisan), 11, 33, 52, 55, 64, 82, 93, 106–109, 111–112, 115–116, 125, 144, 156, 207, 547, 641–643
Bushmans River, 93, 144
Bushveld Complex, 15, 24, 26, 30, 636
Butha-Buthe, 123
Buthelezi Commission, 392
Buthelezi, Mangosuthu, 392–393, 398–399, 405, 410, 427, 429–433, 504, 516
Butler, Jonathan, 566
Butterfield, Herbert, 434
Buxton, Thomas, 90
Buys, Coenraad (de), 651
Buys, Flip, 490
Buys, Michael, 650–651
Byrne scheme, 588

Cabo da Boa Esperanca (Cape of Good Hope), 41
Cabo Tormentoso (Cape of Storms), 41
Caesar, Julius, 413
Caetano, Marcello, 353, 361
Calata, James, 320
Caledon, 48, 104
Caledon, Earl of (governor), 81–82, 85–87, 90, 93, 133
Caledonians, 590, 608
Caledon Square, 382
Caledon River, 116, 121, 137, 152, 164
California, 463, 479
Calueque, 419
Calvinia, 64, 255, 552, 564
Calvinism, 612
Cameron, Trewhella, 10
Cameroon, 36
Campbell-Bannerman, Henry, 259
Campbell, John, 63, 109–110
Canada, 244, 299, 342, 449, 452, 462, 469, 479, 480, 586, 589, 595, 625
Canis familiaris, 36
*Canis lupus arab*s, 36
Cape Agulhas, 87

Cape Chinese Exclusion Act, 543
Cape Colony, 11, 47, 50, 52–53, 56–57, 60, 66–67, 76, 79–80, 88–90, 92, 96, 101, 103, 106–108, 111, 113–114, 118, 120, 122–123, 125–126, 131, 146, 149, 151–152, 154–155, 157–160, 164, 167–171, 182–183, 185, 190, 199, 203, 205–207, 209, 212–213, 216, 226, 229, 230–231, 234–235, 237, 240, 243–244, 246, 248, 252–253, 255, 258, 260–262, 264–266, 291, 302, 313, 315, 455–456, 548, 588–589, 593–595, 597, 648, 650
Cape Coloured Association, 266
Cape Corps of Infantry and Cavalry, 88, 97
Cape Flats, 47, 331, 548, 563–564, 570, 572
Cape Herald, 564
Cape of Good Hope, 41, 43
Cape of Good Hope Printers' and Bookbinders' Society, 479
Cape of Good Hope Printers' Protection Society, 479
Cape of Good Hope Savings Bank, 210
Cape Mounted Riflemen, 88
Cape Native Voters' Association, 273
Cape Patriots, 62
Cape Peninsula, 44, 80, 318, 381
Cape Town, 48, 50–51, 54–55, 61, 64–66, 68–71, 73, 75, 81, 83–84, 87, 89–92, 94, 97, 155, 160–161, 199–200, 210–211, 225, 229, 236–237, 262, 266, 270, 279, 282, 285, 290–293, 307–308, 318, 331, 334, 340, 342, 344, 349, 359, 375, 382, 386, 394, 400, 408, 412, 479–480, 482, 533–534, 547–548, 550–551, 553–554, 556, 558, 560, 563–565, 567–569, 572, 579, 589, 613, 617, 624, 645
Cape Town Minstrels, 554
Cape Town, University of, 225, 534, 558
Cape Regiment, 81, 85, 88, 97–100
Cape Times, 289, 437
capitalism, 308, 387, 442, 444, 478, 501, 590, 597
Capra aegagrus, 36
Capra hircus, 36
carbon dioxide, 22–23, 470
Carnarvon, Lord, 176, 183, 239
Carnegie Corporation, 304
Carnegie investigation (poor whites), 304
Carolus, Cheryl, 571
Carshagen, Carina, 223
Carter, Jimmy, 368
Casalis, Eugène, 124
Casey, William, 415
Cato Manor, 582
cattle (farming), 34, 36–38, 44, 47, 50, 52, 60, 64, 70, 84, 93–96, 102, 112–113, 115, 123, 128, 130, 134, 138–140, 142–144, 158–159, 166, 189, 196, 199, 213–216, 256, 450, 530, 643–644, 646, 648, 651–652, 656
Cenozoic Era, 18, 25
Central Intelligence Agency (CIA), 415
Cetshwayo, 160–161, 179, 265
Chamberlain, Joseph, 185, 204, 236–237, 240–241
Chambinga River, 419
Champion, A.W.G., 483
Chapman, 102
Charterists, 504

Chase, John Centlivres, 103
Chase Manhattan Bank, 475
Chatsworth, 582, 587
Chavín, 647
Chavonne, 83
Chennai (Madras), 576
Chile, 438
China, People's Republic of (Beijing), 397, 518, 537, 542–543, 635
China, Republic of (Taiwan), 369, 462, 518, 543
China, Sam, 583
Chinese, 12, 37, 195, 542–544
Choro, 44
Christian (Christiandom), 42, 50–51, 54–56, 58–59, 66, 73–74, 86–87, 89, 111, 133, 159, 224, 229, 258, 282, 300, 306, 340–341, 353, 548–550, 553, 556, 574, 576, 579, 587, 610, 612, 614–621, 623–624, 626–628, 630, 646
Christian Institute, 391, 620
Christian National Education (CNO), 282
chrome, 26, 470
Chua, Amy, 442
Chungwa, 93
Churchill, Winston, 249, 321
Church Street bomb, 516
Cillié, Piet, 436–437
Cilliers, S.A., 280
Cilliers, Sarel, 48, 137, 146, 227
Ciskei, 355, 392, 407, 430
citizenship, 86, 115, 236, 239–240, 246, 270, 346, 350, 355, 365, 392, 407–408, 614
Citizen, The, 372, 396
civil service, 102, 233, 235, 258, 276, 286, 289, 301, 310, 397, 408, 490–491, 506, 509, 523, 538–540
Claas Das, 44
Claasen, Jonathan, 572
Claasz, Armosyn, 74
Clanwilliam (Jan Disselsvlei), 82, 107, 131, 453
Clark, Alured, 65
Clerk, George, 153
climate (change), 22, 27–28, 35, 84, 213, 507, 637, 647, 655, 660, 662
Cloete, Henry, 149
Cloete, Jan, 52
coal, 28, 30, 193, 200–201, 216–217, 324, 354, 454–455, 458, 468–470, 578
Cobbing, Julian, 118, 646
Cobbing theory, 118
Cochoquas, 49
CODESA (Convention for a Democratic South Africa), 500, 504, 630
Coetsee, Kobie, 497
Coetzee, Alistair, 568
Coetzee, Jacobus, 60
Cold War, 353, 387, 517–518, 521
Colenso, 243, 246
Colesberg, 106, 114, 137, 189–190, 244
Colley, George, 177–178
Collins, Richard, 82, 87, 94, 97
Collins, W., 554–555
colonialism (colonists), 11, 68–71, 73, 80, 103, 159, 169, 387, 446, 573, 576, 591, 613, 645

Colour Bar Act, 326, 427, 481, 484–485, 556
Coloured Advisory Council, 279, 357
Coloured Persons' Representative Council, 358–361, 370
Coloured People's Organisation, South African, 343, 378, 559
Coloureds, 9–10, 12–13, 45, 85, 94, 106, 123, 128, 130, 136, 138, 143, 145, 157, 195, 224, 231, 254–255, 260, 262–263, 265–267, 272–276, 279, 293–294, 298, 331, 359–360, 370–371, 411, 547–572, 592
commando system, 51–53, 55, 62, 64, 83, 93, 98, 113, 128, 141, 143, 252, 592
Commonwealth, British, 267–268, 340–342, 387, 415, 433, 449, 452, 454, 462, 477, 559, 601–603, 605, 607–608, 614
communism (communists), 225, 296–298, 319, 322–325, 343, 349, 353, 366, 374–376, 380, 384, 410, 418–419, 421, 483, 486–487, 489, 494, 497, 499, 506, 518, 527–529, 580, 582, 615, 622, 628
Company garden, 83
concentration camps, 9, 247, 249–251, 257, 281, 594, 657
Concordia, 196
Congella, 149
Congo (DRC), 342, 345, 519, 542, 545
Congress of Democrats, South African, 343, 375, 378–379, 582
Congress of South African Students (COSAS), 394, 532
Congress of South African Trade Unions (COSATU), 394, 423, 488–489, 491, 494, 501–502, 504–505, 507, 528–529, 536, 585, 670
Congress of the People (COPE), 530, 589
Congress of the People (Kliptown), 377–379, 560, 617
Congress of Traditional Leaders of South Africa (Contralesa), 511
Conservative Party (CP), 406, 424
Consolidated Gold Fields of South Africa, 194
constellations of states, 360, 399
Constitution (ANC), 320
Constitution (Cape Colony), 171, 233, 266, 594, 596
Constitution (democratic South Africa, 1996), 382, 421, 423–430, 435, 489, 493, 495, 497, 500, 509, 511, 521–522, 526, 538, 540, 555, 587, 630, 660
Constitution (tricameral parliament, 1984), 267, 370, 405–407, 585
Constitution (South West Africa, Namibia), 363
Constitution (Natal), 171
Constitution (Natalia, 1838), 147, 150
Constitution (Orange Free State), 175, 233
Constitution (Union of South Africa, 1909), 261–263, 265–266, 268, 270, 286, 288, 299, 315, 333–335, 562, 601, 611, 615
Constitution (ZAR, 1857), 175
Coornhoop, 45
copper, 26, 37, 44, 188–189, 210, 212, 216, 455, 466, 470
Corner House mining group, 593–594, 597
Cornwall, 479
Coronationville, 331
Corps Bastaard Hottentotten, 51

Corps Pandoeren, 52
Cory, George, 145
Cosselin, Constant, 124
Cottesloe, 619–620, 632
cotton production, 76, 171, 214, 463
Council for Scientific and Industrial Research (CSIR), 658
Council of Non-European Trade Unions (CNETU), 324, 486
Council of Unions of South Africa (CUSA), 488, 670
covenant (Blood River), 227
Covid-19 pandemic, 671, 674
Cradle of Humankind, 32
Cradock, 107, 114, 134, 393–394
Cradock, John, 82–83, 86, 94, 97
Cradock four, 393–394
Cradock Youth Association (CRADOYA), 393
Craig, James, 65
craton(s), 15, 22–24, 26–27, 29–30
Cressy, Harold, 556
Creswell, F.H.P., 268–269, 482, 484, 597, 601
Creusot gun (Long Tom), 186
crime, 422, 435, 514–515, 517, 523, 526, 531, 544–545, 583, 587, 609, 631
Crocker, Chester, 417
Crocodile River, 39, 120, 453
Cronin, Jeremy, 502
Cronjé, Andries, 252
Cronjé, Piet, 178, 186, 240, 243–244, 246, 248, 252
Cuba, 365–366, 391, 417–420, 513
Cuito Cuanavale, 418–419
Cuito River, 419
Cullinan, 28, 30, 454
Cullinan Commission, 456
Cupido from Bengal, 55
Currie Cup, 592
Curtin, P.D., 77
Curtis, Lionel, 262
customs (agreement, union, act, duty), 81, 83, 221–222, 262, 272, 456–457, 471, 548
Cuyler, Jacob, 82, 94, 100

Dadoo, Yusuf, 325–327, 388, 580–582
Da Gama, Vasco, 41
Dairy Board, 451
dairy farming, 61, 194, 199, 486
Dalai Lama, 542
D'Almeida, Francisco, 41
Damaraland, 135
Daniell, Richard, 102
Daniëlskuil, 110
Daniels, Pieter Johannes, 224, 551, 555
Danster, Dawid, 109
Dar es Salaam, 389
dark energy, 20
dark matter, 20
Daumas, François, 124
Dawood, Ayesha, 582
De Beaulieu, Augustin, 42
De Beers (Consolidated Mines), 190, 192, 212, 454, 466, 470
Debe Nek, 95
De Broglio, Chris, 561

De Bruyn, Pieter, 60
De Chavonnes, Mauritz Pasque, 59
De Clercq, Sara (Du Toit), 56
De Cuellar, Xavier Perez, 397
Defiance Campaign, 343–344, 376–377, 380–381
De Gaulle, Charles, 445
De Graaff, Nicolaus, 42
De Jong, Cornelis, 54
De Jonge Thomas, 60
De Kalk, 189
De Kiewiet, C.W., 154, 445
De Klerk, Theunis, 100
De Klerk, F.W., 420–427, 429–433, 493–495, 497, 503, 516, 585, 631
De Klerk, Willem, 351
De Kock, Gerhard, 476
De Kock Commission, 464, 476
De Koning, Anna, 57
Delagoa Bay, 41, 118–120, 137–138, 184, 200, 211, 217, 222, 240, 649
De Lange, Adriaan, 99
De la Rey, Koos, 180, 243, 245–246, 248, 252
Delft, 42
De Lille, Patricia, 504, 534, 673
Delport, Petrus, 62
Delportshoop, 189
Delville Wood, 599
Demas, Desmond, 564
De Mist, Augusta, 57
De Mist, J.A., 57, 59, 66, 81, 148
Democratic Alliance (DA), 466, 503, 525–526, 532–534, 537, 546, 664–667, 672–673
Democratic Party (DP), 369–370, 503, 533
Democratic Turnhalle Alliance (DTA), 418
dendroclimatology, 647
Denmark, 42
Deng Xiaoping, 397
depression, 209–212, 219–220, 305, 451–452, 454, 456, 486, 525, 536, 538, 546, 556, 564, 601
Derby, Lord, 179
De Savoye, Jacques, 48
De Suffren, Pierre André, 61
De Villebois-Mareuil, Georges, 245
De Villiers, Dawie, 427, 660
De Villiers, J.E., 295
De Villiers, Johan, 11, 41, 76, 79, 676
De Villiers, M.L., 302
De Villiers, W. Brückner, 273
De Villiers, Wim, 467
De Waal, J.H.H., 293
De Wet, Christiaan, 180, 245–246, 248–249, 252, 295
De Wet, Johan, 337
De Wet, Olof Gotlieb, 81
De Wet, Piet, 252
Dhlomo, Oscar D., 145
diamond (fields, industry) 15, 24, 28, 30, 158, 166, 175–176, 179–183, 188–193, 195–203, 206–208, 211–212, 215, 217–221, 228, 232, 449, 454–455, 466, 470, 479
Dias, Bartholomew, 41
Dicke, B.H., 649

Didiza, Thoko, 511
Diefenbaker, John, 342
Difaqane, 116–117
digger(s), 180–181, 184, 188–193, 212
Digoya, 39
Dimawe, 166
Dingane, 120, 142–148, 297, 422
Dingiswayo, 119, 647
Dinizulu, 161, 179
dinosaurs, 25, 30
Dippenaar, Laurie, 477
District Six, 331, 562–564, 613
Dithakong, 112, 124
Dlamini-Zuma, Nkosazana, 513, 668, 671
Doctors' Pact, 327, 581–582
D'Oliveira, Basil, 560–561
Doman (Anthonie), 44
Dominium Party, 601–603, 605
Dominiums, British, 268, 270, 299, 595, 600–601, 604–605
Dönges, T.E., 279–280, 330–331
Donkin, Rufane, 102–103
Doornfontein, 193, 202
Doornkop, 186
Doorn Nek, 94
Doppers, 175, 283, 288
Dordt, Synod of, 73
Drakensberg, 15, 30, 34, 38, 107, 119, 121, 137, 148, 152, 156–157, 177, 639
Drakenstein, 47–48, 52, 58
Driefontein, 193
Drommedaris, 43
drought, 36, 114, 126, 195, 211, 219, 305, 453, 465, 636–638, 640, 642, 645–648
Drought Commission, 652
Dube, John, 314, 316–317, 611
Duinhoop, 45
Duminy, Johanna, 57
Duncan, Patrick, 270, 595, 602–603
Dundee, 480
Du Pisani, Kobus, 12, 349
Du Plessis brothers, 256
Du Plessis, J.C., 329
Du Plessis, Wennie, 328
Du Preez, A.B., 617
Durban, 137, 142, 199–200, 211, 214, 217, 262, 327, 354, 403, 412, 480, 488, 526, 530, 571, 578–580, 582–584, 605, 608
D'Urban, Benjamin, 134
Durban-Westville, University of, 583
Dutch, 45–47, 51, 54, 56–57, 59, 66–67, 75, 81, 84–85, 89, 109, 136, 170, 223–226, 228–231, 233, 236, 263, 273, 283–291, 293, 300, 479, 549–550, 552, 556, 584
Dutch East India Company (VOC), 42, 74, 542, 574, 647
Dutch Reformed Church (NG Kerk), 68–69, 104, 175, 416, 610, 613, 616, 618–620, 624, 629–631
Du Toit, Guilliaume, 48
Du Toit, J.D. (Totius), 285, 616
Du Toit, S.J., 179, 228–231, 290
Du Toitspan, 189–190

Earth, 11, 17-18, 20-23, 25-31, 634, 636, 658
East Africa, 18, 25, 31-32, 34-36, 578, 599, 640
Eastern Cape, 38, 98, 104, 106-107, 113, 124, 156, 169, 199, 204, 206-210, 226, 231, 292, 313-314, 324, 376-377, 393-394, 412, 543, 588-590, 607, 640, 645-646, 651
Eastern Province Bank, 210
East London, 200, 211, 483, 561, 563-564, 571, 602
Ebenezer mission station, 87
Ebner, Johann, 65
Eckstein, Hermann, 194
ecology, 22, 191, 200, 633, 637-638, 642, 647, 659, 662
Economic Freedom Fighters, 664-666, 672, 673
Economist, The, 438
economy, 12, 37, 53, 70, 82, 84, 89, 107, 112, 155, 184, 188, 191, 194, 197-198, 201, 205-208, 210, 212-215, 218-220, 222-223, 235, 254, 287, 303-305, 308, 329, 338, 347, 354, 356, 394, 400, 402-404, 408-409, 426-427, 434, 438, 440, 442, 444-446, 448-477, 490, 507-508, 521, 525, 534-535, 538-539, 554, 564, 574, 608, 635, 645, 653, 657
education, 59, 65-66, 84, 91, 105, 139, 155, 169, 179, 184, 229, 232, 254, 261, 274, 279, 282-283, 291, 298, 304, 306, 314, 323, 330, 332-333, 379-380, 390, 393-394, 401-404, 406, 428, 432, 437-438, 440, 444, 450, 459, 490, 500, 502, 512-514, 523, 530, 533, 551, 556, 558, 567, 570, 575, 579, 583, 591, 611-612, 615-616, 618, 623, 630, 663
Eersteling, 181, 192
Eerste River, 47
EFF (see Economic Freedom Fighters)
Effendi, Ahmed, 551, 555
eGabeni (Kapain), 120, 141
Egg Board, 451
Egypt, 36, 61, 542
Eier, 564
Eighth Army, 605
Eiselen, Werner, 336, 338
Eksteen, Hendrik, 51
ekuPumuleni, 120
Eland, Ron, 560
Elandsfontein, 193, 196
Elandslaagte, 243
elections, 159, 175, 231, 261, 324, 333-335, 356, 358-359, 364-365, 424, 432, 441, 500-501, 510-511, 528, 531-532, 554, 585, 596, 630
electricity, 188, 200, 303, 411, 455, 458, 469, 506, 522, 535, 586
Elim mission station, 87
Elizabeth II, 607
Ellis Park, 391
Elphinstone, George Keith, 65
Elsenburg Agricultural College, 450
Elsevier, Samuel, 48-49
emergency, state of, 341, 344, 382, 385, 392, 395, 412, 414, 441, 474, 489, 619, 627
emHlahlandlela, 120
Empire Day, 602
Employment Equity Act, 508, 544
End Conscription Campaign, 620, 622
England, 102, 197-198, 466, 499, 543, 578, 587, 589-590, 592, 608

England, Bank of, 197-198
England, Sons of, 590, 608
Engelgraaf, Daniel, 59
engineering, 118, 221, 458, 471-472, 480, 486, 490, 556
English, 72, 81, 102-104, 134, 136, 169-170, 180, 224-226, 228-233, 235, 237, 242, 252-253, 258, 261-264, 267, 275-278, 281-293, 296, 300, 303, 305-306, 309, 311-312, 328, 333, 340-341, 350-352, 364, 371-372, 405, 410, 417, 428-429, 453, 499, 503, 512, 552, 556, 560, 573, 576, 588-610, 613, 616, 620-625, 631-632, 647
Engen Oil, 521
Enon mission station, 87
Environmental Conservation Act (1989), 661
Erasmus, Daniël, 245
Erasmus, Frans, 278
Erasmus, Jacob, 98
Erasmus, Rudolf, 373, 396
Erasmus Commission, 373, 396
Erwin, Alec, 507
Esau, Abraham, 255, 552, 570
Escher, Alfred, 363
Eskom (Escom), 201, 303, 458, 540, 666
Estcourt, 144
Esterhuyse, Willie, 498
Ethiopia, 31, 34-35, 264, 383
Eurasia, 28, 35-36
Eureka diamond, 189
Europe, 32-33, 42, 55, 59, 61, 66, 69, 75-76, 79-80, 82, 84, 124, 188-189, 194, 203, 205-206, 208-211, 216-217, 219-221, 247, 272, 274, 280, 287, 308, 333, 353-354, 362-363, 369, 435, 439, 442, 450, 469, 479, 483, 500, 521-522, 537, 547-550, 576, 597, 633, 646-647, 652
European Union (Community), 363, 522, 537
Euwe, Max, 561
Eva (see Krotoa)
evangelical churches, 627, 629
exports, 83, 198, 208-212, 215-218, 220-221, 232, 234, 303, 318, 354, 402-403, 442, 449, 451, 454, 459, 463-466, 468-472, 474-475, 518, 537, 650, 652
Express, De, 227, 232
Eybers, Elisabeth, 300

Faber, Cornelis, 99-100
Fagan, H.A., 329, 335, 613
Fagan Commission, 329, 335, 613
Fairbairn, John, 103, 590
Faku, 121
Fanon, Franz, 386
FAPLA (Angola), 366
Farrar, George, 194, 596
Faure, Abraham, 85
Fauresmith, 217
Fauresmith Bank, 218
Fawcett, Millicent, 251
Federale Mynbou, 460, 467
Federale Volksbeleggings, 308, 460-461
Federal Party, 358
Federasie van Afrikaanse Kultuurverenigings (FAK), 301-302, 307

INDEX 699

Federation of Non-European Trade Unions (FNETU), 486
Federation of South African Trade Unions (FOSATU), 394, 488
Federation of South African Women (FSAW), 379
Federation of Unions of South Africa (FEDUSA), 490, 505
Ferreira, G.T., 477
Ferreirasdorp, 202
Fichardts, 199, 233
Ficksburg, 123
Financial Mail, 444-445
First Afrikaans Language Movement, 230
First National Bank, 477
First Rand Group, 477
First World War, 272, 281, 294, 296, 317-318, 449, 454, 456, 578, 598-600, 604-605
Fischer, Abraham (premier), 233, 596
Fischer, Bram, 385
fish industry, 542
Fish River (Great, Upper, Lower), 60, 83, 93-97, 102, 107, 113, 126, 354, 453
Fitzpatrick, Percy, 594, 596
Fivaz, George, 509
Flag Bill, 601
Flanders, 599
Fleck, Abraham, 81
Florisbad, 33
FNLA (Angola), 365
Fokeng, 39, 112, 117-118, 121
Fordsburg, 202
Fort Armstrong, 157
Fort Beaufort, 111, 128
Fort Hare, University of, 344, 496
Fort Knokke, 83
Fortuin, Bernard, 570
fossil(s), 22, 24, 27, 30, 32-33
Fouché, Willem, 253
Fourie, Jopie, 295
France, 32, 42, 47, 79-80, 186, 194, 198, 205, 239-240, 245, 247, 353, 368, 387, 445, 448, 545, 599
franchise (vote), 147, 159-160, 169, 170-171, 185, 187, 231, 236-237, 241, 253-254, 258-259, 261-263, 267, 271-272, 274-278, 306, 314-315, 321, 327, 333-334, 350, 375, 399, 440-444, 551, 555, 558, 562, 576, 578, 592-596
Franchise Action Council (FRAC), 375
Fransch, Anton, 572
Franschhoek, 47
Fraser, George Sackville, 88, 94-95, 99
Fraser, Tibbie, 233
Fredericks, Mark, 557
Fredericks, Matt, 555
free blacks, 46-47, 51, 55, 59, 69, 75-76, 108-109
Free burghers, 45-49, 54-55, 58, 60, 74, 76, 134
Freedom Alliance, 388, 430
Freedom before education slogan, 512
Freedom Charter, 343, 377-380, 391, 422, 439, 441, 444, 499, 504, 506, 560, 617
Freedom Front Plus, 664, 666, 672
Freemasons, 590
free trade, 62, 66, 302, 448, 455, 520

Frelimo, 365, 386, 415-416
French Revolution, 56, 90
Frere, Bartle, 161
Friedman, Bernard, 280
Friends of the Earth, 658
frontline states, 361-362
Frykenius, Sijmon, 62
fynbos, 29, 637-640, 652

Galant, 91
Galata, 93
Gallus gallus, 36
Gambia, 76
Gamtoos River, 142
Gandhi, Mohandas, 254, 266, 326, 376, 543, 576-579, 581
Gang of 8, 389
Gardiner, A.F., 143
Gariep River (see Orange River)
Gariep dam, 354, 453
Gatsrand, 246
Gauteng, 38, 393, 455, 587, 639, 662
Gaza kingdom, 120
Gazankulu, 355
Gcaleka, 96-97, 136, 159-160
Gear programme (Strategy for Growth, Employment and Redistribution), 501, 507-508, 528-529
Gebhart, Wilhelm, 91
Gelvandale bus protest, 564
Genadendal, 59, 85, 87, 553
Gencor, 521
Gender Equality, Commission for, 493
General Mining, 460
General Motors, 457, 475
Genootskap van Regte Afrikaners (GRA, Society of True Afrikaners), 169, 223
George (town), 100, 636
George VI, 606
Gerdener, Theo, 369
Gereformeerde Kerk (Reformed Church) 154, 175, 610, 612-613, 631
Germany, 87, 186, 194, 198, 203, 205, 239-240, 247, 250, 278, 281, 294, 309, 326, 368, 409, 417, 435, 448, 458, 533, 559, 598, 603, 658
Germiston, 193
Geskiedenis van ons land in die taal van ons volk, Die, 229
Gesuiwerde (Purified) National Party, 276, 305, 603
Ghana, 76, 339, 342, 647
Ghetto Act, 326, 581
Giliomee, Hermann, 10-14, 68, 223, 281, 396, 411, 434, 517
Gini coefficient, 535
Glen Grey Act, 160
Global Organisation of People of Indian Origin (GOPIO), 586
God save the Queen/King, 591, 607
Goede Hoop, 43
Gogosoa, 44
Gokhale, G.K., 577
gold (mines, fields, price), 26, 37, 39, 76, 181, 184-185, 188, 192-201, 203-204, 206-208, 211-212,

216, 219–222, 234–236, 239, 257, 259, 296, 305, 324, 338, 446, 449, 452, 454–456, 460, 465–470, 477, 479–481, 486–487, 535, 543, 567, 589, 593, 650, 662
Gold Coast (Ghana), 76, 338, 647
Goldman, P.L.A., 250
gold standard, 197, 305, 452, 454, 456
Goldstone, Richard, 426
Gomas, John, 558
Gonaqua, 60, 93
Godongwana, Enoch, 674
Gondwana, 23–25, 27–28, 30
Goniwe, Matthew, 393
Gonnema, 44, 49
Gool, Zainunissa (Cissie), 325, 558
Goonam, Dr, 580
Gorachouqua, 44
Gordonia, 158
Gordon, Robert Jacob, 60, 64
Gore, Al, 522
Goringhaicona, 44
Goringhaiqua, 44
Government of National Unity (GNU), 410, 427, 433, 493, 495, 500, 660
Gqozo, Oupa, 430
Graaff, De Villiers, 352, 405
Graaff-Reinet, 79, 107, 113–114, 132–135, 139, 146, 237, 253
Graham, John, 88, 94
Grahamstown, 92, 96–97, 107, 140, 210
Graham's Town Journal, 140
grand apartheid, 331
granite, 21, 26, 470
Great Britain, 12, 61, 79–81, 88, 90, 101, 135, 151–152, 157, 162, 166, 170, 172, 176, 179, 182–183, 185–186, 188–190, 194, 197–198, 203–206, 209, 213, 217, 220–221, 224–225, 227, 232, 235–237, 239–242, 247, 254, 259, 261, 266–268, 270, 277–278, 281, 285, 287–288, 293–294, 299, 302–303, 308–309, 312, 316–317, 334, 341, 353, 363, 368–369, 383, 387, 409, 415, 433, 449, 450, 452, 454–455, 458–459, 475–476, 478–482, 500, 520, 576, 589–591, 593–594, 596, 598, 600–608, 610, 614, 658
Great Trek, 101, 104–106, 125–128, 131–132, 135–136, 153–154, 165, 174, 206, 226, 302, 307, 559, 589, 603, 648–649
Great Zimbabwe, 37, 644
Greece, 479
Green Market Square, 83
Greenpeace, 658
green revolution, 633
Greig, George, 103
Grey, George, 159, 163, 226
Grey, Henry, 82
Grey College, 232
Greyling, Abraham, 100
Griekwastad, 109, 157
Griqua(s), 11, 55, 63, 88, 106, 108–113, 115–116, 118, 120, 151–152, 156–158, 179, 182–183, 189–190, 232, 547
Griqualand East, 157, 160

Griqualand West, 158, 182–183, 190, 203, 553
Grobler, Jackie, 11–12, 155, 313, 374
Groblersdal, 120
Groenewald, Pieter, 672
Groenkop, Battle of, 248
Groote Kerk, 58, 83
Grootvadersbosch, 101
Groot Vlug, Die, 293
gross domestic product (GDP), 212, 440, 444, 462
Group Areas Act, 271, 330, 343, 346, 402, 563, 614
Group of Ten, 390
Grove Primary School, The, 533
Gudaos (Skaapdrif), 60
guerrilla warfare, 245–246, 249, 254–255, 265, 362, 363, 366–367, 383–384, 388–389, 391, 399, 403, 415–416, 418, 655–656
Guguletu, 394
Guinea, 46
Gujarat, Gujarati, 575, 587
Gumede, Josiah, 319, 322
Gunn, G.H., 580
Gun War, 164
Gupta family, 586, 666–667, 669
Guy, Jeff, 647
Gxarha River, 646

Haas, Paulus (Daalie), 85
Habana, 93
Haffejee, Hoosen Mia, 582
Hain, Peter, 561
Hallett, Robin, 347
Halstead, Thomas, 142
Halt All Racist Tours, 567
Hamis, 65
Hananwa, 39
Hanekom, Derek, 511
Hani, Chris, 500
Hankey, 88
Hanover, 79
Hanover Park, 563
Hantam, 52, 64, 137
harbours, 80, 83, 138, 195, 199–200, 211, 214, 216–217, 219, 234, 314, 318, 415, 468–469, 472
Harris, John, 385
Harris, Karen, 12, 533
Harris v Minister of the Interior, 562
Harrismith, 217, 280
Harrison, George, 181, 193
Hartebeespoort Dam, 453
Hartebeesthoek, 354
Hartenaars, 111
Harts River, 111, 182
Harvard College, 155
Hasselt, 46
Havenga, N.C. (Klasie), 280, 309, 328
Hawkes, Abiathar, 94
Healdtown, 496, 611
Heath, Willem, 514
Hebrew, 227, 291
Heidelberg, 177, 216
Heidelberg Tavern attack, 572
Heilbron, 138, 657

helium, 19
helots telegramme, 241, 594
Helpmekaar Vereniging, 295–296, 459
Hemel-en-Aarde, 87
Hendrickse, Allan, 571
Hendricks, Krom, 553
Hendriks, Hendrik, 111
Hendrik Verwoerd Dam, 453
Henning, Harold, 584
handsuppers and joiners, 252, 261
health care & matters, 76, 196, 202, 404, 478, 490–491, 502, 507, 513–514, 544–545, 553, 580, 660
Here XVII, 42–43, 46–49, 58, 61–62
Herenigde (Reunited) National Party, 605
Herry the beachcomber (see Autshumao)
Herschel, 199
Herstigte (Reconstituted) National Party, 351–352
Hertzog, Albert, 351
Hertzog, J.B.M., 261, 267–270, 273–274, 276–279, 283, 286–289, 294–295, 298–299, 305–306, 308–309, 329, 448, 550, 556–559, 596, 598, 601, 603
Het Kaapsche Grensblad, 101
Het Nederduitsch Zuid-Afrikaansche Tijdschrift, 85
Het Volk Party, 261, 263, 282, 543, 596, 597
Het Volksblad, 290
Heunis, Chris, 406, 413
Heyns, Johan, 625, 630
Highland water scheme (Lesotho), 520
high treason, 100, 253, 265, 344, 380, 384, 496
Highveld Steel and Vanadium, 472
Hind Swaraj, 577
Hindu, Hindi, 291, 574–575, 587, 610
Hintsa, 96
Hitler, Adolf, 278, 308, 445
HIV/AIDS, 498, 502, 513–514, 523, 531, 544–546
Hlakwana, 112
Hlubi, 119, 121, 161–162
Hobhouse, Emily, 251
Hobson, J.A., 263
Hoernlé, Alfred, 436
Hoffman, Josias, 153, 163
Hofmeyr, Hoffie, 12, 443
Hofmeyr, Isabel, 650
Hofmeyr, Jan Hendrik (Kleinjan), 277
Hofmeyr, Jan Hendrik (Onze Jan), 170, 231–232, 234, 236, 261, 284, 298
Hofmeyr, J.H., 298, 306, 443, 459
Hofmeyr, W.A., 459–460
Hogan, Barbara, 545
Hogge, W.S., 151
holism, 267
Holkrans (Mthashana), 256
Holomisa, Bantu, 504
Holocene Epoch, 18, 29, 31, 35
homeland policy, 271, 337–340, 346, 349–350, 355–357, 359–360, 363, 385–386, 390, 392, 397–399, 407–409, 413–414, 429, 431–432, 437, 464–465, 510, 586, 615–616, 653–654, 659
hominid, 32
Homo erectus, 32, 35
Homo habilis, 32, 35
Homo sapiens, 33, 35, 640, 642
Homo sapiens sapiens, 33, 35

Hoogenhout, C.P., 229
Hooper, James, 90
Hoop van Suid-Afrika, Die, 285
Hoorn, 42
Hope, Christopher, 607
Hopetown, 179, 189
Hop, Hendrik, 60
Houd den Bul, 45
Houghton, 202, 533, 587
Houphouët-Boigny, Félix, 353
Hottentots-Holland, 47, 67
Hottentot (see also Khoekhoen/Khoikhoi), 11, 42, 45, 51, 100, 547
Huguenots, 47–48, 56, 58
Huisgenoot, Die, 290
human rights, 347, 352, 429, 515–516, 518–520, 524, 541
Human Rights Commission, 493
hunter (-gatherer), 32–34, 52–53, 60, 93, 96, 107, 109, 118, 156, 167–168, 215, 640–643, 647, 650
Huntington, Samuel, 440–441
Hurutshe, 39, 117–118, 120, 124
Hüsing, Henning, 48
hydrosphere, 17, 21–23

I am an African speech, 497
IBM, 475
Ice age (s), 28–29, 31, 35
ICU yase Natal, 483
Idutywa, 499
Immorality Act (1929), 329
Ireland (Irish), 90, 102, 170, 206, 242, 268, 589
immigrant(s), 101, 170, 206–207, 213–214, 229, 232–233, 292, 345, 449, 479, 481, 543, 545, 586, 588
imperialism, 80, 176, 204, 231, 234, 245, 260, 269, 287, 422, 596, 612
Imperial Light Horse Brigade, 594
import trade, 81, 186, 198, 200, 208–212, 221, 459, 461, 471, 602
Imvo Zabantsundu, 272, 315
Independent Democrats (ID), 504, 533
India, 25, 28, 36, 41, 43, 68, 80–81, 171, 182, 214, 284, 327, 342, 346, 358, 376, 537, 542, 574–579, 581, 586–587, 635
India, Council of, 43
Indians, 10, 12–13, 41, 81, 170–172, 189, 195, 202, 214, 254, 265–267, 271, 273–274, 293, 311, 313, 322–323, 325–327, 330–331, 333, 341, 343, 346, 357–358, 360–361, 370–371, 376, 380, 390–392, 398, 405–407, 409, 411, 421, 432, 434, 438, 444–445, 448, 473, 482, 490, 496, 503, 528, 538, 557, 563, 568, 571–572, 574–587, 592, 605, 612–613, 627
Indian Congress, South African, 327, 380, 387
Indian Council, South African, 358–359, 361, 370, 376, 378–379, 583
Indian Ocean, 147, 636
Indian Opinion, 577
Indonesia, 291
Industrial and Commercial Workers' Union (ICU), 298, 318, 482

Industrial Conciliation Act (1924, 1925, 1956), 272, 292, 332, 370, 457, 473, 484, 489
Industrial Development Corporation (IDC), 458, 461, 471
Industrial Revolution, 80, 181, 188, 204–205, 478
Industrial Workers of Africa (IWA), 482
industry, 26, 32, 35, 47, 155, 180, 185, 191–196, 198–199, 201, 204, 207, 212, 214, 216–221, 240, 303, 324–325, 332, 369, 394, 403, 417, 451, 454–456, 458, 460–461, 463, 465–472, 479–480, 484, 490, 518, 536–537, 543, 583, 593, 604, 635, 650, 658
Infanta River, 42
influx control, 337, 345, 356, 407–408, 474, 615
Information scandal, 372–373, 396
Inkatha (Freedom Party), 392–393, 398, 412, 423, 426–427, 429, 493, 517, 531, 627, 664–666, 672
insurance industry, 210, 214, 295, 459–460, 476–477
International Defence and Aid Fund, 387
internasionalists, 519
Iran, 369
Iron Age, 15, 34, 36–37, 39, 644
Isaacs, David, 554
Isaacs, Henry, 569
Ismael, Aboobaker, 516
Israel, 369
Italy (Italian), 194, 205, 413, 479, 603
ivory trade, 37, 39, 63, 112, 168, 215, 650, 662
Ivory Coast, 353, 542

Jabavu, John Tengu, 272, 314–315, 551
Jacobs, Katie, 70
Jagersfontein, 190, 212
Jameson, Leander Starr, 185–186, 236, 240, 595, 597–598
Jameson Raid, 170, 183, 204, 233, 236, 240, 594
Jansen, E.G., 336
Janse van Rensburg, J.F. (Hans), 309
Janssens, Jan Willem, 66–67
Jansz, David, 44
Jansz, Leendert, 42
Japan, 43, 439, 462, 469, 569, 635
Java, 43
Jeffery, Anthea, 517
Jeppe, 202
Jesus, Motjie, 564
Jews, 105, 216, 250, 479, 597–598, 607
João II, 41
Johannesburg, 26, 156, 181, 184, 186, 188, 194–196, 198, 202, 211, 216, 221, 240, 297, 301, 316, 318, 320–321, 324–325, 332, 337, 342–343, 346, 375, 378, 382–383, 385, 391, 412, 421, 466, 468, 472, 480, 482–483, 486, 496, 510, 533, 543, 570, 580, 593, 605, 617–619, 623, 626
Johannesburg Stock Exchange, 468, 472
Johannesburg Soviet (Provisional Joint Board of Control), 480
Johnson, Lydia, 554
Jones, D.I., 482
Jones, Rheinalt, 611
Jonker, W.D. (Willie), 629–630

Jordan, Pallo, 660
Joris, 90
Joubert, Christiaan Johannes, 194
Joubert, Isaac, 94
Joubert, Jan-Jan, 12–13, 525
Joubert, Piet, 176–178, 184, 242, 245
Jozini Dam, 453
Jupiter, 20–21
justice system, judiciary, 61, 66, 69, 100, 130, 132, 148, 226, 232, 260, 266, 311, 345, 409, 429, 433, 540, 555, 587, 608, 625, 632

Kaapmans, 44
Kaapvaal Craton, 15, 22–24, 26–27, 29–30
Kabega Park, 543
Kabwe, 389
Kadalie, Clements, 273, 298, 318–319, 482–483
Kajee, A.I., 579
Kalahari, 31, 34, 121, 156, 636, 639
Kalanga, 40
Kalden, Petrus, 48–49, 58–59
Kamdeboo, 64
Kamiesberg, 63, 110
Kanna Hy Kô Hystoe, 569
Kareeberg, 53
Karoo, 15, 29–31, 87, 114, 636–638, 640–641, 652
Kassa, 93–94
Kathrada, Ahmed, 582
Kat River, 93, 95–97, 111, 156–157
Kaunda, Kenneth, 362
Keate, Robert, 182, 190, 203
Keert de Koe, 45
Keet, Bennie, 614
Kei River, 96, 159–160
Keiskamma River, 60
Kekana Ndebele, 39, 167
Kelly, Michael, 90
Kemp, Jan, 295
Kenya, 31, 34–35, 435, 560
Kenyanthropus platyops, 35
Keppel-Jones, Arthur, 443
Kestell, J.D. (Vader), 307
Keys, Derek, 427, 495
Kgalagadi, 39, 124
Kgatla, 39, 117–120
Kgosana, Philip, 382
Khama, 124
Khami, 37
Khan, R.K., 579
Khoe, 43
Khoekhoen, Khoikhoi (also see Hottentots), 11, 33–34, 44–46, 49–53, 55, 58–60, 63, 81–82, 84–88, 93, 96–97, 100, 106, 111, 115, 156–157, 217, 313, 634, 643, 651
Khoisan, 53, 547, 564
Khumalo, 120
Khunwana, 124
Kies, Benjamin, 559–560
Kijkuyt, 45
Kimberley, 28, 30, 180, 188, 190–191, 196, 198–202, 209, 211–212, 224, 228, 232, 243–244, 258, 454, 466, 480, 543, 551, 553

Kimberlite magma, 15, 24, 28, 30
Kindergarten (Milner), 595
King William's Town, 386
Kirkwood, 134
Kirstenbosch, 45
Kissinger, Henry, 362–363
Kitchener, Horatio Herbert, 247–248, 250–252, 255, 257, 655–657
Klaarwater, 63, 88, 109–110
Klaassmits River, 107
Klipdrift, 343, 378, 617
Kliptown, 340, 373
Klomphaan, Willem, 75
Knersvlakte, 638
Kock, Jan, 243
Kodak, 475
Koeberg, 90, 353–354, 391, 400
Kok, Adam, 55, 62, 109–110, 112, 115–116, 123, 151–152
Kok II, Adam, 110–112
Kok III, Adam, 112, 157
Kok, Cornelius, 109–110
Kok II, Cornelius, 110
Kok, Kort Adam, 111
Kololo kingdom, 121
Kommagas, 158
Kommissieraad (Commission Board, Natal), 148
Koonap River, 96, 107, 128
Koöperatiewe Wijnbouersvereniging (KWV), 451
Korana, 11, 106, 108–112, 115, 118, 120, 156, 158, 182, 189–190
Koranta ea Becoana, 258
Kotane, Moses, 323, 325
Kotzé, J.G., 228
Kraaipan, 243
Kriel, Ashley, 570, 572
Kritzinger, Pieter, 255
Kromdraai, 32, 193
Kroonstad, 217, 245, 329
Kropf, Albert, 117
Krotoa (Eva), 44–45, 56
Krugel, Willem F., 100
Kruger, Jacob, 108
Kruger National Park, 659
Kruger, Paul, 10, 174–176, 178–179, 183–187, 198, 200–201, 204, 216, 228, 234, 236–237, 239–241, 247, 256, 303
Krugersdorp (Mogale City), 176, 193, 227
Kruithoring, Die, 279
Krygkor, 472, 474
Kuiper Belt, 21
KwaMashu, 341
KwaMatiwane, 143, 147
KwaZulu (homeland), 355, 392, 398–399, 412, 423
KwaZulu-Natal, 38–39, 106, 118–120, 160, 393, 504, 526, 528, 531, 587, 640, 647
Kwena (Bakwena), 39, 117–118, 124, 166

labour (market, laws), 46, 48, 53–54, 68, 70, 76, 79, 82, 84–92, 105, 118, 130–132, 136, 156, 164, 166, 171, 180, 191, 193–197, 200–202, 204, 207–208, 212–214, 217–219, 226, 253, 258–259, 262–264, 268, 296–297, 303, 324–325, 329, 332, 336, 356, 370, 380, 400, 402–404, 404, 414, 428, 439, 441–446, 448, 453–454, 457–458, 465, 467, 469, 470–471, 473–474, 478–491, 499, 502, 504–505, 536–537, 542–543, 545, 554, 556, 558, 564, 571, 574, 577, 579–580, 586, 592, 598, 619, 646
Labour Party, South African, 263, 268–269, 271, 297–299, 305, 482, 596–603, 605–606
Labour Party (Britain), 369, 545, 607
Labour Party (Coloured), 358, 360, 406, 571
Labour Relations Act, 489, 505
Labour Union (Witwatersrand Mine Employees' and Mechanics' Union), 479
Ladysmith, 243–244
Lagden Commission, 263–264
La Guma, James, 483, 486, 558
Laing, Sandra, 330
Laingsnek, 177–178, 243
Lala, 38
Lambert, John, 12, 558
Lambert, Kent, 567
Lamoela, Peter, 569
Land Bank, 451, 464, 540
Landbouweekblad, 290
Landless People's Movement, 541
Landman, Karel, 146
land reform, 495, 510, 540–541
Land van Waveren, 48
Langa, 341, 344–345, 381–382
Langalibalele, 161–162
Langa Ndebele, 39
Langenhoven, C.J., 283, 285, 289–290, 302
Langlaagte, 181, 193, 202
Language Monument, Afrikaans, 364
language rights, 428, 608
Laubser, J.H., 461
Laurasia, 23–25, 27
Lawrence, Harry, 605
Leballo, P.K., 380, 384–385, 389
Lebowa, 355
Lee-Metford rifle, 244
Leeuw, Eddie, 571
Lee-Warden, Len, 344
Leipoldt, C. Louis, 298
Lekota, Mosiuoa, 534
Leliefontein, 158, 255
Lemba, 38, 40, 106, 117
Lembede, Anton, 321–322
Lenasia, 587
Lenders, D.J., 555
Leon, Sonny, 360
Leon, Tony, 503
Lesotho, 34, 37, 39, 162, 191, 232, 254, 384, 415, 519–520
Le Sueur, Franciscus, 58
Letaba River (Klein & Groot), 192
Lewis, Gavin, 554
Lewis, Isaac, 201
Liberale nasionalisme, 300
Liberal Party (Britain), 255, 259, 543, 596

Liberal Party (South Africa), 378, 382, 608
liberalism, liberty, 59, 61, 64, 66, 175, 225, 262, 266–267, 271, 277, 306, 332, 335, 352, 354, 365, 367, 370, 386, 432, 434–436, 440–446, 466, 493, 496, 498, 503, 521, 525, 533, 548, 551–552, 556, 585, 589, 592, 609, 612, 615, 629
Liberty (Standard Bank), 476
Libya, 542
Lichtenburg, 180, 454
Liebenberg family, 138
Liebenberg, Chris, 595
Liesbeek River, 45
Lilliesleaf, 346, 383
Limpopo (River, Province), 31, 36, 38–40, 106, 135, 164, 168, 188, 377, 455, 532, 628
Links, Barnabas, 255
lithosphere, 633
Lloyd George, David, 255
Lobatse, 383
Lobedu, 167
local government, 43, 81, 114, 133–134, 148, 271, 356–357, 407, 411–412, 485, 510, 662
Lojale verset, 300
Lombard Bank, 82
Lomba River, 418–419
London, 65, 80, 92, 98, 103, 132, 168, 179, 197, 201, 233, 244, 266, 268, 270, 299, 331, 387, 491, 555, 560, 576, 580, 591, 601
London and South African Bank (LSAB), 210–211, 215, 217–218, 220
London, Convention of, 239, 241
London Missionary Society, 65, 87, 97, 109
Loskop Dam, 453
Lötter, J.C., 253
Louis XIV, 47
Louis from Bengal, 47
Louis from Mauritius, 90
Lourenço Marques, 137
Louw, Adriaan, 90
Louw, Mike, 417, 420
Louw, M.S., 460
Louw, N.P. van Wyk, 300, 309, 425
Lovedale, 314, 611
Lowveld, 37, 39, 450, 655
Lubbe, William, 570
Lusaka, 417
Lusaka Manifesto, 350
Lutchman, Arthur, 561
Lutherans, 58, 629
Luthuli, Albert, 336, 344, 377–378, 381–382, 384, 387, 619
Lydenburg (see Mashishing)
Lyster, Thomas, 94

Mabhudu, 119
Mabuza, David, 668–669, 672, 674
Machadodorp, 246
Machel, Samora, 415–416
MacKay, Ensign, 98
Maclons, Kulu, 568
Macmillan, Harold, 340–341, 345
MacMillan, W.M., 125

Madagascar, 25, 28, 46, 54, 68, 548
Madeley, Walter, 601, 604
Madlathule famine, 648
Madoersrif (Spring Valley), 99
Madonsela, Adv. Thuli, 664, 667
Madras, 81, 574, 576
Mafeking (also Mafikeng, Mahikeng), 124, 243–244, 256, 258, 431, 538
Magaliesberg, 120, 150, 172, 174
Magellan, Straits of, 43
Magersfontein, 243
Magmoed, Shaun, 572
Mahabane, Z.R., 319
Maharaj, Mac, 582
Maha Sabha, Hindu, 575
Mahlangwe, 649
Mahomed, Hajee, 575
Mahomed, Ismail, 587
Mahomo, Nana, 389
Mahura, 651
Maimane, Musi, 665, 673
Maitland, Peregrine, 152
maize production, 171, 191, 209, 213–214, 216–218, 450, 463–464, 647–648, 656
majority rule, 353, 373, 421, 424, 585
(A)Majuba, 177–179, 227, 239, 593
Makapansgat (valley), 32, 167
Makatees (Mantatees), 123
Makgatho, Sefako, 317–319
Makiwane, Tennyson, 388–389
Makonde, 40
Makuleka community, 649
Makwana, 138
Malacca, 56
Malan, D.F., 269, 276–278, 280, 284, 288–290, 293–295, 299–300, 305, 308–311, 329, 581, 603, 605
Malan, F.S., 236, 284, 298
Malan, Nico, 359
Malan, Sailor, 334
Malan, Wynand, 253
Malawi, 40, 318, 350, 482
Malays, Cape, 55, 68, 89, 547, 549, 556, 574
Malema, Julius, 525, 532, 546, 673
Malherbe, E.G., 298, 304
Malvern, 202
Mamathola, 377
Mamelodi, 394, 398
Mamelukes, 61
Mamre, 82, 85, 87
Manala Ndebele, 38
Mandela, Nelson, 321, 330, 344–346, 377, 382–384, 410, 413, 415, 417, 420–423, 425, 428–430, 432–433, 438–439, 444, 494–501, 509, 511, 513, 518–519, 523–524, 530, 541, 585, 611, 619, 628, 670
mandoors, 54
manganese, 26, 455, 470
Mangope, Lucas, 430–431
Manifesto, Lusaka, 350
Manifesto, Non-European People's, 326
Manifesto, Piet Retief's, 140
Mannenberg – 'Is where it's Happening, 565
Manthatisi, 121–123

INDEX

Manuel, Trevor, 497, 507–508, 571
Mao Zedong, 445
Mapungubwe, 36–37, 40
Maputo, 39, 119, 137, 184, 200, 649
Maqoma, 97
Marabastad, 192
Marais, B.J. (Ben), 614, 618, 631
Marais, Eugène, 284
Marais, Jaap, 351
Marais, Jannie, 290–291
Marais, Jan S., 461
Marais, Peter, 572
Marais, P.J., 192
Marais, Willie, 351
Maria from Bengal, 55
Marico, 113, 172, 174, 186, 216, 377
Marico River, 39, 120
Marikana massacre 536, 671
Maritz, Gert (Gerrit), 131, 137, 139–142, 144, 146, 148
Maritz, Manie, 255
Maritz, Susanna Maria, 139
Marketing Act, 451, 465
Marks, J.B., 323–325, 486
Marks, Sammy, 193, 195, 201
Marquard, Leo, 298
Mars, 20–21, 436
Martindale, 337
Masakhane Project, 510
Maseru, 384–385, 571
Mashaba, Herman, 673
Mashabela, Reneiloe (MP), 665
Mashishing (Lydenburg), 119, 150–151, 165, 181, 192, 216
Matabele, 39
Matanzima, Kaiser, 385
Mathakgong, 256
mathematics, 333, 512
Matiwane, 117, 119, 121, 123–124
Matthews, Joe, 322
Matthews, Z.K., 344, 378, 438
Mauch, Karl, 192
Mauritius, 90, 214
Mauser rifles, 186
Maximov, Yevgeny, 245
Maya civilisation, 647
Mayfair, 202
Mayibuye, 388
Mayibuye, Operation, 384
Maynardville, 331
Maynier, Honoratus, 62–64
Mbata, Congress, 322
Mbeki, Epainette, 499
Mbeki, Govan, 346, 384
Mbeki, Thabo, 420, 493, 495, 497–502, 507, 513–514, 520–524, 526–531, 538–539, 542, 544–545, 587
Mbekweni, 341, 384–385
Mbenga, Bernard, 10–11, 68
Mbewuleni, 599
Mbholompo, Battle of, 124
Mbo, 38

McIntyre, William, 577
McKenzie, Precious, 554
Mda, A.P., 321–322
Mdlalose, Frank, 531
Meat Board, 451
mechanisation, 101, 453, 464, 490
Meer, Ismail, 587
Meiring, Georg, 431, 433
Melrose Hose, 248
Melvill, John, 111, 118
Memoirs of the Boer War, 282
Memorable Order of Tin Hats (MOTHS), 604
Mentzel, Otto, 70, 73
M.E.R. (M.E. Rothmann), 235, 288
Mercury, 21
Merriman, John X., 261–262, 266, 554, 592, 594–597
meteorite(s), 15, 20, 25, 29, 31
Methuen, Lord, 243
Methodist Church, 496, 590, 611, 616, 618–619, 621–622, 625–629
Mexico, 76, 647
Meurant, Louis, 101, 140
Meyer, Andrie, 11, 17
Meyer, Andries, 99
Meyer, Leon, 571
Meyer, Lukas, 179, 245
Meyer, Pieter, 48
Meyer, Roelf, 427, 504
Mfecane, 11, 105–107, 109, 112–113, 116–124, 130, 207
Mfengu, 121, 199
Mfolozi River, 119–120
Mgungundhlovu, 139, 143
Mhudi, 258
Mianmar (Burma), 541
Middelburg (Mpumalanga), 136
Middelburg (Eastern Cape), 253, 394
migrant labour, 191, 196, 254, 336, 407, 445, 467, 483, 619
migration, 11, 105, 109, 113–114, 116–117, 139, 206, 336, 564, 578, 586, 638, 644, 648–649
military service, 52, 85, 252, 255, 272, 278, 599
Mills Report, 359
Milner, Alfred, 186–187, 204, 221–222, 237, 240–241, 251, 259–262, 264, 282, 555, 594–596
minerals & mining, 20, 22–24, 26–27, 29–30, 153, 160, 182–183, 188–204, 206–207, 213–214, 216, 218, 221, 235, 264, 340, 353, 379, 387, 402–403, 454–456, 458, 463–465, 467, 469–471, 473, 477, 479, 483, 492, 527, 530, 535, 543, 588, 649, 660
Mines, Chamber of, 196, 296, 325, 482, 484
Mineworkers' uprising (strike, 1922), 296–298
Minority Front, 526
Minutes of Understanding (1992), 427
Miranda, Michael, 572
Mitchell, Brian, 561
mixed marriages, 277–278, 329, 357, 401, 414, 435, 614
Mkaliphi, 138, 141
Mkwatleng, 123
Mlanjeni (War), 156, 158

706 INDEX

M.L. Sultan Technical College, 579, 583
Mmabatho, 360
Mmalebôgô, 246
Modder River, 115, 189
Modjadji, 168
Modjadjis Kloof, 167
Moffat, Robert, 65, 112, 118, 124
Mogoeng Mogoeng, Chief Justice, 667
Mokgatlha, 124
Mokone, Mangena, 314
Mokôpane, 167
Moletsane, 122–123
Molopo River, 39, 119, 167
Molotsi, Peter, 389
Molteno, 387
Molteno, John Charles, 166, 232
Molteno, J.T., 232
Mondale, Walter, 363
Montague, Ivor, 561
Montreal Protocol, 635
Montshiwa, 122, 166
Moodie, Benjamin, 101
Moordspruit, 144
Moor, Frederick R., 261
Moosa, Valli, 587, 660
Moravian Missionary Society, 51, 59, 82, 87
Moritsane Hill, 39
Morogoro, 388
Moroka (Soweto suburb), 321
Moroka, Chief, 124, 138–139, 151
Moroka, James, 323, 343, 375, 377
Mosega, 113, 120, 141
Moshoeshoe, 106, 116, 122–124, 151–153, 162–164
Mosielele, Kgosi, 166
Mossel Bay, 41, 646
Motlana, Nthato, 390, 591
Motlanthe, Kgalema, 530, 539, 545, 671
motor industry, 457–459, 469, 471, 475, 486, 488, 490
Motsoaledi, Aaron, 545
Mouille, 83
Mount Prospect, 178
Mozambique, 38–39, 68, 117–120, 184, 191, 196, 222, 240, 353, 361, 365–366, 386, 389, 391, 403, 409, 415–416, 519, 548, 650
Mpande, 160, 164
Mpangazitha, 121
Mpanza, James, 320
Mphephu, Chief, 168
MPLA (Angola), 365–366
Mpondo, 38, 117, 121
Mpondomise, 38
Mpumalanga, 38–39, 106, 164, 167, 181, 188, 455, 636
Mthatha, 360, 496, 499
Mthatha River, 117, 124
Mthethwa, 119
Mugabe, Robert, 520–521, 541
Muizenberg, 65
Mulder, Connie, 372–373, 408
Mulder, Pieter, 673
Mulholland, Stephen, 445
Munnik, Gerrit, 51
Murray, Andrew, 104, 589
Murraysburg, 253
Muslim (Islam), 55, 58, 66, 76, 229, 546–547, 549, 574–575, 579, 587, 610
Myburgh, James, 498
Mzilikazi, 39, 106, 109, 112–113, 116, 120, 122, 124, 138, 141–144, 165
Mzimkulu River, 157
Mzimvubu River, 38, 142–143, 145, 147, 157
Mzinyathi River, 120

Naicker, Monty, 326–327, 580–582
Naidoo, H.A., 580
Naidoo, Jay, 585
Nair, Billy, 582
Nama, 34, 88, 156, 158
Namaqua, 44
Namaqualand, 60, 65, 158, 212, 454, 638
Namibia, 60, 64–65, 135, 264, 294, 341, 361, 363, 366, 418–420, 454, 636, 639
Namib desert, 637
Nantes, Edict of, 47
Napier, George, 148, 152
Napoleon Bonaparte, 79
Napoleonic wars, 82–83, 97, 101, 107
Nasionale Pers, 290, 517
Nasrec, 668–669, 671, 673
Natal (also see KwaZulu–Natal), 11, 42, 106–107, 135–137, 139, 142, 144–145, 147–150, 152, 154–155, 160–161, 170–172, 177–178, 182, 188, 196, 199, 206, 208, 210, 213–215, 219, 221–222, 226, 233, 243–244, 246, 248, 252–254, 258, 261, 263–265, 267, 269, 271, 276, 288, 307, 315, 326, 392, 397, 399, 412, 423, 450, 453, 455, 482–483, 574–579, 584, 588–594, 597, 601–602, 606–608, 627, 649–650, 653, 655
Natal Bank, 214–215
Natalia, Republic of, 147, 150
Natal Indian Congress, 326–327, 361
Natal Indian Organisation, 326
Natal Native Congress, 315
Natal, University of, 386
National Anti-Corruption Forum, 514
National Assembly, 427, 493, 526
National Association for Clean Air, 658
National Bank, 215
National Bank of the Orange Free State, 218
National Convention, 263, 265–266, 286, 315–316, 596
National Council of Provinces, 494
National Council of the Non-European Unity Front (NEUF), 580
National Council of Trade Unions (NACTU), 488
National Democratic Revolution (NDR), 539–541
National Environmental Management Act, 661
national executive committee (NEC), 320, 323, 378, 388, 499, 670
National Health and Allied Workers' Union (NEHAWU), 491

National Intelligence Service (NIS), 417, 420, 516
nationalisation, 379, 441, 443–444, 506–507, 532, 536
National Liberation League (NLL), 558–559
national parks, 34, 36, 634, 659, 662
National Party (NP), 12, 224, 267, 271, 281, 287–288, 298–299, 311, 328, 345, 349, 351–352, 374, 396, 435, 451, 453, 464, 484, 493–494, 525, 532, 560, 562, 572, 581, 585, 598, 600–601, 612–615, 657, 660
national prosecuting authority, 513, 531, 674
National Scouts, 252
National Socialism, 309
National Union, 594
National Union of Mineworkers (NUM), 394, 467, 488, 536, 670
National Union of South African Students (NUSAS), 386
National-Minded Bloc, 375
National Water Act, 661
Native Life in South Africa, 258
Native Refugee Department, 257
Native Building Workers Act (1951), 332
Native Convention, South African, 266, 316
Native Labour Regulation Act (1911), 271
Native Labour Settlement of Disputes Act (1953), 332, 488, 558
Native Laws Commission (Fagan Commission), 329, 335, 613
Native Representation Act, 276–277
Native Representative Council, 277, 315–316, 336, 615
Natives (Abolition of Passes and Co-ordination of Documents) Act, 337
Natives Economic Commission, 652
Natives Land Act (1913), 258, 264, 271–272, 317, 610
Native Resettlement Act (Black Spots Act, 1954), 337
Native Trust and Land Act, 277
Natives Urban Areas Act (1923), 319
Natref, 354
nature conservation, 640, 659
Naudé, Beyers, 619–620, 631
Nautilus, 102
Nazi Germany, 250, 278, 309, 417, 435, 533, 603
Ncapayi, 149
Ncome River (Blood River), 146–147, 227, 307
Ndebele, 38–39, 106, 108–109, 112–113, 116, 120, 122, 124, 138–139, 141–143, 165–167
Ndlambe, 93–97, 158
Ndlela, 143, 146
Ndwandwe, 119–120
Ndzundza Ndebele, 38, 167
necklace murders, 392, 412
Nedbank, 220, 475–476
Nederburgh, Sebastiaan, 62
Nederlandsche Bank voor Zuid-Afrika, De, 220
Nederlandsche Zuid-Afrikaansche Spoorweg-Maatschappij (NZASM), 184
Nehru, Jahawarlal, 342
Nellmapius, Alois, 201

Nel, Willem, 99
Nelson, Joan, 440–441
Nelspruit, 249
Nena, 22, 24, 27, 29
Netshitenzhe, Joel, 507
Nevirapine, 514
New Age, 375
Newcastle, 472
Newclare, 337
New History of South Africa, 10, 14, 68
New National Party (NNP), 493, 495, 503–504
New Partnership for Africa's Development (Nepad), 521, 523
New Republic, 161, 179
New Republic Party (NRP), 370
New Rush mine, 190
New Testament, 416, 614
New York Accord, 391
Ngangelizwe, 160
Ngema, Mbongeni, 586
Ngqika, 93–97, 99, 158, 651
Ngqueno, 93
Ngubane, Jordan, 321
Nguni (speakers), 11, 38, 60, 106 107, 116–117, 158, 160–161, 164, 646, 648
Ngwaketse, 118
Ngwane, 119, 121, 123–124
Nhlanganu, 39
Nico Malan theatre, 359
Nieuwe Haerlem, 42
Nieuwoudt, T.K., 255
Nigel, 193, 371
Nigeria, 519, 545
Nixon, Richard, 353
Nkandla, 530, 664
Nkomati Accord, 391, 409, 416
Nkomo, Joshua, 388
Nkrumah, Kwame, 342
Nkuna, 39
Nkwinti, Gugile, 540
Nobel Peace Prize, 497
No Easy Choice: Political Participation in Developing Countries, 440
Nokwe, Duma, 322
Non-European People's Manifesto, 326
Non-European United Front (NEUF), 325–326, 558–559, 580
Non-European Unity Movement, 325, 559
non-governmental organisations (NGO), 630, 635, 658
Nongqawuse, 159, 646
Nooitgedacht, 248–249
Northern Cape, 179, 294, 468, 636
North West Province, 118, 166, 628
Norway, 635
Ntungwa, 38
Nujoma, Sam, 363, 418
Nuwe Orde (New Order), 300–310
Nxaba, 120
Nxele (Makhanda, Lynx), 96
Nyabela, 167
Nzimande, Blade, 529

Nzobo, Dambuza, 143, 146
Nzobo, Ndlela, 143, 146

Obama, Barack, 435
Obasanjo, Olusegun, 519
Oberholzer, Michiel, 152
Obiqua, 53
Odendaal, André, 265–266
Ohrigstad, 150, 165
Okavango, 113
Olafsson, Jon, 42
Oldasoa, 44
Old Guard (United Party), 352
Old Mutual, 476
Old Testament, 73
Olifants River (Cape), 87
Olifants River (Mpumalanga), 192, 453
Oliphant, 43
Oldupai (Olduvai), 32
Omar, Dullah, 587
Onderstepoort, 450–451
Onrust River, 87
Ons Eerste Fabrieken, 216
Ons Land, 236, 290
Oorlogsdagboek, 235
Op die vooraand van apartheid, 311
Operation Carlota, 366
Operation Mayibuye, 384
Operation Savannah, 365–366
Ophirton, 202
Oppenheimer, Harry, 445, 466–467
Oppenheimer, Ernest, 466
Opperman, D.J., 300
Orange Free State, 317, 455–456, 555, 590, 650
Orange Free State, Republic of, 153, 155, 162–163, 175, 183–184, 186, 190, 199, 200, 204, 215–218, 226, 231, 241, 261, 305
Orange River (Groot River, Gariep River), 53, 60, 64, 106–107, 136–137, 140–141, 151–152, 172, 231, 453
Orange River Colony, 248, 252, 259, 261, 265, 282–283, 315, 596
Orange River Colony Volunteers, 252
Orange River Sovereignty, 151–152, 162
Orangia Unie, 261, 282, 596
ORC Native Congress, 315
Orderson, Derrick, 568
Ordinance 50 (1828), 128, 130, 133
Orex line, 468
Organisation of African Unity (OAU), 350, 353, 362, 365–366, 368–369, 388–389
Oriental Bank Corporation, 210
Orlando, 320, 380–382
Orrorin tugenensis, 31, 34
Ossewabrandwag (OB), 309–310
ostrich farming, 200, 209, 216–217
Othello, 331
Oudtshoorn, 200
Ovis aries, 36
Ovis orientalis, 36
Owen, C.M., 151
Owen, Francis, 142–143
ozone, 635

Paardeberg, 178, 244, 246, 248, 252
Paardekraal, 176, 193, 227
Paarl, 47, 223, 228, 280, 292, 295, 334, 364, 384, 460, 497
Pacaltsdorp, 88
Pact government, 268–269, 274, 298–300, 303, 451, 484–485, 601
Pahad, Essop, 587
Palace of Justice, 184
Palestine, 105
Pan-Africanist Congress (PAC), 344–345, 350, 380–382, 384–389, 421, 432, 504
Pan-African Parliament, 520
Pangaea, 22–24, 27, 30
Pannevis, Arnoldus, 229
Paraguay, 369
parallel development, 357, 359–360
Park station, Johannesburg, 385
Paris, 197, 387
Paris Evangelical Society, 124
Parys, 138
pass law system, 128, 130, 180, 197, 270, 317–318, 329, 337, 343–344, 356, 376–377, 379, 381, 401–402, 407, 414, 417, 481, 615, 618, 653
Patel, Ebrahim, 570
paternalism, 70–71, 257, 386
Paton, Alan, 328, 617
Payne, Jill, 645
Pedi, 39, 117, 119–120, 122, 164–165, 191, 255, 313
pedosphere, 634
Pegging Act, 326
Peires, Jeff, 646
Pelindaba, 354
Pennisetum glaucum, 36
Pennisetum typhoides, 36
People's Liberation Army of Namibia (PLAN), 363
Peru, 57, 76, 647
Peter and Paul, 49
Peters, Sandra, 570
Phalaborwa Complex, 15, 24, 26, 30
Phanerozoic Eon, 18, 23, 25
Phijffer, Johannes, 48
philantropists, 90–91, 131, 140
Philip, John, 88, 91, 111
Philippolis, 111, 115, 123
Philipps, Thomas, 102
Philips, 458
Phillips, Lionel, 188, 530
Phiring, 165
Phoenix, 577, 582, 587
P(h)ongola River, 119–120
Phosa, Mathews, 501
Phuting, 112
Piekenierskloof, 52
Pienaar, Francois, 494
Pienaar, Petrus, 64–65
Pietermaritzburg, 148, 214, 227, 382, 608
Pietersburg (Polokwane), 181, 184, 628
Pieterson, Galima, 571
Pieterson, Hector, 367
Piet Retief (emKhondo) (town), 330

INDEX 709

Piketberg, 52, 62, 64
Pilanesberg (volcano), 15, 24, 27
Pilgrim's Rest, 181, 192
Pillay, Milo, 560
Pinnock, Don, 562–563
Pirow, Oswald, 277, 309
Pitt, William, 79
Plaatje, Sol, 256, 258, 316
platinum, 26, 455, 466–467, 469–470, 536
Player, Gary, 584
Pleistocene Epoch, 18, 28, 31, 35
Plettenberg beacon, 107, 114
Pliocene Epoch, 18
Pluto, 21
Pniel, 258
police, 69, 71, 171, 196–197, 264, 294, 296–297, 318, 325, 330, 341, 344, 346, 367, 375–376, 378, 381–386, 389–390, 393, 397, 400, 412, 414, 421, 426, 433, 482, 487, 509, 515–516, 533, 536–537, 545, 564, 570–572, 578, 618, 624, 628
Political Council, 58, 65
Politie, Raad van (Council of Policy), 141
Pollsmoor, 497
Polokwane (also see Pietersburg), 181, 184, 527–529, 628
Pol Pot, 445
pom-pom gun, 186
Pondoland, 160, 377
Pongolapoort Dam, 453
Pongola River, 543
Ponnen, George, 580
poor whites, 194–196, 202, 304
Popham, Home, 67
Population Registration Act, 330, 414, 543, 614
populism, 441, 529
Poqo, 345, 384, 385
Port Elizabeth, 200, 211, 217, 457, 561, 563–564, 566–567, 608
Port Elizabeth Bank, 210
Porter, William, 262
Port Natal (also see Durban), 137, 142, 149
Portugal, 80, 249, 353, 361, 363, 409
Portuguese-India, 41
Portuguese, 10, 37, 39, 41–42, 76–77, 118, 137–138, 184, 189, 194, 221–222, 361, 365–367, 389, 403, 479, 550, 647
post apartheid, 446, 568, 585–587
Postma, Dirk, 175
Potchefstroom, 148–150, 152, 172, 177, 216, 283, 424
Potgieter, Andries, 162, 165
Potgieter, F.J., 649
Potgieter, Hendrik, 136–138, 140–142, 144–146, 149–152, 165, 168, 172, 174
Potgieter, Piet, 167, 174
Potgietersrus (Piet-), 167
poverty, 75, 79, 84, 90, 156, 158, 185, 195, 204, 210, 215, 248, 252, 259, 293, 303–304, 307, 347, 356, 407–408, 413, 439, 445, 501, 506, 514–515, 523, 530, 537–538, 555–556, 559, 564, 579–580, 586, 599, 631–632
power sharing, 371, 399, 406, 423–425, 494–495

pragmatists, 519
Preller, Gustav, 145, 284, 286, 298
Presbyterian Church, 104, 590, 611, 614, 616, 622, 626
President's Council, 407
press (newspapers), 85, 103, 140, 170, 202, 224–225, 227, 229–232, 236–237, 241, 247, 266, 272, 285, 289–290, 292, 303, 314–316, 323, 326, 351–352, 364, 367, 371–373, 390–391, 396–397, 426, 432, 437, 440, 498, 517, 522, 533, 577, 590–591, 593–594, 597, 601–603, 608, 620, 623
Pretoria, 29, 38, 106, 120, 165, 175–178, 183–184, 186, 216, 227, 240, 245, 248–249, 252, 257, 270, 282, 284, 285, 288, 301, 307, 317, 324, 343, 379, 385, 391–392, 394, 400, 415, 430, 451, 454, 472, 513, 515–516, 518, 544, 614, 622, 655, 656
Pretoria, Convention of, 239
Pretoria, University of, 451
Pretorius, Andries, 146–148, 150–151, 153, 172, 174–175
Pretorius, Fransjohan, 12, 14, 239
Pretorius, M.W., 167, 174–175, 182
Prieska, 453
Pringle, Thomas, 102–103, 590
Prinsloo, Dionē, 14
Prinsloo, Hendrik Petrus (Kasteel), 99–100
Prinsloo, Marthinus (Anglo-Boereoorlog), 246, 248
Prinsloo, Marthinus (Graaff-Reinet), 64
Privy Council, 270
Progressive Federal Party (PFP), 370, 406, 466
Progressive Party (PP), 345, 354, 369, 466, 533, 595, 608
Progressive Reform Party (PRP), 369, 466
Prohibition of Mixed Marriages Act, 329, 357, 614
Promotion of Bantu Self-Government Act, 339, 616
Proot, Matthijs, 42
prostitution, 201–202
protectionism, 448, 453, 459, 471
Protection of State Information Act, 665

Proterozoic Eon, 18, 22, 24

Quinlan, S.C., 603
Quinn, Jackie, 571
Quinn, Leung, 543
Qulusi, 256
Qwaqwa, 355

Radio Freedom, 388
railways, 155, 184, 195, 199–200, 211–212, 215, 221–222, 240, 246, 249, 262, 297, 302–303, 354, 362, 376, 416, 449, 455, 458, 468, 485–487, 490, 553, 563, 655
Ramaphosa, Cyril, 394, 467, 488, 501, 668–674
Ramayana, 575
Ramos, Maria, 508
Ramsamy, Sam, 582
Rand Merchant Bank, 477
Rand Central Electric Works Limited, 201
Rand Club, 202
Rand Daily Mail, The, 444, 533

Rand Easter Show, 342
Randlords, 194, 201–202
Rand Mines Limited, 194
Rangasamy, G.K., 561
Rapport, 223, 337
Rarabe, 93
Ras, Catharina (Trijn), 56
Rasnick, David, 514
Rautenbach, P.S., 659
raw materials, 80, 210, 449, 459, 468
Read, James, 87
Reader's Digest Illustrated History of South Africa, 10
Reagan, Ronald, 418–419, 475
Rebellion, 1914–1915, 294–295, 422
Reconstruction and Development Programme (RDP), 495, 501, 507
redistribution of wealth, 421, 441, 507
Red Oath (Africa Oath), 604
rainbow nation, 104, 494, 524, 631
referendum, tricameral parliament (1983), 391, 406
referendum, constitutional (1992), 424–425, 430
referendum, Natal, 265
referendum, republican (1960), 341–342, 607
Reform Committee, 186, 240
Reformed Church (Nederduitsche Hervormde Kerk), 175, 610, 612–613, 617, 624
Reform League, 593
Reijger, 43
Reitz, Deneys, 244, 296, 298
Rembrandt Group, 308, 460
remonstrantie (report), 42
Renamo, 415–416
Renoster River, 138
Researches in South Africa, 88
Reserve Bank, 464, 475, 669
Retief, Piet, 48, 128, 130, 139–148, 286
Retief-Dingane treaty, 143, 145, 147–148
Reuters, 591
Revolutionary Council (ANC), 388
Reynders Commission, 474
Rhenish Missionary Society, 87, 549
Rhode, Abraham, 564
Rhodes, Cecil John, 170, 185–186, 192, 194, 204, 212, 230, 234, 236, 240, 551, 594, 596
Rhodes Cup, 553, 560
Rhodes, Frank, 185
Rhodes University, 611, 617
Rhodesia (see also Zimbabwe), 222, 361–363, 366, 373, 388, 403, 418, 608
Rhodesia, Southern, 222
Rhoodie, Eschel, 372–373
Richards Bay, 354, 468–469
Richardson, Lallam, 564
Richtersveld, 34, 158, 638
Riet River, 128, 152
Ricketts, Colin, 566
rinderpest, 195, 652
Rissik, Johann, 194
Rivonia, 346, 383–384, 496, 564
Road to South African Freedom, 388
Robben Island, 158, 162, 386, 422, 496, 530, 582
Roberts, Lord, 178, 244–247, 249–250, 259, 655

Roberts, W.A., 554
Robertson, William, 104, 235
Robinson, John, 594
Rodinia, 22, 24, 27, 30
Rolland, Samuel, 123
Rolong (Barolong), 39, 109, 112–113, 117–119, 121–122, 124, 138–139, 151, 166, 182, 190, 252, 256, 258
Roman Catholics, 58, 610–611, 620, 622, 627
Roman-Dutch law, 226
Rondebosch, 45
Roodepoort, 186, 193
Roodewal, 245
Roodezand, 52, 58
Rooigrond, 179
Roos, Tielman, 269
Roosevelt, Franklin D., 321
Rorke's Drift, 161
Rose-Innes, James, 104
Round Table, 309
Rousseau, lieutenant, 98–99
Rousseau, P.E., 461
Roux, Paul, 47
Royal African Company, 76
Royal Air Force (RAF), 604–605
Royal Flying Corps, 599
Royal Navy, 591, 599, 602, 604
Rubicon speech, 413, 421, 628
Rubusana, Walter, 314
Rudd, Charles, 192
Rupert, Anton, 308, 312, 417, 460
Rupert, Johann, 477
Ruskin, John, 577
Russia (USSR, Russians), 105, 194, 245, 247, 323, 326, 366, 418, 479, 537, 542
Rustenburg church discussions, 628
Rustenburg Declaration, 629
Rustenburg (Z.A.R. and North West Province), 27, 81, 83, 120, 175, 215, 256, 536
Rwanda, 519, 542, 545

sabotage, 309, 346, 383–384, 400, 422, 487, 496
Sabotage Act, 487
Sadie, Jan, 445
Sahelanthropus tchadensis, 31, 34
Sak River, 53
Saldanha Bay, 42, 47, 468, 472
Saldanha steel, 354
Salisbury, Lord, 236
Saloojee, R.A.M., 587
Saloojee, Suliman, 582
San (see Khoisan, Khoikhoi)
sanctions, 368, 399, 413–415, 471, 473–475, 489, 585, 659
Sandile, 158
Sand River, 121, 151
Sand River Convention, 151–153, 166, 172, 174
Sanlam, 295, 308, 459–460
Sannaspos, 245
Santam, 295, 459
Sasol, 354, 391, 400, 458, 461, 472, 474
Sastri College, 579

INDEX 711

Saudi Arabia, 635
Sauer, Jacobus W., 271
Scheepers, Gideon, 253
Scher, David, 12, 260, 328, 467
Schlebusch Commission, 352
Schmidt, Georg, 51, 59
Schoeman, Hendrik, 245
Schoeman, Stephanus, 174
Schoemansdal, 150, 168, 172, 650
Scholtz, Leopold, 419
Scholtz, Piet, 166
school boycott, 375, 393–394, 399, 570
Schreiner, Olive, 226
Schreiner, William P., 170, 266, 555, 592, 594
Schuinshoogte, Battle of, 177
Schwarz, Harry, 369
science, 17, 285, 451, 512, 635, 658
scorched earth policy, 281, 594, 612, 646, 654–655
Scorpions, 514, 526, 564
Sebetwane, 121
Sebokeng, 412
Sechaba, 388
Sechele, Kgosi, 166
Second World War, 250, 278, 281, 308, 312, 318–321, 323–324, 326, 334–335, 339–340, 362, 417, 435, 439, 446, 448, 452, 454, 457, 461, 466–467, 486, 559, 562, 603–604, 634, 653
Security Council (United Nations), 363–364, 368, 519, 541
Seekoei River, 106–107
Sewgolum, Papwa, 584
segregation, 12, 174, 201–202, 263–264, 266, 270–272, 277–280, 306, 317, 319, 326, 329, 335–336, 402, 434–438, 517, 553–554, 557, 559, 573, 578, 581, 592, 606, 613, 621, 653
Seidenfaden, Johannes, 65
Sekonyela, 122–123, 142–144
Sekhukhune, 165
Sekwati, 122, 164–165
Selborne, Lord, 222, 261, 555
Selborne Memorandum, 261, 315, 555
Seme, Pixley, 316, 319
Senate, 66, 81, 104, 269, 276, 332, 334–335, 494, 562
Senzangakhona, 119
Separate Amenities Act, 331, 357, 616
separate development, 338–340, 342, 349, 356, 359–360, 373, 471, 612, 614, 624, 660
Separate Representation of Voters Act, 334–335, 343, 357, 376, 562
separate residential areas (group areas), 271, 278–279, 330, 343, 376, 398, 437
Sephton, Hezekhiah, 102
September, Reginald, 388
Serfontein, Divan, 568
Settlement Land Acquisition Grant Scheme (SLAG), 511
Sexwale, Tokyo, 501
Shaik, Schabir, 526–527, 531
Shaka, 106, 118–120, 122–123, 647
Shakespeare, William, 258, 331
Sharpeville, 341, 344–345, 380–383, 496, 582, 618–619

Shashi River, 40
Shaw, George Bernard, 235
Sheba Reef, 192
sheep and wool farming, 34, 36–37, 44, 48, 53, 70, 82, 84, 93, 102, 114, 118, 139, 157, 189, 199, 209–211, 215–218, 221, 232, 449, 463–464, 638, 643–644, 652, 665
Shell, Robert, 11, 14, 68
Shembe, Isaiah, 314
Shepstone, Theophilus, 171, 176, 592
Shiloh Mission Station, 157
Shilowa, Mbhazima, 534
Shivambu, Floyd, 673
Shona, 38, 40
Shoprite Checkers, 521
Sijmon in 't Velt, 44
silent diplomacy, 498, 520
silver, 76, 216, 470
Simond, Pierre, 47
Simons Bay, 65, 80–81
Simon's Town naval agreement, 369, 602
Sishen-Saldanha railway line, 354
Sisulu, Walter, 322–323, 343, 346, 384
Scotland (Scottish), 101–102, 104, 225, 483, 589–590, 619
Slagtersnek Rebellion, 98–101
Slave Lodge, 50, 54–55, 68–69, 74, 83
slaves (slavery), 11, 14, 46–47, 50, 53–59, 61–62, 65–66, 68–77, 79, 82–83, 88–96, 102, 115, 118, 125, 131–132, 171, 207, 224, 229, 231, 241, 275, 288, 319, 438, 499, 542, 547–550, 566, 574, 594, 646
slaves, desertion of, 46, 54, 56, 130
Slovo, Joe, 388
Sluysken, Abraham Josias, 62, 65
Small, Adam, 569
smallpox epidemic, 50, 56
Smit, Erasmus, 122, 139–140
Smit, Nicolaas, 179
Smith, Andrew, 135
Smith, C.S., 580
Smithfield, 212, 267
Smith, Harry, 150–153, 168
Smith, Ian, 361–362
Smith, Nico, 624
Smith, Richard Jon, 566
Smith, T.C., 149
Smith, Terence, 568
Smuts, Jacques, 85
Smuts: A Reappraisal, 280
Smuts, Jan (J.C.), 252–253, 261–262, 267–270, 275–276, 278–280, 282–284, 287–288, 295, 297–299, 303, 305–306, 308–309, 324–326, 328–329, 480, 484, 523, 529, 556–557, 559, 578, 595–598, 600–606
Sneuberg, 52, 64
Snyman, Kootjie, 245, 256
Sobukwe, Robert, 322, 344, 381, 384–385, 618–619
socialism, 303, 309, 322, 439, 444, 500, 558
Sofasonke, 320
Soil Conservation Act, 653–654
Solidariteit, 490
Solomon Commission, 578

Solomon, E.P., 596
Somalia, 545
Somerset, Charles, 91, 95, 97–98, 100–104, 225
Somerset, Henry, 78, 98
Somerset East, 107, 131, 134
Somerset West, 48
Somme River, 599–600
Sundays River, 453
Sonde met die bure, 285
Sonqua, 53
Sons of England, 590, 608
Sophiatown, 337, 617
Sorghum bicolor, 36
Sorghum verticilliflorum, 36
Soshangane, 120
Sotho, Basotho (speakers), 11, 38–39, 106, 108–109, 111–112, 116–119, 122–124, 151–152, 162–164, 180, 191, 196, 199–200, 208, 218, 232, 610
South Africa Act, 265, 272, 316, 334–335
South Africa First policy, 287–288, 598
South Africa House, 270
South Africa, New, 9, 223, 425, 544, 573, 609
South Africa, Republic of, 259, 343, 413, 433
South Africa, University of, 496
South African Breweries, 289
South African College, 225
South African Coloured People's Association, 551
South African Commercial Advertiser, The, 103
South African Communist Party (SACP), 367, 375, 385, 388, 394, 419, 421, 489, 494, 501–502, 507, 528–530, 582, 628
South African Congress of Democrats, 375
South African Congress of Trade Unions (SACTU), 379, 487–488
South African Council of Churches (SACC), 516, 618, 620–622, 628–629, 632
South African Council of Sport (SACOS), 567–568, 584
South African Democratic Teachers' Union (SADTU), 491
South African Employers' Consultative Committee on Labour Affairs (Saccola), 473
South African Engine Drivers' and Firemen's Association, 480
South African Federation of Trade Unions, 487
South African Fire and Life Assurance Company, 210
South African Indian Congress (SAIC), 327, 582, 615
South African Indian Council, 358–359, 361, 376, 583
South African Institute of Race Relations, 517, 611
South African Iron and Steel Industrial Corporation Limited (Iscor), 303, 354, 457, 461, 472
South African League, 551, 594–595
South African Military Nursing Service, 604
South African Mineworkers' Union (MWU), 480–482, 487, 489–490
South African Municipal Workers' Union (SAMWU), 491
South African National Defence Force (SADF & SANDF), 365–366, 418–419, 430, 500, 509, 624

South African Native Convention, 266, 315
South African Native National Congress (see African National Congress)
South African Non-Racial Olympic Committee (SANROC), 561
South African Party (SAP), 261, 269, 273, 275, 287, 298–299, 554, 597, 605–606
South African Party (Cape), 596–597
South African Police Service (SAPS), 509, 515
South African Railways and Harbours, 458
South African Students' Organisation (SASO), 386, 391, 569, 670
South African Teachers' Union, 282
South African Trades and Labour Council (SAT&LC), 486
South African Trade Union Congress (SATUC), 486
South African Trade Union Council, 487
South African Typographical Union, 479
South African War (also see Anglo-Boer War), 12, 242
Southern African United Front (SAUF), 387
Southern African Development Community (SADC), 519–520
South Korea, 439, 462
South West Africa (see Namibia)
South West Africa National Union, 387
South West Africa People's Organization (Swapo), 363–366, 418–420
S(Z)outpansberg, 27, 30, 40, 136–138, 168, 172, 215, 280, 650
Soweto, 321, 341, 347, 360, 367–368, 370, 381, 389–391, 396–397, 401, 403, 408, 412, 474, 512, 584, 617–618, 621, 623, 627
Soweto youth uprising, 370, 389–390, 401, 403, 412, 512, 623
Soviet Union (see Russia)
Sparrman, Anders, 50, 61
Speaking Together, 378
Spioenkop, Battle of, 243–244, 246, 254
Spoorbond, 485
sport, 202, 249, 301, 329, 351, 357, 359, 399, 433, 494, 523, 526, 538, 545, 551–553, 560–562, 565, 566–569, 573, 579, 583–584, 586, 592, 599, 608
Springboks (sport), 494, 545, 560–561, 567–568, 592
Springbok Legion, 600, 606
squatters (informal settlements), 85, 317, 320–321, 408, 537, 564
Squires, Hilary, 526
Sri Lanka (Ceylon), 248
State Security Council, 414, 516
Stalin, Josef, 445
Stallard, Charles, 601, 604
Stallard Commission, 261
Standard Bank, 210–211, 215, 217–218, 220, 460, 475–476
Star, The, 289, 298
Star of South Africa (diamond), 189
Starrenburg, Johannes, 49
"state capture", 665–668
State of Capture (report), 667

INDEX 713

Status Act, 299, 601
Steelpoort River, 38–39, 165
Steenhuisen, John, 673
Steinberg, Jonny, 563
Steinkopf, 158
Stellaland, 179
Stellenbosch, 47, 49, 56, 58–59, 107, 113, 145, 224, 273, 288, 290–292, 450, 553, 563
Stellenbosch, University of, 145, 290–291, 450
Stem van Suid-Afrika, Die, 302, 307
Sterkfontein, 32, 35
Steyn, Hermanus, 62
Steyn, President M.T., 186, 233, 240–242, 286, 288, 294, 364
Steyn, Justice M.T., 364
Steyn, Phia, 633, 649
St Helena, 81, 248
Stockenström, Anders, 94, 97
Stockenström, Andries, 96–98
stock exchange, 43, 155, 197, 212, 451
Stofberg, Louis, 351
Stone Age, 15, 29, 32–35, 640
stone tools, 25, 32–33, 35, 53, 642
Storm, Christiaan, 90
Stormberg stream, 107, 114
Stormjaers, 309
Strandley Pool, 22
Strauss, E.R., 280
Struben, Fred, 181, 193
Struben, Harry, 181, 193
struggle, liberation against apartheid, 9–10, 259, 265, 323, 343, 345–346, 350, 353, 360–361, 363, 367, 378, 380–381, 391, 393, 398–399, 412, 417, 420–423, 427, 494, 496, 504, 506, 517–518, 525–526, 531, 561, 572, 582, 615, 620, 627, 630
succulent Karoo, 29, 637, 640
Sudan, 36
Sudan, South, 542
sugar, 76, 171–172, 209, 214, 257, 450, 463–465, 490, 574–575, 578, 580, 653
Suid-Afrikaanse Akademie vir Wetenskap en Kuns, 13–14, 285
Suid-Afrikaanse Federasie van Vakbonde, 487
Suid-Afrikaanse Konfederasie van Arbeid (SAKVA), 487, 489
Sultan, M.L., 579
Suppression of Communism Act (1950), 343, 374, 376, 487, 615
Sutherland, 354
Sutherland, Henry, 104
Suzman, Helen, 533
Swadeshi, 577
Swanson, Charles, 553, 563
Swartbooi, 189
Swart, Christie, 570
Swart, C.R., 329, 343
"swart gevaar", 557
Swartkei River, 107
Swartkoppies, Battle of, 152
Swartkrans, 32
Swartland, 58, 90
Swazi, 117, 160, 162, 164–165

Swaziland, 37–38, 106, 120, 162, 241, 254, 415, 636
Swellendam, 57, 62, 86, 101, 131, 235
Switzerland, 409, 423
Symons, Penn, 243

Taaibosch, Koos, 108
Table Bay, 42–44, 60–61, 80, 208, 318
Taiwan, 369, 462, 518, 543
Talana, 243
Tambo, Oliver, 321, 344, 387–388, 412, 417, 420, 422, 438, 496, 499–500
Tamil, 574, 587
Tanzania, 32, 35, 117, 120, 361, 385, 387–389, 519
Tarka (River), 93, 99, 134, 137
Tas, Adam, 48
Taung fossil site, 32
Taung, 109, 120, 122–123, 138
Tautswe Hill, 39
Tavernier, Jean-Baptiste, 42
taxation, 55, 62, 85, 90, 114, 134, 171, 174, 184–185, 204, 208–209, 214, 221, 230, 264, 404, 411, 421, 441, 446, 508, 510, 532, 534, 535, 537, 546, 576–578, 585, 593, 651
Teachers' League of South Africa (TLSA), 555–556, 573
Techipa, 419
Teenstra, Marten, 89
telecommunications, 477, 490
Telegu, 574, 587
Tembe, 39
Terre'Blanche, Eugène, 431
Terrorism Act, 386
Thaba Bosiu, 106, 116, 123–124, 162–164
Thaba Nchu, 137–140
Thatcher, Margaret, 415, 475
The Hague, 66
Thema, Selope, 375
Theron, Danie, 246
third force, 426
Thom, George, 104
Thomas, Cornelius, 568
Thompson, Leonard, 10, 267, 443
Thorneycroft's Mounted Infantry, 244
Thukela River (Tugela), 145, 243, 656
Tibet, 542
Timol, Ahmed, 582
Tlhaping (Batlhaping), 112, 119, 121, 124, 166, 180, 182, 188–191, 199–200, 651
Tlharo, 124
Tlokwa, 116, 121–123, 142
Tloome, Dan, 323
Tobin, John, 554–555, 572
Tolstoy, Leo, 577
Tomlinson, F.R., 338
Tomlinson Commission, 338, 616
Tonkin, 43
Torch Commando, 334
Tosh, Peter, 566
Totius (see Du Toit, J.D.)
Trade and Development Co-operation Agreement (TDCA), 522
tradesmen, 46–47, 89, 101, 206–207, 457

Trade Union Council of South Africa (TUCSA), 487
trade union movement, 12, 194, 197, 272, 292, 297, 318–319, 324–325, 332, 354, 357, 370, 375, 379, 394, 400–403, 408, 426, 440, 447, 457, 473–474, 487–502, 505, 527, 529–530, 536, 539, 581, 584–585, 597
Trafalgar, Slag van, 79
transformation, 59, 117, 121–122, 130, 134, 155–156, 278, 366, 400, 443, 452, 497–498, 506, 509, 511, 523, 539, 577, 630–631, 634, 651, 660
Transgariep, 107–108, 113–116, 121–122, 172, 649
Transkei, 159–160, 345, 349, 355, 359, 377, 385, 398, 407–408, 421–422, 496, 499, 504, 616
Transnet, 540
transport riders, 180, 200, 215
Transvaal (see also Zuid-Afrikaansche Republiek), 150, 162, 166, 172–177, 179–186, 192–194, 197–198, 204, 211, 213–217, 220–222, 226–228, 230–236, 239–243, 245–246, 248–251, 254–255, 259, 261, 263, 265, 269, 271, 276, 282–283, 288, 294, 296–297, 301–302, 315, 318, 324–327, 344, 351, 375, 377, 380, 412, 430, 450, 455, 480, 483, 496, 543, 553, 555, 575–578, 581, 588–590, 593–598, 617, 619, 649–651, 655–657
Transvaal Indian Congress (TIC), 326–327, 581
Transvaal Miners' Association, 480
Transvaal Freedom War (see First Anglo-Boer War)
Transvaler, Die, 311
Travels in South Africa, 109
Tregardt, Louis (Trichardt), 128, 136–138, 649
trekboers, 11, 55, 86, 106, 108, 113–116, 118, 122, 125, 152–153, 644
Treurnicht, Andries, 364, 406, 409, 424, 617
tricameral Parliament, 391, 406–407, 409, 411–412, 429, 432, 571, 584
tripartite alliance (ANC, SACP, COSATU), 394, 489, 501–502, 504–505, 507
Trojan horse incident, 572
Truro, 574
Trust Bank, 461, 475–476
Truter, Anna Maria, 57
Truter, Christopher, 570
Truter, Johannes, 81
Truth and Reconciliation Commission (TRC), 393, 426, 515–518, 631, 667
tsetse fly, 168, 643, 649–650
Tshabalala-Msimang, Manto, 514, 544
Tshangana, 39
Tsonga, 38–39, 117, 191, 196, 649
Tshwane, 38
Tswaing impact crater, 29
Tswana (speakers), 11, 38–40, 106, 108, 111–113, 116–119, 124, 165–167, 179, 255–256, 258, 349, 610
Tucker, Frederick, 243
Tulbagh, 48, 64, 66, 91, 107, 246
Tulbagh, Elizabeth, 56
Tulbagh, Rijk, 56, 60
Turnhalle conference, 363
Tutu, Desmond, 494, 516, 621, 629–632
Tweebosch, Slag van, 248

Tyali, 98

Uhuru, 339
Uitenhage, 57, 66, 82, 87, 93, 104, 131, 135–136, 142, 412
Uitlanders (foreigners), 181, 184–187, 194, 204, 236, 239–241, 593–595
Ulundi, 161
Umkhonto we Sizwe (MK), 345–346, 367, 383–384, 388, 391, 422, 496, 509, 530, 571–572
uMvoti mission reserve, 336
Union of South Africa, 259, 262–263, 265–267, 269, 286–287, 302, 311, 315–316, 331, 333, 336, 340, 386, 402, 482, 597, 599–611, 616
Unionist Party, 271, 273, 292, 296, 299, 597–598, 600–601
Union Jack, 269, 275, 296, 591, 601–602, 607–608
UNITA (Angola), 365–366, 415, 418
United Association of South Africa (UASA), 490
United Democratic Front (UDF), 391–395, 412, 414, 504, 571, 584
United Democratic Movement (UDM), 504
United Nations (UN), 350, 377, 388, 397, 418, 435, 475, 517, 541, 581, 635
United Party (UP), 276–277, 303, 305–306, 308, 329, 345, 352, 405, 443, 466, 562, 605, 613
United States of America (USA), 194, 198, 205–206, 220, 314, 316, 321, 353, 362–363, 366, 368, 386–387, 435, 438, 442, 450, 463–464, 467, 469, 475, 479, 520–522, 534, 537, 617, 633, 657–658
Universe, 11, 17–21, 23
unskilled labour, 84, 89, 92, 171, 185, 191, 194–196, 208, 212, 259, 305, 397, 402, 405, 440, 457, 481–482, 485, 543, 545, 564
Unwin, Herbert, 244
Ur, 22–23
uranium, 353–354
Urban Areas Act, 271–272, 319, 337, 343
urbanisation, 201, 212, 259, 401, 474, 515, 640
Utrecht, 173, 216
Uys, Dirkie, 145
Uys, Piet, 136, 144–146

Vaal Dam, 453
Vaal River, 26, 32, 39, 106, 122, 136, 138–139, 149–153, 166–167, 172, 182, 189, 211, 232, 453–454, 636, 651
Vaal River, Battle of, 138
Valentijn, François, 50
Van Aardt, Willem, 100
Van Arckel, Joannes, 58
Van de Graaff, Cornelis, 57, 61
Van de Graaff, Reinet, 57
Van den Bergh, Hendrik, 373
Van der Bijl, H.J., 461
Van der Elst, Jacques, 9, 14
Van der Heiden, Jakobus, 48
Van der Hoff, Dirk, 174
Van der Kemp, J.T., 87
Van der Lingen, Aart, 88
Van der Merwe, Johan, 433
Van der Ross, Richard, 279, 335, 547–548, 551,

INDEX 715

555–556
Van der Stael, Pieter, 59
Van der Stel, Frans, 48
Van der Stel, Maria, 57
Van der Stel, Simon, 47–48, 52, 189
Van der Stel, Willem Adriaan, 48–49, 54, 57
Van Eck, H.J., 461
Van Eeden, Elize, 12, 633
Van Emmenes, Albert, 49
Van Goens, Rijckloff, 45
Van Jaarsveld, Adriaan, 64
Van Kervel, Adriaan, 82
Van Lier, Catherina, 57
Van Lier, Helperus Ritzema, 57, 59
Van Meerhoff, Pieter, 56
Van Niekerk, Schalk, 189
Van Plettenberg, Joachim, 60
Van Reede, H.A., 55, 74
Van Reenen, Dirk, 64
Van Reenen, Sebastiaan, 64
Van Rensburg, Lang Hans, 136
Van Riebeeck, Jan, 10, 43–46, 58, 376, 615
Van Riebeeck (De la Quellerie), Maria, 45, 56
Van Ryneveld, Daniël, 82
Van Ryneveld, Willem, 81, 86
Van Schalkwyk, Marthinus, 503, 660
Van Wyk, Amie, 630
Van Zyl, Kylie, 645
Vavi, Zwelinzima, 529
VBS Mutual Bank, 673
vegetable production, 43, 45, 69, 194, 199, 209, 214, 216
Vegkop, 139
Venda, 38, 40, 106, 117, 168, 313, 355, 392, 407
Venter, Al J., 548
Venter, Bill, 472
Vereeniging, 193, 195, 201, 260, 344
Vereeniging, Peace of, 248–249, 256, 258–260, 315
Verenigde Oos-Indiese Kompanjie (VOC), 42–43, 45, 58, 61–62, 64, 83, 113, 133, 574, 644
Vergelegen, 48, 54
Verhoef, Grietjie, 11, 12, 205, 448
verkramptes, 351–352, 364
verligtes, 351–352, 364
Vermaak, J.A., 55
Verwoerd, Betsie, 433
Verwoerd, H.F., 332–333, 336–342, 345–346, 349, 354, 365, 382, 444–445
Vet River, 138, 141
Victoria College, 290–291
Victoria, queen, 159, 170, 227, 241, 554, 591
Victoria Falls, 362
Victor Verster prison, 497
Vierkleur, Transvaal, 269, 296
Viervoet, Battle of, 151
Vigna unguiculata, 36
Viljoen, Ben, 249, 656
Viljoen, Constand, 430–433, 500
Viljoen, Gerrit, 423, 427
Virodene, 513
Visagie, Jan, 11–12, 105, 125
Visser, Wessel, 11–12, 188, 478

Vlakfontein, Battle of, 256
Vlok, Adriaan, 516
VOC (see Verenigde Oos-Indiese Kompanjie)
Vogelstruisfontein, 193
Voice of Women, 388
Volksangbundel, 301
Volkskas, 460, 475–476
Volkskongres, First Economic, 460
Volksrust, 211
Volksstem, De, 227
Volkwyn, Jan 331
Voortrekkerhoogte, 400
Voortrekker Tabakmaatskappy (Voortrekker Tobacco Company), 460
Voortrekkers (Trekkers), 11, 48, 112–113, 115, 122, 124–126, 134–154, 162, 165–166, 168, 172–174, 205–206, 213–214, 226–227, 297, 307, 649–651
Vooruitzigt, 180
Vorster, B.J., 310, 349–357, 359–373, 385, 390, 396, 405, 418, 561, 620, 622–623
Vorster, Koot (J.D.), 617
voters' roll, separate, 277, 406
voters' roll, common, 271, 275–276, 279, 333–335, 375, 558, 562, 615
Vreemdelingekorps (Foreigners' Corps), 240
Vrededorp, 202
Vredefort Dome (impact crater), 15, 24, 26, 30
Vryburg, 179
Vryheid, 179, 256
Vryheidsfront, 431–432
Vukani Bantu – The Beginnings of Black Protest Politics in South Africa to 1912, 265

Wage Act, 457
Wage Board, 457
wage labour, 156, 164, 197, 201, 207–208, 213–214
Wagenmakersvallei, 47
Wakkerstroom, 176, 216
Waldheim, Kurt, 363
Walker, E.A., 125
Walker, George, 181, 193
Wales (Welsh), 200, 479
Walvis, 43
Warden, Henry Douglas, 151–152
Warmbad (Aigams, Namibia), 60, 65, 88
Wasbankspruit, 146
Washington, 387
Washington, Booker T., 314
Washington Post, The, 397
Waterberg, 30, 216
Waterboer, Andries, 109, 111–112, 157
Waterboer, Nicolaas, 182, 190
Waterson, Sidney, 605
Waterwich, Robert, 572
Wellington, 47, 199, 211
Welsh, David, 432
Welwitschia mirabilis, 639
Wenkommando, 146–147
Wepener, Louw, 163
Western Cape, 29, 89, 113, 157, 230–231, 292, 326, 344, 384, 432, 450, 503, 526, 530, 533, 537, 570, 592, 640, 652
Western Cape, University of the, 335, 358, 566, 569

Wessels, Leon, 427
Westminster, Statute of, 270, 299, 601
Wetton, 331
wheat production, 47, 50, 70, 87, 89, 102, 138, 180, 199–200, 209, 216–218, 230, 302, 450, 463, 652, 656
whites, 106, 145, 162, 168, 170, 174, 194, 196, 202, 254, 271, 274, 293–294, 303–304, 322, 326–327, 331–332, 335, 356–357, 362, 371, 376, 378, 380, 398, 400, 406, 408, 411, 414, 417, 425, 481, 485, 552, 556, 563, 572, 586, 591–593, 607, 609, 614–615, 623, 651, 653–654
Wiehahn, Nic (Wiehahn Commission), 370, 473, 488–489
Wijlandt, Willem, 58
Wilberforce, William, 90
Wilcocks Commission, 278–279, 559
Wildlife Society, 658
Wilgespruit, 193
Williams, Coline, 572
Willshire, Thomas, 96
Wilson, Harold, 353, 369, 567–568
Wilson, Monica, 10
Winburg, 138, 148–150, 152
Winds of change speech, 340–341, 345
Windhoek, 363, 419
Windvoël, "General", 256
wine industry, 44, 47–48, 50, 70, 82–84, 89, 199, 209–210, 230–231, 302, 451, 463, 537
Winterberg, 99, 107, 140
Winterhoek, 93
"Winternag", 284
Witbank (eMalahleni), 201, 472
Witsieshoek, 377
Witwatersrand, 26, 39, 181, 184–185, 188, 193–196, 201, 203, 211–212, 219–220, 234, 239, 296, 318, 320–321, 375, 385, 423, 466, 479–481, 484, 496, 589, 593
Witwatersrand, University of the, 496
Witzenberg, 52
Wodehouse, Philip, 164
Wolmaransstad, 656
Woltemade, Wolraad, 60–61
Wood, Evelyn, 178
Wood, William, 143
Woordeboek van die Afrikaanse Taal, 291
Worcester, 91, 104, 211, 537
Workers' Herald, The, 318
work (job) reservation, 194, 457, 473–474, 481–482, 484, 486, 488–489, 619, 623
World Bank, 474
World Cup (rugby), 494, 545, 568
World Cup (soccer), 546

World Council of Sustainable Development, 663
World Alliance of Reformed Churches, 625
World heritage cites, 26, 32, 34, 36–37, 662
World Council of Churches (WCC), 388, 617–619, 632
Wragg Commission, 576
Wupperthal, 87

Xanthium spinosum, 652
xenophobia, 545, 587
Xhosa, 38, 60, 64, 82–83, 93–99, 101, 117, 121, 124, 128, 151, 157–160, 313, 345, 349, 384, 408, 432, 527, 592, 610, 646, 651
Xuma, Alfred, 320–321, 323, 327, 581
Xuma, Madie, 320

Yamato 691 meteorite, 20
Yeoville, 202
Young Turks (United Party), 352

Zacharias, Jan, 55
Zambia, 121, 361–362, 387–389, 466, 500
Zandvliet, 59
Zeeland, 42
Zeerust, 377, 530
Zeko, 98
Zibhebhu, 161
Zille, Helen, 525, 532–533, 672, 673
Zimbabwe, 15, 24, 27, 29, 36–40, 113, 117, 188, 362, 388, 498, 502, 520, 541, 545, 609, 628, 644
Zimbabwe African People's Union (ZAPU), 388
Zondo, Raymond, Deputy Chief Justice (Zondo Commission of Inquiry), 667–668
Zuid-Afrikaan, De, 224
Zuid-Afrikaansche Republiek (ZAR), 11, 151, 155, 157, 162–163, 165, 167–168, 170, 173–176, 178–179, 182, 184, 186, 190, 192–195, 197–198, 200–201, 204, 211, 215, 217, 226–227, 233–237, 239, 240, 297, 302, 480, 575, 593–594, 649–650, 656
Zuid-Afrikaansche Zendelings Genootschap, 51
Zulu (Zululand), 39, 106, 117–120, 122–123, 142–147, 149, 160–161, 164, 171, 179, 196, 208, 213–215, 227, 254, 256, 265, 313, 336, 349, 355, 392, 399, 431, 480, 528–530, 574, 577, 586, 588, 610, 647, 651
Zululand, University of, 390
Zulu Rebellion, 577
Zuma, Jacob, 513–514, 525–532, 539, 545, 586, 661, 664–671
Zuurveld, 82, 93–95, 99, 101–102, 590
Zwagershoek, 93, 100
Zwangendaba, 120
Zwide, 119–120, 647